Firepower: Making 21st Century Warfare Decisive

Firepower: Making 21st Century Warfare Decisive

John Musgrave

ISBN (Hardback): 978-1-913012-41-0
ISBN (ePub): 978-1-913012-42-7

A full CIP record for this book is available from the British Library.

Published in association with Riverside Publishing Solutions, Salisbury, UK
www.riversidepublishingsolutions.com

Designed and typeset by Riverside Publishing Solutions, Salisbury, UK
www.riversidepublishingsolutions.com

Printed and bound in the UK.

Contents

Foreword

In the Officers' Mess in Larkill, the home of Britain's Royal Artillery, is a rather magnificent Statue of the Patron Saint of Artillery – Saint Barbara. Inscribed very simply are two words – 'Armed Science', a theme which permeates Colonel John Musgrave's excellent new book. Saint Barbara is also celebrated by Artilleries across NATO and a good deal of the Commonwealth. This international fires network of innovators and integrators, led by the United States, is increasingly significant in an era where great power competition is once again a reality and where Alliances ever more crucial. However, this is not a book on Gunners for Gunners, far from it. John has produced a a lively and fascinating read for anyone interested in Defence and the dilemmas which democratic countries face in relation to the threat of, or use of, lethal force – ultimately militaries' unique selling point.

After a generation of counter insurgency, John Musgrave's book argues, the West has fallen into a historical trap of undervaluing the utility of firepower, particularly Army firepower, in the ability to defend, deter and, ultimately, defeat potential adversaries. These are highly relevant discussions, not least as NATO looks to operationalize the capstone Concept for Deterrence and Defence of the Euro Atlantic area (DDA) and as Defence forces across NATO assess their multi-domain mix of capabilities and effectors. John's book challenges the reader as to the role of firepower in the changing character of warfare in the 21st century, discussing what effects and capabilities will be most effective as instruments of policy – all interwoven brilliantly with anecdote and vignettes. Artillery already has ranges into the 100s of kms bracket, hypersonic weapons will offer an order of magnitude change again – arguably a paradigm shift in how we may fight in the near future.

In the Larkhill Mess building are other historical reminders of the value brought by thought leading Gunners such as Shrapnel, Congreve and Alanbrooke, to which this book makes a highly significant contribution. John concludes with 50 propositions – highly relevant questions, liking strategic considerations to tactical developments at the end of an excellent and highly entertaining read. In these resource challenged times, the very least we must do is to think deeply and boldly about change within our profession of arms.

Major General John Mead OBE

Appreciations

I was lucky to have Jonathan Bailey as my first battery commander in a regiment with Michael Charlton-Weedy and Chris Nicholls, who all imparted in me an appreciation of the need for soldiers to study their professions. The Royal School of Artillery has been a constant feature in my service and its institutional excellence makes demands upon all Gunners to live up to its standards. Key to the production of this book has been Peter Thompson, who has corrected both wayward grammar and my logic. John Cresswell has also challenged and improved my writing. Dicky Winchester has also added to the creative process. Malcolm Prior has provided invaluable assistance with the graphics. And Olivier Fort has provided many insights over the years. And of course thanks to Major General John Mead for his belief in the need for such a book and of course for the foreword.

Disclaimer

The views expressed in this book are the authors and do not reflect views of the British Army or any part of the UK government. For the sake of brevity and readability he/him/his is used, it refers to both male and female.

Introduction

'Repeatedly since the Cold War, our armed forces have defeated enemies on the battlefield, only for our governments to fail to translate those battlefield successes into advantageous, enduring strategic outcomes[1]*'.*

David Kilcullen, Strategist

Despite being identified in both the popular mind and the academic sphere as resistant to change[2], the West's militaries have over the last quarter century discarded their tried and tested way of war in favour of novel, and so far, unproven methods. This traditional way of warfighting probably originated with the Ancient Greeks and led to the West's geopolitical dominance from the 1500s. It realised war's political purpose through closing with and overthrowing the opposition, in either a decisive battle, or a series of battles, leading to World history being written in terms of decisive battles. The switch away from this has been led by the dominant military power, and America's operational art has been largely adopted by its allies. This includes countries such as South Korea and Japan, which have only become part of the Western military tradition in the last seventy years. Max Boot characterised the new method as being based on precision firepower, in contrast to what Russell Weigley had previously identified as an attritional approach[3]. This precision can be seen as the weaponising of information age technology and theory. From a military technical perspective this new way of war has overpowered opposing militaries. However, in a series of post-Cold War conflicts against second and third rate powers it has failed to deliver the decisive military success that leads to enduring political outcomes.

Why is this so? The convenient answer is to see political factors as the cause of failure in the Iraq, Libya, the Balkans and Afghanistan conflicts. Instead, this analysis spreads the responsibility to the West's new approach to warfighting and its rejection of seeking decisive victory through a range of methods, but culminating in close ground combat to overwhelm an adversary. Despite once promising 'Shock and Awe', the West's new strategic approach has seen moderation in the application of force, so elongating the conflict and allowing opponents to develop counters. The West's new *ways* primarily seeks to minimise casualties, including those inflicted on the opposition. The *means* are similarly straitened; rather than the classic default of overwhelming force, arbitrary force levels are set, in particular of in-theatre ground forces[4]. Politicians may have set wholly unrealistic *end states*, but their militaries have not only been guilty of accepting these but of making these even more unattainable through the *ways* and *means* employed[5].

Instead of overwhelming an adversary, in this new approach, victory is sought through exploiting information dominance, leading to carefully calibrated precise targeting of lethal and non-lethal force. Whilst the West's new way of war has achieved military excellence over the last three decades, this has not been of a form that easily translates into achieving war's political purpose. Instead, it has led to drawn-out insurgencies or frozen conflicts, neither of which provide a ready pathway to their political resolution.

Given its failure to deliver decisive political outcomes against, at best, regional powers, it is reasonable to question the new way of war's utility in addressing the West's new warfighting paradigm of facing peer opponents[6]. Two decades ago, the American sponsored liberal international order seemed to be going from strength to strength. Now this order is in crisis, and the future is up for grabs[7]. America's conventional warfighting advantage is now challenged in the air, maritime, space and cyber domains, where the West has long assumed guaranteed superiority.

The crucial advantage of applying precise firepower through airpower is that it minimises own casualties through making close combat anticlimactic and through allowing Western armies to face opponents whose combat power has been significantly reduced by airpower prior to close combat. When this is not the case, plentiful close air support could compensate. As close combat is no longer expected to be the decisive act, Western armies have significantly reduced their capacity to fight without airpower's assistance. In particular this has led to major reductions in their organic firepower.

Against peer opponents, airpower cannot be expected to inflict significant attrition before ground forces meet in close combat, nor can it be expected to provide much close air support. This should not be a surprise as this book's historic survey will show: airpower has always been the form of ground fire support that is the easiest to counter. Nor can a quick-fix to this be expected. Western air forces may have adapted to the proliferating threat of hard-to-suppress man-portable missiles by operating at medium altitude, but altitude loses its relative safety against the modern sensors and the long range missiles that peer opponents deploy. Defeating such systems is possible, but it is likely to take time, and this will be at the expense of providing direct support to ground forces. So a peer challenge exposes the vulnerability of a land warfighting approach that is now is largely reliant upon aerial firepower.

This emphasis upon conventional warfare may appear passé, but this book contends that it is only through open conflict that the most significant political issues can be resolved. Unfortunately, this is likely to include a rising China's place within East Asia (and so its global position as this region becomes the epicentre of the World economy) and a restored Russia's relationship with the other USSR successor states, and hence NATO and the EU. In addressing the most meaningful political challenges, land combat remains uniquely effective. While land warfighting cannot occur in isolation, only armies can capture or disperse a belligerent's armed forces, physically occupy territory and subsequently control a population.

This emphasis on warfighting does not mean neglecting the many tools used in state competition below the threshold of conventional combat. This can include: diplomacy, economic aid, military-training assistance, intelligence sharing, and arms supplies. Regimes can be pressurised by: sanctions, restricting access to global institutions, travel bans, sponsorship of insurgent/dissident groups, and covert action by special operations force. All of these have recently been eclipsed in the public consciousness by cyber and information operations, which have become the chosen mediums by which a state's interest can be pursued without risking overt armed conflict. In comparison to these methods, open violent political conflict (war) is likely to remain rare. And of course, great powers have not openly clashed since World War Two.

This has led to the view that in imitation of authoritarian states, the West's primary security focus should be on constant competition in this 'gray zone' between peace and war. The strategist David Kilcullen is the most persuasive advocate for this latest rationale for side-lining decisive combat. In his view a state's aims can effectively be achieved by operating below the threshold of open conflict and leveraging their economy, society and technology to dislocate regular forces[8]. However, underpinning Russia and China 'gray zone' activity are the substantial conventional forces that can demonstrably win on the battlefield, even against first rate powers. Their fielding of massed tanks and artillery leads to little debate of their combat worth. Unfortunately, the West lacks a similar capability[9]. The main danger of a doctrine that identifies that the West's political objectives can be achieved without being prepared to employ conventional force is that it undermines the need for stronger land forces.

Bolstering the West's land forces needs to start with increasing organic firepower, as this dominates conventional warfighting. Stressing firepower, and the role of humble cannon and mortar in 21st century warfare may appear backward-looking. Gunpowder artillery has passed its thousandth year on the battlefield; superficially it remains the same – a tube or rocket using a propellant to launch a projectile – but as a system-of-systems it continues to exponentially increase its lethality. But this appears to be insufficiently revolutionary for militaries such as the Americans, who are acclimatised to dramatic technology driven change. Hence the stressing of the potential of a strategic cannon with a 1000 mile range over their more mundane modernisation of their field artillery.

For over a century, tube-launched exploding projectiles have been the major cause of combat killing and wounding; with small arms coming a distant second. Airpower, even in World War Two, when the aerial bombardment of civilian populations was mostly considered legitimate, has not challenged the lethal dominance of these relatively simple weapons[10]. Firepower's lethality has forced those that enter Ares' arena to adapt their tactical employment to prioritise their battlefield survival over all other considerations. This creates an empty battlefield, as ground forces seek to avoid becoming a target by blending into the landscape and seeking its physical protection. At first this empty battlefield was limited to the line of sight of direct fire weapons. Artillery and mortars, coupled with modern sensors, now make any overt military activity problematic up to tens of kilometres behind the line of contact. With sufficient resources and a favourable air situation, aircraft can extend this over the whole theatre, though of course without the persistence of ground forces separated by a contested no man's land. Such has been firepower's dominance that overmatched opponents have sought to close with their adversaries to distances that may make direct fire deadlier, but restrict the lethality of artillery and aerial firepower. Firepower's battlefield dominance can be understood as follows:

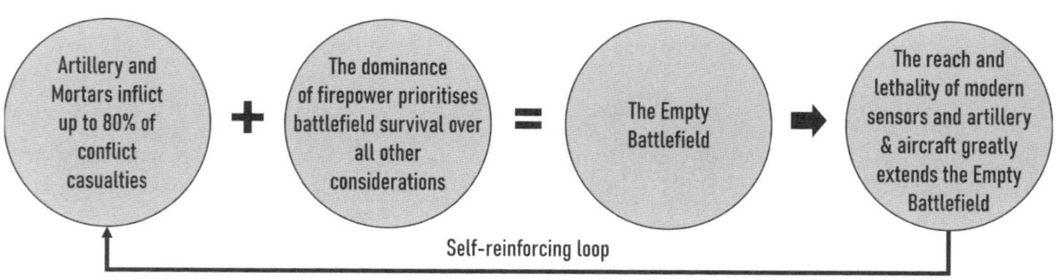

Killing may not be the key objective in war, but despite the optimism of the proponents of successive new ways of warfare, attrition has often provided the route to victory. This is generally indirectly, as battlefield deaths and wounding are seldom so disproportionate between belligerents as to make the difference decisive. Ground combat invariably becomes decisive by either forcing the opposing soldiers to flee, or turning them into prisoners of war[11]. On its own, firepower achieves physical and psychological attrition. When firepower is combined with the close assault of tanks and infantry it becomes the primary means of breaking an opponent's will to fight, through overcoming their primary group cohesion and thus their ability to resist. Even the threat of close combat, particularly when this comes from an unexpected direction, can be sufficient to convince an opponent to surrender or flee. These are generalisations, as the factors leading to a belligerent losing the will to resist remain contentious[12]. But few would dispute that decisive ground combat is largely the outcome of combining of fire and manoeuvre, with the suppressive effect of firepower allowing the movement necessary to close with an opponent.

As well as making conflict more decisive, capturing a significant proportion of an opponent's forces aids war's political objective. At conflict termination, there is a considerable difference between a captured combatant, and an opponent who has been uninvolved in the fighting. The latter may not have psychologically accepted defeat, because they have not gone *under the yoke*. Of course, it requires prisoners of war to be treated honourably for this to assist in persuading the losing belligerent to accept a conflict's political outcome. When the West is true to its chivalric traditions, it has been significantly more humane to captured combatants than most other cultures.

History shows that a subsequent peace is more likely to be successful if the manner of a defeat is decisive and follows from a 'stand-up fight'. With a 'good fight' being a contest in which psychologically there is no shame in accepting defeat. The need for a contest appears to be hardwired into *homo sapiens*, leading to the dominance of stand-up fights that test comparable forces upon the battlefield. To the ancient Greeks this contest was called the Agon and it could only be properly satisfied by evenly matched hand-to-hand combat between heavy infantry (hoplites)[13].

Combining a 'stand-up fight' with turning combatants into prisoners not only supports a conflict's termination, it also aids the translation of this into peaceful relationship between former enemies. The Great War is the most famous example of the failure to do this. The Armistice meant that the German Army was not forced to accept the verdict of the battlefield, thus allowing the 'stab in the back' myth to gain credence. In any future peer conflict, between nuclear armed powers, achieving early decisive tactical victory will probably be key to avoiding further escalation[14]. In traditional Western warfighting the relationship between the conduct and termination of conflict can be understood this way:

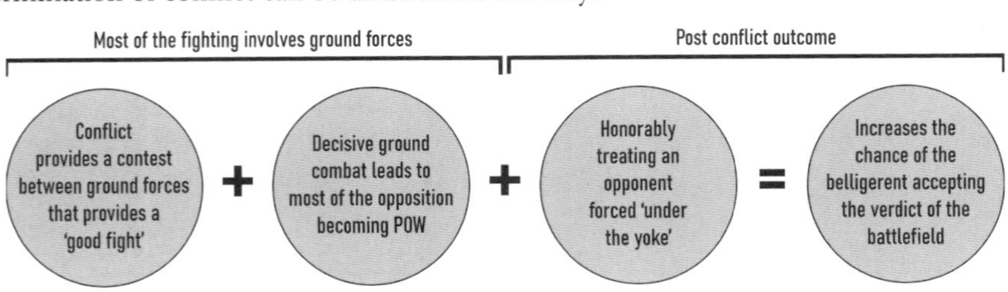

By relying upon airpower to do most of the fighting the West has failed to provide a contest in most of its recent conflicts. In addition, airpower dominated warfare provides limited opportunity for opposing forces to surrender, leading to most of an enemy's casualties being killed or wounded. In the 2003 Iraq War this led to defeated Iraqi forces escaping, rather than becoming prisoners of war. Their opponents at times actively conspired in this. Western militaries when faced with detaining prisoners of war can choose to avoid the challenge, in part through wishing to avoid losing momentum in an advance, this also avoids subsequent media and legal scrutiny[15]. For the 2003 Iraq War, this approach fuelled the insurgency, leading to some belligerents being known as 'Pissed Off Iraqis': young men who just wished to regain their honour[16]. In addition to failing to provide a 'good fight', reliance on airpower meant that at conflict termination, Coalition ground forces lacked both the numbers and the military standing to provide a physical threat that would overawe any opposition to the occupation. The practical outcome of this approach can be understood in this way:

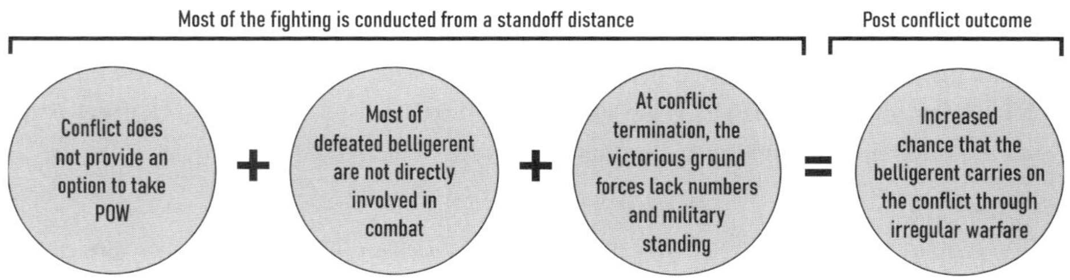

So how did the West get to this new way of war? The West's post-9/11 style of conventional warfighting was the culmination of changes in force employment (Stephen Biddle phrase that encompasses '*the doctrine and tactics by which forces are actually employed in combat*[17]) that began at the end of the Cold War. The key step in the transformation was the 1991 Gulf War, this was a hybrid between new and old approaches to warfighting. The Coalition assembled a large artillery park, but initially almost totally relied upon the firepower provided by airpower. The conflict proceeded on traditional lines, proving the effectiveness of airpower against an opponent willing to deploy in the open, and then the artillery/mortar and tank/infantry combined arms team made this decisive in close combat. However, the timing of the ceasefire, after four days of ground warfare, was largely driven by the perceived need to avoid further casualties in the Iraqi forces fleeing on Highway 80. Letting them escape, instead of continuing the slaughter, was the only option, because despite identifying the Republican Guard as vital to the preservation of Saddam's power, Coalition ground forces were not postured to cut-off their retreat.

The defeat or better yet the capture of Saddam's most loyal and military capable forces would have allowed a significantly different political outcome. The historian Victor Davis Hanson identified that the West's '*bloody past suggests to us that enemies cease hostilities only when they are battered enough to acknowledge that there is no hope in victory – and thus that further resistance means only useless sacrifice*[18]'. In rejecting this orthodoxy, the Gulf War's truncated ending led to a political impasse. Despite this, for some, the conflict proved that technology-led changes to the character of conflict made ground firepower and manoeuvre largely unnecessary. Crucially, precision aerial firepower appeared to offer a more humane style of warfighting, that significantly reduces own casualties and with this, reduced domestic political risk.

Visibly demonstrated by the 338,000 troops of Group Soviet Forces Germany, the Cold War imposed an intellectual clarity on NATO that resulted in an empirical approach to force employment. Freed of this constraint, responding to the demise of a peer threat and emboldened by the 'lessons of the Gulf War', in the nineties new age theories of war proliferated. By this time, following the lead provided by the post-Vietnam War, American Army doctrine had become the 'sport of generals' as opposed to the distilled lessons from conflict[19]. The outcome was novel theories of war that sought to reflect the new paradigm. These were influenced by the broadening of military thought that resulted from engaging with other traditions, notably the Chinese one, popularised by Sun-Tzu's 'Art of War'. The Middle Kingdom's approach stresses indirect means, the employment of non-violent methods and a more drawn-out approach to conflict. Carefully calibrating force is central to the Chinese military tradition; crudely this trades a reduced chance of total victory for a significantly reduced chance of defeat[20]. As such, it contrasts with the West's traditional or Napoleonic approach, which emphasises the maximum use of force to impose one's will upon an enemy in a stand-up battle. Dr Henry Kissinger analyses the difference by looking at the games played, by the two cultures:

> *Chess has only two outcomes: draw and checkmate. The objective of the game ... is total victory or defeat – and the battle is conducted head-on, in the centre of the board. The aim of go is relative advantage; the game is played all over the board, and the objective is to increase one's options and reduce those of adversaries. The goal is less victory than persistent strategic progress*[21].

The influence of non-Western ways of war has led to the view that ground forces should primarily be employed as a means of 'communicating meaning', rather than seeking to overthrow their opponents through close combat[22]. Though this has happened before: the Italian *Condottieri* and the armies of the Age of Reason often prioritised avoiding casualties and the chance of defeat over seeking a decisive outcome.

The retreat from the orthodox use of firepower with ground manoeuvre was accelerated by the security challenges of the immediate post-Cold War period. In Europe the demise of the peer threat was followed by ethnoreligious conflicts in the Wars of Yugoslavian Secession. General Sir Rupert Smith identified in his book 'The Utility of Force'[23] that intervening Western forces faced a new form of conflict, whose character was defined by underlying historical grievances, leading to conflict more tribal in nature, with wars being fought by and amongst the civilian population, rather than by armies on the battlefield. At the time this was seen as a wholly new character of conflict to conventional state-on-state war of the Western military tradition, leading to a debate on the actual usability of traditional warfighting methods, and even its underlying theory. This included the questioning of Clausewitz's interpretation of the role of politics in war, which is a central in most Western military thought[24]. A summary of the pathway to this rejection of orthodox force employment is:

The new doctrine saw information dominance translated into military effect through precisely targeting largely air delivered munitions against identified vulnerabilities; leading to carefully calibrated effects designed to bring the enemy to a state of 'cognitive-strategic collapse'; and, resulting in behavioural change in an opponent's strategic leadership that achieves the war's objective. As well as computing, the key enabling technologies were precision guidance and GPS. This allowed munitions to achieve sub-metre accuracy despite being delivered from standoff distances that largely outrange retaliatory weapons. When coupled with easily obtained air supremacy, this approach made Western forces effectively invulnerable in the wars of the 1990s. This appeared to make obsolete the more orthodox warfighting approaches of the World's other militaries. The historian Victor Davis Hanson confidently predicted in 2003: '*Any time the Western way of war can be unleashed on an enemy stupid enough to enter its arena, victory is assured*[25]'. In the narrow sense he was right in that American led coalitions had military superiority, but this did not translate into significant materiel damage if an opponent took effective counter measures, so preventing technological superiority being translated into the desired political outcome. And even if physically defeated, this did not always lead to a stable peace.

All this apparent change resulted in some identifying these years as representing a revolution in military affairs[26]. The counterview was that technology on its own cannot lead to revolutionary change. This being an apparent lesson of previous revolutions in military affairs[27]; which despite being associated with significant technological change, such as gunpowder, feature changes to all the social, political and economic aspects of war. In addition, ground warfighting may be uniquely resistant to technological change because of its enduring nature. This Clausewitz identified as being the realm of: '*danger, physical exertion, intelligence and friction as the elements that coalesce to form the atmosphere of war, and turn it into a medium that impedes activity*[28]. This friction is at its greatest in the land environment due to the impact of human and physical terrain. This also leads to the fog of war, which the German theorist quantified as three quarters unknown to a quarter known. This nature makes land warfare significantly more difficult to transform than the air and maritime domains. And so, we should be wary of extrapolating changes in these environments into ground combat. Despite this, the bolder proponents of war's transformation stated that technology significantly reduced war's fog and friction[29]. This has not proven to be the case when faced by opponents who are not as obliging as Saddam's Army.

As well as being susceptible to counters, experience has shown that advanced technology can add new forms of friction[30]. This is both physically – the result of Moore's Law increasing modern military equipment's vulnerability to Murphy's law – and through making decision-making more challenging. Command can be hindered by too much information, particularly when data has indeterminate fidelity and latency[31]. Experience shows that much information is irrelevant when making a choice. This particularly applies to time-constrained, chaotic, and uncertain situations when the human brain defaults to intuitive or naturalistic decision-making[32].

The weaknesses of this new way of war were not immediately apparent. Its employment in the Balkans were technical successes, but Bosnia and Kosovo have effectively become frozen conflicts. Post the overthrow of Gadhafi, Libya has effectively become a failed state. The apparently decisive invasions of Afghanistan and Iraq descended into insurgencies. Turning battlefield victory into a sustainable political outcome is not a novel challenge. Thucydides identifies the fundamental tragedy of the Peloponnesian War as Athens' unwillingness to accept the verdict of the battlefield and instead returning to the fight in 431 BCE[33]. Instead of reverting to conventional fighting, the loser now usually changes the character of conflict away from conventional warfare. The greatest Western military theorist, Clausewitz, was the first to systematically examine irregular warfare. Identifying that people's war was the means for European nations to carry on the struggle after their battlefield failure in the Revolutionary and Napoleonic Wars[34]. He also identified that overwhelming battlefield success could forestall this. Conversely people's war is stoked by any setbacks to the occupying force. Referring to Britain's First Afghanistan War (1839–42): *'The Duke of Wellington thought that the difficulties would start as soon as the military successes ended'*[35].

The increased prominence of irregular warfare can be seen as *'the West has become the victim of its own conventional military success*[36]'. This is usually linked with questioning conventional warfare's decisiveness[37]. This book will show that irregular warfare remains at its historic proportion of conflict, that it has not become the most effective form of organised violence[38], and that orthodox conventional warfare retains its decisiveness. And when used correctly, conventional warfare can still pre-empt an insurgency by an overwhelming application of force. As well as making it more likely that they will face an insurgency, the West's new way of war, through side-lining ground combat, compounds the challenge Western armies face in becoming effective counter-insurgents.

War amongst the people follows similar grammar to the other forms of war. When fighting an insurgency, individual battles are rarely decisive, but this does not mean that the pathway to victory lies in the minimum application of force. Conventional forces have historically been successful through employing firepower and manoeuvre to separate the insurgent from the population. Combat power is required to achieve the spatial and population control that is necessary to allow the successful implementation of the non-military aspects of combating an insurgency. Lacking an unrelenting combat focus, in both Iraq and Afghanistan Coalition ground forces instead pursued the non-military lines of operations: economic, political or social. This of course contravenes established military principles, in particular concentration of force, leading to the emasculation of most of the advantages of a conventional military force[39]. It also rejects the lessons of almost every successful counter-insurgency, including the often-quoted Malayan Emergency. When faced by an established insurgency, successful campaigns, initially at least, have made significant use of firepower to separate the guerrillas from the people. Failing to achieve this, and provide basic security for the people, has been a causal factor in recent failures[40].

The other reason that Western militaries should concentrate upon military operations is that an insurgency is fundamentally a civil war – with a non-state group (or groups) trying to either overthrow the government or secede from a country – and so in the eyes of the population intervening external powers lack legitimacy. To avoid becoming a third party in the conflict, successful interventions have operated through indigenous governments[41]. Successful campaigns have also featured the graduated handover of the military campaign to indigenous forces, following a successful mentoring, train and equip programme. This engagement enables Western countries to encourage the host government to address an insurgency's underlying causes; this contrasts with trying to impose developed world norms[42]. This approach to counter-insurgency is unglamorous and painstaking, and it requires a long term political commitment. Unfortunately, the product of America's strategic culture and national character is an unwillingness to govern what they conquer[43]. Of course, even with the best strategy, resolving civil wars is inherently more difficult than inter-state conflict, as the combatants cannot simply lay down their arms and go home[44]. Following the intervention to support a failing government an idealised campaign plan, against the usual counter-insurgency lines of operations, could progress as follows:

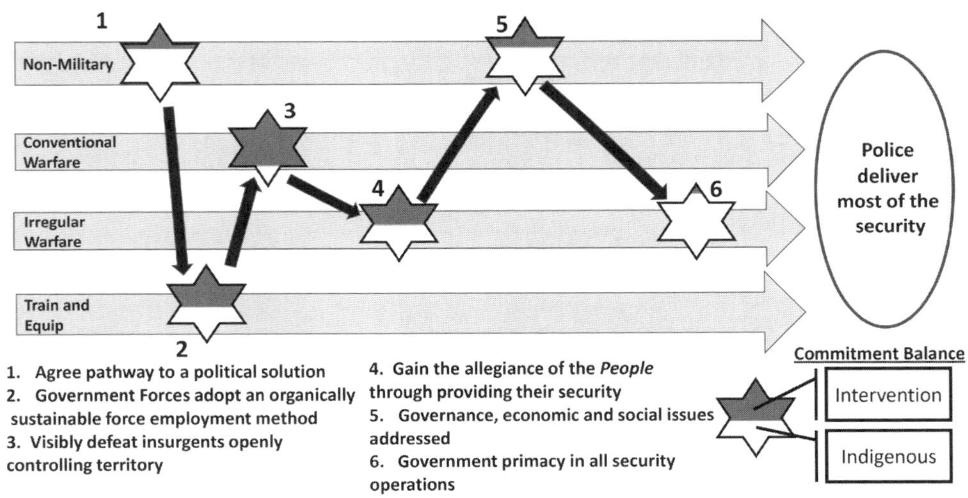

Traditional ground combat may appear to be an outmoded way of addressing 21st century threats, but it is how the so-called Islamic State was defeated. The application of overwhelming conventional force against Islamic State fighters, the destruction of much of Raqqa and Mosul by firepower and the subsequent physical occupation resulted in the 'Caliphate's' end. This was largely accomplished by regional forces using mainly artillery firepower; in contrast Western forces carefully calibrated their use of force and achieved significantly less effect. Despite the confident predictions of Western pundits, currently (2020) the major post-conflict challenge is dealing with captured Islamic fighters and not a resurgence in irregular warfare that was a predicted outcome of occupying the territory of the so-called Islamic State.

In contrast to this decisive use of conventional land warfare, the new Western way of war has incrementally led to the greater use of military force at reduced strategic effect, leading to America being constantly, rather than decisively, engaged. Despite this, it remains attractive because it offers politicians less risky conflict, particularly in terms of casualties, through employing airpower and special forces rather than conventional ground forces. This encouraged Western politicians, usually abetted by their military advisers, to resort to warfare without sufficient clarity on how to realise war's political purpose. Clausewitz identified the temptation to take '*the first step without thinking what may be the last*[45]'. At the zenith of liberal interventionism, Madeline Albright, the 64th US Secretary of State, reflected this paradigm by asking: '*What's the point of having this superb military … if we can't use it?*[46]'. The outcome of three decades of Western military superiority are armies institutionalised into continuous engagement in low intensity warfare. This comforting norm presents commanders with constant employment in tackling unchallenging tactical problems; in contrast, the new geopolitical paradigm requires nuance and strategic insight. The new Western Way of War in the *Pax Americana* years set a low bar for military intervention and failed to bind the liberal-democracies into a series of conflicts that were, arguably, injudiciously embarked upon:

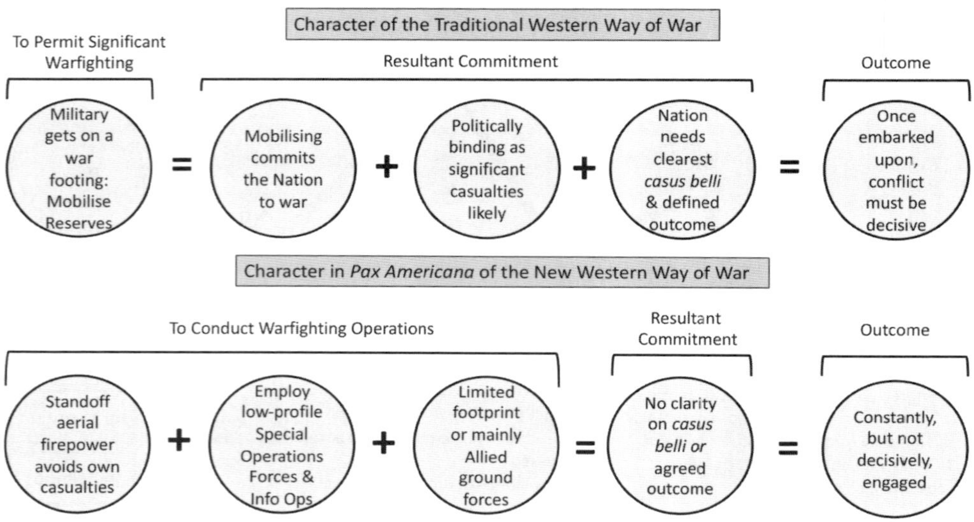

While the West has been fixed by continuous conflict, the other major military powers have expended most of their resources on modernising their warfighting forces. Russia understands that it is its overwhelming combat power that deterred its neighbours from effectively responding to its false militias, surrogates, cyberattacks, fake news and 'little green men' (non-uniformed Russian personnel). China adds to these methods the seizure and fortification of strategic shoals. If the West restored its conventional warfighting capability then future 'little green men' could be killed or captured[47]; of course, knowing this, Russia would not employ them. Pending this, the following dynamic applies:

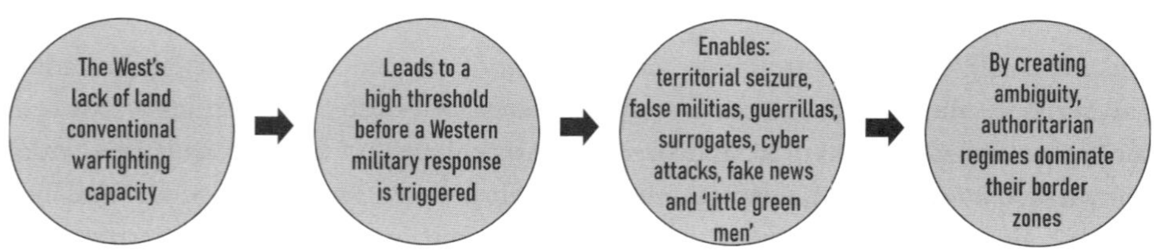

Russia's ability to operate below the threshold of conflict has been identified as representing a novel security challenge that requires specific counter. But there are historical parallels, most obviously Hitler's seizure of the Rhineland, Austria and piecemeal acquisition of Czechoslovakia. Western powers were unwilling to risk war in part because they: *'were hypnotised by Nazi braggadocio and pageantry rather than [by] examination of precise armament output and relative quality of weapons*[48]'. Re-armament was key to finding the resolve to draw a red line on further German expansion, but unfortunately it was not sufficient to deter it.

Some reconstitution of the West's conventional warfighting capability is on-going. The American Army's 2019 military budget had an 88% increase in spending on artillery systems, and placed an emphasis on replenishing their depleted munitions stocks[49]. In contrast, the US Marine Corps are planning to reduce their aircraft and artillery holding (cannon batteries from 21 to 5, though they are fielding more long range rockets) as they focus on what they perceive as the literal challenge in the western Pacific Theatre[50]. Of course, specialising their force structure on a single predicted character of conflict both limits their ability to adapt in contact against an unexpected Chinese threat and their employability elsewhere. The Europeans have identified the need for change, but of course they are not addressing this with the same focus as the Americans; often choosing to invest in bureaucracy, rather than battalions; seen in the creation of EU capabilities that replicate NATO ones[51]. Current NATO plans are challenged because their militaries are so accustomed to guaranteed air support that they do not realise their ground forces relative firepower deficiency.

Publicly the Russian military are confident that they can dislocate Western airpower. Without air support they are unlikely to see NATO's ground formations as a creditable opposition. The authoritarian regimes superiority in long range attack missiles is similarly destabilising. The rocket forces fielded by China, Russia and Iran are not just to wage war against other land forces, they can coerce neighbouring states and can contest regional access. The ports and airfields, that are the traditional gateways into overseas theatres, are easy targets for precision missiles, this has attracted the phrase of anti-access/area denial, or A2/AD.

Of course, this book seeks to focus on tactical land conflict, but it cannot ignore the strategic impact of the operational challenge branded as A2/AD. Western military planners have become fixated upon the ability of their potential adversaries to deny land, air and maritime power access, principally achieved through recent advances in missile and target acquisition technology, leading to the geographic representation of the coverage provided by missiles from bases such as Kaliningrad or one of the newly created island in the South China Sea[52]. While the lethality of these weapon systems has increased, the grammar of peer and near-peer conflict has not significantly changed. It was only in the very final stages of the Second World War that Anglo-America airpower operated over Germany with the relative impunity that has been the norm for the current generation of Western airmen. In the Pacific Theatre, American carrier battlegroups could not maintain continuous air operations, as has been the norm since the Korean War. Instead they manoeuvred to limit the threat posed by land-based airpower. In any future conflict, to survive, modern Western aircraft carriers will have to exploit gaps in their adversaries' all-weather, satellite based, surveillance system and employ weather fronts to mask strike operations. While the focus has been on anti-aircraft and anti-ship missiles, land operations will be challenged by the ability of long-range cruise and ballistic missiles to attack lines of communications and static logistic facilities. Again, advanced missile technology makes this a significant challenge, but it is not a novel one, merely a new manifestation of airpower; whose impact may be as much psychological as physical. Grown used to operating with air superiority, in most cases since 1943, Western armies have neither invested in adequate active, nor have effectively trained for passive, air defence. This, plus assuming that entering a theatre to be the uncontested activity it was in *Pax Americana*, is no longer an option.

By fighting at range, the Americans intend to set up the conditions for successful close combat. However, we can expect Russian forces to exploit their significant firepower edge in the close battle, as they are likely to have the initiative, and it is always easier in warfare to destroy order than sustain it. Meaning that the Russians are likely to impose their way of war in any conflict with NATO's frontline states, as the Red Army initially did against Poland in 1920, and could again do on the same terrain[53]. Even if Western airpower eventually overcomes the opposing air defence, Russian doctrine relies upon rapid penetration of opposing forces, so making them a challenging target for airpower.

Washington's refocused attention on great-power competition recognises that with the end of *Pax Americana* the West currently lacks an effective deterrence to conventional land warfare[54]. Despite this intent, America keeps getting dragged back to every Middle East *crisis de jour*; the region President Trump calls 'sand and death'. This challenges the desire to reset and retrain for peer conflict, and then husband their 'force in being' to deal with the most important and appropriate challenges. The West must avoid Britain's historic mistake of fielding an effective army too late to deter a war, but in sufficient time to survive after comprehensive defeat in the first battles[55]. In any future challenge to America's preeminent position, the initial engagements are likely to be the only ones, as these are likely to redefine the new great power balance. As it is difficult to envisage a protracted conventional conflict between nuclear armed great powers. Russia and China have demonstrated their willingness to fight short sharp wars to redefine power relations, though of course this so far has been limited to resolving their regional aspirations. Simplistically, the West's challenge is to make its armies resilient enough to hold while airpower-led joint warfighting acts at the operational and strategic levels.

In tackling these issues this account will unashamedly stray from the wholly necessary into what its author finds interesting. The narrative's weaving allows events and concepts to be revisited in multiple contexts. At times it may appear polemic in its desire to restore the West's military capability, on battle-proven conventional warfighting lines, with force decisively employed to achieve a defined political purpose. As will now be clear, the author believes that the West no longer has the luxury afforded by the lack of peer competition to follow unsound theories and unsuitable force structures. Finally, this book relies heavily on quotes, hopefully not to be decorative, but to support and enhance the narrative. It recognises the validity of Barbara W. Tuchman's view that *'nothing so comforts the military mind as the maxim of a great, but dead general*[56]*'*. But quotes, plus the considerable use of notes, are designed to ensure that this serving officer sticks to open source material. Of course, no book is ever the last word on any topic; but if it serves any purpose, it is the need to recognise the requirement for further study into 21st century ground warfare.

Chapter 1: Firepower's Role in the Current Character of Land Warfare

'For after all allowances have been made for historical differences, wars still resemble each other more than they resemble any other human activity. All are fought, as Clausewitz insisted, in a special element of danger and fear and confusion. In all, large bodies of men are trying to impose their will on one another by violence; and in all, events occur which are inconceivable in any other field of experience. Of course, the differences brought about between one war and another by social or technological changes are immense[1]*.'*

Professor Michael Howard

This chapter seeks to describe the current character of land warfare and advances some tools as to how it can be best understood. It does not seek to advance a general theory of war; instead it provides a methodology to analyse firepower's role in land warfare. This is necessary, as current Western theory and force employment has marginalised close combat and organic firepower, especially in counter-insurgency operations.

Our best guide to the future is the past: there is almost four millennia of warfare to study[2]. Even though we have only a hundred years to draw upon, this maxim holds true for the study of joint firepower in land warfare. Failing to rely upon past evidence significantly increases the chance of error in predicting the future character of conflict. Therefore, we should be wary of the easy criticism that militaries prepare for the last war. Equally, we should be cautious of seeing future warfare as a linear continuation of current trends. We can be sure that despite counter-insurgency's recent dominance, it is no longer the main driver for most militaries. Nor should we be too eager to see conflicts as having a fixed character. The war in Iraq and Syria against the self-proclaimed Islamic State terrorist organisation, has combined novel asymmetric technology and tactics with an increasingly conventional character of conflict. The Battle of Mosul was the largest land tactical engagement since the 2003 Iraq War and the physical damage inflicted on this city, and the ferocity of urban fighting, have rivalled previous total wars.

The hundred years of joint fires' history provides a variety of characters of conflict. The most dangerous to the current world order is great power conflict, this has had many obituaries. Famously, World War One occurred despite the fervent contemporary belief that major conventional war was inconceivable. Self-evidently this was more about what contemporary minds could conceive, rather than what was actually possible. What four thousand years of warfare shows is that conflict between major powers is rarely premeditated, and that general war is always improbable, until it actually happens. Part of the reason that major conflict is rarely expected is because it often occurs when major powers are drawn into conflict by their allies[3]. The historical comparison to the current American reliance upon the Chinese to manage the North Koreans, is the pre-World War One expectation that Germany would control the

Austro-Hungarians, while the Russians managed the Serbians[4]. Disputed territory can be equally inflammatory; in the 2012 Sino-Japanese crisis, the Americans were concerned that the disputed Senkaku Islands could be a modern version of Sarajevo in 1914[5].

An Information Age Revolution in Warfare?

> *'In the 1990s … We assumed that advances in information, surveillance technology, technical-intelligence collection, automated decision-making tools, and so on were going to make war fast, cheap, efficient, and relatively risk free – that technology would lift the fog of war and make warfare essentially a targeting exercise, in which we gain visibility on enemy organisations and strike those organisations from a safe distance. But that's not true, of course*[6]'.
>
> Major General HR. McMaster

Land warfare's pre-eminent battlefield challenge of surviving firepower is being contested by the view that warfare has been transformed by the information age. This has led to network-centric warfare and similar competing theories identifying that the manipulation of information is now war's decisive element. Proponents of the view that information technology represents a radical break from the past have identified a revolution in military affairs, which is viewed as either radically changing war's character, or its very nature. Presumably these theorists also expect a new type of clock to be able to change the nature of time. More usefully, these theories also identify that the traditional air, sea and land domains have been joined by conflict in the space, cyber and electromagnetic environments.

No one can argue that information technology has not considerably changed modern warfare. But some believers in a revolution in military affairs have been guilty of identifying anything that is novel in the *way* a military does things as transformational, seemingly regardless of whether the actual *outcome* changes[7]. Assessing the information age's actual impact on warfare is challenging; it requires an individual to master both the transforming technology, with its scientific complexity, and the practical breadth and scope of its impact[8]. Of course, we must also recognise that while rapidly changing technology catches the eye, it can blind us to continued dominance of older equipment and techniques. This particularly applies to expensive capital intensive items, such as the Boeing 747 which first flew in 1969. New widebody airliners may come every generation, but it soldiers on. The challenge of replacing expensive platforms particularly applies to the military sector, leading to armoured vehicles being upgraded rather than be replaced, making them multi-generational. Even the most modern militaries have aircraft, ships and tanks significantly older than the personnel that operate them[9]. In contrast to the continuation of legacy bespoke military equipment, the West's opponents have shown the effectiveness of militarising everyday technology: commercial airliners, fishing trawlers, cheap commercial drones and trucks[10].

We should also be cautious of assuming that we are living in an age of accelerating change driven by technological innovation. Of course, the 2010s have produced astonishing advances in technologies such as artificial intelligence (AI), virtual reality and facial recognition that have direct security application. But the iPhone – the smartphone that put a computer in almost everyone's pocket – is almost 15 years old and subsequent versions have been effectively marketing exercises. It is now largely accepted in academia that the slowing down in innovation is linked to the reduced productivity of research; this has been in decline since at least the 1970s[11]. There are more than 20 times as many Americans engaged in R&D today as there were in the 1930s, but their average productivity has declined by a factor of 40. So without a gamechanger to research, such as AI, reducing innovation should be expected. This means that the current unequal change will probably continue:

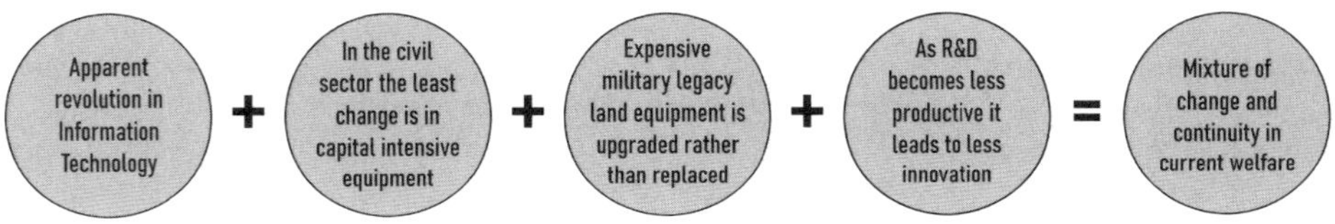

War's complexity is why the Clausewitzian trinity, in its rejection of the mono-causal, is regularly cited as offering the most sophisticated explanation of political conflict. As war's complexity makes it resistant to a single cause of change, this leads to the question as to whether technology on its own is sufficient to create a revolution in military affairs. The historian John Lynn identified that armies made choices within a menu of possibilities consistent with necessity and technology. For Lynn these choices are determined by a military's values, expectations and preconceptions about war[12]. The need for a cautious approach is supported by previous revolutions in military affairs featuring significant political, economic and societal change. It is noteworthy that the French Revolutionary and Napoleonic Wars saw no significant change in military technology, and yet in almost every other respect, land warfare changed. Change in individual technologies (tanks and dive bombers), were less significant in what would be known as the *Blitzkrieg*[13], than the organising of panzer divisions and an effective tactical air force. This force employment was required to deliver a new form of warfare that met the geopolitical imperative of quick, decisive wars that avoided protracted conflict on two fronts. Those opposing the Nazis often had an edge in individual technology, but they had not undertaken a transformation of the state, its military capability and their tactical force employment, that the Germans saw as necessary to achieve their revisionist political outcome. The *Blitzkrieg* years show that technology was less important than a combination of the weaknesses of the opposition, especially in terms of national morale and ethos, and the superior German doctrine, morale, training and leadership.

Historically a Revolution in Military Affairs occurs with the achievement by a military of overwhelming force employment superiority. This is caused by a confluence of a rare strategic advantage, plus a willingness to redefine armed force in a way that makes it difficult for a competitor to imitate without a similar radical change. Militaries and their states are forced to adapt or they will perish. This relationship can be understood:

Despite the lack of historical provenance, continuing the paradigm established in the 1980s with the AirLand Battle doctrine, the American military and their suppliers see maintaining the technological edge as the key to military dominance. They expect robotics, quantum computing and artificial intelligence as offering a Third Offset Strategy – nuclear and precision weapons were the first and second[14]. For this to be so, history shows that this needs to be supported by equally radical change in the other contributors to military capability.

Recent societal changes may prove to have a greater impact than advances in technology, this includes many post-modern Western societies becoming significantly less bellicose. Certainly, the traditional leading military powers – most notably Western Europe and Japan – have a significantly reduced appetite for war. In contrast, in the Developing World, the militarisation of societies has resulted in significantly greater violence and a willingness to employ the most extreme methods in conflict. These include suicide bombs and the militarising of women, children and even the physically and mentally disabled. These societies have also embraced the most extreme forms of peoples' wars and in some cases, have a religious-ideological element largely missing from Europe since the Thirty Years War[15].

Whether these societal developments change war's strategic context is a lively debate, as is its influence on state-on-state conventional warfighting[16]. In 2015 William S Lind expressed the view that the decline of the state – due to a political, moral and social revolution – is changing the character of conflict[17], leading to a return to the pre-Westphalian political order, as this better reflects the post-9/11 wars than the current state-based political paradigm[18]. Others suggest a change in the state's nature. Including a shift from defending the nation's sovereignty and territory, to a 'market state' that seeks to maximise the opportunities for its civil society and citizens within a transnational World[19]. Against this, the recent coalescing of radical Islam into a state structure shows the continuing appeal of this form of organisation. Even in the old states, the rise of populism should make us wary of the view that the state is altering its nature.

Many would opine that the challenges of the 2020s are best suited to the institution that was created in conflict. Certainly, the nation state has led the response to Coronavirus (COVID-19). It is wise to recall Charles Tilly's observation: '*war made* the *state* and the *state made war*[20]'. Leading to the state been defined as the body with a monopoly upon the use of force, which is enshrined in international law[21].

A possible guide to deciding whether a revolution has occurred or not, is to determine if militaries are actually doing new things, as opposed to doing the same things differently. In the commercial sector, the information age has flattened hierarchical organisations and has created wholly original businesses, catering for previously unimagined markets. It is difficult to detect such 'digital disruption' in land forces, whose structures and culture retain most of their traditional form. Digital evangelists may opine that this is due to intransigent militaries being too conservative to reform, this being the modern version of the relatively consistent academic viewpoint that militaries, by their very nature, are resistant to invention and innovation[22]. The alternative perspective is that the current military approach, with adaptation, will suite warfare in the information age, as new technology has not significantly changed war's character, let alone its nature. And, that four millennia of armed conflict have made military structures appropriate to war's nature and able to adapt to its evolving character. This careful approach is not restricted to the military; many businesses which originated in analogue times have successfully adopted digital technology without significantly changing their structure. In management terms, these have kept their existing business model while embracing new technical competences[23]. Most have proved to be sufficiently competitive to avoid being 'Amazoned'[24].

It is difficult, when it comes to warfare, to detect wholly new information age 'products'. One possibility is multi- or all-domain operations, which some in the American military see as the ability to simultaneously operate through and across all domains to overwhelm foes by presenting them with multiple challenges. Information technology certainly enables greater simultaneity of effects across the discrete domains, but it is inaccurate to see these domains as suddenly becoming contested. Control of the electromagnetic spectrum has been disputed since World War One; space was militarised from the first. Warfare in cyberspace[25] is new, but is probably likely to have its greatest impact in the wider national and international security environment than in land warfighting. It is already one of the chief means to coerce – along with social media and more traditional non-lethal tools – in the current *unpeace*[26] between rival countries. As conflict in the cyber and space domains is unprecedented, it is easy to envisage it escalating out of control. Perhaps its most significant impact is to potentially increase the chance of major power rivalry tipping over into open warfare[27]. All-domain operations aspire to deliver a: '*computer-coordinated fight across land, sea, air, space, and cyberspace, with forces from satellites to foot soldiers to submarines sharing battle data at machine-to-machine speed.*, seeking to synchronise whilst preserving decentralised execution based on mission-type orders. However, these aspirations are dependent upon the delivery of technology which is as yet unrealised, even in the most advanced areas of the civil sector. When considered beside the glacial pace of military procurement, these aspirations will almost certainly not be realised before a new doctrinal concept is realised. Multi-Domain Operations can be visualised as the seeking to converge effects across domains and the levels of warfare:

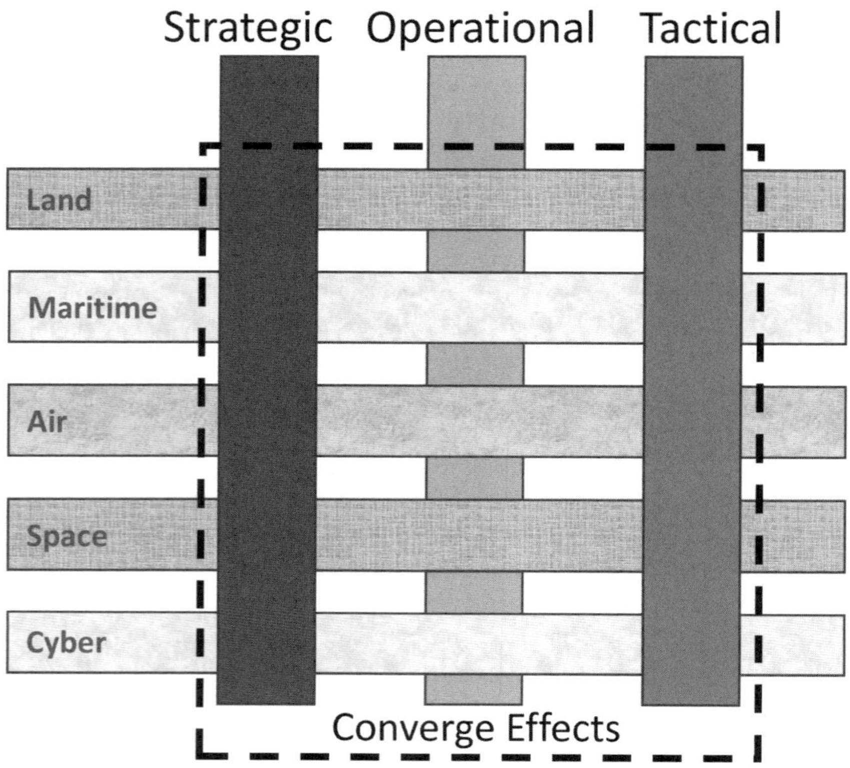

There is of course danger in seeking to mimic leading-edge technology when this is at the expense of the tried and tested. The concepts behind much of the West's military transformation draws on the experience of recent warfighting; this has been largely uncontested in the air and maritime domains, with only limited challenge on the ground. Significant changes to force structure and employment based on this experience probably represents a greater risk than moderate adaptation. Therefore, we need to be wary of the *certainty* of views such as '*future warfare will centre on personnel using remotely controlled unmanned and autonomous equipment*[28]'. There are precedents of armies changing too fast, or by too much. This happened to the British Army in the 1930s, with their 'pure of breed' tank formations, and the American Army in the Pentomic era[29]. There are also naval and air examples, notably the premature abandonment and then restoration of gun technology in both environments[30]. The unifying factor was the propensity for military bureaucracies to overreact to what was seen at the time as revolutionary technology. The same driver has led to established commercial companies over-reaching themselves: Marconi/GEC was the UK's largest engineering company until it precipitously shifted into information technology in the 1980s.

The supporters of a transformation in warfare place the gaining and exploiting of information at the centre of warfighting. In fact, the practitioners of warfare have always been well versed in the need to fight for information, and then turn it into actionable intelligence, whilst simultaneously dealing with the uncertainty that is an enduring feature of conflict[31]. Commanders of previous ages might be surprised with the following 'novel' insight:

> *'The degree of information superiority that one side might be able to achieve over the other is, potentially, what most needs to be measured for effectiveness in the Information Age … gaining knowledge is as much a contest as is manoeuvre or the effective application of firepower in military operations … the superior side achieves "information dominance"[32].'*

Self-evidently there is a great deal of value in improving information and its flow. This includes the great strides made by the dynamic targeting of joint fires systems. But addressing one aspect of warfighting is not a revolution in warfare. We are probably on safe ground in identifying that information flow will have its greatest impact upon militaries through changing the political environment in which they operate. This means that getting the narrative right is crucial to avoid falling foul of what was originally termed the 'CNN effect' – the 24-hours news cycle's ability to rapidly sway opinion, largely through images. This particularly applies to those societies that feel that their military actions should be constrained by legality and legitimacy. Authoritarian regimes, less concerned with their domestic audiences, can seek to exploit these concerns through carefully crafted counter-narrative and disinformation campaigns. Employing information as a weapon is of course as old as conflict. The recent advances in technology merely make this more pervasive. The perceived impact of the media on strategy is not unprecedented; in the 'press wars' that preceded World War One politicians and soldiers were confronted by the emergence of a mass media that catered for their newly literate population. The decision-makers of those years considered that they were uniquely challenged by a plethora of sources of information. These newspapers tended towards extreme views – as they were competing with each other – leading to extreme volatility in public opinion[33].

This book, while recognising change due to the information revolution, will largely argue for land warfare's overall continuity, particularly in force employment and organisation. This recognises that it is problematic to identify a revolution in warfare without any peer level conflict; history's other revolutions have occurred in major inter-state conflict. In its overall conduct, land warfare will continue to be the most conservative of the domains where conflict occurs. This means that the modern system of ground warfare, which is the outcome of the enhanced firepower that has dominated warfare since 1914 will continue, with adaptation to the information age technology. This should be expected, given the tactical and technological maturity of most land firepower systems leads to incremental change, rather than a radical break with the past[34].

The Nature and Character of War

> *'It is extraordinarily hard to predict the conditions of war. For each war it is necessary to work out a particular line for its strategic conduct. Each war is a unique case, demanding the establishment of a particular logic and not the application of some template[35].'*
>
> Aleksandr Svechin, Soviet military scholar

While this has already been touched upon, to ensure that readers understand this book's approach, it is unashamedly Clausewitzian in differentiating between the enduring nature and a changing character of war. War's nature is violent, interactive, and fundamentally political; without any of these elements it is not war. As a believer in the unified nature of war, a sceptical view is taken of those that see significant divisions in warfare beyond those descriptor terms that are needed to aid understanding. As General Carlos Ospina, the architect of the counter-insurgency campaign that defeated the Revolutionary Armed Forces of Colombia, stated when asked about his methods: '*war is war*[36].'

Until recently, on-going operations to contain Jihadism led the leading Western armies to assume a future dominated by counter-insurgency against opponents using irregular or unconventional warfare tactics. A view supported by the apparent rarity post-1945 of conventional inter-state war. The actual quantity of inter-state conflicts does not wholly support this assertion, as there have been at least twenty-five since World War Two[37]. One study concluded that over the last two centuries, inter-state war accounted for 20% of all conflicts[38]. A quick reckoning identifies around a hundred inter-state wars since 1648, showing that the proportion of conventional conflict is consistent, at around a fifth of the total. Therefore, we should be cautious of insights such as '*there is no doubt that irregular warfare campaigns will be the norm rather than the exception in the future*[39]'. Actually, the current numerical dominance of non-inter-state conflict is entirely consistent with the established historical pattern of the Westphalian order.

It is safe to conclude that despite its low proportion in the total number of wars, conventional inter-state conflict, in terms of scale and decisiveness of outcome, will continue fulfilling its historic role, alongside economics, of largely determining geopolitics. That it has a healthy future is demonstrated by what Russia has gained from the recent conflict on the Donbas. Russia has dismembered a rival state and redefined its global position, specifically with the EU and NATO[40]. It has at least paused the further eastward expansion of these two alliances. This follows a policy of what one historian has described as 'strategic relativism', a Machiavellian approach by which Russia gets stronger if its adversaries get weaker[41]. Russia's masking of its involvement and use of novel means to sow dissension and polarisation within alliances, countries and institutions may have caught the eye, but these are ancillary to conventional military power. It follows that we should expect conventional inter-state war to continue in its historic role of addressing political situations that otherwise cannot be resolved. For Chinese leaders this could involve a Bismarckian approach of not shying away from a conflict if that is what they perceive as necessary to rejuvenate their nation[42].

While we may take solace in the declining frequency of conflicts between major powers since 1648, when they do occur they have set a pattern of increasing lethality. In terms of strategic history, what has been unusual post-World War Two has been the absence of direct major power conflict. As an explanation, realists would identify the constraining effect of nuclear weapons, and since 1989 the pre-eminence of America, due to its conventional military superiority. Those of a more liberal disposition might identify progress made towards a better geopolitical structure, that constrains competition between states through international laws and conventions. Other theories include: democratic peace theory ('democracies do not fight democracies'); increased economic inter-connectivity; changed human nature; war's diminishing utility as a vehicle of state policy; and the lingering impact on the major powers of the bloody short century: 1914–45. Simplistically the two views can be described as follows:

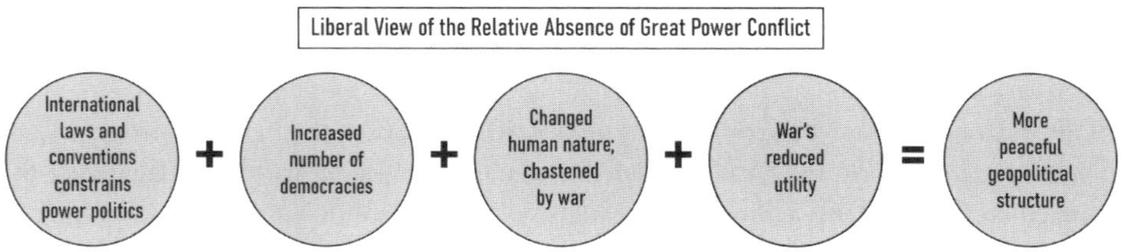

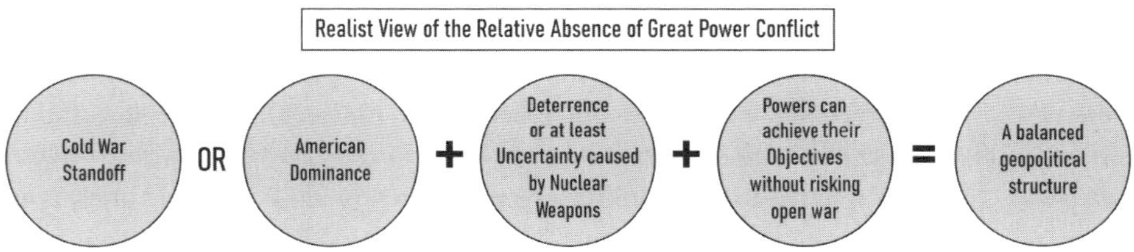

As Bear Braumoeller pointed out in his book *Only the Dead*, the wars of recent decades may have been relatively small in scale, but there is little reason to expect that trend will continue indefinitely[43]. The views of the philosopher Norman Angell caution against too much optimism[44], he saw changing human nature and greater inter-connectivity as key factors in preventing major war, but his ideas preceded World War One by five years. The German sociologist Norbert Elias, argued in 1939 that the Western World had undergone a 'civilising process', driven by the expansion of the absolutist state, in which individuals came to prize restraint and self-control. Emanuel Kant proposed his ideas on perpetual peace immediately before the French Revolutionary and Napoleonic Wars. It might almost be inferred that major wars are most likely when they are conceived to be impossible.

To add to the uncertainty, non-state actors are now capable of inflicting significant damage upon even strong states and can also successfully conduct conventional warfighting. Given the nature of political organisations such as Hezbollah and the self-proclaimed Islamic State, reason or state policy may be losing traction to less rational factors as the cause for conflict[45]. It follows that this book assumes that the strategic context is not that predicted by Steven Pinker of gradually reducing violence[46]; instead, it favours the Colin Gray and Lawrence Freedman interpretation that a downward trend of a few decades means nothing, as history is made in its discontinuities.

Irregular warfare's popularity is due to it enabling an outmatched belligerent to remain in the struggle; insurgencies feature a protracted struggle for the population that challenges an adversary's power, influence, and will. As this takes time, this tests the resolve of militaries, states and their strategic partners[47], making defeating an insurgency problematic and seldom quick, with time usually being seen as on the side of the insurgent. As Henry Kissinger famously identified: *'The guerrilla wins if he does not lose. The conventional army loses if it does not win*[48]. This, plus recent failures, have led to the questioning of the ability of regular forces to expeditiously conduct counter-insurgency[49]. However, recent failures need to be balanced against numerous counter-insurgency successes, though liberal democracies may not approve of some of the methods used[50]. American special operations forces can be largely proud of their successful assistance in low-profile counter-insurgency victories in Asia and Latin America.

The apparent efficacy of irregular warfare has led to the view that it is the stronger form of war, and so it could form the basis of a defence strategy for smaller nations[51]. The Baltic States have prepared for a guerrilla campaign in response to the Russian threat. However, a nation-state relying upon irregular warfare for defence must first surrender its national sovereignty. Without conventional forces, an invader is not effectively opposed until it has occupied a nation's territory. This consideration forced the so-called Islamic State to conduct conventional warfare to defend its 'Caliphate'. The occupying force's subsequent removal involves inflicting upon a nation the horrors of a protracted people's war. As Friedrich Engels, the nineteenth century revolutionary theorist identified: *'never play with insurrection unless you are fully prepared to face the consequences of your play*[52]'. This has resulted in successful insurgencies often being Pyrrhic victories, notably the physical destruction inflicted by the French and American Wars on Indo-China; and the militarisation to expel Napoleon led to Spain's 19th century instability.

A resurgent Russia and a rising China (the Peoples Liberation Army has accounted for 60% of the total increase in defence spending since 1990[53]) means a decline in the American alliances' relative conventional military superiority. These revisionist rivals present America with a geopolitical challenge that has become known as the 'Thucydides' Trap'. This is named after the historian who recorded the 5th-century BCE clash between the rising power of Athens and the established military hegemon Sparta[54]. One study identified that the result of an emerging power confronting a ruling power has historically been war in 12 out of 16 cases over the last 500 years[55]. However, this plays out, what can be deduced with some certainty is that the Jihadist threat is no longer the dominant security concern of America and her allies. Equally redundant is liberal interventionism; current and future American Presidents will probably follow John F. Kennedy's post-Cuban Crisis approach of seeking a World tolerant of diversity of political systems[56], rather than Woodrow Wilson's aim of making it safe for democracy or Clinton's equating of the new world order with American values.

The new American administration is likely to continue President Trump's re-prioritising away from secondary theatres – in particular the Middle East, but also Africa – to concentrate upon Europe, East Asia and the Pacific. Despite proposed troop reductions, Europe remains the priority for American ground forces[57], but this will no doubt be a temporary anomaly. East Asia's growing economic dominance makes it irrelevant if the Middle Kingdom just wants to dominate this region or the entire World; as the latter will follow from the former. This means that East Asia will become the World's cockpit for conflict and no doubt it will follow the European precedent by drawing-in all the major powers. This means that conflict on the other continents are likely to be more common, because they lack the geopolitical importance of East Asia.

A Framework to Understand the Current Character of Conflict

'In broadest definition, political warfare is the employment of all the means at a nation's command, short of war, to achieve its national objectives. Such operations are both overt and covert. They range from such overt actions as political alliances, economic measures (e.g. ERP – the Marshall Plan), and "white" propaganda to such covert operations as clandestine support of "friendly" foreign elements, "black" psychological warfare and even encouragement of underground resistance in hostile states[58].'

George Kennan, Cold War American diplomat

As has been established, the purpose of this book is not to offer a general theory of war, but analysing joint fires' place within land warfare requires an established framework. It is orthodox to see conventional and irregular warfare as being on a linear spectrum; adding a third element adds depth to the interpretation, so aiding the understanding of war's character[59]. The term political warfare was widely used in the Cold War following George F. Kennan's famous invocation of 'measures short of war' that laid out a range of diplomatic, political, economic, and other means of competition within a broad national security strategy[60]. Political warfare is not now in common usage, despite its reintroduction being championed by Benjamin Jensen[61]. General Carter, the British Chief of the Defence Staff, in his 2019 annual lecture, identified that *'the idea of political warfare'* had returned[62]. Concern over its use include whether it meets the violent part of the Clausewitzian definition of war (the others being adversarial and political purpose), as there is a natural desire to restrict warfare to actual fighting, so distinguishing it from all other forms of conflict and competition[63]. Instead of direct fighting, political warfare engages an adversary with: sabotage, espionage, subversion, information operations, psychological warfare, economic pressure, cyber warfare, media operations, criminality and various forms of intimidation. In Clausewitz's own day naval blockades did not lead to immediate casualties, but food shortages had a deadly impact; hence they were seen as part of warfare, despite their lack of direct and immediate lethality[64]. Following this analogy, this study sees political warfare as part of war, even if it is not directly lethal[65].

Most aspects of political warfare are as old as war. One of the most effective information operations was the future Emperor Augustus' undermining of his rival Mark Anthony prior to their decisive clash at Actium. This sought to separate his rival's *power* – the number of legions – from his *authority*, by portraying him as an oriental despot, under Cleopatra's malign influence. A couple of centuries earlier, the Spartan's drove some of their helot slaves into the Achaean League's territory to create a banditry problem that would undermine their neighbours prior to a conventional invasion.

The West's current failure to effectively compete in this medium is identified as an outcome of largely abandoning high-level political warfare operations at the end of the Cold War[66]. In contrast, the Russians continue to excel at political warfare. They specialise in near constant pin-prick attacks – including kidnappings and land snatches – to destabilise their neighbours; these strategies are key to sustaining a series of frozen conflicts[67]. The Chinese anchor their political warfare in Maoist theory; they emphasise public opinion warfare, psychological warfare, and legal warfare; the – 'Three Warfares Doctrine' – which these are defined by the effect they are designed to achieve. The First Warfare attempts to shape public opinion both domestically and internationally. The second attempts to influence foreign decision-makers and how they approach China's policy. The third seeks to shape the legal context for Chinese actions, including building the legal justification and using domestic laws to signal Chinese intentions[68]. Despite being an authoritarian state, the Chinese Communist Party see the key importance of mobilising their public. Central to the Chinese approach to war is nuance, this is captured in the term *Shih,* which is a holistic idea that refers to the advantage gained from the manipulation of context.

In political warfare, apparent willpower and ruthlessness usually trumps actual diplomatic, economic, political or military clout. Technological advances, in particular the internet, have changed the scope and arena of political warfare through allowing information to be stolen in vast quantities and spread anonymously, with much of this disinformation being out-sourced to the victim society. It follows that authoritarian regimes have intrinsic advantages in political warfare that allows them to blur the distinction between peace and war. The challenge for democracies is how to conduct political warfare, and specifically respond to disinformation[69]. This does not mean that the democracies cannot more effectively compete. Israel, which of course faces a clear existential threat, in its public strategy recognises the need for 'campaigns between wars'. These are a series of operations with a unified strategic logic, that are aimed at weakening and reducing the enemy's strength[70]. Underpinning this policy is an open security dialogue with their electorate.

All wars include elements of the conventional, irregular and political forms of warfare. Of the major 20th century conflicts, World War One was probably the most dominated by conventional warfare, with irregular warfare being limited to the Balkans, the Middle East and Africa, though fear of facing a guerrilla campaign – their Franco-Prussian War experience – led to the German atrocities in Belgium and its profound political impact. There was limited political warfare; but it could have significant effect, such as the German transportation of Vladimir Lenin home to Russia, and the Anglo-French winning narrative that facilitated American participation in the conflict[71]. World War Two had more peoples' wars, and widespread use of special operations forces and partisans. Political warfare was instrumental in setting the conditions for the Blitzkrieg's dramatic success. As the war progressed, as Eric Hobsbawm observed in Age of Extremes[72], it became effectively a struggle between three secular religions: fascism, communism and liberal democracy, all engaged in a battle of ideas. Subsequent conflict has seen a growth in political warfare. Irregular warfare proliferated with the end of the colonial empires and has featured in the conflicts following the collapse of European communism; this has been interspersed with much more decisive conventional operations. Below is an attempt to diagrammatically represent the overlapping nature of the three forms of warfare. A conflict's position relative to these three circles identifies which form of warfare had the greatest impact upon its character of conflict.

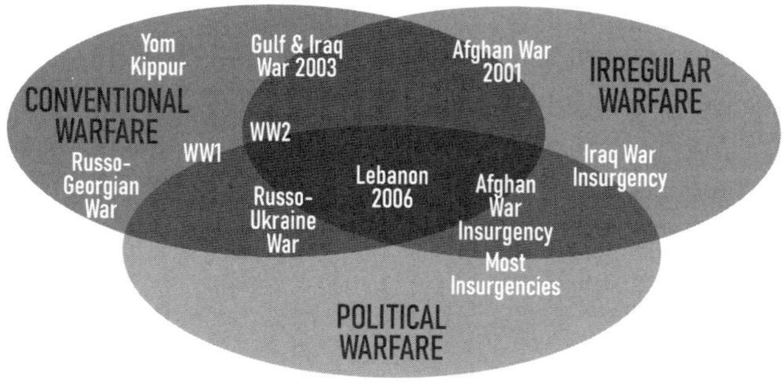

In this analysis, the Hezbollah resistance to the Israelis in Lebanon in 2006 is identified as achieving an equal weighting in all three forms of warfare. In addition to their usual irregular and political warfare, Hezbollah recognised that they could achieve an asymmetrical advantage through confronting Israeli forces with conventional tactics; this achieved surprise and exploited the Israelis' neglect of combined arms training. Their approach has been identified as something new[73], attracting the term 'hybrid warfare'. Hezbollah achieved a character of conflict that initially confounded the Israelis; their employment of high technology weapons and some novel tactics was impressive, but this was not a new form of warfare.

However, the term 'hybrid warfare' now has standing; it has been joined by shadow, gray zone[74], ambiguous and 'sub-threshold' conflict. All of which are described as employing seemingly novel techniques, when most are established political warfare tools. The following techniques are attributed as fitting into the space between peace and war:

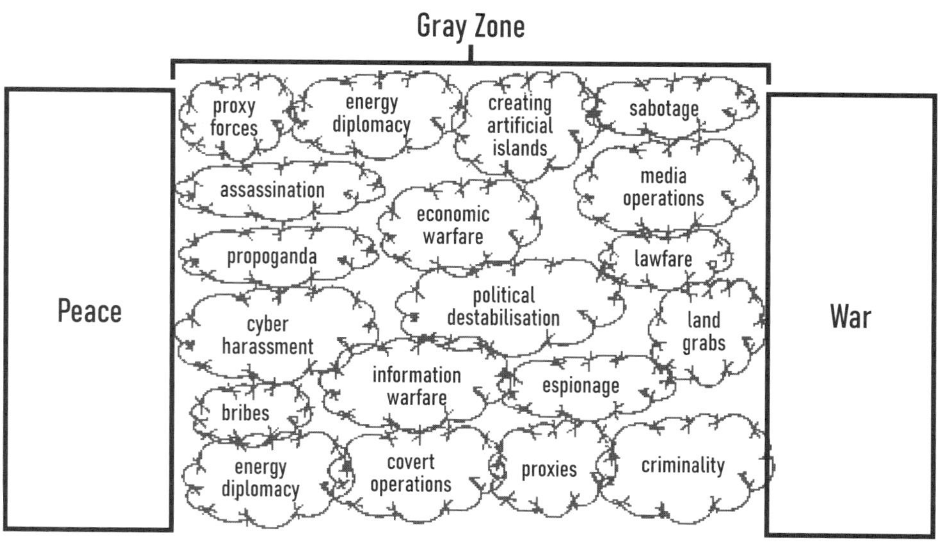

The main issue with these theories is their acceptance of a binary distinction between peace and war. Actual experience shows that belligerents can repeatedly cross into fighting before retreating from lethal means, and that war can have a spectrum of variation in intensity, capability and attribution. Furthermore, almost all the gray zone methods are equally usable in war. Certainly, the West's adversaries do not recognise this crisp division. One of Russia's leading theorists, Yevgeny Messner opined: '*We must stop thinking that war is when people fight, and peace when they are not fighting. You can be in war without fighting*[75]'. The Russians use a variety of phrases for their balancing of conventional, irregular and political warfare, most frequently 'New Generation Warfare'. In the West the colloquialism 'Gerasimovism', after the Russian Chief of the General Staff of the Russian Federation, has become popular[76]. Much of Russia's capability is exaggerated by their propaganda, but they have demonstrated a greater ability than NATO to synergise conventional, irregular and political capabilities, allowing them to exploit the West's false distinction between peace and war, and exploiting this to ensure they do not break the threshold that automatically triggers a response.

Tailoring state or non-state actions to remain below the detection and response threshold of an opponent is considered a characteristic of gray zone conflict. This is done through the careful calibration of military activity to create an environment which encourages alliances and individual states to avoid making an unpalatable response to aggression. This recognises that the burden of decision-making usually rests with the victim and not the aggressor. Echoing the *realpolitik* of his age, Clausewitz identified that the defender who resists an invading force is the initiator of conflict. Powerful states have always attempted to achieve their objective while operating below the threshold that provokes an armed response. In Clausewitz's time this included the largely peaceful partition of Poland by Prussia, Austria and Russia. An act that reflected Thucydides' Melian Dialogue: '*the strong do what they can and the weak suffer what they must*'[77]. The Russians may have followed a strategy of ambiguity, but the Ukrainians were clear that it was the threat of overwhelming conventional force that prevented them from taking robust measures to counter 'little green men'.

Advocates of seeing hybrid or gray zone conflict as a new form of conflict identify ambiguity as a novel feature; certainly, it is in terms of scale – the Russians have weaponised denial. The desire for vagueness over direct Russian involvement in the Ukraine may have been a factor in more easily deniable artillery being used for fire support rather than the Russian Air Force. Though practically this also robbed NATO of the possibility of enforcing a 'no-fly zone'. None of this ambiguity is new – proxies were a distinct feature of the Cold War, starting with the Greek Civil War in 1946[78]. A few years later, disguised Russian pilots clashed with American pilots in the Korean War.

In contrast to Russia obfuscation, there can be nothing more obvious than constructing artificial islands in the South China Sea; but again, the Chinese ensured that this did not provoke a direct response[79], mainly achieved by an incremental approach. The aim of this steady cumulative pressure was to force an opponent to recognise a *fait accompli.* Given the stakes (ultimately the threat of nuclear conflict), the Cold War saw considerable use of the incremental approach in geopolitics. This was described by Thomas Schelling in his 1967 Arms and Influence, and attracted the term 'salami slicing'[80].

The authoritarian state's key advantage is that they know they are in the midst of inter-state competition; in the same way that the West knew it was in an existential struggle during the Cold War. Current geopolitics prevent such clarity. In addition, Western countries make themselves vulnerable to authoritarian regimes employing political warfare by creating an environment around war that avoids confronting the *plain* truth. This can be seen in the use of military euphemisms that rarely serve clarity of understanding and they encourage ethical blindness[81]. The Vietnam War was the watershed for democracies in their relationship with their electorates through the fourth estate. Currently, amongst the democracies, only Israel, and to a lesser extent India, maintain a clear public dialogue on defence (which can also be seen as another euphemism), and in particular the offensive use of force.

If this study rejects the various categories of hybrid warfare, it must also cast off the American compound warfare. This is a combination of conventional and irregular or counter-guerrilla warfare, so it limits itself by failing to fully examine the role of political warfare[82]. The apolitical nature of Western armies encourages soldiers to restrict themselves to purely military considerations, despite this being at odds with war's political character. The individual American Army officer is thoroughly educated in Clausewitzian theory, and yet in application their officer corps can be profoundly uncomfortable with war's non-military aspects[83]. This is compounded by the continuing legacy of General MacArthur's discredited creed that politicians should state their long-term goals and then 'get out of the way'. This approach is particularly short-sighted in addressing counter-insurgencies, as these conflicts can be more political than military[84]. This results in officers being educated in doctrine that fails to address the first order issues of the politico–strategic context; leading officers into concentrating upon second order issues at the military–operational level[85]. Much of the academic criticism of the West's current counter-insurgency doctrine centres upon failing to address the dominance of politics in this character of conflict[86].

In addition to understanding the balance between conventional, irregular and political warfare, our analytic framework needs to recognise the importance of the conflict's political purpose in determining the character of conflict. Clausewitz's 1827 realisation that the implication of war being an act of policy meant that a more limited type of conflict was equally valid[87]. Previously he assumed all wars were Napoleonic in scope: annihilating the enemy through decisive battle, then dictating the peace. The alternative was a more calibrated approach, to achieve limited political, social, economic, or psychological objectives, with the outcome being settled by genuine negotiation. Of course, these are theoretical poles, and most real wars occur between these two extremes. In addition, to identifying the mechanism by which a conflict's character can change, such as the adoption of guerrilla tactics due to conventional defeat – he also identified that its political purpose can change. This can either be through rational choice, or in response to war's self-reinforcing dynamic towards escalation. Evidenced by the escalation in the peace terms deemed acceptable by the Great War's combatants, driven by the death toll.

The problem with compartmentalising war is that it obscures the inter-dependencies. In the case of Russia's operations in Ukraine it was its overwhelming superiority of conventional force that was key. Of course, dividing-up war can assist understanding, but it fails when despite significant intellectual effort, there has been no agreed conclusion as to which historic and ongoing conflicts fit into this new category between peace and war. It follows that this work rejects this sub-division of war. Instead its sees conflict as a continuum between war and peace, with conflict's character largely being determined by its mix of conventional, irregular and political warfare, modified by its political purpose.

War Without Land Warfighting

'More than most other forms of military power, politicians find airpower easy to manipulate, to employ or withhold, in the hope of achieving nicely measured political effects[88]*.'*

Eliot A. Cohen, Political Scientist

Standoff precision attack, predominantly delivered by airpower, against an opponent with limited capacity to directly retaliate, is obviously militarily and politically attractive; especially when it promises to be decisive through directly targeting an opponent's leadership and so convincing them to acquiesce with a war's political objective. Unfortunately, while airpower provides a tempting option it, alone, it cannot achieve a war's political objective when this is beyond the limited coercion ('gun boat diplomacy') that is the forte of both air and maritime power[89]. Perhaps the most telling criticism of this approach is David Betz's assertion that it is another deviation from the historically successful Western way in war. It replaces closing with the enemy to achieve a decisive battle that leads to peace, with the more drawn-out Eastern approach, with combat being largely conducted at distance[90]. These campaigns become protracted because the promised decapitation by airpower using precision technology has consistently failed, as it did on six occasions in between the end of the Cold War and 2003[91].

Despite both theoretical and practical criticism, the political attractiveness of standoff warfighting has led to a diminished role for Western ground forces. While not immediately decisive, airpower dominated the Gulf War of 1990–91, NATO's interventions in the Wars of Yugoslav Secession and the conventional phases of the Afghanistan and Iraq Wars. The need to translate military success into peace then led to the occupation of these territories. In the case of Afghanistan and Iraq this led to unsuccessful counter-insurgencies and the further questioning of the usability, and even the utility, of Western land forces.

There is longevity in this Western desire for a form of warfare in which they largely provide the much safer combat enablers, while avoiding the chancier business of ground warfare. President Dwight D. Eisenhower in the 'New Look' policy identified that this would be the basis for America's military's relationship with its allies[92]. This was the initial approach in America's involvement in Vietnam; it is a methodology associated with powers seeking to maintain the *status quo,* rather than becoming more powerful through the decisive employment of military force. As a result, Presidents Eisenhower, Nixon and Obama have all been identified with a policy of *'retrenchment, through limiting America's ground commitment*[93]'. All three having taken office during or after America's involvement in significant land combat: Korea, Vietnam and the post-9/11 Wars. The same rationale also applied to President Trump, who was ahead of his national security establishment in his desire to disengage from a series of operations and deployments that fix America's forces in secondary theatres.

The key advantage of employing aerial firepower without ground forces is that it significantly reduces the probability of own casualties; its second advantage is that firepower is not fully committed when it engages the enemy. At war's tactical level, firepower is easily manoeuvred around the battlefield, unlike forces committed to the direct fire battle. In the military-strategic space, it is politically easier to disengage without 'boots on the ground', especially if these are not engaged in close combat. Thirdly, for some regimes, firepower also has greater deniability; avoiding responsibility is significantly more challenging with ground forces committed to close combat.

Solely employing airpower is the lowest level of overt military commitment in an intervention. If supporting allied forces on the ground, ideally this should be against a set of targets away from the front line to avoid fratricide. While this can constrain its effectiveness, the mere presence of airpower will hinder the opposition and provide moral support to allies. The deployment of joint fires terminal controllers and fires staff integrated into the allied ground forces' command structure makes aerial fire support to the close battle significantly more effective. This is the next level of commitment, with troops on the ground, but largely avoiding close combat. The next escalation is the deployment of artillery, a step taken by the Americans, French and Russians in operations against the Islamic State and in the recent Syrian Civil War. As well as becoming involved in combat, ground forces can also provide training support. When combined with re-equipment, this can significantly improve an ally's military capability. The hierarchy of political commitment and military effect can be understood as follows:

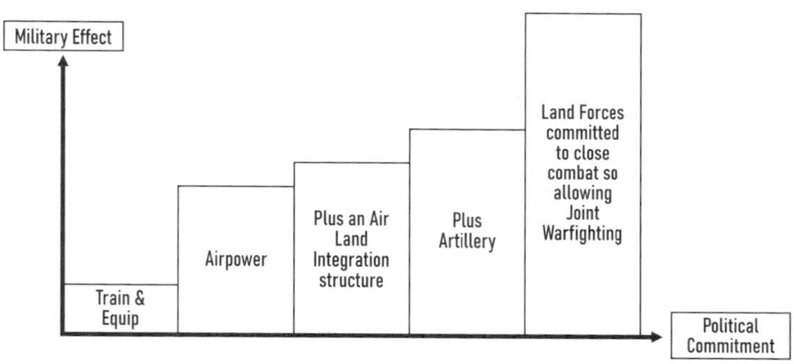

Relying upon indigenous land forces significantly restricts a major power's influence on a conflict's political outcome. In Afghanistan in 2001, America's allies the Northern Alliance, having overthrown the Taliban regime, were unwilling to risk the casualties required to destroy al Qaeda. As this was America's war aim, this led to the belated deployment of American ground forces. CIA Director George Tenet noted that:

> *'They had put their fate in the hands of the Afghan tribals, who were going to act at a time, place and pace of their own choosing. They had their own issues, endgames, ambitions and internal power play … That was the price of admission when it was decided at the front end that the tribals were going to do the bulk of the ground fighting and not the US military'*[94].

Furthermore, creating an indigenous land force through the arming of warlords led to a rival ground forces, that subsequently undermined the chances of a stable Afghanistan. The same happened in Libya. In Syria, America has largely been unable to control the forces that it has expensively armed and supported: the Syrian Democratic Forces, the Rojava-based anti-Isis coalition dominated by Kurdish fighters and the rebel groups fighting with Turkey in

Afrin. America may have achieved its objective of defeating the so-called Islamic State and in conducting counterterrorism operations against al Qaeda; but Turkey, Iran and Russia, through employing significant ground forces, have determined the endgame of the Syrian Civil War.

The primacy of land power in shaping the post-conflict settlement is an enduring historical lesson; it was the rationale that determined the political settlement after World War Two. As General Secretary Joseph Stalin explained in his conversation with Yugoslavian Communist Milovan Djilas: '*This war is not as in the past; whoever occupies a territory also imposes upon it his own social system … as far as his army can reach*[95]'. It was the Red Army's occupation of Eastern Europe that determined the post-World War Two political settlement, not Western maritime power airpower, even with a monopoly of atomic weapons. Land power as the final arbiter of war's political outcome is one of Rear Admiral J.C. Wylie's four guiding strategic principles:

> '*The ultimate determinant in war is a man on the scene with a gun. This man is the final power in war. He is control, he determines who wins. There are those who would dispute this as an absolute, but it is my belief that while other means may critically influence war today, after whatever devastation and destruction may be inflicted on an enemy, if the strategist is forced to strive for final and ultimate control, he must establish, or must present as an inevitable prospect, a man on the scene with a gun. This is the Soldier*[96].'

As only land power can impose control upon an opposing territory it will always be employed when a truly decisive political outcome is required. Which is not the same as assuming that land power is a suitable tool for all security challenges, regardless of the political temptation to use it. Armies must balance ensuring that they are usable across a spectrum of possible security challenges, with maintaining their conventional warfighting capability to settle geopolitical challenges. For major powers the latter must have primacy, but adroitly using ground forces in tasks such as capacity building may assist with the avoidance of conventional war.

So, in conclusion, not all security challenges are of the same importance. The most important ones redefine global power relationships. A political purpose that important will almost inevitably involve the taking and holding of ground, by land forces conducting conventional warfighting. America and her allies face two major security challenges that will redefine geopolitics. The rise of China and its desire for dominance within its historic sphere of influence (a Chinese Monroe Doctrine?); and a resurgent Russia aiming to overturn the post-Cold War settlement. The question is determining how land fighting power will assist with addressing these challenges, whilst continuing to try and counter Islamic Jihadism.

Joint Firepower in Land Conventional Warfare

> '*The tendency towards under-rating fire-power … has marked every peace interval in modern military history*[97].'
>
> Liddell Hart

Gil Eliot identifies in his book 'The Twentieth Century Book of the Dead' that artillery was the twentieth century's biggest killer and dominated World War Two even more than World War One[98]. Shells and bombs inflicted 58% of British casualties on the Western Front in World War One, and in World War Two's North African desert the percentage rose to 75%. When the fighting shifted to Europe and close country, this percentage slightly reduced. Soviet artillery inflicted approximately 70% of the German Army's casualties on the Eastern Front. The Soviets lost 51% of their casualties to artillery and mortar fire, this was despite the German Army's relative lack of investment in indirect fire. Artillery inflicted a higher percentage of casualties in World War One than World War Two on American forces. This was due to them facing the full weight of Imperial German artillery in 1918 with limited active and tactically rudimentary passive counters. In Korea, nearly 60% of Americans killed in action fell to blast or fragments from artillery or mortar shells. However, militaries have limited institutional memory, leading to firepower's historic role of inflicting the most casualties being questioned. The West's recent experience of counter-insurgency has led to the *perception* that the Improvised Explosive Device is the greatest killer on the modern battlefield. However, there can be no doubt that whenever effective artillery is fielded, it is the big killer, and this has been the case since the widespread use of modern artillery in the Russo-Japanese War[99]. This remains the case, with between 70–80% of casualties attributed to firepower in the Russo-Ukraine War. In this, as with most conflicts, the proportion increases in static combat, and reduces when the fighting becomes mobile.

It is therefore safe to conclude that, as firepower has increased its ability to inflict casualties throughout the joint fire century, there are no reasons to suppose this trend will not continue. Hence, the Russians expect artillery's dominance to endure[100]. Certainly, this is the view of the American Army's Futures Command; their wargames attribute 82% of kills to artillery, 12% to manoeuvre forces and 6% to air and aviation. Firepower's ability to both aid and hinder manoeuvre has also proportionately increased in the last few decades. Its greater relative combat power is the result of its superior rate of technological development when compared to manoeuvre forces, who are constrained by limitations of cross-country movement and line of sight target engagement.

As well as inflicting casualties, firepower delivers the suppression that enables manoeuvre forces to close with and force the opposition to capitulate. The role of the 'stand-up fight' and the importance of forcing capitulations has already been established as crucial in the process of turning military success into a long term political outcome. History shows that adequate suppressive firepower makes possible battlefield manoeuvre, but the view that the assembling of a large park of artillery reduces the tempo of military operations is an enduring proposition. As Clausewitz identifies[101]:

> *'An excess of artillery is bound to cause operations to partake more and more of a defensive and passive character … A shortage of artillery will, on the contrary, enable us to let the offensive, mobility and manoeuvring predominate*[102]'.

One strand of this belief is that there is negative correlation between firepower and the moral factors that underpin successful offensive operations; this is not borne out in actual conflict.

In the American Civil War, the Army of the Potomac had three guns per thousand men; the opposing Confederates often had a significantly higher proportion. Despite this, the Confederate forces were more agile and aggressive. The more mobile Western Theatre employed fewer guns. The Union commander General Sherman identified that this was a reaction to his veteran troops having a reduced need for artillery to provide moral support. An alternative explanation is that the West had a different character of conflict, particularly its logistic challenge[103]. Britain's General Haig stated, in the initial stages of World War One, that an over-reliance on artillery would cause a loss of morale, surprise and initiative[104]. This was before he oversaw the creation of arguably the War's most effective artillery arm. World War One followed the historic trend of successful militaries finishing the conflict with a significantly larger artillery park. Without the imperative of conflict, armies revert to the traditional peacetime undervaluing of the role of firepower. This leads to politically acceptable reductions in artillery and mortar force structures, and significant savings in munitions stockpiles.

Failing to assemble sufficient artillery and mortars, together their ammunition, has on occasion led to Western armies conducting conventional warfighting with entirely inadequate organic firepower. The Americans in the South West Pacific in 1942, and in Afghanistan in 2002, provide examples of fighting wholly without artillery. This occurred through the belief that assembling sufficient materiel would thwart an otherwise 'sound' military undertaking, and they rationalised this approach by the belief that aerial firepower would provide an adequate substitute. More common is the initial employment of inadequate organic fire support; to be corrected following a reminder of the realities of war. This was the case in the 1982 Falklands War's first battle at Goose Green. Subsequently, battalion attacks were sequenced and timed to assemble sufficient artillery, mortars and ammunition.

Militaries schooled in a Marxist-Leninist derived approach to warfare, with its attendant prescriptive firepower norms, tend to avoid being militarily unsound. This 'scientific' schooling leads to an understanding of the complementary relationship between manoeuvre and firepower[105]. For example, the Soviet response to NATO's fielding of anti-tank guided missiles was not to increase their number of tanks; instead, they increased their holdings of mortars and artillery by 40% between 1971 and 1985[106]. They recognised that the missiles' longer ranges meant that more possible firing points needed to be suppressed. Most of this additional firepower was armoured artillery, designed to accompany the break-through and exploitation force through the greater depth of NATO's anti-tank defence. Despite this schooling, the Russians employed inadequate quantities of firepower in the First Chechen War; they have more than compensated in their subsequent wars.

Joint Firepower in Irregular Warfare

'[The Viet Cong attempted to] 'surprise the Americans and separate them from their firepower and the battle becomes an even match [both restricted to direct fire weapons][107].'

General Scales

The heyday of insurgency was the end of the European colonial empires, yet back then irregular warfare lacked the prominence it now has. This stems from the current users of such tactics being, at least until the last few years, *the* major security threat to the World's dominant military power. This period has passed, but any future inter-state conventional conflict is likely to include irregular warfare through their proxies and special operations forces. Alternatively, given the risks of conventional warfare, the major powers might determine that a character of conflict that mixes political and irregular warfare is the correct means of pursuing their political objectives. Avoiding the risks of conventional warfare will particularly appeal to those educated in the Chinese military tradition, which favours avoiding defeat over the chance of achieving an overwhelming and potentially destabilising victory. As the concept of *shih*, predicts that the strategic configuration of power inherent in a system will endure[108].

Firepower may have a lesser role in counter-insurgency than conventional war, but some attrition will always be required. If it were otherwise then it would not be warfare and it could be solely conducted by civilian agencies. For the insurgent, inflicting defeat on government forces may not always be their primary tactical objective, but ultimately, they have to physically replace them and become the state's new armed force.

Irregular warfare tactics seek to exploit physical and human terrain to avoid becoming a viable target. This means that in war amongst the people, employing firepower can result in collateral damage, either through accident or by the deliberate actions of the insurgents. As the prize is the allegiance of the people, collateral damage incidents will directly affect campaign success. In contrast, the killing of non-combatants and the destruction of non-military property may be regrettable in conventional warfare, but it is usually not vital to the successful conduct of military operations. Whatever the character of conflict, incidents of collateral damage can undermine the campaign's narrative and influence public support in the intervening troops' homeland and in the wider global community. The significance of collateral damage varies considerably between liberal-democracies and authoritarian states. This leads to the employment of firepower being at the heart of Western concerns over the efficacy, legality and legitimacy of their conduct of counter-insurgency operations[109]. In contrast, authoritarian regimes have repeatedly shown their willingness to use firepower to impose obedience through terror[110].

All counter-insurgencies try to separate the insurgents from the people. The distinction between counter-insurgency doctrines hinges on whether this is mainly done by defeating the insurgent, or by gaining the allegiance of the people through inducements. Authoritarian regimes usually focus on employing combat power against the opposing combatants and then using it to impose their control over the population. An approach that echoes the West's colonial conflicts; CE Callwell, the doyen of Victorian small war theory, identified the use or threat of violence as necessary to gain moral ascendency over an opponent[111]. Defeat can cause a belligerent to lose his standing; this can be decisive in the competition for the people's loyalty[112]. The key is to exploit a successful battle or battles' sphere of influence by consolidating control over the people. The wily insurgent can use time and space to recover, as Mao famously did in the Long March to Jiangxi province.

Unless employed by a regime willing to use terror as a weapon of war, firepower needs to be carefully calibrated to avoid it reinforcing an insurgency's standing. The historian Victor

Davis Hanson identified the challenge of balancing campaign legitimacy with the need to visibly inflict defeat on the insurgency:

> *'How the military is to reconcile the irreconcilable facts of modern liberal concern for the mayhem of war with the need to demonstrate manifestly the defeat of an adversary, I am not altogether sure'*[113].

Western armies have consistently misused firepower in their counter-insurgent tactics by incorrectly focussing on its ability to inflict casualties. Even more so than in conventional warfare, firepower needs to combine with manoeuvre; employing it on its own is usually counter-productive. Manoeuvre in irregular warfare is infantry based (regardless of their means of transportation), with these often reinforced with embedded military specialists, civilian agencies and with host nation support. Once security is established, these agencies can proceed with: governance reform, improvements to public services, physical reconstruction, economic development and social amelioration.

The successful Malayan Emergency and the Vietnam War provide ready comparators of the use of firepower. This is not to equate the challenge of the two conflicts, as regardless of tactics, the desired political end state in the Vietnam War was probably not achievable, as this was driven by the perceived requirements of US domestic and foreign policy[114], while the strength of the communist opposition overmatched the ways and means that America was prepared to employ[115]. In the Malayan Emergency firepower was usually part of a combined arms team tasked with separating the insurgent from the people. Experience showed this was most effectively done by the highly visible defeat of communist guerrillas in a given area. The attrition inflicted was usually secondary to the impact on insurgent morale and their credibility as a replacement government. Firepower in other circumstances, regardless of the attrition achieved, was often irrelevant to winning the battle for the people. This British force employment in the Malaysian Emergency largely followed this relationship:

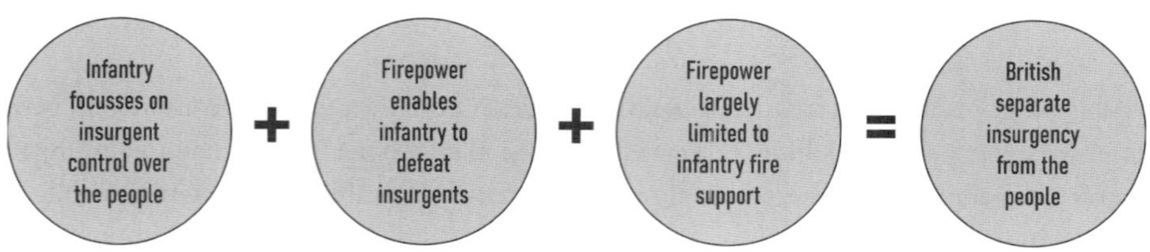

In comparison, American firepower in Vietnam rarely supported ground manoeuvre. Much of it was relatively indiscriminately employed on prophylactic harassing and interdiction fire missions. At the time the Americans had an unshakable belief in their way of war with its emphasis on mobility and firepower; later General Scales identified that: *'no amount of technology or firepower will make secure a region unless the support of the population has been gained*[116].' True to their doctrine, American manoeuvre forces attempted to come to grips with the North Vietnamese and Viet Cong through *search and destroy* missions. They would have had a superior chance of bringing their opponents to decisive battle through challenging the insurgent's grip on the villages. This follows the principle successively relearnt by navies in the World Wars that defending merchant convoys is a more effective way of engaging an opponent than searching the oceans.

Following the overwhelming defeat of the Tet offensive, and the transition to more effective counter-insurgency tactics, the Vietnam War may have become more winnable from a military perspective. However, this offensive demonstrated to the American people the communist's ascendency through attacking targets in zones previously considered to be under firm government control. This provoked even more indiscriminate use of firepower by the Americans and South Vietnamese, including the destruction of the ancient city of Hue. This reinforced the belief in a significant proportion of the American people that the war was either unwinnable or could only be won at price they were unwilling to pay[117]. The American force employment in the Vietnam War largely followed this relationship:

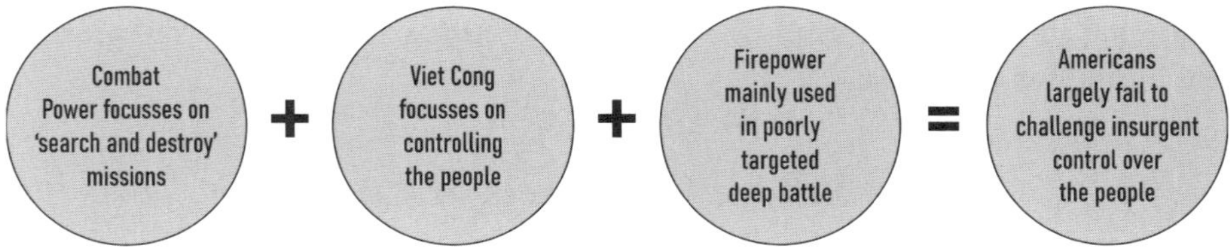

Airpower has significantly increased regular force's combat power relative to the insurgents. Its importance has been evident from the first. American airpower in Nicaragua, during the 1927–33 insurgency, was credited with the defeat of insurgents when they tried to employ regular warfare tactics[118]. This is at odds with the views of Christopher A. Lawrence, who stated that: '*I am struggling to think of a single insurgency that was defeated by airpower, primarily defeated by airpower, or even seriously undermined by airpower*[119]'. He is of course narrowly correct, but this fails to identify airpower's key ability of preventing an insurgency from progressing to conventional warfighting. The latter is the necessary step before becoming the government, as this provides the means to take and hold ground, specifically state apparatus[120]. When this transition is attempted in the wrong circumstances, firepower is able to inflict a severe defeat. At the tactical level, aerial firepower is also key in preventing troops dispersed on counter-insurgency operations from being vulnerable to being defeated in detail. Plus, of course, it enables ground forces to exploit the third dimension in both manoeuvre and logistics. Finally, not being fixed defending vulnerable land lines of communications releases considerable ground combat power from mundane security tasks.

Precision terminally-guided munitions, in concert with special operations forces and a more sophisticated targeting process, have resuscitated the view that firepower's attrition can be decisively employed separate from manoeuvre. This technology and techniques make the targeted killing of the insurgency leadership seem more legitimate, especially if it is equated to defeating terrorism. There may be doubts of the effectiveness of decapitating terrorist leadership, but it tends to be a popular political option. It promises the pursuit of justice and reassures populations that their governments are acting. Societies who have suffered from terrorism tend to support the employment of lethal force when the arrest and trial of terrorist leaders is impractical. Furthermore, as special operation forces largely conduct these attacks, they come with the advantage for Western democracies of reduced scrutiny[121].

Employed in this fashion, special operations forces exhibit the characteristics of firepower rather than conventional ground forces. Strike teams are inserted, have an effect (usually kill or capture), and then extract. Their limited time on the ground means that they do not have the psychological effect that conventional ground manoeuvre exerts upon an opponent and the people by their persistent presence. Despite mixed results, 'decapitation strategies' are now a central tenet of Western counter-insurgency and counter-terrorism[122]'. The Israelis probably remain the leading state user, with some 2,700 targeted killings of their enemies[123]. Of course, this is dwarfed by insurgencies, who often systematically target 'enemies of the people'. Ho Chi Minh's National Liberation Front carried out at least 36,000 assassinations during their struggle.

Despite this new faith in the primacy of 'decapitation strategies', historical examples of the defeat of guerrilla movements show the requirement for a long-term, multi-faceted approach, aiming at inflicting a 'creeping death'[124], with firepower being a key element in the separation of the insurgent from the people.

Likely Future Characters of Conflict?

'Victory smiles upon those who anticipate the changes in the character of war, not upon those who wait to adapt themselves after the changes occur [125]*.'*

Giulio Douhet

Given the end of *Pax America,* competition between the major powers will no doubt have a healthy future. Much of this will probably remain below the threshold of open conflict, with relatively anonymous, or at least deniable, cyber-attacks being the most popular weapon. However, 21st century nations will participate in ground conflict when their political need – whether rationally, irrationally or non-rationally determined – overcomes its price. As ground conflict is the most casualty intensive character of conflict, the major brake on the Russians and Chinese may well be their sensitivity to fatalities. This follows from the former's declining life expectancy and the impact of the latter's one child policy.

Some senior military personnel tend to see this great power rivalry as a return to familiar Cold War practices, but the character of warfighting moves on, and *'no man steps in the same river twice, because it is not the same river or the same man*[126]'. It is difficult to envisage future conventional conflict that does not have significant elements of irregular and political warfare. We must also recognise that there has been a thirty year hiatus since preparing for peer-on-peer conventional conflict has dominated most Western soldiers' education. This challenge is compounded by a failure to systematically record Cold War warfighting practices in formats that could educate future generations. As the Russians recognise: *'What is completely forgotten is brand new'*[127].

As conventional warfare will remain the most decisive form of conflict most major armies will primarily prepare for this character of conflict. The increased lethality of irregular tactics probably represents a permanent shift in warfare; consequently, militaries will not turn their backs on the doctrine and practice of irregular warfare, as the American Army did after the Vietnam War[128]. However, the outcome of optimising for conventional conflict means that armies will have to accept that an effective counter-insurgency capability may have to evolve in conflict. This may result in early reverses, but this should be seen as an acceptable risk given irregular warfare's lack of immediate decisiveness. The key task being to get the strategy right, recognising that successful tactics can be developed in contact.

In preserving their counter-insurgency expertise there is a danger that this could undermine the restoration of conventional warfighting capability; this is compounded by a range of factors that make many Western militaries institutionally resistant to restoring conventional capability. Following the post-Cold War peace dividend Western armies lack both front line strength and reserves to absorb casualties; allied with this is a perception that their societies are intolerant of casualties. In addition, many senior officers continue to see conventional peer-on-peer land warfare as a feature of the previous industrial age, whose character is at odds with their personal operational experience; in which the application of force has been characterised by being: own- and enemy-casualty averse; stymied by legality and legitimacy concerns; and intensely politically aware. All of these characteristics are heightened by constant media scrutiny; this contributes to a risk-averse culture, which practically translates into a reluctance to employ firepower. In particular, this applies to non-precision munitions, employed using offensive rules of engagement, in the hurly-burly of land close combat. This is exactly the capability required for success in conventional conflict. A legacy of decades of peace-support and counter-insurgency operations also hinders innovation in conventional warfare; as what can be imagined is conditioned by what individuals already know[129]. The outcome is that Western militaries may be ill-prepared for a peer conflict. Historically failing to prepare for the correct character of conflict has led to even highly professional armies being uncompetitive in the first clash of arms. The historian John Shy identified '*The peculiarity of first battles lies mainly in the lack of recent, relevant combat experience*'[130]. For Western armies the following outcome could result:

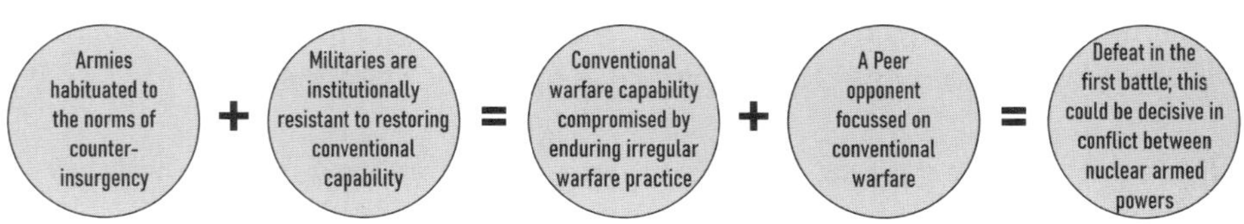

Victorian colonial armies had to regularly adapt to radically different characters of conflicts, but this combat experience did not necessarily prepare them for major conflict. Garnet Wolsey was Britain's pre-eminent late nineteenth century soldier, his speciality was commanding small imperial expeditionary operations, leading to decisive battles, that were made one-sided by the disparity in combat power. But he was well aware that '*what in our little army we call a battle*[131]' was of a different order of magnitude to the real warfare and major battles which had just occurred in the 1870 Franco-Prussian War. Unfortunately, realising this did not make it easy to address. Accustomed to fighting significantly less sophisticated foes, the Victorian British Army initially failed to cope with the tactical challenge of the Second Anglo-Boer War. The Boers were equipped with the latest Mauser rifles and Krupp artillery, which they employed using advanced Western tactics coupled with their native resourcefulness. This was a significant change in the character of conflict for a British Army whose last major warfighting had been against the largely spear armed Dervish intent on creating a melee.

Even the most professional armies can be guilty of failing to analyse the likely future; particularly when they are successfully conducting military operations[132]. The Israeli military theorist Brigadier General (Retired) Shimon Naveh identified that his country's armed force had become *'addicted to the present fight'*[133]. Denis E Showalter identified that the failure of the German Army to adapt to the challenges of the Eastern Front was due their previous overwhelming success, which:

> *'left the German soldier neither the time nor the inclination to consider any changes except those they predicted. As had been the case in 1914, the army found itself forced to revert to increasingly random improvisations when its original bag of tricks emptied in 1941 somewhere between Smolensk and Moscow*[134]'

Most of the Wehrmacht's historians concentrate upon their tactical successes, rather than the abject failure to adjust to the character of conflict that the Soviets forced them to fight. The former is gallant, the latter more institutionally challenging for any military. The revisionist states and transnational jihadist organisations that are adopting state-like structures have already identified the West's lack of land conventional warfighting capability as an opportunity. Mixing this with irregular and political warfare tactics, and adding to this ambiguity over the status of combatants, results in a complexity that seeks to counter the West's technologically sophisticated approach. Key to this is dislocating Western airpower; both actively through integrated air defence systems and passively through not presenting viable targets. The conflicts on the Donbas, Syria and Iraq may not be definitive, but they certainly signpost the character of warfare that a future adversary is likely to seek. Marine General Krulak was an early advocate of the belief that in the right human and physical terrain, a more primitive approach can succeed, or at least ensure that the conflict is so drawn-out as to prevent a clear result:

> *'They've seen the might of our technology. They're not going to fight us straight up. We're not going to see the son of Desert Storm anymore. You're going to see the stepchild of Chechnya*[135]'.

Adjusting to a future vision that has more to do with 'Blade Runner' than '2001: A Space Odyssey' presents a challenge for high technology societies and their militaries. These are conditioned to 'mirror image', leading to them focusing on a possible opponent's most sophisticated warfighting capabilities. As a result, Western militaries concentrate on Russia's relatively few long-range precision missiles, whilst largely overlooking its primitive, but significantly more potent tube and short range rocket artillery. The key, as Frederick the Great reminds us, is the need to ask '*What design would I be forming if I were the enemy?*'[139] and field capabilities accordingly. If military establishments were more adept at this they would avoid been surprised by enemies who employ simple technologies creatively[137].

Being technologically focussed can lead to a failure to understand the role in war played by societal and cultural factors. This led to suicide attacks – the Developing World's precision weapon – being both unanticipated, and their impact on the character of the conflict being under-appreciated. This has happened before; in World War Two, the US Navy faced *Kamikaze* tactics. As both were out with the West's paradigm of conflict, they had a psychological impact in excess of their physical. Ralph Peters presciently observed: *'Technologies come and go, but the primitive endures … In this age of technical miracles, our military needs to study mankind*[138]'. Of course, military intelligence prefers to focus on technology and orders of battle, over the challenge of gathering and analysing the actions of individuals. The novelist William Gibson is attributed with observing that *'The future is already here – it's just not very evenly distributed'*; an observation that required a recognition that the future character of conflict will have much in common with the arc of violence surrounding the prosperous West. Western powers will also have to abandon the strict distinction between peace and war, and recognise the need to distinguish between the different kinds of competitions and identify appropriate response to disparate forms of aggression[139]. Firepower will rarely be the direct response to political warfare, but it underpins the military power that frames any 'sub-threshold' conflict.

Whether largely conventional or irregular in character, the next conflicts are almost certainly going to require a greater employment of firepower. A safe prediction with four millennia of precedent for war's character seeking decisive methods[140]. America and its allies have been bogged down in Afghanistan, Iraq and most recently Syria without gaining geopolitically. They embarked upon what General Bradley identified seventy years ago as *'the wrong war, at the wrong place, at the wrong* time, and with the *wrong enemy*[141]'. These campaigns were a tragic luxury that were not strategically punished due to *Pax Americana*; consuming Western land power in tertiary theatres would be a very dangerous option in the current multi-polar World order.

The next three chapters will, through examining the character of conflict over the joint fires century, identify that land force employment has always been in a state of flux. This is largely the result of disequilibrium, or the absence of a state of balance between the forces acting on a system. Identifying which factors will drive change in the future is problematic. Most militaries assume that technology will be the main engine of change; it certainly is for conflict in the air and sea. But on land, when a technology provides a tactical advantage, an opponent's counter need not necessarily be through technology. It follows that uncertainty of the future character of conflict necessitates building flexibility into force structures to enable rapid adjustment. This follows Professor Sir Michael Howard advice:

> *'No matter how clearly one thinks, it is impossible to anticipate precisely the character of future conflict. The key is to not be so far off the mark that it becomes impossible to adjust once that character is revealed*[142]'.

Chapter 2: Firepower Dominated Total War

'The chief utility of history for the analysis of present and future lies in its ability, not to point out lessons, but to isolate things that need thinking about ... History provides insights and questions, not answers'[1].

Geoffrey Tilly, Historian

This and the next two chapters are the exception to the book's thematic approach. They chronologically survey the key conflicts of the last hundred years, seeking to emphasise those that signpost firepower's future. In contrast to Clausewitz's 'On War', which heavily favoured the most recent conflicts, lessons are drawn from the totality of the joint fire's century. This chapter covers firepower in land warfare up until the end of World War Two.

Not only does an historical survey provide context, it can also challenge the comforting assumption of a linear progression to current practice. This is surely important, as it is difficult to be certain of the merits of the lessons of the West's most recent conflicts, given their lack of reciprocity between combatants. This needs to be balanced against assuming a complete disconnect from recent conflict, as Air Marshal Sir John Slessor identified:

'If there is one attitude more dangerous than to assume that a future war will be just like the last one, it is to assume that it will be so utterly different that we can ignore all of the lessons of the last one[3]*.'*

Gunpowder was first militarised in the 10th century; it became essential at sieges in the 15th century and in pitched battle a century later, when it became sufficiently mobile. It was only in the 15th century that gunpowder significantly surpassed the previous tension, torsion and counter-balance artillery. These forms of artillery had been around for millennia but they had not redefined conflict because they made only an occasional, and infrequently decisive, impact in open warfare. Gunpowder artillery's late arrival means that employing its firepower has been an indispensable component of land warfare for less than a tenth of the history of organised violence[2]. The joint fires system is barely 100-years old; in its complete form it dates to the mid-1960s, with the fielding of attack helicopters.

World War One saw in their nascent form, the introduction of most of the constituent elements that make up modern land warfare. Firepower was employed in both the close and deep battles; the separation of firepower's terminal controller from the means of delivery – indirect fire – became the dominant means of employment; airpower went from technical infancy into being a decisive element in combat. These developments meant that the 'empty battlefield' extended significantly beyond the range of direct fire weapons, forcing the adoption by successful armies of the modern tactical system to counter firepower's dominance.

World War Two was the last time that the great powers clashed directly in open warfare. Out of fashion for over fifty years, the battlefield rocket made its reappearance in World War Two. Its ability to deliver a heavy weight of fire, together with its greater range, meant that it was soon on the pathway to supplanting the cannon in the deep battle. The nature of the deep battle was changed by airpower, from one that was relatively shallow, to one where – at least in Western Europe – air interdiction was prosecuted over almost the whole theatre. The years 1939–45 also saw the fielding of reliable wireless communications, making fire support significantly more responsive and effective; radio-equipped forward air controllers could speak directly to the airborne pilot, making possible immediately responsive close air support[4]. In contrast to the Anglo-American manoeuvring of firepower, the Soviets perfected their distinctive form of ground and air combined arms warfighting; this is still employed by their successor states, notably Russia, as well as some former allies.

The intent of the three historical chapters is not to be a general account of joint fires, but to provide lessons. These lessons can provide an empirical guide to assist the understanding of those currently wrestling with the challenge of the 21st century battlefield. Or as RG Collingwood expressed it: *'We study history in order to see more clearly into the situation in which we are called upon to act*[5].' Identifying the key lessons is important as military history shows that warfare invariably evolves faster than even the most adaptive militaries expect.

These historical chapters are followed by two chapters that advance theory, using the Clausewitzian methodology of balancing an analysis of history with the development of theories. This recognises that history has only so much to teach, and caused the Prussian theorist to bemoan: *'Why is history so lacking in useful examples?*[6]'. In this study, the key lack of examples results from an absence of recent major power conflict. This leads to the challenge of determining the impact of a 'technological revolution' in joint fires that has not been tested in peer-on-peer conflict.

The Emergence of Indirect Fire

'How odd it was [in the Seven Year War] to have a lieutenant–colonel as Inspector of the entire artillery of an army [Prussian] locked in war with five-sevenths of Europe!'[7]

C Decker, Historian

Frederick the Great observed in his 1768 Military Testament that battles are won by superiority of fire, but this logic was not followed in the organisation and practices of Enlightenment Europe's armies. Subsequently, artillery came to dominate warfare in the Napoleonic Wars, through its ability to manoeuvre on the battlefield and deliver decisive massed firepower from beyond the range of smooth bore muskets. The French were the most successful at this due to creating a separate artillery chain of command. This was an impossibility in Frederick's Prussian Army, as artillery officers were invariably not gentlemen and so could hardly be expected to exercise independent command[8]. Even in less rigid armies, artillery formed a distinct element, in part due to the arm's novelty, but also because its technical training separated its officers from their contemporaries in the traditional arms.

Napoleon's aggressive artillery generals sited their grand batteries on the battlefield at the point of decision, or even more aggressively, led artillery charges that would see guns fire and manoeuvre to close to the decisive range of canister shot. It required aggressive leadership to achieve Jomini's view that *'Artillery is an arm equally formidable both in the offensive and defensive*[9]'. This dominance led to counters, perhaps the most effective of which was the Duke of Wellington's use of the cover provided by reverse slope positions. This approach largely negated preparatory fire from French fixed batteries and dislocated the Napoleonic combined arms battle. This led ultimately to the Battle of Waterloo being a series of separate infantry, cavalry and artillery attacks.

The root cause of the inability of artillery in the American Civil War to provide effective offensive support was the failure to resource a separate chain of command; one army corps had its guns commanded by a lieutenant[10]. This led to talented artillery officers transferring to the infantry; the pre-war 3rd US Artillery Regiment included, at one time or another, the following great names: Meade, Sherman, Thomas, Reynolds, Bragg, Early, and Burnside[11]. General George McClellan named Colonel Hunt as the chief of all artillery in the Army of the Potomac, but his successors in command of this army rarely allowed him to exercise effective control over the reserve artillery, let alone authority over brigade- and division-level batteries[12].

Artillery's challenge in the American Civil War was made greater by a series of technical innovations. The widespread use from around the 1850s of rifling and then breech-loading infantry weapons meant that artillery, especially when manoeuvring in the open, became vulnerable to infantry firepower. Riflemen could accurately engage from ranges well beyond that achieved by canister (about 350m), which was then the most effective artillery anti-personnel round. This was compounded by artillerymen, presenting an upright target when serving their guns, while infantrymen could take cover. Subsequently, rifling and breech loading, when applied to artillery, led to a longer-range weapon with a higher rate of fire. Furthermore, artillery's anti-personnel effect was partly restored by the widespread use of shrapnel shells. However, being limited to direct fire, artillery could not always expect to outrange riflemen. This vulnerability to small arms fire meant that late 19th century artillery largely lost its offensive capability as this necessitated movement in the open; a vulnerability that unfortunately repeatedly led to disaster, as demonstrated by the British at the Battle of Colenso in 1899[13].

In response to the lethality of firepower, from the mid 19th century infantry made greater use of battlefield dispersion and cover. This made it significantly more difficult for artillery to suppress defensive positions before an assault. Of the major powers, the British were the least prepared for this tactical challenge; as their army was structured for Imperial policing it could not generate the quantity of firepower required on the modern battlefield. Field Marshal, The Earl Kitchener, in the Boer War identified what will be an enduring theme, the under-provision artillery: '*My God! I can scarcely credit their taking the fearful responsibility of sending us into the field practically unarmed with artillery*[14]'.

Starting with the 1904–5 Russo-Japanese War, artillery began to regain its battlefield pre-eminence. The employment of indirect fire[15] from concealed positions allowed firepower to be manoeuvred independently of the gun's movement. The separation of the observer from the means of engagement is one of joint fire's chief advantage over the direct fire weapon system. Direct fire needs an uninterrupted line of flight from the barrel to the target. Separating the source of the firepower from its control allows a joint fires observer to employ the best means of acquiring a target; this may be as simple as the occupation of an elevated observation post to improve the field of view. This ultimately led to balloons and aeroplanes being recognised as the ideal surveillance platforms.

Most of the technologies and procedures that were to dominate World War One were trialled in the Russo-Japanese War, most prominently: indirect fire, machine guns, barbed wire and trenches. Most observers agreed that the primary tactical lesson of the Russo-Japanese War was the dominance of quick-fire artillery. Major J M Horne, a British officer who was attached to the Japanese Army, identified:

> *'The greatest impression made on me by all I saw is that artillery is now the decisive arm and that all other arms are auxiliary to it. The importance of artillery cannot be too strongly insisted upon, for other things being equal, the side which has the best artillery will always win … so strongly am I convinced of the immense importance of artillery that it seems almost a question for deliberate consideration whether artillery should not be largely increased even at the expense of other arms'*[16].

American observers identified that the casualties caused by artillery greatly exceeded any previous conflict[17]; initiating the dominance of shells and bombs in inflicting casualties that continues to this day.

Needless to say, this lesson was not heeded, not least by the Japanese; who despite their experience in the Russo-Japanese War, retained an absolute faith in the primacy of infantry. This reliance on moral qualities came from their cultural viewpoint; or as Allan Millet and Williamson Murray put it, their *'notions of spiritual strength and cold steel*[18]'. Not having gone through the profound tactical transformation caused by World War One's firepower, the Japanese entered World War Two as a 1914 vintage army. Their initial success showcased the fighting qualities of their individual soldier, but their tactical inferiority was cruelly exposed by opponents using combined arms tactics, most brutally by the Soviets in the 1945 Manchurian campaign. Only where terrain and weather diminished the impact of combined arms tactics did they obtain much success after their initial string of victories. For the other major armies, a belief that moral qualities surpassed other tactical considerations largely died in the trenches.

World War One: Artillery Dominance and the Emergence of the Deep Battle

> *'The war of 1914–18 was an artillery war: artillery was the battle-winner, artillery was what caused the greatest loss of life, the most dreadful wounds, and the deepest fear*[19]'.
>
> John Terraine, historian

Despite the Russo-Japanese War, whose lessons were largely repeated in the two Balkan Wars (1912–13), all belligerents entered World War One believing in the infantry's pre-eminent tactical role. While doctrines varied between the armies, all to an extent expected that moral qualities could overcome massed firepower; it took the verdict of the battlefield to force change on these militaries. As Charles de Gaulle identified *'tactically the realisation of the German firepower made nonsense of the current doctrine*[20]'. Its late entry into the War meant that America, the most mechanised country in World, preserved in its 1918 Army Field Service Records, this 1914 viewpoint:

> *'The infantry is the principal and most important arm, which is charged with the main work on the field of battle and decides the final issue of combat. The role of the infantry … is the role of the entire force*[21]'.

The doctrine of infantry primacy led to most artillery equipment being designed for close support, primarily employing open sight engagements. The most extreme in this approach were the French, who in 1914 fielded 3,840 of their superb 75mm guns to only 384 heavier guns. This resulted in 58 heavy batteries against 665 field and horse artillery batteries. France's heavier guns were older and technically inferior to what the Germans fielded. They were mostly 155mm 'Rimailho' cannons that had to be broken down in two sections for movement, and had a maximum range of only 6,300m. Even the French had begun to react to lessons of the Balkan Wars and had ordered 220 of the long-barrelled 105mm Schneider (L13S) Field Gun[22]. But the ethos of the French Army can be gauged from a staff officer's response to their lack of heavy artillery: '*Thank God we don't have any. What gives the French Army its force is the lightness of its cannon*[23]'. And how could this view be wrong if Napoleon had decreed in 1809 *'that I could do as well without howitzers*[24]'. After experiencing British reverse slope tactics and fortified farms in the 100 Days Campaign, the former Emperor had changed his view during his final exile. The initial French approach was:

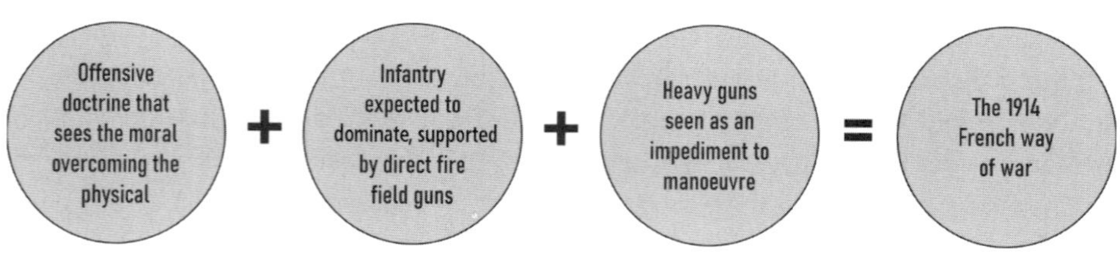

In contrast to the French, the pre-War German analysis determined the need for heavy mobile cannon that were able to defeat the Franco-Belgian frontier fortifications. German field artillery was average, but in 1914 they had a four to one advantage in their superb Krupp and Skoda (borrowed from the Austrians) heavy guns and howitzers. Crucially, by making this deductive leap, they found it easier to adapt to the World War One's character of conflict and the need for a firepower centric approach. As the historian John Terraine identified the German Army was the 'motor', the driving force of the war[25].

World War One's widespread fielding of mortars was not envisaged by any belligerent. It could not have been predicted because trench warfare stretching across a continent was unimaginable, until it had actually happened. These circumstances meant that this traditional niche siege weapon became the essential infantry direct support weapon; the mortar provided a means of delivering a heavy weight of fire, with a steep trajectory, from a light and simple to operate platform. In World War One, there were three main types: firstly, purpose-built designs that were effectively mini artillery pieces (a pre-War German innovation like their mobile heavy artillery to overcome frontier fortifications). Secondly, improvised weapons, often only sufficient to lob a bomb into a nearby enemy trench; and finally, designs based on the brutal simplicity of the British Stokes mortar, the ancestor of most modern mortars. In addition to providing direct support, from 1915 mortars were integrated into artillery fire plans, where they were usually tasked with engaging forward enemy trenches, a mission that suited their range and trajectory.

Aircraft were used from the opening engagements as reconnaissance platforms. The French had gained valuable operational experience of employing aircraft in this role in Morocco in 1913. German initial success against the Russians was made possible by aerial reconnaissance; as their commander, Field Marshall, Paul von Hindenburg identified: '*Without the airmen no [Battle of] Tannenberg*[26]'. The Royal Flying Corps could have made a similar contribution, but the British commander, General Sir John French, despite personally meeting the pilot, was unwilling to accept that the bulk of the German Army was advancing through Belgium. It was through reconnaissance and target acquisition, in particularly spotting for artillery, that aircraft made their greatest contribution. This extended to observing the movement of own forces; once an offensive was launched forward elements were rarely in communication with their HQs, leading to aircraft being tasked with maintaining contact and reporting progress[27]. Their rival was the observation balloon; obviously, these needed to be at a safe distance behind the front line, but from a vantage point of 3,500 feet, they could identify a man on the ground five miles away or a vehicle 10 miles away[28]. Balloons provided persistent coverage, while fixed wing aircraft could range over the target area and employ aerial photography. Photographic interpretation soon became vital in overcoming counter-surveillance measures.

Airpower's most direct impact on ground operations was in strafing with their one or two machine guns, this usually being more effective than their limited bomb load. While pilots could receive a mission brief while on the ground, they usually had to acquire their own targets. Given the static nature of much of the warfare, separating friend and foe was not usually challenging. In mobile operations pre-arranged markers could designate friendly forces, alternatively aircraft could engage all targets in front of the lead artillery barrage; primitive wireless ground-to-air communications prevented close air support being any more flexible. Employed in mass, airpower could have a significant impact on ground operations. At the Battle of Cambrai in November 1917, 289 aircraft of the Royal Flying Corps first achieved air superiority, then attacked targets in front of the barrage, and even conducted ammunition aerial resupply. In March 1918, airpower helped plug the gaps torn in the British lines by the German offensive; the hundred British fighter aircraft that covered the open flank of the British Third Army could claim sole responsibility for repelling an infantry attack.

The lessons of the employment of airpower in World War One have largely endured. Airpower's greatest impact was against moving ground forces. In 1918, when the fighting had become more mobile, artillery could fail to keep up with the pace of operations, leading to aircraft temporally becoming the principal source of firepower[29]. Employing tactical airpower against HQs and logistic hubs, usually up to a depth of 30km behind the front, was pioneered by the Anglo-French; they used modified bomb-carrying fighters, as depth targets were less vulnerable to strafing. While the Imperial German Air Service conducted air interdiction, their focus on direct support meant that this was done on a more limited scale. In the summer of 1918, by attacking supply columns and effectively isolating the battlefield, air interdiction played a significant part in the collapse of Turkish forces in Palestine. This foreshadowed the dominance airpower would exert upon subsequent desert operations; it also showcased airpower's disproportionate impact on morale. In contrast to artillery and mortar fire – which arrives with little warning – visible aircraft represented a more personal, and thus psychologically challenging threat[30].

The Allies, and in particular the British, believed in relentless offensive action to achieve and maintain control of the air. By mid-1916, the British Army had recognised that air superiority was a prerequisite for realising effective tactical air support[31]. In contrast, the Germans were content to achieve battlefield air superiority as and when required. A succession of technically innovative fighters gave them local air superiority, which they invariably wasted, notably at Verdun: *'limiting themselves to protecting German observation balloons … and later to ineffective patrolling*[32].' The aim of constant patrolling aircraft was to enforce a *Luftsperre* or aerial blockade[33]; meanwhile their opponents sought to contest control of the air on both sides of the frontline, along its entire length. Through choosing to engage only with mass and employing elite fighter squadrons, the Germans achieved superior kill ratios. In contrast to these local tactical successes, general Allied air superiority enhanced the overall fighting power of their armies – largely through superior target acquisition for the artillery – and allowed them to gain a moral ascendency in the air. This approach was later enshrined into Western airpower doctrine, which sees air superiority as being the precursor to the effective employment of airpower. This approach to air warfare mirrored the constant contesting by Anglo-French artillery of fire superiority. Again, the Germans were usually content to achieve the localised defeat of the opposing artillery system to facilitate their offensives.

Artillery's employment largely determined World War One's character of conflict. This artillery revolution was not driven by technology, most of this was in place before 1914. However, what was technologically possible could not be implemented because of the pre-war doctrine and culture. It was the tactical challenge of trench warfare that led to fundamental changes in force employment that would otherwise have been unimaginable; notably opposition to indirect fire due to the belief that guns should be *seen* to support the infantry[34]. Artillery was not uniquely resistant to change: an example was the adopting uniforms that suited concealment: *'red trousers are France'* declared Eugene Etienne, the Minister for War in 1913[35].

In the initial war of manoeuvre almost all of the artillery was controlled at brigade level and employed in direct support of the infantry and cavalry battalions. Overcoming an entrenched defensive system based on machine guns and artillery led to the command of artillery becoming centralised. It rapidly became the orthodoxy that massed firepower had to physically destroy all the defending weapons. This became the purpose of the divisional, corps and even army level fire plans. Despite its increased quantity and quality, initially artillery could not achieve the levels of destruction that this approach required. At first the answer was simply more and more artillery and ammunition, aiming at achieving greater and greater destruction[36]. The effect that General Henry Rawlinson set for the 1916 Somme Bombardment was that: '*Nothing could exist at the conclusion of the bombardment in the area covered by it*[37]'. By focussing on a smaller area and with sufficient materiel, by late 1916 it was practically possible to effectively achieve destruction through artillery fire. In response, the defenders changed their force employment to reduce firepower's effectiveness; the Germans led the way with their adoption of defence in depth following the Verdun and Somme Battles. They also led on developing offensive techniques, which was considerably easier on the Eastern Front with its greatly reduced force densities. The Germans repeatedly proved their ability to penetrate Russian defences through massing their artillery. On the offensive, half their artillery park routinely was heavy guns and howitzers to smash Russian field positions. In the middle years of the War the following applied:

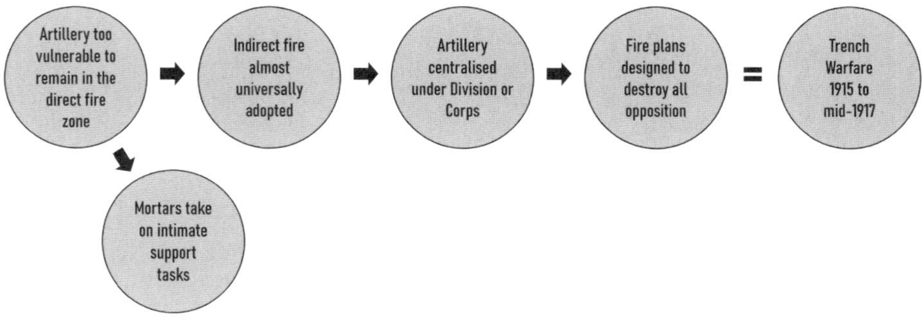

By late 1917 the Germans, French and British had all concluded that, in the attack, the key role of artillery was to neutralise, not destroy, the enemy defensive system. Once the opposing indirect and direct firepower was neutralised, the infantry could capture, and subsequently hold, their objectives. It was the increasingly scientific application of artillery that was key to any successful offensive, regardless of whether these also featured tanks and infantry using infiltration tactics. Addressing the inherent errors in the indirect fire system meant that massed fire could be predicted, rather than requiring the time-consuming registering of individual batteries onto their targets. In contrast to the start of the War and the infantry's preeminent role, by 1918 the preparation time required to launch an offensive was determined by the need to identify targets, write and disseminate the fire plan and assemble the artillery park and its munitions.

Artillery had three main offensive roles in this new all-arms battle; first preparatory fire, which, ideally with sufficient resources, was short and intense – concentrations of firepower aimed to systematically neutralise the enemy's command, control and firepower systems. Artillery fire was usually needed to breach the protecting barbed wire, though armies with sufficient tanks could dispense with this part of the preparatory fire and thus achieve greater surprise. Integrated into these fire plans would be chemical strikes, with the most persistent agents being employed against locations that would not be immediately assaulted, such as HQs, logistics and artillery.

Secondly, covering fire was then required to get the infantry onto their objective. The scale and sophistication of World War One defences meant that not all enemy positions could be identified with any accuracy, necessitating the use of barrages[38]; this was especially true when facing a defence in depth, when defenders used their mobility to avoid firepower, including abandoning their prepared positions to use the cover created by the attacker's preliminary bombardment. Barrages ensured that firepower covered any possible enemy positions, as a single unsuppressed machine gun or artillery observer could have a devastating effect. Most offensive barrages advanced in small increments, usually 100 yards every few minutes, moving forward at the pace of the assaulting infantry. The barrage was also a visible demonstration of firepower, providing the moral support that facilitated the infantry closing on an objective. As already identified, it was highly visible from the air, providing airpower with a ready delineation of hostile and friendly forces.

At their most sophisticated, a barrage consisted of a cocktail of high explosive, shrapnel and smoke. By 1918, the British standard ratio was 4:5:1 respectively; but there was national preference, the Australians favoured high explosive fuzed instantaneous, while the Canadians preferred shrapnel[39]. By the end of the war, most fire plans featured multiple barrages aimed at different enemy lines of defences, interspersed with concentrations against known enemy locations. With this fire support, resolute attacking infantry could break into almost any defensive position. Barrages were, however, expensive in shells, difficult to coordinate with both infantry and tanks, and dissipated, rather than concentrated firepower. The proportion of firepower devoted to barrages, rather than concentrations of fire onto identified enemy locations, directly reflected the level of certainty over the enemy's dispositions[40]. Certainty of target location remains an enduring theme; it is central to the debate of how much of modern firepower can be precision, allowing it to be employed against point targets. As opposed to how much needs to have an area effect, to suppress likely, but not individually acquired, enemy locations.

Continuous fronts and an inability to exploit a breakthrough made deep manoeuvre impossible in most theatres. As a substitute, linking firepower with advances in target acquisition created the firepower deep battle. The longest-range World War One guns fired around 20km (leaving aside oddities, including the famous Paris Guns) and, as identified, tactical air forces usually limited themselves to 30km behind enemy lines. In addition to these physical limitations, there was initially a reluctance to vigorously fight the deep battle. As already noted, the Germans were particularly reluctant; notably failing to attack the *Voie Sacrée* during the Battle of Verdun[41]. Initially this was a deliberate design: leaving the line of communication open was necessary to ensure that the French continued sending troops into what the Germans considered to be a killing area. However, the German failure to achieve a favourable rate of attrition should have triggered a change in operational approach to one that used the deep battle as a means of shaping the close battle. The deep battle was further restricted by the primitive nature of technical target acquisition. Firing batteries could usually be located through flash spotting and sound ranging or aircraft, identifying other targets was more problematic. The deep battle may have been quite shallow and relatively ineffective, but World War One was the start of the permanent split of land firepower into fire support and deep fires.

Denying the enemy the opportunity to use their firepower through counter battery fire became almost a prerequisite of a successful battle[42]. The British led in the locating of hostile batteries through technical means, in particular sound ranging; they vigorously conducted the counter battery battle. Commenting on the last hundred days of the war, the British Official Historian noted:

> *'The British artillery throughout had the upper hand of the German batteries, whose fire, if not quickly subdued, was gradually lessened directly they disclosed their positions by fire*[43].'

The creation of the firepower deep battle subjected soldiers to the stress of conflict over a significantly greater duration, as they were targets not just when on the front line, but whenever they were present in the arena of conflict. This led to the shell shock being the descriptor of the new form of warfare's psychological assault on combatants[44]. This was not new as a phenomenon, but it was in terms of scale and duration. A century before, Clausewitz had recognised that battles could exhaust morale, and that *'soldiers, after fighting for some time are apt to be like burnt out cinders*[45]'. From now on, the challenge was one of constant rather than fleeting danger, requiring the management of a different kind of psychological pressure.

World War One saw marked national differences in the application of artillery. The Germans, under their famous artilleryman Colonel Bruchmüller[46], engaged the whole depth of the enemy's position with sudden and concentrated preparatory fire. They made extensive use of gas and employed more tubes per target than the Western Allies, in part to offset the inferior accuracy of the German guns. In their Cambrai-St Quentin offensive of 21 March 1918, the Germans employed 6,473 guns and 3,532 mortars, exploiting their traditional General Staff expertise in the assembling of this mass of artillery whilst maintaining surprise. This was a traditional German strength that, when coupled with Stormtrooper infantry trained to fight their way forward, unlocked first the Russian, and then the British and French defences:

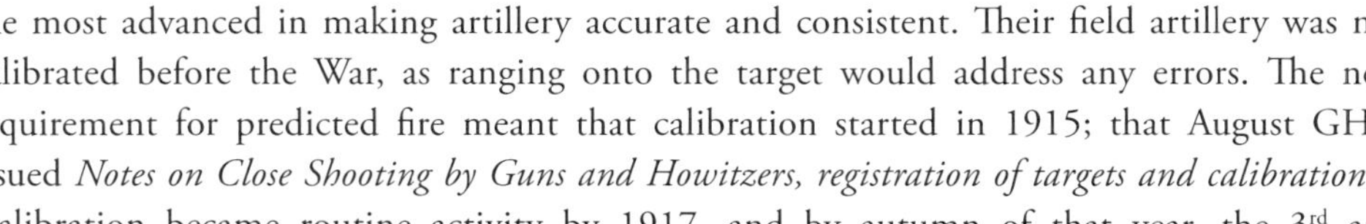

The British superiority in specialist artillery techniques and training meant they were the most advanced in making artillery accurate and consistent. Their field artillery was not calibrated before the War, as ranging onto the target would address any errors. The new requirement for predicted fire meant that calibration started in 1915; that August GHQ issued *Notes on Close Shooting by Guns and Howitzers, registration of targets and calibration*[47]. Calibration became routine activity by 1917, and by autumn of that year, the 3rd and 4th Armies in France had permanent calibration ranges in their rear areas. The geographic position of the Allies on the Western Front meant they were better placed to make allowance for the prevailing weather when calculating their firing solutions. British batteries measured surface meteor data and the Royal Flying Corps estimated wind velocity. Allied survey was significantly more scientific in determining accurate location for both targets and batteries; Field Survey Companies were held at army level[48]. In contrast, the Germans produced a single correction for meteorological data and calibration, whose use was still being debated in 1918. Their methods of employment continued to make allowance for the need to adjust predicted fire during the bombardment or shoot out the error through mass[49].

This scientific gunnery allowed the British to dispense with the lengthy preliminary bombardments that were central to German's 1918 offensives. As early as 1917, the British were putting at least an equal emphasis on delivering neutralising covering fire as on the preliminary bombardment[50]. These innovations led to the Battle of Cambrai; this began at dawn on 20 November 1917, with preparatory fire by 1,003 guns on German defences, quickly followed by smoke and a creeping barrage. The silent registration of batteries enabled a wholly predicted bombardment, this achieved suppression with surprise. The possession by the British of significant tank support further de-risked this approach; tanks on the first day of major attacks (few were serviceable by day two) were able to breach the barbed wire obstacles and provide intimate fire support. The predicted fire plan starting at or just before H-Hour (when the assaulting infantry left their trenches) became the standard British tactic. This approach was made possible by more accurate guns and a superior deep battle capability that could rapidly silence hostile batteries. The decisive Battle of Amiens in August 1918 was supported by just over two thousand guns, but these were probably more effective than the greater numbers of guns used by the Germans five month earlier in their Spring offensive. By 1918 the pre-war hippophile Royal Artillery was now the technical master of modern artillery[51]; except against the most heavily defended German positions, their usual approach was:

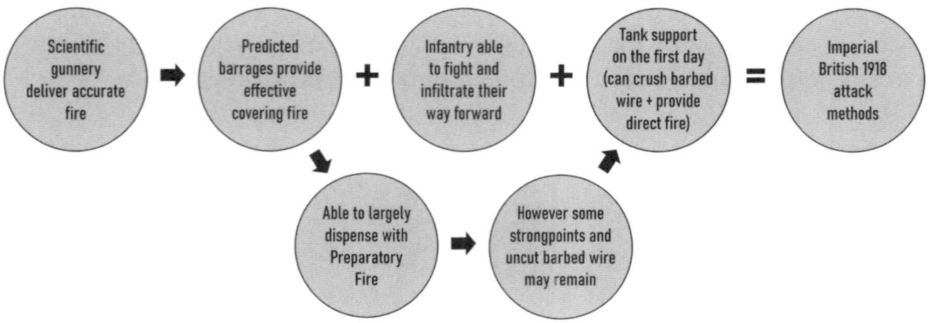

The British varied their approach to match the tactical challenge. Breaking through the Hindenburg Line in September 1918 required the barrage to be preceded by preparatory fire in the German style; this aimed at destroying defences and reserves.

By 1918 it was the French that perhaps expected the most from their artillery; casualties having dissipated their traditional *élan*. More so than other armies, variation in tactics became associated with individual senior commanders; in contrast to the other belligerents they had a significantly greater divergence in character and background than is usual in self-selecting military elites. True to his family heritage of Napoleonic service, Marshal Foch was noted for the decentralisation of heavy artillery and his reliance upon systematic counter-battery fire, supported by air observation to achieve target acquisition. Marshal Petain, who was considered by his fellow commanders to be too cautious and casualty-concerned, preferred to mass his artillery to achieve destruction; Colonel Repington of the London Times observed that he:

> *'tried to make his heavy guns supple so that they could quickly concentrate their fire on different objectives and destroy them by feu d'écrasement [obliteration fire][52]'.*

Prior to the 1917 mutinies, the protestant and half English General Nivelle emphasised fast rolling barrages; however, the failure of this approach (due to technical rather than tactical shortcomings) largely resulted in a reversion to Marshal Petain's more conservative approach. This was aided by the formation of a general reserve artillery to facilitate massed fire. By mid-1918 the French Army's morale had largely recovered from the mutinies, and their lower risk, more attritional approach was replaced by more modern methods. However, they retained a greater emphasis on destruction than the British. They led in tank design, the Renault FT is recognisable as the predecessor of the modern tank, but French combined arms doctrine was too cautious to exploit its potential as a means of swarming over German defences. French adaptation to the conflict's character should not be under-estimated, as can be seen in the reversal of their pre-War capability decisions; in 1918 they fielded 4,968 75mm guns to 5,128 pieces of heavy artillery[53].

The Americans largely followed French tactics, but with their newly raised artillery's requirement for simplicity they put even more emphasis on the technically easier preparatory fire, because, despite French tuition, they initially had difficulty with complex rolling barrages and predicted fire. This resulted in prolonged bombardments – which had to be sufficiently long to allow the Americans to adjust the rounds onto the target – preceding often poorly-supported infantry attacks. Even when they began to master modern gunnery, General Pershing's infantry-centric approach prevented the full exploitation of combined arms tactics. This approach is in direct contrast to the subsequent firepower-orientated American way of war and the views of the Civil War Private Edgerton of the 107th New York:

> *'There is one thing that our government does that suits me to a dot. That is we mostly fight with artillery. The rebels fight mostly with infantry[54].'*

Up until the Armistice, the American Army continued to expect their infantry to fight their way forward without effective fire support. The failure to tackle German firepower can be seen from 87% of American casualties in the Great War being inflicted by artillery[55].

Barrages were rarer on the Eastern Front, in part due to its lesser defences and more mobile character, but also because usually only the Germans had the technical skill to effectively coordinate a moving barrage with their infantry. The Tsar's army despite its experience in the Russo-Japanese War fielded relatively few howitzers; instead they largely relied upon relatively light guns like the French Army[56]. Once the initial manoeuvre phase ceased the Russians seem never to have evolved beyond their belief in the need to maximise destruction through a preliminary bombardment, with the only limitation being the amount of materiel available. This was the Tsar's army's major challenge; by 1915 they were forced to reduce their number of field guns per division by a third. Their initial one-to-eight ratio of heavy to field guns proved inadequate, and an improvised park of heavy guns and howitzers was assembled from fortresses, converted naval guns and from their allies.

By the final stages of World War One, correctly employed artillery allowed infantry to break into the strongest defensive position. However, the depth of penetration was limited to the range of the guns. It was only in exceptional circumstances that sufficient fire support could be provided by moving forward artillery and mortars. As the subsequent Soviet analysis identified:

> *'the concentration of artillery suppressive assets could not in the final analysis overcome the firepower-intensive front. In fact, suppression affected only the forward defensive belt, leaving the defensive depths largely untouched. Offensive artillery was incapable of reaching into the entire tactical depth, for artillery lagged behind the attacking infantry. This was not a question of suppressive firepower, but a question of the mobility of suppressive assets, which confronted battlefield obstacles that were insurmountable for wheeled and horse-drawn conveyances. For attacking infantry, the tragedy lay in the fact that after 3–4 hours of a successful attack, only a small number of the 100 supporting pieces continued firing. At this point, the exhausted attack was suspended[57].'*

The tank should have provided the Western Allies with their best close support direct fire weapon; however, their lack of reliability meant they were rarely available after day one of any battle. They certainly were not an exploitation force. The same applied to the few tracked self-propelled guns fielded. General Alexei Brusilov's Russian offensive in the Ukraine, in the summer of 1916, employed light guns with his exploitation forces; in the more congested battlefield of the Western Front, similar measures were employed, but it was rare for anything other than man-portable support weapons to make it across no-mans-land. The French fielded three 37mm guns per regiment from 1915. These were designed for open sight direct fire up to a range of 500m[58]. The major limitation was that guns that relied upon soldiers to drag them across no-man's-land lacked the weight of shell to defeat modern strongpoints. The answer of course was to: make artillery and mortar fire support responsive to observers in the front line with radio communications, exploit the advances being made in tracked cross-country vehicles and make close air support more responsive to impromptu tasks. This technology would be ready for the next major war.

Despite the technical limitations of artillery, mortars, tanks and airpower, World War One saw the transformation of war from one that was the dominated by the infantry and assisted by the support arms, into the modern combined arms battle. General and historian Jonathan Bailey identified that:

> *'three-dimensional conflict was so revolutionary that the tumultuous development of armour and air power in 1939–1945 and the advent of the information age in the decades that followed amount to no more than complementary and incremental improvements upon the conceptual model laid down in 1917–18[59]'.*

Despite their proven utility, there remained considerable resistance to combined arms tactics. Prominence was subsequently given to the elite infantry who were the tip of the spear in the 1918 fighting; these included the German Stormtroopers with their infiltration or 'Hutier' tactics[60]. In World War One, these were successful when employed in concert with powerful artillery. Between the wars, some German soldiers rejected *materialschlacht* in favour of approaches that through re-emphasising the moral aspects of warfare restored the central role of the *warrior*. This led the Germans to seek a novel tactical solution to the 'riddle of the trenches'. Combined arms warfare's dominance would resurface in the next World War, but only after an initial period of success by armies that sought to deny its logic.

World War Two – Artillery's Tactical and Airpower's Operational Dominance

'Renown awaits the commander who first restores artillery to its prime importance on the battlefield from which it has been ousted by the heavily armoured tank[61]*.'*

Sir Winston Churchill

World War One started with all the belligerents convinced of the primacy of infantry, supported by the other arms; World War Two started with armies following radically different forms of force employment. The Between the Wars period saw a rejection of 1918's successful combined arms approach, largely in favour of the dominance of a single arm. Unfortunately the victorious powers were the least inclined to undertake a scientific study of the Great War to determine its lessons when determining their doctrine.

For the British, the return to *proper* Imperial soldiering led to the introduction of the 1920's aptly-named 'Small War' infantry battalion establishment that saw a rejection of firepower in favour of restoring the pre-war dominance of the rifleman. Two light machine guns were retained per platoon, and the disbandment of the Machine Gun Corps saw medium machine guns and mortars go through a myriad of re-organisations before becoming divisional level weapons[62]. Field artillery regained its dominance over heavier ordnance, aided by the disbandment of the separate Royal Garrison Artillery. Traumatised by the Great War, the British hoped that they could avoid land warfare and rely upon their air force, navy and allies.

The British were probably the most culpable in failing to study the Great War; the Kirke Committee did not assemble until 1931. Its report was effectively shelved until a bowdlerised version was circulated 30 months later, for thought and discussion rather than action. Like many lessons learned publications it was strong on what should be done, but weak on actually how it could be done, because identifying actual change upsets the vested interests that exist within any complex organisation. Hence it largely stayed clear of forthright views on controversial topics, such as mechanisation. In contrast to the official lack of force development, the 1930s were a time of original thought in newspapers and books. Some of it innovative and prescient, some merely novel and militarily unsound; the proponents of armoured warfare fell into both camps. Except for aerial firepower, the largely British 'mobility theorists' downplayed the requirement for firepower. The limited British contribution to the Battle for France showed that they doctrinally were inadequately prepared for modern warfare; however, being fully motorised they were better at retreating, the standard British Army manoeuvre at the start of a continental conflict.

Marginalising firepower was not the German General Heinz Guderian's view: *'armour and mobility are only two of the important characteristics of the tank; the third and the most important is firepower'*. The Germans developed a novel form of combined arms warfare that was light on artillery firepower, which history would know as Blitzkrieg. In contrast, their allies the Japanese continued to follow the pre-1914 doctrine in expecting their infantry to morally dominate the battlefield.

The Soviet analysis was closest to the real lesson of the final 100-days on the Western Front, in identifying the supremacy of the combined arms close and deep battle over other approaches. They also recognised its limitations resulting from World War One's technology. Adding to the 1918 combined arms approach a mechanised force able exploit the break-in battle; this was made possible by advances in mobility and communications. A doctrine they would initially be unable to employ as Stalin's purges had removed much of the Red Army's leadership.

France entered World War Two with an artillery-led attritional defensive approach to warfare, which they saw as the key lesson of World War One. However, this was derived from the first three years of the war rather than 1918, with its restoration of the power of the offensive. Hence French doctrine did not feature: predicted artillery fire plans aiming at achieving neutralisation, massed tanks and aeroplanes or infantry equipped and trained to fight through defences. The Fall of France was at least equally due to non-military factors, but a doctrine based upon centralised command and control to synchronise firepower did not prepare their army to face the challenges presented by the Blitzkrieg. The French Army's employment of artillery-dominated methods of 1916/17 reflected their state's determination to take a low casualty approach. This resulted in the *cul-de-sac* that led to the Maginot Line and an Army wholly unfit for modern warfare[63]. Their Air Force became independent in 1933 in a deal that has been described as *'a masterpiece in contrived ambiguity*[64]' that stymied effective joint operations. This meant that Army was almost totally reliant upon the firepower of its artillery.

To learn the lessons of the Great War, the Americans convened the Hero Board in December of 1918, named after Brigadier General Andrew Hero. It was tasked to: *'to make a study of the experience gained by the Artillery of the AEF [American Expeditionary Force] and submit recommendations based upon such study*[65]'. This made some prescient deductions on their future artillery and mortar capability requirements; unfortunately, Americas isolationist strategic position meant that initially these could not be fully resourced. Officially American doctrine continued to be infantry dominated, but their wartime experience created the conditions for innovative development; in particularly by their artillery school in the 1930s.

By 1939 the balance between the deliverers of joint fires had changed from in 1918. In contrast to World War One, reliable direct fire 'accompanying artillery' could be provided by tanks, assault guns and self-propelled artillery. Technically more capable aircraft were able to take over some of the artillery tasks; in particular those requiring greater range and weight of munition. Portable wireless radios delivered the greatest change, allowing land and air forces to inter-communicate, and artillery fire to be rapidly moved around the battlefield[66]. This meant that in contrast to the previous war, World War Two's fire plans could flexibly adapt to the changing battle. The mortar could now support mobile operations, rather than merely provide fire support from established positions. The Soviets and Germans led on the rocket's return to the battlefield; prizing its ability to rapidly deliver a heavy volume of fire and its superior mobility, the result of their light platform. The rocket's greater dispersion of fire compared to tube artillery was not a significant issue for the Soviets with their belief in massed firepower. While some detractors saw his views of warfare as being through a World War One prism, ultimately Churchill was right in his view that an Allied victory would principally be achieved by firepower. And that artillery would deliver most of this firepower on the land battlefield; mastering both the German armour-led combined arms, and the Japanese light infantry, ways of war.

Between the wars, faced with the evident need to rebalance between air and surface-to-surface fires, nations took different approaches. Despite the experience of World War One, the Anglo-Americans failed to identify the need for a complementary relationship between artillery and airpower in their doctrine. Institutional interests ensured that doctrine developed in isolation. The American Army Air Corps' pre-war doctrine actually precluded the use of aircraft to attack targets within artillery range[67]. Despite the Americans and the British determining that aircraft had largely replaced heavy artillery, both failed to define how actually to employ airpower in the deep battle. This practical problem did not interfere with this policy's chief benefit: it avoided the expense of procuring new heavy artillery. The British did little more than fit pneumatic tyres to their few remaining World War One heavy guns and howitzers. Fortunately, the Americans were not as short sighted, and through Lease Lend they were able to equip the British with modern ordnance.

The Germans entered World War Two with a clear, agreed, air/land doctrine. In a rejection of their World War One approach the Germans saw airpower as setting the conditions for successful land warfare through gaining overall air supremacy, preferably through surprise attacks on airfields before the start of formal hostilities. The Luftwaffe would then switch to air interdiction[68], and when ground fighting reached its decisive point, German aircraft massed overwhelming firepower on the battlefield[69]. Unlike other air forces in the early years of the War, the Luftwaffe recognised that: '*there would be moments ... where air power could provide the margin on which victory or defeat turned*[70]'. This doctrine was developed in the Spanish Civil War; it was then refined in the less challenging Polish and Norwegian campaigns, before its triumph in the Battle for France. The High Command suffered from personal and inter-service disputes, but despite the actions of their masters, at the tactical level German forces invariably achieved effective air and ground cooperation. This was assisted by the Luftwaffe's organisation largely paralleling the army's command and control. The Luftwaffe's air signals liaison parties were attached to army HQs from the regimental level upwards.

At the time, the Ju-87 Stuka dive bomber symbolised German aerial firepower. In fact, these aircraft, with their specialist training, made up less than 15% of the Luftwaffe's aircraft in 1940[71]. Their prominence has led to a continuing misconception of German airpower's role in the Blitzkrieg years. Despite recent scholarship, the fallacy endures that the Luftwaffe were the Wehrmacht's flying artillery[72]. As they demonstrated at the start of each campaign, the

Luftwaffe's first priority was to achieve air superiority, before switching to air interdiction and terror bombing of civilian targets. While this was on-going only the specialist dive-bomber units were regularly tasked to provide close air support. The Stuka was actually designed to be the equivalent of the mobile heavy artillery that Germans fielded in World War One to break through Belgian and French fortifications. It was a dive bomber in order to attack point targets; the Stuka was less suited to engaging deployed units, but they proved to be effective in this role because of their air/land integration training. However, the dive bomber's performance trade-off and method of attack rendered them vulnerable in contested airspace to both effective anti-aircraft guns and any fighter aircraft.

True to their doctrine, at the decisive moment of the campaign, all available Luftwaffe aircraft were switched to attacking the opposing land forces. To support the crossing of the river Meuse during the Invasion of France, the following order was produced:

> *'On the 13th of May [1940] the point of main effort of our Western Offensive lies in the sector of Group von Kleist. Almost the whole of the German air force will support this operation[73].'*

The Luftwaffe attacked the French X Corps and in the 8-hours prior to the planned river crossing; they defeated the formation's artillery, command and control, and logistics, thus unhinging the French infantry defending the river line. The Luftwaffe liaison teams attached to the assaulting panzer divisions identified the targets and communicated them to the airfields, allowing the targeting information to be disseminated through pre-flight mission briefing. Coordination between air and ground forces was achieved by using the river as the dividing 'bomb-line'. The lack of direct communication between ground and air prevented aircraft from providing covering fire in the assault across the river. Instead this was provided by organic direct and indirect fire weapons. This approach proved successful against a largely passive enemy. Impressive as this concentration of aerial firepower was, other German forces crossed the Meuse without receiving any air support[74]. The force employment of the German air force in 1939–41 was:

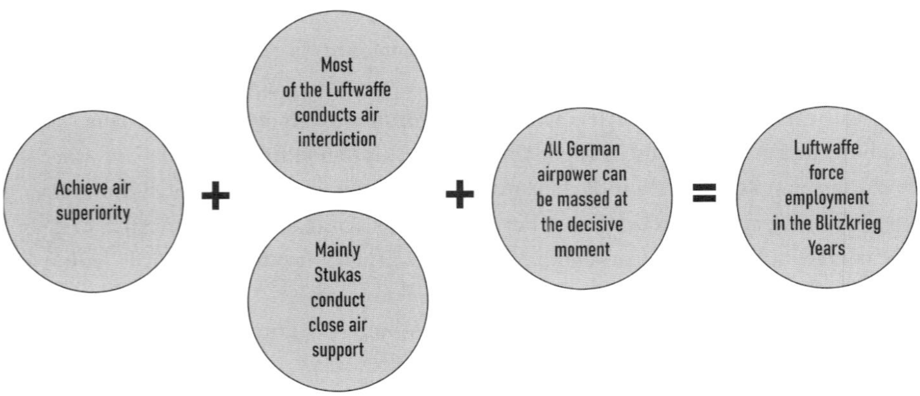

The French campaign, and their subsequent ones leading up to the invasion of the USSR, convinced the Germans that they had sufficient firepower to support the decisive manoeuvre that would shatter their opponent's will to resist; leading to mass capitulations. However, in the early years of the War the Germans faced weak and dislocated defences. They also benefitted from the superior fighting ability of German soldiers and airmen, which made them per capita World War Two's most effective military[75]. Unfortunately for the Wehrmacht, as Frederick the Great discovered after the Battle of Zorndorf in 1758: '*It is easier to kill these Russians than defeat them*[76]'; leading to the limitations of their warfighting approach been exposed in the second half of the war.

The Germans remained the masters of mobile operations, but after initial successes in Russia they were rarely successful in attacking set defence. In contrast, the Soviets were able to break-through properly structured German defences and then conduct operational level exploitation. They were able to do this in the winter months from 1942 and in all conditions from mid 1943, despite this being the time when the German military was at its peak of effectiveness. The key difference between the two tactical systems was in their use of firepower. Soviet doctrine expected firepower to systematically neutralise an enemy's defence throughout its entire depth as a pre-requisite to a successful offensive. Once a breach was achieved, accompanying artillery and aircraft maintained the advance's momentum. In contrast, the Germans were generally dependent upon either identifying an existing weakness in a defence, or generating one through rapid manoeuvre. When faced with a set defence, they expected an armoured wedge, led by their heavy tanks to bludgeon their way through.

Soviet doctrine saw artillery as the primary provider of firepower in the combined arms battle that also included airpower. Airpower was entirely subordinate to ground operations, with their initial task being engaging targets outside artillery range, before switching to supporting advancing mobile forces[77]. The World War Two Soviets did not distinguish between close air support and air interdiction, referring to both as support of the ground forces[78]. Their emphasis was effect on the battlefield: devoting 40–50% of sorties to this task[79]. By the Battle of Stalingrad, the Soviet Air Forces had adopted a new air offensive doctrine, which effectively is still in force. This had two phases: pre-planned aerial preparation attacks, and air support which accompanied the breakthrough force. The first phase required the achievement of local air superiority over the battlefield[80]. Airpower then compensated for the Soviet artillery's short range; 70% of which was under 100mm calibre and could only engage targets up to an average of 5km behind the forward line of enemy troops[81]. The need to neutralise German defences throughout their full depth led to the few longer-range bombers (actually these were medium bombers by contemporary Anglo-American standards) being assigned to targets immediately behind the front line. Targeting followed the doctrine articulated by 1930s Red Army Marshal Mikhail Tukhachevskty that airpower should be:

> '*employed against targets beyond the range of infantry, artillery, and other arms. For maximum tactical effect aircraft should be employed in mass, concentrated in time and space, against targets of the highest tactical importance*[82].'

By 1944 it was usual for two fighter divisions to cover a tank army employed as the breakthrough force. These divisions had between 1,500–2,500 combat aircraft. Mass was achieved through denuding other sectors of the front. The norm was for 90–95% of available aircraft to be allocated to an offensive. Aiding this massing of firepower was the progressive strengthening of the Air Corps of the Stavka Reserve. This was formed in 1942; by January 1945 it comprised 43% of all Soviet combat aircraft[83]. Many of these aircraft were Il-2 Shturmovik which could roam over the battlefield with relative immunity and acquire their own targets along the axis of advance. This compensated for the Soviet inability to dynamically control airborne air support. Aircraft were essential in the Soviet firepower system, as once ground forces had broken-through, they were beyond the range of any artillery that was not accompanying the exploitation force.

The Soviet definition of air superiority was the ability to deploy overwhelming airpower over the area where their ground forces were seeking to achieve a decision. So, they did not systematically attempt counter air operations to achieve theatre-wide air superiority. As a result, despite the growing dominance of the Soviet Air Force, the Wehrmacht was largely free to operate unhindered behind its front line, with partisans posing a greater threat than airpower. Hence, in contrast to operations against the Western Allies, the Germans retained the ability to conduct armoured operational level manoeuvre on the Eastern Front until the end of the War[84]. This was the Soviet approach to airpower in their Great Patriotic War:

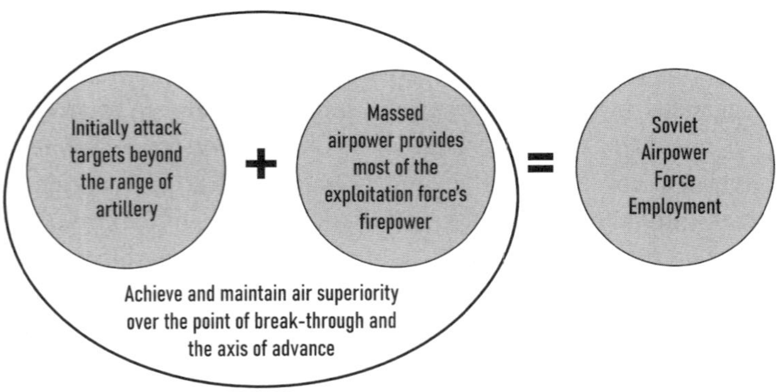

The Soviet lack of interest in achieving air superiority, except over the battlefield of a major offensive, allowed German aircraft, including the obsolete Stuka, the freedom to continue inflicting significant loses on Soviet forces. With ground based air defence often being the only significant challenge to their operations. This different character of air operations is rarely mentioned in Anglo-American centric airpower studies, but is necessary to understand Russia's current approach to the air/land battle[85].

Faced with this challenge, by 1943 the Germans also largely focussed their airpower on the land battlefield. The Luftwaffe's principal role became defeating armour, seeking to engage single vehicles, rather than the area targets which better suit bombs[86]. This led to their concentration on developing airborne gun systems, where they achieved a substantial technological lead over the Allies. The inability of the Luftwaffe from 1943 to interdict a battlefield was as much to do with their doctrine and equipment, as the relative numbers of aircraft. Though of course contemporary sources focussed on the lack of materiel.

At Operational Citadel, or Kursk, Generalleutnant Hermann Plocher identified that the Luftwaffe were inadequate to the task:

> *'Because the Sixth Air Fleet (and Fourth Air Fleet) lacked sufficient force, particularly suitable units, and because its operational area was so vast, it was unable to seal off the probable area or to annihilate the enemy concentrations*[87]*.'*

The Germans elected to fight a set-piece battle without recognising that its supporting airpower, which had become focussed on directly supporting the close battle, was unsuitable to its preliminary task of isolating the Kursk salient through air interdiction. Once the attack began, Soviet resistance on the ground was so fierce that the Luftwaffe almost totally switched to emergency close air support. The Soviet response to this switch in German airpower tactics was to mass their air defence artillery in the front line and take risk elsewhere. At the Battle of Kursk, these guns inflicted four times the Luftwaffe losses that Soviet fighters achieved[88]. Except for the elite tank hunting cannon armed aircraft, this threat largely forced the Luftwaffe to operate above 7,500 feet. Providing accurate close air support required them to dive from this safe altitude, through a wall of flak[89].

The outcome of the Luftwaffe's failure to conduct effective air interdiction was that Soviet forces were free to manoeuvre, as they demonstrated by counter-attacking once the German attacks had culminated. Being fixed in providing close air support also hindered the delivery of other aerial tasks. Quite rightly the effectiveness of the Soviets at *maskirovka* – the art of camouflage and deception – is lauded, but the Luftwaffe's failure to systematically conduct tactical reconnaissance and maintain battlefield surveillance was a significant factor in the Wehrmacht being consistently surprised by Soviet attacks.

Following the Battle of Kursk, with the initiative lost, the Luftwaffe was tied to an overall German strategy whose objective was attrition. This expected the Soviets to collapse due to their heavy losses[90]. In practice, the Luftwaffe was reduced to the role of a close air support 'fire brigade', fixing fighter-bombers to this task meant that they could rarely compete for air superiority over a Soviet breakthrough. In the 'flying artillery' role the Luftwaffe inflicted considerable damage, but through the dispersion of their effort, German airpower lost its ability to decisively contribute at the theatre level of war. To the German Army, the logic of fixing German airpower to supporting the close battle was inescapable. Soviet tanks presented the most direct threat to German ground forces, and therefore all available weapon systems should be used against them. The institutional dominance of the German Army prevented the emergence of any rival views to fixing airpower to the close battle[91]. Western airpower aided this blinkered approach by drawing German fighters away from the Eastern Front. By 1943, the Luftwaffe's air superiority priority had become the sky over their own homeland; a fight that they were to lose in 1944 to the American long-range P-47 and P-51 fighters.

Initially the Anglo-Americans misinterpreted the German approach of their Blitzkrieg years; incorrectly they identified close support of ground forces as being the Luftwaffe's primary mission[92]. It took time for the correct lessons of German success to be identified and counters implemented, but this is not unusual in the lesson identification process. General Maresciallo

Badoglio, Chief of Staff of the Italian Army, perhaps provides the finest example of the obduracy that can be second nature in militaries. When handed a perceptive intelligence analysis of the German tactics in the Battle for France, he said '*We'll study it when the war is over*[93]'.

In 1940 the British Army were so totally outclassed that the myth of the dominance of close air support, and specifically the Stuka, took hold as a means of excusing the defeat. German airpower was contrasted with what was seen by the Army as the failure of the RAF. This was despite their effective contesting of air superiority during the Dunkirk evacuation and subsequently in the Battle of Britain. Their challenge in the Battle of France was operating as an expeditionary air force from temporary facilities, as part of a losing coalition. Bowing to the resultant political pressure, the RAF created the Army Co-operation Command to apply the key 'lesson' of 1940: the importance of close air support, delivered by specialist aircraft, under the control of land forces[94]. This was classic confirmation bias – the tendency to recognise what confirms existing views and deny what doesn't. This is a phenomenon that in particular be-devils military decision-making, due to its hierarchical bureaucracy[95]. In this case the bias was due to the British Army having not fully reconciled itself to the independent air force. Inevitably they saw the 1940 campaign as justifying the need to reassert control over air assets that they believed was essential to deliver effective air support.

The Anglo-American force that invaded North Africa in Operation Torch initially followed the flawed doctrine of the Army Co-operation Command and its American equivalent. This resulted in the parcelling out of tactical aircraft to various tasks, giving the Luftwaffe the opportunity to achieve air control over the initial decisive engagements[96]; this approach was already obsolete. The British Desert Air Force were practising what subsequently would became the standard force employment of Western air forces[97]. Its essential features were the employment of multi-role fighters under a unified command, cooperating with, rather than being controlled by, ground forces. As the British ground commander, General Montgomery identified:

> *'Nothing could be more fatal to successful results than to dissipate the air resources into small packets placed under command of army formation commanders, with each packet working on its own plan*[98].'

By 1943, the Anglo-Americans had evolved airpower significantly beyond the German Blitzkrieg approach. Firstly, air superiority over the whole theatre was sought. Secondly, the initial belief, not wholly overcome even by 1943, was that aircraft losses outweighed the benefit of direct air support on the battlefield. This led to an emphasis on air interdiction and measures to make close air support more survivable. These included technical innovation, such as the fielding of rockets that gave aircraft greater standoff. In addition, the suppression of enemy air defence systems become a standard artillery task. Made easier by the third factor: the use of forward air controllers, including airborne ones, in and over the front line, to make airpower more responsive and lethal. In addition to controlling airstrikes, these could nominate and mark targets, de-conflict airspace and brief attacking aircraft on the ground forces schemes of manoeuvre. This added greatly to the synergizing of the ground and air attack team. Fourthly, air interdiction was extended over the theatre rather than being restricted to immediately behind the battlefield. Of course, this was possible due to the American fielding of longer-range tactical aircraft, but neither the Germans nor the Soviets fully exploited the range of even their shorter-endurance aircraft. The reach of Anglo-American airpower allowed them to conduct a deep battle different in its nature and scope to what had come before. It stretched German anti-aircraft resources to cover from their front line to their homeland. Finally, airpower was used separately from land power to conduct strategic attacks on an enemy's homeland; this reserve of firepower could also be employed in set-piece land battles. Its components can be understood as follows:

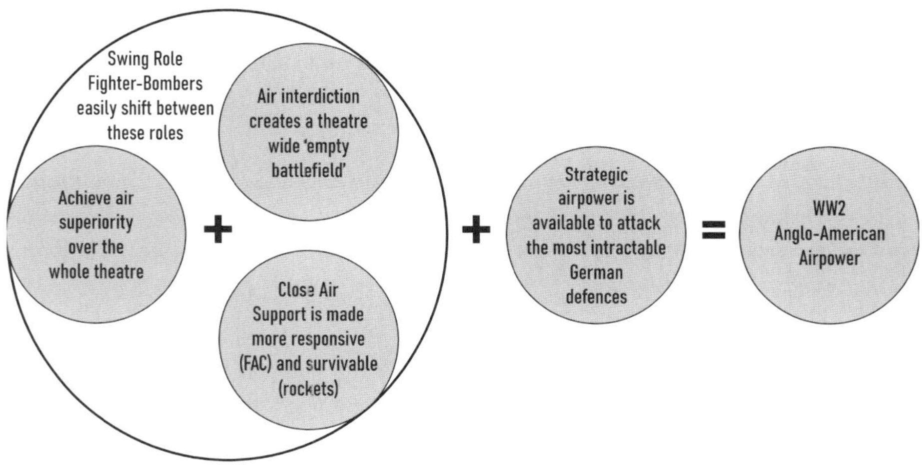

Despite the significant advances in aircraft technology, as in the Great War, the effectiveness of airpower significantly increased when the enemy postured themselves as a viable target. In the close battle, airpower's contribution was at its greatest in manoeuvre operations, it was least effective in positional warfare. Through sheer mass, strategic heavy bombers overcame airpower's unsuitability against ground forces defensively postured. The most famous example was the use 1,800 heavy bombers, 396 medium bombers, and over 350 fighter-bombers to bombard a 4 by 2.3-mile section of the German line, for 80 minutes, at the start of the Operation Cobra offensive. Once the aircraft had departed, American artillery took up the fight. The German defensive and tactical reserve positions received a weight of firepower well in excess of what artillery on its own could have delivered. However, strategic bombers were a blunt weapon: inaccurate bombs inflicted significant casualties upon American forces.

Air interdiction's impact was significantly greater than the few tanks and guns it directly destroyed; only at night and in poor flying weather could Axis troops and supplies safely move in a zone of up to 200km behind the Battle of Normandy's front line. A tank without fuel or spare parts is out of the fight; air interdiction achieved this through directly destroying more trains than tanks[99]. For the RAF in the Normandy campaign, 60% of their sorties were tasked as armed reconnaissance, hunting their own targets, 25% were allocated targets in pre-mission briefing, and the remaining 15% were held in cab-ranks or air alert. These aircraft remained on station for a period determined by their endurance. If they did not receive an impromptu close air support request, then they would head to pre-arranged armed reconnaissance areas rather than returning with their ordinance to their airfield[100].

Perhaps the Army Co-operation Command's greatest contribution was its joint development with the Royal School of Artillery of airborne forward and artillery air controllers. Placing an airborne forward air controller or artillery controller in a Stinson L-5 Sentinel spotter aircraft allowed them to be significantly more effective at acquiring and engaging targets[101]. These airborne observers kept the enemy forward areas under constant surveillance throughout the daylight hours. Field Marshal Erwin Rommel attested the effect of the combination of these forms of interdiction; identifying that they *'pinned my army to the ground … denying both supplies and the ability to freely manoeuvre'*[102]. Allied airpower was undeniably effective, however as this USAF study identified:

> *'Evaluations of German officers, almost universally and most emphatically, credit Allied air power with their defeat in Western Europe … This testimony must be discounted as to some extent as self-serving, coming as it did mostly from Army officers who were searching for an excuse for the failure of the German Army on the ground*[103]*'.*

World War Two's tactical airpower could also provide fire support when artillery firepower could not keep up with the tempo of operations. The failing was usually due to being unable to assemble sufficient shells, rather than physically deploying the guns or constructing the fire plan. The Germans pioneered this approach in their 1940 invasion of France, logistically prioritising fuel over ammunition and expecting airpower to make up the firepower deficiency. The British applied the same methodology at the Mareth Line battles in March 1943 when 54 medium bombers led the attack, before handing over to 26 fighter-bomber squadrons. The aircraft initially attacked likely enemy positions on their own, before switching to engage targets in front of a weak artillery rolling barrage; this acted as much to delineate the battlespace as achieve any impact on the Axis defenders. This improvised use of airpower enabled a successful outflanking operation without the need to assemble an orthodox level of artillery support. By this stage of the war, the level of air and ground force cooperation allowed this hastily planned attack to be quickly and successfully conducted[104]. When battlefield movement was restored following the break-out from Normandy, having achieved air superiority, the Allies had sufficient aircraft to maintain between four and twelve aircraft above and in front of their lead armoured columns. Ideally the aircraft dealt with threats that otherwise would have forced the column to slow down; more often ground forces were required to get the Germans to unmask. In these circumstances a tank-mounted forward air controller used VHF to direct the fighter-bombers to their target. The effectiveness of armoured column air cover should be measured by its assistance in sustaining armoured tempo, rather than just targets destroyed.

Despite the advances made through the War, air support remained a blunt instrument; 'blue on blue' incidents were regrettably common. The rule seemed to be that whenever the ground war was fast moving and fluid, the number of friendly casualties from air action greatly increases, a lesson that probably endures[105]. Hence the request by the Commanding Officer of a Gordon Highland battalion to his General during fighting in Normandy in 1944: *'the one thing that I cannot afford is to have the RAF operating anywhere within 50 miles of me*[106]'.

Compared to the Great War, the aircraft of World War Two carried a significantly greater payload, in more challenging weather, and at greater range; this enabled them to both mass an unmatched weight of fire, and operate over the whole theatre. In comparison to airpower's leap forward, artillery made only incremental improvements in range and lethality between the Wars. World War Two's real artillery revolution was in its command and control, enabled by wireless communications, or cybernetics as it was subsequently called[107]. The aim of cybernetics was to greatly increase fire mobility; the ability to shift firepower around the battlefield. This could empower observers to engage lucrative targets of opportunity with concentrations of fire, which for the most important tasks could be all the guns in range, or 'fire mission all available'[108].

The Germans and Soviets effectively did not participate in this command and control revolution. This is understandable for the Soviets who had developed a crude, but effective, means of providing fire support that built upon their Tsarist heritage, and made effective use of traditional Russian mass. In contrast, the German Army had initially led in the application of firepower in World War One with: mobile heavy artillery, mortars, and from 1917 fire plans designed to achieve the neutralisation of a defensive system throughout their entire depth. Their World War Two successors failed to carry forward their legacy and did not undertake any significant innovation. Of course, the terms of the Treaty of Versailles interrupted German artillery development, but it spurred innovation in the other combat arms. The fault may partly lie with Colonel Georg Bruchmüller, whose individual genius dominated the German application of firepower in the Great War, possibly at the expense of stifling the growth of an institutional basis for sustained innovation. The British Royal Artillery innovation in World War One was subsequently sustained through its artillery school and gunnery instructors. The American artillery pioneered the modern artillery command and control system in the 1930s despite their lack of resources[109]. The Americans were clear as to the opportunities presented by improved wireless communications; as this 1921 article in the Field Artillery Journal identified:

> *'Although these developments in radio will render it of enormous value to the Army as a whole, it is believed that it will be of especial and utmost importance to the Field Artillery in particular – especially to Divisional Artillery. It is believed that the greatest problem of Divisional Artillery will be solved by the aid of Radio; i.e. the accompanying of the Infantry with fire*[110].'

The Germans superficially were similar to the other major combatants in having an artillery officer at each level of command, but these did not act through a separate artillery chain of command [111]. The Germans were determined in 1939 to avoid being drawn into an attritional conflict defined by massed artillery. Instead of centralisation, each German level of command had its own indirect and direct firepower; their task was to quickly suppress opposing defences to enable high tempo manoeuvre. Their early success convinced them that they could further reduce their need for massed firepower. Following this logic, in the summer of 1941 the

Germans broke up their corps artillery and allocated it to their divisions, and prior to the invasion of Russia, the Germans reduced their shell production by 70%[112].

The Germans and Soviets started with a similar quantity of artillery on the Eastern Front, 6,000 and 7,000 respectively. The German artillery park was soon eclipsed by Soviet production, not least in terms of available ammunition. Once the Soviets had ceased retreating, German weakness was compounded by the Red Army's superior ability to concentrate firepower; in part due to their superior mechanisation made possible by American trucks. They massed almost as high a proportion of artillery as aircraft to support the decisive battle, while ruthlessly taking risk on the less important sectors of the front. Soviet all arms divisions were progressively stripped of guns as the war progressed; their increased mortar holdings only partly compensated, as they lacked the range to cover extended front lines. The benefiters of the reorganisation were the artillery formations in the *Stavka* Reserve. In 1941, roughly 20% of Soviet artillery was outside the all-arms divisions; by 1944, more than 65% of their artillery was in artillery divisions and brigades. This command and control system facilitated the massing of 17,000 rocket systems, artillery and mortars for Operation Bagration in June 1944, leaving 7,000 pieces for the rest of the front.

The Soviets' deep battle doctrine required unity of command at the Front level of command, and not the echelons below; this allowed the parallel artillery chain of command to centralise control of firepower in the set-piece battle. Once operations became mobile, control over artillery was delegated down to individual rifle and tank battalions. Lacking sufficient forward observers, radio equipment and mechanical calculators the Soviets could not participate in the cybernetic revolution. In part this was because the artillery lacked the skilled personnel – despite receiving the choice of recruits after the NKVD (the state police) and the air force[113]. Instead they relied upon pre-planned artillery fire plans, with mass compensating for any lack of accuracy. It was a blunt instrument, but as their massed artillery exceeded in terms of tubes, rocket launchers and ammunition anything seen on the Western Front, it was effective.

Soviet artillery doctrine did not identify any need to switch artillery between the close and deep battle. Instead their direct and general support artillery had specific roles in the fire plan, so allowing the simultaneous engagement of the whole of the enemy's defensive area. This inflexibility led to this German observation of the World War Two Soviet artillery:

> *'The divisional artillery, consisting of artillery battalions of various calibres, is in the habit of engaging in observed fire for the direct support of the infantry, while the artillery battalions of the GHQ [General HQ] artillery, which are uniform in calibre, are inclined – no matter whether they are parts of GHQ artillery regiments, brigades, or even divisions – to undertake unobserved fire and fire with the aid of sound-ranging, flash ranging, balloon and aircraft observation, and radio direction finding, and to engage in concentrations and rolling barrages*[114]'.

No doubt a Great Patriotic War Soviet artilleryman's rejoinder would be that what the Germans considered as flexibility was an unscientific application of firepower that concentrated on close fire support, and that the Germans, by neglecting the engagement of deep targets, failed to systemically neutralise opposing forces.

The Germans could not compete with Soviet mass, but they could employ cybernetics to rapidly concentrate their in-range artillery at the decisive point. The 18th Artillery Division was an attempt to replicate the fire mobility achieved by the Western Allies; this division lasted 9-months before being dispersed to deal with a series of individual crises. It was doomed because the prevailing German warfighting approach was one of decentralisation, improvisation and *ad hoc* battlegroups[115]. In February 1944, the Germans introduced a fire control battery for each Volks Artillerie Korps, groupings that had replaced the corps artillery structure; again, this failed through lack of resources. The 6th Panzer Army had only one fire control battery during the Battle of the Bulge. The lack of an empowered institutionally-distinct body of artillerymen, answering directly to the commanding general, is both a symptom and a cause of this German mis-appreciation of firepower's centrality in modern war. Without a separate artillery chain of command, firepower tends to be dissipated to address the most urgent individual tactical problem that is faced by each level of command[116]. Despite German failings, such is the power of artillery, that of the 10 million soldiers that the Soviet Union lost in World War Two, half were killed by indirect fire[117].

Following the early successful fighting against the Italians in the Western Desert, the British Army's failure against German forces led to them abandoning orthodox military science and replace it with novel and unproven structures and doctrine. This reflects a military culture schooled in small wars and wary of the hard fighting of peer warfighting. Experiments included: forsaking all arms cooperation and mass, emasculating artillery, and neglecting air/land cooperation. The corps and divisional levels of command were effectively discarded, with the permanent allocation of most of their assets to brigades. This was both a false imitation of the German approach, and an unnecessary adaptation to desert conditions. In contrast, the Germans combined arms tactics usually achieved combat superiority through massing their organic firepower at the decisive point. The British could not match German tactical excellence; and having abandoned their conventional structure, they could not compensate with their traditional strengths of massed artillery and airpower. Success came though returning to traditional structures that enabled the execution of a firepower dominated combined arms doctrine that served the British from El Alamein until the end of the War. Reinstating an orthodox firepower organisation required strong-willed commanders, as subordinate commander prefer to have their own artillery and airpower.

The Second World War British had more artillery in their divisions than any other army, holding a lesser proportion above divisional level in brigade-size groupings called Army Group, Royal Artillery (AGRA). Unlike the Soviets they were not reliant upon bespoke artillery formations to reinforce the main effort; instead they had perhaps the most sophisticated command and control system fielded in the war, if this is judged by the ability to shift artillery fire and mass on priority target. They were also perhaps the most ruthless in denuding less important forces of fire support[118]. As British casualties mounted and war weariness set in, they also expected their artillery to do more of the fighting than any other military.

The US artillery entered the War with a system of fire direction centres designed to make multiple battery fire missions their standard means of target engagement[119]. These batteries, being geographically spread could have significantly different times of flight; this is also the case with batteries with different equipment. The Americans overcame this by using time on targets (TOT) as their principal means of fire control. After initial reverses in North Africa, the Americans perfected their centralised control of artillery and airpower; this included the absorption of infantry guns into the divisional fire control system. The American divisions had fewer guns than the British, but significantly more were in non-divisional artillery battalions. These accounted for about half of the American field artillery in the European War and about a quarter in the Pacific theatre. Only the Soviets had more reinforcing artillery. The difference between the theatres resulted from the divisional level conducting most of the fighting against the Japanese, though corps level operations took place in the Philippines and Okinawa[120]. Unlike the British, the Americans were less willing to even temporally denude divisions of their organic artillery to support a higher priority, instead they weighted the main effort with their non-divisional artillery battalions.

The Free French forces provide a contrast with the firepower orientated Anglo-American approach. Being based on the North African regular army they did not follow the metropolitan defensive artillery doctrine. Notably, under General Juin at the Battle of Cassino, they proved to be willing to aggressively advance, over challenging terrain, with limited fire support[121].

The Anglo-Americans in Europe and North Africa were clear on how to employ firepower. Airpower could significantly add to the preparatory fire, but artillery and mortar firepower dominated once soldiers had begun the assault. Reaching a similar consensus took longer in the Pacific Theatre; in the New Guinea and Philippines campaigns an air commander confidently stated that *'in this Theatre artillery is delivered from the air'*[122]. This was despite the technical inadequacy of airborne firepower to support troops in primary jungle, not least the challenge of target identification, as well flying in very testing meteorological conditions[123]. That this gained credence was due to the logistic challenge of providing adequate organic land fire support; this made attractive any more expedient approach. This led to Australian and American forces deploying to New Guinea without their direct support artillery and with a reduced quantity of mortars[124]. This view was in accordance with contemporary American doctrine, which did not see a significant role for artillery in the jungle:

> *'Field Artillery guns are unsuited for use in the jungle. Pack howitzers, though more suitable in design and transport, are limited by their weight, bulk, and ammunition requirements. In addition to the limitations imposed on these weapons by their own bulk and weight and that of their ammunition, the dense jungle greatly confines the burst of their projectiles. Also, the advantages of their long range will ordinarily be lost because of the impossibility of ground observation and the limited effectiveness of air operation*[125].

This approach was corrected, World War Two proved that jungle fighting, like that in all other terrain, was a combined arms activity. The fighting quality of the Japanese Army was such that defeating them invariably required lavish firepower followed by hand-to-hand fighting. One example from the Burma campaign illustrates this:

> *'the impact of 100 bombers, 100 or so guns, eighty 3-inch mortars and 100 tanks followed up by well-trained, determined infantry was too much even for the most fanatical and determined foe in his village position*[126]'.

Such was the strength of Japanese fortifications that bunker busting often required 5.5-inch or 155mm calibre artillery firing over open sights. The Anglo-Americans saw this as an unusual adaptation, unlike the Soviets, who not only designed their guns to be equally adept at indirect and direct-fire, but also articulated which method of engagement to employ depends upon tactical circumstances, leading to their fire plans tasking Soviet heavy guns to conduct direct fire against individual German strongpoints and buildings. The British 25pdr gun-howitzer proved to be effective direct fire anti-tank weapon, but this was seen as a mis-use of its capability, unlike its Soviet equivalent, the 76.2mm ZiS-3 which was designed to be dual role. The Germans expected firing over open sights to be the normal means of engagement for their heavily armoured assault and infantry guns. The Soviets saw their assault guns as vital to defeating bunkers and field fortifications, and more effective than tanks in urban warfare. More general fire support was provided by field guns mounted on converted tank chasses. Rather than accompanying the assault, when employing direct fire, these occupied overwatch position 1–2km from the objective. In both armies, these vehicles soon took on an anti-tank role.

In contrast to the Germans and Soviets, Anglo-American self-propelled artillery was primarily designed for indirect fire, only in mobile operations could direct fire become a regular means of engagement. Self-propelled guns proved their worth in challenging terrain; often being the first guns ashore in amphibious operations and through being able to provide their own platform they could deploy in almost any urban and jungle terrain. Their versatility convinced the Western nations that the self-propelled gun should be the standard support weapon in armoured warfare. The Soviets did not implement this until the 1970s.

Many of World War Two's more important battles were fought within cities[127], including Stalingrad, Leningrad, Ortona, Caen, Berlin and the two most devastated cities: Manila and Warsaw. The Soviets proved to be skilful at this form of warfare. They employed their standard approach of mixing direct and indirect fire, combining centralised preliminary fires with the subsequent apportioning of tube, rocket and mortar artillery down to company level. Their key tenet was to ensure that their individual assault teams achieved fire ascendency prior to moving. While urban fighting on the Western Front lacked the scale of the Eastern Front, firepower also dominated this combat. During the 19-day battle for the city of Aachen, American forces fired an average of 9,300 artillery rounds a day, with the German defenders firing an average of 4,500 rounds in response[128]. In contrast to the Soviets, the Anglo-Americans attempted, where possible, to avoid collateral damage, in particular when attacking occupied cities such as Groningen, where the Canadians largely restricted the use of their artillery to outside the inner city, and only requested fire support when faced with the stiffest resistance[129].

The war rocket returned to the battlefield because its unmatched weight of fire provided the shock effect and destruction favoured by Soviet artillerymen. This led to the final organisation of the World War Two Soviet Breakthrough Artillery Divisions having almost as many rockets and mortars as guns and howitzers[130]. The war rocket was also widely used by the Germans, with the Western Allies making more limited and specialist use (such as 'shooting-in' amphibious assaults). The German use of the weapon presaged its subsequent use in irregular warfare. It was a means of delivering a high volume of fire before departing the launch site to avoid the inevitable retaliatory fire from the very effective Anglo-American counter fire organisation.

In both the infantry support role and as a substitute for medium and heavy artillery, the mortar proved to be an essential weapon; in the most challenging terrain it became the most common fire support weapon. As with rockets, mortars provided the Germans with a more survivable form of fire support than tube artillery. The Soviets valued its impressive striking power compared to its platform weight, its importance reflected the terrain challenges of the Eastern Front, leading to them being the main support weapon in the Pinsk Marshes. From 1943 the Soviets were almost always on the offensive, which meant that the mortar's lack of range was often unimportant, as they were able to site their batteries in range of their future objectives. It was this that led to the Soviets deploying a significant proportion of heavy mortars in their artillery division. In contrast, field artillery and lesser calibre mortars remained the standard support weapon for the Soviet rifle divisions tasked with ground holding. The 76.2mm ZiS-3 field gun's greater range provided coverage over the infantry positions and it also had an impressive anti-tank capability. Hence the resistance to its centralisation at the expense of supporting infantry divisions.

Anglo-American artillery, like their air forces, sought fire superiority across the whole frontline. The effectiveness of this approach has already been noted, with German tube artillery being eclipsed by more survivable mortars and rocket launchers. Matching their view of air superiority, Soviet artillery only sought dominance at the point of decision; here they assembled sufficient firepower to ensure that the German artillery could not interfere with their break-in and exploitation. Soviet weight of fire often achieved destruction, but the effect desired was neutralisation; the destruction of German artillery was a task for mobile forces following the break-through. With their emphasis upon counter battery operations, the British and American led the development of target acquisition, perfecting existing technology as well as introducing weapon locating radars. Rather than relying upon technical means, the Soviets employed ground reconnaissance parties as their primary target acquisition resource; these had the dual role of target acquisition and terrain reconnaissance for the breakthrough forces.

Naval gunfire provided the firepower necessary to get an amphibious force established ashore, with effective spotting, it was significantly more accurate than airpower. Naval guns provided a heavy weight of fire, though even battleships did not have the weight of ordnance to rapidly silence coastal guns mounted in concrete fortifications. In contrast, aircraft could drop a powerful enough bomb, but could rarely hit the target[131]. Naval firepower was usually required to provide protective fires in the initial few days following the landing, as the defenders often reinforced at a greater rate and with more mechanised forces, so achieving superior combat power. The heavy guns of the battleships may have provided the most impressive firepower, but it was the cruisers and destroyers with calibres equivalent to heavy and medium artillery, coupled with the rate of fire of field artillery, that often provided the most effective fire support.

Dedicated naval gunfire observers and an effective bombardment planning staff proved their utility in both European and Pacific Theatres. It was the Pacific Theatre that perhaps witnessed the greatest advances in the synchronisation of joint fires. Hard-won experience allowed the Americans at the invasion of Okinawa in April 1945 to achieve:

> *'the interlocking of naval, air and tank and artillery support and the Interchangeability of Marine and AAF [Army Air Force] aviation and Marine and Army artillery demonstrated that the American services had made tremendous progress in joint operations during the course of the war'*[132].

As a comparison to this synchronicity, a British Brigade Commander on the 6th June 1944 in Normandy struggled with responsive fires: a battalion artillery shoot took 15-minutes, naval bombardment 30-minutes and air support took at least two hours due to the complicated chain of command[133].

The sophistication of American preparatory naval fire was largely frustrated by the Imperial Japanese Army's excellent field craft, fortifications, coupled with fanatical discipline and bravery. The massed air and naval firepower employed in a preparatory bombardment of the eight square miles of Iwo Jima, may have killed as few as 200 of the 21,000 defenders. Even more firepower was employed in the three-month Battle of Okinawa, where 2.6 million artillery rounds were fired, a quarter of these were the heavier naval calibres. Japanese defences countered this firepower through extensive underground constructions that were usually sited on reverse slopes and were always meticulously concealed. The Japanese planned to limit their above-ground movement to night attacks; however, their occupation of caves made them vulnerable to American infantry assaults that sealed their entrances and this forced the Japanese infantry to counter these assault teams on the surface, so becoming exposed to American firepower[134].

Individual armies varied in their understanding of the actual purpose of firepower. The British in the European Theatre stuck to their World War One approach of seeing neutralisation as enabling manoeuvre. Airpower undertook much of the preparatory fire, with artillery focussing on covering fire. In contrast, destruction was deemed essential in operations against the Japanese, given their reliance upon heavily fortified bunkers, coupled with an unwillingness to surrender. However, in Europe, such was the weight of firepower, particularly when aerial fires were added to the mix, that the actual effect, on occasion, was destruction. In Operation Veritable the British XXX Corps effectively 'blasted' their way through the Siegfried Line as there was little room to manoeuvre[135]. In contrast, the Soviets and Americans always emphasised preparatory fire over covering fire. US doctrine in 1944 stated:

> *'In an attack on an organised position, the artillery must batter the enemy strength to the point of complete collapse before friendly infantry is committed to the assault*[136].'

The Americans tended to elongate their preparatory fire as the war progressed, especially before amphibious assaults. Two weeks became the standard time for a naval bombardment in the

Pacific War; this is in contrast to the landing at Tarawa in November 1943, these were proceeded by two and half hours of preparatory naval fire[137].

Most artillery was fired in concentrations but, when they had sufficient artillery, on the offensive the British usually employed rolling barrages. In contrast, the Americans had largely discarded this distribution of fire when fighting the Germans[138]. Initially few Soviet artillery units could technically master simple barrages, let alone moving ones. By 1944 the Soviets were making extensive use of rolling barrages to counter the German elastic defence practice of moving between defensive positions to avoid the full weight of the fire. The Germans learnt that defending through strongpoints rather than manoeuvre merely provided an easy static target for Soviet artillery concentrations[139]. From mid-1944, pioneered by the 2nd Belorussian Front, static barrages were extensively employed to protect penetration corridors against counter-attacks[140]. The technical improvement of Soviet artillery is illustrated by their employment of a rolling double barrage at the Battle for Berlin, including one that advanced over a kilometre[141].

All the Allied armies employed massive quantities of firepower in the break-in battle. As Soviet deep battle theory[142] in effect saw this as a preliminary operation, they prioritised their fire support around the decisive phase, the break-in battle's exploitation. The effectiveness of Soviets in exploiting their breakthroughs contrasts with the lack of preparation for the pursuit displayed by the Western Allies[143]. Soviet firepower's task was to achieve the forward passage of the mobile exploitation forces without them losing momentum. Despite the fielding of a greater proportion of long-range artillery in the Breakthrough Artillery Divisions, the greater depth of German defences from 1943[144] meant that much of the Soviet artillery could be out of range. As a result, the insertion of mobile forces was the cue for the Red Air Force to enter the battle in mass; usually through the employment of corps of five hundred specialist ground attack aircraft. The Soviet breakthrough battle used firepower in following sequence:

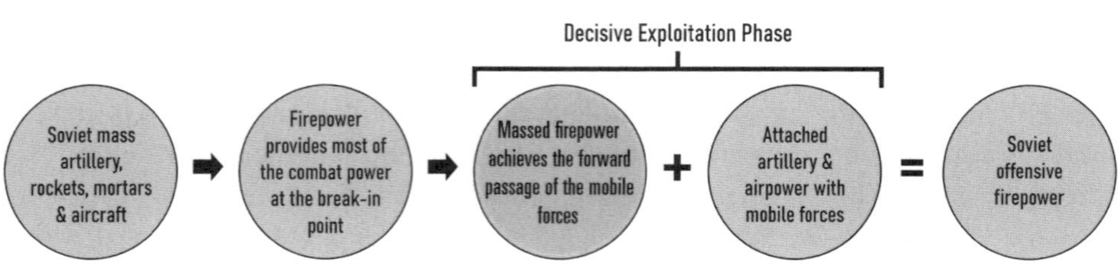

The mobile group spearheading the exploitation echelon, was tasked with provoking a 'systemic operational shock' through deep penetration into the enemy force's rear areas[145]. The mobile group's artillery was usually excused from the break-in battle's fire plan, so that it was fully provisioned and rested for this task. The artillery marched in the manoeuvre unit's column; in order to preserve tempo, ideally fire support was provided without ever leaving this formation. A successful forward passage of the mobile forces placed them in their opponent's vulnerable rear area of HQs, artillery, repair and supply facilities. This forced by-passed German infantry units to retreat to avoid being cut-off; once these were outside their prepared positions they were highly vulnerable to mechanised attack. Below is the sequence of a Soviet set piece battle:

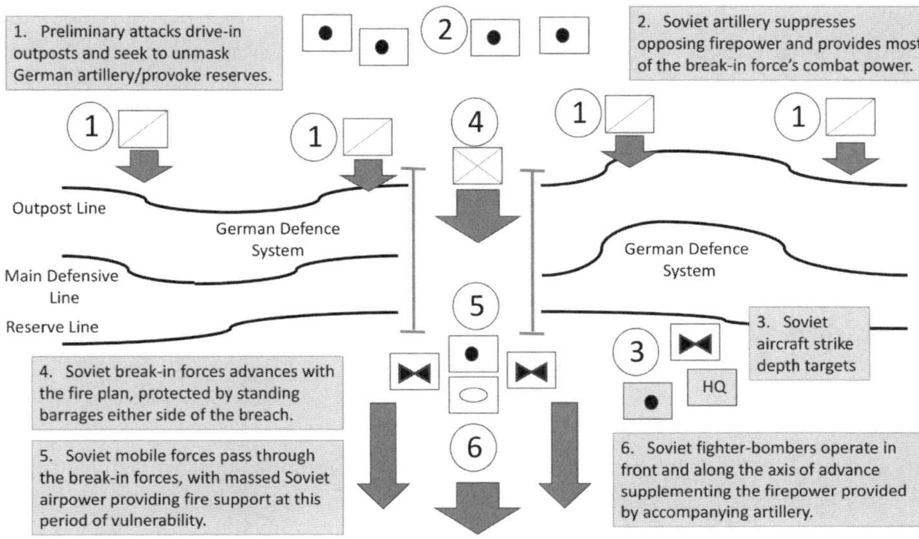

In contrast, the Western Allies focussed their firepower planning on the seizure of the immediate tactical objective. With their more flexible command and control system, the Anglo-Americans expected that support to the subsequent exploitation could be largely improvised; this often led to the Western Allies failing to correctly site their guns to provide fire support for the exploitation force. The usual outcome was that this armoured force was largely reliant upon their accompanying artillery and on-call close air support. An extra challenge was caused by expecting artillery organic to Anglo-American armoured divisions to contribute to the initial fire plan. This required the direct support artillery to stop firing and join their division once it entered the breach in the enemy defences. At best, this policy resulted in these guns been short of ammunition and crewed by physically tired soldiers; when war's friction intervened, the exploitation force could lose its organic fire support.

At Operation Goodwood, in the Normandy Campaign, true to their doctrine, all available British artillery fired in the break-in fire plan. Subsequent traffic jams prevented the armoured divisions' direct support artillery from joining their tanks in seizing of Bourgebus Ridge. This was always likely as only half of the British armoured divisions' artillery was armoured and tracked, thus making it vulnerable to being held up by enemy action[146]. Unlike Soviet doctrine, in the Goodwood offensive there was no pre-planned use of airpower after the break-in battle. The air commanders mooted a second strategic air force bombing attack against the likely German depth positions on Bourgebus ridge, delivered late on the first day or early on the second day of the offensive, but this was declined by the ground commanders. As a result, British armour, having outstripped its supporting artillery, was held by the unsuppressed German defences on the ridge.

The Soviets may have been effective at providing fire support in the break-in and breakthrough battles, but their exploitation forces' relative lack of firepower made them vulnerable to counter attacks. This was because Soviet artillery ceased being centrally controlled and so tank and rifle battalions could only call upon the fire support of their attached guns and rockets. In contrast, the Anglo-American artillery command system functioned in the pursuit, and it allowed any gun in range to support the exploiting force. The Anglo-Americans also made much more effective use of airpower in open fighting, with the aircraft overhead of the advancing columns being directed by the forward air controllers mounted in tanks. The Soviet lack of ground-to-air radio communications meant that aircraft were usually limited to acquiring their own targets on the axis of advance.

In summary, Western artillery and airpower benefited from a revolution in command and control that enabled them to both mass and provide responsive, decentralised firepower. The Anglo-American deep battle used persistent observation by aircraft and ground sensors to cue artillery and aircraft strikes. They extended the deep battle through theatre-wide air interdiction, preventing the Germans from conducting armoured manoeuvre with the freedom that they enjoyed on the Eastern Front.

In contrast, the Germans marginalised firepower and subordinated it to manoeuvre; this proved inadequate after the Blitzkrieg years. What is inexplicable is that after 1942 it was obvious that the Germans were locked into the attritional conflict that they had sought to avoid, and yet they failed to adjust their methods to this reality. This failure to correctly appreciate the grammar of the conflict continued in the two post-War memoirs of the German Generals, Guderian and von Mellenthin, which have most heavily influenced Western views of the Russo-German War[147].

The Japanese belief that moral factors could overcome firepower proved unfit even in jungle warfare; in open terrain they were totally overmatched by modern combined arms armies. This was underscored when they faced battle hardened Soviet formations in the Manchurian campaign. Hence, their firepower doctrine can be discounted as anachronistic. This leaves three principle means of employing firepower in this war. These are the Western or Anglo-American centralised system, the Soviet system and that employed by the Wehrmacht. The characteristics of these three systems are best understood by them being outcomes stemming from trying to balance different goals:

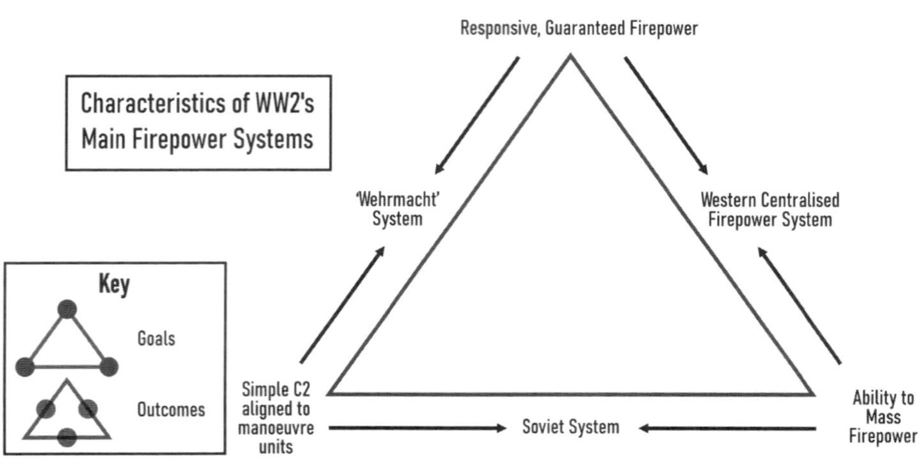

The Eastern Front was dominated by Soviet artillery; airpower's role was supporting, but becoming more important once the majority of artillery lacked the range to support the exploitation force. The Soviets flipped the Western orthodoxy: seeing firepower as the decisive element in the close battle, while mobile ground forces, with supporting aircraft, were the principal means of conducting the deep battle. Soviet confidence in their approach and the almost 'canonisation' of the Great Patriotic War meant that other views were stymied, particularly those that sought a greater air force role[148]. Leading Marshal of Aviation Vershinin in 1949 to state that World War Two had proved that success could only be won by all services working together, by which he meant tactical airpower being under the Front Commander[149].

It was to be the Western Allies' form of warfare, with its greater balance between the various forms of joint fires and its decentralised approach that was to prove more successful in the various post World War Two conflicts. Through America's dominance, especially of NATO, this firepower approach became the Western orthodoxy. The Soviet centralised combined arms approach, with its rigid integration of all forms of firepower into a fire plan that determined the manoeuvre plan, may well have proved superior if the Cold War had gone hot. Where World War Two was decisive was that the belligerents went to war with at least six force employment approaches; by 1945 this had crystallised into a binary Western and Soviet division. Both of these recognised that firepower dominated the conventional battlefield. The German system failed because it did not.

Chapter 3: The Firepower's Continued Dominance in the Cold War

'from the 1950s the fire-power equations were unbalanced by nuclear weapons.[1]*'*

Shelford Bidwell and Dominic Graham, Gunners and Historians

Direct great power conflict ended with World War Two, despite this the World was kept busy with a series of conflicts of varying character. The majority of this chapter's analysis is of state-on-state conventional war, an approach justified by this remaining the most decisive form of conflict. Of the Superpowers, America was the most heavily engaged, fighting conventionally in Korea and against both an insurgency and conventional forces in Vietnam. They also enforced the Monroe Doctrine in interventions that add little to this study. These conflicts allowed America to perfect a highly responsive and flexible fire support system. The Korean War confirmed that despite nuclear weapons conventional firepower still ruled the battlefield. The limitations of using firepower without manoeuvre against opponents employing irregular warfare tactics was demonstrated in America's Vietnam War and Soviet operations in Afghanistan. Perversely both Superpowers saw attrition through firepower as the means to their victory.

As they involved relatively matched armies, the Arab-Israeli Wars provided the main arena for the advance of military science in conventional warfare. The Israeli Army's force employment changed throughout its six conventional inter-state wars, culminating in a combined arms approach with a powerful artillery park and very extensive use of mortars; while Arab conventional armies mainly employed Soviet equipment and doctrine.

The Vietnam War saw the extensive fielding of armed helicopters, and then dedicated attack helicopters, which added the final element of the joint fires system-of-systems. However, no country has matched America's enthusiasm for attack helicopters, and many choose to operate without this capability. Doctrinally Western airpower focussed on air superiority and interdiction; with the Americans leading in the use of airpower in close support. The Soviets favoured employing attack helicopters, seeing the Hind helicopter as a direct replacement for their Great Patriotic War armoured ground attack aircraft.

Limited War in Korea: The Dominance of Conventional Firepower

'Americans excelled at this kind of war, in which the American preponderance in artillery, air power, and heavy firepower of all kinds was employed to its maximum. Americans always have been outstanding in swapping high expenditures of ammunition and bombs for casualties[2]*'.*

Bevin Alexander, American military historian and Korean War Veteran

The Korean War showed that the major powers could conduct conflict below the nuclear threshold and that conventional firepower would continue to dominate. For analytical purposes it can be divided into a war of movement (June to November 1950) that brought out no new lessons, followed by a static phase that lasted until July 1953. The conflict's character was defined by politics rather than technology and force employment. The need to avoid escalation led to the war being geographically limited to the Korean Peninsula, resulting in the purely tactical employment of airpower. Avoiding Western casualties led to an extreme form of the mantra that 'shells save lives'. The fighting and ceasefire negotiations were contiguous for much of the conflict, talks began on 10 July 1951, so from a political standpoint losing ground was not an option, leading UN forces to adopt a strictly attritional positional defence. Elastic defence in depth might have been more effective, but it could not guarantee that lost ground would be retaken. The defeat of the Communists did not need to be outright, merely sufficient for them to agree a political settlement. Hence both sides used their offensives to gain territorial advantage in the ongoing negotiations.

UN firepower superiority gave them the edge in inflicting casualties. The result was that in the static phase, the Korean War replicated a high-tech version of World War One's attritional warfare; with holding ground being the defining characteristic, both sides used field fortifications as the main counter to firepower. This led to destruction rather than neutralisation becoming the desired effect of both artillery and airpower[3]. The unique character of the conflict reinforced the American way of war's emphasis upon synchronised firepower to achieve attrition. This path led to failure in Indo-China almost a quarter of century later.

World War Two artillery tactics and equipment needed little adaptation to this character of conflict. As destruction was often the required effect, divisional artillery usually engaged as a single fire unit; this accentuated America's traditional favouring of destructive preparatory fire rather than neutralising covering fire to enable manoeuvre, it also led to prominence being given to the larger calibres. The rate of fire and the danger close capability of 105mm howitzer fire was essential in halting enemy massed infantry attacks, but 155mm howitzers and guns, together with 203mm and 240mm howitzers, were required to defeat Communist field fortifications[4]. The War's character led to significantly more shells being fired than was the norm in World War Two; the rate of fire of individual batteries at the Battle of Soyang was four times greater than the Battle of Bastogne seven years earlier[5].

Air support saw the real innovation in joint fires technology and procedures. Helicopters were widely used by American-led UN forces, but they had not yet been armed; jet aircraft dominated the conflict, but their air speed made them less suitable for close air support. This, together with the USAF's formation as an independent service, led to a series of disputes over air support. Fuelling the dispute in this firepower-orientated, casualty-averse war, was a negative impression of the air force contribution. This was probably because, as General MacArthur's Congressional hearings identified, '*too much was expected of the air*[6]'.

The UN's forces emphasised interdiction over close air support (337,913 interdiction sorties were flown compared to 131,395 close air support sorties[7]). This being the orthodox means of employing airpower, especially when the opposing ground forces are largely entrenched. Air attacks destroyed much of North Korea's infrastructure and made resupply more hazardous and laborious for the Communists. However, they adapted to the challenge and conducted most of their logistics at night, when they relied upon difficult-to-interdict human and animal transportation. The physical and psychological impact of air operations behind the front line certainly had a profound impact on North Korean Lieutenant General Nam Il (their chief delegate at the armistice talks):

> *'It is owing to your strategic air effort of indiscriminate bombing of our area, rather than your tactical air effort of direct support to the front line, that your ground forces are able to maintain barely and temporarily their present positions* ...[8].'

Though, as with the Germans in World War Two, we must be wary of totally accepting this, as the General also saw UN airpower as the excuse for his '*powerful and battle-skilled ground forces*[9]' not being victorious on the ground.

Interdiction did have a impact, but this was largely unappreciated at the time, as the commanders of the newly independent air force had over-promised by undertaking to deliver a 'knock-out blow'. In what would become an enduring theme, the West's opponents had constructed a character of conflict that largely negated airpower's operational and strategic impact, while largely countering its tactical effect. They achieved this by presenting close air support with heavily entrenched and dispersed targets, and air interdiction with a largely infrastructure-agnostic logistic system. The resultant political frustration led to the USAF's constant attempts to widen the theatre of operations to allow them to engage targets on the other side of the Yalu River, in Chinese territory. President Truman was not prepared to escalate the conflict, even when this required the sacking of General MacArthur. This would not be the last time that air force commanders, in search of a decisive target set, would challenge a limited war's political bounds.

The controversy over close air support became an inter-Service dispute through X Corps (a mixed Army and Marine formation supported by 1st Marine Air Wing) being identified as a better joint warfighting team than the rest of 8th Army. The key difference was that X Corps, largely through using US Marine resources, had a superior air/land integration structure. Each battalion had a forward air controller and all HQs above brigade had tactical air control parties (TACP). As in the World War Two Philippines Campaign, the Army-led X Corps was content with the USMC lead on air/land integration. It was this structure, and not who flew the mission, that was important; as the whole of the force was supported by the American Air Force, Navy and Marine aircraft plus allied air contingents. The USAF agreed that this air/land integration structure was more effective, but they refused to meet the resource bill required to roll it out across 8th Army. Cynical ground officers opined that this was also because they believed it would generate more close air support requests, which could divert aircraft from the air force's priority, the interdiction campaign[10].

Close air support was vital in avoiding the overrunning of isolated UN forces in the War's mobile phase; later it provided the weight of ordnance necessary to destroy Communist entrenchments. Even B-29 Superfortresses were employed against ground forces, but they failed to have the impact strategic bombers had in World War Two due to less suitable targets, less effective air/land integration and their reduced familiarity with close formation conventional bombing[11]. Counter flak fire missions were common in World War Two set-piece battles; in the Korean War, they almost became a prerequisite to executing close air support. Plentiful fire support made this possible, but it was also necessary because radar directed anti-aircraft guns were significantly more lethal[12].

Both sides saw the superiority of firepower as the conflict's key lesson. The US Army's focus upon attrition came at the expense of manoeuvre, and ultimately in its next conflicts the Army's offensive spirit. The North Koreans effectively fought the mobile phase of the war without indirect fire. In the static warfare they steadily built up their tube and rocket artillery in terms of quantity and technical ability. The monthly highpoint of their artillery ammunition expenditure was 220,880 rounds in October 1952[13]. This was employed through rigid fire plans that required batteries to be individually adjusted onto a target, so massed fire could not be improvised against opportunity targets. Faced with superior firepower, the Communists sited their guns well back, in concealed and fortified positions, making extensive use of caves and tunnels, to increase their survivability. As in World War Two the mortar proved to be more difficult to defeat than artillery, resulting in the US artillery conducting twice as many counter mortar, as counter battery, missions[14].

The North Koreans nowadays see their artillery as not just a battlefield weapon, but a strategic one, due to the ceasefire line being so close to their opponent's capital[15]. This threat is made more dangerous with their fielding of longer-range artillery and South Korean housing developments that have put more civilians within range[16]. Much of their artillery firepower continues to be emplaced in hardened underground bunkers; these may be vulnerable to modern accurately-delivered bunker-busting bombs, but the North Koreans have also developed counters to the guidance systems that make this precision possible.

One of the War's legacies was the American Army's perspective that their air force was not providing adequate support; they identified that the new jet fighters were too fast to effectively acquire and engage ground targets, while strategic bombers were now focussed on the nuclear role. The Army's preferred solution was of course a bespoke close air support aircraft. Their second concern was that the Air Force's institutional preference for deep air interdiction made them resistant to providing close air support. The third complaint was the air force's inadequate resourcing of the air/ground integration structure. All this led to the Army redoubling its efforts to create its own helicopter-based air support.

In understanding the Korean War's broader context, Stalin was probably the most prescient when he identified to Mao that:

> *'[a] drawn out war gives the possibility to the Chinese troops to study contemporary war on the field of battle and in the second place shakes up the Truman regime in America and harms the prestige of the Anglo-American troops[17].'*

America was to fight its next Asian war with a significantly superior close air support system, but their opponents could draw upon the Chinese experience of countering airpower. Western forces would also discover that firepower can be Janus-faced in a counter-insurgency.

The Indochina Wars – The Attack Helicopter Completes the Joint Fire System-of-Systems

'Mass application of firepower, as in Korea and WW2, was felt to be the most efficient methods of generating an enemy body count while minimising US casualties[18]'.

Andrew F. Krepinevich Jr., 1986

The French and American Indo-China Wars lasted from the end of World War Two until 1975. The Communists largely set both the tempo and the character of the conflict; varying this between irregular and regular warfighting, and making extensive use of political warfare techniques. The Communists correctly recognised that the will of the French and American people to continue the struggle was the decisive factor. The French and American forces usually fought well, the latter were never defeated in a significant pitched battle, but they both lacked a strategy to deliver a favourable political outcome. A simplistic analysis of their tactical shortcomings identifies that the French failure was as a result of being overmatched by Viet Minh firepower, while the American failure was in not understanding how to correctly employ their superior firepower.

Facing non-linear tactics, the French covered Vietnam with *'positional artillery, spreading its net across the vital points so it would always be ready to fire*[19]'. France's 'artillery of intervention' was meant to provide additional support to mobile forces, but the lack of airlift meant that it was tied to the limited road network. This deficiency in mobile organic firepower could not be overcome by French airpower; making French forces vulnerable when operating outside the range of their positional artillery. The dynamic can be understood as follows:

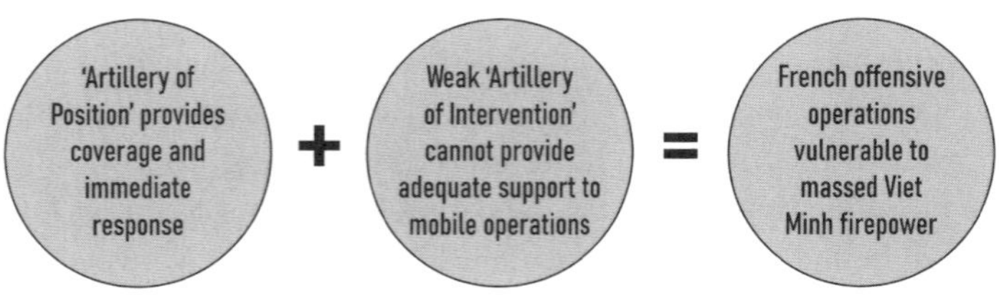

Despite this, the French embarked upon the Dien Bien Phu operation with the intent of creating an artillery fort that would bring the Viet Mihn to decisive battle and defeat them. The French deployed 30 guns, spread around the base's wide perimeter, in open positions that provided maximum coverage for their patrolling infantry. The Vietnamese managed to assemble around 200 guns and mortars, with sufficient ammunition to sustain a daily rate of fire of around 2,000 rounds. This required somewhere in the region of 100,000 porters to maintain the 600km line of communications[20]. Having the initiative, the Vietnamese guns were sited to engage only the sector of the French position they intended to assault; the dispersed French guns lacked the range to provide massed fire at the threatened point of the perimeter. Their lack of protection meant that they could not survive counter battery fire; in contrast Vietnamese guns and mortars were well concealed and were usually dug-in with overhead protection.

The French Air Force lacked the numbers and doctrine to compensate for their Army's firepower deficiency at Dien Bien Phu. Before this decisive battle they had over-specialised in counter-insurgency. Their P-63 and B-26 aircraft relied upon strafing with machine guns and cannon; this was the right response to dispersed guerrillas, but it led to them largely discounting bombs[21]; this meant that they lacked the weaponry and skill to take on entrenched artillery. Reliance on low level strafing made French aircraft particularly vulnerable to the twenty-four 37mm anti-aircraft cannon, plus 740 weapons between 12.7mm and 20mm calibre, that the Viet Minh deployed at Dien Bien Phu.

Defeat in this battle need not have led to French capitulation: they lost only 4% of their overall Theatre strength, while the Viet Minh suffered around 50% greater casualties. But the Viet Minh, in achieving their political objectives, were prepared to accept greater casualties than the French. In addition, being out-gunned in a conventional battle through being tactically inept had a considerable psychological impact. As President Eisenhower unsentimentally observed:

> *'Who could be so dumb as to put a garrison down in a valley and then challenge the other guy, who has artillery on the surrounding hills, to come out and fight[22]'.*

Despite this set back, this French way of warfare in being light on firepower, and over-reliant upon the most easily countered form – low level close air support – would often be the pattern for subsequent counter-insurgency in the retreat from Empire.

Initially the Americans attempted to fight their Indo-China War with airpower, military advisors and special operations forces, plus non-military support. This led to the USAF having the dual mission of training the South Vietnamese Air Force and supporting their ground forces. The latter soon became the priority; as a result, American air liaison officers and forward air controllers were deployed to South Vietnamese Army HQs[23]. The Americans assessed that airpower could not achieve military success without equally competent ground forces; army and marine units arrived in 1965. Given the terrain, the strength of the opposition and the current level of airpower technology, this was probably necessary to prevent a Communist takeover. However, rather than seeing this as a temporary arrangement, pending the building-up of indigenous forces, the Americans took over the War and marginalised their ally.

Taking up the grid system from the French, the Americans covered Southern Vietnam with fire bases. Their primary function was to provide highly responsive fire support to the forces operating in their area of responsibility[24]. Their disadvantage was that in achieving coverage they dissipated firepower; in addition, they could provide an opportunity for the Communists to mass firepower and manpower to overrun individual fire bases. However, in contrast to the French, the Americans were never significantly outmatched by their enemy's firepower. As well as lavish air support, in 1969, the Army fielded 61 artillery battalions to support their 59 infantry battalions in South Vietnam. This general war ratio of an equal numbers of artillery and infantry battalions was partly offset by America's allies being predominantly infantry. The result was that attacks on fire bases usually provided the Americans with an opportunity to fix their elusive enemy and then employ their superior firepower[25]. The most famous instance of this was the siege of Khe Sanh in 1968, which was probably an attempt by the Communists to replicate a Dien Bien Phu style decisive battle. Instead, it provided the Americans with an opportunity to demonstrate the complete superiority of their firepower over both North Vietnamese regulars and their Viet Cong auxiliaries. At times the communists degenerated into effectively human-wave attacks supported by wholly inadequate supporting firepower.

One downside of fire bases is that they tended to fix Americans to cautiously operating within range of their artillery; this led to what their commander, General Westmoreland, described as a *'fire base psychosis*[26]*'*. To counter this, General Westmoreland attempted to fight the war through search-and-destroy sweeps designed to bring the Communists to battle; it was a counter-insurgency approach that largely ignored the concept of the people being a prize to be contested. Responding to a question posed by a reporter on civilian casualties caused by friendly fire, the General replied *'it does deprive the enemy of population'*[27]. In Westmorland's time, of the American forces, only the Marines with their Combined Action Platoons, devoted significant resources to securing the people. Starting in 1965, these aimed at securing nearly eighty villages, each with small garrisons of around 13 Marines and 35 Vietnamese militiamen; for 1.5% of the total Marine manpower this had a disproportionate effect. Despite this, General Westmoreland's view that it was a waste of resources, as it diverted troops from search-and-destroy missions[28].

Except for specific surge operations, the dispersion of guns prevented artillery achieving the mass required to first fix and then defeat the Communists. Artillery was invariably the first responder and provided guaranteed, all weather, fire support, but it was air and aviation firepower that was usually decisive. Weapons able to engage close to own troops were at a premium, as the Communists sought to nullify American firepower through closing with, or better yet, intermingling with the anti-Communist ground troops. As a result, 105mm calibre weapons dominated; the self-propelled version was kept in service even when the 155mm M109 had replaced it in other theatres. A key advantage was that in its towed form, the 105mm howitzer was easily helicopter transportable. Use was also made of the 155mm howitzer, the 175mm gun and 203mm howitzer. When 105mm and heavier guns were located in the same fire support base, the former were preferred for the direct support of troops in contact. The latter were used when the smaller calibre cannon lacked the range, and when engaging targets away from own troops, such as during harassing and interdiction missions. The North Vietnamese made effective use of their long-range 130mm guns to harass and distract American artillery. This resulted in artillery duels that usually only the American 175mm guns had sufficient range to join. While the threat posed by the 130mm gun challenged American artillerymen, the Communists, in what has become a standard tactic in irregular warfare, derived most of their firepower from man-portable rockets and mortars.

The only joint fires weapon system on the American side to diminish in importance was the battalion level mortar. Its principle advantage of guaranteed fire through ownership was undermined by American infantry invariably operating within the coverage provided by at least one fire base, leading to artillery support being almost always available. In addition, aviation fires could be safely employed closer to own forces than the mortar; this often made the carrying of their own means of indirect fire support superfluous to the already heavily burdened infantry.

As with the Korean War, most of the innovation was in aerial firepower, with the fielding of two new types of aircraft. Firstly, the AH-1 Cobra, the World's first attack helicopter; and secondly the gunship with its laterally-mounted direct fire armament. The arming of the Huey utility aircraft with guns and rockets preceded the bespoke AH-1 Cobra; aerial rocket artillery was employed in mass as a supplement to artillery fire, or if this was out of range, as a replacement. This enabled manoeuvre outside the range of fire bases without the requirement to preposition artillery and shells to provide fire support. The helicopter's machine guns, cannon and grenade launchers allowed it to excel at danger close fire support. This led to the helicopter becoming an essential element in America's fire support system. As the Army Chief of Staff General Creighton Abrams observed in April 1973: '*the attack helicopter's unique ability to provide precise close-in fires to the engaged infantryman is essential*[29]'.

Gunships were created when the USAF fitted the C-47 transport aircraft with three 7.62-mm miniguns in their cargo compartment, with the aircrew directing these through an electronic targeting system. In 1967 the more modern version, based on a C-130 airframe, was deployed. This upped the armament (this could include, in addition to machine guns, 20mm, 40mm and 105mm cannon) and used a target system that made it suitable for danger close engagement. Despite being vulnerable – six were lost in the War – the aircraft's firepower, loitering ability and accuracy made it very popular in the close air support role.

The conflict's character accelerated the fielding of fighter-bombers that were more capable of carrying heavy weapon loads, such as the F-4 Phantom. It also led to the retention in theatre of obsolete piston aircraft that were sufficiently robust and slow to acquire and engage targets at low level. Partly motivated by an institutional need to prevent any further growth in the Army's attack helicopter capability, the USAF commissioned a dedicated close air support aircraft, this resulted in the A-10. The strategic bomber was again employed in direct support of ground forces with the B-52 Stratofortress delivering a weapon load of up to eighty-four 500- and 750-pound bombs.

Lack of investment resulted in most aerial munitions employed in the 1960s being of World War Two vintage. Eventually the conflict led to the fielding of better conventional designs, plus cluster and precision munitions. Perhaps the most significant technical development of the Vietnam War was the perfecting of precision guided air-delivered weapons. This development set airpower on a different path to the other providers of joint fires and involved shifting from area to point targets, and achieving this without the need to close with the target. This traditional means of achieving accuracy of course made the aircraft vulnerable to even the most primitive air defence systems. Over the last fifty years, precision technology has radically changed how air and aviation operates, while in contrast artillery and mortars still largely remain an area fire capability employing unguided munitions.

The true lesson of the famous 13 May 1972 attack with 2,000lb laser guided bombs on the Thanh Hoa (Dragon's Jaw) Bridge was that its destruction was achieved from the safety of medium altitude. In contrast previous attacks on the bridge, even when undertaken by strike packages as large as 79 aircraft, were ineffective because air defences precluded low-level weapon release which would achieve the necessary level of accuracy. When flying over North Vietnam, American aircraft faced with ground fire, surface-to-air missiles, and enemy MiGs, followed a 'rule of fives': 500 knots, 5,000 feet, and pulling 5-G (5 × the force of gravity) through violent manoeuvre. This largely precluded precise bombing with unguided weapons.

Bridges have always been targeted by airpower trying to interdict land operations. In World War One, the cutting of the pontoon bridges across River Piave was instrumental in the Italian defeat of the Austro-Hungarians in June 1918[30]. With unguided weapons, it required a significant commitment in resources and a willingness to take casualties. The American 9th Air Force in June 1944 cut or effectively blocked 19 out of 35 bridges on the River Loire, directly costing 12 aircraft and requiring the employment of 2,923-aircraft sorties[31]. Prior to D-Day all of the River Seine bridges south of Paris had been dropped[32]. The ability to relatively safely and efficiently destroy pinpoint targets was a milestone. However, we should be wary of assuming that the destruction of a target intrinsically has value. The objective of the Thanh Hoa Bridge attack was to interdict supplies flowing into South Vietnam, however, as the official Air Force history acknowledged:

> *'The destruction of virtually every known major bridge in North Vietnam had no discernible effect on the convoys that clogged the country's roads every night and, in the northern route packages, by day as well[33].'*

The ineffectiveness of air integration, despite precision attack, in the Vietnam war can be understood as follows:

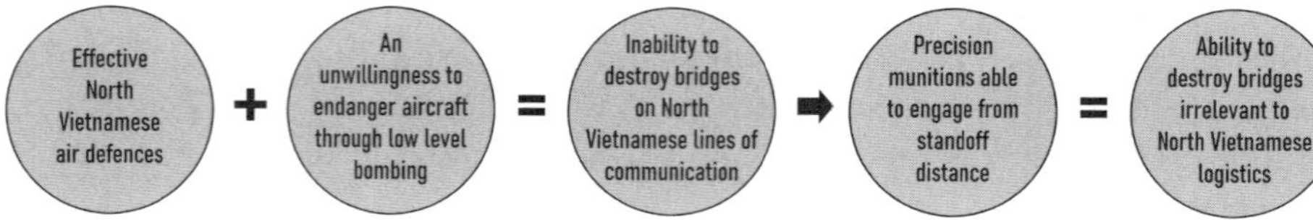

Airpower showed its dominance when the character of the conflict became conventional in the 1972 Easter offensive. Aircraft destroyed in the order of 227 North Vietnamese tanks, 25 of these were by Army helicopters. As the other benefiter of precision was the attack helicopter, whose successful use of the TOW anti-tank guided weapon against North Vietnamese armour pointed the way to its future principal role in the Cold War. Standoff engagements by attack helicopters was seen as a way of reducing their vulnerability: 270 of the 1,100 AH-1 Cobras deployed to Vietnam were lost. However, in terms of attrition per sortie, all forms of airpower were significantly more survivable than any previous wars[34].

Compared to Korea, the Vietnam War's command and control of airpower did not cause significant inter-Service friction. Following established American joint practice, airpower was centralised under the Air Force; their Tactical Air Support Element was embedded in the Military Assistance Command Vietnam that ran the War, and this directed the USAF's Tactical Air Control Centre. This harmony was aided by an initial absence of targets other than ground support –

until the bombing of the North was politically authorised[35] – and a surplus of aircraft over tasks. Through providing TACPs down to brigade level, the USAF resourced air/land integration at the scaling the Army had wanted in Korea. The increased fielding of forward air controllers included airborne ones, who flew a series of more capable observation planes. One of the conclusions subsequently drawn from the War was that '*the rapid evolution of close air support will emerge as the outstanding airpower achievement of the war*[36]'.

The conflict developed most of the modern joint fires command, control and battlespace management procedures. This was triggered by the challenge of synergising the full range of joint fires with the other significant users of airspace – in particular helicopters, who were the normal means of manoeuvre and logistics. Detrimentally this emphasis on synchronising combat elements encouraged over-command, evidenced by stacks of command helicopters circling over troops in contact[37]. A phenomenon, identified as a '*commander under pressure regressing to his previous level of competence, a tendency American generals repeatedly showed in Vietnam as they became squad leaders in the sky*[38]'.

The Battle of Hue gives an example of the challenge in coordinating firepower:

> '*In the battle for Hue .... [each] brigade had their normal supporting artillery – three direct support batteries, a medium battery, and, during the latter periods of the attack, an 8-inch battery. Those units ... fired 52,000 rounds. In addition, 7,670 rounds of 5-inch to 8-inch naval ammunition, and 600 tons of Air Force delivered munitions were expended in the area*[39].'

The result of this firepower was the destruction of 40% of the city; which was justified at the time as it minimised ground force casualties[40]. Throughout the war, only a small proportion of firepower – perhaps 15% of artillery and as few as 4% of aerial bombs – actually supported ground forces in contact[41]. Much of the remaining fire was unobserved and highly speculative. This led to considerable civilian casualties and the undermining of support for the South Vietnamese government. This indiscriminate use of firepower paradoxically both strengthened the insurgency and undermined America's national will to sustain operations; furthermore, dud munitions provided the Communists with a significant proportion of the explosives they needed to continue the fight. The excessive use of unobserved firepower, separate from any attempt to secure the allegiance of the local population, is difficult to reconcile with any logical application of a counter-insurgency strategy. Eventually budgetary pressure, rather than tactical considerations, led to a reduction in the quantity of harassment and interdiction fire. Before 1968 this unobserved fire accounted for nearly 40% of US Army artillery ammunition, declining to just over 29% of ammunition expended in July 1968[42].

In the Vietnam War, the US military can be accused of losing sight of a strategy beyond the application of firepower. Firepower can win conventional battles, but it cannot win wars; the whole confused and bloody enterprise that is war cannot be reduced to the apportionment of firepower to targets[43]. So entrenched was the pre-eminence of firepower in the contemporary American way in war, that at a press conference, General Westmoreland's one-word answer, as to how to defeat the insurgency, was: '*firepower*'[44].

The Tet Offensive provided an opportunity for the Americans to make their use of firepower more decisive. When it was over, between 45,000 and 58,000 North Vietnamese and Viet Cong were dead compared to American and South Vietnamese losses of around 9,000[45]. This outcome was an opportunity for government forces to seize control of the people. Hanoi's official history of the War identifies this as a point in which: '*The political and military struggle in the rural areas declined and our liberated areas shrunk*[46]'. General Abrams, who took over in the aftermath of the Tet Offensive, switched the emphasis from attrition to pacification and protecting the population. The Americans could have followed a classic enemy-centric approach to counter-insurgency in exploiting the highly visible defeat of the Viet Cong through seizing control of the people. Unfortunately, the American Army was no longer a military instrument that could implement such tactics. General Maxwell Taylor, former Army chief of staff and chairman of the Joint Chiefs of Staff quipped that '*the Army had been sent to Vietnam to save that nation, but the Army had to be withdrawn in order to save the Army*'[47]. Even if the American Army and Marines had been capable, their nation was not behind them.

Recognising this, the Americans adopted 'Vietnamization' as their exit strategy; but given their late start, they were unable to create South Vietnamese forces with the necessary combat power to defeat the subsequent Communist conventional attack. The failure of the United States to leave behind in South Vietnam an armed force capable of standing alone is due to many factors, many of which are deeply rooted in Vietnamese society[48]. But two factors were the responsibility of the Americans; first, the failure to recognise that building up a viable South Vietnamese state, including effective armed forces, was the key to mission success; second, the unrealistic attempt to replicate the American approach to warfare in the South Vietnamese forces. This Army lacked the organisation, culture, resources and technical ability to successfully employ joint fires in the American way. This led to the South Vietnamese forces relying upon American airpower to the detriment of developing a sustainable organic firepower system. The sequence that led to this was:

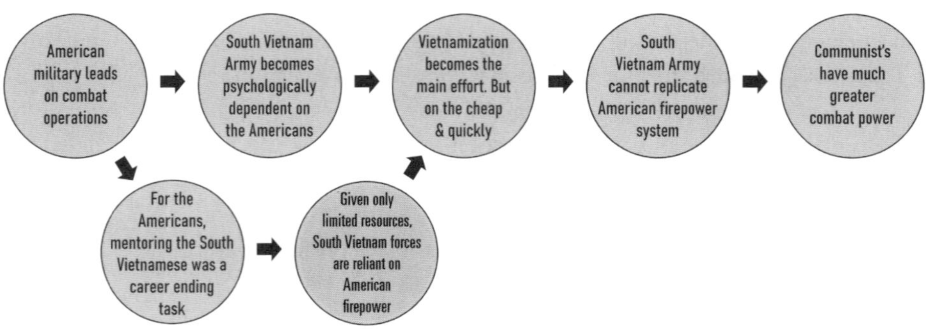

American airpower was able to stave off defeat following the assault that began with six hundred Soviet and Chinese supplied tanks crossing the Demilitarised Zone on Easter Sunday 1972; but even then, America's joint fire system was beginning to breakdown as their armed forces unravelled. A ban on firing artillery for fifteen miles around the location of a downed

USAF pilot during a rescue mission proved to be a low point in air and land cooperation. Its impact was to provide a corridor for the North Vietnamese armour to advance[49]. South Vietnam's collapse in spring 1975 might have been avoided if American air power had been available, but even if this was practical, further support was politically impossible. As will be seen in subsequent American interventions, the failure to create a viable host nation joint fires system will be a recurring theme.

The Arab Israeli Wars – The Increasing Dominance of Firepower

'artillery has always seemed to me to be something we can win without, perhaps because it doesn't do much harm to tanks[50].'

Israeli Brigadier Avigdor Kahalani's (77th Armoured Brigade) view until the Yom Kippur War

The Arab-Israeli Wars through their regularity and sophistication, have proved to be, in the Cold War years, a test bed for new equipment and tactics. In its short history, the Israeli military has evolved from being a light infantry army, to one based around the tank, to a genuine combined arms army. A consistent development has been the growth in power of the Israeli artillery and the increased ability of the air force to directly support ground forces.

The Israeli Army made limited use of firepower in their first two wars[51]. In the 1956 War after the initial breakthrough battles, artillery and heavier mortars (the most common support weapon even at brigade level) were largely left behind. This was in part due to the terrain, but also because the Israeli Army's force employment stressed mobility, surprise and night attacks. This led to 80% of infantry attacks in the War of Independence and the 1956 Sinai Campaign being at night. This ethos was at odds with the time-consuming process of organising fire support. There was also a shortage of suitable mobile equipment, only one battery, with the 27th Mechanised Brigade, had 105mm self-propelled howitzers on AMX-13 chassis[52]. In addition, they had 25pdr and 34 M-50 French 155mm towed howitzers, and around 300 120mm towed mortars, plus many smaller calibre ones. In contrast, Arab armies were well equipped with modern largely Soviet supplied towed artillery, giving them a significant firepower advantage that the Israelis tried to dislocate through their high tempo manoeuvre and operating at night. Benefiting from the assistance provided by the British and French air forces, the Israeli air force exploited air superiority through concentrating on air interdiction, but it also provided some close air support.

By 1967 the Israelis had modified their view on the role of their firepower, this was to achieve and maintain armoured manoeuvre through short intense concentrations of fire to stun Arab defensive positions. Israeli artillery rarely conducted deep fires; rather than getting into an unequal artillery duel, tanks, infantry and airpower were employed to defeat Arab artillery. Every effort was made to avoid set-piece battles, but when this was necessary, at least under

General Sharon's command, the Israeli Defence Force showed its ability to conduct combined arms deliberate operations:

> *'Sharon's division [at Abu Ageila] … fought a meticulously planned set-piece battle whose delicate combination of fire and movement would have delighted any staff officer addicted to sand tables and war games. Sharon combined heliborne paratroopers, foot infantry, tank battalions and concentrated artillery fire in a concentric attack totally unlike anything the Israeli Army had ever done before. The conduct of the battle was rigidly centralized, unplanned movements were ruled out, and there was very little scope for command initiative except at the very top*[53]'.

In contrast to the Sinai theatre with its space for manoeuvre, the seizing of the Golan Heights in 1967 required more traditional measures, including a preliminary artillery and air bombardment of some 100 hours duration. This may not have destroyed many of the fortifications, but through interdicting daylight movement, it prevented Syrian commanders from getting around their men, so reducing fighting effectiveness.

While Arab armies have seen airpower as the decisive element in Israeli battlefield success, its greatest impact was at the operational level. As General Uzi Narkiss, a commander in the Six-Day War put it:

> *'The IAF [Israel Air Force] was very important … but not so much for the ground battles. Mostly for morale and for the absence of Arab air strikes that they gave us*[54]'.

For the first two days of the 1967 conflict the Israeli ground forces received limited air support, as the Israeli Air Force was still gaining air superiority. Subsequently, relentless Israeli air pressure was credited with turning the defeat of the already retreating Egyptians and Jordanians into routs[55]. As in previous desert wars, air interdiction was particularly effective against supply trucks, but most Arab combat forces did not really have the opportunity to run out of fuel, ammunition and food before they began their retreat. The impact of airpower appears to have been largely psychological, causing Arab command paralysis and undermining morale.

Compared to their American contemporaries, the Israelis' close air support capability was limited. The former Israeli Defence Force Chief of Staff General David Elazar emphasised this approach: *'before 1973 [Yom Kippur War] I considered the subject of close air support the last priority of the Air Force'*[56]. As their airpower task was to first achieve control of the air, and then become the primary means of defeating their adversaries at the operational level, the Israelis favoured swing-role fighter-bombers. As a result, they never saw the need for a specialist ground attack aircraft.

In the 1969/70 War of Attrition, Egyptian forces, reinforced by Russian 'advisors', employed an integrated air defence system. By preventing Israeli airplanes from penetrating beyond the Suez Canal, this limited Israel's ability to impose its national will through airpower[57]'. Even though the War of Attrition was effectively a draw, it should have alerted the Israelis that their approach to warfighting was being countered. As most of the ground fighting was artillery duels, the Israelis' recognised their need for more powerful and survivable artillery[58]. They doubled their artillery holdings, fielding modern self-propelled M109 155mm and M107 175mm guns[59].

The modernisation of artillery in the War of Attrition could have resulted in a degree of rebalancing of the Israeli combined arms tactics; but under the influence of General Tal, the Israeli way of war in conventional warfighting became even more focussed on the tank, with armoured infantry and artillery being marginalised. 81mm mortars were removed from tank battalions, but despite this, the Israelis continued to make more use of the mortar than any other Western army[60]. General Tal actually questioned the need for twelve 155mm guns in Israeli armoured brigades if the tanks provided over a hundred 105mm guns. This was a short-sighted view, as in addition to offering the ability to suppress area targets, given their lack of infrared sensors, artillery illumination was needed by the Israeli tanks to effectively fight at night.

In the 1973 Yom Kippur War the Arab offensives across the Suez Canal and onto the Golan Heights were supported by traditional Soviet-style massed artillery. Israel was soon to discover that their unsupported tanks were countered by the Soviet-supplied anti-tank guided missiles and rockets, in the same way that surface-to-air missiles and cannon had nullified their fighter-bombers.

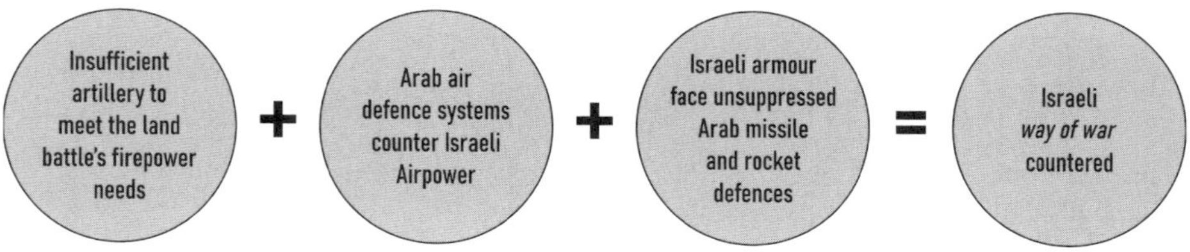

The principal Israeli ground forces lesson was to relearn combined arms tactics. This did not mean additional vulnerable infantry mounted in light armoured personnel carriers, but suppressive fire covering all movement in the open. The idea that mechanised infantry by their mere presence could unlock this challenge was characterised as *'11 men behind one inch of armor protecting four men protected by 11 inches of armor'*[61]. The unsupported tank attacks of the first days of the War were replaced by a more orthodox approach:

> *[In 1973 on the Golan Heights] 'No longer did the tanks charge on their own; instead they moved inside an artillery "box" formed by thousands of exploding shells while they and their accompanying APCs [armoured personnel carriers] raked every rock capable of offering shelter with machine-gun fire*[62]*.'*

The Israeli artillery's key lesson of the conflict was the superiority of the self-propelled gun, due to its survivability and mobility. Israeli guns moved position between five and fifteen times a day[63]; Arab towed guns proved to be much more vulnerable to counter-battery fire. This lesson may have spurred the Soviets to hasten the replacement of towed with armoured self-propelled guns in their lead formations.

The Israelis also identified the need for their guns to be sufficiently robust to be able to sustain a high rate of fire. By the end of the War's first day, only one out of 48 guns could fire on the Egyptian front[64]. This was the result of an unprecedented rate of fire; once this was realised, it led both NATO and the Warsaw Pact to revise significantly upwards their artillery ammunition holdings. Briefly there was renewed interest in ensuring that cannons remained within their designed rates of fire, before this lesson was lost in the steady routine of peacetime training.

While mortars showed their usefulness in the direct infantry support role, their lack of range was exposed, as the Israelis did not always hold the initiative and therefore could not always site them in positions from which they could provide fire support. As a result, while valuing the mortar as an organic fire support weapon, the Israelis, ceased to see them as a substitute for artillery. Furthermore, the mortar's lack of range prevented them from being effectively massed, and the Israelis had learnt the need for massed fire. They routinely used 36-gun concentrations on the Sinai Front. In the Valley of Tears Battle, the Israeli 7th Armoured Brigade was supported in the decisive phase of the fighting by 21 batteries of guns. This was the result of the brigade direct support battalion assuming command of successive reinforcing artillery battalions as they arrived on the Golan Heights. By the third day of the battle, only the 17 tanks were defending the ramp, but they were supported by 84 guns and rocket systems.

The importance of mass renewed their interest in multiple barrelled rocket systems. In the 1973 War the Israelis used two battalions of captured BM-24 systems and the MAR-290 rocket system, a copy of Soviet technology. Subsequently they began to develop their own system in the 1970s; this resulted in the LAR 160 and the even more sophisticated American MLRS entered Israeli service in 1982. The latter fired cluster munitions, which also equipped their 155mm systems (the American M483A1 Dual Purpose Improved Conventional Munitions); to increase their lethality against armoured targets.

The Israelis saw the key combined arms lesson of the 1973 War as the need for more artillery, not infantry[65]. Following war, Israel's 25 artillery battalions, with a variety of captured and often outdated equipment, were replaced by 87 battalions, equipped mainly with the American M109, M107 and M110 cannon. In 1973, the Israelis had about 300 artillery guns, many towed; by 1982, they had more than 958[66]. In 1973, the artillery brigades of each of the six tank divisions usually had two or three battalions of 155mm self-propelled howitzers, a battalion of self-propelled 160mm mortars and two battalions of self-propelled 120mm mortars. By 1977, there were nine divisional artillery brigades, most with four battalions of self-propelled 155mm howitzers and one battalion of self-propelled 160mm mortars. In addition, many manoeuvre brigades had an organic battalion of 120mm mortars and both tank and infantry battalions had 81mm mortars[67]. Furthermore, by the 1980s every main battle tank and many other armoured vehicles mounted a 60mm mortar.

The Israeli Air Force had been significantly enhanced following the Six Day War, with a 77% increase in the quantity of fighter-bombers and a 350% increase in deliverable payload. Despite more materiel, being opposed by an integrated air defence system, it could not achieve the dominance it had achieved in the 1956 and 1967 Wars. By their doctrine, the Israeli Air Force should have achieved air superiority before conducting other operations. However, the ground situation, particularly on the Golan Heights, necessitated immediate direct attack on the

Arab ground forces. Forced to conduct this against unsuppressed gun and missile air defences, this led in the first three days of the 1973 War, to the Israelis losing an unsustainable 30–40% of their aircraft undertaking ground attack[68].

It was Israeli ground forces, particularly on the Egyptian front, who were to initially lead on the defeat of the opposing integrated air defence system, aided in this by the introduction of American air-to-surface guided weaponry, including the AGM-45 Shrike anti-radiation missile. These missiles could engage the radars of the surface-to-air batteries; while tanks and artillery fire could asymmetrically attack all the elements of the Egyptian and Syrian integrated air defence systems[69]. This was so successful that by the end of the War, the Israeli loss rate per sortie was a third lower than in the Six Day War[70]. Defeating the Arab integrated air defence system had the following impact:

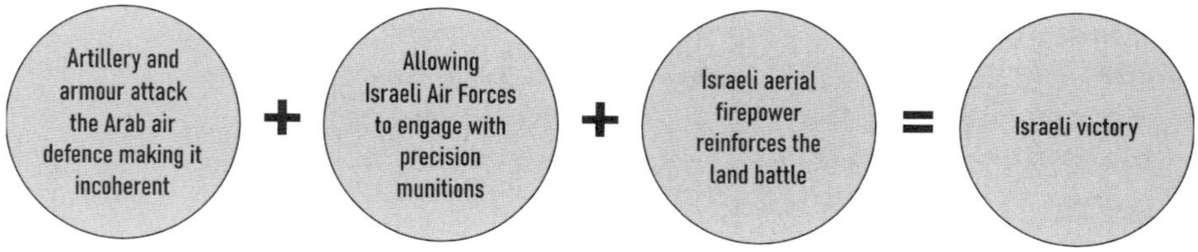

The conclusion of Rafael Eitan, the Former Chief of the Israeli Defence Staff was that ground forces needed more firepower in order to become more self-reliant, because:

> *'The Air Force must not be involved in support missions for the land forces until it has assured itself reasonable freedom of operations by destroying the enemy's missile network. This being so, the land forces must be prepared to bear the burden in the war's opening stages, and not to pin their hopes on the performance of aircraft*[71].

The fielding of helicopters armed with the TOW guided anti-tank missiles provided the Israelis with an effective means of employing airpower against armour from standoff distances. Arab anti-aircraft weapons were largely rendered ineffective by the TOW missile's range (3,750m) and its employment at low level to maximise terrain masking. This allowed some 15–18 Israeli helicopters (UH-1D, Alouette II and III) to destroy dozens of the 21st Egyptian Division's armoured vehicles without loss[72]. This established for the Israelis the superiority of helicopters over fighter-bombers when engaging tanks, as these would always be guarded by effective Soviet-supplied air defence. This led to the procurement of specialist attack helicopters – first the AH-1 Cobra in 1975 and subsequently the AH-64 Apache.

In the Israeli Defence Force's next significant operation (the First Lebanon War, which started on 6 June 1982) they overmatched the opposing Palestinian Liberation Army and regular Syrian forces. Equipped with the best American aircraft, the F-15 Eagle and F-16 Fighting Falcon, armed with effective standoff precision-guided munitions, and innovatively cued by unmanned aircraft, the Israelis quickly achieved air superiority. They rapidly destroyed Syria's entire air defence array in the Bekaa Valley, including at least 19 air defence batteries, before turning on the Syrian air force, which lost between 80 and 100 aircraft shot down[73].

The invasion was supported by 32 artillery battalions that deployed into Lebanon, with a further 18 battalions supporting from the Golan Heights. The Israelis demonstrated their new attachment to massed artillery fire through firing a 20-battalion TOT mission[74]. Their technical excellence was shown at the Battle of Sultan Ya'akob, when eighteen and a half battalions of 155mm and 175mm cannon, plus MAR-290 290mm rockets, fired a TOT, danger close, box barrage to cover the retreat of an Israeli tank battalion. On reaching Beirut the War bogged-down; the Israelis were content to avoid further significant casualties, by substituting firepower, including divisional artillery fire missions against single rocket launchers. They accepted the resultant collateral damage and gained a reputation for callousness, increased through the widespread use of bomblet ammunition. In the siege, seven artillery battalions were deployed in the direct fire role; with three times the explosive content of the tank round, the 155mm artillery shell could destroy most buildings, the 175mm shell was required to destroy the most modern concrete buildings.

By 1982 the Israelis ground force's tactical evolution had created an unassailable conventional superiority over the neighbouring Arab armies. This was based around the firepower provided by self-propelled tube and rocket artillery and the fielding of proportionally more mortars than any other army. Mortars provided battalions with most of their intimate fire support, this allowed artillery to be massed against the most important targets. The air force had an increased close support capability, but its primary function was to gain air superiority and then aid the ground war through air interdiction. Attack helicopters were seen as the most effective anti-armour capability. Unfortunately for this military, it would be faced by challenges that sought to dislocate its excellence at conventional warfighting.

Soviet Warfighting: Firepower Dominated Counter-Insurgency in Afghanistan

'Absolute supremacy of firepower did not guarantee victory. Native knowledge of the terrain and detailed study of a known adversary offset that advantage[75]*.'*

Ali Ahmad Jalali and Lester W. Grau

Successive reforms throughout the Cold War increased the Soviet Army's capability on the lines established for successful warfighting in the Great Patriotic War[76]. The challenge of fighting an enemy largely using irregular warfare tactics in the remote mountainous terrain of Afghanistan, would have led most armies to reduce their reliance upon artillery, leading to greater employment of light infantry and airpower. However, artillery was the Soviet's principal arm and it dominated their force structure. Initially they used it in their traditional way, with standard preparatory timed fire plans that usually lasted 18–35 minutes and fired the prescribed norms. This firepower may have hindered Afghan guerrilla manoeuvre, but without adequate targeting intelligence, and facing an elusive foe, most rounds were almost certainly wasted. This meant that the subsequent linear assault by Soviet infantry was rarely decisive[77]. The Soviets needed firepower to do most of the fighting as the force level they chose to deploy could never dominate the country through manoeuvre[78]. Technology sought to offset their limited footprint, and led to seismic sensors being placed on routes to automatically trigger indiscriminate artillery fire[79]. Lack of numbers was compounded by the limited fighting skills displayed by Soviet infantry, especially when on their feet[80].

The Soviets realising their tactical failings, replaced centralisation with the decentralised firepower doctrine that they used in mobile conventional warfighting, shifting from battalions to batteries, and even platoons, as the standard fire unit[81]. They often engaged over open sites, making artillery fire quicker to respond and more accurate. At the time this accompanying artillery was identified as an innovation, rather being recognised as them applying a standard conventional warfighting practice. The same reaction has occurred to the Russian practice in Ukraine. Soviet doctrine recognised that decentralised artillery especially suited mountain warfare; they employed a battery of guns and one of mortars in direct support to each battalion fighting the Japanese in the Manchurian mountains in 1945. Firepower could still be centralised for set-piece battles when this suited the tactical situation, but this was adjusted to the nature of the opposition, such as box barrages to prevent the Afghan guerrillas from escaping[82].

Mortars suite mountain warfare because their high trajectory allows them to fire over peaks and penetrate into deep crevices[83]. As the Soviets also wanted direct fire, this led to the combination gun-mortar being widely fielded. The towed Vasilek 82mm gun-mortar with its fast rate of fire (up to 120 bombs per minute) could rapidly win most fire fights, but it was vulnerable to even small arms fire due to its lack of armour, and its bomb lacked blast against entrenched opposition, leading to it been supplemented by the 2S9 120-mm self-propelled armoured gun-mortar. This excelled at supporting motorised forces and was deployed in either battery or battalion strength. The conventional mortar was still required as its light weight allowed it to be airlifted into position, together with an adequate quantity of bombs, to support dismounted troops. This stalled the shift towards larger mortar calibres and led to a lighter 82mm mortar (the 2B14) for the airmobile forces. As Soviet aerial firepower rarely operated at night, these mortars were often the only guaranteed fire support for airmobile forces when they operated outside artillery coverage.

The accompanying artillery and mortars were supported by less mobile positional artillery sited in the Soviet equivalent of firebases. These tended to be more temporary than those in Indo-China, with extensive use of mines substituting for a more formal defensive perimeter. Their primary task was to safeguard routes, with only the largest and best-equipped being designed to provide fire support to an area of operations. Most were manned by Afghan Government troops, often with the obsolete M-30 122mm howitzers[84]. The most important bases had the long-range 130mm guns and rocket launchers. One unusual use of positional artillery was the three battalion-size firebases around the resistance-held city of Kandahar. Unlike a traditional siege battery trying to achieve a breach in order to capture a town, these guns and rockets sought to denude the city of its population through indiscriminate bombardment. Employing firepower to permanently drive away the population is a standard approach in previous and subsequent Soviet and Russian wars amongst the people.

True to their conventional doctrine, initially firepower was rarely effectively coordinated below battalion level. Pressure of operations led to a greater fielding of artillery and mortar controllers, with company level fire support teams been fielded by the elite airborne forces. While in theory, all Soviet combat arms officers were trained to adjust indirect artillery fire; in reality this was rarely effective, there were instances of fire support requests from infantry commanders being refused in Afghanistan[85]. This reluctance to trust non-artillerymen to control fire missions was in part due the mujahedeen seeking to close with Soviet forces to negate firepower. This necessitated as standard the use of danger close procedures – dropping the first rounds at a safe distance and then walking the fire closer – a technical mission probably best left to a full-time observer. Shortage of controllers led to direct fire becoming the default means of engagement, this also included rocket artillery.

Initially most air support was pre-planned attacks conducted by fixed wing aircraft; this largely proved ineffective against an elusive foe. The Mi-24 Hind attack helicopter was particularly valued because its persistence allowed it to provide overwatch and then react to attacks. In comparison, fighter-bombers had a much more limited loiter time before heading back to base to refuel. When helicopters provided convoys with over-watch their presence usually deterred attacks. In the early years of the war, before the introduction of effective surface-to-air missiles, the Hinds' effectiveness led to them being called *Shaitan-Arba* or Satan's Chariot. Despite employing flares, beacons, and exhaust baffles the Hinds lacked wholly effective technical counter-measures to the CIA-supplied Stinger anti-aircraft missile, leading to them being forced to change their tactics[86]. This resulted in helicopters either operating at very low altitude to prevent early lock-on, or very high, beyond the range of the Stinger missiles. This reduced their effectiveness and prevented them from loitering with impunity over the battlefield.

The Soviets lost less than 350 helicopters in Afghanistan, and more than half of these occurred before the arrival of the Stinger; in contrast, the Americans lost 5,042 helicopters in the Vietnam War[87]. However, the effectiveness of air defence should not be solely judged by quantity of aircraft destroyed; more important is the ability of air defence system to reduce the effectiveness of aircraft by forcing them to adopt force protection measures that reduce their impact on the land battle. Despite popular perception, the countering of attack helicopters did not decide the conflict, as the first Stingers arrived in September 1986, which was after Gorbachev, the General Secretary of the Communist Party of the Soviet Union, had decided to withdraw from Afghanistan.

What the impact of the Stinger missile did demonstrate was the risk of over-reliance upon a single joint fire capability. The Soviets did not have an integrated network of firebases that could provide reinforcing firepower to the accompanying artillery and mortars; nor could Soviet fighter-bombers provide really close fire support, so preventing them from replacing attack helicopters. Even when the Hinds were effectively countered, fixed wing aircraft usually limited themselves to bombing civilian populations and providing preparatory fire, at a safe margin in front of ground forces. Indicative of the limited confidence in the ability of fixed wing close air support was the fielding of only two squadrons of the specialist ground attack Su-25 Frogfoot; their lack of range resulted in only a partial coverage of the theatre. This deficiency in fixed-wing support was the outcome of faulty conventional warfighting doctrine that led to a very limited air/land integration structure. This was designed to engage pre-planned static targets and in conventional mobile operations aircraft were expected to identify their own targets either to the side or in front of an axis of advance. The few forward air controllers that were capable of dynamically directing aircraft were usually fixed in staff appointments within regiment and higher HQs.

The Soviets rarely attempted to synergise joint fires to make its impact greater than the sum of the individual effects, they deconflicted by time and task; this resulted in sequenced fighter-bomber, helicopter and then artillery/mortar fire strikes. Indicative of the rudimentary nature of fire support was the physical separation of joint fires and ground forces; a 200m separation between own troops and attack helicopter fire was enforced to the very end of the war. The Soviets instead relied upon artillery, gun-mortar and tank direct fire to provide close fire support. In the last years of the War, the elite units were challenging this orthodoxy, resulting in significantly improved coordination between the various sources of joint fires, airborne forces. The Soviet firepower system can be understood as follows:

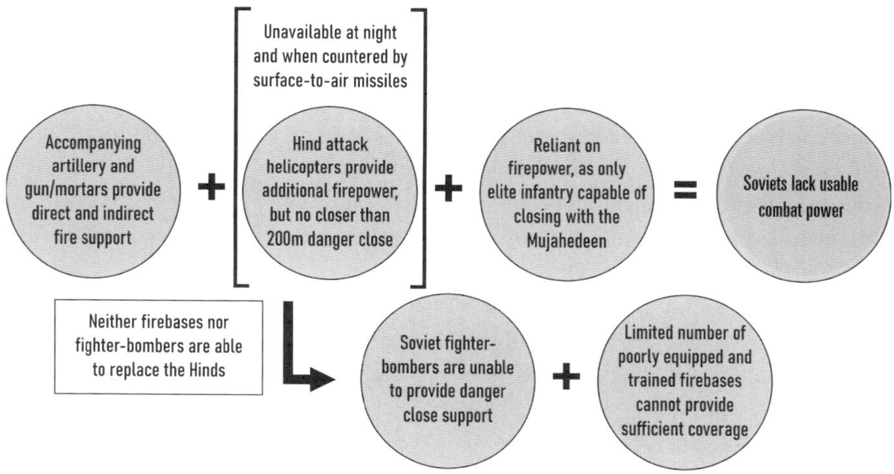

At the operational level the Soviets' approach was to replace their combined arms battle with firepower. In part this reflected political sensitivity to casualties and the unsuitability of their manoeuvre forces, which lacked mass and had limited combat power in Afghan terrain; but the major factor was their applying of a conventional warfighting doctrine to an irregular warfare character of conflict. As a result, Soviet operations in Afghanistan were characterised by a lack of restraint in the application of fire. This was partly a rational policy, stemming from an extreme approach to counter-insurgency that countenanced the wholesale depopulation of Afghanistan's second city, Kandahar. However, it was also because the Soviet forces were incapable of a more sophisticated approach. Similar callous force employment would be a trade mark of Russian forces in the Wars of Soviet Secession and then in Syria.

Joint Fires in Light Infantry Conflict: Africa, Falkland Islands 1982, Iran-Iraq War 1980–88

'At Darwin and Goose Green there was not enough artillery and insufficient ammunition because the helicopter lift was inadequate. The battle was nearly lost as a consequence[88]*'.*

Commander of Britain's 3rd Commando Brigade

In the majority of the World's conflicts, particularly in Africa, infantry have dominated operations because militaries lack the expertise to effectively employ joint fires. This often leads to artillery and mortars conducting direct fire, with individual weapon crews acquiring and engaging their own target. When employed, indirect fire invariably lacked accuracy, consistency and the ability to mass a number of barrels let alone batteries onto the same target. Firepower, and especially airpower, has rarely supported mobile operations, instead it has engaged large static targets, at a very safe distance from own troops. Instead of covering these types of operations, this section restricts itself to those conflicts where the level of military aptitude leads to useful lessons being identified.

France's war in Algeria began four years after their Indochina War, resulting in them following their established practice of siting artillery mainly in firebases. Outside the fire support coverage of these bases, airpower rather than 'accompanying artillery' was used to support mobile operations. Of course, only airpower had the reach to provide support in a country four times the size of France and against the elusive Armée de Libération Nationale guerrillas. As these could never muster the conventional combat power of the Viet Minh there was a reduced requirement for danger close fire support. In addition, this emphasis upon airpower probably stemmed from the French commander for the crucial phase of the war being Air Force General Maurice Challe.

France did not deploy modern aircraft; which proved to be an advantage as their lack of range resulted in the air force being fully integrated into local ground operations. Initially their standard aircraft was the converted trainer T-6G Harvard, armed with three 0.30 calibre machine guns and with pylons to carry a variety of bombs and rockets. These were supplemented by the higher performance World War Two P-47 Thunderbolt fighter-bomber. Increased insurgent anti-aircraft capability saw these replaced by the more capable, but still propeller-driven, A-1 Skyraider. All these were rugged aircraft able to operate from improvised strips that were sufficiently close to ground operations that close air support could usually respond within 30 minutes. The conflict also saw the first deployment of helicopters as fire support platforms; this was noteworthy through being first rather than for its impact[89]. This was not a conflict dominated by technology, as the US Concepts Division, Aerospace Studies Institute identified:

'without the benefit of exotic hardware, or perhaps because of a lack of it, an effective counter-guerrilla Air Force was in being [in Algeria] by 1959[90].'

The theatre was divided into three geographic joint commands, formed by combining an army corps and a tactical air command[91]. This decentralised employment of airpower matched the counter-insurgency principles espoused by the theorist Jerome Klingman:

'given a reasonable STOL capability, light armed surveillance aircraft should be attached to and deploy with small ground combat units. Fixed-base operations from large built-up facilities outside the combat area should be avoided. Aircraft should be immediately available to the ground force commander as assigned or attached resources of the counter guerrilla attack or reconnaissance unit. When the unit moves, the aircraft moves with it[92].'

South African and Cuban forces clashed during the Angolan Civil War of 1975–6 and the South African Border Wars of 1987–8. Initially the South African Defence Force's World War Two equipment was out-ranged by more modern Warsaw Pact supplied equipment. This provided the impetus to produce their own systems; these principally focussed on delivering long range[93], leading to the G5 and G6 guns, and the Valkiri 127mm multiple-rocket launcher. From 1987, when the conflict was resumed, the superiority of South African armoured forces was decisive[94]. These were supported by effective artillery pieces and forward observation officers, who defied convention by effectively attaching themselves to their target, rather than moving with their own infantry. Both conflicts were fought with Cuban/Angolan air superiority; the South Africans partly countered this by engaging their air strips with artillery fire. Most of the actual close combat was undertaken by UNITA, South Africa's Angolan allies, but with South African armour and artillery support, whose superior morale and training allowed them to outmatched equally well-equipped Cuban forces. However, UNITA could not exploit these battlefield successes, partly because their South African ally operated under the political imperative to avoid casualties, leading to them avoiding urban combat. As a result, UNITA offensives were reliant upon towns falling into their hands without a fight.

In contrast to the South Africans, the Rhodesians had limited artillery – ageing 25pdr gun/howitzers – that only proved useful on the rare occasions when their opposition decided to hold ground. Most notably, when they defended their base camps in Mozambique against the September 1979 incursion. As a result, the Rhodesian tactics stressed manoeuvre, including vertical envelopment, this was predominantly done by parachute due to the shortage of helicopter lift. This tactic became known as 'fireforce'. It relied upon uncontested airpower – only a few helicopters, and no Dakota transport planes were shot down in this conflict – and infantry that once it was on the ground was able to manoeuvre, despite the challenging terrain, to fix the guerrillas as a target. Two fixed-wing squadrons and an armed helicopter squadron provided the fire support[95]; helicopters were armed with either a 20mm cannon or twin machine guns. While more sophisticated jet aircraft were available, the Cessna Skymaster armed with machine guns, rockets, locally made cluster bombs, and 450lb blast and napalm bombs were more effective at acquiring and engaging guerrillas. This firepower totally overmatched their foe who were at best armed with mortars, rocket launchers, light machine-guns and automatic rifles.

The Falklands campaign featured a series of battalion-sized attacks, all planned to culminate before dawn. Firepower was initially underappreciated, as befitted the British Army's schooling in post-colonial policing. 2nd Battalion, The Parachute Regiment's first battle at Goose Green was a superb feat of arms and a tribute to the fighting power of airborne infantry; but this heroism was made necessary by wholly inadequate fire support[96]. The only supporting warship, HMS Arrow, suffered mechanical failure in its 115mm gun soon after the attack began, leaving only three 105mm Light Guns with 960 rounds and two 81mm mortars with 300 bombs to support the attack[97]. Air support, at the loss of one Harrier (a predicable victim to an unsuppressed anti-aircraft gun), only became available in the closing stages on the battle.

After the Battle of Goose Green, the battalion attacks were sequenced to concentrate firepower. Despite this, inadequate helicopter lift could prevent batteries from being repositioned to be in range, so that not all of the 30 British guns could be massed to support each attack. This sequencing also allowed battalion mortars to be detached from their parent infantry battalion to increase the firepower of an attacking unit. When this was combined with air support, naval gunfire and limited armoured support, the British battalions had firepower superiority over the Argentinian defenders.

World War Two fire planning procedures were employed, partly modified by the greater flexibility provided by superior communications. Most fire plans had their targets 'on call', awaiting an order from a forward observer to engage. It was soon established that the challenge of movement over very inhospitable ground precluded the use of timed fire plan schedules. While the British infantry initially favoured silent fire plans – targets were not engaged until the defenders opened fire – the impact of effective fire on the Argentinian defenders was soon recognised:

> *'They only had to shell us for a few hours for many to beat it, starting with officers and NCOs ... If they the professionals are going back ... we're [the conscripts] going too*[98]*.'*

These psychological factors led to a British battalion commanding officer making the following appreciation *'we decided to make this a noisy attack rather than a silent one, because second-rate troops do not like being shelled'*[99]. The conflict also reaffirmed the maxim that firepower steels the soldiers it supports, with effective fire restoring momentum in advances that had been stalled by incoming fire[100].

The most reliable British fire support was provided by 105mm Light Guns, as the infantry's 81mm mortar suffered from the soft ground not being able to absorb its recoil forces. The RAF Harriers were primarily armed with cluster bombs and cannon for low level attacks. This may have been an effective counter to Soviet integrated air defence systems, but it made them vulnerable when conducting close air support against Argentine radar-directed anti-aircraft guns. This led to the adaption of standoff tactics, including using laser-guided bombs, to improve survivability and to the engagement of targets behind the front line, rather than close air support[101].

The aim of this deep battle, Operation Tornado, was to undermine the morale of Argentinian soldiers. Naval fire was the principal means of delivering harassing fire. Firing up to 750 rounds per raid, warships kept the main Argentinian positions around Port Stanley under nightly bombardment. Argentinian airpower meant that the ships had to retire before dawn. The Royal Navy also had to be careful of their target. The Argentinian's deployed the 155mm L/33 cannon, with a supporting targeting radar, that could engage the British frigates at 18km, before these could get within their 12km firing range. Ground based Exocet missiles soon proved to be even more effective coastal artillery. The British could not risk losing ships on what was in effect a secondary task. Not being able to provide a continuous bombardment may have been an advantage, as post-war interviews suggest that the harassing fire was psychologically successful through being short and sharp, as this prevented Argentinian soldier from becoming acclimatised to enduring fire.

The Argentinians deployed more guns than the British, but made ineffective use of their Ota Melara 105mm artillery. This was out ranged by the Light Gun, but instead of aggressively closing the distance, these guns passively awaited counter battery fire. Throughout this conflict the Argentinians were short of artillery ammunition, hence they hoarded their limited stockpile for what they expected to be the decisive battle around Stanley. This was one of the reasons why they did not interfere with the British advance[102].

As per Argentine counter-insurgency doctrine, the Pucara, their dedicated close air support aircraft, was forward based with the army on the islands. This made them vulnerable to being attacked on the ground, including by the Special Air Service in their original World War Two role. Inexperience in operating without air superiority led to the British presenting the Argentinian Air Force with the occasional lucrative target, such as at Bluff Cove when the British attempted to move massed forces in daylight. But as in most wars, the winner is the one who made the fewest mistakes. Key to the British success was the combining of firepower with their aggressive infantry; this meant that every assault was successful, creating a unstoppable momentum; meanwhile their deep battle undermined the whole enemy force's will to resist.

After an initial indecisive phase of combined arms manoeuvre, the 1980–88 Iran-Iraq War turned into a largely static infantry and artillery dominated conflict. The Iraqis relied upon a deep, integrated fortified zones of barbed wire and trenches designed to absorb the momentum of attacks, for their defeat by artillery. Iraq's superiority in guns and rocket launchers (quadrupling their number to over 4,000 in the course of the war) more than offset Iranian numbers, regardless of their fanaticism. Iranian forces could not cross these fortified zones quicker than Iraqi mobile reserves could reinforce a threatened sector. The result was World War One-style attrition, which at the time was seen as a possible indicator that modern firepower – including the extensive use of chemical munitions – had achieved supremacy over manoeuvre[103]. On reflection, the stalemate was the result of these armies being unable to combine firepower with manoeuvre forces to achieve a rapid breakthrough of the extensive defensive positions[104]. So the conflict reflected a retrogression in military science. With its greater access to outside assistance, the Iraqi Army was better placed to re-establish orthodox military practice. Iraq's victory in the decisive fifth Battle of Karbala was due to orchestrating fire and manoeuvre in the Soviet style. Iraqi fire support was centrally controlled, largely through timed programmes, with assaulting troops being rehearsed to match their movement to the fire plan.

One of the features of this conflict was the use of artillery to bombard urban areas, to attack civilian morale. Ballistic missiles – their first use since World War Two in this role – and airpower were also employed against cities. Being better able to buy aircraft from the global arms market and sustain them with spare parts, Iraq relied more on airpower. The Su-25 Frogfoot was the mainstay of direct air support. Saddam Hussein's decoration of all his Su-25 pilots with Iraq's highest national military award indicates their effectiveness[105]. The conflict saw history's first air-to-air helicopter combat, conducted at distance with guided missiles designed to engage tanks and at close range by cannons and machine guns. The final tally may have been 10 Iranian Sea Cobras and 6 Iraqi Mi-24s destroyed. Iraqi helicopters rivalled fixed wing aircraft in the provision of close air support; but in the featureless terrain they were vulnerable to Iranian anti-aircraft cannon, and they lost an estimated 250 helicopters in the conflict. Responding to this, Iraqi helicopters resorted to employing their rocket in indirect fire from behind what limited cover was available.

After a wearing out fight and a World War One style gaining of military competence, the Iran-Iraq War confirmed that firepower coordinated with manouevre remained decisive upon the battlefield. After experimenting with tank primacy, by the 1980s the Israeli combined arms doctrine also expected firepower to provide its orthodox function of dominating the battlefield and enabling manoeuvre. The Americans in Vietnam and the Soviets in Afghanistan expected firepower to provide the route to victory. They both compounded this over expectation with failing to integrate it with manoeuvre so that they could offer the local people a viable alternative to the insurgents.

This chapter ends in 1989 with the fall of Soviet communism. For land warfare the watershed is several years later, with the end of the consensus that firepower dominates conventional warfighting, through the emergence in the West of a rival view: that warfare would be dominated by the information age technologies and techniques. The impact of this will be taken up in the next chapter.

Chapter 4: The Post-Cold War Divergence into the Firepower and Information Centric Warfighting Approaches

'The Goliath of totalitarianism will be brought down by the David of the microchip[1]*.'*

President Ronald Reagan, 1989

Post-1989 Western armies have progressively deviate from a force employment approach that had previously proved its worth against peer opponents. In retrospect, it is evident that it was the threat provided by Soviet forces that enforced professional clarity upon NATO's soldiers. Without it they have strayed from orthodox military science, most blatantly in reducing their organic firepower. This has partly been replaced by a greater reliance upon airpower; leading to close air support reaching a new level of sophistication. The most significant technical develpoment was firepower's new levels of accuracy. Still largely aircraft delivered, precision munitions can now provide a virtually guaranteed ability to hit point targets.

Western militaries have proved to be adept at militarily defeating third rate powers – Iraq, Bosnia, Kosovo and Afghanistan's Taliban regime – through either conventional warfighting or the coercive use of airpower. But as has been identified, turning this military success into an enduring political outcome has proved elusive, especially when conventionally defeated opponents revert to irregular warfare to carry on the conflict. Equally problematic has been the effective fire support of indigenous forces when the West limits its involvement to providing airpower.

The Israeli experience has proved particularly informative. Their reduced conventional warfighting ability being exposed by Hezbollah in 2006. Subsequently they have restored and enhanced their ability to effectively support ground manoeuvre with firepower, whilst still minimising collateral damage. They retain an enduring belief in the requirement for ground forces to use unguided munitions to attack area targets, as do the Russians; by their metrics they have been successful in a series of conflicts, attributing much of this to land firepower. They continue to modernise a traditional warfighting structure with more lethal and longer range artillery.

Persian Gulf 1990–91: The Airpower Revolution?

'Enemy forces were fielded largely in terrain ideally suited to armour and air power and largely free of non-combatant civilians[2]*'.*

Secretary of Defense Cheney's
introduction in the interim war report

At the time, the Gulf War was seen as marking a paradigm shift in warfare, and specifically in joint fires; subsequently this view has been questioned. Central to this re-evaluation was that, in effect, only one side really fought. Hence the charge made by Angelo Codevilla: '*Magnificent. But was it war?*[3]. At the time it appeared to be a flawless high-tech display, but subsequent analysis has cast doubt upon surgical interpretations derived from TV strike imagery[4]'. Violence on a state does not in itself make a war in the Clausewitzian sense of a contested duel to deliver political ends. Of course it was a war, but it was an unusual one because of the limited political ends being sought, the disparity of forces, but mainly because Saddam Hussein gave the Coalition the opportunity to fight in the way that exploited all their advantages[5].

Overturning the Iraqi conquest of Kuwait required a 41-day air campaign followed by a 100-hour air/ground war. The air campaign was supplemented by naval gunfire, cruise missiles, and a series of artillery raids, including the firing of thirty-six Army Tactical Missile System (ATACMS). In a conscious rejection of the gradual build-up of firepower of the Vietnam War; the air campaign was dubbed 'Instant Thunder' to differentiate it from the previous conflict's 'Rolling Thunder'[6].

Airpower displayed its increased ability to destroy ground forces when they are made vulnerable though being badly postured. While terminally guided bombs and missiles got most of the plaudits, between 93% and 95% of the ordinance dropped was unguided[7]. These benefitted from the advances in computer-aided bombing that allowed unguided munitions to be accurately engage area targets[8]. The most effective anti-armour weapons were the unguided cluster munitions. The Iraqis partly countered laser-guided bombs by igniting the oil fields to create sufficient obscuration to break weapon lock-on. In these circumstances GPS guidance was required to engage point targets; few of these munitions were available; this limitation to Western airpower was not fully rectified until 1997.

Improved individual munitions were but one factor in airpower's greater lethality, modern aircraft were able to carry greater payloads and operate in most weather and at night. Open desert terrain, by making target acquisition easier, had always made airpower more lethal; in addition, it created a thermal contrast between individual armoured vehicles and the desert that aircraft with thermal imaging sensors could exploit. At the other end of the spectrum, the Joint Surveillance Target Attack System (JSTARS) provided a theatre-wide capacity to detect moving targets. Despite contemporary plaudits, the conflict did not represent a revolution in airpower's lethality: '*Coalition aircraft only achieved an armoured fighting vehicle killed to sortie rate of about 0.039*'[9]'. This was two and a half times less lethal than in previous recorded conflict, these had between 0.1–0.3 armoured fighting vehicle-killed-per-sortie-rate[10]. It was time and its unchallenged application that allowed airpower to be decisive. The result of the initial defeat of Iraq's primitive integrated air defence system allowed Coalition aircraft to operate with relative immunity between 10,000 to 15,000 feet above ground level. To improve the attrition rate, two weeks into the air campaign the air commander decreased the attack altitude to between 4,000 and 7,000 feet, an acceptable risk given the ineffectiveness of Iraqi air defence[11]. Below 4,000 feet, the difficult-to-suppress machine guns, anti-aircraft artillery and man-portable missiles can be effective.

It was the Iraqi Army's deployment posture, rather than a revolution in airpower's capability, that led to their devasting losses. The Iraqi leadership behaved as if they were wholly unaware of the challenge of fighting a modern air force; their only personal air warfare experience was the 1981 Israeli air strike on their nuclear facility, plus a few attacks on Iraqi air bases at the start of the Iran-Iraq War. In the latter conflict, the Iraqis gained air superiority by default, as the Iranians could not maintain their American-built aircraft. It is difficult to identify any previous or subsequent army that has been so accommodating in its own destruction by contravening what military theorist Steven Biddle described as the 'modern system' of land warfare.[12] This consists of taking measures designed to nullify the enemy's firepower, while seeking to maximise the impact of one's own firepower. The relationship between these factors can be understood as follows:

The orthodox application of centralised airpower proved its worth in the 41-day preparatory bombardment. Ground commanders argued for *their* own dedicated sorties, but General Norman Schwarzkopf, as the Theatre or Joint Commander, personally identified himself with centralised airpower: '*It's all my air, and I'll use it any way I please*[13]'. Lieutenant General Charles Horner, the Joint Forces Air Component Commander, exercised direct command of all air assets (except helicopters flying below 500 feet and aircraft over water). The other component commanders nominated tasks and targets, but the air component largely determined their validity, priority and how to execute them. This was then promulgated in the Air Tasking Order (ATO). This central planning was considered essential by the air force:

> '*to ensure the use of available air power does not revert to a Vietnam–Tactical Air Command view when it was seen as little more than aerial artillery in support of the Army*[14]'.

In contrast to World War Two, Korea and Vietnam – when the pre-planned mission cycle against deep targets required 24-hours to complete – the 72-hour ATO cycle appeared unwieldy. Specifically land commanders found the target nomination and prioritisation process unresponsive. There were mechanisms to short-cut the process and more dynamically engage targets. However, the complexity of marshalling such an air campaign resulted in the ATO being 300-pages long, and so flexibility was not easy to achieve[15]. This was a factor in the lack of agility demonstrated in the Battle of Khafji. Coalition airpower was focussed on deep targets and so was incorrectly postured to detect and engage the initial attack. Subsequently, given time, it effectively isolated the Iraqi three-division spoiling attack, starving it of support[16].

The Battle of Khafji was a blip in the air campaign's overall measured efficiency. The proficiency by which airpower was applied in the 41-day bombardment was in stark contrast to the inadequate coordination of land and air power during the ground war. The root cause was an inability of air and land forces to cooperate in dynamic conflict. This resulted in a failure to dynamically delineate battlefield responsibility between the two components. The true test of who should control battlespace is which component is best placed to advance the joint mission. Instead the ground force's control of battlespace hindered the air component's ability to attack escaping Iraqi forces. Moving the fire support control line that effectively separates air and land primacy is the gift of the ground commander. This can hinder the joint mission, but it should not have in this case, as General Schwarzkopf was both land and joint commander. Of course, it was war's friction that prevented sufficiently prescient movement of this line. Rather than achieving a 4-star decision, it proved easier to use 'kill boxes' that allowed aircraft to acquire and destroy targets; these continue to be the mainstay of subsequent air and land integration.

Prior to the ground war, there were Army and Marine concerns over the resourcing of close air support, focussing on the guaranteed use of the specialist A-10 and Harrier platforms. Actually, the success of the preparatory air campaign led to an excess of aircraft sorties over targets. The result was that the air component allocated a peak of 50 sorties per hour to a battle front that was at times only 125 miles wide. A surfeit of aircraft on the ground war's first day resulted in a third of A-10 and even a higher percentage of Marine Harrier sorties failing to employ their weapons. More targets became available on subsequent days, as the manoeuvre of ground forces unmasked suitable targets and the air/land integration structure became more effective through practice. Few of these sorties were actually used for genuine close air support, instead the assigned aircraft were usually employed beyond the close battle. As a result:

> *few situations presented themselves as "troops in contact" to test how well close air support by US fixed-aircraft or attack helicopters could be synchronised with ground-fire systems*[17]'.

Iraq's artillery was its premier arm; in terms of quantity of ordnance and munitions it significantly out-gunned the Coalition. Individually most of its pieces were not up to Coalition standard, however they fielded the excellent South African G5 155mm gun and Soviet-built multiple rocket systems. These had impressive reach and lethality, and so they were a priority target in the air campaign. While the preliminary air campaign was effective, many of the batteries were only located when Coalition ground manoeuvre resulted in them unmasking. An efficient combination of rockets, supported by heavy and field cannon, cued by weapon locating radars, proved effective in defeating them or fixing them for destruction by airpower. Iraqi artillery failed as a system-of-systems due to deficiencies in doctrine, target acquisition and command and control. Its artillery park was effective against static Iranian targets, but it could not cope with a mobile modern army with a counter battery capability.

Coalition forces massed their firepower to breach the Iraqi defensive position; the American 1st Infantry Division planned on a 180-minute preparatory fire plan, but the lack of opposition reduced this to 30-minutes. As a result munitions were not expended at the expected rate. The US elements of VII Corps fired 12,821 shells, and 5,659 rockets in the 100-hours ground war. In comparison, over a shorter time scale, during Operation Cobra in World War Two, 21 field artillery battalions (around 1,000 guns) expended 140,000 rounds. Anglo-American fire plans in the later World War Two sometimes fired over 1,000 rounds per field gun, and proportionately fewer for medium and heavy guns as their calibre increased. But given superior targeting and accuracy, Coalition artillery was probably more lethal[18].

As the air and then artillery preparatory fire was so effective, there was little need for significant covering fire support during battalion level attacks; this suited the highly centralised fires system that the Americans and British had developed in response to the Soviet threat. Critics of this system have identified that this came at the expense of responsive fire support to brigade and battalion manoeuvre; this being the outcome of artillery prioritising targets that created the highest attritional pay-off'[19]. The concern over the balance between deep fires and fire support also surfaced over the employment of cluster weapons on targets that were subsequently to be assaulted. As well as creating a quantity of unexploded ordnance that led to friendly casualties, their considerable danger close distance meant that their impact could rarely be exploited by assaulting forces.

Without constantly moving forward, 81mm and 120mm mortars lacked the range to support the infantry and armour that were fighting through the very large Iraqi defensive positions. In addition, mortar platoons often suffered from a mobility differential, as they were often mounted in vehicles a generation older than the tanks and infantry fighting vehicles. In addition, coming into action and being ready to fire was a slow process, due to its reliance upon manually surveying individual mortars before computing firing data. The challenge faced by battalion mortars in providing intimate fire support to high tempo armoured operations has yet to be addressed by certain Western armies.

Apache attack helicopters fired the first shots of Operation Desert Storm, destroying Iraqi air defence in a deep strike operation. Despite its centrality in AirLand doctrine this was the only significant deep strike of the conflict. In addition, the 101st Airborne Division conducted a series of air assaults that dominated Highway 80, the Basra to Baghdad road. The open desert terrain allowed Apaches to exploit the range of their sensors and missiles, achieving a standoff in close combat which allowed them to engage with relative impunity. Only one AH-64 was lost to enemy fire, but its crew was recovered; sand was the major enemy, causing serious mechanical problems. The Army was so confident of its ability in this terrain that it deployed 45% (274 aircraft) of its AH-64 fleet. These destroyed a disappointing equivalent number of Iraqi vehicles as the quantity of attack helicopters fielded. Other variants of attack and missile equipped armed helicopters were even less successful. Despite this, at the time the attack helicopter was seen as a real success story; in hindsight, the brevity of the ground war and the paucity of Iraqi air defence may have provided a false sense of optimism of the attack helicopter's survivability, especially in deep attack[20].

The Gulf War illustrates the truism that militaries rarely seek actual lessons and instead often selectively identify what validates their existing institutional trajectory; crudely this translates into justification for their pre-war capability shopping list. In hindsight, the chief lesson of the Gulf War was the failure to look beyond the immediate conflict to the post-war political outcome. The escape of most of the Iraqi Army was decisive in the continuation of Saddam Hussein's regime, the conflict may have achieved its stated purpose in liberating Kuwait, but not its wider political purpose. The design of battle meant that Coalition Forces could either complete the destruction of Iraqi forces through firepower, which was considered politically unacceptable, or let them escape. A plan designed to capture a significant proportion of the opponent's forces would have better set the conditions for the Iraqis to accept the conflict's political outcome.

It was those who could expect to be on the receiving end of Western firepower that learnt the most from the conflict. The initial Russian interpretation was that the Coalition incorrectly applied airpower in the 41-day air offensive; instead this should have been husbanded for the 'decisive' combined arms ground war[21]. On reflection the increased lethality of deep strike and precision standoff weapons was recognised[22]. Both Russia and China concluded that they needed to enhance their airpower and to partly embrace precision munitions; they also recognised that given their lack of resources they could not compete as equals in this latest iteration of firepower-based attritional warfare. For these countries and non-state actors opposed to the West, the principal challenge was to reduce firepower's impact, chiefly through avoiding becoming a viable target. For the Russians this meant strengthening their ability to operate in the political warfare space as this offered a means of applying force without triggering the intervention of American led Western airpower.

Perhaps the Gulf War's most dangerous effect was to engender a belief in Western political establishments that technology meant that decisive wars could be fought without having to risk much equity, particularly in terms of own casualties. Any objective study of the conflict would have identified that military technology remained secondary to force employment. This was evidenced by the less well-equipped US Marine Crops achieving a similar kill-ratio to the US Army. The South African-built guns were technologically a generation ahead of Coalition artillery, and yet were ineffective because the Iraqis were deficient in a myriad of human factors that lead to their effective combat employment[23].

Arab-Israeli Conflict – From Political and Irregular to Hybrid Warfare

'Pinned down by Hezbollah anti-tank missiles, direct fire weapons, and mortars, the infantry soldiers of the Nahal Brigade were hard pressed to lend support to the tank column ... Incredibly, there was no coordination whatsoever between the infantry and the tanks, and frantic calls from the trapped tank command for artillery and air support were denied by Northern Command due to concerns over fratricide[24]'.

Lieutenant Colonel Scott C. Farquhar report
on the 2006 Hezbollah-Israeli war

Between 1948 and 1982 Arab armies, largely using Soviet equipment and tactics, failed to defeat Israel in conventional conflict. Recognising that they could not overcome this conventional superiority, Arab nations henceforth either came to a political understanding with Israel or avoided symmetrical warfare. For those continuing the struggle, Israeli firepower would be negated through hybrids of political, irregular and conventional forms of conflict. Lacking a peer opponent, the Israelis began to see standoff airborne precision firepower as their principal means of coercing their neighbours. The lack of an external threat and the internal security challenge led to the Israeli ground forces losing its conventional warfighting focus, leading to them being outfought by Hezbollah ground forces in Israel's 2006 invasion of Lebanon. Learning from this, Israel's current doctrine recognises the need to seize terrain through close combat in order to defeat their sub-state opponents.

Hamas and Hezbollah have developed distinctive ways of war to negate Israeli firepower, whilst their mortars and rockets provide a persistent threat to Israeli civilian targets. The Israelis have sought to counter these by a combination of detect and warn systems that allow civilians to occupy rocket-proof shelters, and interceptors to shoot down the rockets. However, technology cannot guarantee to defeat these primitive weapons; resulting in this 'strategic harassing fire plan' provoking the Israelis into ground offensives against Lebanon and the Gaza Strip. Israel has launched five major offensives against Hamas and Hezbollah in the last fifteen years[25]. Following the logic of the Western Allies when faced with German V1 and V2 weapons in World War Two; that the seizure of the launch sites is the only totally effective counter to highly-mobile missile launchers. Militarily these ground offensives have had mixed results, all have resulted in considerable political fallout[26].

Entering the new millennium, with their unbroken series of successful wars, the Israelis were justifiably confident of their conventional superiority over any potential opposition; this led to an assumption that a future threat would mainly be an asymmetric one, of opponents using irregular warfare tactics. This over-confidence led to the 2006 invasion of Lebanon – also known as the Second Lebanon War – being poorly planned and the Israeli forces being incorrectly prepared for the challenge:

> *'prior to the war most of the regular forces were engaged in combating Palestinian terror. When they were transferred to Lebanon, they were unfit to conduct combined forces battles integrating infantry, armoured, engineering, artillery forces, and other support forces ... This was particularly apparent with field artillery and air forces who were used almost exclusively for attacks on pre-planned targets and rarely in support of ground manoeuvre[27]'.*

Hezbollah achieved tactical surprise through occasionally choosing to employ conventional tactics, precisely the challenge the Israelis were ill-prepared to counter; they fought from concealed, village based, fixed positions that were often linked by underground tunnel complexes. They skilfully combined indirect and direct firepower, and employed modern Russian anti-tank missiles that could defeat the latest Israeli tanks. Firepower was needed to either destroy, or more realistically suppress, these positions to allow ground manoeuvre. Complacency led to many Israeli infantry battalions deploying without their mortars[28], the mortars and artillery that deployed were unresponsive to firepower support request; hence the Israelis lacked the organic firepower to enable manoeuvre.

The Israeli's Artillery Corps had compounded this lack of conventional warfighting practice by doctrinally focussing on rivalling the air force in the deep battle; this came at the expense of their key role in the close battle. The Israelis did not stint on firepower, expending some

173,000 artillery shells and rockets; this was significantly more than the Yom Kippur War of 1973[29]. But little of this fire was delivered as part of the combined arms battle; instead it was relatively indiscriminately fired into built-up areas. As well as being militarily ineffective, this resulted in condemnation from the international community. Part of the problem was inadequate target acquisition, but given Hezbollah's skill at concealment, Israeli artillery were unlikely to have a target until their ground forces were engaged in close combat in a prepared killing area[30]. In these circumstances, artillery needed to assist their tanks and infantry in winning the firefight through suppressing likely firing points with explosive and smoke shells. Even when this was effectively applied, the lack of fire and manoeuvre coordination often resulted in fire lifting before the Israeli infantry were close enough to successfully assault[31].

As with the Japanese in World War Two, Hezbollah's fortifications largely negated fire aimed at achieving a neutralising effect. In previous wars, medium artillery had shells with sufficient explosive content, but in this conflict even a near miss from a 155mm round could be ineffective against Hezbollah bunkers and tunnels. This led the Israelis to conclude that heavier firepower, ideally precision guided, was required in the close fight. The Israelis turned to their air force and rocket artillery to destroy modern reinforced concrete bunkers; faced with a similar challenge in the City of Grozny, the Russians gave this role to their 240mm mortars.

The conflict showed the Israeli Air Force that Hezbollah were not going to present viable air interdiction targets. This is the result of Israel's non-state opponents choosing to fight from well-stocked prepared positions, so negating the need for: conventional lines of communications, HQ complexes, or gun and mortar battery positions. Nor were the fanatical Hezbollah fighter vulnerable to the psychological pressure of operating under pervasive airpower – this being their normal 'peacetime' experience – so there was not the command paralysis or willingness to retreat that had previously characterised regular Arab forces. In response, the Israelis changed their emphasis from air interdiction to close air support. The outcome for these two militaries was:

At the root of the Israeli military's shortcomings was a failure to appreciate that the Hezbollah had migrated from being an insurgency that was only capable of irregular warfare tactics. It was now an established military, able through changing its tactics to vary the character of conflict. Furthermore, the 2006 conflict showed that a non-state entity's rudimentary domestic technology base is not a barrier to effectively employing high tech weaponry. Nor is the lack of state-recognition a barrier to becoming a first-class army capable of conducting all arms tactics. As a UN observer in the Lebanon commented on Hezbollah: *'What was really significant is the amount or quality of staff work that goes into their activities that renders them different from*

any other guerrilla outfit[32]'. Accepting this would have meant that the Israeli military would have been better prepared for the challenge[33]. Learning from this, before their next conflict the Israelis re-energised combined arms tactics, including artillery and aircraft regularly live fire training with ground manoeuvre forces[34].

Improved air and land coordination was evident in Israeli operations against Hamas in 2008. In this clash they were able to fully synchronise manned and unmanned aerial systems, guided and unguided artillery and ground manouevre. Following incessant Hamas rocket fire from the Gaza Strip, on the 7 July 2014, Israel initiated a ten-day operation that began with a series of standoff strikes. To aquire targets throughout the conflict up to forty air platforms operated in the congested airspace over Gaza. Given their greater endurance, unmanned aircraft identified most of the 6,000 designated targets and by establishing the pattern of life they allowed the strikes to be cued at times that minimised collateral damage. The imagery that these drones provided was essential to preserving legitimacy and countering inevitable accusations of excessive force. Despite its sophistication, this standoff assault failed to significantly impact on the rate of rocket fire; as a result, Israel launched a ground attack, as it needed a decisive political outcome not an inconclusive firepower duel.

As well as underground tunnels, the Gaza Strip's urban terrain allows the construction of over-ground tunnels by linking buildings with passage ways. This provided Hamas fighters with movement routes totally concealed from overhead sensors. As these fighters also ensured that they had an insignificant electronic signature, the Israelis were almost totally lacking in timely tactical intelligence. As a result, it proved virtually impossible to locate Hamas fighters before they engaged Israeli forces in close combat, which was when Israeli ground forces needed responsive area target fire support at danger close distances; this could only be provided by artillery and mortars. At the Battle of Shejaia the reconnaissance battalion of the Golani Brigade found themselves surrounded by Hamas fighters who had just emerged from their tunnel complex. Overmatched, the Israeli soldiers retreated into their heavily armoured personnel carriers (the Namer) and called in the fire from three battalions of 155mm artillery effectively on top of their own positions. After 20-minutes of firing, the Israeli infantry emerged as Hamas had broken-off the engagement[35]. More than 14,600 unguided artillery shells were fired into the Gaza Strip, providing massed area fire support in circumstances where precision weapons could neither provide a timely response nor the volume of fire required.

Despite showing the continued utility of tube artillery with unguided munitions, by 2020 only around half of the Israeli artillery personnel operate cannons. An active forces divisional artillery brigade now has only two battalions of M109. As it seems that battalion strength may have been reduced to 12 tubes, a division has only 24 conventional artillery tubes spread across the close and deep battles. Even if restricted to the close battle, 24 tubes will be challenged to provide suppressive fire against both long-range anti-tank missiles, and shorter-range man-portable anti-tank launchers[36].

Active forces divisional artillery also have one battalion of MLRS launchers firing guided and unguided rockets, and one battalion of non-line of sight missile launchers. The MLRS battalion employs both 227mm and 122mm rockets and target acquisition systems. The Israelis first fielded non-line of sight missile systems in 1986, employing two guidance systems:

the laser-guided Nimrod and the Tammuz, which had a man-in-the-loop directing the guided missile by data link. The Spike non-line of sight missile has replaced these; with its relatively low yield warhead and man-in-the-loop guidance it minimises the chance of collateral damage. The Israelis fielding of the 122mm precision-guided rocket reflects their emphasis on danger close fire; its 20kg warhead offers a significantly smaller danger area when compared to the 90kg of the MLRS Unitary munition[37].

The 2014 conflict also showcased Israel's improved close air support capability, F-16 fighter-bombers were dedicated to individual ground forces brigades to build trust and understanding. In previous conflicts, aerial fires were rarely brought closer than 1,000m of friendly troops, in this conflict, at least one precision bomb was delivered to within 350m of friendly forces. Improved responsiveness resulted in close air support regularly being provided within 30 minutes; and in some cases, 20 minutes. In this character of conflict, fighter-bombers provided better support than attack helicopters because their precision munitions had sufficient destructive power to destroy Hamas fortifications[38]. The changed Israeli Air Force approach can be understood as follows:

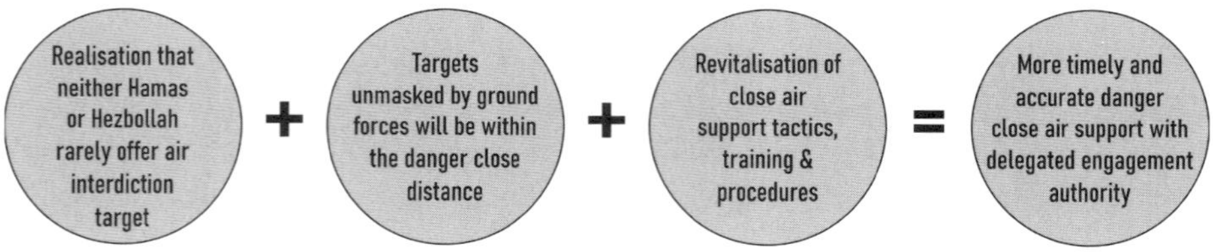

The 2014 conflict highlighted the current disconnect between the practical rules governing the application of deep fires and that supporting the close fight. Israeli deep fires achieved a high level of discrimination; this was through sophisticated target acquisition, an ability to choose when, or even if to engage, and then the use of precision munitions. The type and yield of the munitions were carefully calibrated to achieve the desired target effect, whilst minimising the chance of collateral damage. This is a complete contrast to circumstances in which fire support to ground manoeuvre is forced to operate. In close terrain, the opposition invariably determines the place and time of combat, this often allows them to engineer collateral damage concerns. Fire support needs to be immediate and in sufficient mass to achieve decisive effect, this often effectively precludes the use of precision munitions that require either individual coordinates or the designation of point targets. The contrast with the level of discrimination that deep fires achieved increased concerns over the Israeli use of unguided artillery munitions. This point of difference was unfortunately highlighted by the Israeli Air Force's Chief of Staff: *'one hundred per cent of the targets we attacked had constant [visual intelligence] above them before, during and after attack*[39]'. Of course, Hamas' actions were designed to prevent the surgical application of firepower in close combat, for both military and political reasons. However, the Israeli population, who are well informed of military realities, were overwhelmingly behind the conduct of the operation[40].

Despite Israel's attacks, Hamas continued firing missiles. Their resilience was due to the efforts they had put into countering Israeli firepower through protecting their military infrastructure, chiefly their offensive and defensive tunnels[41]. They were also aided by the Israeli military operation's predictability: this opened with an air offensive and was followed by ground attacks along obvious routes. The military goals chosen for this operation could not inflict sufficient damage to force Hamas to stop firing rockets and thus restore the *status quo ante bellum*[42]. As a result, this style of limited operation will most likely need to be repeated when either Hezbollah or Hamas rocket fire requires a political response.

Recent conflict has led the Israeli Artillery Corps to return to their roots of prioritising fire to enable manoeuvre; from which they derive their motto *'Without support the infantry won't move'* (which in Hebrew rhymes). Brigadier General Roy Riftin, commander of the Israeli Defence Force's Artillery Corps in 2014 identified this priority:

> *'[we] needed to view ourselves first and foremost as a supporting organisation to enable the Army to achieve its objectives ... In parallel, we will build capabilities to enable accurate means of standoff attack*[43]*.'*

Despite the Israeli Air Force's significantly improved close air support capability the need for greater quantities of organic fire support is recognised; this has led to the reintroduction of mortars into armoured as well as infantry units[44]'. The need for superior bunker busting capability has led the Israelis to field guided rockets for their American-made MLRS. The continued requirement for the massed area firepower, that only tube artillery can deliver, has resulted in the Israelis seeking a replacement cannon for the venerable M109. Amidst this innovation, the Israeli military experience has demonstrated how easy it is to forget the basics; in particular the need to practice in demanding training the delivery of timely, massed and accurate firepower integrated into the combined arms battle.

Russian Warfighting: Firepower Dominated Conflict in Chechnya, Georgia, Ukraine and Syria

> *'Within that space [300m close combat zone] Chechen forces 'hugged' Russian forces to avoid Russian supporting artillery and airstrikes while Chechen small arms and RPG fire exacted a blood tax on those same Russian forces*[45]*'.*

The Wars of Soviet Secession have featured a series of conflicts whose character has ranged from state-on-state conventional through to insurgency. Whatever the character of conflict, the Union's successor armies, and the Russians in particular, have stressed the primacy of artillery within the combined arms battle. Following the Gulf War there was a slight shift towards seeing an independent role for airpower, this has now been corrected; however, this may be challenged as a result of the Russian Air Force's operations in the Syrian Civil War, where they are learning different lessons from those that the ground and airborne forces are acquiring in the Ukraine conflict. Despite its apparent military strength, continuity in methods may be partly due to modern Russia's weak institutions preventing any constructive challenge; it has been described as a regime posing as a state[46].

In the years immediately following the fall of the Soviet Union, the disintegrating Russian Army was only capable of applying firepower crudely. Firepower was indiscriminately and ineffectively used in the First Chechen War (1994–96), aircraft and artillery preparatory fire wrecked the City of Grozny; this was treated as a large 'free-fire' zone, but ineffective targeting left the defenders relatively unscathed. During the assault, fire support was not aligned with manoeuvre; as a result, the unsupported attacking armoured columns were defeated in detail. The Russian failure to effectively employ their weapon-locating radars allowed the Chechens, at crucial times, to achieve local fire superiority with their limited numbers of howitzers, rockets, and mortars.

When they resumed the conflict three years later, the Russians were significantly better prepared. Centralised timed artillery fire plans were used during the approach to Grozny and to capture the city outskirts. To tackle the Chechen capital the Russians assembled a modern siege train, including the thirty-barrelled 220mm Buratino rocket system's, whose thermobaric warhead creates a sustained blast wave that is especially lethal against personnel in buildings, tunnels and bunkers. This munition technology was also employed in aerial bombs and conventional surface-to-surface rockets. 240mm mortar batteries, with their dedicated laser designator-equipped observers, provided responsive precision firepower whenever a Chechen strongpoint held up the advance. Following Soviet doctrine, in the urban fighting the Russians employed most of their artillery under command of their motor rifle battalions. Each battalion was supported by a platoon of tracked 2S1 122mm howitzers, two platoons of 120mm Nona-K towed gun-mortars, and a platoon of 82mm mortars[47]. Direct fire was the preferred means of employing artillery as it was easier to coordinate with motor rifle forces; this decentralisation, plus the employment of precision mortar bombs and the use of thermobaric munitions (which are less prone to cratering) allowed the Russians to avoid the indiscriminate massed artillery fires that creates rubble and improves defensive positions.

In the open terrain of the advance to Grozny Russian attack helicopters could employ their sensors and weapons at close to their maximum range. Once in the city, helicopters could rarely achieve standoff engagements, making them vulnerable to missile and cannon air defences. Fixed wing aircraft were more survivable, but their effectiveness was limited by poor cooperation with ground forces. As aircraft usually had to acquire their own targets they had to operate at altitudes and airspeeds that made them vulnerable to Chechnyan air defences; this led to the Su-25C becoming the principal aerial source of firepower. Its armour and self-defence suite allowed it to survive while flying slow enough to find its own targets, this also made it sufficiently manoeuvrable to achieve an attacking profile.

In the Second Chechen War, the Russian mixed the traditional with the new. The conventional elements included: timed set piece fire plans, artillery providing direct fire support down to platoon level, and the use of armoured close air support aircraft. The new elements were the use of artillery precision and thermobaric munitions, these increased the lethality of joint fires in urban combat without creating the destruction of buildings that would prevent manoeuvre. Chinese military observers considered Russian operations to be worthy of imitation. Highlighting that the unified command and control ensured that each joint fire system had its own specific role, and so provided a coherent response to Chechen tactics. They recognised that this was a different approach to the American synergising of firepower[48].

Most commentators on the five-day Russo-Georgian War of 2008 emphasise the Russian integration of conventional combined arms with information and cyber operations. More significantly it demonstrated the inability of their single services to work together. The Russians won because the Georgians were even less competent; while the Russians had the edge in conventional warfighting capability, this was compounded by poor Georgian leadership and inadequate planning.

The Russians do not appear to have implemented either a traditional Soviet combined arms battle plan, with airpower integrated with ground forces, nor a Western-style joint campaign plan to coordinate air and land operations. This failure led one source to suggest that *'Russian ground and air forces actually fought two different wars without much knowledge as to what was going on in the other sphere*[49]'. This doctrinal confusion was compounded by the 1998 transfer to air force command of helicopters; these being the most effective Russian close air support platform.

Air force staff officers were embedded in ground HQs, but these had no direct communications with the 4th Air and Air Defence Army commanding the air assets, preventing timely fixed and rotary wing close air support. Post-War Russian analysis identified the inability of the air force to integrate into combined arms operations as the key weakness; one review argued for at least one forward air controller per battalion, and the return of full control of tactical aviation to the ground commanders[50]. The inability to operate airpower at the operational level, as in the Western approach, led one American commentator to identify that Russia had a *'remarkably limited capacity to wage air combat for a country aspiring to be a military great power*[51]'. In contrast, Russia's Black Sea Fleet was clear about its role: it established sea control and provided naval gunfire support.

Following Soviet doctrinal practice, the Russians did not initially attempt to achieve air superiority over Georgia. Russian airpower and ballistic missiles engaged a series of static command and control facilities and military infrastructure targets, but these were ineffective, due to a lack of intelligence-led targeting. These targets were attacked in the conventional way, as aircraft lacked the precision weapons to conduct standoff engagement, or non-contact warfare to use the Russian term. Six aircraft were lost due to a combination of Georgian ground air defence, their own 'friendly fire' and lack of airworthiness. This led the Russians several days into the conflict to undertake the suppression of Georgian air defences.

We should be wary of judging the Georgian War from the perspective of how a Western joint force would operate. The traditional Soviet style operational-level insertion of ground manoeuvre forces to conduct the deep battle eventually proved to be successful – they seized all their objectives – but, there were flaws in the enabling break-in and break-through battles. These were principally due to the Russian inability to fully suppress Georgian artillery – which was armed with effective cluster munitions fired from Israeli supplied rockets. In the fight for Tskhinvali, reportedly, the Georgian multiple barrel rocket launchers fired for 14-hours unopposed[52]. This failure was attributed to the inadequate numbers of weapon locating radars and unmanned aerial vehicles, their inept handling, plus the constant movement of Georgian artillery[53]. Russian multiple-launch rocket systems were equally effective, delivering '*demoralisation and retreat*[54]' upon poorly motivated Georgian troops.

For the Georgians, the key lesson was the requirement to re-posture their forces towards national defence against a conventional threat. Their previous emphasis had been supporting the Global War on Terrorism through expeditionary forces schooled in countering irregular warfare. For Russia, this was the last war of the legacy force inherited from the Soviet Union; its poor performance drove modernisation[55], leading to a new structure that swept away the half-hearted reforms that partly sought to adopt Western airpower techniques.

Russian information operations have cast the Ukraine conflict as valiant, independent insurgents defending their language and culture from nationalist bullies; in reality the former imperial master has reasserted its regional authority[56]. The conflict has shown how effectively Russia addressed the failings highlighted in their war with Georgia. Russian counter battery, electronic warfare and unmanned aerial vehicles were ineffective in the Caucasus conflict, they are now key Russian strengths[57]. The conflict has showcased the improved target acquisition capability of unmanned aerial vehicles, and the increased lethality of massed fires, in part due advanced munitions. Airpower has had an insignificant impact because the Russians have chosen not to use it, and their air defences have largely prevented the Ukrainian air force from entering the battle. Despite this absence, firepower has dominated the conflict, inflicting up to 80% of casualties. The low force ratios, the lethality of the deep battle and the decentralisation of fire support have been identified as indicating the future character of conflict, when actually these are all continuations of Soviet/Russian conventional warfighting practice.

As would be expected from two ex-Soviet armies, artillery has dictated the fighting. Unused to how firepower dominates positional conventional operations, one American observer identified that a period of static fighting was '*World War I with technology*[58]'. Russian regular forces, Eastern Ukrainian separatists and the disparate groups of Russian volunteers and mercenaries; which operate at various degrees of distance from the Kremlin, have all proved effective in their use of indirect fire[59]. The Ukrainians have steadily improved their technical and tactical handing of artillery, ceasing using their artillery to achieve attrition in stalemate situations: shelling cities such as Luhansk for weeks, achieving limited military effect, but through creating images of damaged buildings, they have furnished their opponents with useful propaganda[60].

The character of the conflict has led to an emphasis on long range and destructive fire; this has increased the importance of rocket systems. The conventional Russian ratio is one rocket battalion to two or three tube artillery battalions; the ratio on the Donbas in 2014 was three rocket artillery to four tube artillery battalions. The requirement to engage Russian batteries sited well behind the front line led to the Ukrainians fielding the old, but long ranged, towed 2A36 152mm guns. On the Russian side self-propelled and towed 152mm and 203mm guns – including the new 2S35 152 mm self-propelled gun/howitzer – have been favoured. Long range Russian artillery has found itself immune from counter-fire by remaining on their side of the international border. Because following the logic of limited war, the Ukrainians recognised that firing into Russia could be a pretext for their increased intervention. These dynamics resulted a move to larger calibre weapons:

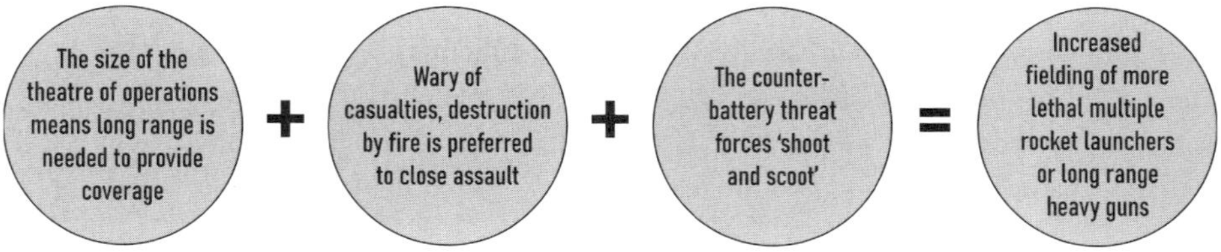

Short-range 2S4 240mm heavy mortars were used when the Russians could site them in range of a static target, such as the defences of the Donyetsk and Luhansk airports occupied by Ukrainian airborne forces. These battles ended in defeat for light infantry, inevitable when the occupants of single fixed position face modern firepower. Field fortifications have been successful in limiting the effect of firepower, but only when combined with dispersion and deception. The multiple entrenched positions currently occupied by the Ukrainians are designed to prevent firepower being concentrated on individual positions.

To support the close battle, both sides employ the Soviet practice of attaching artillery to tank and infantry battalions. The 122mm 2S1 was designed for this role: it is highly manoeuvrable – particularly in soft soil and marshy areas – and is adept at direct fire. On the offensive, the Russians tend to site their 2S1 in over-watch positions between 1 and 6km from Ukrainian strong points, with the primary task of suppressing anti-tank defences. Lacking anti-tank weapons, the Ukrainians have also had to employ their 2S1 to counter Russian and separatist tanks[61]. In mobile operations, Russian and pro-Russian separatist Battalion Tactical Groups have had their usual allocation of mortars and 122mm guns further reinforced by 152mm tracked 2S3, towed D-20 152mm howitzer and the BM-21 multiple rocket launcher. This has been identified as a reaction to the combination of massed firepower with a low-density battlefield (force-to-space ratio). The Soviet practice of battalions receiving enhanced fire support in special circumstances – such as urban and mountain warfare – may now also extend to abnormally dispersed combat[62]. These Battalion Tactical Groups have received considerable attention in Western reporting, but the Russians are moving back to the divisional level of command for their forces facing NATO. This recognises the need for centralisation of the control over firepower when facing set defences.

Despite the efforts made by both sides to counter its effects, artillery's lethality continues to increase: inflicting 70% of Ukrainian casualties in the manoeuvre phase of the war and around 80% once the conflict became more static[63]. Increased deadliness is due to a combination of: significantly improved target acquisition, advances in individual munition lethality, and platforms capable of delivering more rounds, accurately onto a target, in a short period that prevents it taking cover. The ability to fix mechanised targets with remotely delivered mines allows repeat volleys of cluster and thermobaric munitions. This range of munitions includes some that NATO nations have abandoned or never developed. The major limitation of these advanced munitions is their cost when compared to the normal high explosive round. This means that they have represented only 5–10% of the rounds expended on the Donbas. They have been reserved for major operations, when they could form a quarter of munitions expended. The conflict's duration has required the careful husbanding of all types of shells. This allows the occasional intense firing periods, when batteries have fired 300–400 rounds per tube in a day.

Casualty concerns has led to the Russians to use firepower without manoeuvre; the most intense period of this was mid-July 2015, when Russia launched 53 intense fire strikes on 40 different positions over a six-week period. The Potomac Foundation's president Phillip Karber – who has extensively visited the Ukrainian battlefront – identified the impact of one of these as being:

> *'In a three minute period … a Russian fire strike wiped out two mechanised battalions with a combination of top-attack munitions and thermobaric warheads*[64]*.'*

The most effective fire strikes were against formations behind the front line. This was due to the Ukrainian failure to make themselves less vulnerable through employing the means of minimising the effects of firepower – concealment, cover, movement, dispersion and deception. These have been common in close combat since the start of the 'empty battlefield' in the 19th century; due to modern sensors and the lethality of artillery fire, this rationale now applies to the whole force.

The lethality of artillery munitions when effectively massed makes the employment of the lightly armoured vehicles problematic[65]. Brigadier Ben Barry surely draws the correct conclusions in that:

> *'It's possible to concentrate artillery fire of such density that it can knock out light armoured vehicles. I don't think this factor has really sunk in with NATO armies or for that matter with Western [defence] manufacturers*[66]*.'*

Rather than participating in the assault, their prescribed doctrinal role, given their vulnerability, BMP and BMD infantry fighting vehicles in both armies usually adopt over-watch positions, supporting the dismounted infantry assault with fire, so, sacrificing tempo in the attack for vehicle survivability. In World War Two dislocating the combined arms team was achieved by artillery fire separating tanks and infantry; armoured personnel carriers and infantry fighting vehicles were introduced to prevent this. Now, given the vulnerability of these vehicles to advanced artillery munitions, the current combined arms team may also be being superseded[67]. The new separation is between the heavily armoured main battle tank and the rest. To prevent this, the Russians and Ukrainians are joining the Israelis in fielding an infantry fighting vehicle with the protection of a main battle tank[68]. In addition, most of their fighting vehicles have received increased armour protection on the top of vehicles. The Russians are fielding vehicle protection systems capable of engaging indirect fire, and air defence systems capable of intercepting indirect fire rounds in flight (one system is deployed to protect one of their Syrian bases). This is in addition to electronic warfare capabilities that can disrupt the fuzing or accuracy of munitions.

Russian air defences have largely prevented the Ukrainian air force from entering the battle. For Ukrainian Hind attack helicopters '*survival requires flying extremely close to the ground*[69]'. Their vulnerability has resulted in Hinds firing rockets from behind cover, in a primitive form of indirect fire (this was also a practice of the Iran-Iraq War). In contrast to not employing manned aircraft, the Russians have made extensive use of drones. Their unmanned aircraft were ineffective in the Georgian War, as the Russian-made Pchela unmanned aircraft was vulnerable through flying low and being noisy; following this conflict, the Israelis provided the technical assistance to address this deficiency[70]. On the Donbas at the company level, unsophisticated quadcopters provide near persistent surveillance; on finding something interesting, they can cue larger, more capable systems that are able to accurately locate a target[71]. In contrast to the Western approach, the Russians use their unmanned aircraft to find targets for their cannons and rockets to strike.

This is the first conflict in which both sides have made extensive use of drones. The Russians have countered the less numerous usually unsophisticated Ukrainian systems with mobile jammers that break either the command link with the aircraft, or its link with their satellite navigation; either can lead to the aircraft crashing. The Ukrainians have tried the same approach, but less successfully, due to their limited technical resources. Leading to them to largely relying upon passive air defence: the use of camouflage, cover, dispersion and unpredictable movement to avoid becoming a viable target. The Ukrainians are currently closing the technical gap and should be expected to become a leading supplier of this technology.

The Russians have also tactically employed cyber warfare, including, according to some sources the X-Agent, a Trojan horse that penetrated Ukrainian fire control systems and provided targeting information on their battery locations. While the veracity of this is questioned, the Ukrainians are certainly very wary of reliance on networked solutions[72]. Russian fire plans synergistically link lethal firepower with electronic attack. They seek to defeat command-and-control networks by jamming radio communications, radars and GPS signals, so dislocating any response. Leading to this lesson being identified: '*If your radars don't see incoming fire, you can't coordinate counter fire*[73]'.

In addition to their Soviet-vintage equipment, the Ukrainians have fielded American weapon locating radars able to detect mortars. These initially were highly vulnerable through employing tactics and procedures better suited to counter-insurgency operations, where they could emit for long periods from the same location. As their counterfire capability is outmatched, Ukrainian artillery has learnt that once it fires or electronically unmasks, it must move within a matter of minutes.

In comparison to the liberal use of firepower in support of the Eastern Ukrainian separatists and in their previous conflicts, Russian operations in Crimea largely avoided the public use of lethal force. This is obviously a deliberate approach aiming at, if not legitimising the takeover of this territory, then at least creating a cognitive dissonance within Western decision-makers over how they should respond. The conclusion that can be drawn from the Crimean operation, is that Russia's relatively indiscriminate firepower in other circumstances are equally conscious decisions, as they have most recently shown in their intervention in the Syrian Civil War.

By relying upon airpower, including cruise missile strikes, the Russian Air Force has become the lead service in Syria, rather than being a supporting player within combined arms armies.

This independent use of airpower could be a significant development in the Russian way of war. The Russian Chief of the General Staff Valeriy Gerasimov, identified that:

> *'today [Russia is] acquiring priceless combat experience in Syria. It is essential for this to be analysed in the branches of service and the combat arms at both the operational and tactical levels, and for a scientific conference to be held on the results of the military operations.*[74]'

However, as the ground forces were fighting in Ukraine while the Air Force operates in Syria, whatever lessons are learnt, this is unlikely to be a catalyst to Western-style joint warfighting.

To negate mobile air-defence systems, Russian aircraft in Syria have conducted the majority of their engagements from medium altitude (usually above 5,000m), achieving with unguided bombs a reported accuracy of 200–300m[75]. This is a considerable improvement on the view of previous Russian Chief of the General Staff, who in 2009 identified that his air force: *'can run bombing missions only in daytime with the sun shining, but they miss their targets anyway*[76]'. Limited use has also been made of satellite and laser precision guidance to engage the very highest value targets.

Lacking the West's concern with avoiding the unintended consequences of using firepower, the Russians employ a highly responsive sensor-decider-shooter linkage that does not insist on the high level of target development that is the Western norm. This leads to the Russians not seeing a requirement to establish a 'pattern of life' to reduce collateral damage before engaging. While militarily efficient in speeding up engagements and making effective use of sensors, this approach is more prone to errors, some could lead to unintended consequences. Of course, the Russians have a different perspective, favouring effective firepower over such concerns, and they see policy advantages in being relatively indiscriminate. As their Soviet predecessors did in Afghanistan, the Russians appear to have employed firepower to displace the civilian population through terror; targeting those unlikely to support the Assad regime due to their religious identity. This approach may also have a sophisticated trans-national dimension, in seeking to displace the Syrian population to cause a refugee crisis for the European Union[77].

The initial Russian Air Force deployment was mainly fixed wing aircraft. With the primary task of bombing the entrenched rebel forces around Aleppo. Against the more mobile Islamic State forces, attack helicopters have proved more useful, providing 'over the shoulder' fire support to assaulting Syrian troops. This led to more Mi-35 Hinds and the more modern Mi-28 Havoc and Ka-52 Alligator replacing most of the Russian fighter-bombers. In addition to these helicopters, by March 2017 the Russians had mainly had air superiority aircraft (Su-30 and Su-35S) and a few Su-24 bombers. Making it clear that Russians, despite fielding fourth and fifth generation fighter-bombers (the Su-57 has had a limited deployment to Syria), continue to see attack helicopters as the primary close air support platform.

Despite official denials, mixed in with the usual stream of fake news, Russian soldiers in Syria man at least one battery of the 2A65, their newest 152 mm towed howitzer, and have also provided trainers and advisors[78]. This assistance, plus modern Russian equipment has significantly improved Assad's artillery[79]. It is now employed on traditional Soviet and Russian lines, as Konstantin Sivkov, who often speaks on behalf of the Kremlin identified:

> *'the success of the Syrian Army in the first day offensive in Hama province towards Idlib was partially due to the method that is called "fire wave". This means very dense artillery shelling, using 300 or more artillery pieces per 1km of the frontline. The fire is aimed at the defence lines and is moved forward as the troops advance. This method consumes a lot of ammunition, but it is very effective in getting through fortifications[80].'*

Pending any possible doctrine change due to the Syria deployment, in peer-on-peer conventional operations Russian airpower is likely to be integrated into the combined arms plan. The Russian Army remains convinced that land warfare continues to be dominated by firepower, leading to significantly more organic firepower than Western armies. Set-piece operations will continue to be fought with highly-centralised timed fire plans aimed at rapidly passing manoeuvre forces through defended areas to deliver operational-level exploitation. These fire plans coordinate cyber and electronic attack with artillery, mortar and air fires. In mobile operations, the Russians will continue to decentralise firepower and employ direct fire; in part this is to overcome their ground forces *institutionalised* inflexible command and control. Political warfare has always been a part of the Soviet/Russian combined arms approach, its relative prominence may have increased in recent years. Western commentators readily identify the Russian cyber capability, but they also employ techniques *'unchanged since the Great Patriotic War,'* including loudspeaker broadcasts in foreign languages and leaflet drops[81].

In terms of platforms, the Russians are rebalancing towards greater use of long-range rockets and missiles and more capable 152mm guns. The gun-mortar has largely displaced the traditional mortar and may replace the 122mm gun in the close battle. They have established an edge over NATO in terms of munition lethality; crucially munitions such as thermobaric and cluster are highly lethal, but they rarely destroy buildings, which would hinder urban operations. They have revolutionised their target acquisition through employing layered sensors, in particular unmanned aircraft. If the replacement of fixed wing aircraft with attack helicopters in Syria is a guide, then the Russians continue to believe that helicopters are a superior close fire support platform; this includes the provision of overhead fire support in front and each side of an axis of advance in conventional warfighting.

The Bosnia and Kosovo Wars – Apogee of Airpower?

> *'I didn't want to change my beliefs, but there was too much evidence accumulating to stick to the article of faith. It does look as if air power has prevailed in the Balkans, and that the time has come to redefine how victory may be won[82]'*
>
> The Historian John Keegan

For the Western nations that intervened in the Wars of Yugoslav Secession, these were always conflicts of choice, and were embarked upon with limited liability, resulting in military means that ensured that there was little prospect of friendly casualties. They also sought to avoid, where possible, civilian and even undue enemy casualties; this led to NATO's warfighting being bedevilled by concerns over legitimacy and legality. Advances in airpower provided a warfighting approach that met this challenge through medium altitude precision bombing; ultimately, this constrained application of airpower delivered NATO's military objectives in both the Bosnian and Kosovo conflicts. At the time, the Kosovo air war was seen as a significant evolution in warfare, as a result of airpower being seen to be decisive without requiring warfighting assistance from ground forces. On reflection the Kosovo conflict demonstrated the effectiveness of counters to aerial firepower; resolving the crisis required a significant air armada and almost three months to coerce a small, isolated country. This made NATO's approach to warfighting vulnerable to those willing to fight closer to *real war* in the Clausewitzian sense[83].

The 1990s Balkan Wars, in addition to showcasing airpower as the means of imposing NATO's political will, also reconfirmed the dominance of artillery in the indigenous military operations. Artillery was employed conventionally against rival forces, and in what has become the norm in wars amongst the people, directly against civilians. In the Croatian theatre, artillery proved decisive in Operation Storm, the 4 August 1995 offensive by the Croatian Army against the Republic of Serbian Krajina. The lack of Serbian artillery was considered to be the prime reason for Croatian success[84]. In Bosnia, the Serbian advantage in artillery and mortars more than compensated for the superior infantry numbers of their opponents; this allowed the Serbs to both hold ground and subject the Bosnian Muslim and Croatian populations to persistent bombardment. As with the Soviets in Afghanistan, the purpose of this was to displace the civilian population and achieve 'ethnic cleansing'.

Western intervention in Bosnia can be divided into the UN and NATO phases. The UN made some use of airpower and artillery, usually cued by weapon locating sensors. This was limited by a narrow view of their own self-defence and their obligations to defend designated safe areas. NATO's intervention began with a modest air campaign, delivering 1,026 bombs against 56 Bosnian Serb military targets – most of these were locations of batteries – this was less than half the munitions used on an average day against Saddam's army in the Persian Gulf War. Aided by minor support from NATO artillery, this attrition of Serbian artillery was the most significant military factor in tipping the balance in the Bosnian War[85]. Airpower was successful despite at times challenging weather. The Serbs proved to be less accommodating opponents than the Iraqis, but their artillery dominance had led to them disregarding survivability measures: they largely occupied static, poorly concealed, over-concentrated battery positions.

Serbian ethnic cleansing of the Kosovo Albanians led to a 78-day air campaign and ended with another NATO ground force occupation; over 1,000 planes conducted 27,000 combat sorties. Serbian ground forces were initially seen as the only legitimate and legal target by NATO's 19 members, as these were directly involved in ethnic cleansing[86]. Understandably the air component commander wished to attack Belgrade as this was a more lucrative target for airpower than dispersed ground forces. The predictable ineffectiveness of the latter led NATO to incrementally expand its bombing to include strategic targets in Serbia, aiming at more directly influencing President Slobodan Milošević and his leadership group.

The aerial bombardment achieved NATO's goal, summed up by a spokesman as: *Serbs out, peacekeepers in, refugees back*. This led to the view that this was the first war won solely by airpower, and so achieving Giulio Douhet's theories, as articulated in Command of the Air[87]. Others have identified factors in addition to airpower: the growing political isolation of Serbia, declining Russian support, and the presence of NATO armies poised over the border to intervene.

What could not be debated was the failure of airpower to inflict significant damage on Serbian ground forces. The consensus now seems to be that NATO bombing killed around 1,000 soldiers and destroyed 22 armoured vehicles. This is in direct contrast to what was believed at the time[88]. Inadequate battle damage assessment continued after the war; in 2000, the US Congress was told that 246 Serb tanks and other armoured fighting vehicles had been destroyed[89].

Due to collateral damage concerns, 69% of weapons dropped were precision guided, as opposed to 5–8% in the Gulf War[90]. Precision weapons may have allowed accurate medium level engagement, but the principal challenge was locating Serbian ground forces in tree-covered mountains and in urban areas, and then differentiating them from civilians; this needed to be to a level of certainty that satisfied NATO's rules of engagement. Foul weather added to the challenge, as did the Serbian employment of smoke screens to thicken industrial smoke. As well as challenging sensors, sufficient quantity of particles in the air could counter laser guided munitions. Coordinate-seeking munitions were widely used, but these increased the targeting challenge as they required precise target locations.

In retrospect, the conflict actually highlighted airpower's limitations rather than heralding its supremacy. NATO aircraft flew 7,000 attack sorties of which 3,400 were against Serb ground forces[91]. If this figure is used, this works out as an armoured fighting vehicle-kill-per-sortie rate of 0.07, if the loss rate claimed in the Department of Defence's Report to Congress is used. If the more generally accepted 22 Serbian vehicles destroyed figure is used, then it leads to an armoured fighting vehicle-kill-per-sortie rate of 0.006. Both are well below historic norm 0.1 to 0.3 of armoured fighting vehicle-killed-per-sortie[92]. This makes airpower a very inefficient means of waging war; as in the Gulf War it succeeded through mass and time[93]. In order to increase its lethality, twenty-four AH-64 attack helicopters were deployed to Albania[94]. However, employing them was not considered to be a justifiable risk when fixed-wing aircraft were operating with relative immunity from medium altitude[95].

In contrast to those who saw the campaign as the realisation of airpower theory, those likely to oppose Western airpower would have identified exploitable weakness. These learnt how effective the skilful use of cover, concealment, dispersion and deception was against even modern aircraft. Active counter-measures to sensors and guidance systems, coupled with preserving the threat of air defence systems through avoiding engaging, could significantly reduce the effectiveness of an air campaign. The absence of ground forces was the key factor in allowing the Serbians to largely dislocate aerial firepower. A land threat would have forced them to concentrate to avoid defeat in detail, so making them vulnerable to airpower. The West's reliance on precision was also exposed as a double-edged weapon – it leads to a public expectation that wars can be fought without the unintended consequences of collateral damage. It also encourages an approach that sees warfare as an exercise in targeting. This reductive approach, having identified that the Serb ground forces in Kosovo were either conducting or shielding ethnic cleansing, saw them the only legitimate target. A more nuanced approach would have identified the various levers available to coerce the Serbian government into withdrawing from Kosovo, leading to its replacement by a NATO force.

The Serbs were initially willing to absorb the punishment, even if they lacked the means to oppose it. Perhaps if they had not been so isolated – even their traditional ally Russia failed to materially support them[96] – they could have outlasted NATO's political will to continue the bombardment. As Clausewitz noted, an enemy's power of resistance equalled *'the product of two inseparable factors, videlicet the total means at his disposal and the strength of his will'*[97]. The rationship between these factors can be understood as follows:

Despite the challenges, NATO always possessed escalation dominance. The restrictions on the air component's targeting could always be relaxed; they could also have employed the full range of joint fires, having rocket and tube artillery available as well as attack helicopters. And while a land attack on Kosovo was a daunting prospect given the limited attrition inflicted on Serbian ground forces, pursuing more limited ground manoeuvre aimed at 'shaping' Serb formations into a suitable target for joint fires was a viable option.

While NATO may have achieved its military objectives, the outcome for both Bosnia and Serbia/Kosovo has been *frozen conflicts*. In part this was due to Western airpower failing to inflict a visible defeat on the Serbian and Bosnian Serb ground forces that would have helped them to politically accept the outcome of the fighting. In fact, the Serbian forces leaving Kosovo saw themselves as undefeated, and as having exposed the relative impotence of NATO airpower. The inability of NATO air forces to dynamically engage elusive targets independently of fixing ground forces would next be exposed in the Afghan campaign[98].

The India and Pakistan Conflicts – Firepower-Dominated Mountain Warfare

Devastation caused by extremely accurate and timely fire assaults in most difficult and inhospitable terrain greatly facilitated the capture of key objectives. Innovative use of guns and MBRLs [multiple barrel rocket launchers] in direct firing role at long ranges added a new dimension in application of fire[99].

Lieutenant General S. Padmanabhan

The dominance of firepower has increased with each Indo-Pakistan conflict. These armies combine a belief in massed fires, as should be expected from forces whose initial doctrine was British, with a long-standing conviction of the worth of large calibre cannon[100]. Long range 155mm guns have been the decisive weapon in the border disputes in Kashmir, some of the most challenging mountainous terrain in the World. Faced with these conditions, most armies might choose a low firepower approach, using smaller calibre guns and mortars, and relying upon infantry. Instead the Indian Army employed massed firepower to shoot their infantry onto the objectives.

Initially the successor states to the Raj followed the British command and control system, this allowed the 9th Battalion of the Madras Regiment, Indian Army, to attack at the Battle of Ichhogil Bund in 1965 supported by the whole of the divisional artillery plus brigaded mortars from uncommitted infantry battalions. Like British Imperial forces in World War Two's Burma Campaign heavy preliminary fire proceeded the covering fire plan. In this assault the bombardment started 20 minutes before the H-Hour when the assaulting force crossed their start line.

Of the sub-continent's wars fought at high altitude, the Kargil War of May-July 1999 provides the most lessons. In this, Indian and Pakistani forces clashed at altitudes of up to 6,000 metres (20,000 ft) on the Kashmir Line of Control. High altitude and weather conditions limited bomb loads and made aerial engagement extremely challenging. The practical physical difficulty of bombing was compounded by poor coordination between the Indian Army and Air Force; some see this as an enduring problem, that was particularly evident in India's 1962 War with China[101]. Certainly, Indian Air Force doctrine focusses on counter-air operations, and in the Kargil War it was initially reluctant to risk undertaking close air support against targets with air defence. The Indian pilots were effective in strike operations, when they did not need close coordination with the Army.

The Indian Mi-24 attack helicopters were unable to fly at these altitudes due to their low power to weight ratio. As a partial substitute, Mi-17s were armed with rocket pods and machine guns, until the loss of one to a Pakistani shoulder-fired missile suspended further flights[102]. In addition to these practical and doctrinal challenges both sides preferred not to rely upon airpower. To ensure that the conflict remained localised, reliance was placed on 'tactical' artillery rather than 'operational' airpower[103]. So for both sides artillery, supported by mortars, provided most of the fire support.

As the conflict was initiated by Pakistani infiltration into Indian controlled territory, they were able to occupy an easily defended location that offered good observation of the battlefield. This gave them superior visual target acquisition, which they supplemented with weapon locating radars and unmanned aerial vehicles. The challenging terrain limited the effectiveness of these sensors, but they provided a significant edge over the Indians (who largely lacked them) in the counter battery fight, leading to the Indians subsequently acquiring Israeli drones.

Faced with this challenge, the Indians assembled 300 guns, mortars and rocket systems, including the highly effective Bofors FH-77B field howitzer. This park recognised that only the artillery could provide the firepower necessary to suppress the Pakistani positions[104]. The limited available space was the chief deployment challenge, guns were placed on any available ground, presenting the unique survey challenges of accounting for significant altitude difference between the individual guns within a battery. The superior range and lethality of the Bofors gun more than compensated for its limited mobility and the challenge of finding sufficient deployment space[105]. In this conflict of limited objectives, fire mobility proved superior to platform mobility. The conflict also reinforced the requirement for high angle fire to engage targets over intervening terrain; an advantageous feature of the Bofors gun was that it can elevate to 70 degrees.

Indian artillery fired more than 250,000 rounds, bombs and rockets over the course of the whole campaign, significantly more than the Israelis expended in the Yom Kippur War[106]. Massed fire was employed in support of each assault. 120 guns and mortars, plus a troop of BM-21, supported the final assault on Tiger Hill, expending 9,000 rounds, bombs and rockets. During the peak period of assaults, each Artillery battery fired, on average, over one round per minute for 17 days continuously. A radio interception from a Pakistani soldier on the receiving end of a 9,000 rounds bombardment was *'hell has fallen on us.*[107]'

When engaging mountainous positions with indirect fire, rounds can easily range over the peak and fall ineffectively into the dead ground behind; to avoid this, where possible, the Indians employed direct fire. The terrain allowed the Indians to conduct direct fire from up to 10km away. Rocket launchers in normal situations cannot conduct open sight engagements, but the discrepancy between launcher and target altitude allowed Indian BM-21 multiple-rocket launchers to engage with direct fire[108].

Given the character of the conflict and the physical challenge of the terrain, quite rightly overwhelming firepower was employed to ensure that the objective and supporting positions were completely neutralised before each assault. In the words of one artillery commander they were *'cracking a nut with a sledgehammer'*[109]. The conflict restated the need in mountainous terrain for well-trained and equipped light infantry. They are the only force capable of decisive manoeuvre, but they need heavy volumes of responsive firepower to seize positions, and they must be trained to assault just behind the artillery fire.

Despite the mass of artillery deployed by the Indians, through their lack of sensors, they were not able to silence the opposing artillery. The Pakistanis superior weapon locating radars provided a distinct edge in acquiring and destroying Indian guns. India's ineffective counter battery capability led to Pakistani artillery inflicting the bulk of Indian casualties (80%) in the Kargil campaign. Addressing this was a key lesson of the conflict[110], prompting the fielding in each divisional artillery brigade of a targeting battery; though arguably the Indian Regiment of Artillery still remains out of balance, with too many guns for too few means of target acquisition[111].

Building on this defining experience, the historic influence of the British Army, and after 1948 contact with the Soviet and then Russian militaries, the Indian Regiment of Artillery began to redefine its role. One expert on the Indian approach believed that artillery firepower now dominated the battlefield:

> *'[Originally] a "supporting" arm, whose firepower "neutralised" … artillery has now graduated to a full-fledged combat arm that dominates the battlefield with its accurate fire power that causes telling destruction …artillery will launch fire assaults or "attack by firepower" … With its ever-increasing range and lethality, the artillery is now capable of simultaneously fighting the contact, intermediate and deep battles*[112]*.'*

Supporting this view was the identified requirement for more guns of higher calibres. *'We are going for "mediumisation" – guns of over 130mm calibre,'* said Lieutenant General Madan Bhandari, Commandant of the School of Artillery after the conflict[113], at a time when more than half of the Indian artillery was made of Indian Field Guns of 105mm calibre. Initially more 130mm calibre guns were introduced, these were subsequently up-gunned to 155mm.

Despite this rebalancing, the terrain and infrastructure in India is not always suitable for employing conventional medium guns, or at times anything other than mule-transported pack artillery. This led to each infantry division having a specialist 105mm light regiment (battalion sized), in addition to the field guns supporting the brigades and the divisional medium regiment. If the 1971 War's practice still remains indicative, then the additional batteries of these light regiments can be attached to directly support infantry battalions, often through firing over open sights. The Indian Army's fielding of the M777 155mm howitzers shows their concern with retaining platform mobility to cover their long land frontier, while providing the superior destruction of the medium calibre shell. The mountain divisions currently retain lighter 105mm guns and 120mm mortars as their standard ordnance. There are 12 mountain divisions in the Indian Army's total of 40 Divisions, so unless these field the M777 to support their brigades – which will require a further substantial purchase – there will remain a significant quantity of lighter artillery.

Afghanistan 2001 and 2002 – Western Air with Northern Alliance

'we were forced to use the close air support ... to provide suppressive fires for our ground forces because we were unable to get our mortars into action, on that first day at least [when only half the mortars and no artillery had deployed][114]'.

Major Dennis Yates, fire support office on Operation Anaconda

America's wars of limited liability ended with the destruction of the Twin Towers. Despite this, at first America tried to achieve its political objective – the defeat of the Taliban regime and the destruction of al-Qaeda – without conventional ground forces. When these were belatedly deployed they initially went into battle without their supporting artillery and most of their mortars. The fallacy that airpower, with precision munitions, could replace organic artillery and mortar firepower in the close battle was soon exposed.

Despite the popular perception of an absence of conventional close combat, the Taliban were defeated in a series of conventional ground battles. Northern Alliance forces made the Taliban into a viable target for airpower, but they still had to do most of the hard fighting[115]. American special operations forces provided the forward air control and targeting data to deliver air and land coordination. Perhaps the most famous example of the coordination challenge was the Battle at Bai Beche, on 5 November, 2001. The Uzbek leader Rashid Dostum's cavalry decided to attack Taliban forces despite special operations forces simultaneously conducting an air strike. This turned into very effective covering fire as the bombs landed seconds before the cavalry arrived, allowing them to overrun the stunned defenders[116]. The deployment of conventional American ground forces was necessary once it became apparent that the Northern Alliance's war aims differed from the US when it came to the destruction of al-Qaeda[117].

This led to perhaps the most controversial American battle in recent years, Operation Anaconda, which was fought in March 2002 in the Shah-e-Kot valley, southeast of Kabul. It had the aim of encircling the al-Qaeda and Taliban forces escaping to neighbouring Pakistan. An air assault force drawn from 10th Mountain and 101st Airborne Divisions was tasked to seize a series of mountain passes to block their enemy's retreat, so allowing their Afghan allies and airpower to inflict further attrition[118]. No sooner had the American troops landed than they found themselves fixed by artillery, mortar, rocket grenade and heavy machine gun fires, as the al-Qaeda and Taliban forces had already taken command of the heights. Deploying without guns and only a limited number of mortars, they lacked the necessary resources to win this fire fight.

Effective cooperation between the army and air force is rarely in place at the start of a conflict; it usually requires the imperative of combat to overcome single service intransigence. Throughout, Operation Anaconda was impaired by poor air/land integration planning[119]. This resulted in the preparatory air strikes, which the assault force thought was scheduled for an hour, lasting only five minutes; the opposition remained concealed and undamaged until the actual air assault. Once the troops were on the ground, the divisional HQ was overwhelmed by air support requests and it lacked an efficient air/land integration structure to address them. The thirty seven USAF Joint Terminal Attack Controllers inserted in the operation subsequently received most of the criticism. There were failings, but they certainly provided sufficient coverage: this amounted to one controller per grid square. The greater problem was the lack of coordination of their efforts that an effective air/land integration structure could have provided. In its absence, aircraft were double-tasked, targets were double-targeted, and lacking low level airspace management, aircraft nearly collided[120].

Even the most effective air/land integration structure could not compensate for the lack of organic firepower. American airpower was designed to deliver precise munitions to point targets (56% of the munitions that were dropped in February 2002 were precision guided[121]) and not to provide persistent suppressive area firepower; nor was aerial fire support optimised for time-competitive close combat. The division's deputy fire support coordinator identified that *'PGMs [Precision Guided Munitions] take too long to arm and deliver to attack small mobile targets and targets of opportunity*[122]'. The fleeting attacks by fixed wing aircraft were effective, but no substitute for persistent organic firepower. Throughout the battle aerial firepower became progressively less effective, as the Taliban learnt to hold their fire when aircraft were overhead. Greater persistence and area firepower should have been provided by the supporting AH-64 Apache helicopters; however, the terrain prevented them from occupying standoff firing positions, making them vulnerable to intense ground fire from all directions, including from above. Only one Apache was still flying at the end of the first day.

General Hagenbeck's decision not to deploy the 10th Mountain Division's M119 105mm cannon, appears, with the benefit of hindsight, to represent a considerable risk[123]. He may have thought, as was becoming the orthodoxy at the time, that aerial firepower could substitute;

however, this was a considerable gamble given the division's lack of a worked-up air support system. The imperative behind this decision was the shortage of helicopter lift in the air assault, leading to the prioritising of riflemen over fire support[124]. In the absence of their M119 howitzers, the division was reliant upon 81mm and 120mm mortars to provide a guaranteed area target suppression capability; despite this, no attempt was made to centrally control their deployment. The brigade conducting the blocking mission had a total of 34 mortar tubes. One infantry battalion deployed with only one 120mm mortar (which was almost immediately knocked-out), but with its full complement of 81mm mortars in the initial assault. Other battalions assaulted with no mortars[125]. The mortars' lack of range resulted in them deploying too close to enemy positions; one mortar platoon only had the time to fire 16 bombs before being suppressed by enemy fire. Even if they had been correctly sited, they would have been outranged by Taliban rockets and a Soviet vintage D-30 122mm howitzer[126]. As the blocking infantry battalions could not occupy a continuous front, the conventional wisdom was that this necessitated the maximising of organic fire support weapons[127]. In this terrain, given the dead ground, indirect fire is essential to dominating the ground between isolated positions. The need for support weapons was soon realised, but additional mortars did not reinforce the deployment until nearly eleven hours after the start of the operation[128]. The fire support challenge can be summerised as:

Whatever tactical mistakes were made under operational pressure, the employment of ground forces with inadequate or no organic fire support is a recurring theme at the start of a conflict. Not knowing the opposition's combat worth or the character of conflict compounds this risk. Of course, the safest option is the combined arms approach, where a multiplicity of arms provides the flexibility to adapt to the enemy's action[129]. An effective close air support system significantly adds combat power, but it cannot replace the responsiveness, persistence, and ability to provide danger close fire support of cannons and mortars – these are the essential fire support attributes required by light infantry in complex terrain. Airpower can complement organic area fires though destroying point targets; in some Western militaries the flawed assumption still endures that airpower can make up for any level of deficiency in organic fire assets. The current belated priority being given to artillery is not due a rejection of this view, instead it is a recognition that against a peer opponent, who will contest airspace, close air support will become rare.

Despite the tactical setbacks that prevented America achieving the attrition it sought, the bases from which al-Qaeda had planned and prepared the 9/11 attacks were destroyed. Its people had been killed, captured, or driven out across the Durand Line into Pakistan. One of the reasons that the Americans failed to achieve the attrition sought during Operation Anaconda was that airpower became fixed on the blocking force's close fight. This prevented airpower from fulfilling its *actual* role in the operation: engaging the al-Qaeda and Taliban forces retreating towards Pakistan. Instead of declaring victory and moving on, America now changed its political objectives and an insurgency emerged from the four years of flimsy peace following al-Qaeda's expulsion from Afghanistan.

Iraq 2003 – 'Shock and Awe'

> *'By applying mass simultaneously at key points, rather than trying to push a broad, slow conventional advance, we throw the enemy off balance. We saw this in Afghanistan – rapid, fast maneuver. This creates momentum. We put our forces deep into the enemy's territory, moving so quickly that the Iraqis will not have time to react. When they finally do move, they become targets for the air component. Speed and momentum are the keys*[130]*'.*
>
> General Franks, leader of the Invasion of Iraq

The transformation of a controversial military concept – *Shock and Awe*[131] – into a popular aphorism through its use by key personalities in the build-up to War, helped shape the political direction for the Iraq invasion. This was despite the term being largely discredited by orthodox defence professionals. But it was politically popular because it reflected a view that warfare had been transformed[132]. Like the Afghan War, the Iraq War was heralded as a new form of warfighting based on the transformative effect of the latest information technology and the potential of precision weaponry. This justified General Frank's political superiors mandating the employment of considerably smaller forces than the military professionals considered appropriate.

The 2003 invasion of Iraq broke from the recent American way of war through simultaneously applying fire and manoeuvre. In conflicts since World War Two, the Americans have used time to maximise the effect of firepower. This led to the Gulf War 's sequenced battle design that saw the use of aerial firepower as a discrete activity to achieve a desired level of attrition. The Iraq War was different through a mix of conscious design, the imperative for accelerated action imposed by the Secretary of Defence, Donald Rumsfeld, and the unique circumstance of the no-fly zone. The latter had allowed Coalition airpower to conduct a preliminary bombardment stretching over years. The result was the destruction of almost any target of military worth; the ground offensive was required to set up further worthwhile targets. General Frank's strategy was largely a targeting exercise. He identified a targeting matrix made up of nine slices of the Iraqi centre of gravity. The actual focus of the campaign was the capture of Baghdad. This, it was assumed, would lead to the fall of the regime, and its replacement by a government friendly to the US[133]. Unfortunately, true to Maximilian Robespierre's view that *'no one welcomes armed liberators'* this did not happen[134].

A commonly-identified criticism of political interference in the campaign is that this resulted in a lack of ground forces for post-conflict operations; equally serious was its impact upon the conventional warfighting. Lack of ground forces, and in particular organic firepower, barred the American-led coalition from fighting in a way that would have made it easier for Iraqi society to reconcile itself to defeat. Events would subsequently show that the Iraqi Army should have been the campaign's centre of gravity. This army may not have had much conventional military capability, but it was crucial in terms of its moral authority within the Iraqi state. Simply bypassing Iraqi forces rather than physically forcing them to surrender created a problem that would be subsequently compounded by the post-war decision to disband the whole army. The result was that most of the Iraqi Army simply did not accept that they had been defeated, and so were unwilling to acquiesce to the political outcome the American-led coalition sought to impose. This led directly to the insurgency and the failure to achieve a stable political outcome.

Implementing this faulty strategy was an operational plan that became in effect a race for Baghdad. Despite being seen at the time as transformational, much of the technology employed was not new, and what was new was largely employed in traditional ways. In many ways, the campaign was a modern version of Blitzkrieg; not least in the relative combat capacity of Saddam's conventional forces compared to the Coalition. Overwhelming firepower and rapid ground manoeuvre were designed to break the enemy's will to fight, in accordance with classic manoeuvre warfare theory[135]. This led to armoured thrusts that by-passed Iraqi formations and cities in order to strike at what identified as the political heart of Saddam's regime. Aircraft flew in front of armoured columns to enable a high rate of advance; ground forces fixed the opposition for airpower. Both echoed the Battles of Mortain and Falaise, and the subsequent advance across France in 1944. Attack helicopters were primarily employed in the close battle, as they had been in the Vietnam and Gulf Wars, rather than in the deep battle, as had been predicted in Cold War AirLand doctrine. Aggressively-handled armoured artillery employing direct and indirect fire provided most of the danger close fire support. The missing element was the encirclement of the opposing ground forces, which resulted in the Germans capturing millions of prisoners in the Blitzkrieg years.

The American Army embarked upon this operation with the lowest proportion of artillery to manoeuvre arm battalions of any campaign in a century[136]. Both the 101st Airborne Division (Air Assault) and 3rd Infantry Division (Mechanized) went into battle with only their organic divisional artillery. The orthodoxy was that a division committed to combat should expect one or two reinforcing artillery brigades[137]. As this was not available, reinforcing the brigade on the division's main effort meant reallocating the artillery battalion from another manoeuvre brigade[138]. This was especially risky in non-linear conflict because at any time a following brigade could find itself in close combat, without its artillery fire support.

The doctrine of 'rapid dominance', from which 'shock and awe' was derived, promised that firepower would be significantly more effective through employing sophisticated targeting that exploited the potential of precision munitions[139]. This military doctrine saw overwhelming power and force as the means to paralyse the enemy's perception of the battlefield, and so destroy their will to fight. This approach was designed to leverage America's '*superior technology, precision engagement, and information dominance*[140]'. Information superiority would result from: improved satellite observation; signal and communication intelligence gathering; and significantly more persistent airborne sensors. The latter included a new-generation of manned and unmanned aircraft employing optical, infrared and radar surveillance. These were meant to provide an information flow which would supplement, if not replace, traditional ground and aviation reconnaissance. However, for the brigades in contact this proved to be almost wholly unfounded, and they were forced to rely upon their organic find capability. RAND identified a stark contrast between relatively static divisional HQs and their subordinates:

> *'What we uncovered in general in Iraq is, there appeared to be … a digital divide … At the division level or above, the view of the battle space was adequate to their needs. They were getting good feeds from the sensors … But among front-line army commanders … Everybody said the same thing. It was a universal comment: "We had terrible situational awareness"*[141]*.'*

This digital divide resulted in similar limitations in target identification, collateral damage estimates, and bomb damage assessments[142]. Lacking an adequate flow of information from the divisional level of command, the brigade relied upon their reconnaissance patrols, plus their counter-mortar and counter-battery radars.

Air and land cooperation benefitted from a 'run-out' in Afghanistan and the subsequent review of close air support procedures – largely driven by the US Marine Corps[143]. As already identified, the war had some of the characteristics of the high-speed advance across France in 1944, resulting in similar tactics: combat column formations, operating on a single route and employing an overhead 'close air support stack'. The superior sensors and firepower of modern aircraft often allowed them to defeat Iraqi forces ahead of the column, so that the ground advance did not lose momentum. Again, like the Blitzkrieg, almost all aerial fires took place in front of the direct fire zone, with the aircraft themselves finding their targets or being allocated them by airborne controllers, who were a real force multiplier. The USMC airborne controllers excelled in their control of kill boxes and notably employed air force jets that otherwise would have returned home with their ordnance[144]. This meant that fighter-bomber firepower was rarely employed within danger close distances. The lack of practice at proper close air support procedures meant that both the US and UK identified the need for post-War work to further refine and practice integration[145].

With the ground forces unmasking targets for airpower, the war showed the complementary nature of air and land components. As V Corps commander, Lieutenant General Wallace, observed:

> *'There were episodes in the fight when operational manoeuvre caused the enemy to react; when the enemy reacted, it allowed us to employ joint fires against him, which, in turn, allowed our operational manoeuvre to be more successful. For example, around Baghdad, manoeuvre caused the enemy to move out of his defensive positions, and when he was moving, the Air Force identified him and we attacked him with aircraft and long-range rockets. The complementarity between fires, manoeuvre and reconnaissance was evident at the corps level down to the tactical level*[146]'.

However, despite improved situational awareness – largely the product of more capable airborne sensors – the battlefield had not suddenly become transparent; even above brigade level, it remains the realm of Clausewitzian fog and friction. This was demonstrated by unobserved movement around Baghdad of three Iraqi Republican Guard divisions. Despite being within the coverage of airborne sensors, these were not engaged by airpower until they contacted American ground forces. The 3rd US Infantry Division fought the largely intact Iraq Medina Division, despite this having been classified as totally destroyed by airpower[147].

As fixed wing aircraft were rarely employed within danger close distances, direct support artillery and mortars, reinforced by attack helicopters, provided most of the fire support in the close battle. Artillery was usually at the front of the column, sometimes a battery behind the lead company, with the rest of the artillery battalion in range of the lead elements. Digitised survey technology reduced from eight minutes to 30 seconds the time for 155mm howitzers to be ready to conduct indirect fire[148]. These timings are considerably superior to what was achieved at the National Training Centre for hasty occupations, a difference largely due to removal of peacetime safety restrictions[149]. In summary, the high speed advance was due to:

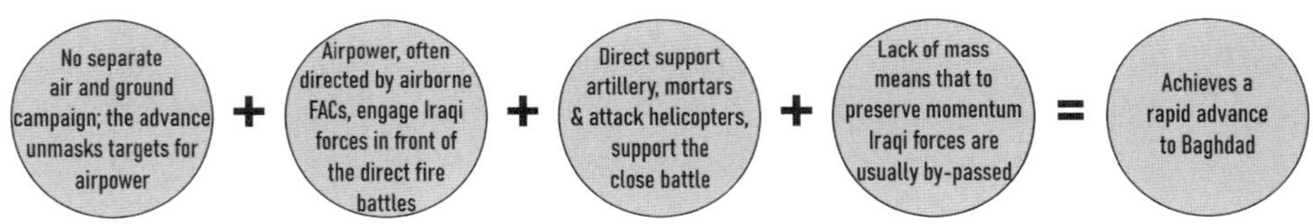

Prompt target acquisition in the close battle was aided by the US Army mounting armoured fire support element in bespoke Bradley fighting vehicles that provided the same protection and manoeuvrability as the rest of the force. The British were equally well provided, the USMC were not. Artillery fire support could be extremely fast, with a fire mission being ordered, cleared (at least one formation relied upon the target grid being broadcast over the manoeuvre command nets, with silence being consent to engage) and delivered within two minutes[150]. Having the guns close behind the lead elements resulted in short times of flight and more accurate fire; in addition, the low trajectory and an easily understood gun to target line greatly aided de-confliction with air and aviation. Keeping the guns close to the observers also made for reliable communications.

Bold handling by the American artillery exploited the M109's mobility and protection; this compensated for its lack of range when compared to more modern guns, in a way that the USMC's M198 towed gun could not[151]. The Marines' overall lack of armour led to them employing a more deliberate tactical approach[152]. This featured more preparatory and extended covering fire, resulting on one occasion in a 30 minutes long preparatory fire plan, an approach that had been common in World War Two[153]. Despite seeing a further increase in the proportion of precision to unguided aerial munitions, post conflict studies focussed on the need to suppress area targets in the close battle. These identified the greater effectiveness of massed fires over precision weaponry when engaging area targets[154].

As in the 1990–91 Gulf War, an effective counter-battery system, based on howitzers (but supported by aircraft and rocket artillery) and weapon locating radar, soon rendered Iraqi artillery ineffective. It was the availability of sensors, rather than insufficient available firepower, that usually delayed the defeat of hostile batteries. During Operation Peach, the crossing of the

Euphrates, it took an hour for the Americans to site a radar that could trigger counter fires to silence a 152mm battery[155]. In the 3rd Infantry Division's area of operations alone, there were almost 1,800 occasions in which Iraqi artillery was acquired, and 74 counter fire missions were conducted in response[156]. Radars were also used to cue aviation to track and engage batteries that were 'shooting and scooting'.

Manoeuvre commanders were reluctant to authorise cluster munitions, particularly on objectives they were due to assault, or into urban areas. Coalition air forces dropped nearly 1,500 cluster bombs, but these were on targets largely away from Iraqi civilians. These cluster bombs were mainly course-corrected, only 32% of air-dropped munitions in the conflict were wholly unguided. The Coalition's military capability was so overwhelming that any reticence to employ cluster weapons was not militarily significant.

Mortars again proved to be more survivable than the other means of Iraqi fire support. The Coalition used 60mm mortars at the company level, in the bipod and tripod modes, and either 81mm or 120mm for battalion fire support. The conflict highlighted what was already recognised: the 81mm and 120mm mortars' lack of range, and the time it takes to be ready to fire after moving, restricted their utility in mechanised operations. The 81mm bomb's small payload limited its effectiveness, as the Iraqis usually fought from field fortifications or buildings.

Both the British and the Americans recognised the imperative to enter urban areas if the War was to be swiftly concluded. Their doctrine interpreted their World War Two experience as urban operations being centred on infantry, with intensive house-by-house and street-by-street fighting. This also saw armour and firepower as having a limited role, despite World War Two operational research and experience showing the need for a combined arms approach[157]. An infantry-led approach to urban operations would have largely conceded the technological advantages of Western armies, and would have led to unacceptable casualties. Modifying their doctrine, the Americans instead sought to exploit their advantages in firepower and armoured manoeuvre[158]. This led to a series of armoured raids called Thunder Runs aiming at destroying Baathist symbolism, to convey the 'regime change' message. The first Thunder Run lasted 2 hours and 20 minutes and involved a 17km traverse of southwest Baghdad. Artillery was not employed; instead the American armour relied upon their direct fire weapons and overhead air support. Lessons were learnt, and in subsequent Thunder Runs artillery fire was directed at vulnerable points, including overpasses on highways that allowed the Iraqis to fire down on the armoured columns.

The Coalition sought to be highly discriminate in using firepower in urban areas. As well as seeking to reduce collateral damage, it also aimed at avoiding creating rubble. Operational analysis has determined that this can be as effective as prepared defences, increasing attacker casualties by about 50% and halving the rate of advance[159]. This led to the Coalition mainly using precision munitions, often with low yield warheads, against urban targets. Some 7,114 GBU-12 Paveway laser-guided 500lb bomb were used; when even a 500lb bomb was overkill, inert concrete munitions were used. In urban conflict, helicopters came into their own, due to the ease with which they could achieve the best angle to attack buildings while employing low danger are a munitions[160]. When all of these methods proved inadequate to further reduce the unintended consequences of firepower, A-10s risked flying at 2,000–3,000 feet over Baghdad to conduct strafing runs with their 30mm cannon. Unmanned aerial vehicles were primarily used for reconnaissance and target acquisition, but Predators still fired twelve Hellfire missiles in the conventional warfighting phase. Their endurance allowed them to loiter over the target, allowing them to choose the moment to engage based on minimising collateral damage with their low yield munitions. Facing even less opposition, the British used a more infantry-focussed approach to urban fighting, and could afford to be even more restrained in their use of firepower.

The new AH-64D, with the Longbow millimetre wave fire control radar and matching fire-and-forget Hellfire missiles, was expected to be very effective in Iraq's open terrain. While the weapon system performed well, its contribution was overshadowed by controversy over how aviation was employed. The US Army deployed two divisional and one corps aviation brigades; the latter's chief purpose was deep strikes. The corps aviation brigade conducted a two-battalion (34 Apache) deep strike on the evening of 23–24 March 2003, to destroy a brigade of the Iraqi Republican Guard Medina Division[161].

Little opposition was expected, leading to the helicopters employing the same ingress and egress routes. 31 ATACMS were fired to suppress air defence on the route, with another 30 missiles reserved for targets of opportunity[162]. The ATACMS were scheduled to fire 30 minutes before the arrival of the attack helicopters. A delay in the brigade's transit resulted in a further 90 minutes being added to the gap between the missiles landing and the helicopters transiting[163]. Compounding this fire support miscalculation was the helicopters taking the same route back without any scheduled covering fire. Artillery should be significantly easier to integrate with aviation than fixed wing aircraft, yet the aviation brigade completely failed to coordinate fire and manoeuvre. However, whatever the tactics employed, it is difficult to see how Iraqi air defences could be systematically suppressed as they relied upon ground observers with mobile phone or low power radio, who alerted machine gunners reliant upon optical tracking. Moreover, flying helicopters in a single column along a single route was never going to be a great target acquisition challenge. The only certain counter was to avoid flying low over enemy-occupied territory[164]. One Apache was lost and all the other aircraft received damage, making the brigade combat ineffective.

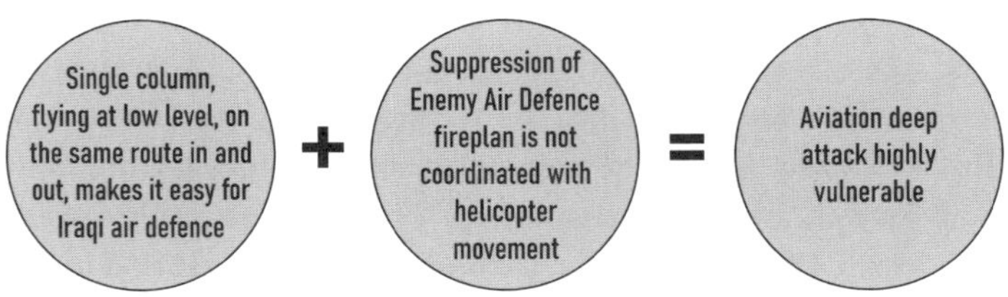

Despite moderate successes by divisional aviation in smaller deep strike operations[165], there was a switch away from this AirLand doctrine despite it being the institutional preference of Army Aviation:

> *'While the U.S. Marines have consistently emphasized the use of attack helicopters in small elements as part of the combined-arms team, most [US] Army attack aviation emphasises larger-scale deep attack missions in preference to close-combat attack, with battalions of attack helicopters*

penetrating deep into hostile territory to strike en masse against enemy force concentrations. Advocates argue that a few large-scale deep attacks will have more impact on the enemy than a larger number of smaller attacks in close combat will. The Air Force's traditional preference for strategic attack and AI [Air Interdiction] over CAS [close air support] is based on the same rationale[166]*.'*

In concert with fixed wing airpower, attack helicopters proved their worth, directly supporting 3rd Infantry Division's swift advance on Baghdad. They employed the full range of their sensors and missiles to fire from positions already cleared by ground forces; this significantly improved their force protection. 101st Division centred their combined arms force on the attack helicopter; whether providing fire support, reconnaissance or deep strike, as a result they were usually well synchronised with the other arms and the Air Force. A further blow to the massed deep attack doctrine was the decision later in the conflict to forgo night landing and take-off to avoid accidents. As the 101st Airborne Division determined the:

'Enemy did not present a massed target array; consequently risks (especially night desert landings) of conducting deep attacks outweigh potential effects on target[167]*.'*

Commanders realised that in a conflict, where the outcome was never in doubt, the risk simply did not justify the reward. The same applied to air assaults of infantry and limited supporting arms into Iraqi-controlled territory ahead of advancing ground forces.

Aviation's nap-of-the-earth flying and pop-up tactics were developed in the Cold War to reduce the helicopter's vulnerability against sophisticated integrated air defence systems. Employing them against a foe reliant upon small arms or grenade launchers, occasionally supplemented by man-portable surface to air missiles and anti-aircraft artillery, probably increased the helicopter's vulnerability. Against such a foe, fixed wing aircraft are a superior means of engaging depth targets, given that they can fly at safer altitudes, at speed and often with stealth. Once in the target area, they can employ weapons with greater standoff distance. The War led to a questioning of aviation's deep attack role, which has been a major part of Army doctrine since the 1980s; however, the discussions of the relative merits of maintaining an aviation deep attack capability were soon overtaken by events. America transitioned into more than a decade of counter-insurgency operations; in this attack helicopters were primarily employed providing fire support in the close fight[168]. Even without this, any examination of the lessons of the conflict would have led to a recognition of the Army's minor contribution to the deep battle. In addition to the limited success of deep aviation attacks, only 414 of the Army's long-range rocket – the ATACMs – were fired. In contrast the Coalition air forces flew 20,733 sorties that struck 15,592 land targets[169].

America fought with a third of the artillery pieces they employed in the Gulf War; despite this, sufficient battlefield firepower was achieved[170]. Ineffective opposition, plus greater ground and air synergy, led Lieutenant General Wallace, the V Crops commander, to opine that the Army could manage with less general support artillery. However, he caveated this view with the need for guaranteed air support[171]. The character of the War appeared to validate the emerging American view that the divisional level of command should take on an oversight role, leaving the conduct of the fighting to the brigades. This led to them taking command of assets previously controlled at the corps or divisional level.

The outcome of these conclusions and financially-driven downsizing was the disbandment of much of the US Army's corps level artillery. Both the corps and divisional artillery HQs were disbanded as they were not needed to control the employment of firepower to support the commander's main effort. Their remaining functions were assumed by the reduced number of fires brigades, who were too few to support all the higher HQs requiring their expertise[172]. Field artillery battalions became organic to manoeuvre brigades, this hindered their ability to be massed on the main effort, as well as having profound effects on their training governance and thus professional competence.

The aim of these reforms was to deliver *'fires with the agility required to support manoeuvre units during operations in a fast-paced non-linear environment*[173]'. The post-Iraq War American Army in many ways replicated the Wehrmacht, both in its deficiency of artillery mass[174] and its lack of an effective artillery command structure able to centrally employ firepower. This approach suited opponents such as the Iraqis in 2003, but historically it has not been effective in conventional war between peer adversaries.

Iraq and Afghanistan – Fighting the Insurgency

When you're facing a counter-insurgency war, if you get the strategy right, you can get the tactics wrong, and eventually you'll get the tactics right. If you get the strategy wrong and the tactics right at the start, you can refine the tactics forever, but you will still lose the war[175].

Colonel Robert Killebrew, 2006

Despite employing irregular warfare tactics to negate the Coalition's firepower superiority, joint fires had a significant role in fighting the Afghan and Iraqi insurgencies. These conflicts were pursued with a degree of sophistication that avoided the Vietnam War's direct equating of the application of firepower with the defeat of the insurgency. In both Iraq and Afghanistan, the American-led Coalitions largely followed people-centric insurgency doctrine[176], but this failed to deliver the security necessary to gain and retain the allegiance of the people. Particularly in Afghanistan, Coalition forces failed to tactically integrate firepower with manoeuvre to visibly defeat the insurgents. Separate from ground force operations, special operations forces pursued a leadership targeting or decapitation strategy that aimed at killing or capturing the insurgent leadership; this employed both precision joint fires and special operations forces direct action. This sophisticated form of attritional warfare was seen by some as an opportunity to 'mow the grass' of global jihadists[177]. Optimistically, leadership decapitation was seen as a means to reduce the intensity of the violence through decreasing the insurgent's capacity to mount attacks, leading to an opportunity for the non-miltary lines of operation to work. However, it became a replacement for offensive operations by conventional forces that could have delivered a secure environment for the prize in counter-insurgency, the people.

The American military's shift away from relying upon organic fire support assets was always likely to be challenged by an effective insurgency. When insurgents can usually choose the moment to engage, there is a premium on guaranteed, responsive firepower able to operate at danger close distances. As in other Western counter-insurgency operations, field artillery and mortars were mainly deployed in forward operating bases in platoon or battery strength, to provide responsive fire support to patrols and convoys. Dispersion to achieve coverage resulted in an inability to mass firepower onto an individual target[178]. This led to artillery being the first responder, followed by aircraft and aviation who provided the weight of fire to win firefights.

The most useful aircraft were those whose endurance allowed them to stay on station; the B-1, B-2 and B-52 bombers, especially when supported by tankers, combined endurance with payload, but these were rare assets. Despite their relatively limited payload, unmanned aircraft's endurance made them the conflict's premier close air support and reconnaissance platform. The fighter-bombers' lack of persistence was partly compensated by their high speed, allowing them to quickly aid troops in contact. Aviation was chiefly employed in reconnaissance and fire support. Constant force generation of brigade combat teams led to multi-function aviation task forces replacing the divisional structure. To support this, aviation staff migrated from divisional to brigade level[179]. On operations, attack helicopters primarily operated in pairs[180], usually in concert with ground forces.

Only when coalition forces conducted set-piece operations was there the opportunity to mass firepower and target acquisition sensors. In the Battle of Sadr City, the assaulting brigade was reinforced with: two MQ-1 Predator and two RQ-7B Shadow unmanned aircraft, six AH-64 Apache attack helicopters, fixed-wing close air support, and guided multiple launch rocket systems. These were in addition to the organic mortars, howitzers, scouts, weapon locating radars, plus aerostat and tower mounted cameras[181].

While the improvised explosive device (IED) was the chief insurgent weapon, both the Iraqis and Afghans made use of indirect fire, particularly to attack security force bases. Rockets and mortars were favoured as these combined a heavy weight of fire with simplicity, ease of concealment and mobility. The initial Coalition response was the targeting of firing positions with artillery or mortar fire, largely cued by weapon-locating radars. As the insurgents, particularly in Iraq, became more sophisticated, this resulted in firepower being wasted on unmanned or vacated firing points, or causing collateral damage that could be exploited in the battle for the people. In response, the Coalition forces networked their radars, allowing them to cross-cue aircraft, these could track or engage the rocket or mortar teams escaping from their firing point.

The fielding of sophisticated counterfire systems led the insurgents to favour rockets, as these had longer ranges than mortars and did not require complex platforms; rockets without fins can be launched from any slope pointing in the direction of the target, making the Chinese-designed 107mm rocket the most popular weapon. This small rocket could be easily man-carried, often on the back of a motorbike. Other rockets had longer range, better accuracy and a more lethal warhead. With longer range comes a higher trajectory, making it easier for weapon locating radars to detect. In contrast, the 107mm rocket's low trajectory allows it to mix with ground clutter. Sophisticated simultaneous multiple fire points attacks add to the weapon locating challenge.

As well as the being the mainstay of the counterfire battle, weapon locating radars provided sufficient warning of incoming fire for those within in the target area to take cover. They could also cue close range defensive weapons – such as the Phalanx 20mm Gatling Gun – to shoot down the incoming rocket or mortar. Their final task was orchestrating the post-attack response, through establishing the quantity of incoming rockets, and if this differs from the number that have exploded, direct the specialist teams to deal with the unexploded ordnance.

Counter-insurgency operations increased the proportion of artillery troops devoted to surveillance and target acquisition, at the expense of those manning firing systems. These sensors operated across the electro-magnetic spectrum to provide a layered coverage. Most of these sensors were sited in Coalition bases, either in towers or tethered aerostats, and were networked via point-to-point communications. Where the terrain was suitable, and the bases mutually supporting, they could deliver a high degree of persistent wide area surveillance over the intervening terrain. Troops operating away from these sensor clusters were reliant upon less effective organic sensors, reinforced by airborne platforms. In previous Western counter-insurgency campaigns, patrols have tended to be restricted to within range of the fire support bases. In Afghanistan they could become tied to the sensor coverage. This could be more restrictive, because unlike indirect fire it is largely reliant on line of sight.

Special operations forces largely took on the offensive role in both theatres, achieving most of the attrition through direct action and joint fires strikes. Special forces usually employed force within offensive rules of engagement. Managing the 'risk to reward' calculation in these two campaigns led to increasingly sophisticated collateral damage measurement. Contrary to perception, legal advice in Western countries has usually tended to facilitate rather than obstruct strikes. The real obstacle is risk-aversion at the military strategic and political levels, when legal differences can provide a rationale for indecision[182]. This reinforces the key political advantage of employing special operations forces: their greater anonymity in applying force. However, special forces attrition could seldom be decisive as it was rarely combined with securing and maintaining the allegiance of the people. In both Iraq and Afghanistan, the land and special forces component were rarely coordinated:

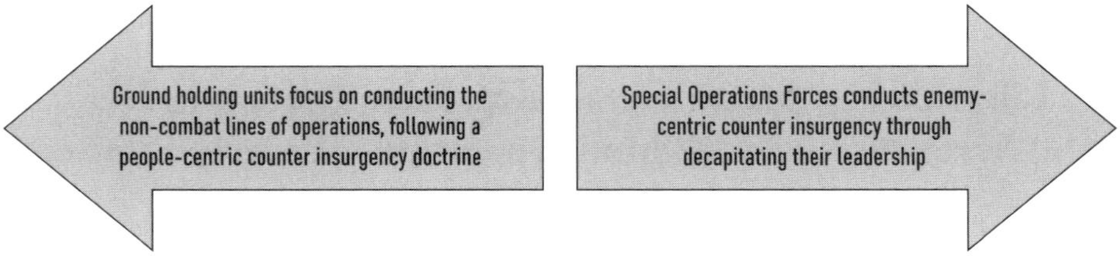

As in the Vietnam War, the creation of a viable indigenous military was left too late. Again, the prevailing view was to maximise resources to defeat the insurgency, rather than recognising that the intervention forces would inevitably hand-over the fight to indigenous forces without a clear victory. Despite being promoted publicly, the US Army's culture, as reflected in its personnel management system, placed a low priority on the advisory mission[183]. This was compounded by the inability of the two nations to effectively cooperate once US combat forces left Iraq at the end of 2011. After this date only a small office of military cooperation was left, so there was not an effective train and assist mission in place until June 2014, when the Iraqis were challenged by the so called Islamic State.

The historical pattern is clear; the withdrawal of foreign forces allows the primacy of indigenous security forces, and this results in greater government legitimacy. Ultimately this assists in the insurgency's marginalisation and to gradually the police becoming the lead agency. As with South Vietnam, providing Iraqi and Afghan armies with adequate firepower was not a priority. Iraqi units had nothing above the 60mm mortar as late as 2009[184]. As with the final stages of the Indo-China Wars, once the anti-government forces no longer faced overwhelming firepower, they adopted regular warfare tactics. These better served their objective of quickly imposing their rule, leading to the Islamic State conducting conventional assaults, and overmatching Iraqi government forces acclimatised, trained and equipped to conduct counter-insurgency operations.

In summary, the American-led Coalition in both Iraq and Afghanistan focussed their special operations forces on decapitating the enemy's leadership. In parallel the ground forces largely pursued a people-centric strategy that rarely sought to decisively engage their opponents. As a result, firepower was rarely used within a combined arms operation framework to visibly defeat the insurgents, and so secure territory and the allegiance of its people[185]. That attrition on its own cannot be effective in defeating mature insurgencies has been well established by the Israelis. Despite this, it proved to be attractive for factors unconnected with achieving the right political outcome for Iraq and Afghanistan. Finally, the failure to develop indigenous firepower allowed insurgents to transition to a more decisive character of conflict once the Coalition disengaged. Addressing this asymmetric advantage was a high priority once Coalition forces, led by America, re-engaged with Iraq. Responding to the errors of Iraq and Afghanistan, the US Army's latest operating concept seeks greater tactical balance[186]. This identifies that raids and precision strikes rarely decisively affect a conflict's human and political drivers. American doctrine now recognises the centrality of building-up the host-nation's military forces, recognising that this represents the only means of successfully ending the intervention. However, institutionally any army with warfighting ethos will see this as a secondary task; in contrast, properly regulated private military companies have excelled in this function[187].

Libya 2011, Operations Against Islamic State in Iraq and Syria, and France's Mali Operation – Largely Limited Liability Warfare

'Airpower is an unusually seductive form of military strength, in part because, like modern courtship, it appears to offer gratification without commitment[188].'

Eliot A. Cohen, American political scientist

Chastened by their experience in Iraq and Afghanistan Western nations were reluctant to deploy ground forces in Libya and Syria. Instead seeking to support indigenous ground forces with airpower. The limitations of employing airpower tactically, without an effective air/land integration structure, were again exposed in the West's operations in Libya, and initially in operations against the Islamic state. The French operations in Mali benefitted from their continuous engagement since colonial days, resulting in a political willingness to deploy ground forces and a well-established working relationship with Malian forces.

In Libya, a NATO Coalition employed the 'Afghan Model' of an aerial intervention to support indigenous rebel ground forces with very few Western *boots on the ground*[189]. Only the Americans had the capability to 'open the door' to allow the effective employment of airpower against ground forces at virtually no risk. This they did, even though they were 'leading from the rear', by using their most capable aircraft, together with Tomahawk cruise missile, to defeat Libyan air defences. This allowed fighter-bombers with inadequate defensive aid suites (i.e. non-American) and the low performance A-10 and AC-130 Spectre gunships to operate. In addition, they provided 70% of intelligence collection and targeting assets[190].

The first targets hit were the ground forces advancing on the opposition capital Benghazi, and the Libyan leadership centred on Muammar Gaddafi. These two target sets were initially considered the only legitimate means of employing airpower. Throughout, highly restrictive rules of engagement stymied the campaign; positive target identification before engagement was very difficult to achieve in close combat without Coalition forward air controllers embedded in rebel forces. This, coupled with air interdiction's traditional advantage in desert warfare made the deep battle more productive, notably in preventing the reinforcement of regime forces in Misrata. Another key airpower success was the disruption of government command and control through targeting Gaddafi. While airpower could rarely locate and destroy regime artillery, its overhead presence forced it to stop firing and maintain constant movement that reduced its accuracy and availability.

Given the inability to effectively conduct close air support without Western forward air controllers, attack helicopters were deployed onto French and British warships. The same lack of an air/land integration structure meant that helicopters were unable to effectively cooperate with rebels. Consequently, attack helicopters could not achieve force protection through operating 'over the shoulder' of friendly ground forces and employing standoff engagements. Instead they were forced to conduct deep attacks, despite force protection concerns due to their inability to fly above the ceiling of surviving anti-aircraft defences. This led to targets been attacked – including a static undefended radar installation – that were more suited to fixed wing aircraft. This nervousness extended to British Apache helicopters missions being given fast jet cover[191]. A total of 22 Apache missions were conducted. With an equal number cancelled, largely due to a lack of situational awareness of the relative locations of pro- and anti-regime forces[192]. French Tigre and Gazelle helicopters were more aggressively employed, benefitting from their experience of African conditions and less restrictive rules of engagement[193]. As a result, they destroyed 'technicals', tanks, artillery, anti-aircraft-artillery and radar installations, from their first operational sortie.

The creation of a 16-mile buffer zone around Misrata was a more suitable mission, but this was probably beyond aviation's capacity given that the available helicopters could not maintain a persistent presence and the inability of NATO sensors or indigenous ground troops to cue strikes. The Russians in Syria showed how effective attack aviation can be in this type of conflict; however, they have the advantage of being in theatre and embedded in the regular Syrian Army. This provides a liaison structure able to coordinate ground and aviation fire and manoeuvre. Achieving this with an improvised Libyan rebel force, and with helicopters working off unfamiliar improvised helicopter carriers, was an order of magnitude more difficult. Whatever its tactical failings, the Coalition, largely through airpower, were largely effective in preventing Gaddafi's regular forces being used against their own population.

After initial difficulties, almost a hundred naval fire support missions were carried out. These included: shows of force, neutralisation, harassment, interdiction and defensive barrages to halt the advance of the troops loyal to Gaddafi's regime. There were issues of unfamiliarity in integrating naval fire into the joint HQ's campaign design, the staff being more familiar with targeting airpower. The warships' key advantage over airpower was persistence, in contrast, Gaddafi's forces tended to hold their fire to avoid detection when aircraft were overhead[194].

Of course, the absence of ground forces prevented the Coalition from imposing a political settlement which could have avoided Libya's current endemic instability. Libya is now a failed state.

In June 2014, America and its allies chose to rely upon airpower to support their Iraqi and Syrian allies against the Islamic State. Again, this led to problematic synchronisation between aerial firepower and ground manoeuvre. Collateral damage concerns led to the Coalition being reluctant to train and authorise Iraqis as forward air controllers. The Iraqi Security Forces and Kurdish Peshmerga militia both saw air strikes as vital, but without embedded controllers these took far too long to call in. This was exploited in the early stages of the conflict by the lightning-fast mechanised assaults by Islamic State suicide bombers and heavily armed militants[195].

Learning from previous conflicts, once Central Command had time to effectively respond, they deployed forward air controllers; initially these were provided by the special operations forces[196]. An American Army divisional HQ subsequently provided a robust support and mentoring structure, including an effective air/land integration structure. This addressed the close combat challenge; surprisingly given their effectiveness in the 2003 War, forward air controllers (airborne) were not widely employed to apply airpower in depth. The explanation may be the capability's marginalisation in the years of counter-insurgency operations[197]. In the Libyan conflict instead of using airborne forward air controllers, Long Range Patrol aircraft were given the task of Strike and Armed Reconnaissance Coordinators. Mounting a certified controller within an aircraft with the sensors, communications and endurance of a maritime patrol aircraft certainly helps and it is a viable option in uncontested airspace. But their job was to maximize the effectiveness of air interdiction and armed reconnaissance assets; in contrast airborne controllers seek to find targets, for air-to-ground attacks, that will support the ground forces[198].

Once the Islamic State advance culminated, the conflict went into a drawn-out attritional phase in which airpower was unable to deliver decisive blows. In its application of force, America has been accused of following a strategy of '*creeping incrementalism*' rather than employing overwhelming firepower[199]. This was partly due to targeting constraints that can only be met through sufficient time and resources devoted to target development[200]. This led to around two-thirds of targets struck being Islamic State ground forces, with the remaining attacks being on buildings and other fixed infrastructure. This was despite the Islamic State occupying territory and setting up some of the apparatus of a regular state; this should have made it more vulnerable to air attacks than other insurgencies. The attacks on its oil supply got off to a slow start, and by mid-2015 these only accounted for 130 targets struck, less than 3% of the total. By 2016 these were having an effect on the oil-dependent economy. The Islamic State were skilful at denying air interdiction viable targets; their logistical support and troop movement blended into normal civilian traffic. This made attacks on bridges and roads a more productive target, yet these represented less than 2% of the total sorties. Due to their choice to only employ precision munitions, there was the possibility that mid-campaign Western air forces could have run out of these weapons before the Islamic State ran out of manpower.

Despite a desire to avoid using land forces, once the conflict became a succession of urban battles, a limited quantity of Coalition artillery was also deployed. These provided a persistent source of firepower at minimum risk to Western personnel. The Battle of Mosul, which began in October 2016, was the largest conventional land battle since the capture of Baghdad in 2003. Around 8,000 Islamic State fighters were opposed by approximately 75,000. The failure to properly re-establish a unified Iraqi military led to their assault being on three axes. The Iraqi Army led in the north, the Iraqi Special Operations Forces in the centre, and the Federal Police, a paramilitary force, in the south. In addition, there were other militias and Kurdish forces.

Adding to the city's inherent physical challenge, Islamic State fighters made extensive use of tunnels, both through buildings and underground. More active methods to defeat Coalition firepower included the use of smoke from burning tyres to obscure visibility and defeat laser guided weapons. In addition, the thousands of civilians stuck in the middle of the fighting were used as human shields. This physical and human terrain largely enabled these experienced fighters to freely manoeuvre around the urban battlefield with little chance of being attacked. The Coalition response was the persistent stare provided by unmanned aerial vehicles to identify any fleeting opportunities to strike. If these drones were armed, they had a chance to engage during the short window of time that Islamic State fighters met the Coalition's targeting threshold.

The close battle re-confirmed the requirement for all urban movement to be covered by suppressive fire on known and suspected enemy battle positions. The challenge was to achieve this whilst, where possible, avoiding the civilians trapped in the city becoming casualties. This led to smoke munitions being the favoured means of tackling likely enemy locations. Every move required guaranteed on-call firepower, which only artillery and mortars could provide. Concern with avoiding collateral damage initially restricted the employment of area firepower, but as casualties mounted, the Iraqi government from December 2016 significantly loosened its restrictions on artillery. This obviously came at the cost of civilian lives and the physical destruction of Mosul, further hindering friendly movement and improving the insurgent's defences. In contrast, firepower from Western nations was tightly controlled, with artillery being largely restricted to the outskirts and aerial firepower being rigorously targeted. Despite this the French alone conducted 2,500 fire missions with their Caesar guns.

The Islamic State supplemented their mortars and rockets with improvised firepower. Islamic State fighters routinely wore suicide belts; in addition, they relied heavily upon suicide car and motorbike bombs and at the height of the campaign produced these at a rate of five per day. They conducted around a thousand of these attacks in the Battle for Mosul, making their production facilities a high priority target for Coalition airstrikes. Suicide car bombs inflicted severe casualties on Iraqi Humvee convoys, forcing the Iraqis to deploy their heavy armour. But these also suffered avoidable losses through lack of effective infantry support. Adapting to urban conflict, the Iraqis started:

> *'fighting on foot, street by street. We entered the neighbourhoods by night, in seven-man sections. [The Islamic State] tried to use suicide cars against us, but on foot we were able to conceal ourselves, to use subterfuge, to enter homes for shelter, and so on*[201]*.'*

Another improvisation by the so-called Islamic State was the weaponising of commercial drones with 40mm grenades, delivering primitive aerial firepower capability at relatively little cost[202]. These proved difficult to counter, with both jamming and trying to shoot them down being only partially effective.

The outcome of this challenge is that the Iraqi artillery has now been equipped with self-propelled guns and rocket launchers; it is on its way to being restored as the premier arm. Given the importance of urban fighting, they have fielded the Russian Buratino which has thirty 220mm rockets with thermobaric warheads mounted on a T-72 chassis. Iraqi airpower is undertaking a staged development aiming at the fielding fighter-bombers. The Iraq Army is no longer a counter-insurgency force that offers an asymmetric advantage to any opponent that comes at it with a conventional warfighting capability. It has hard-won experience in urban combined arms fighting, and has demonstrated a willingness to ruthlessly apply firepower.

In late 2012 France rapidly reinforced their forward-deployed African garrisons with combat power sufficient to challenge a Jihadist insurgency threatening Mali. The Mali deployment is a significant exception to the post-Afghanistan War avoidance by Western nations of employing their soldiers in ground close combat. It should be seen as part of France's traditional policing of its informal sphere of influence.

Effective use of joint fires in support of manoeuvre was a key element of the operation; however, there were challenges in synergising ground and air forces. For fire support the French used: the truck-mounted 155mm CAESAR howitzer, 120mm mortars, the Tigre attack helicopters and fighter-bombers. In line with their experience in Afghanistan, their doctrine made the artillerymen supporting the battlegroup commander responsible for fire support. Resisting this centralisation of joint fires under an army officer, the air force deployed additional officers to Mali, attaching them to army battlegroups, but they reported directly to the air commander[203]. A further challenge was the lack of flexibility in the control of airspace, which manifested in the need to individually clear each artillery and mortar fire mission. This was regardless of whether any aircraft were actually using the airspace. Given that guns and mortars could provide fire support 24/7 and the air force provided, at best, a few hours of support each day, there should have been a more rational approach to airspace management.

At the heart of these tensions is a culture clash between an Army whose training and outlook is expeditionary, with an Air Force that is more metropolitan in outlook. The French Army sees certain advantages in scarcity of materiel resources. This builds upon a military culture that has always believed in a uniquely French approach to war that places *'an emphasis upon the human qualities of the soldier and the Army*[204]'. This culture of make-do is called *système D* (derived from *débrouille*, meaning 'resourcefulness'). This approach prevails despite the Army's Afghanistan experience, where the American materiel way of war dominated[205]. The predominant French Army view sees close combat, properly supported by joint fires, as the primary means of defeating the enemy. And that this is best achieved through resourcing and trusting local commanders. In contrast, the French Air Force is more comfortable with warfighting being reliant upon centralised command and control.

The political outcome of the Iraq and Afghanistan conflicts has been an unwillingness to deploy Western forces in ground combat; for reasons already identified, Mali is an exception. France's enduring political and emotional commitment to Africa means that this operation cannot serve as a model for other countries seeking to rapidly employ combat forces; France also has strategic patience, though at the time of writing this open ended commitment is being questioned. French forces have recaptured Northern Mali, they should now be handing over to local forces. With some allied support it is embarked on an enduring commitment of a 5,000 strong force to combat Sahel's Islamists. A major challenge for Western militaries is making the joint firepower that their politicians are willing to employ more effective in supporting allied ground forces. The Islamic State experience shows that this is best achieved through embedding an air/land integration system. Airborne forward air control offers the means to more effectively employ aerial firepower beyond the line of contact. Though their persistent observation, these controllers can separate friend and foe and mitigate collateral damage. This is best done from an unmanned aircraft. Significantly enhancing the fighting power of allies also requires terminal controllers with their ground forces and a joint fire staff structure[206].

The 2020 Nagorno-Karabakh War – Drone Victory?

'The first lesson that the Azerbaijani-Armenian clashes showed is the vulnerability of traditional land units – armoured, mechanized, and motorized formations – in the face of advanced drone warfare weaponry and concepts[207].'

Doctor Can Kasapoglu, Turkish scholar and military analyst

The clear military victory by Azerbaijan over Armenia and the Republic of Nagorno-Karabakh in their 44-day conflict was something of a surprise to the casual observer of affairs in the Caucasus. In previous conflicts the Armenian Army had proved itself to be superior: it had better officers, more motivated soldiers, and more agile leadership – as well as a committed general population. However, the local economic balance of power shifted decisively in the second decade of the 21st century towards Azerbaijan. Now a wealthy petro-state it was ready to spend that wealth on Turkish, Russian and Israeli technology in a manner that decisively dislocated the expected advantage of Armenian troops in close combat[208]. This was aided by the Russian decision to stand aside in this conflict, in contrast to the first (late 1980s to May 1994) and second wars (2016). This opening allowed Turkey to provide air superiority for the Azeri forces – uncontested by the Armenian air force despite flying Su-30s previously provided by Russia. Yet while the Azeris had the edge in most military capabilities, it was their employment of drones that has been heralded as decisive. This capability will be covered in more detail below, but a note of caution should be sounded here – we should be wary of drawing too much analysis from the combat footage available on social media. Other battlefield systems, notably artillery, lack similar live video feeds and so their contribution can be under-estimated.

Azerbaijan employs a modern unmanned aerial fleet featuring: medium-altitude, long-endurance drones, such as Hermes-900 and Heron; loitering munitions such as Orbiter 1K, SkyStriker, and Harop; and the Turkish Bayraktar TB2 unmanned combat aerial vehicles. These were effectively given free-rein, as, in addition to not contesting the air with their fighters, Armenian ground-based air defence was similarly impotent, reliant as it is on 1980s Soviet-era air defence systems designed to engage manned, fixed wing, aircraft. The Azerbaijan unmanned aircraft flew too slow and presented too small a radar cross-section for these systems to acquire them as a target. The inability of conventional air defence to cope with modern drones was illustrated by the Turkish supplied Bayraktar TB2 destroying – with impunity – both the S-300 PT and PS series and the 9K37M Buk-M1, with their laser-guided Roketsan MAM-L missile. This aircraft had already demonstrated its suppression of enemy air defence credentials in the Syrian and Libyan conflicts, and this now appears to be its standard role – hence naming it as an unmanned *combat aerial vehicle*. Armenian forces did not have a jammer able to interrupt the signals linking the drones to their guidance stations. Even if they had, Azerbaijan had acquired the IAI Harop anti-radiation loitering munition that can autonomously home in on radio emissions.

This conflict, and similar operations in Syria and Libya, illustrates that the diffusion of remotely operating systems is outpacing effective counters. Unmanned aircraft are considerably cheaper and easier to employ than the defensive systems needed to counter them. And not only can drones destroy targets worth many times their own value, the cost of an air defence missile capable of intercepting them can also exceed the value of its target.

Yet the purchase of these systems is not enough in itself – their effective deployment was underpinned by newly acquired tactical expertise; the Azeris appear to have benefitted from Turkish tactical advice in employing their unmanned aircraft. Only a minority of drones engaged with their own weapons – most missions directed tube and missile artillery. While the Bayraktar TB2 unmanned combat aerial vehicles has, as in recent Turkish operations, featured heavily on social media, the decisive capability appears to have been the networking of sensors and shooters. Unmanned aircraft cued massed artillery, because few of the unmanned Azeris' aircraft were armed; and those that had munitions lacked the lethality to destroy entrenched positions and infrastructure; hence the drones cued artillery with its range of munitions, as opposed to employing the limited quantity fitted to an aircraft prior to launch.

As successor states to the USSR, both sides had strong artilleries. Cannon were the mainstay of the close battle; in the deep battle, long-range tube artillery, was supplemented by multiple rocket systems and ballistic missiles. The Armenians had a materiel advantage in the quantity of long-range missiles[209]; however, this was not translated into a decisive edge due their lack of accuracy and a shortage of equally long-range sensors. It was the superior targeting of Azeris drones coupled with precision weapons – including the Israeli-made LORA ballistic missile – that was decisive. The Azeris employed their missiles to destroy chokepoints in this mountainous terrain, such as bridges and defiles. Destruction of a bridge connecting Armenia with Shusha, apparently by a LORA missile, was key to the fall of this city. The Armenian mountain positions, whilst superficially strong, were vulnerable to their lines of communication being interdicted; reliant upon a single supply road, Azeri unmanned aircraft could keep these routes under persistent observation, preventing both resupply and reinforcement. In addition, Armenian fixed positions were not sufficiently hardened to offer protection against modern artillery strikes. Greater survivability could have come from fighting from new positions, rather than continuing to occupy what they had held during the ceasefire. Knowing their exact location, the Azeris fire strikes overwhelmed each isolated Armenian positions leading to them one by one falling to close assault.

Faced with defeat through a combination of the incrementation attrition of their fighting vehicles and the isolation of their forward positions, the Armenians retaliated by engaging easily targeted Azeris infrastructure and population areas with their ballistic missiles. This indiscriminate use of firepower was a response to lacking a modern targeting capability and accurate weapons.

The high level of attrition of armoured vehicles – made more impactful due to the combat footage on social media – has led to questioning of the continued viability of the tank on the battlefield. However, the consensus amongst militaries is that armour has always been vulnerable to air attack, made more so in this case by poor tactics and old equipment. In addition, as in all decisive land warfare, this conflict was ultimately decided by the seizing of ground, and tanks are the least vulnerable weapon system capable of achieving this.

Instead of attributing the destruction of armoured vehicles to operating in the face of air superiority, a more nuanced analysis attributes this attrition to the effective combining of unmanned aerial systems with indirect fires. This has also been a lethal feature of the Russo-Ukraine conflict; it is but a modern version of the linking of artillery with airborne spotters. This has dominated in positional warfare in both World Wars, and its impact was perhaps at its most pervasive in the Korean War. What is making artillery more lethal is the pinpoint targeting of advanced sensors coupled with the greater lethality of anti-armour munitions.

So what are the lessons that should be drawn from this conflict? A key one is the need for a robust air defence architecture, and the inability to conduct any form of movement, whether armoured manoeuvre or resupply, without its protection. The assumed air defence solution is a sophisticated network that is equally capable across a range of air threats. Such systems will be procured as long as armies to see manned aircraft as the greatest threat. However, low, slow and small drones present a unique challenge through their ability to operate in the ground clutter that interferes with radars, which are often the primary sensor of integrated air defence systems. Quadcopters, with their ability to hover behind cover, are probably the most challenging target. Low flying drones will be highly survivable, even when an opponent has conventional air superiority at higher altitude through a combination of fighter aircraft and an integrated air defence system. Responding to the threat of small unmanned aircraft requires more localised protection; this probably needs to be organic to manoeuvre forces. This capability will need a range of sensors and probably a combination of kinetic and electronic means of engaging aerial targets. If drones are free to operate, then in combination with artillery, they will provide a distinct edge in the close battle and could dominate the deep battle.

In sum, the Nagorno-Karabakh War is a continuation of the trends of recent conflict, in particular the power of joint firepower when effectively targeted. It has highlighted the vulnerability of fixed location to precise firepower and the danger of massed manoeuvre without adequate force protection. It also showed the 'un-usability' of advanced airpower; neither side were willing to risk their expensive aircraft in this conflict. Artillery and drones provided the Azeris with an effective substitute; for the Armenians defeat was preferable to losing their air force.

Enduring Themes of a Century of Joint Fires

'To define future threat is, in a sense, an impossible task, yet it is one that must be done. The only sources of empirical evidence accessible are the past and the present; one cannot obtain understanding about the future from the future[210].'

Colin S Gray

Apart from an interlude in the Blitzkrieg years, centralised firepower employed in mass, has dominated the last century of conventional warfighting. In addition, it has been effective in operations against irregular forces. Even though individually it is the greatest killer, on the battlefield this dominance has been in concert with manoeuvre, with firepower enabling ground forces to decisively close with the enemy. After a century of almost continuous conflict, there remains considerable variety in the organisation and force employment of joint fires. Broadly there are now the Western and Russian approaches to the centralised employment of artillery and airpower. However, lavish their use of firepower, the Soviets/Russians usually combine fire with ground manoeuvre. In contrast the American way of war from the second half of the 20th century expected more and more from firepower on its own. The Soviets/Russians have also partly taken this approach in Afghanistan and Ukraine due to casualty concerns.

There are two forms of permanently decentralised firepower; the most common form seeks to boost infantry firepower, usually with organic company and battalion mortars, the second provides organic firepower at all levels of command. This force structure aims at facilitating manoeuvre by providing each commander with guaranteed suppressive fires; this approach was initially successfully employed by the Wehrmacht in World War Two. Despite its artillery being the creator of much of the centralised firepower system, this approach has gained traction in the American Army; since 2004, artillery battalions have been organic to the American Brigade Combat Team, leading to the marginalisation of the divisional artillery. The Americans are restoring their artillery chain of command and with it some ability to mass all their firepower[211].

The Western centralised firepower system has exploited cybernetics to improve its ability to seamlessly manoeuvre fire between formations and the close and deep battles. Ensuring firepower is centrally controlled to support the commander's design of battle. For many Western ground forces, this skill has atrophied due to the priority being operations other than peer conventional warfighting. Western armies are restoring their conventional warfighting capability with a belated priority being given to artillery, largely driven by the recognition that a peer opponent will contest airspace. Such an opponent will prevent airpower from sufficiently weakening them before close combat, and will then impede close air support from providing a substitute for an opponent's lack of organic firepower. Despite this geopolitical imperative, most Western armies remain heavily influenced by a generation of mainly peace support and counter-insurgency operations. Their doctrines retain concepts from this experience and the theories supporting an information revolution in military affairs.

The result is that most Western armies almost wholly lack corps and divisional artillery. They employ a targeting system primarily designed to avoid collateral damage rather than defeat an elusive opponent. They have marginalised their firepower staff and any artillery commanders that remain. Operationally they have often fail to identify the need for combining fire and manoeuvre in close combat to decisively defeat opponents as a precursor to achieving a stable post-conflict political settlement. In addition, firepowers role in gaining the allegiance of the people in an insurgency is not systemically exploited, nor reflected in doctrine.

The Russian system follows orthodox 20th century warfighting practice in terms of organisation and doctrine. They couple this with a significant lead in artillery and gun/mortar technology – in particular range and lethality – gained while the West was fixed by counter-insurgency operations. Their artillery is centralised under a separate staff for set piece operations, subsequently they decentralise to provide fire support to mobile operations. Airpower is part of the combined arms battle. The set-piece battle requires the scientific application of centralised firepower to prescribed norms; ideally, they avoid it as their aim is to exploit a fragmented battlefield. This requires units to be self-sufficient in firepower. When fighting is fluid, the Russians continue their historical practice of allocating mortars, gun-mortars, rocket launchers and howitzers down to company and battalion level. Their purpose is to gain the initiative through fixing an adversary with firepower, thus allowing decisive manoeuvre. The Indians use the centralised Russian approach, but combine it with the greater flexibility of a Western command and control system.

There has always been the belief that shells can substitute for hard fighting, but firepower was elevated in the Korean War to being the way to victory, seeking a return to the total dominance artillery briefly had in the middle years of World War One. Achieving a decision through close combat, that combined fire and manoeuvre, could result in significant friendly casualties. This was at odds with the political context of America's limited wars in the period 1945–89. Instead the manoeuvre force role switched to fixing the enemy for their destruction by firepower, then if necessary they occupied the territory. At its most extreme in the Vietnam War, this methodology simplistically equated war with the application of firepower; equating what could be hit and destroyed with what was important to securing war's political purpose. This force employment failed to recognise firepower's double-edged impact, particularly in war amongst the people. Despite its failure in Indo-China, the conflict developed revolutionary technology and techniques that would make the American firepower system significantly more lethal in conventional warfighting.

The removal of a peer threat with the end of the Cold War provided an opportunity for an even greater emphasis on avoiding decisive close combat. The reduced role of ground manoeuvre led to a lesser need for fire support; this elevated target effect above firepower's ability to integrate into the all arms team. This marginalising of close combat suits airpower and rockets over tube artillery and mortars. A further advantage of employing aircraft-delivered precision firepower from the relative safety of medium altitude, was that it was politically attractive. It promised both the minimising of friendly casualties by avoiding significant ground combat and a more sanitised form of conflict that limited collateral damage. At its best this American way of war proved irresistible, especially when the opposition failed to adopt measures to effectively counter firepower. It made airpower decisive before ground forces engaged in the Gulf War, and relegated them to being peacekeepers in the Kosovo War. The belief that technological advances was so significant that a revolution in military affairs had resulted let to a proliferation in information theory and doctrine. It is difficult to determine the practical effect of this literature on the actual fighting. Most practitioners have experienced the opposite to that promised, that technology often contributes to the fog and friction of war.

Though ultimately successful through time and overwhelming force, the Kosovo conflict signposted the effectiveness of the counters to standoff fires. This coincided with a re-emphasis on fire support, leading to the 2003 Iraq War being a pragmatic mix of the deep and close battles. Ground forces at the operational level sought to set up Iraqi forces as targets for airpower, resulting in fire support coordination measures that provided the greatest freedom for aerial firepower. Airborne forward air controllers ensured the efficient employment of aerial firepower; whether in kill boxes or immediately in front of advancing armour. This left mortars, artillery and aviation to provide fire support at danger close ranges. The limited American conventional operations in Afghanistan had similarly re-established the primacy of fire support over deep fires. Counter-insurgency operations in Iraq and Afghanistan likewise emphasised danger close fires.

So where does this leave the role of the individual joint fire systems? In the joint fires' pantheon, tube artillery remains the primary fire support weapon. Its position is secure because of its generalist ability; it can fire a wide range of munitions, at both intense and sustained rates and with sufficient range to cover a divisional-sized deployment of ground forces. With unguided munitions it is sufficiently consistent to provide covering fire up until the last couple of hundred metres of an assault, and these characteristics also enable it to provide close defensive fires. Almost all infantry and some armoured battalions supplement artillery support, which is usually controlled at brigade or divisional level, with their own organic mortars. These excel in providing the most rapid and closest fire support to troops in contact. Rockets and aircraft have largely replaced tube artillery in the deep battle, exploiting their superior range and ability to deliver a much heavier weight of fire. Unguided rockets can also deliver overwhelming preparatory firepower in the close battle; however, their extended danger area prevents them effectively providing covering or defensive fire. Guided rockets and aerial precision munitions have permanently changed the character of positional warfare with their ability to destroy almost any strongpoint or urban structure. Precision guidance, plus its large warhead makes, the Russian 240mm mortar the premier modern-day siege gun. The American guided MLRS provides Western armies with a similar capability.

The expectation following the Gulf War was that airpower would continue to increase in its ability to destroy fielded ground forces. This justified the reduction in the quantity of artillery and mortars in the West's order of battle. Actually, in successive conflicts since the Cold War, less damage has been inflicted per sortie. It is the effectiveness of active and passive counters that make airpower the most easily frustrated form of firepower in the land battle. The Russians, and armies that take their lead from them, have not undertaken a similar re-balancing from artillery to airpower; instead they continue with the 20th century norm of almost one artillery battalion to each infantry or armoured battalion. They do not accept that airpower can provide a substitute for mortars and artillery; nor do they accept that the users of firepower can be agnostic of its source, and need only to be concerned with target effect. This fallacy has been exposed throughout the joint fires' century, most obviously in Afghanistan's Operation Anaconda, when aircraft could not provide the guarantee and persistence that is required to support light infantry manoeuvre.

The overwhelming historical experience is that in conventional warfighting, few ground support sorties are actually genuine close air support, instead aircraft are employed beyond the close battle. Traditional close air support has a role against irregular opponents, in terrain that allows an opponent to get within danger close distance, and in extremis when ground forces are being overrun. The Israeli experience has been illustrative – facing conventional state enemies their air force emphasised the traditional gaining of air superiority, followed by air interdiction. Their current Hamas and Hezbollah enemies rarely provide suitable depth targets and have become adept in getting within the danger close distance, leading to the Israelis becoming expert at close air support. For the same reasons, since the Cold War, most Western air forces have also significantly increased their close air support capability; however, in peer conventional warfighting broader aircrew skills will be required, with most air support being forward of the close combat zone.

Attack helicopters are now the most lethal direct fire weapon system in the close battle; they have largely replaced fixed wing aircraft in providing the closest aerial fire support. Despite the attraction of resuscitating AirLand doctrine, conventional combat experience has shown the vulnerability of massed helicopters in the deep battle. In lesser numbers, infiltrating into an opponent's rear area, helicopters have proved a significant nuisance, and even a pair of modern helicopters have sufficient organic firepower to inflict considerable physical damage. In contrast, in a succession of conflicts, the more survivable fighter bombers have proved to be a superior means of engaging depth targets. Beyond counter battery missions Western long-range rockets have yet to make a significant contribution in the conventional deep battle; this was most recently demonstrated by their limited use in the Iraq War where airpower dominated. In contrast they are the primary Russian means of conducting their relatively shallow firepower deep battle. But again this is not combat proven against a peer opponent.

Most air forces operate as an independent component, with the most capable seeking to achieve air superiority and then flexing resources across the tactical, operational and strategic levels of war. This centralisation allows, when the situation dictates, ground forces to be supported by the totality of airpower. This also allows airpower to become the decisive element in the Western joint warfighting approach that seeks to synergise all the environmental components. Russia appeared in the 1990s to have structurally dallied with its airpower exercising a more independent role, before reasserting Frontal Aviation being a subordinate element of combined arms operations. By limiting airpower's role in the Great Patriotic War, the Soviets excelled at the tactical integration of aerial firepower with ground manoeuvre. In the Wars of Soviet Secession, the Russians have not shown anything close to the same expertise. While driven by broader policy considerations, on the Donbas the Russians have effortlessly fought without airpower. The Russian Air Force is effectively operating on its own in Syria; but this does not seem to be leading to a more independent approach; the 2018 force replacement of fighter-bombers by attack helicopters shows that Russian airpower essentially remains tied to ground operations.

There are also distinct Soviet/Russian and Western methods in the deep battle. World War One created the firepower deep battle, this was initially restricted to the range of the guns and primitive target acquisition systems. As aircraft became more capable, the deep battle has elongated. In World War Two the Western air forces ranged hundreds of miles beyond their front line, dominating the deep battle. On the Eastern Front, the firepower deep battle was shallow; instead the Soviets relied upon achieving a breakthrough into the German rear areas to conduct deep ground manoeuvre, though much of this exploitation force's combat power came from escorting Soviet ground attack and fighter-bomber aircraft. In the Soviet combined arms battle, aerial firepower has always had its greater role in mobile operations. Heavily armoured attack helicopters are now seen as the natural successor of the World War Two Il-2 Shturmovik. In conventional warfighting they operate in front and to the flanks of an axis of advance; in counter-insurgent operations they provide fire support and protect convoys.

Casualty concerns have led the Russians to embrace the firepower deep battle in their more recent conflicts. In the Russo-Ukraine conflict this relies upon rockets; the result is an empty battlefield that extends significantly beyond that imposed by direct fire weapons. In any future conflict Western airpower will attempt to impose its reach over much of the operational theatre. The Russians with their superiority in artillery and tactical sensors (particularly drones) will seek to dominate the area immediately behind the line of contact, at the point they intend to breakthrough.

The result of this difference of approach is that the Russians see artillery and air superiority as an activity bounded physically and temporally by the need to insert mobile forces into the deep battle. This makes the Russians more vulnerable to counter fire than Western militaries, with their need to achieve the local systematic suppression of the opposing firepower systems. In 2008, the Georgians demonstrated this by disrupting the Russian advance with their rocket systems. Conversely, Western military have been guilty of seeking absolute superiority, whether in air or artillery, at the expense of making the most efficient use of resources.

The proportion of casualties inflicted by artillery and mortars has steadily increased over the joint fires' century. In the first fifty years firepower was mainly a man-killer, as indirect area firepower was an inefficient means of killing tanks and troops in field fortifications. Fighter-bombers were most effective against soft skinned vehicles and trains, hence the dominance of air interdiction over close support. It took aerial rockets and cannon to provide an anti-tank capability, leading to the A-10 being built around its 30mm cannon. Munitions have significantly increased their lethality since the 1960s. For aircraft, cluster bombs provided the most lethal capability against massed armour. Guided missiles provide a high probability of destroying individual vehicles. Artillery have benefited from cluster, mine, and sensor-fuzed as well as improved high explosive munitions. Other factors in increasing artillery lethality include: the switch to larger calibres while retaining high rates of fire, improved ability to mass batteries, and superior first round accuracy.

The Russians have demonstrated in the Ukraine that massed artillery, with the correct cocktail of munitions, can devastate lightly armoured mechanised forces, making problematic the battlefield survivability of all light and medium armoured vehicles. The mounting of infantry in lightly armoured vehicles was to prevent artillery fire from separating tanks from their support; the vulnerability of armoured personnel carriers to artillery has now dislocated the mounted armoured combined arms team, leading to most attacks on the Donbas being on foot. Sensor fuzed munitions are now posing a similar survivability challenge to main battle tanks, these are being countered by defensive aid suites and enhanced roof armour.

A succession of Ukrainian 'sieges' has again demonstrated the inability of static defences to withstand firepower. Combining mobility and improvised protection, including exploiting rubble created through the bombardment of urban areas, has proved to be a tactically superior approach to holding ground. This avoids providing firepower with an obvious target that will be destroyed regardless of how well protected. A comparison can be drawn with World War One, when defenders moved into the shell-holes in no-mans-land rather than occupying known positions. Urban terrain provides the greatest opportunity for this approach, as demonstrated by the Chechens who ceased relying upon strongpoints due to Russian firepower, and instead adopted mobile teams operating between temporary firing points. Conventional light infantry and irregular warfare tactics are merging in order to dislocate firepower. Turkish operations in Syria and Azebaijan forces in the 2020 Nagomo-Karabakh War have displayed the power of firepower linked to effective airborne sensors; in these conflicts unmanned aircraft provided this capability, in previous wars it was light aircraft with air or artillery terminal controllers.

The Soviets and Russians have applied an enemy-centric approach to counter-insurgency, and have largely relied upon their accompanying artillery to provide fire superiority. This is in direct contrast to Western counter-insurgency practice, where decisive firepower comes from the air. Western artillery and mortars have usually been located in a latticework of fire support bases. Defending these bases absorbs considerable resources, and despite this, they have historically proved to be vulnerable. Previously they were prone to being overrun, this is less likely given the effectiveness of modern firepower, but this can result in airpower being fixed in providing this support. Now they are vulnerable to be isolated by encircling IEDs and fixed by harassing rockets and mortars. The Russians have occupied firebases in their campaigns, but they are not fixed to operating within their artillery range, because of their accompanying artillery. The reduction of organic firepower in Western armies has been accelerated by their experience of counter-insurgency when most of the attrition has been accomplished by special operations forces pursuing a decapitation strategy. Russian counter-insurgency remains wedded to the overwhelming requirement to inflict attrition, resulting in firepower unsupported by manoeuvre, similar to the Americans in Vietnam, where it significantly contributed to their defeat.

As well as restoring its peer warfighting capability the West's most immediate requirement is making effective the use of air superiority when it is unwilling to deploy ground forces. Operations against the so called Islamic State have shown that embedding an air/land integration system will significantly increase airpower's lethality when operating with allied ground forces. Given the number of times that Western airpower has faced this challenge, establishing such a capability is probably a necessity in the NATO force structure, as is restoring the 'slow' airborne forward air controller capability.

Below is a summary of the balance between individual capabilities in the firepower system-of-systems:

Illustrative Balance between the Joint Fires Systems by Conflict

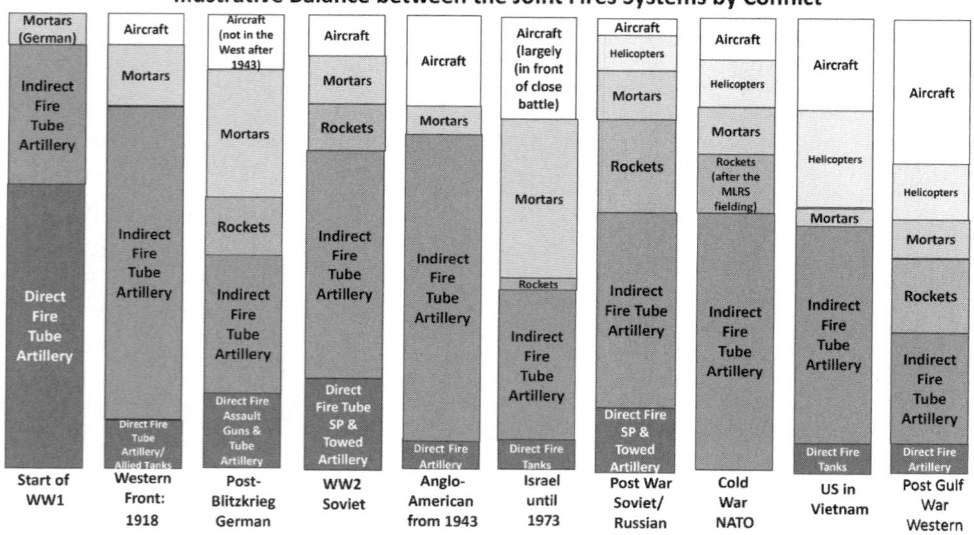

Chapter 5: Firepower's Grammar and Challenges

'the whimsicality you find amongst all of the gunners in Europe, which leads them to raise pointless difficulties[1]*.'*

Frederick the Great

Firepower practitioners stand apart from land warfare's mainstream. Their late emergence forced them to make an accommodation with pre-existing military structures and cultures. Their separation from the traditional ground warfare arms is maintained by through bespoke professional technical training. The disconnect between commanders and their 'scientific' artillerymen was particularly noticeable in the opponents of Napoleon, history's greatest gunner, giving the French a distinct edge[2]. Two of his greatest opponents: Archduke Charles and the Duke of Wellington maintained fractious relationships with their artillerymen[3]. The Iron Duke extended his distrust of artillerymen to include their technical innovations – Congreve rockets, shrapnel shells and carronade guns. His view was that the midst of the Napoleonic Wars was not a: *'proper time period to alter the equipment of the army or try experimentation*[4]*'*.

The requirement for specialist training is at its lowest with infantry-operated mortars, and at its greatest with military flying. Adding to the friction is the specialists' tendency to seek out differences. Leading to some artillerymen seeing their calling as a 'black art', whose 'secrets' needed to be preserved. At times, approaching this with the same energy as the original guild of multinational, largely itinerant, and nepotistic master gunners who plied their trade among the rulers of medieval and renaissance Europe. Bruchmüller, the World War One German artillery maestro, may have been the last artilleryman of this breed[5]. He personified the advanced artillery tactics of the later stages of that war. In comparison, his contemporaries in opposing armies were more systematic in their organisation, method and means; this involved working through multi-disciplinary teams, and crucially they focussed on establishing easily-imitated processes. This is the point when the talented individual gives way to the system[6].

The slow assimilation of artillerymen into the military mainstream was as much a social and cultural phenomenon as a professional one. A key event in this process was the combining the training of artillery officers, together with the military engineers with whom they were usually grouped, with their 'social superiors' from the cavalry and infantry. Enabling this process of assimilation was the demise in European armies of separate ordinance boards, whose primary responsibility was acquisition of cannon. A further stimulus was provided by modern war's proliferation of new technical corps. This included the creation of air forces, which soon evolved from being a branch within one of the existing army technical corps, to being their own corps, and finally in most militaries to becoming independent services. Non-European armies have generally had less historic baggage to overcome in their integration of the technical arms[7].

For some armies, operating artillery has meant a separate career structure, training and education establishments; it can also lead to a discrete staff organisation, distinct from the General Staff, whose primary function was the control of the traditional manoeuvre arms. The Soviet and now the Russian forces have preserved the greatest separation between arms in their education and training, despite recognising that this is to the detriment of all arms cooperation[8]. The trend in Western militaries is for a reduction in the independence of the artillery staff, this is paralleling the reduction in of the quantity ordnance. This has led in some armies to the ceding of firepower leadership to air forces, resulting in aerial techniques and procedures gaining traction in the land warfare.

While gunners have joined the professional mainstream, they still preserve a distinguishing grammar, articulated through unique vocabulary. This can be the necessary expression of their distinct approach, which is rarely understood by non-practitioners, hence Frederick the Great's accusation of 'whimsicality'. Despite their short history, the airman's vocabulary is already extensive; this partly articulates the need to operate in a new environment, but much of it can fairly be described as a means of reinforcing their separation from non-aviators. Hopefully avoiding this distraction, Chapter 5 will cover the vocabulary and grammar necessary to understand joint firepower.

Target Effect: Destruction, Neutralisation and Suppression

'the main advantage derived from artillery fire was its power of neutralising the hostile rifle, machine gun and artillery fire, as opposed to the destruction of trenches and obstacles[9].'

Major Brooke in 1917 (Later Field Marshal Alanbrooke)

Area firepower aims to suppress or neutralise a zone, the destruction of individual targets is effectively a bonus. The effect sought is psychological as *'the ultimate limiting factor for the maintenance and endurance of organised and competent forces on the battlefield is man[10]'*. Suppression is the preventing of a target fulfilling its mission, and most armies define it as lasting as long as the fire is delivered. Neutralisation achieves the same effect as suppression, but most militaries interpret this as extending beyond the fire being applied. These terms are rarely precisely used. Destruction is the physical rendering of a target combat ineffective. The definition of what level of physical damage is required to achieve destruction varies between armies, with the Russians favouring the most overkill. Suppression, neutralisation and destruction are the three effects identified in NATO doctrine[11]. Additional effects in common usage include harassment and damage to physical terrain features.

World War One's heavy artillery soon demonstrated its ability to rapidly destroy any defence works that made themselves obvious targets. Given sufficient munitions, this was regardless of the quantity of protecting steel and concrete. The ineffectiveness of the Belgian fortifications at Liege, Antwerp and Namur was soon repeated on the War's other fronts[12]. This led the French to abandon their observable permanent fortresses at Verdun in 1915 to occupy improvised field fortifications capable of exploiting dispersion, concealment and cover. The same logic applied to coastal engagments, it was the Turkish mobile batteries that posed the greatest threat to the Anglo-French fleet in the Gallipoli Campaign. This also largely applied in World War Two, when aircraft had replaced heavy artillery as principal means of destroying fortified targets. The ability to destroy identified targets has been significantly reinforced by precision guidance, this both allows the optimum placement of high explosives and significantly reduces the quantity of munitions required to hit the target.

With unguided munitions, achieving suppression is significantly less resource intensive than destruction; that destruction takes ten times the quantity of shells as suppression has been established by operational experience. The barrage at the Battle of Messines in 1917 aimed at achieving destruction; it required 383,000 rounds per mile of front. A year later at Amiens the lesser effect of suppression was achieved with 43,000 rounds per mile of front[13]. With this quantity of shells, the effect on the target probably continued for some time after the bombardment lifted. So achieving an effect in excess of the NATO neutralisation definition. Or an effect midway between destruction and neutralisation. This has been termed extended neutralisation, it is the result of high-intensity fire that continues to have a psychological effect for hours after the fire has lifted[14].

Extended neutralisation is usually linked with larger munitions with their greater blast effect; in World War Two Anglo-Americans associated this effect with air-delivered firepower. The Wehrmacht exploited this phenomenon in their reliance on intense bombing to stun encircling Soviets, so enabling German troops to escape. The Soviets and Russians have achieved this effect with massed artillery in a manner that other armies would consider to be inefficient overkill[15]. Soviet and Russian ammunition norms are based on a 90% probability of achieving either destruction or neutralisation[16]. As destruction is defined as destroying at least 50% of a target's combat power, a very significant weight of fire is required. Even when seeking neutralisation, they employ significantly more firepower than Western armies[17]. The Soviets also believed that the effects of fire drops off rapidly after five minutes. Therefore, they specify that between a third to a half of the ammunition allocated to the mission must be fired in the first 3–5 minutes.

A different approach to NATO definitions is taken by General Bailey in his breaking out of the four individual effects accruing from firepower. First, the neutralising effect of preventing or impeding movement, observation, and equipment use. Secondly the materiel effect, which is the destruction of an opponent's equipment. Thirdly the lethal effect, which is the inflicting of personnel casualties. Finally, the morale effect that results in the shock and demoralisation that occurs among soldiers under fire[18]. It is the last that is the most difficult to quantify in terms of inputs and outcomes. The key variable, individual human reaction, is difficult to quantify:

> *'Bursting [high explosive] shells do seem to have a curious effect on people. Some are sort of mentally paralysed, and some physically so. I've seen a man alive and unhurt, but absolutely incapable of lifting a hand or speaking. Its curious*[19]*.'*

Ultimately it is unproductive to attempt any separation of firepower's individual effects. As Clausewitz observed: '*The effects of physical and psychological factors form an organic whole which, unlike a metal alloy, is inseparable by chemical processes*[20]. While precisely determining the actual effect of fire on an enemy's morale is highly problematic, operational experience and research, mainly from World War Two, provides norms. Despite this, there remains considerable debate on the relative effectiveness of different forms of firepower. Specifically, is it the individual weight or the quantity of munitions that counts? In other words, does a single 100-pound shell have the same impact upon the recipient as four 25-pound shells?

There is no universally accepted methodology for determining equivalence between the effectiveness of various calibre of munitions. World War Two British operational analysis determined that the square root of the weight of the explosive filling was a good approximation of relative effect when facing men crouching in slit trenches[21]. This methodology works on the assumption that the effectiveness of fragmentation is largely proportionate to the detonation velocity that a shell imparts, this being a product of its explosive content. Of course, this methodology provides a rough approximation, and does not consider many of the advances of munition technology. These include: improved explosives, superior shell case material and preformed fragmentation. Nor does it make any allowance for the impact of ground, such as the boggy ground during the Falkland Island campaign, which successfully absorbed much of the fragmentation[22].

The conclusion in World War Two was that it was the number of bangs and not the size of bangs that counted; this has not subsequently been seriously challenged[23]. But modern armies are not as energetic in exploiting this as were the World War Two British, who superimposed 'pepper pot' groups, consisting of machine guns, mortars, anti-aircraft guns and even tanks, to supplement conventional artillery fire[24]. The key effect of this increased number of bangs was to prevent commanders from getting around their men; recognising that preventing personal leadership was the key factor in undermining a unit's will to fight.

This British view is supported by the Soviet analysis; this is consolidated into their weight of fire tables. These tables identify the quantity of shells needed to suppress a given target. An infantry target in the open required sixteen 85mm shells, fourteen for both the 100mm and 122mm shells and eight for 152mm shells. It is the relationship between the different calibres of shells rather than the actual quantity that is important. The Soviet firing tables support the contention that smaller shells are, proportionate to their weight, more effective than larger ones.

Experience shows that achieving an effect on hardened targets required an initial heavy weight of large calibre munitions, followed by a reduced amount of fire to maintain suppression. During the World War Two Battle of the Rhineland, rocket and medium guns initially engaged concrete-protected targets, before handing over to field guns[25]. At the same time the Red Army combined the shock-effect of BM-31-12 300mm rocket with the steady pounding of their field artillery[26]; neutralisation could not always be achieved. British research in 1943 concluded that the concrete-protected casement guns '*could only be neutralised through destruction*[27]'. Airpower could provide the initial heavy weight of fire before handing over to artillery to extend the neutralising effect. In the Canadian attack of 8 August 1944 in Normandy the heavy bombers dropped 3,458 tons over thirty minutes, before handing over to 144 5.5-inch guns (100lb shells) and 216 25pdr gun/howitzers. The guns could sustain a rate of fire which delivered 11 tons of high explosive per minute. The artillery extended the neutralisation achieved by the air attack, allowing the eight attacking armoured columns to penetrate the enemy position and begin the 'dog-fight' before the defenders could effectively respond. The assault was also aided by the obscuration caused by such a weight of fire[28]. Unfortunately for the Canadians, there was an undetected antitank screen that was outside the area of the initial bombardment. This was beyond the range of the majority of the supporting artillery, nor could it be systematically neutralised by the supporting fighter-bombers, so the initially successful attack was halted. This illustrates that against combat-hardened troops firepower's neutralising effect only affects those directly on the receiving end, rather than the whole defensive system.

Achieving an effect upon a target is not solely a product of the munition type; the delivery means also has an impact. The morale impact of visible airpower was evident from the first (though it must also be remembered that aerial munitions have also always been, proportionate to their weight, more lethal). This was illustrated by the historian of the Bavarian List Regiment (Corporal Hitler's unit) who recorded that:

> *'Twenty-five, thirty or more aircraft suddenly appear [and] each drop forty bombs. We do not worry anymore about infantry fire [and] we have become used to artillery, but these aircraft drive the troops to distraction. We literally climb up the trees, in order to avoid the fearsome low trajectory projectiles from exploding bombs'*[29].

Historian Phillip Maligner's view was that Trenchard, the first commander of the British air force, believed that *'although its material effects were great, airpower's psychological effects were far greater*[30]'. This view was widespread, leading to the Stuka dive-bomber being fitted with the *Jericho-Trompete* (Jericho trumpet) wailing sirens designed to further enhance their impact on morale.

How battle-hardened troops are to receiving an air attack, rather than the weight of firepower delivered, appears to be the key variable in determining airpower's psychological impact. Even a small quantity of munitions coupled with considerable strafing was sufficient to rout French troops at the Battle of Sedan in 1940[31]. As will be discussed later, for those on the receiving end, strafing is, by a margin, believed to be the most effective air-to-ground weapon. The greater psychological effect of airpower may be due to low level aircraft presenting an obvious visible threat, in contrast to the anonymity of artillery and mortars. As air attack is an unequal struggle, it justifies ground forces taking a safer, life-preserving, course of action. This was the rationale used by even a combat-hardened Panzer commander to excuse his division's failed counterattack in Normandy 1944:

> *'they [fighter aircraft] came in hundreds, firing their rockets at the concentrated tanks and vehicles. We could do nothing against them and we could make no further progress*[32].'

In contrast, at the Battle of Monte Cassino, very heavy area bombing of the defenders seems to have had a limited impact. Not least because pauses in the application of fire allowed German commanders to visit their soldiers:

> *'on entering a position immediately after a bombardment one would find that, aside from a few exceptions, the guns, machine guns and observation instruments were intact, and that even the*

effect on the men's morale, which initially had reached critical proportions, wore off after the initial experience … Apparently an air attack accomplishes its objective only to some extent if its effect on morale is immediately exploited by a ground attack[33].'

The British in World War Two considered it essential for assaulting troops to follow up an air bombardment by strategic bombers within an hour of the final bomb. With the intervening time being filled by artillery fire. In contrast, two minutes was the specified time between artillery fire lifting and the troops being on the objective. This could be extended, for an unspecified time, by really heavy fire[34].

Conditioned by the restrictions of peacetime safety, modern armies rarely effectively practice assaulting an objective before defenders can recover from a bombardment. In peacetime, firepower from different sources is seldom synchronised to elongate the neutralisation achieved by an initial heavy weight of fire. Some armies rationalise that simulation can replace, rather than supplement, live fire training. This is not the view of the best trained armies. Though too many tend; to use much of their live fire training allocation on special to arms exercises, rather than training with manoeuvre forces. As a result, most soldiers are not exposed to danger close firepower in their peacetime training, making them more vulnerable to its effects on operations. While their officers lack practical experience in the integration challenge.

Point and Area Fires

'There was a concentrated amount of fire during the course of a complex battle [Shejaiya in northern Gaza,]. We responded with massive fire in order to paralyse the sources of fire firing on us … [precise munitions cannot provide the] mass of fire that at times is necessary[35]'.

Unattributed Israeli artillery officer

Directing firepower precisely against identified enemy locations is obviously the most effective approach. Armies have striven for this, but have had to make compromises to war's nature and character. In World War One and World War Two, the inability to identify all sources of enemy resistance led to the employment of moving barrages, as these would cover all of the ground where the enemy might be concealed. Against this, barrages are expensive in shells, complex to deliver and inflexible, and crucially they dissipate firepower rather than concentrating it upon known enemy positions. Consequently, barrages were usually combined with concentrations of fire onto identified enemy locations. The split of firepower between barrages and concentrations directly reflected the level of certainty over the enemy's dispositions[36]. As target acquisition capability improved, barrages have been abandoned. The American artillery almost wholly abandoned them in the European Theatre in World War Two, but not in the Pacific where, largely due to the terrain, there was less certainty about the opposition's defensive positions. The same rationale led to their extensive employment by the Soviets in their Afghanistan War.

The tension between the merits of employing artillery in barrages or concentrations has its modern equivalent in the point target versus area target debate. When there is certainty of an enemy's location, precision munitions can be individually employed. When there is only a general suspected location, then multiple munitions need to be employed to cover the area of the target. The key advantage of area fires over point engagement is its greater tolerance of error in determining the target's location. As only a general target location is required, engaging an area usually remains the most effective way of employing firepower in the conventional close battle. Of course, multiple terminally-guided precision munitions can also be directed at individual points to provide an area coverage over a location suspected of containing the enemy. With long range fire precision guidance is necessary to offset the dispersion caused by range and so effectively engage an area target with a battery or battalion.

It is easy to achieve individual target accuracy with fixed infrastructure, whose exact location can be determined. It is this that has made precision weapons employed by Western airpower an order of magnitude more effective against air interdiction targets. Against land forces stationary in the open aircraft have been equally effective. Acquiring and engaging with individual precision weapons mobile targets, that exploit ground clutter, is challenging. In these circumstances, warheads that can identify their own target within a designated area are the most effective. The most common type in land warfare are sensor fuzed munitions – these can be deployed by bomb, rocket or shell. They are fired at a target area, where they individually acquire their own target and defeat them with an anti-armour warhead. These expensive and relatively easily-countered munitions currently require a high contrast target – such as a tank – to be effective. The target accuracy challenge of area and point engagement can be understood as follows:

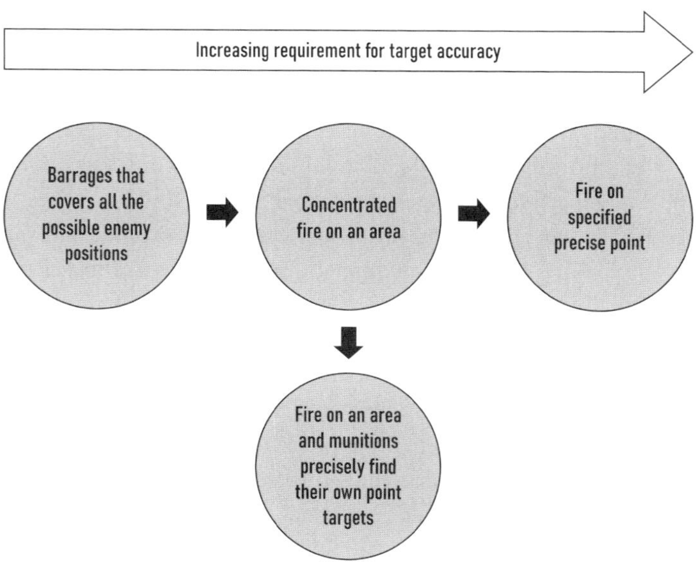

Precisely matching firepower to targets will of course achieve the desired effect at a fraction of the firepower previously considered necessary. It is seen by the proponents of a revolution in military affairs as the primary means of exploiting the information revolution in combat. This leads to view that: *'When mass is needed for offensive or defensive purposes, it needs to take place at*

the point of impact[37]'. Colonel Phillip S. Meilinger, one of airpower's leading theorists, takes this approach to its logical – if impractical – conclusion:

> *'One could argue that all targets are precision targets – even individual tanks, artillery pieces, or infantrymen. There is no logical reason why bullets or bombs should be wasted on empty air or dirt. Ideally, every shot fired should find its mark*[38]*.'*

Engaging a point target in land warfare needs to address three elements. First, acquiring the target with sufficient accuracy to determine its precise location. While possible, this runs counter to land warfare's enduring nature. In the friction and fog of war, except in the most barren terrain, it is close to impossible to identify and accurately locate every individual battlefield target. If land warfare was uncontested – which by our Clausewitzian definition means that it isn't actually war – technically this should be possible. In reality, the transparent battlefield remains unachievable as the advantage lies with the side trying to spoil, spoof and confuse[39]. Secondly, firepower needs to be correctly apportioned to achieve the desired effect; doing this in a timely manner is the main challenge. Processing power is less of an issue than communication bandwidth, given the frequencies that are required to overcome ground clutter. The third requirement is the accurate delivery of the munition. This is close to guaranteed on a peacetime range, but not on a cluttered battlefield with an opponent trying to counter the munition's guidance. Technology may not provide the answer: Artificial Intelligence's (AI) ability to overcome these constraints will be limited by most militaries seeking to retain at least an element of human oversight; furthermore, when it comes to target identification, currently AI is significantly easier to fool than the human brain[40].

Land component joint fires practitioners can draw upon the experience of direct fire practice, this recognises the need for both area and point engagement. A sniper (point engagement) and a machine gun (area engagement) are equally valid responses to different targets and the need for different effects. Snipers accurately engage point targets, while machine guns accurately engage area targets. Snipers are: logistically more efficient, less prone to collateral damage, and can usually meet more restrictive interpretations of the laws of armed conflict. But no one is suggesting that snipers can replace machine guns. Both have a recognised place on the battlefield. This is because there is a clear understanding that in a firefight, not all targets will be immediately identified. Nor would it be tactically wise, given the time-sensitive character of this combat, to wait until a sniper can individually engage every target. Instead, the machine gun seeks to achieve suppression of likely firing points through a heavy weight of fire, this also delivers a much quicker rate of killing than individual aimed shots.

Armies have made only limited use of precision artillery and mortar munitions. Conflict amongst the people in Iraq and Afghanistan should have suited these weapons and led to greater use of precision indirect fire. However, as the American Army's buyer of equipment identified in 2010: *'We were surprised to find that there wasn't more precision being fired*[41]*.'* As of September 2015, the Americans had only fired nearly 770 Excalibur 155mm shells in combat. Partly due to the reduced target effect of this round, due to space for explosive being sacrificed to achieve precision. Leading to ground forces choosing to employ either unguided munitions or aerial munitions because they better achieve the desired target effect. More have been fired against the Islamic State, but this was not in support of Western ground forces. The main factor against employing precision artillery munitions was that in the time competitive business of ground combat there is rarely sufficient time to determine a precision grid reference. In comparison, the Western air forces have almost wholly switched to terminally-guided munitions. Point-target engagement capability suits air interdiction, and in the absence of a precision grid reference, they can also provide precision close air support with laser designation.

The recent Israelis experience of close combat against determined opposition has led to them continuing to see unguided area firepower as essential. They see terminally-guided precision weapons as a supplement and not a replacement for area target land firepower, so guided rockets supplement their 155mm cannon. The Israelis use precision munitions to make firepower significantly more effective, particularly against bunkers, and more *usable* in the urban environment. But they also understand that precision munitions cannot provide timely, massed, coverage over an area target. So against a determined opponent, in the time-competitive business of close combat, unguided artillery fire remains essential. In part this was a political statement as the Israelis are determined that Hamas and Hezbollah do not dictate the character of conflict:

> *'asymmetric warfare cuts in two directions, and that its militia enemies should not be able to dictate the style of combat or the rules of engagement*[42]*.'*

The Russians do not see precision guidance as reducing the requirement for area firepower. They see precision weapons' greater accuracy as a means of achieving overwhelming firepower, rather than as a means of being more discriminating in their use of firepower. Hence the Russian Chief of the General Staff's view that: *'the application of high-precision weaponry is taking on a mass character*[43]'. Their procurement has emphasised sensor-fuzed munitions as they require the target accuracy of an area engagement and deliver considerable lethality against armoured targets. Their expense is justified to destroy high value fighting platforms. The Russian Air Force's modest fielding of laser-guided and coordinate-seeking (using their equivalent of GPS) munitions corresponds to their limited interest in engaging fixed-point targets in air interdiction. Rather than relying upon airpower the Russians main point-target capability in ground combat is the 2S9 mortar. This 240mm weapon employs laser-guided munitions, and has mainly engaged strongpoints in urban warfare; previously such targets required massed direct fire.

The cost of precision munitions and their manufacture lead-time will always limit the stockpile; making the retention of unguided weapons an economic inevitability[44]. The expense of precision munitions largely prevents their employment during training; as even the most advanced simulation does not fully compensate for live fire; this challenges their effective integration into the combined arms battle. In contrast, peacetime live fire training allows troops and their commanders to gain confidence in employing unguided weapons.

The major Western armies have invested in munitions whose precision guidance allows them to home onto a grid reference to within a metre of accuracy. These characteristics mean that these munitions should have been widely and successfully used on operations against the insurgencies in Iraq and Afghanistan. As the major factor limiting these weapons is their inability to provide an immediate response with a heavy weight of fire, then they are likely to be even less usable in conventional conflict. If a comparison can be drawn to another era of warfighting, it is the unsuitability of immature rifled artillery to the American Civil War's character of conflict:

> *'these guns have enviably high accuracy, but lamentably low killing power – precisely the opposite qualities to those most needed to stop a massed attack*[45]'.

The right type of precision munitions for mobile peer-on-peer conventional warfighting are sensor-fuzed munitions. These are able to: engage multiple targets, with a high level of lethality and achieve rapid target engagement by employing an area target location. Their ability to engage battalion and company sized area targets makes them a key anti-armour weapon, hence they are particularly favoured by the Russians. For positional warfare it is large calibre rocket, mortar or aerial bombs able to destroy strong points.

Firepower in the Attritional and Manoeuvreist Approaches to Warfare

> *'Fire without movement is indecisive. Exposed movement without fire is disastrous. There must be effective fire combined with skilful movement*[46].'
>
> The Infantry Journal Infantry in Battle, 1939

Richard Simpkin referred to manoeuvreist and attritional (also known as synchronised or positional[47]) warfare as *'the two main theories of war*[48]'. This can be seen as an enduring division in warfare, that was first articulated in Homer's epic poem the Iliad, with the split between the contrasting qualities represented by Achilles and Odysseus. Respectively they personify *bie* (strength) and *metis* (cunning)[49]. Unimaginatively interpreted this polarity leads to a simplistic binary doctrinal division; used intelligently it aids understanding, as manoeuvreist and attritional represent the ends of a continuum. As pure examples of either style of warfare cannot exist, the key is finding the point along the continuum that suits a given character of conflict. This point is not fixed, and can shift within conflict as it moves to a different phase[50]. It can also vary with the level of war, with different approaches being taken at the tactical, operational and strategic levels. The Wehrmacht may have been tactically manoeuvreist on the Eastern Front, but from 1943 they saw their way to strategic victory as being through attritional defeat of the Red Army.

Over the joint fires' century, the balance between these two approaches has shifted as new force employment overcame the current dominant form of warfare. The British military theorist and historian General Fuller described this dialectic as the 'Constant Tactical Factor'; this describes the process by which improvements in warfare are checked by counters[51]. This leads to swings in advantage between offensive or the defensive, and the balance between firepower and manoeuvre. The difference between this and the Marxist dialectic is that an external challenge, rather than internal contradictions within the system, is usually the engine of change. As a result, militaries can have ineffective ways of war that remain unchallenged until conflict.

The effectiveness of firepower in the attritional approach can be easily measured; this is not just in terms of enemy force elements destroyed. At the tactical level, if it is competently applied, there is invariably a positive correlation between the quantity of firepower employed and the resultant reduction in friendly casualties when seizing an objective[52]. As a result, the attritional school of war is usually considered to be firepower's natural home. Actually, firepower is vital to both approaches to warfare. As SLA Marshall observed, it is *the* essential enabler of manoeuvre:

> *'Fire is the key to mobility. To fire is to move. Weapons when correctly used will invariably bring decision. But without superior firepower, mass and velocity can never win a war*[53].'

Firepower's role in manoeuvre warfare is clear: it is to enable and sustain manoeuvre; attrition, while often advantageous, is a secondary to achieving this. This is because manoeuvre theory's essence is defeating the enemy's will to fight rather than their physical ability to fight. In the attritional school, objectives are concentrations of enemy combat power or geographical features; these need to be defeated or seized. In the manoeuvreist approach objectives are effects that lead to an enemy's defeat; ideally this does not require significant attrition[54]. A reasonable test of the extent to which an army actually employs the manoeuvreist approach is whether in its tactical training it seeks to by-pass enemy locations. A commander following an attritional approach will almost automatically assault these, to create further attrition and make the battlefield 'tidier', even if these opponents are no longer militarily relevant. In the manoeuvreist approach, the defeat of by-passed forces is usually achieved when they surrender, as further resistance is untenable through being isolated from any support.

Clausewitz identified that defence is the stronger form of warfare, but it achieves the lesser aim, while the attack is the weaker form of warfare, but it has a positive aim[55]. This is a useful concept when analysing the employment of firepower within these two theories of war. Attrition theory employs firepower with the lesser aim of the incremental defeat of an enemy through systematic destruction; it favours a centralised command system to systematically match firepower to targets. This cautious approach can enable an army to remain 'balanced', so allowing it to counter an opponent's tactical adjustments. General Montgomery recognised that in the British Army he had a force that could not compete with the Germans in manoeuvre warfare; therefore, he was determined to prosecute his campaigns and battles (Operation Market Garden aside) in a manner which prevented his more agile opponents from exploiting any mis-step. He sought through attrition to fix (unbalance) and defeat his opponents. Montgomery stated: '*my military doctrine was based on unbalancing the enemy while keeping well-balanced myself*'[56]. This was an effective means of war, suited to the geopolitical circumstances and the character (limitations) of the British Army. The impact of this form of force employment was to make the British Army very deliberate and unable to exploit fleeting opportunities. The attritional approach is the stronger form of war because it is both easier to execute and it incurs less risk. Edward Luttwak identified the dangers of taking this approach too far:

'In the extreme case of pure attrition, there are only techniques and tactics, and there is no action at the operational level. All that remains are routinised techniques of reconnaissance, movement, re-supply etc. to bring firepower-producing forces within range of the most conveniently targetable aggregations of enemy forces and supporting structures[57].'

In contrast, manoeuvre warfare is the weaker form of employing firepower; it requires a high level of skill to execute and when this is not expertly done it creates vulnerabilities. It requires commanders to elevate their thinking from mere destruction, instead seeing how firepower best serves defeating an opponent's will to fight[58]. This can be seen in the actions of Montgomery's most famous opponent; as a small unit commander fighting the Romanians in World War One, Erwin Rommel choose to rely upon a lesser form of firepower at the decisive point (mortars), as these did not have the danger close distance of heavy artillery, nor did they produce craters that would slow down the assault:

'Our artillery began to plaster Mount Cosna … [with] 210mm and 305mm shells … as prearranged, the breakthrough place … was free of artillery fire. Here our mortars did excellent preparatory work[59]'.

Instead of merely massing firepower to inflict attrition, Rommel sought to defeat the Romanian will to fight by enabling his assaulting force to rapidly penetrate their defences. On a larger scale, in the same war, Colonel Georg Bruchmüller also partially embraced a manoeuvreist approach. He identified that the role of artillery was to enable decisive close combat: *'We desire only to break the morale of the enemy, pin him to his position, and then overcome him with an overwhelming assault[60].'*

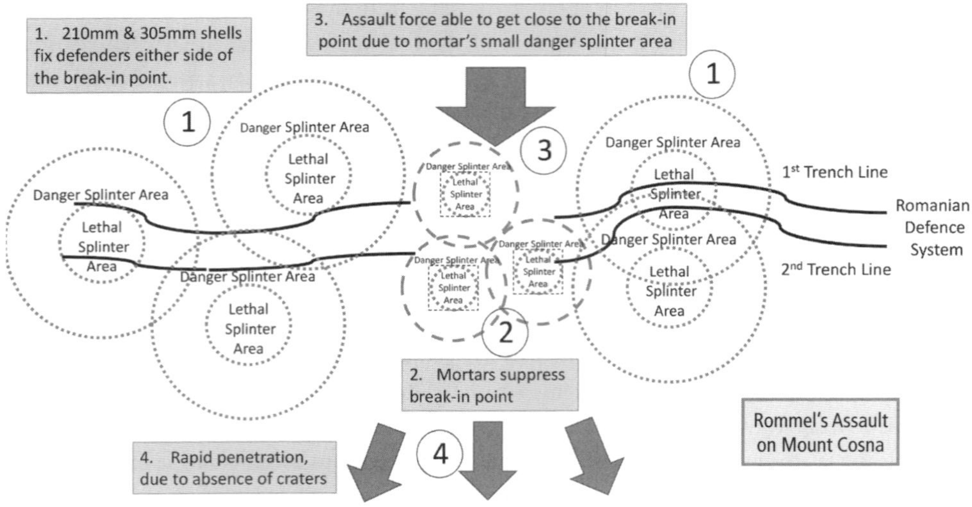

As well as requiring a high level of skill, employing firepower in a manoeuvreist way necessitates a level of decentralisation in decision-making that some armies find uncomfortable.

The two theories of war can lead to differences in determining the importance of a target. A manoeuvreist might consider an individual machine gun as a worthwhile target if it is holding up an advance, and so preventing the execution of the mission; the attritionalist would discount this, as a single machine gun has negligible combat value. This latter view stems from the belief that the defeat or destruction of a target has a value largely independent from the current tactical situation. This leads to measuring firepower's effectiveness by its reduction of an opponent's military capability through the destruction of high value targets. A manoeuvreist might argue that destroying things is at best a measure of performance not effectiveness, and in some circumstances, it may not even be that. It is context that provides the determinant of actual military value. An extreme example of this was the isolated World War Two Japanese island garrisons by-passed by American maritime forces. Destroying these would be a negative measure of performance, as it would consume American combat power, and their futile, but heroic, resistance could have reinforced the Japanese warfighting ethos.

As these two theories of war are usually seen as opposite 'magnetic poles', one is often equated as being a rejection of the other. Most military doctrine describes the manoeuvreist approach in this way, rather than identifying its own advantages. Armies have described themselves as manoeuvreist, effectively identifying one theory of war as their binding principle, so discarding other approaches. This Manichaean approach hinders Western militaries' understanding of the merits of the two theories. An attritional approach may suit a conflict's character when technology offers the West almost risk-free standoff precision warfighting against lesser foes. It also provides a low risk means of achieving the political objective of a conflict that does not require the total defeat of the opponent's armed forces. Furthermore, as already identified, practically delivering manoeuvre warfare is challenging, this may be beyond the capability of an individual army or a hastily formed coalition.

Delivering effective manoeuvre warfare was considerably easier in the age of horse and foot. This was partly due to the ease of command and control; the main factor was artillery being a direct fire weapon system. This made the coordinating of its firepower with infantry and cavalry movement relatively easy.

World War One's single greatest tactical challenge was integrating indirect fire with manoeuvre. This was essential to overcoming field fortifications held by the power of machine guns and the ability to cue artillery defensive fires. Given the war's primitive communications, the coordination of indirect firepower with infantry manoeuvre required centralised control. This resulted in highly-synchronised fire plans that provided little flexibility. By 1918 technical and tactical innovation had restored some flexibility, but it was not until World War Two that radio-based fire control allowed firepower the flexibility to effectively support a manoeuvre warfare approach. The Western allies led in this. The Soviets took a low technology approach during their exploitation of a breakthrough battle in employing their accompanying artillery in the Napoleonic manner, firing largely over open sights. Much of the Blitzkrieg's firepower was also direct fire, greatly simplifying their combined arms coordination.

The difficulty of integrating aerial firepower with ground manoeuvre led General Pete Quesada of the 9th US Army Air Force in World War Two to observe: *'close-in air ground cooperation is the difficult thing, the vital thing, the other stuff is easy*[61].' This has led certain countries to stymie aerial firepower's ability to influence the operational level of war, in order to achieve effective tactical air/ground cooperation in the land battle. This has been accomplished by placing airpower under army command, and fixing them to tasks that directly support tactical ground operations. The World War Two Soviet approach further simplifies this by directing aircraft to engage targets either side and in front of the axis of advance, rather than seeking to directly coordinate with ground forces.

The table below seeks to distil the implications for firepower of the two main theories of war:

Activity	Manoeuvre Warfare and the Manoeuvreist Approach	Attritional, Positional or Synchronized Warfare
Command and Control.	Command retained at the highest level to deliver unity of effort, but control is delegated to the level best able to execute the task.	Employs a methodical and analytical process that assumes that the commander can observe and orient himself to the entire battlefield. This belief is reinforced by modern collection and analytical technology.
How the enemy will be defeated?	Shatter the enemy's cohesion through a variety of rapid, focused, and unexpected actions that create a turbulent and rapidly deteriorating situation with which the enemy cannot cope.	Cumulative destruction of enemy, largely through application of superior firepower.
The primary function of firepower.	Achieve and sustain manoeuvre through extremely violent blows to destroy/ defeat individual force element(s) coupled with neutralisation of the enemy's command and fires system. Meanwhile also denying the enemy's ability to manoeuvre.	Efficient application of fire against high value targets to systematically destroy a significant proportion of the enemy's combat worth.

(*Continued on next page*)

Activity	Manoeuvre Warfare and the Manoeuvreist Approach	Attritional, Positional or Synchronized Warfare
Countering opposing firepower.	At the decisive point, the enemy's joint fire system needs to be systemically incapacitated to prevent it interfering with friendly decisive manoeuvre. If possible, the defeat of the opposing air component delivers a significant blow, both practically and psychologically. Preferably achieved by an asymmetrical approach.	Incremental defeat of the enemy's joint fires system across the whole Theatre. Largely delivered through symmetrical means, such as: air-to-air combat and counter battery 'artillery duels'.
Time and Space.	Simultaneous attack throughout an enemy's depth. Coupled with decentralised firepower command and control to meet the local needs of manoeuvre.	Sequenced application to ensure maximum target effect over all the whole of the enemy's force. Achieving a designated reduction in enemy combat effectiveness is the key consideration.
Characteristics of the joint fire systems.	Prefer firepower systems able to provide a heavy weight of fire in a short time period through quantity and size of warhead. Rockets and mortars are ideal for delivering shock effect at the decisive point. Range can be sacrificed, as holding the initiative allows these weapons to be deployed within range of their target.	Range, persistent rate of fire and responsive fire system. Capable of achieving a large coverage coupled with a range of munitions able to do a variety of tasks. Centralised fire control system able to shift firepower to engage the most lucrative target.
Firepower summary.	The weaker form of war (risky), but with the more positive purpose (shatter cohesion) and systemically incapacitate, to gain greater rewards. This is challenging to execute as it is reliant upon a high level of situational awareness and intuitive decision-making.	The stronger form of war (safer) but with less ambitious purpose (incremental attrition), it offers the lesser rewards. Execution, while complex, is amenable to what militaries do well: routine staff work.

Whatever theory is espoused, the tendency to default to firepower is deep-seated in most military culture; in part because their leadership tends to be risk averse. In 1990 Christopher Bellamy observed that that: '*the US military historically has thrown its manoeuvre-focused doctrine by the wayside and fought battles based on firepower and destruction*[62]'. This may be fair for America's first war with Iraq, but the 2003 operation was more manoeuvreist, mixing bold ground manoeuvre with the application of overwhelming firepower, in high tempo, decentralised operations. However, as the Iraqi opposition was so totally overmatched – where was the risk?

There are good reasons to favour an approach to war that provides greater opportunity for firepower to achieve attrition. The growth in firepower's capability over the last few decades has significantly exceeded any increase in manoeuvre. There have been only minor improvements in the speed of mounting and executing manoeuvre. The latter remains constrained by the limits of the internal combustion engine, physical obstacles and enhancement to man-made counter-mobility capabilities, notably improvised explosive devices[63]. Except for the attack helicopter, direct fire weapons have only made incremental improvements in lethality; this represents a shift in the 'Constant Tactical Factor' away from ground manoeuvre. Theorists in the late Cold War saw rotor technology as the means of returning the advantage to manoeuvre; despite their firepower and mobility, helicopters' vulnerability means that they cannot yet (or ever?) replace ground manoeuvre.

The character of conflict of the Iraq and Afghanistan counter-insurgencies favoured the systematic, centralised control by large HQs of sensors and shooters (including special operations forces). This was in part because technology allowed generals to immerse themselves in the comfort of the sub-tactical, but also reflected the intense political control they were forced to operate within. Information technology can be exploited by both theories of war, but it naturally favours the attritional one[64]. Conflict in the information age encourages control being exercised at the highest level; this is usually manifested as an unwillingness to delegate engagement authority, by employing restrictive rules of engagement. The counter view is that there are opportunities in information technology, which together with firepower's greater lethality, can assist the manoeuvreist commander in psychologically defeating an opponent.

Joint Fires and the Combined Arms Battle

'It is not so much the mode of formation as the proper combined use of the different arms which will ensure victory[65].'

Baron de Jomini

The combined arms approach to warfare recognises that working as a team accentuates each combat arm's strengths and masks their weaknesses. An opponent, through defending against one combat arm, can create vulnerabilities that another arm can exploit. This means that personnel subjected to artillery fire will, by taking cover at the bottom of a trench, become vulnerable to being overrun by attacking infantry. When correctly employed, combined arms tactics create a dilemma for the opposing commander, making the challenge psychological, as well as physical. Lieutenant Colonel Robert Leonard, US Army, called this the 'Alcyoneus Principle[66]', which is the engineering of a situation that makes an opponent vulnerable.

Defence in World War One was significantly stronger than offence because of the dominance of the artillery and machine gun combined arms team when employed in concert with natural or manmade obstacles. This was the principal factor causing the tactical stalemate. To avoid the machine gun fire, infantry caught within its beaten zone sought positions that offered cover; they became a static target for artillery, whose trajectory largely rendered irrelevant most of the cover that was effective against direct fire weapons. On the defensive, artillery and machine guns could be easily integrated through pre-arranged drills, supplemented by reliable communications provided by buried communication lines. The simplicity of this combined arms team meant that it was very difficult to defeat or even dislocate through offensive action.

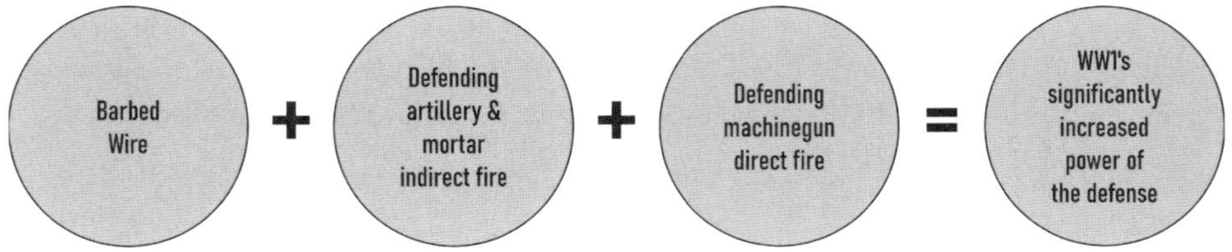

Overcoming the artillery and machine gun's defensive strength required a considerably more sophisticated and powerful offensive combined arms system. First, this needed to negate opposing artillery so removing fire support from the defending infantry. Concealed batteries could only be defeated through a revolution in target acquisition, the processing of this information into fire plans, and an overwhelming superiority in firepower. Key to identifying hostile batteries was air surveillance, which required air superiority. Secondly, the other part of the deep battle was using firepower to dislocate the opposing command and control system, and so hinder the movement of tactical reserves. Thirdly, in the close battle, offensive fire support needed to be coordinated with manoeuvre. In contrast to the reliability of defensive battlefield communications, those that supported mobile operations – optical, surface laid wire, 'portable' radios, runners/gallopers and carrier pigeon – were wholly unreliable. This leads to fixed fire plans for the break-in battle, with the infantry following the movement of the barrage.

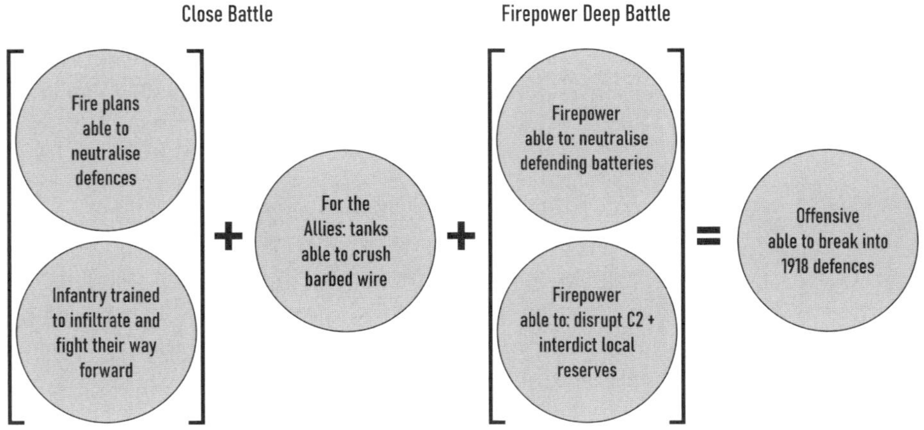

By 1918 this offensive combined arms system, with sufficient preparation and mass, could capture any defensive position. However, the inability to communicate with supporting artillery and aircraft prevented subsequent exploitation. This was compounded by World War One's artillery lacking the range and the cross-country mobility to provide support beyond an assault's preparatory and covering fire. Airpower was too technically limited to provide a substitute for artillery's lack of range; this allowed operational-level reserves to reach a threatened sector before the attacker had fought their way across the defensive zone.

As has already been identified, the physical separation in World War One of cannons from their target acquisition and fire control was primarily a survivability measure: gunners reluctantly took to indirect fire; but it led to the unprecedented massing of firepower, its manoeuvre across the battlefield and the creation of the deep battle. All of which were essential in restoring the power of the offensive by 1918. The historian Bruce Gudmundsson identifies that this has caused a division in how armies fight:

> *Leading to the seperation of 'the guns and their leaders, from the close combat of the infantry and the tendency for a single combined arms battle to divide into two separate struggles*[67]*.'*

Mr Gudmundsson advanced the proposition that artillery commanders actively disengaged from close combat to allow them to independently conduct their own deep fight; while there is merit in this analysis, most artilleries have concentrated upon the close battle, arguably to the detriment of the deep. This dominance is partly tradition and culture, but it is also because of the rarity of conventional war; deep fires are rarely significant in counter-insurgency. In addition, peacetime training tends to emphasise manoeuvre, this makes its fire support the most prominent and prestigious artillery role. It is inappropriate to draw a comparison between the institutional aspirations of most artilleries and Western air forces, who certainly from the first sought an independent role (except the USMC). This is a difference identified by the leading experts on Britain's World War Two artillery:

> *'the artillery commanders had no ambition other than to be allowed to support the army in the field ... By contrast, the question of air support for the Army in the field was fraught with conflicting aims, inter-service rivalries and misunderstanding arising from personal relationships*[68]*.'*

Other analysts, notably Jonathan Bailey, see the separation between fire support and deep fires as a key advance in military science; rather than this being the splintering of the combined arms battle, it is the culmination of it. World War One's creation of the firepower deep battle was the beginning of truly modern combined arms warfare[69]; the next significant step was Soviet deep operations theory, allowing the power of the offensive to be restored through making the close battle an enabler to a deep battle that combined firepower and manoeuvre.

In 1926 Soviet Field Marshal Mikhail Tukhachevsky advanced a theory of war designed to replace World War One's artillery-led combined arms battle. This did not diminish the role of artillery, as it was to provide most of the combat power; tanks, cavalry and infantry provided the psychological threat that makes firepower decisive. Airpower provided the reach to engage the enemy reserves and HQs; the break-in and breakthrough battles became the means to insert mechanised forces (including, he proposed, aerially-delivered force elements) into the enemy's rear areas[70]. The standard Western interpretation of Soviet practice is that firepower only supports the most successful manoeuvre force. When actually, in the Soviet approach, an advance was successful because of the firepower applied, with manoeuvre forces advancing to exploit this success. Direct fire weapons are not expected to provide a significant proportion of the combat power; hence the Soviet commander's key task was the fire plan. Seeing the close battle as in effect a preliminary operation, focussed Soviet armies on engaging the enemy throughout their operational depth; this was initially with firepower, before being joined by mobile forces designed and trained for exploitation[71]. The concept of the artillery offensive was formally abandoned in the 1950s, but this was semantics, and this approach still heavily influences the Soviet successor states and their allies[72].

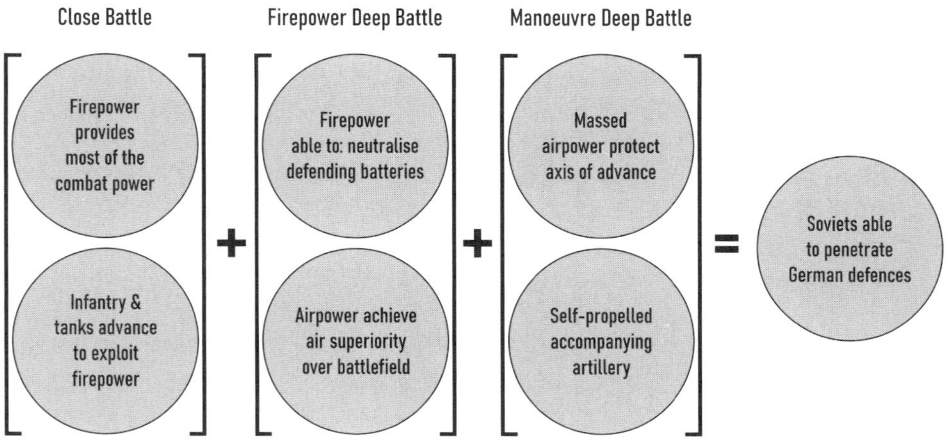

Soviet deep battle doctrine meant that their plans were an order of magnitude more sophisticated than the World War Two Western combined arms approach. Particularly in terms of achieving simultaneity of effects across the depth of a defence, and secondly in setting the conditions for exploitation. The Anglo-Americans relied upon prolonged attrition – the wearing-out fight – largely through air and artillery firepower, to exhaust the Germans in the close battle. This was the precursor to the breakthrough and pursuit; modified by evolving technology, and slightly confused by the advent of nuclear firepower, this became NATO's approach until the AirLand doctrine of the 1980s. This new doctrine featured the re-allocation of firepower from the close to the deep battle. The intellectual reaction to this was led by the former American soldier Robert Leonard:

> *'for many, the field artillery seems becoming more concerned with pursuing independent operations than with supporting the combined arms team[73].'*

His sophisticated analysis advanced the view that artillery had established a fire support system that operated in parallel to the manoeuvre chain of command. This led to it being employed against a largely artillery staff-devised high payoff target list[74]. He opined that this neither fully reflected the commander's needs, nor was sufficiently responsive to cope with the fluid targeting requirements of the hurly burly of close combat.

Despite the impressive performance of fire support in the 2003 Iraq War, American artillery was formally directed to be target, rather than manoeuvre support, focussed. Major General McCaffery gave his divisional artillery in Operation Iraqi Freedom the following instructions:

> *'Don't waste time or ammunition on targets of less than battalion size, but when you do find a suitable target, bring everything to bear with an immediate crushing bombardment – then move out'*[75].'

In other words, artillery was to be massed against targets due to their size and the level of attrition that could be inflicted. If this approach had been exclusively followed, then the high payoff target list would have been prioritised over timely fire support to manoeuvre. However, providing highly responsive fire support is in the American artillery's DNA[76]. Despite this, following the Iraq War, the view that the American artillery needed to focus on fire support led to the close support artillery battalion moving from under command of the divisional artillery to under command of their all arms brigades; the fire support teams became part of the infantry and armour battalion they supported. The cure has proved to be worse than the disease and the Americans have restored their artillery's control over the training of these fire support teams. The need to restore the doctrinal phrase 'fire support', in lieu of 'fires', shows that these reforms have misfired.

When employed individually, firepower cannot achieve the effect of combined arms and present an Alcyoneus challenge. NATO's Joint Air Attack Team (JAAT) seeks to achieve a combined arms effect through employing air, aviation and artillery against a single target. These three forms of firepower are complementary. Attack helicopters and aircraft engaging from standoff distances can pick off anti-aircraft systems at long range; when this is coupled with artillery suppressing the target area, fixed wing aircraft can close with a greater degree of safety. Armoured vehicles that remain in cover to avoid aircraft provide a stationary target for artillery; if they move away from artillery fire, they become an easier target for aircraft and aviation. Coordinating three weapon systems of markedly different characteristics (not least velocity and persistence) is significantly more complicated than employing them individually. Despite this JAATs are probably easier to achieve than combined arms in the close battle, however, practically this is not the case due to the lack of peacetime practice.

Advances in munitions now allow artillery to achieve the Alcyoneus principle through employing a 'cocktail' of munitions. The munition mix could include: scatterable mines, anti-armour sensor-fuzed munitions, thermobaric blast munitions, bomblets, jamming munitions and conventional high explosive. Each munition presents a different challenge, this can overwhelm a target's ability to respond[77]. Tanks seeking to avoid sensor-fused munitions through violent manoeuvring can make themselves vulnerable to scatterable mines. The blast of thermobaric munitions will remove protective cover that might have prevented a bomblet's anti-tank warhead achieving the optimum engagement. Ideally all these weapons should be employed simultaneously. However, the thermobaric and high explosive part of the 'cocktail' needs to be temporally separate from the sensor-fuzed munitions and scatterable mines, otherwise their blast could prevent these working effectively.

Looked at from the perspective of an infantryman in the close battle, the modern joint fire system does not seem to be optimised for combined arms operations. Critics of the current approach correctly identify that mortars are the only indirect firepower dedicated to supporting company and battalion combined arms operations. This is because the remainder of the joint fire structure is a compromise between fighting the close and deep operations; this is a necessity for effective combined arms conventional warfighting at the divisional level.

Land Warfare's Firepower Dualism: Fire Support and Deep Fires

'At the end of the Cold War it was common to regard the deep battle as necessary to set conditions for the decisive close battle. By the early 1990s the deep battle was more commonly seen as the potentially decisive one, success in which obviates the need for a more costly encounter between manoeuvre forces in the close battle[78]*.'*

Major General Jonathan Bailey

Throughout history armies have sought to reduce the effectiveness of their opponents before forces come into close combat; these operations were usually preliminary to armies concentrating for battle. This began to alter in the American Civil War; firepower led to greater dispersion on the battlefield, while railroads and telegraphs made possible dispersed yet coordinated operations across the theatre. Throughout the conflict deep manoeuvre was conducted by raiding forces, but they were initially rarely coordinated with the main army. In General Grant's decisive 1864–1865 campaign, the forces under his personal command fixed General Lee's army, while the armies of Generals Sherman and Banks conducted operations in his rear. World War One invented the firepower deep battle; Soviet deep battle theory combined this with the manoeuvre deep battle, making it their decisive operation[79]. The Russian emphasis on the all arms nature of the deep battle continues; for the West it is largely the domain of firepower.

The deep battle is the engagement of forces not yet committed to the close battle. Geographically it is determined by inter visibility between the firer and his target. In urban and jungle combat, effectively the deep battle can be a couple of hundred metres beyond own forces. Despite the actual divide between the close and deep battles being determined by terrain, armies try to allocate command responsibility for the close and deep battles. Divisions and corps usually have responsibility of the deep battle, with brigades and lower undertaking the close battle. In addition, most Western air forces claim to primacy over the deep battle. This rests upon the proven greater effectiveness of air interdiction over organic land fires in the deep battle. Of course, armies see the deep battle as an intrinsic part of the land battle, and so even if the actual firepower is predominantly delivered by aircraft, they seek control.

Fire support and deep fires require different characteristics in their target acquisition systems, platforms and munitions, and different approaches to command, control and engagement procedures. Western militaries have sought to blur these distinctions, flexing artillery and fighter-bombers between the close and deep battles. Militaries not willing to invest in sophisticated command and control systems choose to field dedicated capabilities over general-purpose ones.

While all fire needs to accurate and consistent, of the two, consistency is more important with danger close fires[80]. Inaccurate artillery and mortar fire can always be adjusted on to the target before troops come into its danger zone[81]; consistent fire allows troops to get within a practical assault distance of an artillery suppressed objective; when holding ground it allows a curtain of fire to be sited to prevent such a close assault; this normally needs to be within 400 meters of friendly positions, as this final protective fire represents the last resort of defensive plans. As suppression is often the effect required, a small munition with a high, sustained rate of fire, is advantageous; this leads to a small danger area and so a reduced danger close distance. The system needs to deliver a high level of guaranteed and prompt fire support, and be easily coordinated with ground manoeuvre. These are the characteristics of the mortar, and small calibre artillery organised to deliver direct support. Accuracy and consistency can be understood as follows:

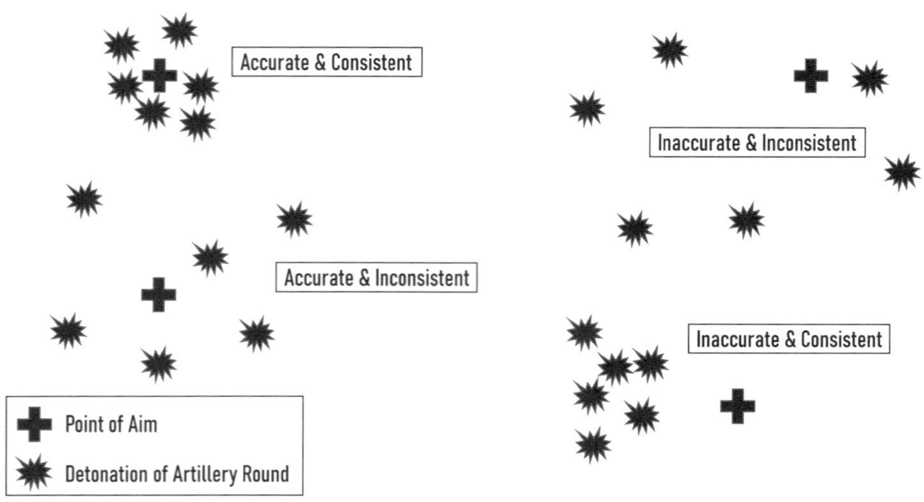

Deep fire requires some of these attributes, but these are usually secondary to range and the necessary weight of fire to achieve the defeat or destruction of a target. This fire does not usually need to be as consistent, capable of an immediate response, or be sustained; this makes the multiple rocket system ideal for engaging deep targets. They can achieve both long range and carry a heavy warhead by employing a larger rocket. This is the reason that rockets have largely replaced tube artillery as the primary depth fire weapon.

Despite these distinct requirements, armies try to meet all their fire support needs with the minimum number of weapon systems. This leads to the compromise 155mm calibre, this is actually too large for fire support, particularly of unarmoured forces and a little too small for most targets in the deep battle and tackling modern concrete reinforced buildings. The Russian and Israeli decision to field rocket launchers capable of firing different calibre rockets provides greater flexibility to support both the close and deep battles with the correct munitions. Western armies see the 155mm calibre's ability to just about deliver both roles as an efficient use of resources, but when these armies have so few guns and rockets, switching them between the close and deep battles is problematic.

In contrast to the West, Russian artillery is divided by task. The artillery brigades are designed to deliver the deep battle; each combined arms brigade has sufficient artillery to meet their close support needs, in most circumstances. With the reintroduction of the divisional level of command the Russians may be moving to greater switching of resources between close and deep battles.

Of course, aircraft can be easily switched between the close and deep battles, however, they best suite the latter; this is because in contrast to mortars and artillery, each aircraft individually determines its point of aim, except when using precision munitions guided to a grid reference. This means that aircraft fire may be individually accurate, but between aircraft it can be inconsistent; which means that unlike artillery and mortars, aerial firepower cannot consistently suppress an objective before an assault. The same limitation applies to danger close defensive fires. Aircraft also lack the weapon load and loiter time to deliver sustained suppressive fire support; aerial firepower's other main disadvantage in the close battle is the large danger area of most aerial munitions. This has not always been the case, up until the Korean War, continuous aircraft strafing with machine guns and cannons was used against danger close targets. This required a significant quantity of aircraft carrying considerable quantities of munitions, and operating at low level. This is no longer an effective use of airpower; in the close battle fighter-bombers are best used to destroy opposing forces prior to own forces closing up to the danger close distance.

Attack helicopters are better able to provide a range of support in the close battle. They can hover in a firing position at a safe standoff distance, initially striking an area with a heavy weight of rocket fire to achieve suppression, and then sustaining this with cannon fire. However, given their limited weapon load, it takes a significant quantity of helicopters to suppress even a company-sized target. This led to a battery of twelve helicopters been the standard fire unit in the Vietnam War's aerial rocket artillery.

Most artilleries recognise that they have a dual requirement to provide both fire support and deep fires, with the former invariably becoming the priority once troops come into close combat. The alternative view is that this dualism is an evolutionary step to a final destination of a decisive deep battle, with the close battle becoming a minor activity. This is the institutional journey undertaken by most air forces and it is one being pursued by some army aviation. With America's retreat from the ideas behind AirLand doctrine (which expected firepower to effectively defeat the Soviet second echelon forces) it is the Indian Army that is the leading proponent of the artillery-based attritional deep battle. With the new millennium India introduced the Cold Start doctrine which required accurate and heavy volumes of firepower, coordinated with combined arms operations including air support[82]; this required sequenced massing against a series of targets; the Indians call this the '100-guns concept[83]'.

The modern joint fire system-of-systems needs to be able to conduct both fire support and deep fires. But this does not mean that all parts of the system need to be equally adept at both functions. Unfortunately, this has not always been recognised, leading to standardisation on generalist capability. Fire support can lose out through the fielding of unsuitable artillery and mortar calibres. Western armies are currently further disadvantaged through their reliance on easily-countered airpower; one recent estimate was that 80% of NATO's firepower was air delivered[84]. Modern aircraft excel at destroying targets, but cannot provide the persistent firepower required to neutralise a defensive system for the duration of a set-piece attack, nor the close in fires to provide a barrier to close assault. The paucity of artillery above the brigade level makes the traditional Anglo-American flexing of artillery between the close and deep battles largely a chimera. Nor does most Western rocket artillery have the necessary munitions to provide effective reinforcing fires to the close battle. In set-piece conventional battles, the most successful warfighting approach seeks to engage an opponent throughout his whole depth; both the Russians and the West seek to achieve this, but only the former have the resources to achieve this with organic land assets.

The Balance between Organic Firepower and Manoeuvre Forces

'I think, perhaps, we've got too much artillery in the force structure, if the Air Force is going to be as available as it proved to be in this campaign. I'm not suggesting we do away with all the field artillery brigades, but I am suggesting that the brigades could be a little smaller[85].'

Lieutenant Colonel TG William Wallace,
Commander V Corps in the Iraq War

The apportionment of resources between firepower and manoeuvre is the product of a range of factors; effective conventional warfighting is only one, an army's internal cultural and institutional factors tend to dominate. Resources devoted to firepower tend to increase in conflict, before being reduced in peacetime cuts. This results in most infantry battalions, over the last century, having between two and six mortar tubes in peacetime, switching to between eight and twelve tubes when fighting. The requirement for brigade, company and platoon level mortars are often entirely overlooked in peacetime; mortars are often sacrificed to avoid manpower cuts in infantry companies, following the rationale that firepower can always be sourced from elsewhere, while riflemen cannot, a view that is the opposite to warfighting experience, when understrength units man their support weapons at the expense of riflemen. This has been an enduring phenomenon; the importance of maximising firepower was recognised in the British Imperial forces in 1918 when actual bayonet strength was secondary to quantity of support weapons[86]; for the US Army in the Vietnam War:

> *'whenever unit strength is reduced, weapon strength must be increased ... as gaps in the line must be closed through more firepower and that fire must be guaranteed and responsive*[87].'

Between 1915–1992, Western armies conducting conventional warfighting against a peer opponent, invariably had an overall ratio of close to one artillery to one manoeuvre battalion; a lower ratio has been employed in some terrain and characters of conflict. The logic of combat soon led to the total number of artillerymen approaching the infantry total, both overall and in individual battles. The British on the first day of the Battle of the Somme, 1 July 1916, had about half the number of artillery personnel engaged as the infantry strength in the attacking divisions. This reached 80% in the Third Ypres Battle in autumn 1917; it continued to rise, reaching 85% during the October struggle for the main ridge[88].

Western armies usually have a battery supporting each infantry or armour battalion. This is usually irrespective of whether this is in the most popular three-battalion brigade ('triangular') or the four-battalion brigade that was common in World War One. At the divisional level, most armies field a single medium or general support battalion. The American World War Two infantry division is illustrative, it had a battalion of 155mm howitzers and three 105mm battalions supporting its 'triangular' structure. Their armoured division had the same quantity of task force level, but this proportionately could provide more firepower, as there were only six manoeuvre units compared to the nine manoeuvre battalions that were in an infantry division. However, unless reinforced by their corps, most armoured divisions lacked a medium artillery battalion.

Modern Western armies largely retain this brigade level ratio, but their undervaluing of firepower has led them to have virtually no divisional or corps artillery. The armies of the World Wars and the Cold War held much, if not most, of their artillery at divisional, corps and army level. Globally, the Americans in World War Two had 2.89 battalions of non-divisional artillery per division[89], although this was unbalanced between theatres due to their distinct characters of conflict. The European Theatre of Operations had twice the non-divisional artillery as the Pacific one. The result being that when fighting the Germans, the Americans had almost as many artillery battalions as tank and infantry battalions. The British Liberation Army that returned to France in 1944 had 65 field, medium and heavy artillery regiments (battalions). 30 were in the 11 divisions and the rest were at Corps and Army level. This was a ratio of slightly more armour and infantry units than artillery ones. To compensate, the British fielded 8-gun batteries. In 1944, the British artillery had 17% of the total army manpower, compared to 16% in the infantry[90]. Of course, the Soviets led the way in both mass and centralisation. By 1944 more than 65% of their artillery was in artillery divisions and brigades; the Soviet artillery and missile troops were numerically the largest element of the army.

Immediately following World War Two, Western armies significantly reduced their artillery park; this cut fell disproportionately on divisional and corps level artillery. The easy rationale for this was that that aerial and nuclear firepower made much of this support superfluous.

The limitations of the former and un-usability of the latter were soon exposed. This reduction was compounded by the replacement of tube anti-tank and aircraft artillery, which could re-role to indirect fire, with missile systems; this was subsequently partly reversed when the limitations of missile technology were exposed. Initially the Americans in the Korean War lacked the non-divisional artillery to achieve their standard World War Two ratio of three or four artillery battalions to support a battalion attack[91]; a year into the Korean War, the quantity of non-divisional artillery battalions equalled those with divisions. By then, the overall quantity of artillery battalions almost equalled the combined total of infantry and armour battalions[92]. Post-World War Two counter-insurgency campaigns employed a lower proportion of firepower. America's Vietnam War, with its significant element of conventional fighting, probably had the highest proportion of firepower; the Anglo-French usually fought with, at most, direct support artillery in the conflicts which saw them retreat from empire.

The 1990–91 Gulf War was the last time the Americans and their allies fought with the orthodox quantity of artillery and its associated command and control. The US Army deployed two corps artillery headquarters, seven divisional artillery headquarters, and seven field artillery brigade headquarters. These commanded the 43 artillery battalions[93]. In comparison there were 53 American Army armour and infantry battalions; in addition, the two armoured cavalry regiments had their organic artillery. The US Marines were not quite as well provided in artillery; they had 18 manoeuvre battalions to 9 artillery battalions, but each of these had four firing batteries. The British took practically all they could, but remained in the judgement of the Americans under-gunned, so they provided a reinforcing artillery brigade. The result for the British was a one-to-one ratio of artillery to manoeuvre battalions[94]. Following the Gulf War there were further significant reductions in the proportion of artillery in the American and their allies' orders of battle.

In the 2003 Iraq invasion, the US Army field artillery deployed one corps artillery headquarters, two divisional artillery headquarters, three brigade headquarters, and eleven battalions; however, the two lead American divisions conducted most of the fighting with only their organic divisional assets. The US Marine Corps had a ratio of five artillery battalions to 15 manoeuvre (including reconnaissance) battalions. The British proportionately had more artillery than the American Army, which they fought at the divisional level, despite not deploying any general support artillery. If the reinforcing American artillery brigades had been able to effectively get into the fight, then the US Army would have had a more traditional ratio. In attacking without their general support artillery, the Americans fielded their lowest ratio of field artillery pieces to troops in combat since either their early battles in World War One, or perhaps even as far back as the Spanish-American War[95].

Most of the firepower in the Iraq War was provided by aircraft. In the preceding years of enforcing the no-fly zone, airpower had achieved air supremacy and had destroyed almost all identified Iraqi military targets. As a result, there were no other significant alternative tasks to ground support. It is difficult to envisage this unique set of circumstances being repeated. This is the context for V Corps commander's remarks in the opening quote. Despite his caveat of the need for guaranteed air support, the conflict was widely seen as defining the future, and justification for further significant reductions in artillery. What is seldom noted is that despite ineffective Iraqi opposition, each of the cannons and rocket launchers delivered a much greater volume and higher rate of fire than in Operation Desert Storm, indicating a relative shortage of organic firepower[96].

Organic firepower is not just a matter of quantity. In World War Two the standard divisional close support pieces were also fielded in the independent artillery brigades and divisions; their task was to reinforce brigades with close support artillery. Western general support artillery now mainly employs rocket systems[97]; these systems have been very effective in counter-insurgency operations through engaging point targets with a low yield warhead; in conventional warfighting they will be similarly effective in urban operations and against bunkers[98]. This convinced the Israelis to replace a divisional M109 battalion with a rocket one; but these rocket systems cannot effectively conduct area suppressive fires. If the only tube artillery is at brigade level, then a brigade needs to lose its direct support artillery to reinforce the commanding general's main effort. When this is considered too great a risk, Western brigades are reliant upon their three batteries of guns, possibly supported by precision rockets and air support, to suppress any opposition to their manoeuvre. World War Two experience shows that three or four artillery battalions are required to suppress identified and potential opposition opposing a single infantry battalion attack. Furthermore, a peer opponent will have a counter-battery capability that will further diminish a brigade's fire support; to avoid destruction a battery will need to move soon after unmasking.

NATO's replacement of artillery with airpower has not been followed by the Russians, Indians, Iranians, some Arab countries and the Chinese; their quantity of artillery reflects the norms of traditional conventional warfare. Despite having a first-class air force, the Israelis have over the years proportionately increased the size of their artillery park, although it is now slightly contracting and shifting away from area fires. Despite the prominence of close air support in recent operations against Hamas (largely delivering precision bombs on point targets), Israeli conventional warfighting doctrine requires their ground forces to fight without air force assistance. This recognises that their air force has initially to gain air superiority and conduct air interdiction.

Throughout the Cold War, the Warsaw Pact increased their artillery numbers and capability. By the late 1980s, Soviet divisions had: seven tube, one multiple launch rocket, and one long-range rocket artillery battalions, equal to the number of motor rifle and tank battalions (nine). In addition, they fielded eighteen artillery divisions. By 2008 the Russians had recovered from the collapse of the USSR and were fielding their New Look brigades; most of these have two tube artillery and one multiple launch rocket system battalions to support their four manoeuvre battalions[99]. In addition, most brigades have an anti-tank battalion with a battery of 100mm guns with an indirect fire sight to allow them to supplement the fire plan; the Russians also train their tank formations in indirect fire. Having two tube artillery battalions means that the brigade could always have a battalion giving fire support, with the other moving to keep pace with the advance, or to avoid counter fire. Alternatively, this level of artillery support allows individual batteries to be allocated under command of tank and infantry battalions, whilst retaining a battalion under brigade command.

At first sight the Russian airborne troops are not as lavishly provided with fire support as their ground forces compatriots. Most airborne troops battalion tactical groups have six 120mm self-propelled gun-mortars and four 82mm mortars. In comparison, a motor rifle battalion could have six 122/152mm self-propelled guns reinforcing its organic holding of up to eight 120mm or 82mm mortars. However, airborne battalion tactical groups have less than half the personnel of their ground force colleges, so they actually have a higher ratio of fire support weapons, but of a lighter calibre[100]. This also applies to divisional artillery, air transportation limits this to: eighteen armoured 120mm gun mortars and twelve D30 towed 122mm guns.

In addition to the artillery in their brigades, Russian ground forces deploy a total of thirteen artillery, multiple launch rocket and longer-range rocket brigades. This is just under a fifth of their total number of all arms brigades[101]. Some of these artillery brigades are just equipped with rocket systems, the majority have two battalions equipped with 152mm gun-howitzers, and one of rocket launchers. These brigades' field some of the best Russian equipment in the 2S19 and Uragan; the preponderance towards 152mm makes them well suited to reinforce the manoeuvre brigades with close fires. Experience of the Russo-Ukraine War has shown the need for large calibre tube artillery; heavy (240mm) mortars and tube artillery (203mm guns), previously in the reserve, they are now in frontline service. These weapons are formed into a specialist artillery brigade with a battalion of twenty-four 203-mm SP 2S7 Pion guns and a battalion of sixteen 240-mm SP 2S4 Tyulpan mortars[102]; this weapon mix allows Russian artillery commanders to match firepower to a broad range of targets.

The outcome of this is that Russian ground and airborne forces match the Soviets' historic norm by fielding as many artillery battalions as manoeuvre battalions. A difference is the greater weighting towards rocket artillery. The current Russian ratio is close to two tubes to one rocket battalion[103]. In comparison, in January 1944 the Red Army had 88,900 towed guns and mortars to only 2,167 rocket launchers[104]. The proportion of rocket artillery is increasing as a further Uragan-1M heavy multiple rocket launcher battalion is being added to the up to seven Russian divisions forming from independent brigades. A possible final divisional structure could be four rocket artillery to six tube artillery battalions; in addition, a division should expect to be reinforced by at least one artillery brigade.

Russian independent brigades have triple the artillery of NATO brigades, and with their battalion of rocket launchers, they have significantly greater ability to achieve shock effect through a heavy weight of fire. This level of firepower is considered by them to be the minimum sufficient for a brigade to manoeuvre in most circumstances without needing reinforcing firepower. The artillery and missile brigades can provide reinforcing fire when this is not the case, notably in the break-in battle against an organised defence; this type of operation requires central control over massed artillery to simultaneously suppress the full depth of an opponent's defensive position, particularly the opposing artillery and command elements. This is identified as one of the drivers behind the return to the divisional structure.

Following wars governments look for a peace dividend; this has always tended to fall disproportionately hard upon artillery and mortars as these have expanded to meet the demands of major combat operations. The NATO organic firepower reductions since 1992 have compounded this historic trend with the influence of the new theories of war. Western armies have come to believe that a single tube artillery battalion per brigade, and a rocket battalion at divisional level, is adequate organic firepower; noting that many NATO armies cannot achieve even this. This leads to a firepower deficit compared to armies that follow orthodox military science and field the historic norm for firepower. Rearmament is happening – the Germans intend to be at one artillery battalion per three armour or infantry battalions by 2030; they currently have a ratio of one to nine, in the Cold War it was one to two.

The 'Empty Battlefield' and Force Densities

'This expansion or "emptying" of the battlefield [in the American Civil War] occurred at virtually the same time as the expansion of the theatre of operations. At both the tactical and the emergent operational levels of war, therefore, the ratio of troops to space began to decrease dramatically[105].'

James J. Schneider, Historian

Modern land warfare's pre-eminent tactical challenge is surviving on the battlefield against firepower. The American Civil War and the Franco-Prussian War were initially fought with massed formations that would not have been out of place on a Napoleonic battlefield. Improved small arms and artillery firepower meant that observable troops rapidly became casualties. The tactical response created the 'empty battlefield', a term that gained traction in military publications from the Franco-Prussian War[106]; it describes a battlefield without visible opponents, the result of enemy action forcing troops in the contact zone to conceal themselves. Even the most open ground can provide sufficient cover to prevent personnel and sometimes vehicles being effectively engaged. Cover's ability to reduce the lethality of weapons is usually more successful with direct rather than indirect fire. The change in force employment was iteratively achieved: closed packed formations gave way to increasingly thin skirmish lines; these were then replaced by highly dispersed platoons and sections squads.

If survivability was not a factor then massed formations are more effective on the battlefield; they offer an easier leadership challenge, superior command and control, increase morale through being part of a visible cohort, offer more efficient logistics, and they aid with the massing and control of firepower. All these factors explain why massed formations were very reluctantly abandoned; in addition, there is also a very human inclination towards crowding together, a tendency which increases with danger. Overcoming this with military training is significantly more difficult than teaching massed formations; failure to instill survivability into solders has led ill-trained troops to spontaneously adopting massed formations, invariably with tragic results[107].

Stephen Biddle's seminal study shows that even first-class armies, with the imperative of major war, cannot easily evolve a modern system that places battlefield survivability over all other factors. This is despite armies identifying that the modern system of warfare is the correct response to the challenge provided by the lethality of firepower. It is challenging because it requires the employment of: '*small-unit independent manoeuvre, and combined arms at the tactical level, and depth, reserves and differential concentration at the operational level of war*[108]'. All of these techniques challenged pre-1914 military orthodoxy and so had to be forced upon reluctant militaries.

Initially the battlefield void extended only over that area of the contact zone that could be covered by small arms fire and direct fire artillery. World War One's invention of the firepower deep battle resulted in the empty battlefield extending behind the front lines[109]. Initially this was limited by primitive ground-based target acquisition; this soon grew in sophistication and a combination of aerostats, aircraft reconnaissance, wireless interception, flash and then sound ranging overcame intervisibility, cover and concealment. This made vulnerable to artillery and air strikes: reserves, HQs, logistic instillations and batteries up to 15–30km behind the front line.

By the next World War airpower had significantly greater reach and lethality. While not as revolutionary, enhancements to sensors, delivery systems and munitions had extended and made more lethal the artillery's deep fire; the combined effect was a significant extension of the danger zone behind the front line. By 1944, Anglo-American airpower's extension of the 'empty battlefield' largely restricted German armoured manoeuvre and resupply to darkness and foul weather. This led to the Germans timing their last operational-level offensive in the West – the Battle of the Bulge – to coincide with blizzards and freezing rain. The extended 'empty battlefield' also hindered generals from personally intervening in the battle, leading to the exercise of command being more HQ based[110].

The Russo-Ukraine War has showcased the advances made in target acquisition and the increased lethality of munitions. Russian multi-layered sensors have been able to acquire targets for their artillery to strike at considerable depth behind the front line. The ability of Russian fire strikes to destroy Ukrainian battalions has been interpreted as being the outcome of indirect fire's improved lethality against armoured vehicles. Of course, this is true, but it is also the failure of the Ukrainians, when well behind the front line, to tactically adapt to the logic of the empty battlefield. Learning from such events, both armies have postured their forces to maximise survivability, this has led to troops only coming together when mass is required for success in close battle. In these circumstances, both sides try to protect their massed forces through achieving local fire superiority, an air defence umbrella, countering opposing target acquisition, and electronic counter-measures.

Airpower could increase the depth of 'empty battlefield' but Russian air defence has denied the Ukrainians the use of their airpower. The Russians have refrained from using both their airpower and longer-range missiles, limiting the area in which they impose the empty battlefield's logic. In contrast, Western airpower has dominated whole theatres of operations, whether in conventional conflict as in the wars against Iraq, or the persistent surveillance and strike that the Israelis impose on Hamas and Hezbollah.

A similar fate to the Ukrainian battalions is likely to be repeated by other armies who fail to adequately adjust to the extended, more lethal, empty battlefield. Without the imperative of conflict, it will be a considerable challenge to impose the changes necessary for rear area forces to survive against modern target acquisition and firepower. Of the occupants of the real estate behind the front line, the artillery has most consistently been exposed to opposing firepower; nonetheless, many artilleries continue to deploy in tight battery positions. These are easy to command, are logistically efficient and offer morale advantages, but they will not survive against an opponent with even a rudimentary counter battery capability. Formation HQs and logistics facilities are even more vulnerable, they generally offer a static, massed and unprotected target. A further vulnerability is armies favouring only a couple of lines of communication routes.

These can be easily targeted, particularly by airborne moving target radars. In contrast, by merging with the existing civilian traffic the Islamic State largely nullified air interdiction. Rear areas forces are likely to remain extremely vulnerable in peer-on-peer conflict until they are forced to change[111]. If the historic lesson of combat troops is a guide, then this will require repeated demonstrations of firepower's lethality.

A feature of the War on the Donbas is the reduced force density; in this it replicates Soviet practice in World War Two when fighting over the same Ukrainian plains. Despite featuring the largest armies, the Eastern Front had significantly reduced force density when compared to the Western Theatre; dispersion was the norm except in the urban sieges and when the Soviets massed their firepower and armour to smash through German defences. The level of dispersion is testified by a US pilot:

> *'While flying over the Ukraine it became evident to me that there were no continuous line of contact between the Soviets and the Germans. There was plenty of evidence of concentrated action in isolated areas. It appeared by concentrating force it was hoped to seize the initiative in local areas. Since either side could use this tactic flanking action was always possible. The defender was always at the disadvantage*[112]*.'*

While the Russo-Ukraine War is not on the same scale, its logic is similar, not least in the inability to maintain a continuous front, and the vulnerability of the less agile forces to encirclement. Even well-prepared positions remain highly vulnerable to firepower, in orthodox military science a brigade has a 10–15km frontage in conventional warfighting; the norm is 50km on the Donbas. The leading Western authority on the tactical aspects of this war, Dr Karber, makes two deductions as a result of the declining force-to-space ratio. First, that it provides greater opportunities for manoeuvre, including the massing of firepower. Secondly, that the increased lethality of massed fires means that remaining static, in the open plain, even if protected by sophisticated fortifications, is rarely a viable option[113]. Mobility even when holding ground is key; Ukrainian artillery constantly move between a number of prepared positions. They have learnt to avoid giving the Russians a static target that they can mass their artillery against. Responding to this increased force-to-space ratio, the Russians have followed their standard practice and have increased the allocation of tube and rocket artillery under battalion command. Yet when a decisive engagement is fought, Russian forces have employed massed centralised firepower. The correct response to the increased force-to-space ratio is to employ mobility to concentrate force; this is more effective than dispersing firepower, as was British practice in the Western Desert in 1941–2. This was when the British Army reverted to its culturally enduring small wars mentality – which has always been more a desire or psychology than a way of war.

The military historian Trevor Dupuy linked battlefield tactical dispersion with the increasing force to space ratio across the whole theatre; he identified a steady increase, since antiquity, of the force-to-space ratio[114]. The global reduction of regular armed forces – including for many European countries the end of conscription – has accelerated this phenomenon. Furthermore, a paradox embedded in the empty battlefield is that the counter-measures to the increased lethality of firepower have actually resulted in fewer casualties for a given time period, this necessitating an increase in the quantity and duration of battles for them to be decisive. However, troops who fail to adopt survivability techniques have been the exception to this.

Most militaries tend to restrict their response to firepower's greater lethality and coverage to their combat arms[115]; this is despite, combat support and service support troops being more vulnerable to the deeper and more lethal empty battlefield. This will not just be in terms of physical casualties; the Israeli experience is that support units face a greater risk of psychological breakdown than combat units when facing firepower[116]. Given the historical resistance that the combat arms displayed in adopting modern methods, we cannot expect the supporting arms to seamlessly adapt to the survivability challenge. For many armies, actual peer conflict will be required to deliver change on this scale. Those on the receiving end of Western firepower have iteratively adapted their logistics and command procedures, in some cases over decades, to make them survivable. With the exception of the British in the Falklands War and the South Africans in Angola, Western armies have for generations fought with air superiority. This has led to the continued employment of practices that will be problematic when facing a peer opponent. Compared to the almost leisurely journey undertaken by combat arms since their 19th century massed formations, the forces in the rear areas will need to rapidly adapt in contact.

Firepower and Manoeuvre's Interchangeability

'Dominant firepower ... will transfer mass, structurally from the combat arm to the artillery, and in the deployment from the direct fire zone (as we now understand it) to the formation and protection of mobile fire bases ...[117]*'*

Brigadier Richard Simpkin

So far, we have considered how the firepower and manoeuvre elements of warfighting can be complementary, now it is time to determine to what extent they can substitute for each other. Central to the Soviet and Russian approach to land warfare is the interchangeability of firepower and manoeuvre, a concept that goes back to the 19th Century[118]. Soviet firepower doctrine at the operational level of war did not differentiate between indirect and direct firepower; at the tactical level, the employment of force was divided into the artillery-delivered 'fire strikes' and the infantry or armour 'troop strikes'. Both forms of attack were expected to achieve overwhelming force to inflict attrition and create psychological shock that paralyses an opponent.

Soviet analysis identified that two deficiencies led to World War One's impasse; first, insufficient firepower to achieve and sustain the manoeuvre that would achieve a breakthrough; secondly, the lack of an effective arm of exploitation, the result of horsed cavalry not being able to advance against even modest resistance, and primitive tanks being simply too unreliable. The solution was partly to simultaneously attack an enemy's whole tactical depth; made possible by combining artillery with longer-range aerial firepower. This theory sought to perfect the offensive methods pioneered by Colonel Bruchmüller at the Battle of Riga. German fire plans aimed at dislocating the opposing defences, and through neutralising defensive firepower provide the stormtrooper with the opportunity to fight their way through the defended zone. The Germans designated the most successful of these attacks as the main axis of advance. Soviet practice in World War Two differed from the World War One German approach through their expectation that firepower would provide almost all of an attack's combat power. Where artillery fire was concentrated defined the most successful attack and the axis of advance; the defenders on either side of this axis, and their reserves, were rendered incapable of interfering with this operation by fire strikes[119]; limited infantry holding attacks could supplement this. On the main axis, Soviet doctrine inverted the traditional relationship between firepower and manoeuvre. Soviet infantry and tank formations did not advance under cover of artillery support; instead they supported the artillery offensive by advancing to seize ground. Their physical presence identified and fixed targets, and through the threat of close assault they provided the psychological pressure to break the defender's will to fight, but they contributed little to the offensive's combat power. In sum:

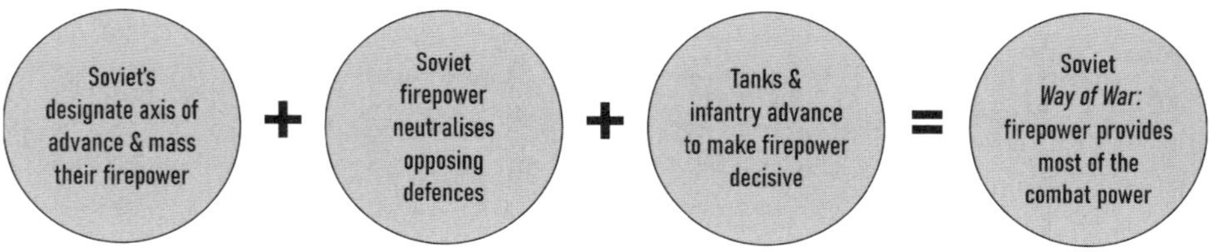

As firepower is not limited by what could be physically massed into a geographic space, the Soviets could achieve overwhelming combat power. Sufficient firepower on their chosen axis rendered all other factors irrelevant to Soviet commanders:

> *'if one has two hundred guns per kilometre of the front, he does not ask about the enemy and do not report about him. Report how far, what objective your units have reached*[120]'.

In effect, the Western Allies in World War Two employed so much firepower in their set piece battles that there was little practical difference with the Soviet approach; however, their intention was always to use firepower to support manoeuvre forces. Whether a wholly organic development, the outcome of firepower's dominance in the Korean and Vietnam Wars, or influenced by the Soviets, the American concept of 'attack by fire' gained considerable doctrinal traction in the 1980s[121]. This sought to exploit their attack helicopters and rocket systems, as well as aircraft employing precision munitions, to achieve the destruction of targets prior to close combat. Previously the Western view was that only massed aerial firepower could economically achieve destruction, and artillery and mortar effect was normally limited to neutralisation and suppression. The proponents of AirLand doctrine believed that the balance between firepower and manoeuvre had shifted: *'The greater amounts and types of firepower available on the battlefield have … brought into question the entire relationship between firepower and manoeuvre*[122].' The Soviets always believed that, in sufficient mass, organic land firepower could achieve destruction.

As well as the Russians, the Indians and Chinese have the artillery quantity and organisation to make firepower interchangeable with manoeuvre in their set-piece attacks. The Indian Army has been heavily influenced by Soviet theory, and now sees massed artillery as being employable independent of manoeuvre forces. They raised their first artillery division in the late 90s and now have four, one per Strike Corps. Like the original Soviet version, the Indian artillery division can apply tremendous amounts of firepower; this is further enhanced by the artillery divisional commander and his staff exercising centralised control over all of the corps' other forms of firepower. This enables artillery to independently degrade or destroy discrete enemy units and formations, creating openings for mechanised assaults. In their border conflicts the Indians have principally relied on massed artillery to provide their combat power, with small assault forces making this decisive through seizing ground.

In addition to the artillery at regimental or brigade level and the divisional level, the Chinese artillery have eight active artillery divisions, each made up of a number of brigades. It seems probable that the Chinese artillery divisions follow Russian doctrine; this would mean that these divisions have the dual role of providing additional firepower and the necessary command and control to conduct simultaneous fire strikes throughout the depth of an opponent's formation[123].

Armies that see firepower and manoeuvre as largely interchangeable field much of their artillery in formations that facilitate independent fire strikes. While firepower cannot totally replace manoeuvre forces, the two are largely interchangeable in generating combat power. As firepower is not limited by what can be physically massed into a geographic space, the assault force on the axis of advance can derive most of its combat power from artillery, mortar and aerial fires. Even a small squad that physically closes with a neutralised enemy is capable of psychologically breaking their will to resist. Firepower is even more interchangeable when holding ground; an outpost line with guaranteed joint firepower can now replace the firepower of battalions of tanks or infantry. Defensive fires provide obstacles that few assaulting troops will cross. Firepower on its own, through stimulating the individual's survival instinct, fixes units.

Danger Close Fires

'[danger close missions] gave us the edge at precisely the moment we needed it...in the risky and uncertain nature of close battle[124]'.

Lieutenant General Harold Moore referring to the
Battle of the Ia Drang Valley

The term danger close was originally an instruction from terminal controllers to guns or mortars that their indirect fire was being applied close to own forces. For certain militaries it has become an all-encompassing description for the employment of joint fires close to own forces and third parties. Two factors have driven the expansion of this term; first, the need to conduct war amongst the people and avoid collateral damage; second, particularly for the West, a character of conflict which has seen an increased use of firepower close to own troops, a response to opponent's tactics.

Danger close has two facets; first, the distance from the fire at which friendly and non-combatants are at risk from that firepower; second, the level of risk of casualties once friendly forces and non-combatants are within this distance. For artillery and mortars this distance is usually known as the 'trigger, danger close or safety distance'. In close terrain it is not unusual for most fire support to be within the 'trigger distance' of friendly forces. As the opening quote identifies, the commander, assisted by the fire support element, needs to manage the risk of using joint fires within the trigger distance to deliver effective warfighting.

The Americans specify the 'trigger distance' as 600 metres for artillery and mortars, and 750 metres for naval gunfire. Other militaries vary their distance to take account of the weight of ordnance and its fuze setting. The Soviets and Russians also formally consider the level of protection of friendly forces – from the most vulnerable troops in the open through to tanks. Operationally the Russians employ a danger close distance of 400m for infantry, 300m for their BMP infantry fighting vehicle and entrenched infantry and 200m for tanks. They also consider the range over which the battery is firing, which they split into above and below 10km[125]. In addition, inadequate mapping and meteorological data can add to the challenge through increasing inaccuracy. All these are valid factors.

The artillery and mortar special procedures used to engage a target within the trigger distance are designed to ensure that fire does not endanger own troops through being inconsistent; crucially an allowance is made for any initial target location error[126]. Employing this drill can be time consuming; as a result, the operational risk of following this procedure may need to be judged against failing to effectively deal with opponents, especially those 'hugging' own forces. In their Afghan War the Soviets discovered that not following danger close procedures – when the need for immediate fire support outweighed other factors – led to a 30% chance of fratricide[127]. It has been common on recent operations to accept greater risk and open at fire for effect within the mandated trigger distance. As the participants of the Battle of Fallujah in Iraq identified: '*rarely were any fires outside of the doctrinal danger-close 600 metres*'[128]. There have been occasions in which danger close procedures have been short-circuited without understanding the inherent dangers. More often it has been a calculated response to modern artillery's improved accuracy, achieved through making greater allowance for the variables affecting indirect fire. This improved accuracy has not led to a revision of the trigger distance. A reduction of the trigger distances by a couple of hundred metres would probably restore the level of risk to that experienced in World War Two, when trigger distances were first determined.

The second requirement is to quantify the level of risk experienced by own forces and non-combatants when they are within the danger close distance. The American risk estimate distances (or REDs) methodology has effectively become the Western standard for determining risk from munitions in combat operations[129]. The REDs tables specify two horizontal distances for each joint fire system. One is based on a 0.1% (1 in 1000) chance of inflicting a casualty[130]. The other distance is that which would cause a 10% (100 in 1000) chance of casualties. These two distances allow the local commander to make an informed risk versus reward decision through extrapolating between these two distances. This balances the resultant risk presented by friendly fire against its likely positive impact on the enemy and the resultant reduction in their firepower.

REDs conflate two factors; first, the munition's consistency around the aiming point; this is calculated as a circular error probability[131]; second, the danger zone of its blast and fragmentation[132]. The danger distances of unguided ballistic weapons – artillery, rockets and mortars – are calculated on the basis that their fire is on-target. This can be through adjustment on to the target, or accurate predicted fire. This results for artillery and mortars in the following REDs:

Mortars and Artillery						
Weapon System	**0.1% (1 in 1000) chance of incapacitation (in metres)**			**10% (100 in 1000) chance of incapacitation (in metres)**		
	1/3 Range	2/3 Range	Max Range	1/3 Range	2/3 Range	Max Range
60mm Mortar	100	150	175	60	65	65
81mm Mortar	165	185	230	75	80	80
120mm Mortar	150	300	400	100	100	100
105mm Gun	175	200	275	85	85	90
155mm Gun	200	280	450	100	100	125
155mm Bomblet	280	300	475	150	180	200
5-inch Naval Gun	450	450	600	210	225	250

So what fire support deductions can be made from artillery and mortar danger distances? Firstly, the contrast between prescribed danger close trigger distances and the 0.1% chance of incapacitation. For 105mm guns the trigger distance is 600m and the 0.1% chance of incapacitation is between 325–425m, depending upon the range. The difference is largely due to the trigger distance allowing for inaccurate fire, while the risk estimate distance assumes that the rounds are hitting the target[133]. Hence when 'guns are shooting to the map', and target locations can be accurately derived, greater risk can reasonably be accepted.

Secondly, when it comes to really close fire support, the 81mm mortar and 105mm gun with their low RED are very effective at getting assaulting troops close to an objective before the suppression needs to be lifted. The 60mm mortar has an edge over both these weapons. However, the mortar's lack of range means that artillery, when close to the troops they are supporting can practically achieve as low a RED[134]. The 155mm gun needs to cease fire, at its usual battle range, 80m before both the 105mm gun and 81mm mortar during an assault. The empirical evidence of World War Two was that assaulting troops had to be on an objective within two-minutes of artillery fire lifting. Assaulting infantry will be pressed to close on an objective within the prescribed two minutes from 280m away. This will result in troops on foot assaulting an objective that is at best is being suppressed by direct fire weapons; this is the rationale for retaining 81mm and 105mm within formations consisting mainly of dismounted infantry.

Thirdly, certain systems are unsuitable for danger close fire support. The American 5-inch – and other naval guns with similar characteristics – are essentially unsuited to firing-in a dismounted assaulting force or providing close defensive fire to protect a position, as is the 120mm mortar, which has similar characteristics to the 155mm gun. This will either have to cease fire on an objective, or start inflicting significant casualties on their own infantry forces as they attempt to close the final 300m during an assault. A combination of 120mm and 155mm fire support is however ideal for troops who expect to close on an objective in their armoured vehicles. While this analysis has focused on the assault, a similar rationale can be applied to danger close defensive fires. Turning to aerial weapons:

Fixed Wing and Rotary Aircraft Missiles, Cannon and Unguided Rockets		
Weapon System	**0.1% (1 in 1000) chance of incapacitation (in metres)**	**10% (100 in 1000) chance of incapacitation (in metres)**
Hellfire AGM 114M Missile	125	40
Maverick Missile	95	35
20mm Cannon M61A1	60	35
25mm Cannon GAU-12	55	30
30mm Cannon GAU-8 (A-10)	65	40
2.75-inch Rockets Aircraft @ medium altitude	365	190
2.75-inch Rockets Aircraft @ low altitude	225	115
2.75-inch Rockets helicopter @ 1,000m	185	100
2.75-inch Rockets helicopter @ 2,000m	305	165

Western aerial firepower lacks formal trigger distances and so generally follow US doctrine and use the 0.1% of incapacitation distance as the determinant of what is a danger close fire[135]. The key deduction from these REDs is that aircraft cannon remains the joint fires weapon of choice in applying firepower very close to own troops. Guided missiles, such as the Hellfire and Maverick, have the next lowest danger area due to their consistent accuracy and small, primarily anti-tank, warheads. This warhead means that they are only really effective against point targets.

Compared to guided missiles and cannon, unguided free fall rockets require a significantly greater safety distance. This can be improved when the firing platform is a hovering helicopter, and through closing the range. At a likely battle distance (2,000m), rockets require a larger danger area than the 2,000lb bomb, this is the largest that is routinely employed in close air support; the rockets' key advantage is that unlike most aerial weaponry they, through having multiple points of impact, are effective against area targets; they can also prolong a suppressive effect through varying the rate of fire. Semi-active laser guidance technology – such as the American Advanced Precision Kill Weapon System – turns a standard unguided 2.75-inch (70mm) rocket into a precision laser-guided rocket. Its attraction is that it is a third the cost of the Hellfire missile; with its claimed accuracy of 0.5m CEP it can defeat lightly armoured vehicles and similar targets with a small warhead that avoids collateral damage[136]. This precision munition, with its small warhead, is likely to have a very small RED; this has not yet been released into open source.

Aerial Bombs		
Weapon System	**0.1% (1 in 1000) chance of incapacitation (in metres)**	**10% (100 in 1000) chance of incapacitation (in metres)**
Cluster Bomb Unit Unguided	265	180
Cluster Bomb Unit: Wind Corrected	155	90
250lb Contact Fuze	135	35
500lb JDAM Contact Fuze	185	55
1,000lb JDAM Contact Fuze	210	75
2,000lb JDAM Contact Fuze	265	80

Sub-munitions spread over an area, rather than a conventional bomb's single point of detonation; this results in cluster munitions having a large lethal zone within the danger area that they suppress[137]. This means that cluster munitions, even without the high probability of unexploded ordnance, are unsuitable for danger close fire support. Air bursting a bomb is roughly equivalent to doubling the size of its danger area, due to its greater effect against men in the open, the criterion used to calculate risk estimate distance.

Aircrafts' range of munitions and their different means of delivery lead to complex decisions on their employment. The chart below seeks to summarise the trade-off between the ability to safely bring fire close to own troops and aircraft survivability:

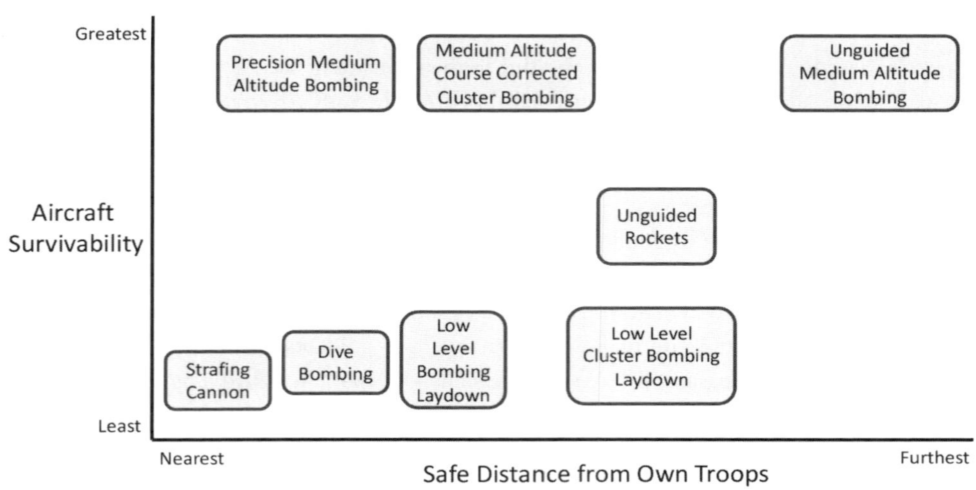

REDs can both guide a commander in determining which firepower to employ and also guide fire support capability choices. In recent conflict the use of REDs has reflected the overriding desire to avoid collateral damage; in earlier conflicts, especially in major combat operations, commanders learnt the penalty of failing to adequately suppress enemy resistance in the assault, or being unable to break up enemy attacks through defensive fires. Only this can inform a risk versus reward decision. As the commander of the American 2nd Battalion, 9th Infantry, observed in Normandy on 1 July 1944:

> *'We must teach our soldiers to remember that when they follow the artillery barrages and air strikes closely, they eventually suffer fewer casualties even though an occasional short may fall on them*[138]*.'*

Modern soldiers have rarely been exposed to this reality. Historically there are numerous examples of defenders calling mortar and artillery fire on to their own positions when this is being overrun. Their training resulted in them being confident that their field fortifications would provide protection from this fire. The Israelis have experienced this in recent years, with their heavily armoured vehicles providing sanctuary while the artillery fire defeated Arab attacks.

The disadvantage of the REDs system is its complexity, which leads to the Americans using a more battlefield friendly systems. The 1,2,3,4,5 rule of thumb provides a reasonable guide to minimum safety distances when modified by local conditions. The 'rule' translates into lifting fire at: 100m for 40mm grenades; 200m for 60mm mortar bombs; 300m for 81mm mortar bombs; 400m for 105mm artillery rounds; and 500m for 155mm artillery rounds or naval gunfire. The purpose of the 1,2,3,4,5 rule of thumb is to impart an understanding of when in an assault, fires need to be lifted to avoid own casualties; it encourages the echeloning of fires.

Despite its importance, optimising joint fires systems for danger close fires is rarely a priority during force design, hence the use of 120mm mortar and 155mm artillery to provide fire support for non-armoured infantry. Recent operations have educated a new generation of officers on the importance of danger close fires able to provide covering fire in the assault and delivering final protective fire that prevents an opponent's close assault. Despite this relearnt lesson, the continuing employment of lighter mortar and artillery calibres is being questioned. Western armies would benefit from re-emphasising the requirement for attackers to close assault a position within the two minutes that it takes defenders to recover from artillery and mortar suppressive fire.

Joint Fires and the Urban Battlefield

> *'Contrary to what is often supposed, urban warfare is not more difficult than other types of warfare. The combat environment is neutral, just like every other environment … [current Western methods] are too positively controlled, too manpower-intensive, too cautious, and cede too much initiative to objectively weaker and less capable opponents*[139]*.'*
>
> David Betz and Hugo Stanford-Tuck,
> the first an academic, the second a soldier

Like much of war's future-gazing, the confident prediction that the future battlefield will be more urban has been generally accepted without the implications of this been followed through in force preparation and design[140]. We can be confident that militaries that are best prepared to leverage this neutral environment will be the most successful; unfortunately, instead of seeing this as an opportunity for their professional, regular armed forces, Western doctrine emphasises the unique tactical challenges; leading to a view that urban conflict needs avoiding. Unfortunately, this view is based on assumptions on urban warfare that are at best equivocal, if not ahistorical. This is particularly the case with firepower's role.

Past urban combat has shown the superiority of direct artillery fire over indirect area fire; this requires tube artillery or a gun mortar. Tracked vehicles are usually essential to get into most direct fire positions in damaged urban terrain; at least 152/155mm artillery or 120mm mortar calibres are required to provide the anti-material effect required by most urban targets. Tanks and other armoured fighting vehicles cannot substitute for direct fire artillery as they lack: munitions with sufficient high explosive content, the necessary elevation to engage high-rise targets, and sufficient rounds, both on the vehicle and within their resupply chain. Of course, our World War Two forebears realised this, and so in addition to assault guns, they always had a proportion of their tanks equipped with larger calibre cannon. These were less suited for long-range anti-tank operations, but were essential in urban operations. Western infantry fighting vehicles are also almost always equipped with high velocity guns to take on other armoured vehicles. As a result, modern infantry may have superior hand-held weapons, but they lack effective anti-material direct fire support from their personal carriers and supporting tanks.

Fortunately the ability to destroy individual buildings and strongpoints with precision munitions is changing the character of urban fighting and reducing the need for direct fire. Once a strongpoint is identified it can easily be destroyed by precision firepower, leading defenders to focus on mobile defence from multiple fighting positions. Improved accuracy should allow the munition to be targeted at vulnerable points; resulting in a lesser blast requirement. However, in the case of the 155mm Excalibur round, guidance resulted in a much reduced payload, leading American troops to favour the guided MLRS munition when assaulting buildings. The medium artillery shell (150–155mm calibre) has traditionally been effective against most material targets, however this has been challenged by stronger civil construction methods. The Russian 240mm mortar and large aerial munitions – 2,000 lbs or larger – are required against the strongest urban structures.

Of course, collateral damage concerns are the principal restriction preventing Western forces from indiscriminately unleashing their firepower, but there also considerable practical concerns; poorly directed area fires will both improve opposing defensive positions, and hinder manoeuvre. Empirical evidence of the impact of rubble is a 50% increase in the defender's effectiveness. Widespread infrastructure damage also prevents the effective targeting of munitions solely reliant upon precision point mensuration. Urban terrain significantly increases the lethality of thermobaric munitions, plus they offer a reduced chance of producing rubble.

Urban terrain multiplies the number of possible firing points; suppressing all of these with direct or indirect firepower is likely to be impossible, this makes screening by mortar and artillery smoke munitions indispensable for above-ground movement. In the Chechen War, considerable use was made by the Russians of white phosphorous against buildings, both in the anti-personnel role, and to start fires, illumination munitions can also be used to start fires, and attackers can exploit the resultant smoke and confusion.

Suppressing ground-based air defences is an even greater challenge in urban terrain. The vulnerability of rotary-wing operations over un-cleared urban areas will chiefly limit them to the urban/rural fringe, or in direct fire support of ground forces firing 'over the shoulder'. Fighter-bombers will favour medium-altitude delivered precision munitions to avoid the lower altitudes contested by easily concealed missiles and guns.

Ground force manoeuvre has historically been the dominant form of target acquisition; this is likely to continue due to urban terrain degrading the effectiveness of technical sensors. Leading to military targets merging into the urban background. In addition to challenging target acquisition, urban terrain challenges munitions that rely upon the strong contrast of a vehicle against the background terrain. This specifically applies to sensor-fuzed munitions with their primitive target acquisition systems. Urban terrain also tests counter-battery operations, as sound ranging is often masked by intervening terrain, and buildings can hide the trajectory of artillery munitions from weapon locating radars.

So how should an army equip itself for urban conflict? First what it does not need is more range; even operations in megacities will allow short ranged indirect fire support to comfortably keep pace with manoeuvre. Most urban fire support will be provided by organic weapons and much of this will be direct fire. Even platoon level assault groups will need field artillery firing over open sights, preferably 152/155mm gun-howitzers, preferably also armoured and tracked. Employing the 120mm gun-mortar as organic battalion fire support provides a similar capability. Indirect fire needs to be dedicated to providing guaranteed support for assaulting infantry. As a minimum, 25% of tube artillery and mortar munitions should be a combination of base ejection and white phosphorous smoke. To engage the strongest structures, larger calibre general support artillery is required; the Russian 240mm mortar has excelled in this role. This system relies upon laser guidance; ideally any future western munition should be dual laser and coordinate-seeking guidance. The Unitary MLRS rocket is ideal as its warhead design is optimised for its blast, so restricting its danger zone; but establishing a sufficiently accurate grid reference in a shell damaged city will be challenging, hence the need for laser guidance.

Aviation should be optimised for close air support with a combination of stand-off anti-material missiles and close-in suppressive cannon and guided folded-fin rockets. As an opponent will rarely provide opportunities to prosecute a deep battle, airpower will primarily support the close battle. Aircraft should employ a combination of coordinate-seeking and laser-guided munitions optimised for danger close (250–500lbs bombs), and the destruction of large buildings (upwards of 2,000lbs bombs). The proven effectiveness of thermobaric warheads should lead to them being the standard rocket and aerial munition in urban fighting.

Target acquisition needs to similarly adjust to the character of urban fighting. In the close battle, most target engagement will be conducted by the fire support teams with the lead infantry companies, often relaying fire missions initiated by the lead rifleman. The firepower deep battle cannot rely upon sound ranging and weapon locating radars; the most effective technical target acquisition system will be unmanned aerial systems. Small hovering un-manned aircraft will be the most survivable, through operating within urban clutter.

Their ability to look behind the building will often make them more effective than sophisticated stand-off surveillance.

Following their doctrine. Western armies will of course try to avoid urban warfighting, and when they become involved they will seek to minimise their use of firepower. However, when the political objective outweighs this concern they will undertake urban conflict, and they need to wage it in a decisive manner. The 'Thunder Runs' of the 2003 Iraq invasion, achieved their immediate political purpose, but they were not decisive in terms of conflict resolution. In contrast, the Battles of Mosul and Raqqa appear to have struck the decisive blows against the Islamic State, at the price of effectively destroying much of these cities. The challenge is to achieve a decisive victory without unacceptable collateral damage. This is possible through an effective target acquisition system linked to precise direct fire and precision indirect fire. If civilians are being used as a human shield, then non-precision indirect fire may well have to be restricted to smoke munitions. Using firepower effectively, and reducing the quantity of assaulting infantry to the absolute minimum, are the keys to avoiding excessive own casualties.

War Without Reciprocity

> *'The British papers' description of sending eight RAF [Royal Air Force] Tornado jets to bomb Islamic State militants in 2014 as "going to war" gives some idea of how far the distortion has gone. Imagine the shock that would result if those terrorists were able to visit similar levels of force on Britain in response*[141]'.
>
> Reporter and Historian Mark Urban

Clausewitz identifies reciprocity as the true mark of warfare. The leading powers have grown used to fighting with such superiority that their opponents' response is limited in means and geography. Through their control of the air (except at the lowest levels) and the sea, the major military powers can largely isolate their ground based opponents. This is being challenged. The Tamils in Sri Lanka were always a partial exception, as they contested the maritime environment; the most capable non-state forces and insurgencies are now effectively using drones; obviously, the 9/11 attacks were by far the most significant exceptions to this rule; they were a strategic use of airpower. The Saudi's have also failed to isolate their operations in Yemen against the Houthi, as the Iranians have provided them with the weaponry (ballistic and cruise missiles plus drones) to strike Saudi Arabia.

Despite this, both the Western nations and the Russians have largely limited their adversaries' ability to directly strike back to terrorism and cyber warfare, or indirectly through media operations. This lack of reciprocity has allowed American-led coalitions to assume that they can define and isolate the theatre of conflict, giving them the freedom to choose whether to engage and disengage; resulting in a limited-liability approach to warfare. The naval strategist Julian Corbett identified that this was also the case in the first age of globalisation, due to the West's undisputed mastery of the oceans:

> *'when the Power desiring limited war is able to command the sea to such a degree as to be able not only to isolate the distant object, but to also render impossible the invasion of his own territory*[142]*.'*

If anything, the less interconnected 19th century offered an even greater degree of isolation than in our current information age, but the dynamic is similar.

In recent counter-insurgencies, through controlling all the domains other than the land one, Western forces have exercised control of the operational level of war; however, dominance at the operational level does not always translate into an easy tactical challenge for the soldier on the ground, as the insurgent can usually initiate engagements on their terms and employs tactics that dislocate the advantages of regular armies – firepower, mobility, logistics and operational coherence. This means that in the contested land domain, it is the insurgents who often have the tactical initiative.

This character of conflict has conditioned Western forces into assuming that the enemy will only intermittently compete above the ground tactical level; this has allowed them to carefully calibrate the application of force to meet domestic sensibilities. This has generally involved a technological approach to conflict that has sought to minimise unintended consequences, particularly in the application of firepower.

Western militaries have grown used to being the sole determinant of escalation, and so are unpractised in dealing with an opponent having this option. In addition, by avoiding a true 'Clausewitzian duel' the West has not experienced war's organic tendency to spiral out of control. Acclimatised to this paradigm, any challenge to the *status quo* is seen as an alarming innovation, rather than warfare re-establishing its true character. Any new development of course provokes military bureaucracies to create new acronyms; in this case, Russia and China's ability to contest the sea and air domains is currently being described as anti-access/area denial, or A2/AD. Of course, from the operational perspective this is a very serious development, but its psychological impact is greater due to the Western nations having grown accustomed to unchallenged dominance in these environments, leading to the acceptance that an area is denied as opposed to what it really is: contested. Failing to understand this is the outcome of not being fully challenged in recent warfighting.[143] As Daniel L. Davis identified:

> *'never since Vietnam has any enemy formation had any chance of inflicting a tactical defeat on U.S. forces. Not in Grenada, Desert Storm, Bosnia, Kosovo, Serbia, the conventional phase of Operation Iraqi Freedom, nor any phase of counter-insurgency operations since 9/11. Not one of our combat opponents over the past four decades has had a capable air force, effective tank, artillery, or infantry force, helicopter fleet, missile force, anti-air capability, or an effective logistic and supply chain*[144]*'.*

Recent non-reciprocity has also encouraged the paradigm of believing that intelligence can accurately predict the enemy's capabilities, and so the character of the future battle. The historical experience has been the need for successful militaries to rapidly adjust to an opposition's unexpected force employment; effective militaries have been those with the flexibility and adaptability to change in contact with the enemy. Building on the work of the British historian Michael Howard, the Israeli former brigade commander and now historian, Meir Finkel, identified the conceptual, doctrinal, cognitive, command organisational and technological elements of successful adaption[145]. The American Army in World War Two stands out as an exceptionally innovative force, as Field Marshal Rommel identified: *'What was astonishing was the speed with which the Americans adapted to modern warfare*[146]*'*. And yet the same Army has been exceptionally slow to adapt to the character of conflict when opposing insurgents. The key factor being that mistakes are rarely as comprehensively punished in insurgency as in conventional war, leading to false approaches enduring rather than been discredited.

One of the results of recent wars' lack of reciprocity, from a Western perspective, is that it reduces the chance of dramatic military reverses. These are often productive engines of change, the maxim 'necessity is the mother of invention' has its counterpart in 'adversity is the father of evolution'. Once militaries are able to fight, regardless of how ineffectively, largely without institutional danger, they lose the driver for change. As the Turkish proverb says: *'one disaster is worth a thousand pieces of advice'*[147]. The Russian defeat in the First Chechen War was a considerable stimulant to military reform, as was the confusion of the first few days of the Georgian War; Israel's continuous conflict with Hezbollah and Hamas has spurred innovation on all sides.

Western Self-Imposed Limitations on Firepower

'allow our swords to grow blunt by and by, through humanitarianism, until someone steps in with a sharp sword and cuts our arms off our bodies[148]*.'*

Clausewitz

The traditional Western way in warfare has focussed on the use of overwhelming force to achieve victory in decisive battle; when this achieved annihilation, it has largely settled strategy. The historian Victor Davis Hanson has chronicled this approach from the 5th century BCE Greek hoplite to this day. Hence his criticism of the current reticence to ruthlessly employ overwhelming force is rooted in historical analysis:

'The way to combat the West is to appeal to either its generosity of spirit or its guilt in hopes that it will call itself off, and thus hand to terrorists and dictators a stalemate that will soon be seen as a victory of sorts, stolen from the jaws of assured defeat[149]*.'*

The Western tradition primarily sees decisiveness in warfare as a means of reducing its adverse impact; twin-tracked with this is a desire to minimise its impact on non-combatants and restrict weaponry, usually unsuccessfully, as in the 12th century ban on the crossbow. This is central to the just war approach and the international laws of armed conflict, which are largely derived from this tradition. How these laws are currently interpreted reflects the West's internationalist approach, with its emphasis on global liberal governance, transnational humanitarianism, development, economic liberalisation, social development and the politics of international security[150]. A tension arises when a desire to minimise human suffering is detrimental to effective warfighting, so preventing fighting from decisively achieving war's political objective. This can prolong conflict and human suffering.

As the West's current warfighting culture has evolved without peer competition their militaries are conditioned to seek a comprehensive approach that employs all the levers of power in achieving conflict's political purpose. Self-evidently, conducting effective conventional warfighting within such a comprehensive approach is by necessity constraining. Some theorists have seen this as highly desirable, with the current Western warfighting practices acting as a driver to the development of a liberal way of war[151]. This development can make the practical employment of lethal force more challenging, not least in its psychological impact on to the traditional warrior ethos[152]; this leads to the embedding of *'civilian modes of warfare' resulting in cultural challenges for the military*[153]'.

The requirement for a comprehensive approach, particularly in counter-insurgency, is incontestable; however, this approach can marginalise the use of force, and specifically that delivered by joint fires. This aversion to the use of firepower has at times gone beyond a rational 'risk versus reward' calculation, particularly given the general lack of understanding of accuracy, weapon yield and likelihood of collateral damage[154]. Aversion to the use of firepower has led to refraining from its use being seen as key to successful 'people-centric' counter-insurgency warfare, leading General Richards, former British Chief of the Defence Staff, to state that: *'in wars among the people, if you are using a lot of firepower, you are almost certainly losing*[155]'.

The West's desire to be more discriminating with its firepower has driven greater precision and greater munition reliability; this leads to more efficient use of firepower in conventional warfighting, as well as making it more usable in counter-insurgency. However, this approach can be taken too far, leading to the equating by some militaries of the employment of precision low-yield weapons with the only 'legal' and 'legitimate' form of firepower, as opposed to recognising that in the laws of armed conflict the binding test is firepower's military necessity[156]. Customary practice on recent counter-insurgency and terrorism operations has been towards a restrictive interpretation of 'proportionality', so limiting the application of force. Operationally this has encouraged a slow build-up of the use of force that has negated much of firepower's psychological impact; this approach can elongate the conflict and can ultimately lead to significantly greater attrition. An extreme exponent of the traditional Western way of war, General Curtis LeMay, held the following views:

> *'If you are going to use military force, then you ought to use overwhelming military force. Use too much and deliberately use too much; you'll save lives, not only your own, but the enemy's too*[157]*.'*

Authoritarian regimes are normally not constrained by a desire to moderate their use of force; hence they continue to employ weapons disavowed by some Western militaries. This current disconnect could result in a potential authoritarian opponent doubting the West's actual willingness to use all the weapons in its armoury. Mao Zedong famously referred to America as a 'Paper Tiger', identifying that the physical possession of military power is irrelevant without a preparedness to use it: '*It is not simply the weapons one has in one's arsenal that give one flexibility, but the willingness and ability to use them*[158]'. An authoritarian opponent could compound this desire for restraint by employing tactics and technology that seek to nullify those technologies that enable the West's improved discrimination. Not only will GPS spoofing directly make Western forces less combat effective, but it could also lead them to questioning whether such weapons can *legitimately* be employed in circumstances where collateral damage would result if their accuracy cannot be guaranteed.

Western militaries have made themselves vulnerable to being dislocated by an adversary through viewing greater precision as almost an end in itself. This has led some adherents of precision warfare to seeing this as an inevitable destination, independent of war's nature and character:

> *'while it has taken US ground forces longer to migrate to precision-centric operations than American fixed-wing air and naval forces, the US Army and Marine Corps appear to be well down this path'* [159].

The chief danger of the 'lowest yield precision munition approach' is that it can lead to the self-denial of the most effective means of warfighting, with this imperceptibly becoming the military norm. This is the rationale behind one piece of American military research only envisaging the use of low-yield air-delivered ordnance (500lb or less) in urban conflict[160]. This is of course not the recent Israeli experience, or that of 2003 when significantly larger ordinance (2,000lb) was vital to delivering operational success in Baghdad and Basra. This is a point reinforced by recent fighting against the Islamic State.

An opponent can accentuate this caution in the use of firepower through ensuring that any 'bombing errors' – whether or not they actually occurred – are widely publicised. The new media of Twitter, Facebook and Instagram is ideal for this purpose, as it has conditioned its audience to have their perceptions shaped by information in sound bites and images. The response to this is the Western military's current emphasis on strategic communication, information activity and the establishment of a coherent campaign narrative; again, the prominence given to this in military decision-making can reinforce the tendency to impose restrictions on the use of firepower. This gives a further advantage to authoritarian regimes, which are largely immune to the media's influence.

In recent conflict, the desire to avoid civilian casualties has been less important than having these deaths directly attributed to Western forces; this rationale led to restrictions on the use of NATO airpower in Afghanistan, which allowed the Taliban to kill more civilians. When the then UK Prime Minister Tony Blair announced his nation's involvement in Afghanistan, he declared: *'The military plan has been put together mindful of our determination to do all we humanely can to avoid civilian casualties*[161].' This of course sets severe limitations on the conduct of military operations. As Murphy's Law dominates war, it in particular restricts the employment of weapons that can be easily attributed through in-built video recording, leading to a significant disconnect between the employment of force by the air and land components, with air forces often being more accountable due to the technology they use. At the same time that the Israeli artillery were using unguided shells against targets in the Gaza Strip, their air force limited themselves to precision guided weapons, directed by a targeting process that minimises the chance of collateral damage[162].

Following the maxim that the only legitimate purpose of war is a more perfect peace, warfighting needs to be conducted in a way that ensures speedy conflict termination, while remaining within the laws of war[163]. Too much restraint could lead to defeat, or more likely, a failure to achieve a military victory that leads to a sustainable peace. This challenge can be compounded by the influence of the comprehensive approach; leading to the setting of political goals for societal change which may meet international liberal norms, but are beyond the means of military forces to deliver. In seeking to employ a liberal way of war, the West has prolonged conflict, giving licence to the other Horsemen of the Apocalypse[164]. This has led to more deaths occurring through famine and pestilence than actual war. As John Stuart Mills observed: '*War is an ugly thing, but it is not the ugliest of things*[165]'.

Joint Fires: A System-of-Systems?

> '*The more important the subject and the closer it cuts to the bone of our hope and needs, the more we are likely to err in establishing a framework for analysis*[166].'
>
> Steven J. Gould, system scientist

Effective employment of firepower relies upon the networking of the munition and its delivery system with information collection, fusion, dissemination, and command and control; this system-of-systems is the iterative result of a century of conflict that has seen constant evolution and rebalancing between each individual form of firepower. Despite this, given that there are five main categories of joint fire delivery system – aircraft, aviation, tube and rocket artillery, and mortars – it is often postulated that there must be overlapping capability. A view that can be articulated as: 'we have five means of putting high explosive onto a target, so we must have too many'.

All five of these delivery means are part of the current firepower system-of-systems because they have proved their worth in a range of characters of conflict. The balance between the providers of joint fire has been tested and refined; inefficient approaches have been discarded in war's Darwinian struggle. What is left is largely mutually supporting, rather than competing; employed together, often their impact can be greater than the sum of their parts. This variety also reflects the need to react to change, particularly in technology, which prevents the overall system from achieving any long-term stasis.

After the evidence of history our best guide to military decision-making is operational analysis that is based upon historic data; however, regardless of the sophistication of the simulation, it is difficult to model the complexity of a system-of-systems. The wargaming models used in most force and weapon development tend to focus on materiel, and rarely adequately account for force employment[167]. The evidence they collect is usually the summation of individual target effect, determined by working back from the target to identify which opposing weapon systems can strike and have an effect; delivering fire in concert with manoeuvre is rarely simulated with any degree of sophistication. This approach fails to adequately model the very things – integration with manoeuvre, persistence, guarantee, consistency of fire and suppressive effect – that make fire support effective. As a result, peacetime operational analysis generally underrates mortars and cannon and usually concludes that a modern combat aircraft can 'service' almost all targets. That there is much more to warfare than engaging targets is one of this book's enduring themes.

Systems theory has been developed to identify the relationship between discrete elements of a closed system, this makes it capable of understanding firepower from an overall system-of-systems perspective through focussing on outcomes. Firstly, it provides a theoretical understanding as to why armies have iteratively developed multiple means of producing firepower. Secondly, it allows us to understand whether this is still a valid approach, or has a particular form of firepower gained predominance, or been supplanted. Thirdly, it allows us to understand the impact of variations away from the established norm, in particular, any unintended consequences.

A subset of this discipline is socio-technical systems theory; this can be used to identify the four constituent elements in this system-of-systems. There are the actors, which are the delivery platforms: artillery, mortars, aircraft and their munitions. Then there are the processes that decide on target acquisition and engagement. Thirdly there is the command and control structures that organise and employ fires. Crucially this includes coordinating fire with manouevre forces. Finally, there are the supporting technologies and tools: the fires command, information and terminal control systems. These four elements divide into social and technical systems as follows:

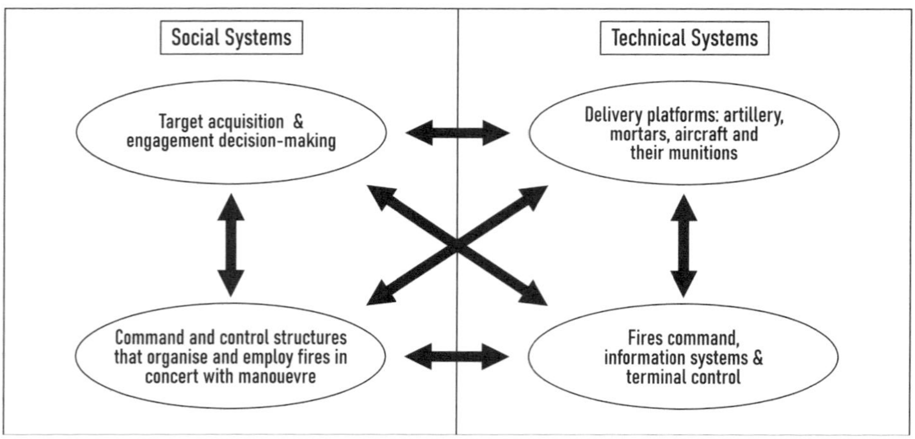

The target-focussed approach that is favoured by most military decision support wargames concentrates on the technical system. Within this it heavily favours the actors, focussing on the platforms and munitions, while discounting the social aspects. This leads to the fallacious view that users of firepower can be agnostic of its source. This is the logical endpoint for those who see warfare as largely an exercise in matching munitions to targets, with the bit in between being a mere 'bag of tricks', to use the air force vernacular. For example, the Hellfire missile can be fired from an attack helicopters, light aircraft, gunship or drone. The differences between these weapon systems in target acquisition, engagement decision-making, terminal control, command, control and information systems almost makes the use of same missile irrelevant.

This system-of-systems approach explains why Western air and artillery fire support systems differ. The target-focussed forward air controller is trained to employ aerial munitions; this leads to an allocation process that puts the controller and the aircraft in direct communication. Effectively utilising aerial firepower in the land battle is a secondary consideration, and in most militaries this skill receives only limited formal training. This approach is effective in ensuring that weapons are accurately and safely put on a target; but this is largely a technical and not tactical exercise. The size of the circles represents the investment that the forward air controller system puts into each element of the firepower system-of-systems:

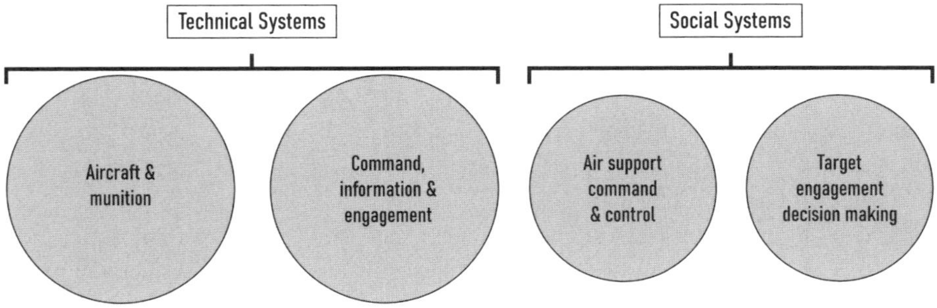

In contrast, the artillery controller is part of a fire support system that is fully integrated into both the artillery and manoeuvre chain of command; this aims at ensuring that firepower is correctly employed in concert with manoeuvre. Most air/land integration structures choose not to invest in the decision-making and command and control structures that would address this. Aware of its chosen limitations, air support systems in many militaries work in concert with the better resourced artillery chain of command, leading to a reliance upon artillery command and control structures to ensure that aerial firepower meets the tactical requirement. The artillery approach leads to a balanced system-of-systems:

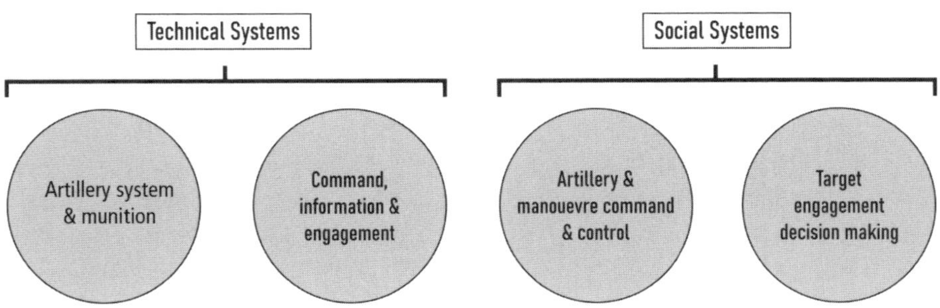

The joint fires system-of-systems has been created by an iterative process, and so militaries must be wary of the unintended consequences of deviating from an established system. Physicist and complexity expert Yaneer Bar-Yam, in *Making Things Work*, identified: '*if we take one part of the system away … how will the rest of the system be affected?*[168]'. In this context, the question is how will a change to one joint fires element have a bearing on the whole system? This means that it is not sufficient to analyse the ability of close air support to replace the target effect of artillery and mortars; instead the question to ask is; what is the impact on airpower's wider contribution if aircraft are used as a substitute for organic firepower? If a systems approach is used to examine Operation Anaconda, in Afghanistan in 2002, then joint fires failed to operate effectively as a system-of-systems. Airpower became fixed in providing fire support for increasingly desperate ground forces, at the expense of them conducting their designated mission: destroying retreating Taliban and Al-Qaeda forces. Routine fire support was a task that could be better performed by howitzers and mortars; freed from this airpower could have used its reach and lethality to inflict the desired attrition on the perpetrators of 9/11.

Taking a systems theory approach provides an explanation of why the whole system matters, and provides a useful tool in analysing the balance within the joint fires system of systems. It provides a theoretical basis for why the processes, structures, tools and technologies matter in fire support; this means that the user cannot be agnostic of the firepower's source. This is why, regardless of how effective a platform and its munitions are at engaging a target, they need to be part of a coherent fire support system.

Of course, all armies aim at a firepower system that requires the least adjustment to the next character of conflict; the most prescient recognise that evolution in conflict will probably lead to them fielding more firepower. The form that this firepower takes is often only revealed in conflict – though, between the World Wars, Soviet theorists with their empirical approach to military science proved to be the most astute forecasters. Systems theory provides modern militaries with the tools to be equally astute.

Chapter 6: Joint Firepower Military Thought, Doctrine and Force Employment

'That we henceforth be no more children, tossed to and fro, and carried about with every wind of doctrine'...

Ephesians 4:14

This chapter surveys land firepower's military thought, doctrine, and finally force employment, or what is actually applied in conflict. It will identify that the considerable body of airpower theory, and its derivative doctrine, is at its weakest in the engagement of land forces; this is probably key to the repeated failure of air/land integration at the start of conflicts. While, despite its longevity, artillery wholly lacks overarching theory; in opposition to Hayek's observation that '*Without theory the facts are silent*[1]', an absence of written theory and doctrine is not seen as an insurmountable hurdle. Instead underpinning theory and doctrine will be derived from analysing practical application[2].

Clausewitz determined that the correct doctrine was one of three factors that could counteract the negative impact of fog and friction on military operations; he illustrated this by describing a battery firing at the wrong target[3]. JFC Fuller called doctrine the '*central idea of an army*[4]. Despite its importance, few armies have specific firepower doctrine. As a result, firepower's overall contribution to warfare lacks an intellectual framework to guide analysis; what there is in Western doctrine tends to focus on fire support, providing only limited guidance on the deep battle and specifically its tackling of the opposing fire system. This does not apply to Soviet/Russian doctrine, which blends firepower and manoeuvre and it sees them as largely interchangeable. With the employment of airpower as a subsidiary element in this all arms battle. This has prevented them from developing an equivalent of NATO's joint warfighting doctrine.

Given the lack of specific joint fires theory and doctrine publications, studying how militaries actually fight is the best approach to determining the conceptual underpinning of the use of firepower[5]. This approach recognises that official doctrine, customary practice, and accepted thought are interwoven elements leading to how a force is employed; even where formal doctrine exists, we must recognise that unofficial or unrecorded customary practice and procedures can dominate a military's culture. This is because cultures are best understood as the socially transmitted pattern of human behaviour within an organisation; this applies to all armies, including the Imperial German Army, despite it being the origin of significant elements of current military practice[6]. It also recognises that a military culture imparts doctrine by shared ambience as much as explicit teaching; this means that it is often counter-productive to try and artificially separate firepower theory, doctrine, tactics, techniques, and procedures. This means that Colin S Gray's definition of doctrine – *'guidance, mandatory or discretionary, on what is believed officially to be contemporary best military practice'* – is too tight a definition to understand joint fires[7]. An example of the challenge of literally applying what is written is that most close air support terminology dates back to World War Two, much of this is still used, but what it is now used to describe has considerably evolved from the original.

Unlike artillery and mortars, airpower has benefited from a significant body of military theory, though it lacks a master theorist of the stature of Clausewitz, Sun Tzu, Corbett or Mahan, though Giulio Douhet comes close. It is a fair criticism that this theory has often been speculatively ahead of airpower's current capability – at times this has been the deliberate intent. The American pioneer General Billy Mitchell controversially identified: *'in the development of air power one has to look ahead and not backwards and figure out what is going to happen, not too much what has happened'*[8]. This rejection of the requirement for empirical evidence contrasts with most orthodox doctrine development, and through promising what cannot practically be delivered, theory's actual impact on real operations has been questioned:

> *'There has been no lack of [airpower] theorists, but they have had only a limited influence in a field where the effects of technology and the deeds of practitioners have from the beginning played greater roles than have ideas*[9]*.'*

Much of airpower theory, and certainly the most speculative ideas, have focussed on the independent strategic and operational role. Lack of theory, plus its lack of status within many air forces, led to close air support practice rarely being treasured[10]. As General OP Weyland, the Korean War Commander of Far East Air Forces, identified:

> *'What was remembered from World War II was not written down, or if written down was not disseminated, or if disseminated was not read or understood'*[11].

Lacking a solid basis in theory, and with often only a cursory coverage in capstone doctrine publications, artillery and mortar publications are usually at the level of operating manuals. The most useful quantify the firepower required to achieve a target effect; this also forms the basis of firepower norms that some armies now embed within their fire control systems. Lacking the grounding provided by a clear conceptual framework with agreed principles, surface-to-surface fires have often proved to be more responsive to fashionable, but unempirical, trends than airpower[12].

Aviation has had a curious mix of theory and practice. American soldier-innovators led prior to and during the Vietnam War, when theory certainly followed practice. Subsequently, in the 1980s AirLand battle doctrine led to aviation's focus on massed deep strike. Some argue that this has been a doctrinal *cul-de-sac*[13]; it certainly has had little bearing on aviation's actual employment on recent operations.

We should not assume that the current prominence of written doctrine has always been the case. It is a relatively modern development which Hew Strachan identified was a product of the post-Vietnam War American Army: *'Doctrine became the one device by which it [the Army] sought to reassert its professional self-worth*[14]'. General William DePuy, the first commander of the

Army's Training and Doctrine Command (TRADOC), made doctrine writing a core function, the business of generals[15]. With general officers leading, there is a greater willingness for armies to change their doctrine; it became part of the competition for career advancement[16], becoming more responsive to the needs of the institution's change agenda rather than being the distilled lessons from the past and resulting in doctrine reflecting an organisation's aspiration. General DePuy identified a very human desire for a break with the past: *'This [AirLand doctrine] manual takes the Army out of the rice paddies of Vietnam and places it on the Western European battlefield against the Warsaw Pact*[17]*'*. As attack aviation illustrates, doctrine can be out of synch with actual force employment; this reinforces the point that the soundest approach is to look at what an army actually does, rather than its doctrinal aspiration.

Understanding a doctrinal approach to the employment of firepower is aided by examining ownership and control. Ownership is firepower's command relationship; this is whether firepower is directly commanded by the commanding general or delegated to subordinate commanders. Direct command of firepower is made possible by a discrete firepower chain of command (usually artillery led) that empowers the commanding general to exercise his authority separate from the hierarchical manoeuvre chain of command. Control over the use of this firepower can either be centralised or delegated; this delegation can be either a forward air controller or artillery observer or for direct fire the pilot or gun commander – the key criteria being who is best placed to conduct the engagement. Below are a series of national firepower systems examined from the criteria of ownership and control:

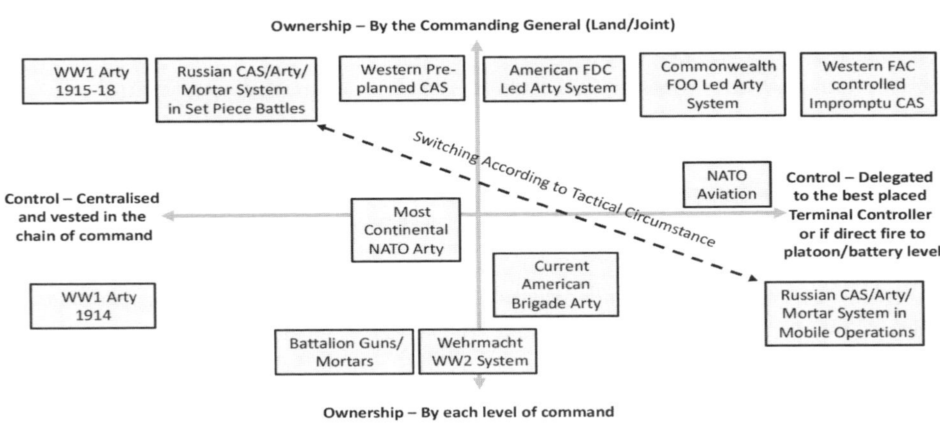

Battalion/Regimental Level Mortar and Artillery Fire Support

'If you want to prevent your troops from manoeuvring, embarrass them with guns ... A line of infantry supported by good, properly established batteries retains its order of battle better[18]*'*.

General Augustin Lespinasse on battalion guns

The close fight requires responsive and guaranteed fires, with the immediate suppression of a target often being valued more than its eventual destruction. Before the introduction of the modern mortar in World War One, tube artillery was the standard means of providing this intimate fire support. From the 17th century most European armies employed a couple of light artillery pieces as 'battalion guns' to provide organic fire support[19]. Napoleon may have achieved most of his victories through massed artillery; but, against General Lespinasse's advice, the decline in quality of French infantry in 1808–12 led to the reintroduction of the battalion guns to boost unit combat power[21]. Without Napoleon's genius and his separate artillery chain of command, massed artillery was largely replaced in the 19th century by direct support artillery at brigade or divisional level; but it remained common practice for a pair of guns to reinforce a battalion or company's firepower when it was occupying a defensive position with an inadequate field of fire, or to shoot-in an attack[20].

The Great War's character of conflict led to artillery's physical withdrawal from the front line, and its centralisation at the corps or army level. Despite their mass and duration, fire plans rarely silenced all the defences. Inadequate communications meant that indirect fire could not be directed against this remaining resistance; this meant that assaulting troops needed artillery firing over open sights to overcome undefeated enemy positions. However, the preliminary bombardment's impact on the terrain usually made it extremely challenging to carry forward heavy weapons. With the return to semi-mobile warfare in 1918, transiting the battlefield became less of a challenge and it became normal practice to allocate guns and heavy mortars to assaulting infantry. The importance of artillery direct fire led the Canadian Corps to specify that when an infantry battalion had a battery under command, four guns provided indirect fire, with a two-gun section firing over open sights[22].

Battalion guns are the simplest form of artillery command and control. They are favoured by armies who see infantry-led operations, rather than combined arms, as decisive on the battlefield. The Japanese were the only major army in World War Two to be heavily influenced by this doctrine, leading to their three divisional field artillery battalions regularly decentralising their batteries to reinforce the two 70mm Type 92 infantry guns in each infrantry battalion. With maximum range of 2,785m (3,060 yards) this cannon was unsuitable for any other task. Similar infantry guns were organic to battalions and regiments of most Continental armies in World War Two; their chief advantage over mortars was their ability to conduct direct fire. But by the end of this war, infantry operated anti-tank guns and recoilless rifles could also fire a munition with an effective high explosive content at undefeated strongpoint, as could tanks, often in the guise of assault guns, in World War Two. At the same time that all these options became available, reliable wireless communications meant that indirect fire had the flexibility to provide timely impromptu fire support; this led to artillery direct fire, in all but Soviet-influenced armies, being less common after 1945 in advanced militaries.

However, armies lacking the ability to conduct indirect fire continued to place their artillery under infantry battalion command. This was the case with most of the Chinese artillery in the 1979 War with Vietnam. People's Liberation Army gunners often did not understand how to correctly conduct reconnaissance, determine accurate surveys, make firing calculations, and communicate with the manoeuvre forces. This limited indirect fire to prominent terrain features or inaccurate fire on smaller targets[23].

Organic battalion firepower can support both the manoeuvreist and the attritional approaches to warfighting. The original battalion guns were designed to boost a battalion's small arms; largely firing canister, an anti-personnel munition that was in effect long-range musketry. Most infantry manned support weapons are direct fire weapons, as these can quickly and efficiently win the fire fight. Placing indirect fire onto the target area may take longer, but it has the advantage of suppressing an area, not just those parts in view. It follows that combining direct and indirect fire effectively suppresses a position, as opposed to the portion that is currently line of sight to direct fire weapons. Suppressing all of the enemy's position is key to preventing them from aggressively reacting to friendly manoeuvre.

The combining of organic direct and indirect fire support to achieve suppression was pioneered by World War One German stormtroopers, the originators of much of modern close combat tactics. At platoon level they employed a combination of machine guns, rifle grenades, light mortars and flamethrowers; company and battalion level had heavier mortars and light field guns able to defeat protected strongpoints. This firepower's aim was to suppress enemy positions hindering forward movement, so negating the requirement for an assault, which would reduce an attack's momentum. By 1917, Allied infantry were fielding a similar range of direct and indirect fire weapons[24]. The need for firepower dominance to achieve manoeuvre led the Australian General Monash's response when his infantry was getting weak in manpower: *'so long as they have 30 Lewis [machine] guns per battalion it doesn't matter*[25]*'*.

Out of World War One came two rival schools of mortaring: the 'trench artillery' approach saw their role as destroying, from short-range, enemy fortifications. The second, and dominant, mortar school saw them as not just the replacement for the tube artillery that had moved behind the front line, but as a general-purpose weapon offering a range of new capabilities. The mortar's' limited range is sufficient for a battalion's battlespace, but insufficient for them to be routinely included into a higher formation's fire support plans; this means they are normally available to deliver the infantry with guaranteed responsive fire.

Who employs them and how mortars are used provides a ready indicator of how manoeuvreist an army actually is. Battalion-level mortars are standard within the infantry; but their employment by tank units is contentious. Arguably this is partly cultural – mortars are seen in most armies as an infantry weapon. Manoeuvreist armies tend to provide all battlegroups, as opposed to just the ones based upon infantry battalions, with integral indirect fire. The requirement for mortars in armoured battalions is actually more compelling than infantry units, as tanks usually lead the advance; particularly in open terrain, as tanks are better suited to achieving and maintaining high tempo manoeuvre. Part of this is ethos, rather than just their superior protected mobility, this is captured in the expression: *'the tank halts between moves; infantrymen move between positions'*[26].

The key physical factor in enabling rapid manoeuvre when opposed by an enemy is guaranteed and responsive fire support. Having a section of mortars permanently deployed ready to fire during an advance allows manoeuvre to be covered by fire. This section is then replaced by another section when the in-place section no longer has the range to support lead forces, this is 'leap-frogging' forward, with the mortars primary purpose being to suppress opposition to allow manoeuvre. An indication of a more attritional approach is not deploying the mortars until an objective is to be assaulted. The counter argument to fielding mortars in armoured battlegroups is: that increasing the span of command to include organic fire support weapons adds complexity, which can be reduce tempo. A view that can be challenged for assuming that movement on field exercises and actual battlefield manoeuvre are synonymous. The need for guaranteed indirect fire support has convinced the Israelis, Russians and Americans to provide their armoured battlegroups with 120mm mortars. The Israelis go one further and fit 60mm mortars to all their tanks, and many of their armoured troop carriers.

The need for a mortar platoon to provide organic battalion-level fire support is almost universally accepted[27]. Task organising additional guns, and occasionally rocket launchers, under command of tank and infantry battalions is seen as the right response to certain tactical situations' for Western armies this can include urban combat; for armies following Russian doctrine, this could be any form of mobile and decentralised operations.

Centralised Western Artillery Doctrine

> *'The command of any body of artillery should be centralised under the highest commander who can exercise control[28].'*
>
> British Field Service Regulations, Volume II, 1935
> (Authored by AP Wavell)

The Napoleonic Wars saw the first systematic massing of firepower at the decisive point. In the preceding wars of the Age of Reason, in battle, artillery was divided into battalion guns and the heavier pieces that were usually spread across the army's front. Napoleon enabled artillery to become the decisive battlefield weapon by massing guns and howitzers under the command of young and aggressive officers in an independent artillery chain of command. Their task was to deploy their pieces in *Grande Batteries* to deliver overwhelming fire at the point that their commander sought to achieve a decision. Massing all available firepower remains the driving principle of the centralised firepower doctrine. This is achieved through a dual firepower and manoeuvre command structure; the firepower command chain allows the commander to control the force's firepower independent of the employment of manoeuvre forces.

World War One's centralised artillery doctrine was a response to the requirement to unlock sophisticated defences and conversely repel modern methods of attack. In pre-1914 doctrine, artillery supported the infantry; in the centralised system, artillery became a partner in the all arms battle[29]. The evolution of artillery doctrine in the conflict can be divided into three distinct systems. Firstly, in 1914 all artilleries were adjusting to an unexpected character of conflict; this saw the employment of indirect fire as a means of allowing batteries to survive, but it took time for artillery commanders and their staff to develop the processes necessary to employ it as a battle-winning weapon.

Secondly, by 1915 artillery was seen as the key to unlocking defences, this led to rigid fire planning; identifying the targets, scheduling the fire, and disseminating the fire plan could take days, and therefore was difficult to adjust to evolving tactical circumstances. The fire plan's aim was to destroy the defenders; this necessitated a long bombardment, which lost surprise and required considerable logistic support. At its attritional extreme, in the middle years of the War, manoeuvre became wholly subsidiary to the fire plan; as summarised in the view from the Battle of Verdun that *'artillery conquers and infantry occupies*[30]'. So artillery became the dominant partner in the construction of the plan. At the expense of prodigious resources, firepower could facilitate the break-in battle; this was in vain, because the telegraphing of the blow (over days and sometimes weeks) allowed the defender to reinforce the threatened sector at a faster rate than the attacking force could cross the shell damaged battlefield. Furthermore, the lack of reliable mobile communications between assaulting troops and the guns, meant that subsequent fire support was limited to those few improvised light artillery pieces and mortar tubes that could be dragged across no-mans-land. Despite more sophisticated methods being used in the final year of the war, the techniques used in 1915–17 have continued to be used. This is because they ensure the most systematic application of firepower to targets, are relatively invulnerable to counters, and minimise the need for investment in communications. Finally, with their systematic and hierarchical approach, they suit the culture of many militaries. This was effectively the Soviet approach to the employment of firepower in their set piece battles in World War Two.

The final firepower doctrine dominated the 1918 battles on the Western Front; this approach featured a more balanced, combined arms approach that became in all its essential features the modern Western form of conventional warfighting. On the offensive the role of firepower shifted from destruction to the neutralisation of the positions to be assaulted, their supporting artillery, and the defender's command and control system. The bombardment became sufficiently short as to avoid the levels of destruction that hindered battlefield movement. This was made largely possible by relatively accurate predicted fire; by avoiding the need to register individual batteries onto their targets this also preserved surprise. Like the 1915–17 system, set-piece battle fire support was provided through timed fire plans, created with the same rigour, but more expeditiously delivered, due to more effective communications. The key difference in the last year of the war was the combining of centralised firepower capable of neutralising the entire depth of an opposing defensive system, with the provision of sufficient organic fire support weapons for assaulting infantry to fight their way forward.

This combination of predicted artillery fire to neutralise a defence with stormtrooper tactics was first employed by the Germans at the Battle of Riga, starting on 3 September 1917, against the Russians. The British employed a predicted artillery plus tank battle plan at Cambrai in November 1917; once this culminated, the British were driven back by a German counter-attack that introduced their new artillery and infantry tactics to the Western Front. By the end of war, except for the Allied advantage in tanks, there was little difference between the combined arms approaches on the Western Front.

Despite its tactical success, after the war the Germans rejected their 1918 doctrine. Instead, they chose an approach that was not reliant on materiel superiority and was better able to exploit what they perceived as the inherent fighting superiority of the individual German soldier. This resulted in largely using artillery to reinforce the organic firepower of infantry and tank units. This was despite improved wireless voice communications making it significantly easier for the fire support to be provided by massed indirect fire.

Despite improved communications, initially the Western powers also forsook their 1918 approach. Instead of exploiting the flexibility made possible by portable radios, the French Army in 1940 employed a 'methodical battle' that rigidly fixed their manoeuvre arm to the progress of the fire plan[31]. This was an extreme form of synchronised warfare that aimed to centralise decision-making and achieve unity of effort by giving French generals a detailed feedback control system. French artillery observers were responsible for the technical execution of the fire plan, rather than the provision of fire support to individual manoeuvre units. For this army, the fielding of portable radios made the methods of 1915–17 more effective. In the right circumstances this could be lethal: on 12 May 1940, the 4th Panzer Division required 8 hours to advance 2km when opposed by a screen of minor elements of 3rd DLM (light mechanised division) supported by 60 guns. German veterans thought the concentration of fire was as intense as they had experienced in the Great War[32].

The British Imperial forces went into World War Two with a more flexible doctrine of centralised artillery firepower, reliant in part, on portable radio. Unfortunately, to preserve operational security, practicing wireless communications was heavily restricted in the lead-up to the German attack in 1940. The resultant emphasis on wire communication between observers and the gun line led to the British artillery being ill-prepared for the war of movement the Germans imposed on them. Over-reacting to this, the doctrine of centralised firepower was discarded in the tactical aberration of extreme dispersion that occurred in the Western Desert Campaign of 1941–42. Subsequently, the tried and tested orthodoxy was ruthlessly re-imposed by General Montgomery. A contemporary Royal Artillery officer described the approach as:

> *'The British system, so simple, so obvious, so flexible and which had taken so long to be accepted rested on (1) reserve of control at a high level, like the Americans; but (2) off-setting this with intimate trust and liaison at each level of command: no one was ever denied fire when he wanted it as a result of centralization; (3) concentration of fire; (4) giving the right to take decisions to the man at the front; (5) an obsession with speed in reply to calls for fire; and above all (6), on maintaining an elaborate system of radio communications linking every user, every agency, and every battery together[33].'*

In contrast to 1918, World War Two British infantry and armour largely became reliant on this firepower to get them onto the objective; this led the British to almost always using timed rolling barrages to provide covering fire; a failsafe approach, that often prevented the seizing of opportunities[34]. Despite professing that its purpose was neutralisation, given their manoeuvre forces' limited combat power, the British often achieved a level of firepower concentration that achieved destruction. By the end of the war, such was their fire superiority that the application of firepower dominated all other tactical methods.[35]

This doctrine of massed firepower could lead to the underestimating of the need for fire support to be decentralised to exploit opportunities; it resulted in the Royal Artillery's senior regiment rejecting using their self-propelled guns to provide direct support to their manoeuvring armoured brigade. Their view was that this was *'the antithesis of the correct use of artillery, the cardinal principle of which is concentration of fire[36]'.*

In advance of the British, the Americans had developed their own centralised command system; fielding fire direction centres in the 1930s, with the specific purpose of massing fire and manoeuvring it around the battlefield. In contrast, the British left much of the decision-making of where to employ firepower to their more senior forward observers. Their HQ based decision-making may have been the factor that led to the Americans largely favouring easier to control preparatory fire and concentrations to providing covering fire.

The exception to the centralisation of firepower in Western armies is the mortar, which continues to maintain the tradition of battalion organic firepower. However, particularly in World War Two, mortars were included in the fire plans supporting set-piece battles, on the understanding that they would then be released when their infantry committed to the fight.

Post-War, Western armies could not deploy the same level of conventional firepower, but the centralised approach remained key to maximising NATO's available artillery. The dominance of firepower over manoeuvre was captured in the American Army's 1949 Field Service Regulations:

> *'Maneuver itself can produce no decisive results, but if properly employed it makes decisive results possible through the application of firepower, through the principles of offensive, mass, economy of force and surprise[37].'*

It was not until 1968 that manoeuvre was elevated in American doctrine to an essential element of combat power; despite this belated amendment, the conventional attritional approach continued to be the NATO doctrine until AirLand Battle doctrine in the 1982. However, the Western artillery system's enabling first principle, the separation of command from control, was during the Cold War a challenge for many of the Alliance's more traditional militaries. Trusting the man-on-spot to make the right decision comes easiest in major conflict when the fog and friction of war makes it essential.

The Western system of centralised firepower is usually considered a more efficient system than the Russian approach. Chiefly because it can – without requiring a binary shift between centralisation and decentralisation – support both set piece and mobile operations, and it can seamlessly switch resources between the close and deep battles. The difference between the two can be overstated. In a deviation from established doctrine, in the pursuit of German forces across France in 1944, all American corps artillery was allocated to the divisions, and heavy artillery was initially kept behind the Seine to increase mobility; centralisation and detailed planning were abandoned to achieve responsiveness[38]. The Soviets and Russians see their system as superior, because its doctrine allows for both centralised massed firepower and the pre-planned need for decentralisation during mobile operations. Achieved by a method that is largely resilient to war's fog and friction.

Soviet/Russian Firepower Doctrine

'The attacker's success depends not so much on the degree of destruction as on the fact that the survivors are unable to fight for some time after the shelling has stopped[39].'

Chris Donnelly, The Russian artillery expert

Czarist artillery doctrine saw artillery as an arm in its own right, rather than supporting the infantry and cavalry[40]. From the 18th century their doctrine set two principal requirements: the massing of overwhelming fire for the main attack, and subsequently the provision of mobile support[41]. This tradition passed seamlessly to the Soviet regime and on to the Russian Federation. The Soviets were clear that achieving concentrated firepower necessitated *'establishing rigidly centralised troop control in the hands of the senior commander initially at critical moments of battle[42]'*. In the Great Patriotic War, the Front Commander and his senior artillery commander immersed themselves in the technicalities of the fire plan for set piece operations; this often including personal forward reconnaissance of the targets. The resultant fire plan scientifically sought to apply firepower to neutralise their opponent through their full depth, whether attacking or defending. It was executed through a fixed timed programme, and with overwhelming mass that usually achieved destruction, despite its failing to apply equal scientific vigour to making their artillery accurate. This, plus the inflexibility in execution, was why their methods had more in common with the techniques of 1915–17 than 1918. This rigidity made their fire plans vulnerable to an opponent who did not wait for its hammer blows. From 1943, a sudden withdrawal became the favoured German approach to negating Soviet firepower. Despite this, the doctrine remained in place. It was the outcome of Soviet military culture, and their practical inability to create a command and control system that fully exploited the possibilities of wireless communication.

To the Soviets, the set piece attack is effectively a preliminary operation to the exploitation[43]. Once firepower, made decisive by tanks and infantry, had achieved the breach, doctrine specified that artillery accompanied the advancing troops through enemy defences, supporting not *'just with fire but also with wheels[44]'*. The major difference from World War One was the ability of mechanised forces to rapidly advance through the breach and be an effective arm of exploitation. At the commencement of mobile operations, centralisation gave way to equally rigorous decentralisation of firepower; in addition to re-gaining control of their own artillery, Front and Army level artillery reinforced the divisions exploiting the breakthrough. Divisions delegated control of artillery all the way down to the company level. By 20–29 August 1944, in the Yassy

Kishinev Offensive, the Soviets had perfected their system. The 3rd Ukrainian Front, during the exploitation and pursuit phase, allocated every infantry battalion with an artillery battalion and in addition, every infantry company had a battery. Only a single artillery regiment was retained at divisional level[45].

The insertion of second echelon mobile forces into the battle and the subsequent change from centralised to decentralised firepower was a moment of vulnerability; to manage this, batteries were forward sited to achieve the range for maximum fire support over the battle handover. Given the limited range of most World War Two Soviet artillery pieces, this meant that batteries often had to conduct a preliminary move to occupy captured ground; this was also the time in which the Soviet airpower maximised its effort. Once the mobile forces were released, their fire support was limited to accompanying artillery and the Soviet Air Force. This approach usually suited the conditions of the Eastern Front after the Battle of Kursk, as this had destroyed the Germans' operational level reserve. On occasion, Soviet forces suffered a local defeat from German mobile forces, as they were vulnerable when not protected by centralised firepower, but the Soviets accepted this risk in return for the greater penetration mobile forces could achieve when directly supported by decentralised artillery. Through to the end of the War, there were instances of Soviet mobile forces being defeated by counter-attacks, but it was usually logistics, rather than the Germans, which halted Soviet advances. Even in Total War, this difference in appetite for risk-taking between Western and Soviet doctrine was unbridgeable.

Faced by superior numbers, German artillery was usually sited in depth, out of range of most of the positional artillery sited for the breakthrough battle. Their task was to dislocate Soviet combined arms attacks, which they sought to achieve by separating infantry and tank forces through their fire; the task was made easier by the Soviet lack of armoured personnel carriers. The Soviets sought to neutralise any battery within range of the break-through by counter battery fire, but they expected their mobile forces to be the major destroyer of German guns.

Recent operations on the Donbas have seen the Russians continue the Soviet practice of decentralising their artillery during mobile operations down to tank and infantry company level. As rocket artillery is now more common, these have also come under battalion and even company command. This has been identified as an innovation; actually, it is in accordance with their doctrine and previous Soviet and Russian practice. Between 1946 and 1957 motorised rifle battalions had an organic artillery battery and a mortar battery, in 1958, the mortar battery disappeared, leaving only a platoon, but the artillery battery remained. From 1966, the artillery was removed leaving only an 82-mm mortar platoon; this was later upgraded to eight 120-mm mortars; this remained the standard organisation of the late Cold War, with some local adaptation in Afghanistan.

If fixating on the organisation table leads to the impression that Soviet battalions lacked decentralised firepower; examining how they trained soon dispels this. In 1989 the Soviet Army Studies Office examined the force composition of 551 Soviet motorised rifle and tank battalion training exercises conducted between 1964 and 1989. The Soviets 'attached' artillery to 77% of motorised rifle battalion exercises and 73% of tank battalion exercises; attachments varied from a battery to several battalions, with an artillery battalion being the most common

(80% of the time). Artillery was 'in support[46]' for 18% of motorised rifle battalion exercises and 13% of tank battalion exercises. Whether 'attached' (the stronger command relationship of the two) or 'in support' 95% of the time Soviet motor rifle battalions trained with artillery. Tank battalions, with their different role, trained at battalion level with artillery 86% of the time[47]. In Afghanistan the operational circumstances made artillery attachments virtually permanent; whether 'in support' or 'attached', the artillery commander and his staff were co-located with the motor rifle or tank battalion commander.

Both Soviet and Russian artillery have primarily employed direct fire when attached to a tank or motor rifle battalion; firing over open sights makes artillery significantly more accurate, particularly against point targets, it also makes fire support more responsive in terms of identifying and getting rounds rapidly onto the target. Firing over open sights and employing a lower trajectory could result in a single figure time of flight; in comparison a 152/155mm gun exploiting its full indirect fire range could have a time of flight of several minutes. In the time-competitive close battle, this time difference in suppressing a target could be decisive. Direct fire was also in part a pragmatic World War Two Soviet response to their lack of trained observers and radios. Russian Missile and Artillery Troops now have sufficient resources to employ a Western-style command and control system; but for the advantages identified above, they continue to decentralise guns and favour direct fire in the mobile battle.

The Russians continue to see artillery employment in a binary fashion: either commanded by the combined arms corps commander and controlled by the artillery chain of command, or decentralised down to company level. This doctrine was recently restated in the Russian Army Digest: '*Artillery will be attached to the combined arms subunits or will provide artillery support under the direction of the senior commanders*[48].' In the sort of battle that the Russians foresee against a peer opponent, their reduced reliance on communications, and extensive employment of direct fire, makes them less vulnerable to the modern battlefield's contested electro-magnetic spectrum. Hence their willingness to inflict fratricide on their own ability to command and control if it equally degrades their opponent's; the same applies to GPS denial.

From the World War Two German perspective, both of the artillery systems they faced were extremely effective. But the Anglo-American system, through its greater flexibility and agility, had a more pervasive effect on their battlefield operations, not just during set piece battles. Anglo-American artillery, in concert with tactical airpower effectively prevented almost any manoeuvre in the open. The 26th Panzer Division failed to recognise the changed character of conflict when it arrived in the Italian Theatre from the Eastern Front. As one British brigade commander put it:

> '*the enemy moved about in front with vehicles and on foot in the open without any covering fire and we shot them to hell with our artillery*[49]'.

The Western system artillery requires considerable investment in command and control, both equipment and skilled personnel. It can also challenge armies whose internal culture requires both the ownership and employment of fire support to coincide. Adopting the most efficient modern approach can require unpalatable trade-offs that historically militaries have been unwilling to accept[50]. This has led many militaries to favour the greater clarity provided by the more hierarchical and delineated Soviet/Russian approach.

Decentralised Firepower Doctrine

'the day goes to the side that is first able to plaster its opponent with fire[51].'

Field Marshal Rommel

Officially the Wehrmacht started World War Two with effectively the same artillery doctrine as the 1918 Reichsheer. This combined centralised firepower that could neutralise the entire depth of an opposing defensive system, with sufficient organic fire support for the assaulting infantry to fight their way forward. Pre-war, massed fire was certainly practiced; in 1938 an exercise on Grafenwöhr training range featured the artillery of six divisions (288 guns) firing at a single target. This preliminary bombardment sought to neutralise the opposing defensive system while platoons, companies and battalions fought their own way forward. However, the Germans lacked the artillery park, munitions and the means of moving guns (horses were the primary source of transportation throughout the war) to systematically implement this doctrine. This was not just due to a lack of resources and time to properly prepare for total war – rearmament started in 1936. The central political and military idea of the Blitzkrieg was to avoid the battle of materiel that Germany had waged in World War One[52]. This went beyond any rational analysis of the military situation; Nazi ideology identified racial superiority as making Germans the best soldiers; their propaganda placed on a pedestal the *Sturmabteilung* battalions that spearheaded Germans attacks in the last year of the Great War. The result was that instead of investing resources in their divisional and corps artillery, the Germans provided their manoeuvre forces with even more firepower than was used by World War One stormtroopers to fight their way forward. Organic heavy weapons at each level of command meant that firepower was guaranteed and responsive; as a result the Germans could often dictate the terms of tactical engagements by seizing the initiative through winning the firefight. This doctrine applied to both their infantry and panzer divisions, the latter's role becoming the equivalent of the World War One stormtroopers.

This Wehrmacht force structure was a triumph of 'proximity bias', with its reliance upon nearby, under command, firepower[53]. The German infantry entered World War Two with organic fire support provided by 50mm, 82mm and 120mm mortars, 75mm and 150mm infantry guns, and their 37mm anti-tank guns could also fire a HE round[54]. From the platoon level upwards, each level of command received heavier calibre fire support; in addition, heavily armoured assault guns accompanied infantry to provide a direct fire capability able to defeat strongpoints. The quantity and skilful use of these infantry support weapons completely outmatched the British infantry in 1940, leading to them to tripling their holding of battalion mortars and requesting infantry guns[55]. If on the main effort, or fighting with the *Panzertruppe*, additional fire support could be provided by tanks and airpower.

This resulted in assaulting forces having significantly greater firepower than in World War One, and so a much greater ability to suppress resistance to manoeuvre. This allowed them to conduct attacks that, according to conventional military science, required an operational pause to assemble sufficient artillery and shells to provide fire support. An example was the crossing of the River Meuse at Houx by the German division led by General Rommel. This was achieved by aggressive infantry tactics and the suppressive effect of direct fire weapons, mortars, infantry guns and the divisional artillery as it came up. But even the best equipped infantry and armour could not fight their way forward against a properly organised and motivated defence without the assistance of massed artillery to neutralise the opposing forces. However, the intent of this doctrine was to avoid set defences, seeking to unhinge these through manoeuvre, through exploiting a boundary, weak spot or better yet a gap in opposing forces. The choice to attack France in 1940 through the Ardennes illustrates a preference for the hazards of difficult terrain over the hazards of combat. Against the British in the Western Desert, through holding the initiative the Germans regularly achieved firepower superiority at the decisive point; a task made easier by British generalship, which until Montgomery, seemed to conspire in the dissipation of their superior resources[56]. Of course, as they discovered on the Eastern Front, it required an opponent who was ill-prepared to face this challenge and without the strategic depth to absorb the Blitzkrieg's initial blows.

When the Germans massed their artillery, their lack of effective targeting plus command and control was exposed. In December 1944 the Ardennes offensive was supported by 1,000 artillery pieces and rocket systems ranging from 76mm to 14-inch railway guns. The initial objective was to defeat the American fire support system; while American artillery command and control was disrupted, only fifteen artillery pieces were lost to German artillery fire[57].

The Israelis are generally seen as taking on the manoeuvreist baton from the Wehrmacht[58]. Initially, like the Germans, they emphasised company and battalion level mortars, valuing their lethality and compensating for their short range through holding the initiative and choosing the point of attack. The limited quantity of artillery directly supported battalion, or at most brigade, level operations; an exception to this approach was General Sharon; he centrally controlled his six artillery battalions at the Battle of Abu-Aguela in the Six Day War. The Israelis started to appreciate the need for more responsive and massed artillery firepower in the War of Attrition, this was confirmed by the Yom Kippur War, leading to the Israelis adopting the centralised Western artillery fire system. They continue to make more use of mortars than any other army, but have fielded a strong tube and rocket artillery park, with a command and control system designed to deliver massed fire.

Despite its success, the Western centralised approach has been successfully challenged in the American Army. Its detractors see the doctrine, in its striving for concentrated firepower, as focussing on inflicting attrition, at the expense of supporting the manoeuvre plan. So, despite previously leading on the creation of the modern centralised control of firepower, the US Army has embraced a more decentralised approach, making field artillery battalions organic to the brigades they support; removing them from divisional control enables the cannon battalion to better provide their brigade with guaranteed responsive support.

The Americans have, to an extent, been here before: their World War One experience convinced them of the need for infantry regiments to have their own organic light field artillery. In 1920, a howitzer company was added to the infantry regiment; lack of clarity of its role led to it being successively equipped with mortars, 37-mm anti-tank guns, and a reduced-range version of the standard 105mm howitzer. The capability was disbanded twice during World War Two, those companies that were manned were absorbed into the field artillery centralised fire support system. This recent partial embracing of a doctrine of decentralised firepower has also led to the fielding of mortars at battalion and company level; the reallocated their field guns to the brigade level of command is despite their guns being designed to be a generalist divisional fire support weapon, linked by a computerised command and control system optimised to deliver massed firepower[59].

The decentralised firepower system is an extremely effective means of supporting mobile forces; however, the lack of centralisation means that firepower cannot be effectively employed to either overcome a set defence or prevent enemy manoeuvre through firepower. Faced with the increased probability of peer-on-peer conventional warfighting, the Americans are rebalancing their firepower system towards greater centralisation, including the re-introduction of the divisional artillery HQ. As of 2020, the authority that the divisional level has over the brigade artillery battalions is still to be finalised. America's 20th century experience of major combat reinforces the need for divisional artillery, supported by reinforcing corps firepower, to be massed in accordance with the commander's priority; divisional fire support is currently limited to rockets. One future option is to employ the new Extended Range Cannon Artillery at the divisional level to provide reinforcing fires to brigades in conflict.

Counter Battery Fire and Deep Battle Doctrines

> *'The experience of modern wars and armed conflicts shows that artillery is still the god of war. Airstrikes cannot replace massed artillery fire. And the most effective way to protect your troops from enemy artillery is to destroy that artillery with counterbattery fire, when enemy artillery positions are detected and instantly suppressed*[60]*'*.
>
> V. Litvinenko and S. Voronkov in [Russia's] Army Digest

From the Napoleonic Wars, the defensive power of emplaced guns had led to artillery's primary offensive role being silencing the opposing artillery prior to an assault; despite this, pre-Great War doctrine did not reflect this requirement. British Army doctrine virtually ignored firing at enemy artillery; *Field Artillery Training* had only seven paragraphs on the topic, and *Field Service Regulations* none. Trench warfare showed that artillery's principal offensive role was to defeat the opposing fire support system that, along with the machine gun, enabled the defender to hold ground. Providing covering fire to the assault was a subsequent task. The employment of indirect fire and the division of land warfare into the close and deep battles necessitated the creation of a system-of-systems to conduct counter battery fire. This required the new discipline of artillery intelligence or information to be invented; the French led the way through forming artillery intelligence units from autumn of 1915[61]. Artillery intelligence personnel soon became the most numerous element of the expanded artillery staff in formation HQs[62]; their task was to obtain and process information about hostile artillery and other depth targets; they then managed the engagement of the opposing fire system, using battle damage assessment as the system's feedback loop.

There are a variety of terms for counter battery operations, distinctions rather than differences, as all seek to destroy or neutralise the enemy's fire support system and thus dislocate an enemy's ability to conduct combined arms warfighting. Ideally this would be done through attacking the artillery system-of-system's weakest points. These usually are: its ammunition trucks, the observer to gun line communications, command posts, and the computers that are responsible for the production of firing data[63]. All recognise the desirability of this approach, however, as Field Marshal, The Lord Kitchener, observed, '*we cannot make war as we ought; we can only make it as we can*'[64]. For counter-battery operations this means that firepower often concentrates upon engaging hostile batteries – often the best protected part of the system – as these are often the only part of the system that can be acquired, through their act of firing[65].

The World War One deep battle rapidly became highly centralised and attritional. In the period 1915–17 the artillery duel extended to weeks in order to silence opposing fire before an attack. If this could not be achieved, then enemy firepower usually prevented the assault from crossing no-mans-land with sufficient combat power to seize and hold a lodgement that could be subsequently reinforced. As well as attacking opposing batteries, deep fires also engaged high value targets such as command posts and logistic sites.

By 1918, the deep battle, and specifically achieving fire superiority at the point of attack, did not need weeks of preparation. Under Colonel Bruchmüller's direction the Germans pioneered the simultaneous employment of accurate massed firepower across an opponent's entire defensive system; no amount of fortifications could protect troops from this firepower, even well protected gun batteries were suppressed by gas shells. If the emotional attachment with holding ground was overcome, then defence in depth could be employed; this allowed main battle positions to be sited out of range of most of the opposing artillery. When faced with the shallow defences employed by the British in Spring 1918, German guns caused the catastrophic failure of the British command and fire support systems, dislocating them from the front line; without fire support and the timely use of reserves, the front line infantry could not hold against the Stormtroopers. The German use of infiltration tactics was prominent in contemporary analysis, but by 1918, on the Western Front, this was the standard approach of at least the elite divisions of all armies. The key to the success of the German Spring offensives was a decisive deep battle, made possible by the British Army's failure to posture themselves to dislocate German artillery. This failing particularly applied to the Royal Artillery, who despite being severely overmatched, failed to prioritise their batteries' survivability over providing fire support to the outpost line; instead they took part in an artillery duel that they could have avoided by being positioned further back.

When the tide turned, the German defences were better suited to survive the modern system of attack; but they could not hold positions against a combination of: artillery fighting deep and close, infantry trained and equipped to fight its own way forward, supported, at least on the first day, by tanks. In these battles, counter battery fire could be expected to neutralise opposing artillery. As the Canadian Corps observed at the Battle of Amiens: '*The enemy barrage at the opening of the attack was fairly heavy, but was quickly smothered by our [counter battery] work and [soon] the enemy shelling decreased almost to zero*[66].' While counter battery fire was effective in neutralising opposing artillery, their actual defeat was usually achieved through the asymmetry of infantry attacking the gun positions. For the German artillery this largely occurred in the general advance of the last months of the war, but without an effective arm of exploitation, this relied upon the disintegration of morale resulting in guns being abandoned, rather than intercepting them while they were been withdrawn.

Learning from the limitations of World War One's shallow firepower deep battle, Soviet doctrine sought to synchronise firepower with deep manoeuvre; achieving this required the simultaneous combining of overwhelming fire at the breakthrough point with the neutralisation of supporting artillery, reserves and HQs. Despite being sited out of range of most Soviet artillery, with their defensive front ruptured, the German cannon were forced to retreat. This led on the Eastern Front to German artillery being largely destroyed by mobile forces, either in their main defensive positions or as they sought to retreat[67], leading to German field artillery being equipped with specialist anti-tank artillery to better defend themselves.

In comparison to Soviet simultaneity, the Anglo-Americans sequenced their World War Two deep battle, employing their materiel advantage to achieve maximum attrition. Instead of the Soviet approach of coordinating firepower with manoeuvre at the decisive point, the Western Allies conducted the deep battle across the whole of the front, and to a greater depth that was made possible by their longer-range aircraft. When undertaking a set-piece attack, particularly in the case of the Normandy Campaign in 1944, firepower was sequenced, employing strategic and then tactical airpower, followed by artillery preliminary fire, before switching to artillery and mortar covering fire. Despite this, Allied firepower rarely targeted German defensive positions to their full depth, firepower was over-concentrated on the close battle, leading to physical destruction which hindered the advance. As a result, the armoured forces designed to exploit the break-in, often ran into unsuppressed depth German defences.

The Western Allies were even more successful than in the Great War at countering German mortars and artillery. As in World War One, the approach was attritional, and it was largely successful in overmatching German tube artillery by 1943, but not their more elusive rockets and mortars. Technology was part of the reason for this greater success, but it was a significantly easier task, as the Wehrmacht did not prioritise a powerful artillery park; in addition, their artillery production had also to meet the requirement of defending the homeland against strategic bombers.

Like World War Two, Cold War NATO doctrine sought to achieve force protection through silencing opposing artillery, but recognising the fire superiority of the Warsaw Pact forces, significantly greater emphasis was placed on survivability. This was achieved through dispersion, cover, concealment, physical protection, deception and above all constant movement. The armoured self-propelled guns provided NATO with a survivability advantage; this was demonstrated by Arab artillery largely failing to silence the Israeli self-propelled guns in the 1973 War. However, Israeli firepower was reduced through being forced to move 5–15 times each day to avoid retaliatory fire. But the Israelis demonstrated with even relatively weak counter battery fire, they could disrupt the combined arms tactics used by armies employing Soviet doctrine. The Soviets did not start to address their survivability challenge until they fielded self-propelled 2S1s and 2S3s in the 1970s; the proliferation of armoured self-propelled guns spurred the introduction of more powerful rocket systems that could achieve the necessary weight of fire before the battery displaced.

Despite the deep battle having being a reality since World War One, it was not formally recognised in NATO doctrine until the 1980s. This was the result of the American adoption of a doctrine designed to face the challenge of multiple echelons of Soviet forces, with their overwhelming superiority in artillery. AirLand doctrine sought to enable artillery, electronic warfare and aviation to join fixed wing aircraft in striking *'at enemy forces that were not yet engaged and destroy enemy capabilities that would have an immediate impact on the close battle*[68]'. AirLand doctrine required a more proactive counter fire battle through the employment of more capable locating and strike equipment. The doctrine recognised that the deep battle could not be seen as an artillery duel. It, like the close battle, was an all-arms affair, but with a greater reliance upon aerial target acquisition and fires; the doctrine sought to synergise the close and deep battles, recognising that Soviet 2nd Echelon forces needed to be defeated, or at least delayed, to avoid NATO forces fixed in the close battle being overwhelmed. This doctrine tried to address the previous failure to effectively connect the close and deep battle. Even the American Artillery's official historian identified that:

> *'corps artillery seemed to fight its own battle at times, while division artillery fought its own … corps artillery and division artillery did not seem to coordinate their efforts effectively and acted relatively independent of each other. Both practices dated back to World War II*[69]'.

In recent conflicts Western nations have not faced a peer opponent with artillery sufficiently competent to justify anything other than a symmetrical and attritional counter battery approach. In the Gulf and Iraq Wars, the Coalition's combination of networked modern sensors, shooters and control of the air easily defeated the Iraqi artillery; this was despite the Iraqis having a quantity and, in some cases, a range advantage[70].

An artillery duel normally requires both sides to participate, as artillery can usually pull back out of range to survive. On World War One's Western Front, the Western Allies attempted to systematically defeat all German artillery through counter battery fire. In the summer of 1916 British artillery claimed the destruction of 13% of the German artillery on the Western Front per month. However, despite this attrition, the Germans could not be defeated as they could disengage from this artillery duel, it was the rapid advance from August 1918 that defeated their artillery. Of course, removing guns from harm's way was not always an option; this was the case at the Battle of Dien Bien Phu, as the French were surrounded in a siege situation.

The artillery counter battery battle should not be criticised due to it primarily being symmetrical, as it is not always possible to achieve asymmetry. For example: the correct asymmetric response to defeating an enemy's airpower is for ground forces to destroy aeroplanes and aircrew at their air bases. However, this is rarely possible; the same applies to locating and engaging batteries that have not unmasked. Airpower is the most asymmetric counter to artillery as it can defeat enemy artillery before ground forces manoeuvre into its range. Initially weak in artillery, the Israelis looked to airpower and ground manoeuvre forces to defeat the opposing artillery. Heliborne paratroopers close assaulted Egyptian artillery in the Six Day War's Battle of Abu Ageila; in the Yom Kippur War, tanks operating effectively as a raiding force on the Western side of the Suez Canal destroyed batteries that assumed they were safe. Airpower is effective against identified static batteries, but its real advantage in the counter fire battle is its ability to track and then engage opponents employing 'shoot and scoot' tactics. This is necessary as rockets employing these tactics are largely invulnerable to artillery retaliatory fire, as they can move from their firing point faster than the combined time required to detect, process the target into a firing solution, and then the time of flight of the counter fire weapon. As a result, rocket launchers are best countered through cueing aircraft into the rough area of the battery. This cueing is best done by persistent wide area sensors – such as weapon locating radars, ground moving target indication radars, or signal or electronic intercept.

When an opponent's artillery is so strong that they cannot realistically be defeated in an 'artillery duel', a more credible objective is to degrade its effectiveness through harrassing fire. On the Donbas, the Ukrainians often sought to disrupt Russian artillery by returning fire with several rounds, before immediately moving to avoid retaliatory fire. As the Russians became more concerned with avoiding casualties, they generally moved their batteries when they came under fire, so limiting their firepower[71]. Pistol guns – individual guns sited away from the main battery location – are used to respond, so allowing most of the Ukrainian battery to remain masked and ready to provide fire support to their infantry.

The disadvantage of instantly retaliating is that it risks provoking a change to the enemy artillery's location; this could result in them not been located until they next open fire. Armies may choose to adopt a passive strategy of absorbing enemy fire without retaliating, in order to acquire as targets the totality of opponent's fire system, allowing them in a single strike to neutralise, defeat or force the displacement of the opposing fire support system. If this is timed with friendly decisive manoeuvre, then an opponent is disadvantaged by having to fight without indirect fire support; this course of action requires friendly forces to absorb a degree of attrition from enemy artillery. Between these two poles, of always and not retaliating, is the selective engagement of those indirect fire assets whose lethality could unhinge the force's operations. This can be the best course of action when facing a peer opponent; this simultaneously protects vital combat power, and allows the defeat of the opposing firepower system to be timed to coincide with decisive combined arms operations.

One of the lessons of 20th century conventional warfare has been the need to achieve fire ascendancy to enable manoeuvre. This does not necessitate the incremental destruction of the enemy's fires system, though over the duration of a campaign this may be highly desirable, removing its effect in a battle through neutralising fire may be sufficient if combined with decisive manoeuvre. Western air forces see the achievement of air superiority as a precursor to the successful application of airpower. The land component should be equally single-minded on the need for fire supremacy over the battlespace where land forces seeks to achieve decisive success. This equates to the Russian rather than the Western view of air supremacy; the latter sees the need for success over the whole theatre, while the former is content to achieve local superiority at the decisive point. When the opposing fire support system is neutralised, decisive manoeuvre is significantly easier. The historical experience is that the decisive defeat of opposing artillery usually follows from the exploitation by manoeuvre forces that follows a break-in battle.

Airpower Doctrine

'until [air superiority] is won, any effort not contributing to it is diversionary and should only be undertaken in emergency situations[72]*.'*

Col John A. Warden II, airpower theorist

From the first, air warfare saw doctrinal differences between belligerents. The World War One Germans largely employed their airpower where they fought their ground battles; in contrast, the British, and then the other Western Allies sought air superiority along the entire front line. By choosing the time and place to contest the air, the Germans could usually achieve superior combat ratios, they further improved their advantage by forming elite air-to-air combat squadrons, leading to them shooting down more aircraft than they lost; in addition, by pursuing the air war over German territory, the Allies lost more aircrew. Despite their casualties, by concentrating on the defeat of the Central Powers' airpower, the Allies achieved general control of the air[73]; and air superiority made aerial photography and target spotting possible. This made artillery – the War's decisive arm – significantly more effective. John Terraine, the conflict's leading historian, identified that by 1917 weather that prevented flying was considered as good as *'putting the gunner's eyes out*[74]'. The doctrine of the Allied Powers led to the centralised command of airpower; in contrast, the French air commander Commandant Jean du Peuty observed that German squadrons operated in watertight compartments without any linkage between them[75]. Control of the air was key to the successful final offensives, including on the Italian/Austrian front, where Allied air superiority was not achieved until October 1918. By 1918, air forces were an essential element of the modern warfighting system, delivering almost all of their current roles, including battlefield resupply and strategic attack[76].

Post-World War One, Western air forces started to become separate services; the US Army Air Corps effectively operated as one from its foundation in 1926[77]. This led to them favouring roles, such as strategic bombardment, that reinforced their institutional independence. They were supported in this by airpower doctrine. Guilio Douhet was the first to express the view that, autonomous of the other elements of warfighting, aircraft could achieve war's political objective[78]. Of the successive revisions of this theory, Colonel John Warden perhaps has had the greatest influence[79]; his five-ring system theory claims to reflect the totality of Western aerial combat experience of World War Two; actually, it fails to adequately cover the tactical employment of airpower. This is inevitable; if the doctrine states that strategic attack can be decisive on its own, then cooperating with the other services can only be a secondary task.

The RAF started World War Two with doctrine that reflected the primacy of strategic attack by bombers, with Fighter Command's primary role being to defend against a German strategic bombardment. Specific air cooperation squadrons had the task of working with the Army; away from the orthodoxy of the home base, the Desert Air Force used the battles in Libya and Egypt to experiment and develop air and land joint operations, developing doctrine that recognised that establishing air superiority enables the other tasks, and protects ground forces. The desert terrain favoured the employment of air interdiction, but particularly in the early years, close air support could be essential to ward off defeat. This was the operationalising of the most prescient pre-war view that air forces should be able to operate across the spectrum of tasks between the two poles of being tied to army support, and independent strategic attack[80]; with centralised command allowing airpower to be flexed in mass across these tasks.

The Americans and British forces that invaded French North Africa in Operation Torch by following their official doctrine dissipated airpower into niche tasks. The importance of gaining control of the air was recognised in American doctrine, but this involved inefficiently flying combat patrols over ground forces. Their debacle at the Kasserine Pass – never waste a good crisis – assisted with the driving through of the necessary institutional change[81]. Characteristically, the Americans adapted quicker than the British forces of 1st Army and their supporting air force. The final piece of the jigsaw fell into place in the Italian and Normandy campaigns, when American and British strategic bomber forces directly supported ground forces, as opposed to conducting strategic air attack[82]. This required national leaders to overrule the Bomber Barons.

By the end of World War Two, in its main characteristics, Western airpower doctrine was complete, but targeting remains the contentious area. Airpower theory and doctrine has consistently failed to make due allowance for the pre-eminence of politics over war, and how this translates into targeting guidance. Politics has led in a series of post-Cold War conflicts to the opposition's ground forces being seen as the only legitimate target[83]. This has resulted in airpower been used as the primary means of defeating an opponent's ground forces; this is not reflected in extant airpower theory and doctrine[84]. Drawing on NATO's experience in the 1990s, Professor Robert Pape identified that airpower's primary function was to coerce an adversary through preventing their military achieving its objective[85]; coercion is a form of negotiation – what Schelling called '*the diplomacy of violence*[86]'. Restrictions on targeting do not just apply to coercion operations; they extend over all characters of conflict. In any future Great Power conflict, it is difficult to envisage a nuclear-armed country's strategic leadership being attacked by conventional airpower, yet most Western airpower doctrine expects the targeting of an adversary's leadership to directly influence their decision-making.

Almost all airpower theorists assume the pre-eminence of Western airpower doctrine, with the other approaches being on a journey to that doctrine; unfortunately, this deterministic approach has hindered the study of airpower. The otherwise excellent *Airpower for Strategic Effect* by Colin S Gray assumes that the most effective employment of airpower requires an independent air force dedicated to achieving air superiority, before then delivering effect at all levels of war. However, historically and currently there are other ways to use airpower. This includes unified land and air operations to achieve combined arms success on the battlefield.

Airpower as part of the Combined Arms Team

[The US Marine Corps Aviation became an independent section] 'primarily for the support of Fleet Marine Forces in landing operations and in support of troop activities in the field[87].'

Robert L. Sherrod, Historian

Employing airpower as part of a combined arms force limits their operational and strategic contribution to joint warfighting – the joint role is sacrificed for the tactical excellence of a combined air and ground team. This has been the approach of the US Marine Corps and the Soviets/Russians, plus those countries that largely follow their doctrinal lead. These militaries' doctrine focus initially on highly synchronised warfighting, respectively amphibious operations and the break-in battle; both follow this with a highly manoeuvreist approach to the subsequent exploitation.

The Marine Corps aviation became an independent section in 1935. It was tasked with providing support in amphibious and subsequent ground fighting. While the Marines would not currently envisage operating other than as a combined arms air and ground team, this has not always been the case:

'Marines would like for everyone to believe that since the birth of Marine aviation in 1912, we have operated as a MAGTF [Marine Air Ground Task Force] … The deployment of the 1st Provisional Marine Brigade to Korea was the first time the FMF [Fleet Marine Forces] went to war as an integrated air-ground team.[88]'

In World War Two, Marine aviation squadrons were largely unsuccessful in their attempts to provide direct support of Marine amphibious landings and campaigns ashore. In the South Pacific Campaign, Marine aviation could operate from their land bases in Guadalcanal, Bougainville, New Britain, and Peleliu. However, in the central Pacific island-hopping, airpower was delivered from aircraft carriers. The Marine fighter – the Vought F4U Corsair – was not initially suitable for carrier-based operations. By the Battle of Okinawa, the final island assault of the War, Marine tactical aviation was able to operate from carriers and then come ashore once airfields were available. This, plus the widespread use of the air-to-ground rocket, allowed Marine Aviation to start rivalling artillery in providing fire support. This was this model of an integrated air-ground team that the Marines took into the Korean War.

The usual explanation for this bespoke approach is that the Marines are a lighter force, with less artillery assets than the Army, hence the need for airpower to provide additional fire support. In reality, the US Marine Corps is not light on direct support artillery. Of course, the Marines have no equivalent of US Army corps-level artillery, but following its latest force structure reductions, the American Army has little of this left. Of course, the Marine Corps' artillery is rarely usable in the initial stages of an amphibious operation, and naval gunfire and air support has to compensate. The Marines have different firepower needs because of their different role, but when both of America's ground forces undertake the same role, they become quite similar. The 2020 1st Marine Division has four artillery battalions: three of 155mm guns and one with the HIMARS rocket system. In prolonged ground combat – World War Two, Korea and Vietnam – an additional artillery battalion was added to the Marine Division's order of battle, resulting in a ratio of five artillery battalions to nine infantry battalions. However, the USMC are currently planning to reduce their artillery pack.

Supplementing their artillery, the Marines prefer the responsiveness and accuracy of their own airpower. The US Air Force's expertise in close air support fluctuates; in contrast, Marine Aviation's institutional commitment to being an air-ground integrated team means they maintain their ground attack knowledge. The Marines would probably prefer to concentrate exclusively upon forming part of a combined arms team; however, the norm is for them to also operate under US Air Force leadership in joint air campaigns. Korea, Vietnam and the wars against Iraq have all seen the joint commander centralising airpower through a single theatre air commander. The Marines have been clear benefiters from centralised airpower. In the defence of Khe Sanh in 1967, they were supported by the full weight of American airpower, when a single air authority planned and executed aircraft allocation, controlled airspace and allocated targets.

Russian armies are always lavishly equipped with artillery. The employment of airpower as part of a combined arms force is not to make up for any quantity deficiency in surface-to-surface firepower. Soviet airpower briefly flirted with Douhet's strategic bombing doctrine in the late 1930s; the Blitzkrieg cruelly exposed the Soviet's muddled doctrine, air inventory and force structure. From May 1942, air army commanders were placed directly under the command of the front commander; the Red Air Force's role was to: drive off German aircraft, provide the reach to suppress the enemy's depth positions in a set piece attack; and then support mobile operations. Stalin recognised that a favourable air situation was the crucial component to success on the ground: '*we can achieve victory over the Germans only if we gain air supremacy*[89]', this led to:

> '*The Soviet understanding of "air superiority" as defined in the peculiar contest of the Eastern Front, differed sharply from the Anglo-American operational practice. Forged in the difficult middle period of the war, Soviet style air superiority meant the capacity to apply at will overwhelming air power in the close support of the ground forces. Air superiority was measured as leverage, largely in the tactical zones, not as a commanding air presence coextensive with the Eastern front*[90]'.

The 2,000km front line and the relative force densities played a part in this doctrine, leading the Germans, to employ a similar approach. The inadequacy of this doctrine was demonstrated in the Luftwaffe's New Year's Day 1945 attack on the Western Allies' airfields in the Low Countries. The aim was to achieve local air superiority over the Battle of the Bulge. It was doomed to failure, as the Anglo-Americans contested air superiority theatre-wide, and thus could easily reinforce a threatened sector[91].

By 1944 the Soviets were employing their specialist ground attack aircraft, the Il-2/Il-4 Shturmovik, in corps strength, as many as 500 aircraft were committed at a time, to a single area. This allowed them to totally overwhelm German forces[92]. Of course, from the physical perspective this was an ineffective use of airpower; too many aircraft compared to targets. From the combined arms warfare perspective, this concentration was usually timed to coincide with the insertion of the second echelon, with airpower compensating for the falloff in artillery support as it became out of range; thus, massed airpower covered a period of unique vulnerability during the mobile force's forward passage through the break-in force. Such overwhelming numbers both overawed defenders and buoyed up the Soviet attackers, increasing the chances of a successful exploitation.

The disadvantage of tying airpower to the combined arms battle was demonstrated by the inability of the Red Air Force to finish off the Luftwaffe in the final year of the war. An independent service could have launched an extensive and sustained counter-air offensive to destroy the remaining 2,000, at most, German aircraft on the Eastern Front[93]. The disadvantage of each Soviet Army having its own aviation army was seen in the Battle of Berlin, with five converging armies, their air forces often bombarded neighbouring Soviet ground forces[94]. Alexander Alexandrovich Novikov may have been Chief Marshal of the Aviation for the Soviet Air Force, but he did not exercise either a command or a coordinating authority in the battle.

Post-War, the Soviet tactical air force (as opposed to national air defence and long-range strike) remained under front or military district command. Forming part of a combined arms team, these air divisions and corps were equipped with a mix of fighter and attack aircraft; these enabled them to protect the front's airspace and support surface operations[95]. Until the nuclear age, the Soviets showed little interest in long-range bombers – they made up only 4% of the total inventory in World War Two – and did not conduct strategic attacks[96]. In the Cold War, nuclear bombers were secondary to the Strategic Rocket Forces; this remains the primary nuclear capability.

In 1998 the Russian Air Force and the Russian Air Defence Forces merged to form the Russian Aerospace Forces[97]. The major factor in the consolidation into a single force was to deliver savings[98], but it was also probably a reaction to the success of the Western unified airpower approach in the Gulf War. Airpower in the Chechen and Georgian conflicts was neither effectively integrated with land operations, nor part of a unified plan, as the Russians lack joint warfighting doctrine and culture; so in this period the Russians became marooned between rival doctrines. The reassertion of military district authority (the peacetime home of front or combined arms army commanders) over the air force chain of command indicates that the Russians have returned to their tried and tested combined arms approach of an integrated ground and air team.

In its short history, Chinese airpower has evolved from primarily air defence of the homeland, to developing a ground attack capability, and now into a service capable of executing long-range strike operations. In the Korean War they limited themselves to contesting the air, largely over Northern Korea. Challenging the World's leading air force spurred their development; in 1959, the People's Liberation Army Air Force published over 300 regulations, including the first elements of China's airpower theory. By 1962 they had identified two forms of air superiority.

Their strategic air superiority was like Western theory in its aim and scope; the second form was tactical air superiority. This equated to Soviet doctrine in being limited to an area, for a short period of time[99]. In the 1979 War with Vietnam, the Chinese largely limited their air operations to maintaining tactical air superiority on their side of the border, this decision was probably not solely derived from doctrine – the impact of the Cultural Revolution on the air force's effectiveness, and a desire to avoid escalation, were probably the driving factors.

Long range strike is a relatively recent development. In 1987 the Air Force formally set out the concept of moving from defending the country's air space to becoming capable of simultaneous offensive and defensive roles. The People's Liberation Army Air Force only received its own service-specific strategic concept in 2004[100]. Like the Russians, they appear to interpret the lesson of the 1990s conflicts as the requirement to move beyond airpower forming part of a combined arms force. They certainly now have the equipment, being behind only the Americans and Russians in their holdings of modern (third and fourth generation) multi-role aircraft[101]. However, the People's Liberation Army Air Force has a rival in the established capabilities of the People's Liberation Army Rocket Force, or as it was formerly known, the Second Artillery Corps, whose ballistic and cruise missiles are designed for the strategic strike missions[102]. This makes it unlikely that they will achieve primacy in the exercise of aerospace power, as is the case with Western air forces[103].

It is questionable whether the Chinese, and for that matter the Russians, either wish to or are capable of adopting Western airpower doctrine. This is not a technical failing; both continue to field fighter-bombers capable of a range of missions. This is indicated by the Chinese decision to replace their specialist close air support aircraft – the Nanchang Q-5 – with significantly more capable multi-role aircraft of indigenous and Russian design. The challenge is probably greatest for the Chinese who, unlike the Russians with their Wars of Soviet Secession, lack the operational imperative to change their doctrine and operating culture. The Chinese emphasis on fielding modern attack helicopters may be in recognition of the fact that these are significantly easier to integrate with land operations than fixed wing aircraft; currently there is no evidence that they deploy forward air controllers below the divisional level, nor dynamically task airborne aircraft.

The employment of airpower as part of a combined air and ground team has produced two effective land warfighting capabilities in the Soviets in World War Two and the US Marine Corps. Having airpower under command makes it more responsive and guaranteed, thus addressing the most significant weaknesses of aerial fire support. The forming of a single team results in a high level of synergy between air and ground elements from planning through to execution, it can remove some of the transactional relationships that can result when independent components seek to cooperate.

The inability of the Soviets and Russians to replicate their Great Patriotic War excellence in air and ground cooperation is not due to a single reason – the post-World War Two conflicts have not suited their combined arms doctrine; attack helicopters are now more suitable than fixed wing aircraft for flying over advancing ground forces and acquiring their own targets. Perhaps the single greatest factor is their lack of demanding operations to overcome the frictions implicit in integrating ground and air forces. The US Marine Corps' near-constant operations, high readiness deployments, and demanding training have prevented the atrophying of air and land integration. At the operational level, they have continued to operate under the US Air Force's joint force control, and have probably benefitted from the peer rivalry.

Independent Airpower Doctrine

'Air warfare cannot be separated into little packets; it knows no boundaries on land and sea other than those imposed by the radius of action of the aircraft; it is a unity and demands unity of command[104] *... The Royal Air Force was concerned to give the British Army the greatest assistance in the most effective way. In order to do this our force had to be under a single control*[105]*.'*

Marshal of the Air Force Lord Tedder

Independent airpower doctrine requires centralised command, by airmen; this enables it to operate at all the levels of war, across the whole theatre; centralisation leads to the most efficient use of airpower through a planning process designed to synchronise hundreds of planes. It is naturally suited to achieving air superiority by shooting down aircraft and the deliberate targeting of fixed facilities and it inherently practices attritional warfare. This doctrine was developed in World War Two and became the USAF's founding principle in 1947[106]. Through NATO, it became the West's predominant airpower doctrine; aided by American leadership and their enforcement of tactics, techniques and procedures. Subsequent modifications, notably by Colonels Boyd and Warden, were largely about refining its employment, rather than organisation and ethos.

The outcome of this doctrinal clarity is that Western air forces have a distinct command philosophy that seeks to synchronise warfare through top-down control, whilst empowering their aircrew; advances in information technology have aided the air component in centralising decision-making and achieving unity of effort. The key tool in achieving synchronisation is the ninety-six-hour cycle of the air tasking order or ATO. Operationally, in its fully developed form, this was employed in the 1991 Gulf War. It had such authority, that it was described as *'a daily articulation of the overall airpower strategy*[107]'. The Gulf War was probably the ATO's apogee as the means by which airpower achieved unity of command. This was due to a confluence of: technology that enabled the level of centralised execution that air forces had always sought[108], sufficient mass of aircraft, and a largely compliant foe. The US Army saw 96-hour cycles as inflexible compared to the twenty-four hours it took to process air requests in the Vietnam War[109]; of course, this is not a totally fair comparison, in the Gulf War airpower was operating across all missions and levels of war, rather than primarily conducting ground support; plus, the ATO has inbuilt mechanisms that provide greater flexibility.

Almost all independent air force doctrine identifies flexibility as a key characteristic or principle; despite this, NATO doctrine has a list of priorities. The originators of centralised airpower doctrine – World War Two's British Desert Air Force – saw offensive action to achieve air superiority as a pre-eminent activity, as this set the conditions for the effective employment of airpower. But, consistent with the principle of flexibility, its commander, Air Marshal Coningham, did not formally list priorities. It was the US Army Air Forces that created what is now the Western standard, stating a formal priority of: air superiority (this now also covers space), strategic attack, air interdiction and finally, close air support[110]. One outcome of this low priority is:

> *'The history of close air support since World War I has been marked by the tragedy of lives lost, unduly protracted conflict, and victory deferred because both air and ground officers have too often failed to benefit as they might from history, from experience garnered and recorded by earlier generations of airmen*[111]*'.*

Independent airpower's centralised approach enables the massing of airpower to support land forces. Of course, the limitations of platforms and air crew prevent Western air forces from seamlessly moving between these different tasks; this is reinforced by the tendency in complex organisations for institutional distinction, this leads to specialism. This has been partly overcome through the post-9/11 Wars making Western air forces well practised in ground support. As a result there has been no repeat of World War Two's strategic bombers acting as an air force within the air forces, with their own command and control arrangements. The dominance of fighter pilots, with the partial exception of the Americans, in senior command positions is a greater concern. At its worst it can lead to an institutional preoccupation with air superiority, preferably achieved through air-to-air combat. The pursuit of the highest guarantee of air control can be at the cost of the joint mission; soldiers specifically see it as a danger to the support of land forces. Seeing air superiority as a condition, rather than a mission, leads to the recognition that it just needs to be *sufficient* to exploit the air domain and preserve freedom from attack on the surface[112].

Western air forces' current close air support proficiency is aided by the convergence of this with the other forms of air attack. Most engagements can now take place from medium altitude, employing guided weapons; traditional close air support skills, such as dive attacks to low level, with aircraft acquiring their own target, and delivering danger close cannon fire support have rarely featured in recent conflict. These skills will still be required when ground units become mixed-up with enemy troops and are in danger of being overrun; this is probably a more likely mission in peer conventional conflict, as the opposition's air defence capability could largely restrict close air support to emergency fire support. This likely scarcity is at odds with current Western doctrine, which routinely expects ground forces to be aided by close air support.

Even with authoritative doctrine, to be effective, the whole system for air/land integration needs exhaustive practice; the challenge of improvising air land integration in contact has been repeatedly demonstrated. One example of practically failing to do this will suffice – on 14 August 1944, the strategic British Bomber Command was tasked to support British forces in Normandy. The British Army's standard means of marking their position was with yellow smoke; this was also Bomber Command's means of indicating a target. Some aircraft bombed friendly positions and *'the more the troops burnt yellow flares to show their position the more errant aircraft bombed them*[113]'. The result was 400 British casualties. Currently peacetime close air support training focusses upon the terminal control of an aircraft's munitions by a forward air controller, rather than testing combined training. The lesson of operations – notably Operation Anaconda – is that the most serious challenges are within the tasking system as a whole, and not the individual terminal controls. Testing the whole system in peacetime requires demanding inter-service training. This is as rarely undertaken with any vigour, as addressing inter-service cooperation is usually unrewarding and is rarely career-enhancing.

A peculiar feature of close air support doctrine is the apparent continuity in organisation, tactics, techniques and procedures from its first articulation in the middle years of World War Two. This continuity is misleading, as the meaning of many of these terms has significantly changed. The most significant is the redefinition of close air support, expanding from forward air controllers using aerial firepower to support ground troops in close combat, to effectively any aircraft directly attacking land forces. In the case of the Kosovo conflict, this happened without any friendly ground forces in theatre, leading to calls for new doctrine to reflect emerging practice:

> *'a new concept of offensive air employment against enemy ground forces was successfully tested in [Operation] Enduring Freedom [Afghanistan 2001]. Although often mistakenly equated with close air support, it was, in fact, something fundamentally new in air power application that entailed direct air attacks against fielded enemy forces who were not in direct contact with friendly troops*[114].'

The desire to see a clean break from the past is implicit in those who identify an information age revolution in military affairs. In World War Two there were cases of airpower inflicting considerable attrition on ground forces not in direct contact with friendly troops. This was not exclusively done by Anglo-American airpower; following their Battle of Kursk counterattack, the Soviets claim to have destroyed 70 tanks from 9 Panzer Division and 240 tanks from the 17 Panzer Division solely by air attack[115]. The highest levels of destruction occurred when airpower was used against retreating forces, when achieving a mobility kill was sufficient for a tank to be abandoned. Against stationary forces the effect is usually limited to extended neutralisation. In the case of the Panzer Lehr Division in the Normandy Campaign, strategic bombers rendered it temporally combat ineffective for a few hours, but it lost only 7% of its personnel and very few armoured vehicles[116]. Western aircraft in the 1990s and 2000s failed to achieve the level of destruction per sortie as their World War Two predecessors, this was despite improved technology and the foolish force posture adopted by the Iraqis in the Gulf War; as a result, the ground operation had to be delayed until the air campaign had achieved the required attrition. More recent opponents of Western airpower have proved to be more elusive, leading to a lower attrition rate. Hence it is difficult to identify from the recent practical application of airpower that there is something fundamentally new. What is needed is accurate taxonomy when using close air support.

A recurring army criticism of independent air forces is their inability to deliver desired level of responsiveness and guarantee. The Post 9/11 Wars have provided the opportunity for Western air forces to improve their ability to dynamically engage ground targets. To achieve this, the American air force is changing its doctrine to empower each level of command, leading to a greater use of mission-type orders; when combined with improved information technology this delivers the synchronisation that is vital in the air domain[117]. The aim is to shift from '*centralised control and decentralised execution*' to '*centralised command, adaptive control, decentralised execution*'[118].

Revised doctrine needs to not only reflect the greater ability of airpower to destroy dynamic ground forces but also its symbiotic relationship with land forces. This goes beyond a ground force's traditional role of *shaping* the enemy into suitable targets, and assisting with the suppression of air defence. The chief integration challenge is ensuring that aircraft, operating on mission command style orders, actually focus on the targets that matter to the land component; this is a significantly greater air/land integration challenge than that faced by the combined arms team – in the latter, airpower operates in support of ground forces. Effective joint operations require truly complementary land and air operations, with multiple shaping and decisive effects, over a significantly greater geographic spread. This probably necessitates reduced air force firepower in the close battle, with helicopter firepower compensating.

Aviation Doctrine

'the presence of substantial aerial firepower in the form of Apaches and Cobras lessened greatly the traditional Army reliance upon the close-in delivery of tactical air power[119]'.

General Scales' observation on the Gulf War

Unlike fixed wing airpower, no one has attempted to develop an overarching theory for the employment of armed and attack helicopters. Richard Simpkin in *Race to the Swift* perhaps comes closest in his examination of what he calls the 'rotary wing revolution'[120]. He takes up General von Senger und Etterlin's concept of the 'main battle air vehicle', seeing this as the next leap forward in battlefield mobility, allowing helicopters to generate most of their combat power through velocity rather than mass. Opining that this would restore the advantage that the Blitzkrieg had over its opponents[121].

In the absence of theory, aviation initially followed technical development; and for many armies, a desire for their own airpower to replace what they perceived as a reduced air force appetite for close air support. Initially America led through a series of innovative practitioners, largely responding to the imperative of counter-insurgency operations. In America's Vietnam War, armed and attack aviation provided escort and intimate fire support for the transport helicopters that conducted much of the troop movement and resupply; aerial Rocket Artillery became the means of suppressing area targets when artillery was not in range and the pure aviation formations were able to fully exploit the speed and reach of helicopters. After the Vietnam War, responding to the Soviet threat, the long-range area fire support role lapsed and divisional aviation units predominantly took on the anti-tank role.

In the 1980s, aviation practitioners handed over intellectual primacy to the developers of the US Army's AirLand doctrine. In 1985 America formed its first corps-level AH-64 attack helicopter brigade, with the specific mission of attacking enemy forces to a depth of 150km; this was to be in concert with long-range indirect fires, electronic warfare, and air force interdiction, but it was the attack helicopter that provided the Army with equity in the air force-dominated deep fight. When many NATO aircraft were daylight only, AH-64 units were to predominantly operate at night to maximise the aircraft's capabilities, and to exploit the enemy's reduced air defence capability.

The primary task of corps aviation brigades became the defeat of the enemy's second echelon armoured forces. Divisional aviation also began to orientate towards the deep fight; in 1986, the deep attack mission cemented army aviation's status as an independent branch[122]. American General Rudolph Ostovich III identified the role as:

> *'Massed attack helicopter formations of brigade size and larger will combine the elements of speed, surprise, and lethality with a marked night-fighting advantage over the enemy ... Massed attack helicopter formations provide the corps commander a manoeuvre asset that can influence the operational level of war, well before ground force engagement is possible*[123]*.'*

The Gulf War began with the Americans conducting a deep aviation operation to attack two Iraqi anti-aircraft missile sites, so creating a safe corridor through the air defence system for the Allied bombing campaign. This strike consisted of nine AH-64 Apaches, one UH-60 Black Hawk and four Air Force MH-53J Pave Low helicopters to act as guides[124]. Key to this success was the lead time, this allowed detailed planning to identify safe ingress and egress routes to the static targets; plenty of preparation time also applied to 101st Airborne Division's air assault operation 155km behind enemy lines. Subsequently the speed of the advance exceeded the ability of aviation units to independently operate in advance of ground units. A comparison can be drawn with the Anglo-American airborne forces that successively planned divisional and corps air assaults in 1944, only for the armoured advance from Normandy to overrun the proposed drop zones. Of course, the mounting tempo of aviation is faster than airborne forces, but in the Gulf War it was not fast enough to mount battalion and brigade level operations in front of a high-speed armoured advance.

Aviation's slow mounting tempo is due to the nature of flying. If tank forces *halt* between *moves,* and the infantry *moves* between *halts*, then aviation *flies* between *briefings*. In addition to pre-flight preparation, a helicopter force has a relatively slow transit time and its restricted endurance results in a limited time over the target. This necessitates the early identification and constant tracking of a suitable target, as helicopters have limited time-on-target, there is little room for error. Battalion and brigade sized attacks add to the challenge, through increasing both the mounting time, and by making a larger target, so increasing aviation's vulnerability to ground based air defences; this can be offset by using multiple routes and massing to engage, but this takes even longer to prepare.

The failure of the US Army's 11th Attack Helicopter Regiment in the Iraq War led to a questioning of the deep attack doctrine[125]; while there were some successes in subsequent deep attacks, the Army fell into line with US Marine Corps approach of using attack helicopters to provide firepower in the close battle[126]. This decision was reached due to a lack of suitable targets, and the vulnerability of helicopters to largely un-suppressible low-level direct fire weapons – RPG-7s, man-portable surface-to-air missiles, machine guns and air defence cannons – when advancing over enemy occupied ground. Employing attack helicopters behind ground forces – shooting over the shoulder – overcomes much of this vulnerability. American aviation also rediscovered the worth of armed reconnaissance, with the small and nimble Kiowa Warrior actually being preferred to Apaches in urban terrain[127]. By the end of the War, the corps commander, Lieutenant General Wallace, determined that aviation had two roles:

> *'The tactic that we settled on was first of all focusing on close support of ground forces with the Apache, which is called "over the shoulder." It's not really over the shoulder but is close cooperation with ground manoeuvre and air manoeuvre ... The other tactic that we have come to employ very successfully is using the Apache doing armed reconnaissance'*[128].

Criticism went beyond performance on an individual operation to a questioning of whether the army aviation's focus on deep operations has led to them seeing themselves as culturally separate from other soldiers, and thus the all arms team[129]; a direct challenge to American aviation's doctrine which specifically states that it operates as part of a combined arms force[130]. The Iraq War both reinforced the need for combined arms operations and demonstrated the requirement for land operations to avoid unduly restricting joint warfighting, because by seeking to maximise the employment of their own organic assets, the American Army limited the ability of airpower to prosecute the overall campaign. Fixed wing aircraft, directed by air force HQs, in the Iraq War again demonstrated their superiority in engaging the enemy in the deep battlespace[131].

In retrospect, massed deep aviation attacks failed in the Iraq War due to a combination of faulty execution, and the employment of tactics that were unsuitable to the character of conflict. The current challenge is that this Cold War doctrine has now been rehabilitated because it is deemed suitable for peer-on-peer conventional warfighting, this is despite its dependence upon a confluence of events that seem improbable in the fog and friction of war. If a doctrinal comparator can be drawn, it is with the American World War Two tank destroyer force, their doctrine was for their mass employment, in pure formations, against enemy armour. This has been identified as *'a doctrinal solution for a problem that did not exist as perceived'*[132], because, instead of massed all-tank attacks, the Germans used all arms tactics.

The conviction that massed armour – originally Soviet second echelon forces – will form a discrete target for a brigade or battalion aviation attack is also unrealistic. Certainly, finding a suitable target has been elusive in recent conventional fighting, there are no reasons to suppose that discrete massed armoured targets are becoming more common, especially given the emphasis in modern force employment of negating the effects of firepower, leading to dispersion made easier by the increased force to space ratio. Even if identified, depth targets are likely to present only fleeting opportunities, almost always beyond the mounting tempo of aviation battalions and brigades; employing artillery, or dynamically re-tasking fixed wing aircraft are more realistic options. The result is that, like the World War Two tank destroyer force, attack aviation has usually provided fire support within combined arms formations.

Despite the practical challenge of reviving the AirLand concept, there are good doctrinal reasons for aviation to evolve beyond just providing fire support to ground forces. The original advocates of aviation manoeuvre saw velocity rather than mass (firepower) as its key attribute, this followed the rationale of the British theorists known as the 'apostles of mobility', that to exploit the tank's speed, all supporting elements need tracked mobility[133]. These thinkers advocated, at their most extreme, a pure tank force; rejecting the combined arms approach, as this would result in operations being conducted at the speed of the slowest arm. The late Cold War aviation theorists used the same logic: helicopters would only reach their full potential through liberating themselves from the speed of ground vehicles, leading to a decisive difference in operational tempo between airmobile and ground forces[134]. It follows that aviation formations, through their superior mobility and firepower, would replace armoured formations as the decisive manoeuvre force[135]. Experience has shown that the helicopter's lack of protection prevents it from replacing armoured forces across the spectrum of its roles; to replace armoured forces in delivering decisive manouevre helicopters need to be able to deliver battlefield shock, as this psychological effect is key to defeating an opponent's will to fight. Achieving it is easiest with forces with superior mobility, as manoeuvre is particularly effective when it comes from an unexpected direction.

There is the view that helicopters cannot achieve this form of manoeuvre, as their inability to remain in a position limits their physical and psychological effect, but the same could be said of the panzer divisions before 1940. Aviation does not need to achieve its psychological impact in the same way that armoured forces do; instead it can capitalise on its much greater ability to operate in an opponent's rear area, achieving the disproportionate effect which Clausewitz identified that '*a small group of skilful raiders*' has through operating in an enemy's rear area[136]. This can be achieved by becoming an arm of exploitation in the traditional light cavalry deep raiding role, but with significantly greater relative lethality[137]. The comparison can be taken further; commanders in previous generations carefully husbanded their light cavalry resources, recognising their vulnerability, in particular in the act of slipping behind enemy lines; they also recognised that if they committed their light cavalry to raiding, then they might not be able to support the close fight. This was the case with General JEB Stuart's raiding Confederate cavalry, who were thus unable support General Lee's infantry at the decisive battle of Gettysburg. The American Civil War is full of such raiding examples, the rule of these operations was to keep moving and never hold ground, as this would make the raiders a target for pursuing forces. This served as inspiration for Ukrainian Colonel Mikhail Zubrowski – a graduate of U.S. Command and General Staff course – who conducted a 450km raid with his 95th Air Assault Brigade (actually an armoured formation) in August 2014[138]. This brigade relied upon infiltration, multiple axes of advance and tempo, all of which also suit aviation operations.

Israel's 1982 Lebanon War provides examples of the effectiveness of formations of two to four helicopters infiltrating into an enemy's rear area. Employing a small force resulted in greater agility, and improved survivability through allowing them to better exploit terrain masking; the Israelis successfully infiltrated 50km behind their enemy's front line. These operations were credited by one source with 60% of the Syrian Army's tank losses[139]. Similarly, Syrian helicopters, despite Israeli air superiority, were able to operate deep within hostile territory, successfully ambushing at least one column[140].

The other way that aviation can exploit its differential in velocity is in concert with ground forces. Aviation can be the 'exceptional force' that operates in concert with a 'ordinary or fixing force'. This was original proposal of the Cold War proponents of airmobility. If we return to our American Civil War comparator, in the 1865 Appomattox campaign, the Union cavalry commander, General Sheridan, convinced General Grant not to send the cavalry off on independent raids[141]; instead their mobility was used to execute flanking operations in concert with the main Union forces. In contrast to the Wilderness campaign of the previous year when slower infantry provided the flanking force, General Sheridan's cavalry pre-empted the Confederate response, and dislocated their resistance[142].

In a quasi-raiding role, aviation benefits from its relative lack of combat power and its need to constantly move; rather than revising Cold War doctrine, aviation's deep battle role could be more effectively delivered by pairs of helicopters task-organised with fixed wing aircraft, long-range rockets and unmanned aircraft. The data transfer ability of advanced fifth generation aircraft would make infiltration much easier through enhancing aviation's situational awareness; drones can scout in front of an aviation force, allowing threats to be identified and either avoided or engaged from standoff distances. Where possible, helicopters should cue artillery and air strikes rather than unmasking their own weapons. In the Cold War a helicopter battalion was necessary to achieve the required attrition to defeat Soviet 2nd Echelon Forces; now even a pair of modern helicopters have the organic and on-call firepower to outmatch most target arrays.

Soviet aviation doctrine draws heavily upon their experience with armoured close support aircraft in World War Two, these were employed as effectively long-range artillery in the set-piece battles, and as a more flexible form of 'accompanying artillery' in mobile operations[143]. This doctrine has led to their helicopters being heavily armoured and primarily armed with cannon, bombs and unguided rockets. As they were seen as an integral part of the exploitation force, their original attack helicopter, the Mi-24 Hind, carried a squad of infantry to seize opportunities; this carrying capacity was particularly useful in Soviet airmobile operations, as these forces were designed to conduct the deep battle in advance of the ground forces breakthrough[144]. The later fielding of helicopters with more in common with Western designs probably represents a shift in doctrine.

With the increased likelihood of peer conventional conflict, American and British armies are showing renewed interest in the deep battle. Cold War style brigade and battalion aviation attacks have resurfaced in their doctrine. The French are also reviewing their doctrine, having previously deduced from recent operations that direct fire support of ground forces is more important than airmobile manoeuvre of autonomous helicopter forces[145]. Somewhat counter-intuitively at a time when the other arms are increasing their dispersion, aviation is favouring mass. In practice, reconstituting massed deep attacks – renamed interdiction attacks – will be challenging due to the atrophy of conventional warfighting skills[146]; this includes flying low and fast to avoid radar threats. In Iraq and Afghanistan, to avoid the enemy's small arms, rocket-propelled grenades and shoulder-fired surface-to-air missiles, helicopters flew higher, diving when required to more accurately engage targets, and then returning to the protection of altitude[147]. Probably more appropriate to modern conditions are more limited deep operations conducted by pairs of helicopters infiltrating into the enemy's rear area. In favourable terrain, or by choosing or creating gaps in ground based air defence, a small helicopter force can expect to ingress and egress unchallenged; if they decide to merely cue fighter-bombers and artillery they could remain undetected. The resultant physical and psychological impact on the enemy is likely to be worth the risk; this is less likely to be the case with a deep attack by a brigade of modern attack helicopters.

Firepower Doctrine in Irregular Warfare

'Two hundred thousand French wishing to subjugate Spain, aroused against them as one man, would not manoeuvre like two hundred thousand French wishing to march upon Vienna[148]*.'*
Baron Jomini, Military Theorist

From the military perspective there is not much that is novel in irregular warfare, as even an occasional acquaintance with the Bible's Old Testament will testify[149]. It is *'a concept as old as warfare itself'*[150]; its counter has equal longevity. Clausewitz had first-hand experience of Russian irregular warfare in Napoleon's 1812 Invasion, and he studied Spanish, Swiss, Italian and anti-Republican French guerrillas. He and the other Prussian military reformers laid plans for the use of these tactics in the 1813 War of German Liberation, though what actually followed was largely regular warfare. Clausewitz's *On War* provided the first Western military analysis of its characteristics, strengths and weaknesses. In effect, concluding that irregular warfare represented a different character of war. His analysis built upon the picket and outpost tactics of the age of horse and musket, which contemporaries identified as 'little war', to differentiate them from pitched battles and sieges. In their character, in particular raiding, these have much in common with current special forces operations[151]; both Clausewitz and his contemporary Baron de Jomini identified that employing irregular warfare tactics largely negates the battlefield dominance of a superior conventional force. They also identified the need for bespoke tactics against such opposition.

Current counter-insurgency doctrine can be most easily understood through the two contrasting doctrines of 'enemy-centric' and 'population-centric'. In addition, to its overall attritional approach, the enemy-centric approach employs two main methods to defeat the insurgents: decapitation (killing or capturing the leadership) and defeating their fielded forces, leading to physically separating insurgents from the people. This doctrine sees the defeat of the insurgent as the precondition to the successful application of the non-lethal elements of the counter-insurgency strategy. Authoritarian regimes tend to favour focussing on the insurgent, as they can employ extreme ruthlessness in their decapitation strategy, and can control the population through the use of terror. In contrast, the population-centric approach sees counter-insurgency as a contest for the people and the environment (physical and informational) they occupy. Gaining the allegiance of the population rather than defeating the insurgent is the main effort. Whichever approach is stressed, enduring success needs a comprehensive approach to achieve the *'agile integration of civil and military measures across security, economic, political and information tracks*[152]'. Recognising that in counter-insurgency, politics permeate all aspects of operations.

Understanding firepower's role in counter-insurgency has been hindered by the enduring belief that its character of conflict is so different that the norms of mainstream war do not apply, this leads to an analysis that emphases the calibrating of the use of force and the imposing of restrictions on the employment of firepower[153]. The West's dominant counter-insurgency doctrine barely covers firepower. The US Army's and Marine Corps' Counter Insurgency Field Manual (Army FM 3–24 and Marine Warfighting Publication 3-33.5), which since its issue in December 2006 has guided operations in Iraq and Afghanistan, mentions artillery and mortars five times, of which three refer to the Laos Insurgency, and only once to its use. The other elements of the joint fire systems are only intermittently mentioned; targeting is covered in attack the network. Quite rightly it exhorts that in using force, the counter-insurgents '*do not create more enemies than you eliminate with your action*[154]', but it fails to balance this by providing any guidance as to how firepower can further a counter-insurgency.

Much of the inspiration for the West's current doctrine comes from the British counter-insurgency operations during their End of Empire. The conventional understanding of this identifies 'minimum force' and 'hearts and minds' as the key lessons; however, for the British, the first step of enacting what was subsequently identified as a 'population-centric' approach was the separating of the insurgents from the people. This could rarely be achieved without fire and manoeuvre. In the Malayan Emergency, which is widely seen as a textbook example of an effective people-centric counter-insurgency, firepower caused considerable attrition; 93rd Field Battery of 25th Regiment Royal Artillery operated at an astounding tempo, sometimes firing hundreds of rounds per day in January 1953[155]. The nine-month operation in the Kuala Langat district of Selangor consumed more than 60,000 artillery rounds and 30,000 mortar bombs[156]. Commanders used artillery bombardments to prevent guerrillas from consolidating their operations in a given area[157]; such was the need for firepower that in 1955 the number of artillery pieces increased to 44 from the 16 of the previous year[158]. A similar increase in aircraft numbers occurred, and of more capable types; this significantly increased the lethality of airpower[159].

The use of firepower in this campaign usually met the 'minimum force' criteria not by its quantity, but how it was employed; it was infrequently used independently of ground manoeuvre. Firepower directly supported infantry tasked with the clearing of insurgents from an area, and was subsequently used to safeguard liberated areas, it was employed in quantity to meet the maxim that '*minimum force is often the maximum possible force, but for the shortest possible duration*'. Firepower could be poorly directed; harassing fire was used, but it was normally coordinated with infantry ambushes[160]. Throughout the conflict, largely independently, the RAF conducted aerial bombardment, much of which was of dubious effect. It was probably lack of resources, as much as policy, that limited the number of non-combatants killed by British bombers in the 12-year conflict to between 670 and 995[161]. This focus on firepower at first sight appear to be at odds with the often-quoted statement by General Sir Gerald Templer: '*The answer lies not in pouring more soldiers into the jungle, but rests in the hearts and minds of the Malayan people*'[162]; however, this maxim applied to the latter years of the campaign. In the initial stages of the Malayan Emergency, there were two critical tasks: the recapture of insurgent-occupied territory, and a political pathway to independence; the latter secured the allegiance of the majority of the people. With the politics in place and the insurgent enclaves defeated through fire and manoeuvre, gaining the allegiance of the disaffected population supporting the Communists became possible through 'hearts and minds' tactics. Between 1952–4, guerrilla strength was reduced by two-thirds, leading to terrorist incidents falling from 500 to less than 100 per month, and monthly civilian and security force casualties reducing from 200 to less than 40[163].

The current misunderstanding of the character of 1950s and 1960s counter-insurgency probably stems from the failure to capture its initial enemy-focussed approach in official doctrine. A failure probably partly due to a '*a traditional British distrust in general principles …*

lessons painfully learnt in one campaign are forgotten[164]'. This chapter's introduction identifies customary practice rather than formal doctrine publications are usually the dominant influence on force employment. Firepower's role in successful counter-insurgency was embedded in practice, without it being formally recorded. Another factor leading to the marginalising of its role is that firepower was rarely employed in the final stages of successful counter-insurgency campaigns, when lessons learnt are usually captured. In addition, what resonates within military culture tends to be what is relatively novel; the employment of firepower was not one of the *new* lessons from these little wars, instead it was seen as an essential component in any military operation[165].

This lack of formal recognition of its role did not matter for those conflicts that immediately followed; firepower was again prominent in the Borneo Emergency[166]. Over time, the British Army's colonial experience diluted and what was remembered was the emphasis on 'minimum force' and the softer side of 'hearts and minds'. This process was reinforced by a desire for distance from the less discriminate use of firepower and the steelier side of 'hearts and minds', including the use of pseudo gangs; these were co-opted insurgents who, through a series of inducements, changed sides and while they remained with the insurgency, they secretly worked for the government. They were used to considerable effect in the counter-insurgency campaigns in Malaya (1948–60), Kenya (1952–60) and Rhodesia (1964–1979)[167].

The British Army's move away from the steelier side of counter-insurgency was reinforced by operations in Northern Ireland. This was almost wholly police support, and not warfare. This prolonged operation initially coincided with America's defeat in Vietnam and the publishing of Frank Kitson's *Low Intensity Operations*; both of which seemed to discredit the enemy-centric approach. In his analysis of counter-insurgency, General Kitson identifies only a minor role for firepower, stating that artillery fire is *only* needed when insurgents '*openly take to the field*[168]'. However, insurgents are invariably visibly in the field at the start of a counter-insurgency, as in the Malayan Emergency, but the General served at the latter stages of the campaign, when this was not the case.

In contrast to the relatively few campaigns considered in the production of Anglo-American doctrine, academics have taken a broader approach. Doctor Christina Goulter identified that there have been numerous successful enemy-centric counter-insurgency campaigns. These include the second (1944–45) and third (1946–49) rounds of the Greek Civil War; Oman (1957–59); Angola (1975–2002); Mozambique (1976–1995); and Turkey (1984–1999). She also identified the crucial requirement for firepower to be integrated with other lines of operation.

> '*during the 'second round' of the Greek Civil War, while air power, tanks, artillery and naval gunfire support were used against Communist insurgent strongholds in Athens, British paratroopers were feeding the local population. In other words, the objects were achieved through fire and manoeuvre, with the latter utilising soft and hard power*[169]'.

As with Malaya, it is difficult to envisage how success could have been achieved in the Greek Civil War without taking on the Communist's armed strength[170]. Michael Burleigh's study of post-World War Two small wars identified that '*hearts and minds campaigns only work once kinetic force – a euphemism for killing people – had achieved population and spatial control*[171]. Not only is firepower essential for splitting insurgents from the people without unacceptable security force casualties, in its visible effectiveness it makes a very compelling argument to the local population that the government is the winning side[172]. This is key in countering the terror used by most insurgencies to gain the allegiance of the people and create a counter-state. The need to achieve moral ascendency over both the enemy and the local population is an essential element in CE Callwell's theories, hence the emphasis on visible confrontation: '*the objective to be sought for clearly is to fight, and not manoeuvre*[173]'. This approach is now rarely followed by Western nations, whose inclination to minimise combat power can result in them being locally out-matched. In contrast to previous Afghan Wars, Britain's initial deployment to Helmand Province was extremely light in firepower; this was then compounded by the dispersion of combat power into platoon-sized garrisons; so instead of being able to overawe opposition from the first, the British were largely fixed by the insurgents[174].

In the current Western approach, conventional forces have largely ceded the defeat of an insurgency's armed strength to special operations forces; these forces conducted kill-or-capture raids, and precision joint fires strikes, on close to an 'industrial scale' in Iraq and Afghanistan[175]. This attrition has been credited by some with having '*opened up space for other measures to advance the pacification of the country*[176]'. Current US doctrine identifies that '*strikes are conducted to disrupt an insurgency, and they can allow other efforts to succeed*[177]'. The effectiveness of this form of decapitation strategy remains disputed[178].

If the population's allegiance is the prize, it is difficult to see how attrition, regardless of how effectively it is done, can significantly assist without actual troops and other agencies on the ground; the permanent presence of these is necessary to win the population's support, chiefly through guaranteeing their security. This approach is grasped by even the most authoritarian regimes, such as the Japanese in China in the 1930s–40s; having seized control of a region, they then maintained a permanent security presence. Subsequently, their *minshin haaku,* or winning the people's hearts, involved reducing feudal dues, providing farmers with seeds and tools and effective local government; of course, this was coupled with extreme ruthlessness against any opposition[179]. This failed because the Japanese could not establish a regime that could reconcile oppressed Chinese peasants with their new masters.

As it has most recently been practised, the current Western counter-insurgency approach disconnects a largely people-centric conventional force close battle from an enemy-centric special operations forces' deep battle. The former generally fails to employ sufficient combat power to demonstrably defeat the opposition, so failing to gain the allegiance of the local population. In contrast, the deep battle inflicts significant attrition, but this is irrelevant in the contest for the allegiance of the people. It is the perceived requirement of the Western democracies to preserve a political mandate for their campaign that leads to this dysfunctional approach. An example of the loss of campaign authority was France's highly effective enemy-centric approach in the Algerian War of Independence; it failed because the French military did not calibrate their use of force with what their own people thought was acceptable. Fearful of this, the Western democracies openly employ a people-centric approach and leave the less publicly-accountable special operations forces to conduct most of the offensive operations. An approach for fighting, but not winning, a counter-insurgency campaign.

Despite this doctrinal confusion, certain conclusions can be drawn about firepower's role in Western counter-insurgency. First, there needs to be sufficient firepower to defeat insurgent enclaves and subsequently to prevent an insurgency from evolving into conventional warfighting. It is the insurgents' decision when to adopt Stage 3 of Mao's Revolutionary War, so the counter-insurgent needs the capability to rapidly transition their fire support to one suitable for conventional warfighting; equal agility is required in shifting to a changed character of conflict if the insurgent de-escalates.

The insurgents will invariably have the tactical initiative as to when and where to engage in combat. To be effective, fire support needs to be prompt, as invariably irregular forces are free to disengage and fight another day. As Philip Caputo observed of his first battle in Vietnam, it was: *'Like so many of the thousands of fire fights that were to follow, it began with an ambush and ended inconclusively'.* Joint fires enable regular forces to stand a chance of winning these initially unequal fire fights.

So secondly, the primary aim of counter-insurgent's firepower is to provide guaranteed responsive fire support. This can be achieved by artillery and mortars dispersing in battery or platoon positions to deliver maximum coverage[180]; this is usually at the expense of mass and thus target effect[181]. These fire support bases invariably require an omnidirectional firing capability. Airpower and to a lesser extent armed aviation – due to its slower speed and lesser weapon load – is usually able to deliver considerable coverage without sacrificing the ability to deliver decisive effect, but it is not a 24-hour, all-weather capability. Against a capable opponent, this usually leads to counter-insurgent operations being limited to artillery and mortar coverage. Operations conducted outside this coverage can be punished by an alert insurgency, especially if weather, time or space to dislocates airpower. The importance of fire support leads to the requirement for joint fires terminal controllers with all combat and logistic elements. This force employment can be understood as follows:

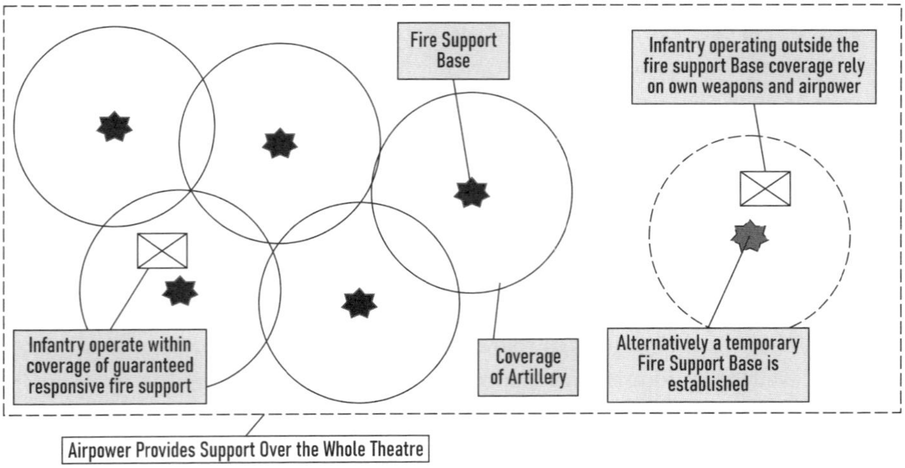

Thirdly, effective use of firepower in counter-insurgency necessitates delegation of the control over firepower. All forms of joint fires, including strategic bombers, have supported individual platoons or sections in recent conflict in Afghanistan. There is debate on whether this decentralisation of firepower's control represents a permanent shift in all characters of conflict, or is limited to counter-insurgency. Firepower's current level of decentralisation is similar to that enjoyed by American forces in the Vietnam War; this was subsequently partly reversed with greater centralisation of firepower to avoid it being dissipated, and so allow it to be massed at the decisive point. The alternate view is that decentralisation will continue because of a confluence of technology and doctrine, as improved communications, and command and control arrangements enable a warfighting approach which seeks to empower the lower levels of command. It is decentralised airpower's command and control that has been the most controversial. This was the norm for the post-colonial wars in the 1950s and 1960s. Belatedly the Americans followed the same logic in November 2010 through empowering the air component coordination element responsible for the Afghan sub-theatre.

Finally, firepower needs to be sufficiently precise to engage the elusive insurgent without inflicting significant casualties on bystanders; this is essential as the population's allegiance is the crucial factor in defeating an insurgency. This is not the case in conventional warfare, when the attitudes of bystanders are rarely decisive in determining a war's outcome. Of course, if non-combatants become collateral damage, it is highly regrettable from the moral perspective and it may have a political impact, but from the practical viewpoint it is of secondary importance to effective conventional warfighting. Against an insurgency, avoiding collateral damage leads to self-imposed restrictions on the employment of firepower; if these are too strict this can neuter one of the counter-insurgents' key strengths. This makes the usability of firepower the key factor; from the technical perspective this is a product of both accuracy and the munition's danger area. This is rarely reflected in official doctrine, but the usability of firepower is an accepted factor in customary thought and practice in Western militaries. At the later, less kinetic, stages of a successful counter-insurgency campaign, precision firepower may be the only usable form of joint firepower. Of course, the chief problem with customary thought is the absence of systematic analysis and peer review; this is the key advantage of authorised doctrine. It leads to unchallenged assumptions, such as only low-yield precision guided weapons have utility in counter-insurgency; this is self-evidently not applicable to all insurgency characters of conflict.

In counter-insurgency the Soviets/Russians largely seek to employ the same principles that govern their use of firepower in conventional warfare. Operationally their use of firepower shares many of the characteristics of the Americans in Vietnam, based on a belief that firepower, largely on its own, can lead to campaign success. The emphasis upon firepower means that that the Soviets and Russians have preceded their counter-insurgency offensives with days or even a week of bombardment, much of it by airpower. Firepower has often been employed without any attempt at manoeuvre, seeking instead attrition and the displacement of certain ethnic groups, rather than the control or gaining the allegiance of, the overall population.

The Soviets/Russians differ from the West in that they make only limited use of fire bases – which they describe as positional artillery – and instead the majority of their guns and mortars accompany manoeuvre forces. As well as providing greater freedom of manoeuvre, this can provide a greater mass of firepower, and a simpler sensor-to-shooter kill chain. Positional artillery is usually a role for second rate troops with obsolete weapons, hence they receive defensive tasks. Russian airpower provides preparatory fire, but only their attack helicopters are usually trusted to conduct danger close fires. The elements of the Russian fire support system in counter-insurgency are as follows:

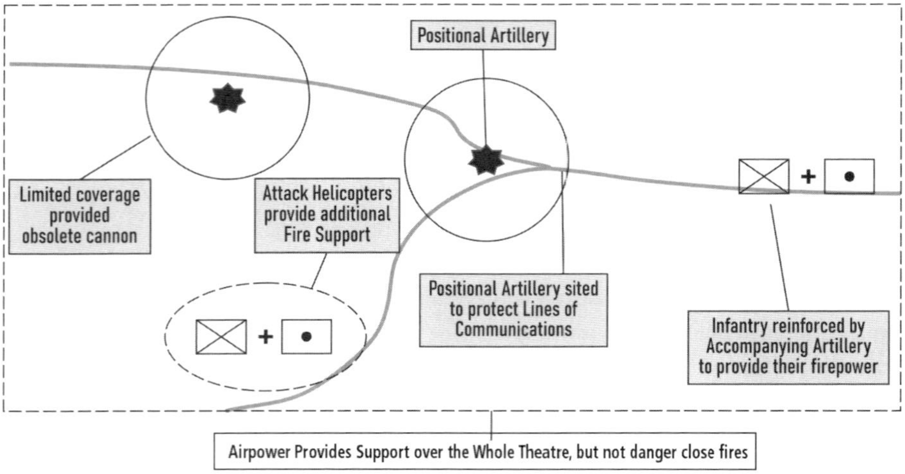

The current Russian approach is similar to that taken by the British in their colonial period when they largely practiced enemy-centric counter-insurgency operations. Hence Callwell's recommendation that the: *'primary duty of artillery in warfare of this nature is to ensure that it is on hand and well to the front*[182].' British artillery followed this tradition through being part of Mobile Outreach Groups in Afghanistan in 2006, but subsequently they adopted an orthodox firebase laydown. The greater weight of fire and speedier engagement of accompanying artillery makes it effective in defeating insurgent forces that are openly holding ground, but it can be less effective in the later stages of a campaign, when control of the population is the objective. This necessitates the dispersal of counter-insurgent ground forces to safeguard the people, this is best supported by a network of fire support bases.

Given joint fires' superior ability to destroy, it can be a double-edged sword, leading to it being the target of the 'strategy of provocation'[183], by which the insurgent seeks to turn firepower into a battle-losing weapon. This can be achieved by seeking to create collateral damage situations, which, with the correct media exploitation, can de-legitimise the counter-insurgency. This can be highly effective when employed in concert with the insurgent's ability to outlast the strategic patience of intervening forces. Avoiding 'own goals' (which caused perhaps 28% of overall civilian deaths) was the significant factor in the restrictions that General McChrystal placed upon airpower in Afghanistan in the summer of 2009[184]. The aim was to reduce the number of civilian deaths that were the Coalition's direct responsibility. Even those campaigning to end the use of NATO airpower in Afghanistan recognised that the overall number of civilian deaths increased, as the result of the restrictions on the employment of NATO airpower was that the Taliban had greater freedom to kill and maim[185].

Notwithstanding the political limitations democracies face when undertaking war amongst the people, the West's counter-insurgency doctrine underestimates firepower's role. There are many reasons for this, but fundamentally it is the result of seeing counter-insurgency's character as being too different from conventional warfare for it to follow the same grammar. In contrast, the Russians make too little allowance for irregular warfare's different character. There is a need for specific counter-insurgent firepower doctrine; it probably needs to crystallise the following truths. Airpower has considerable utility in counter-insurgency due to its ability to achieve coverage without surrendering the ability to provide mass. In contrast, when sited in fire bases mortars and artillery can be much more responsive, but at the price of mass. Delegating control over firepower increases its effectiveness in counter-insurgency; this applies the most to airpower. Throughout the campaign, firepower must remain balanced and able to react, as the counter-insurgent usually has the initiative in escalating and de-escalating violence, either over-matching or dislocating insurgent firepower. Arguably America failed to effectively escalate and de-escalate its use of firepower in the Tet Offensive. Of course, firepower remains a double-edged sword in counter-insurgency, whether accidentally, or when lured, the mis-employment of joint fires can considerably advance the insurgents' cause through collateral damage. But without combining firepower with manoeuvre, a mature insurgency cannot be defeated. This leads to the final deduction – as counter-insurgency is just a different character of war, the deep and close battles must be mutually supporting.

Firepower's Role in Political Warfare

'the Soviets have become masters at combining political, economic, psychological, and other "non-military" forms of struggle with armed conflict[186]*'.*

Raymond L. Garthoff, 1954

The ability to tailor tactics to identified weaknesses has always been an enduring feature of successful warfighting; hence Clausewitz's characterisation of war as being a duel between adversaries. In political warfare – which forms a large part of the current security challenge – the character of conflict sees most of the contest lying outside the traditional military area of responsibility. Countering an adversary operating in this arena requires the full range of state power. The employment of non-military means in conflict comes more naturally to some militaries, in particular those schooled in the Marxist-Leninist approach to war. This stems from the intertwining of military and civil spheres that was evident from the first with Lenin's correction of Clausewitz: *'War is part of the whole; that whole is politics*[187]*'*. Militaries from a more apolitical tradition are more resistant to the need to compete in those activities which in this book has grouped together in the term political warfare. Applying military force without due consideration of political factors has always been problematic in conventional warfighting. This applies even more outside state-on-state conflict; leading one authority to identify that: *' the "First Principle" of counter-insurgency warfare was that the government must have a clear political aim*[188]*.'*

Diplomacy, employing economic power, psychological and media operations can all be gathered under the heading of political warfare. When a conflict has only a small kinetic element, then firepower's predominant role is to avoid own-goals, which can undermine a carefully-crafted campaign narrative. Worst case, collateral damage could furnish a clear justification for the opposition's actions. Hence the need to safely demonstrate force. In Operation Just Cause (Panama-1989) kinetic strikes were offset 500m from a Panamanian Defence Force base to achieve a nonlethal effect, this was supplemented by leaflets and loudspeakers urging surrender[189].

When conflict is limited to political warfare, joint firepower has a restricted number of tasks: first, it needs to preserve a robust warfighting capability to deter any escalation; second, this will often need to be demonstrated. This is easily done by aircraft conducting shows of force. For mortars and artillery, even employing non-lethal munitions such as illumination rounds may be too provocative. In Bosnia in the 1990s NATO ground forces conducted shows of force through regular live firing training, with the purpose of deterring the entities from returning to violence.

In less-kinetic operations, joint firepower's target acquisition capability will often be more important than its strike capability. This is particularly the case within ambiguous three-sided fights, when weapon-locating equipment can provide proof of the source of fire. This can have an important role in countering the opposition's media operations capability. This is not just an issue for the strategic level; land forces will need to identify and counter local media outlets. Identifying and targeting radio stations and mobile phone outlets is rarely practised in peacetime training. These are ideal targets for electronic attack; this is suitable in conflicts where the use of force is highly contained; however, few armies field such capabilities, hence the need for joint support.

Joint Fires' Doctrine

'Why, you may take the most gallant sailor, the most intrepid airman, or the most audacious soldier, put them at a table together – what do you get? The sum total of their fears![190]*'*

Winston Churchill

Self-evidently bespoke firepower doctrine must be joint and applicable to the full range of characters of conflict. For Western militaries, this means that it needs to be part of the joint doctrine that they have been publishing since the 1990s[191]. However, this joint doctrine is rarely sufficiently precise and regulatory[192]. Usually because joint doctrine is the blending of single service doctrine, distilled and diluted to avoid anything too prescriptive, as this could provoke inter-service disputes. Invariably joint doctrine seeks to de-conflict rather than unify effects; its anodyne nature should not come as a surprise as it is inevitably the product of compromises in committee, which, as Churchill observed, are not likely to deliver anything visionary. Even without the joint dimension, a military's peacetime doctrine often includes compromises that mean that it may not reflect the most effective warfighting approach; operational military considerations can be secondary to a service's complex interaction of internal political, organisational and cultural or societal factors. As a result, the most effective warfighting approach may not be possible until warfighting drives the need for change[193].

Joint doctrine needs to unify land and air cultures, which are the products of their discrete operating environments. One of the key differences is in the quantity of individual combat elements, with at least two orders of magnitude of difference between air and land warfare. Land warfare can have tens of thousands of soldiers and vehicles, partly concealed within complex terrain, with often-intermittent communications. In the air domain, at most, there are hundreds of combat aircraft, these are usually easily identifiable within a recognised air picture, and they invariably have guaranteed communications. Given these low numbers and their technical advantages, the centralised execution of airpower is easily achieved; this allows considerable flexibility between mission planning and execution. In contrast, land warfare's 'tyranny of numbers' necessitates decentralised decision-making. With a common approach being formed through doctrine and elucidated in tactics, techniques and procedures. It is these rather than a single authority, such as an air tasking order, that provide unity of purpose[194]. Land forces need common prescriptive practices that apply to the whole hierarchy, between the highest level of command direction and individual execution. The airman, tasked with dealing with a comparative handful of fighting platforms, does not required such regulatory rigour. This can lead to the processes between doctrine and execution being dismissively identified as merely a 'bag of tricks'. This means that by their nature, air forces tend to see doctrine as less binding, and expect a greater degree of improvisation in process when faced with tactical challenges. Faced with these contradictory cultures, it is challenging to establish a common doctrinal approach.

Inadequate coordination between land and air forces is most evident in the conduct of the deep battle. Lack of cooperation is often the root factor in the repeated failure of air interdiction. Dr Richard P Hallion studied four separate conflicts: Operation Strangle (Italy, 1944); the unimaginably named Operations Strangle and Saturate (Korea, 1951–52); French interdiction efforts against Vietminh supply lines, 1952–54; and similar American attempts against the Ho Chi Minh trail network over a decade later. A recurring theme is an inability to agree a joint approach which could see land offensives that increase the enemy's logistic demand being timed to coincide with maximum air interdiction[195].

The near constant operations of Western militaries since 9/11 mean that armies and air forces regularly cooperate; however, this experience will not be directly relevant to a peer-on-peer conventional conflict. Frederick the Great identified that: '*practice, without theory and reflection, dwindles into unsatisfactory routine*[196]'. One outcome of near constant limited conflict is that most air/land training focussing upon forward air control, rather than addressing the more challenging features of air/land warfighting.

Chapter 7: Fixed Wing Aircraft Delivered Firepower

'So long as large armies go to battle, so long will the air arm remain their spearhead[1]*.'*

Cyril Falls, Military Historian

As close air support and air interdiction are but sub-sets of the application of airpower, this chapter is less complete than the subsequent coverage of surface-to-surface fires. It seeks to avoid what has been called airpower's *Icarus Syndrome* – focussing on an aircraft's technical performance rather than its purpose[2]. So this chapter seeks to examine airpower's impact from the perspective of ground fighting. This leads to an examination of weapon accuracy, responsiveness and the level of guarantee, target effect, and survivability against air defences, rather than focussing on an aircraft's flying characteristics.

From its humble beginning in World War One – the armed aircraft used by the Italians against the Libyans in 1911 were significant only in the sense of being first[3] – aerial firepower has come to dominate conventional warfighting. This applies whether it is land or carrier based, manned or unmanned, operating within the atmosphere or from near space, and employing weapons or turning themselves into a weapon as in 'Kamikaze drones'. Within joint warfighting, land component commanders now aim to conduct unified ground and air operations, merging both forces within their operational design. Unfortunately, close air support dominates the inter-service dialogue, leading to militaries being guilty of conflating one means of employing airpower with the totality of merging air and ground warfighting. Within the close air support community, the ongoing debate centres on whether it is an aircraft or a mission. It is probably more productive to consider it as a capability, in which an effective air and land integration structure is as vital as the pilot or the plane. This same structure ensures that other forms of air support – including interdiction which is usually the most effective means of employing lethal airpower – are synergised with land operations.

General Omar Bradley identified the advantage of this convergence for the 12th Army Group's advance from Normandy to Germany:

'the air-armour team is a most powerful combination in the breakthrough and exploitation … The use of this coordinated force, in combat, should be habitual'[4].

General Bradley's operational design aimed at coordinating the two components over the whole theatre, rather than limiting airpower to the close air support of ground forces in close combat. Airpower was used ahead of the armoured advance to break up resistance. Tactical aircraft also had the economy of force mission of providing flank guards. The result was that ground forces did not need to dissipate their strength on this secondary task, so retaining momentum in their advance. This formula was largely repeated in the 2003 Iraq War; but with the air force proving fallible in their provision of a lethal flank guard during operations around Baghdad.

Aircraft made their first impact on the battlefield through spotting for artillery. Modern aircraft are now unrivalled in their ability to survey the battlefield and acquire targets; networking them into other sensor platforms further improves this situational awareness. They have an unmatched weight of firepower, so in the right circumstances aircraft are by far the most effective joint fires system. Even a single aircraft can have a decisive impact on a ground tactical engagement. Aircraft have a range of ordnance that are effective against most ground targets, though precision munitions mean that most Western swing-role fighter-bombers are now optimised to engage point targets; these munitions are ideal against buildings and strong points. In peer-on-peer conventional conflict an area target capability is also required against protected and manoeuvring targets, in the Cold War these targets were attacked with cluster munitions delivered at relatively low altitude; modern cluster munitions have sufficient guidance to get them into the target area from survivable standoff distances. For those nations that have forsaken these weapons, enhanced high explosive can deliver their anti-personnel effect, and precision munitions the anti-tank effect. All of these can be employed from standoff distances. It is not just about munition lethality, as we have already established in chapter 5, the utility of aerial firepower in the land battle is a balance between: lethality, the ability to deliver danger close firepower, and the survivability of aircraft in the attack. As can be seen in this diagram:

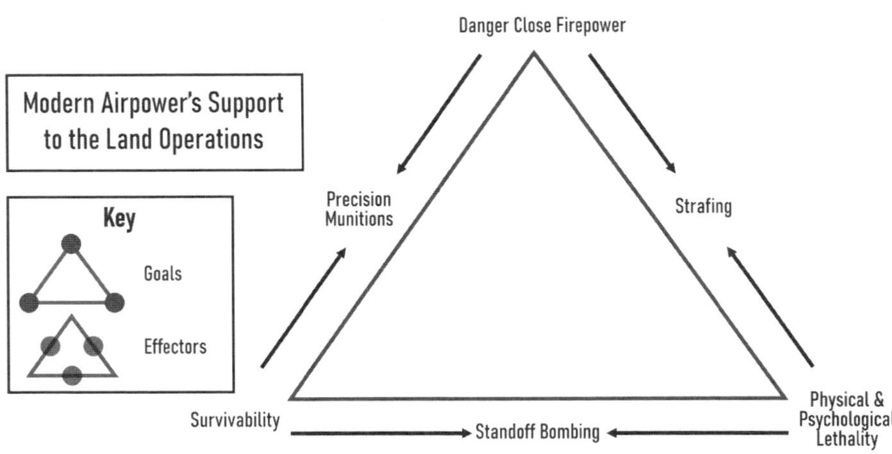

Technology is lessening airpower's enduring limitations, but this is leading to fewer, increasingly precious, aircraft. The willingness to risk these aircraft has become a key factor in determining airpower's role in the land battle, hence the importance of the choice of munition and mode of attack to ensure aircraft survivability.

The disadvantages of employing standoff to improve survivability are a reduced ability to respond to changes in the ground battle and the reduced psychological effect caused by the target not seeing the aircraft. It takes time for ordnance released from a high altitude to arrive on target – even without any horizontal standoff distance, it takes about 45 seconds for a bomb to fall from 32,000ft. This can be crucial against highly dynamic and time-critical targets that are in close combat with own forces. The other advantage of flying close to the target is that the highly visible and intimidating presence of aircraft both supports own force's, and affects the enemy's morale. As has been covered in chapter 5 in its discussion of systems theory, the desire to separate the effect on the target from its delivery platform endures in any discussion of the joint fire system of systems. This 'actor' focussed approach led to Army Secretary John McHugh's view on the proposed retirement of the A-10:

> *'What the soldier wants to see and what the command structure in the US Army wants to happen [is placing] explosive ordnance on enemy positions ... in a timely and effective [manner]'*[5].

Taking purely a target-focussed approach to close air support ignores the impact of an aircraft's physical presence, and that its flying characteristics are key to determining whether explosive ordnance can be placed safely on an enemy position in a way that aids ground fighting.

Evolution of Air Support to Ground Warfare

> *'Close air support is not just a physical act of war. It is, instead, one of the indefinable abstracts of combat that can, by its presence, heighten morale and, by its absence, destroy morale. Moreover, its contribution to battle is immediate, and its results readily apparent to both friend and foe'*.[6]
>
> Susan Mercer Williams and Frank J. Mirande, Historians

The strengths and limitations of airpower's support to the land battle were evident from its first employment in World War One. More than any other form of joint firepower, airpower can be rendered less effective by troops employing cover and concealment. Conversely, its lethality exponentially increases once ground troops move and expose themselves. Trench warfare made spotting, and reconnaissance aircraft, a vital piece of the artillery system-of-systems, while limiting airpower's direct lethality. Trenches may have offered protection, but aircraft could still deliver a suppressive effect, as the German *Schusta* or Protection squadrons did through their systematic strafing of British defensive positions at the Battle of Gavelle in April 1917[7]. The mobile conditions of the German retreat to the Hindenburg Line in spring 1917, and the 1918 offensives, provided the opportunity for aircraft to demonstrate the impact of their bombing and strafing on the Western Front. From the first, the vital importance of air superiority was recognised, it allowed the British, largely unhindered by opposing fighter aircraft, to significantly delay the German advance of 5–21 March 1918 through concentrated airpower[8].

As low-level attacks were the only option, even World War One's rudimentary anti-aircraft artillery and small arms fire inflicted significant aircraft attrition. This vulnerability led to the German ground attack squadrons employing armoured plates to protect the pilot, fuel tank, and usually the aircraft's engine. Aircraft losses led to a view that airpower could be better employed away from the immediate contact zone, through prosecuting a deep battle that sought to disrupt and isolate the fighting echelons. In the favourable terrain and weather of the second Battle of Armageddon, 19–24 September 1918, a combination of British airpower and Arab guerrilla attacks isolated the Turkish defenders prior to the main attack. The bombing of the El Afule telephone exchange completely disrupted Turkish command and control. This and the subsequent pursuit provided a foretaste of airpower's lethality in subsequent desert wars. On one occasion, aircraft destroyed the first and last vehicles of an artillery column traversing a defile, allowing them to subsequently destroy the whole battery with bombs and strafing.

Airpower's deep battle successes led the RAF and the US Army Air Corps between the Wars to conclude that direct attack of ground enemy combat forces was an inefficient use of airpower[9]. The Germans, who had been on the receiving end of the Allies' more effective air attacks, were more enthusiastic supporters of direct support to the land battle. In the *Blitzkrieg*, at the decisive moment the Germans pioneered the shifting of all available aircraft to directly support the land battle. The Western Allies first matched them in their final assault in Tunisia from 5–6 May 1943, when 3,241 tactical aircraft – '*airpower of a different order*' – directly supported ground forces[10].

In Normandy in 1944, fighter-bombers found soft skinned vehicles a relatively easy target, but they were largely ineffective against protected targets; operational analysis showed that it took 3,500 bombs or alternatively 800 rockets to kill a tank[11]. This made the German lines of communication a much more lucrative target than the battlefield. The defeat of German forces in the twin battles of Mortain and the Falaise-Argentan gap can be largely attributed to Anglo-American airpower; most of the German tanks were abandoned due to lack of fuel following the destruction of their supply trucks. While many modern aircraft now have a range of weapons to destroy even the best-protected tank, the interdiction of lines of supply can often be a more efficient approach. This nuance is rarely modelled in operational analysis wargames.

Technical advances have simultaneously increased the warplane's strengths, and reduced the impact of its weaknesses[12]; improved sensors, weapon accuracy and terminal effect has narrowed the gap between suitable and unsuitable targets, allowing airpower to be lethal against even the best protected ground forces. From the 1980s, most modern combat aircraft could operate in darkness, but foul weather continues to hinder air operations. Even partial cloud, snow, rain and fog can significantly reduce the effectiveness of aircraft sensors, including thermal ones through dimming heat contrast; heavy precipitation can block laser guidance. Radar can generally overcome weather, but the heaviest precipitation can block its waves. Bombing from above cloud cover either restricts accuracy or requires self-guiding weaponry, the alternative of going below the cloud level is a riskier option. Across the electromagnetic spectrum, current aircraft sensors are less effective in urban and wooded terrain; even in more open terrain a skilful, low contrast enemy can still limit the impact of airpower. A shrewd enemy with armoured vehicles can still posture themselves to avoid becoming a viable target, as the Serbs demonstrated in the Kosovo conflict, resulting in little damage per sortie; and requiring time to make air attacks effective. Operation Anaconda provides many useful lessons, including the observation that the American Air Force believed it had identified almost half the Al-Qaeda positions prior to the assault, and yet almost all of the ground fire came from previously undetected positions[13]. All this runs contrary to the prediction, confidently made after the Gulf War, that airpower's ability to destroy ground forces would render ground force on ground force combat inefficient[14]. Despite these qualifications, an enemy that fails to actively and passively protect his land forces is becoming more vulnerable to modern airpower. This would have been the case with the Serbians in Kosovo if they had had to posture themselves to defend against a ground attack.

How Aerial Firepower is Employed in the Land Battle

[Most air support in the Vietnam War] '… fell into a grey area between those missions that were clearly close air support in the traditional sense and those that would formerly have been called interdiction'[15].

John Schlight, Official Historian

Airpower's enduring limitation in the land battle is its lack of persistence; reduced aircraft numbers increase this. This means that even the highest contrast ground force elements can operate against an opponent with complete control of the air. In both the Gulf and Iraq Wars, Coalition airpower, on occasion, failed to detect and hinder large-scale Iraqi armoured manoeuvre[16]. While airpower's ability to identify its own targets is increasing, much of its fire support is cued by ground forces; this is due to ground forces' continuous observation, and the fact that through their actions they can create engagement opportunities for airpower. Exploiting this requires an effective air and ground forces cooperation organisation.

Air support to land forces is conventionally divided between close air support and air interdiction or deep air support. In the Cold War, with its linear battlefield, this was further sub-divided:

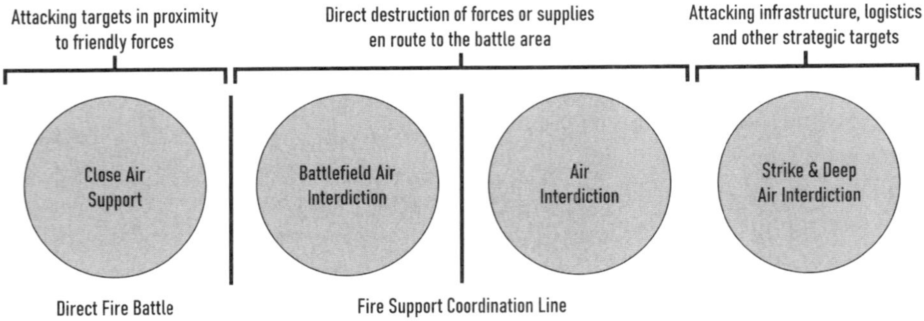

In recent years there has been a tendency to consider all air support within the land component's battlespace as close air support. This recognises that all air sorties, even when not close to own troops, requires some coordination with land forces as they are the permanent occupiers of the battlespace. Close air support within danger close distances continues to require bespoke procedures, with the ground commander needing to accept the risk of employing munitions close to own troops.

Close air support is employed in two main ways: pre-planned and immediate. Pre-planning allows aircrews to conduct detailed mission coordination and planning, as the target's make-up, location and time on target are known. Immediate close air support is a response to an unanticipated target, so preventing aircrews from completing detailed mission planning and coordination before launching. When there is an anticipated requirement, but currently no identified targets, an improved response is achieved by putting aircraft on alert, either on the ground or in the air in a 'cab-rank' holding pattern. Pre-planned close air support is a more efficient use of airpower as preparation allows the aircraft and its munitions to be correctly matched to the target, and force protection measures to be maximised. However, immediate aerial fire support is often more decisive in seizing opportunities and winning ground tactical engagements.

The traditional targets of air interdiction are HQs, logistic facilities, transport vehicles and communication infrastructure, with the aim of isolating the battlefield from further support. Historically interdiction has always been the most effective means of employing aerial firepower against conventional armies; technology may be accentuating this. The challenge for modern aircraft is not hitting a military target but acquiring and then identifying it as hostile. As close air support is more constrained by fratricide concerns, it is air interdiction that can better exploit the lethality of modern sensors and weaponry. The increased power of air interdiction and counter land forces strikes has been evident in the West's most recent conventional warfighting. However, this fact has been obscured by the dominance of close air support in subsequent counter-insurgencies. The legacy of these operations is that many armies remain focussed on close air support; some compound this error through ascribing the favouring of air interdiction to an air force's institutional desire to operate independently of ground forces.

The proportion of Western airpower resources devoted to providing close air support has increased in each conflict since World War Two. In the Korean War the air component devoted between 10 and 15% of its sorties to close air support, translating into an average of 96 sorties for the 8th Army each day. In the Vietnam War, the 7th Air Force peaked at nearly 800 close air support sorties in a day; in Operation Desert Storm, over 600 close air support sorties per day were allocated to the short ground offensive[17]. Despite the impressive quantity of aircraft allocated to close air support, only the minority of these sorties were actually controlled by forward air controllers using close air support procedures. Only 3% of US Air Force sorties in South Vietnam in October 1966 were actually close air support controlled by forward air controllers. During Operation Desert Storm the US Air Force identified that only 6% of their sorties were controlled by forward air controllers[18]. In this conflict, the US Marine Corps air wing cited close air support as accounting for 70% of their missions. On further investigation only 14% of these were on their own troops side of the fire support coordination line that effectively separated land and air component battlespace. Of this 14%, only a proportion would have been sufficiently close to friendly troops to require close air support procedures[19].

In the post-9/11 Wars, with the redefinition of the term, the proportion of airpower allocated to close air support increased. During Operation Anaconda, nearly all of the missions flown were close air support of ground forces in the Shah-e-Kot Valley[20]. Inadequate air and land coordination resulted in much being conducted without forward air control, making it less effective. During the push to Baghdad in 2003, 75% of Navy and Marine air involvement consisted of close air support missions[21]. The US Air Force reported that 79% of targets struck (15,592 of 19,898 attacks[22]) during the campaign were either kill box interdiction[23] or close air support. Of the 1,492 missions assigned to V Corps: 886 were directed to counter land operations within kill boxes, and 606 missions were close air support; however, forward air controllers who could actually see their target controlled only 6% of the close air support missions conducted by V Corps[24]. This did not mean that air and ground forces were neither effectively coordinated nor complementary, land force manoeuvre was essential to force Iraqi forces to expose themselves to aerial firepower, allowing their defeat before they could close with Coalition ground forces[25].

It follows that there is *true* close air support – missions conducted by forward air controllers, using special procedures to manage the risk of employing munitions within danger close range of friendly forces, and there are air attacks that now categorised as close air support because they are on ground forces. The broadening of this categorisation – which is now the NATO standard – is perhaps in part due to American institutional factors. Close air support is the traditional *raison d'être* of the US Marine Corps Aviation; the US Air Force finds it advantageous to describe their direct support to the Army as being of the most committed kind – close air support. To understand aerial firepower's contribution to the land fighting requires the recognition that these two forms of close air support place totally different demands upon aircraft, aircrew and the air/land integration system.

In contrast to conventional warfighting, in recent counter-insurgency much of the fighting was at close quarters. Positive control by forward controllers, supplemented by visual target identification by pilots was often required to employ aerial firepower within danger close distances. Furthermore, recent operations in Afghanistan and Iraq have seen close air support moving from a weapon of last resort to prevent ground forces being overrun, the only time it came close to been guaranteed in the Cold War, to being the principal source of firepower. In addition, in counter-insurgency operations, air cover has been so plentiful as to be used as a preventive measure to deter enemy action[26]. Ground forces preparing for peer conventional conflict should expect to receive limited support from the air, and if the 2003 Iraq War is a guide, as few as 6% of the missions could be *true* close air support.

Air Delivered Weapon Accuracy

'Accuracy to within 50 yards is essential. If it cannot be achieved from heights of 5,000 to 6,000 feet, the target must be attacked from lower level – 500 feet[27]*.'*

Royal Flying Corps HQ Instruction, 1915

Getting closer to the target has been traditional means of improving accuracy. Advances in aircraft design, aircrew expertise and munitions have improved accuracy, so allowing greater standoff from the target, and increasing aircraft survivability. The introduction of munition terminal precision guidance has taken this one stage further through breaking the relationship between range and accuracy.

At the outset of the Vietnam War fighter-bombers were achieving a circular error probability of 750 feet (230m). This was halved in several years of combat, largely through improved training[28]. Most modern aircraft can achieve even greater accuracy through on-board radars and computers that better account for the ballistics of unguided munitions[29]. The media identified a distinct Russian approach in the Syrian Civil War: improving the accuracy of the bomber, rather than the munition[30]. In fact, the Russian SVP-24 targeting system is nothing more than the advances in bombing technology that have been standard in the West for decades. This Russian fake news was designed to obfuscate their less discriminate use of firepower.

Despite improvements in technology and training, the aircraft's attack profile still has a major impact upon accuracy. The steep dive with a late weapon release, to get as close as possible to the target, is the time-honoured means of improving accuracy; World War Two Stukas repeatedly achieved accuracies of 10m in training and, less consistently, this level of accuracy was operationally delivered[31]. When the World War Two Soviets switched to dive-bombing, one air division commander claimed, an almost certainly exaggerated accuracy of 18m circular error probability; as opposed to the 2,000m they had previously achieved[32]. With a high angle dive attack, a modern aircraft with a well-trained crew, with an unguided free fall bomb, can be expect an accuracy of 20–30m circular error probability[33]. The effectiveness of precise bombing with unguided weapons was practically demonstrated by the attack on the Iraqi Tuwaitha Nuclear Reactor; the Israelis achieved 15 out of 16 unguided 2,000lb bomb hits on the target[34].

A modern aircraft, with a well-trained crew, could expect a 100m circular error probability at medium altitude; accuracy similar to dive bombing can be achieved by minimising meteorological errors through releasing almost on top of the target. This necessitates the use of a retard tail or high drag bomb in order to achieve safe separation between weapon and aircraft. Like dive bombing this profile exposes an aircraft to low level air defences. Finally, there is the 'loft and toss' type of attack. The aircraft releases the bomb as it pulls up short of a target so throwing it forward with significantly diminished accuracy, but improved aircraft survivability.

As the opening World War One quote identifies, aircraft have always sought to achieve a point attack capability, the challenge being ground based air defences. By 1944–5 the German flak gunners were expert at their trade, but the commander of the American Ninth Air Force expected a sortie of eight P-47 Thunderbolts to be able to knock-out a defended bridge[35]. By then the linkage between bombing accuracy and the flak threat was well established: it took five and half times more bombs to damage a well defended bridge as an undefended one[36]. A combination of improved ground based air defences and reduced tolerance of casualties has led to a diminished appetite for this approach. Terminal guidance has made this largely redundant, as it allow medium altitude engagement of point targets, with improved aircraft survivability through standoff, and consistency through largely removing operator error.

Direct fire weapons range in their accuracy from multiple rockets that can engage large area targets, to precision guided missiles with a point target capability. Machine guns and cannons combine excellent anti-personnel lethality with accuracy, making them the most suitable aerial danger close weapon. Their accuracy can be reduced by the weapon recoil's impact on an aircraft's stability, which is particularly issue for hovering helicopters. In contrast, a fixed wing aircraft's forward momentum, particularly in a dive, counters recoil. This allows the A-10 to achieve 80% of its shots within a 40-foot (12m) diameter circle from 4,000 feet. The M61 Vulcan 25mm cannon is less accurate, achieving about a 50% greater dispersion[37]. Despite this, in the Vietnam War, cannon fire was routinely directed within 10–20m of friendly forces[38]. But as a F-15E pilot identified about his aeroplane's 20mm cannon *'it's very precise, but you have to get close to the threat to use it'*[39].

Responsiveness of Immediate Close Air Support

> *'One arm of service identifies what needs to be hit; another arm decides whether or not it is going to be hit. As a result, many ground commanders simply do not plan on CAS because they cannot rely on its being responsive unless it has been integrated in detail (and approved) beforehand*[40].'
>
> Raoul Archambault and Thomas M Dean,
> respectively US Army and Navy Officers

Undoubtedly, more capable aircraft and superior use of information technology, linked to a more effective air ground coordination systems, have improved the individual responsiveness of close air support aircraft; but there is a compelling argument that the overall responsiveness has plateaued, due to a reduced overall number of aircraft. Historically the single driving factor in improving responsiveness is actual conflict, as this provides the imperative to address lack of cooperation caused by single service obduracy. Though of course, air and land forces with well worked-up procedures during peacetime are obviously better placed to rapidly improve in conflict.

During the German invasion of France in 1940, *'requests made to the Luftwaffe did not require more than 45 minutes to become effective on the battlefield'*[41]. This became faster as the campaign progressed. By the latter stages of World War Two, American troops on the main axis of advance expected air support within 25 minutes[42]. In the Korean War response time averaged an hour[43]. In America's Vietnam War the average wait for close air support was around 40–60 minutes if ground alert fighters had to be scrambled[44]. Employing already airborne aircraft could get the delay down to 20 minutes[45]. While most sources identify this as satisfactory, some Army sources criticise battlespace management as slowing down the process. They saw this as better reflecting peacetime air traffic control rather than the operational imperative[46]. US Air Force sources, while identifying that the average time from the eruption of a firefight to the first delivery of close air support was over an hour, determined that *'40 minutes of this time was being lost by ground commanders delaying their request for air support'*[47]. Or in other words – if you had asked for it sooner, you would have got it sooner. These single service perspectives fail to adequately account for the other environment's challenges: the soldiers' lack of understanding of the complexity of airspace management; and the airmen's lack of appreciation of the nature and character of ground combat, particularly in complex terrain.

Less than a year before Operation Iraqi Freedom, the Army Chief of Staff, General Eric Shinseki, optimistically identified that about 25 minutes was the normal wait for close air support[48]. For the very highest priority tasks, such as supporting 3/7th Cavalry who were leading the US advance to Baghdad[49], dedicated aircraft got the response time down to 20 minutes. But for the majority of the force, the delay in air support was closer to the historical 45-minute average.

In 2014 Israeli ground forces waited an average of 45 minutes to engage Gaza Strip targets. Throughout, artillery proved to be significantly timelier. When the Gaza Division invoked the 'Hannibal' (emergency kidnapping situation) protocol, within minutes artillery units simultaneously engaged seven targets. The first air-delivered bomb was dropped about 50 minutes after the invoking of the protocol, against a single target. In the extrication operation in Shuja'iyya, the first air strike was executed about thirty minutes after the divisional artillery group completed the engagement of all of their targets[50]. The Israeli aspiration is a response within 10 minutes for the critical targets authorised by a brigade commander; achieving this responsiveness presumably required air alert aircraft. The partial exception to the plateauing of response time is the airborne alert aircraft, which can be more responsive than the historical norm, as digitisation makes them more capable of being rapidly re-tasked; however, air alert aircraft will be less common with declining aircraft numbers.

In 'push close air support', aircraft are launched in the expectation that there will be opportunity targets; pending one being identified, they are 'cab-ranked' on air alert at a convenient distance from the supported forces. This encourages ground commanders, and their forward air controllers, to use their initiative to maximise employment of airpower. Sending forward a continuous stream of aircraft may be an inefficient means of delivering firepower, but, as we have seen, it halves response time. In contrast, the 'pull close air support' system is less resource-intensive, as a command-led process first determines whether an opportunity target represents an effective use of airpower. A compromise is achieved by employing ground alert aircraft; this allows faster engagement of opportunity targets, whilst retaining chain of command authorisation before launch.

The greater endurance of unmanned aerial vehicles and manned aircraft supported by air-to-air refuelling means that they can extend their time over the battlefield awaiting tasking. In recent counter-insurgency operations, this has led for some operations to a near-continuous aerial presence. The slower pace of unmanned aerial systems and gunships means that in larger theatres, fast jets, held at ready alert on the ground, may render more timely support. Of course, when airspace is contested at all altitudes, aircraft will not be able to loiter close to the battlefield; this will further reduce their response time.

This section may appear to be somewhat laboured in showing that airpower cannot, in terms of responsiveness, ever match organic surface to surface. However, what is strange is that this lesson seems to periodically require relearning. This was highlighted in an American task force report following the second battle for the Iraqi city of Fallujah (November 2004):

> *'a big lesson learned is that, even when responsive, close air support is not a substitute for artillery and mortars. It can be very effective, but it is not as responsive as our artillery and mortars*[51]*'.*

Nor should it be expected that greater automation could significantly improve air support's responsiveness. While it will assist, the enduring challenge of air/land integration remains a human one, particularly for close air support. As articulated by the commander of Israel's air-ground cooperation unit who identified the continued human requirement to: *'to supervise the process … so that the bomb does not land on our own forces'*[52].

Finally, the quest for flexibility and responsiveness may be at the expense of effectiveness. One pilot's view of the 2009–2010 surge in Afghanistan was that less than 20% of the close air support missions executed were actually briefed to the aircrew supporting them[53]; airpower had become wholly responsive to Coalition forces being attacked, with aircraft from across the theatre being directed to a contact. This inefficient approach was not penalised in counter-insurgency, given its lack of reciprocity. In conventional warfighting against a peer opponent, the failure to synchronise airpower with ground forces is an inherently less effective approach; inadequate aircrew planning and briefing will add further risk to the employment of aircraft in the land battle. And as already identified, aircraft survivability is the major limiter of close air support.

Specialist Close Air Support

'They [Il-2 Shturmovik] are as essential to the Red Army as air and bread.'

Joseph Stalin

The extent to which close air support of land forces needs specialist aircraft and crews, as opposed to employing any suitably-armed aircraft, remains an on-going debate. The Germans in World War One modified aircraft and trained crews specially for ground attack, though most close air support was conducted by standard aircraft and their crew. Except on the Eastern Front, the swing-role fighter-bomber dominated the delivery of close air support in World War Two; the Anglo-Americans specifically fielded rockets with greater standoff to overcome the vulnerability of their lightly protected fighter-bombers to ground fire. As well as being less versatile, the performance trade-off in creating a specialist close air support aircraft made them vulnerable to opposition aircraft; this usually necessitated the gaining of local air superiority before employing specialist aircraft. As the Anglo-Americans prior to World War Two discounted the need to provide their ground forces with direct support, unlike the Soviets, they did not develop specialist designs. Post-war the more versatile fighter-bomber has dominated. Only America, and to a lesser extent, the Soviets/Russians have fielded specialist close air support aircraft that are suitable for conventional warfare. In addition, low performance jets and turbo-props have proved their worth in counter-insurgency operations. A sub-category of specialist ground attack aircraft is the gunship; this is a conversion of a transport aircraft through fitting a range of direct fire weapons that are largely optimised to engage personnel.

The ideal flying characteristics of the specialist close air support aircraft are: a long loiter time, and an ability to fly low and slow. The latter improves the pilots' ability to acquire targets and discriminate them from friendly forces. Aircraft flying above 350 knots are significantly less effective at strafing. The specialist A-10 strafes at between 300–350 knots, in contrast to the AV-8B Harrier II at 420–480 knots and F/A-18 Hornet at 480–540 knots. In addition, the ability to operate from a rough landing strip allows the aircraft to be close to the fight and thus responsive. Considerable engine power and wing area is required for a large and varied weapon load; a rugged build standard, with armour protecting the aircraft's most vulnerable items is essential in an aircraft designed to go low and slow over the battlefield. Sufficient ammunition and protection enable repeated 'gun runs' when the enemy 'hugs' friendly units to evade bombing[54]. While no aircraft is truly all-weather, a good close air support aircraft needs to able to operate in adverse conditions to improve the guarantee of fire support; this has led to favourable weather being listed as one of the eight conditions for effective close air support in US doctrine[55].

The World War Two Russian Il-2 Shturmovik armoured ground attack aircraft had most of these characteristics. Other aircraft were converted into the role, such as the Stuka; this was originally designed as a dive-bomber to engage fortifications and key infrastructure. Other solidly build dive-bombers – in particular Naval and Marine aircraft – proved equally effective when engaging ground targets. Air superiority aircraft that were too heavy for their primary role, such as the Typhoon, made a more effective contribution. Despite the view put forward by some airpower commentators that World War Two proved the superiority of the multi-purpose fighter-bomber over the specialist aircraft this was not the case on the Eastern Front. The Soviets fielded 35,000 Shturmovik, compared to 54,000 fighters and 16,000 bombers of various types[56]. With the Shturmovik being widely considered to be the Soviet's most effective platform; as the opening quote identifies, Stalin saw them as vital. The Germans built their last of 6,500 Ju 87 Stukas in August 1944; from October 1943 onwards, their specialised ground attack units (*Schlachtgeschwader* or battle wings) were being equipped with a specialist ground-attack version of their Fw-190 fighter.

Post-war the Soviet Union did not field a Shturmovik type aircraft for the jet age, despite having operated this type of aircraft since the 1920s; it abandoned them in favour of the jet fighter-bomber, beginning with the Su-7 Fitter. Obsolete piston and jet fighters took on the ground attack role in the 1950s and 1960s; the reintroduction of the specialist ground attack aircraft occurred in the 1980s with the American A-10 and Russian Sukhoi (Su)-25. Some saw a return to an already discredited approach, others saw it as a recognition that the modern jet fighter's speed made it incapable of 'swinging' to conduct close air support in the way that was possible with its piston engine predecessors.

The Americans at the height of the Vietnam War identified the requirement for a specialist ground attack aircraft; this was the genesis of the A-10 Thunderbolt II, nicknamed 'Warthog' as a result of its rather bulky shape[57]. As it did not enter service until 1984, it should primarily be seen as a Cold War and not a counter-insurgency weapon. This led to it being designed around a 30mm gun that was capable of penetrating almost all tank top armour. Its combination of low speed and excellent downward pilot visibility allowed it to acquire individual targets; this was coupled with sufficient armour to be survivable at low level. Externally it could carry a significant payload of bombs and missiles. Once it was provided with Maverick terminally-guided missiles, it had the option to engage targets from medium altitude, so improving its survivability.

The Su-25 (NATO nickname Frogfoot) was initially thought to be the Soviet version of the A-10. However, the Su-25 is smaller, does not carry as powerful a gun, and flies faster. The Frogfoot could and did fly close air support missions, particularly in Afghanistan; there its straight wing design gave it a greater ability to manoeuvre at slower speeds and deliver a greater quantity of weapons, more accurately, than the MiG-21 and MiG-27 fighter-bombers, but it was primarily designed to engage targets beyond the front line. The Soviets saw the heavily armed, armoured and durable Mi-24 Hind as their primary platform for direct aerial fire support of troops in contact. This was evidenced by the theatre-wide deployment of the Mi-24, while the Su-25 only covered western Afghanistan, where its greater range than the Hind allowed Soviet troops to penetrate further into mujahedeen territory and still remain under effective air cover. Evidence of a wider role is that, the Su-25 pioneered the Soviet employment of precision weapons[58].

The Su-25 suffered most of the losses in Russia's 2008 conflict with Georgia; however, these appear to have been primarily due to inadequate aircraft maintenance and poor piloting skills – the result of years of insufficient funds for flight training – rather than being overmatched by ground fire[59]. No replacement has yet appeared for the ageing Frogfoot; but its deployment to support Assad's Syrian government since 2015 shows that it is valued. Ukrainian Su-25 have made a limited impact due to the strength of Russian air defences; when they have been effective it has been through flying extremely low.

The AC-119 and later the AC-130 are former transport aircraft equipped with a range of heavy machine guns and cannons up to 105mm calibre. These are mounted to fire from one side of the aircraft, enabling them to bombard a stationary target with high accuracy while conducting a continuous turn to circle the target. Their major disadvantage is their vulnerability. Air superiority is of course required, and in addition their slow speed, predictable flight path, size and speed makes them highly susceptible to ground fire; even against rudimentary air defences they are usually restricted to night-time operations.

Against limited air defences, converted trainers can provide a cost-effective alternative to expensive multi-purpose fighter-bombers. Until recently these aircraft have been the preserve of less advanced air forces but in 2009 the US Air Force declared, with the Light Attack/Armed Reconnaissance program, its intent to procure an off-the-shelf observation and attack aircraft. This could mean the fielding of an aircraft such as the A-29 Super Tucanos or AT-6 Texan IIs. America has equipped its Afghan allies with the sturdy, propeller-driven Super Tucano. It is able to operate from austere airfields and is easy to fly and maintain. They can fly slowly while strafing and combine an excellent all-round visibility cockpit with advanced electro-optical sensors and modern avionics. They are armed with two 0.50 calibre machine guns and up to 3,000lbs of munitions, including laser-guided bombs, which the aircraft can self-designate[60]. Ten years on from the programme, USAF have still not fielded an aircraft, indicating a lack of support for this specialist aircraft. In an attempt to resuscitate the program American legislators are attempting to transfer it to Special Operations Command.

Fighter-Bomber and Bomber Aircraft in the Ground Attack Role

'During the Battle of Britain the question "fighter or fighter-bomber?" had been decided once and for all: The fighter can only be used as a bomb carrier with lasting effect when sufficient air superiority has been won[61].'

Luftwaffe General Adolph Galland

As achieving and maintaining theatre-wide air control is the first task in the Western way of airpower; this doctrine requires most, if not all, aircraft and pilots to contribute to air superiority. They can then 'swing' to other tasks, including close air support, once fewer resources are required to maintain air control. All World War Two fighters – the American P-47 Thunderbolt and P-51 Mustang, the British Hurricane and Spitfire, the German Fw-190 and Russian Yak-7 – proved their worth as fighter-bombers[62]. The American P-47 Thunderbolt, designed as a bomber escort, was perhaps the most successful due to its rugged construction and heavy armament: eight 0.50-caliber wing-mounted machine guns, three bomb racks capable of carrying 3,000 pounds of bombs, or ten five-inch rockets. The P-51 Mustang and the British Spitfire rendered good service, but were more vulnerable to ground fire and lacked the P-47's weapon load[63].

As there was not a significant speed difference between the piston-engine specialist ground attack aircraft and the fighter-bomber aircraft, they were both equally effective at acquiring targets and strafing. This would not be the case in the jet age; in the Korean War piston and lower performance jets took on much of the ground attack role; higher performance fighters could only effectively contribute through bombing, as they had become too fast to acquire targets and effectively strafe, this being compounded by their cannons lacking sufficient ammunition to provide effective danger close fire. In addition, to preserve their high performance, these fighters were rarely armoured, making them too fragile to survive against radar controlled low level air defence cannons.

Instead of solely reverting to 'low and slow' aircraft that could deliver traditional close air support, the USAF fielded sensor pods and precision munitions that converted fighter-bombers into a round-the-clock, and almost all-weather, medium altitude strike aircraft[64]. The ability of aircraft to destroy almost any building or strongpoint with large precision munitions (bombs of 2,000–5,000lbs size) has changed the grammar of ground conflict, particularly in urban terrain. The West retains a distinct edge in this technology; the Russian targeting pods lack sophistication when it comes integrating satellite positioning, electro-optical/infrared imaging, laser designation and a video downlink capability. Until the Russian deployment to Syria, the view was that the gap was closing[65]. In Syria, only the newest the MiG-35S has been sighted with the T220 targeting pod; the other Russian aircraft have employed a mix of organic optical systems. Customers of Russian jets have paired them with Western pods: the Indians and Malaysians' Su-30MKI use American and French targeting pods; without targeting pods, Russian aircraft are largely limited to unguided weapons.

The downside of the sophisticated avionics and sensors that allow an aircraft to swing between roles is that this is an expensive capability to buy and maintain and there is a considerable training challenge of multi-skilling their crews; even America struggles to maintain a wholly multi-role aircraft fleet. In addition, given that most aircraft are procured with pre-planned incremental improvement, it is rare for early versions of aircraft to be sufficiently developed to be genuinely multi-role. The F-35 will be a highly versatile aircraft, but its early versions will effectively be single-role.

The specialist bomber has often been pressed into supporting land operations. In the Pacific War the B-24 Liberator Heavy Bomber was regularly employed in direct support of ground forces. In the island-hopping operations in Borneo and the Philippines, when the construction of new airfields could not keep up with the advance, B-24s could be the only land-based aircraft within range. The B-24 operated like tactical aircraft, employing low altitude attacks, with bombs dropped as close as 500 yards from friendly forces[66]. These operations were prosecuted with relatively light losses, something that would not have been possible in more effectively defended European and Mediterranean skies. In these theatres strategic air forces conducted medium level area bombing to stay above most of the flak. These massed attacks required considerable pre-planning and coordination; this could include the withdrawal of friendly forces to a safe distance (unfortunately not by far enough in Operation Cobra when bombs fell on US troops[67]).

From 1967 the American B-52 was used in the Vietnam War in the close air support role. A combination of precise guidance and control techniques, coupled with own troops being static in fire support bases, allowed safe danger close bombing[68]. This was the halfway point in the evolution that was recently completed by the US Air Force's B-1s and B-52s. With their long loiter time (routinely 12 to 15 hours), and considerable payload of precision weapons, they have provided effective danger close air support in the Afghan and Iraq counter-insurgencies. Until 2008 American bombers were limited to bombing on precision grid references. When fitted with the SNIPER Targeting Pod, they could also laser designate their own targets, whether cued from a forward air controller or self-acquired. Modern fighter-bombers carry the same weight of weapon load as the largest World War Two bombers; a modern bomber is a step change from other aircraft. A B-1 carries up to 84 Mk 82 (500lb) free-fall bombs, the B-52 carries about half this load. The Tupolev Tu-160 Blackjack, Tu-95MS and Tu-22M3 Backfire bombers have been key to the heavy weight of ordnance delivered by the Russians in their intervention into the Syrian civil war. The Tu-22M3 Backfire can carry seventy 250kg bombs.

The Argument For and Against Specialist Close Air Support Aircraft

'[The] single most recognizable and feared aircraft at low level was the A-10. Although the actual bomb run was terrifying, the aircraft's loitering around the target area caused as much, if not more, anxiety since the Iraqi soldiers were unsure of the chosen target[69].'

A captured Gulf War Iraqi officer

Equipped with precision munitions and sensor pods, in Operation Desert Storm F-111F and F-15E, America's most sophisticated deep interdiction and strike aircraft, quickly adapted to counter-land missions. Their thermal sensors allowed them to identify Iraqi tanks against the backdrop of a cold desert[70]. Now, due to targeting pods, almost all modern aircraft and their crews can deliver both close air support and air interdiction with precision weapons from medium altitude; delivered this way, close air support is significantly safer, and does not require specialist aircraft, munitions and crews trained in low level attack[71]. Depending on the means of terminal guidance this approach to close air support has been described as: *'bombing on coordinates', 'danger close precision strike'* and *'ground aided precision strike'*[72].

The success of this technology has led to the majority US Air Force view – that *'close air support is a mission, not a platform*[73]*'*. During 2006–13, 67% of the close air support missions in Operation Enduring Freedom in Afghanistan and Operation Iraqi Freedom in Iraq were flown by fighter-bombers, with only 24% conducted by the A-10. The efficacy of these figures is disputed because they count missions flown rather than weapons released. Opponents of this official USAF view identify that in Afghanistan between 2010 and 2014 a total of 121,653 close air support missions were flown, but only 8,691 sorties had weapon-release, or 7% of the total. Furthermore, the data does not distinguish between how close air support was provided, whether it was bombing on grids from medium altitude or supporting troops with strafing[74]. The Air Force commissioned RAND Report identified that A-10s, in the Afghanistan counter-insurgency, were more likely to engage the enemy and employ strafing rather than bombing. The means of attack can be important, as the opening quote identifies, attrition is not the only metric. RAND also identified that the A-10s better met the needs of the ground commanders[75]. This is probably due to specialist close support pilots being better at interpreting the instructions from a forward air controller, and identifying and understanding the impact of any ground manoeuvre upon the mission. A telling argument in favour of the A-10's focus on the ground missions is that currently roughly half of the pilots in a typical Warthog squadron maintain a forward air controller qualification. American fighter-bomber aircrew, who also have to maintain currency and proficiency in other missions, rarely have this qualification[76]. The outcome is that from a system-of-systems perspective A-10 squadrons are much more effective at employing airpower against ground forces than generalist squadrons. They should expect to be even more effective than fighter-bombers when the air/land integration structure is ineffective.

Recent operations have resulted in Western aircrews being well trained[77] and experienced in supporting ground forces. This prompts the question as to whether this will remain true as NATO's air forces react to changed geopolitics by emphasising training for a broader range of airpower tasks. The US Army sees a community based around a specialist aircraft as necessary to advocate for close air support in an air force that doctrinally sees it as its fourth priority. American airpower has previously institutionally turned its back on close air support, as one forward air controller with extensive operational experience was told on being assigned to the Pentagon:

> *'We're trying to purge the Vietnam FAC [Forward Air Control] experience from the fighter corps because we have moved into an era of air combat where the low-threat, low speed, close air support you did in Southeast Asia is no longer valid. And we don't want these habits or these memories in in our fighter force*[78]*'*.

Despite the effectiveness of precision munitions from medium altitude, most Western armies still expect their air forces to provide the traditional form of close air support. Their argument being that the nature and character of ground warfare can prevent standoff engagements being effective. Because in its confusion, ground forces cannot always, in a timely manner, precisely acquire enemy locations, then communicate this target information to the aircraft, for them to either allocate coordinate-seeking or designate laser-guided munitions to each individual target. Faced by the fog and friction of war, aircraft can simplify the sensor and shooter link through acquiring their own targets, identifying friendly and third-party locations and then conducting a direct fire engagement. Ideally this can be done from medium altitude, but when the opposition is intermixed in close combat with own troops, aircraft will probably require low-level flying to acquire targets, and employ guns because friend and foe are mingled. Strafing has always been the traditional means of engaging an opponent attempting to gain immunity from fire through 'hugging' their adversary. Furthermore, when faced by clouds that block laser guidance and most sensors, aircraft need the ability to fly underneath.

Low-level, below-the-clouds close air support with the aircraft visually acquiring their own targets and then employing their guns, has been rare in recent conventional conflict. As we have seen as low as 3–6% of airpower missions supporting American land forces are actually controlled by forward air controllers. This may be proportionately greater in peer-on-peer conventional conflict when, initially at least, air support is likely to be rare, restricting it to exceptional circumstances, such as when ground forces are in danger of being overrun. These tactical circumstances are likely to require aircraft to fly low and slow to allow the pilots to differentiate between friend and foe, and if these are intermixed, strafing is likely to be the best option[79].

The alternative view is that aircraft like the A-10 were designed in a very different era, when the most effective way to deliver precise firepower to troops in contact and engage individual tanks, was through cannon fire[80]. This has led to the ground force's fire support requirement being conflated with the original characteristics of the A-10. The actual aircraft has been significantly developed; they have been retrofitted with sensors and precision weapons that improve their survivability through enabling greater standoff. In ongoing operations in the Middle East, the A-10's eleven weapon hardpoints usually carry only guided munitions and one targeting pod. Even its rocket pods are the new Advanced Precision Kill Weapons System that provides precision guidance to the previously unguided 2.75-inch (70mm) rocket. The A-10 retains the capability to conduct traditional close air support; detractors see this as encouraging the most dangerous approach to providing fire support. Other see this as adding flexibility.

Whether specialist aircraft suffer disproportionate losses – one of the conclusions of the Operation Desert Storm after-action report – is disputed[81]. This data is derived from aircraft lost per sortie, and it does not make allowance for A-10s being significantly more likely to drop ordnance compared to fighter-bombers. Nor are losses balanced against the importance of the task; most would say that preventing the defeat of ground forces justifies the increased danger to the aircraft from ground fire.

There is a genuine concern that the A-10 and the Su-25 may have become the modern Junkers Ju-87 Stuka; an effective close air support platform but lacking the performance to survive in contested airspace. By 1943 the Germans could not operate it against the Anglo-Americans; it was retained to the end on the Eastern Front because Soviet airpower doctrine hampered counter-air operations. Some see the A-10 as fit to operate in Iraq and Afghanistan, but unsuitable for peer warfighting; the more survivable and versatile multi-role fighter is at least the equal of the specialist ground attack aircraft when conducting close air support from medium altitude with precision weapons, and are much more survivable.

The US Marine Corps, who own their own air support, are not as fixed as the American Army on the need for a bespoke capability. They currently operate a mixed fixed-wing fleet: a declining number of specialist ground attack AV-8B, and the F/A-18 and F-35 fighter-bombers. This means that the organisation that is considered by many to be the leading exponents of close air support is content for this to be delivered by a fighter-bomber. Furthermore, despite their historical and emotional attachment to close air support, the American Marines use their airpower in the most effective way to aid the land battle[82]. In operations where the principal task is close air support (Afghanistan through to Syria) the Soviets and the Russian have employed a wide range of aircraft, with only a slight bias towards their specialist Su-25. Their fielding of increasingly capable fighter-bombers, with only limited investment in the Su-25, indicates that this remains their likely direction of travel.

By using the maximum range of their sensors and missiles, helicopters can horizontally standoff a target. When this is combined with terrain masking they are a challenging target; making them a more survivable solution in delivering the danger close air support role in peer conventional warfighting. This appears to be the US Marine Corps approach; attack helicopters are dedicated to rotary close air support rather than employing the Marine's increasingly higher performance fixed wing aircraft to conduct strafing. This allows Marine fixed wing aircraft to concentrate upon the destruction of point targets with precision weapons in the close battle, and engage enemy forces not yet in direct fire contact with own forces. This is essentially the Russian approach, with helicopters taking on closer targets and freeing the fixed wing aircraft to operate in depth. Given the effectiveness of attack helicopters, retaining bespoke fixed wing aircraft to meet the least effective means of employing airpower may well be a capability luxury. The crucial arguments being: concerns over their survivability in general war and the rarity of the requirement to actually conduct low level, danger close, air support.

Airpower: The Most Easily Countered Form of Land Fire Support?

'Anyone who has watched the United States operate understands … that it's to their advantage to deny access into areas, particularly from the air … With air superiority everything is possible, without it nothing is possible[83]*.'*

General Frank Gorenc, US Air Forces in Europe Commander

It is common-place to believe in an ever-increasing ascendancy of airpower in warfare, but there is a counter view that its impact on the land battle is declining. The historian Martin Van Crefeld opined that despite modern aircraft having significantly greater payload, deliverable in almost all weathers, to the highest level of precision, airpower has declined in importance from its World War Two peak[84]. He identifies that this is largely due to the declining quantity of aircraft.

It is a safe prediction that the number of available combat aircraft will continue to decline, as the price of the F-35 indicates; current estimates are in the region of $94–122 million apiece[85]. This continues to be in line with the prediction of the now famous Augustine's Law 16; which opined that due to cost growth, by 2054 it would take the entire US defence budget to procure one aircraft[86]. Even if individual aircraft are significantly more capable, reduced numbers equal a decreased ability to assert their presence over the battlefield; specifically, it prevents any reduction in close air support response times. This means that fighter-bombers largely have a transitory effect; destroying enemy forces, but they cannot provide continuous suppression of likely enemy positions, nor through their persistent presence, restrict movement like their World War Two predecessors.

Attempts to restrict cost-growth have failed and the outcome is an aversion to risking valuable aircraft in circumstances where they can be shot down by a small calibre cannon or machine gun round. The current generation of unmanned military aircraft cannot compensate for declining fighter-bomber numbers, as even the most sophisticated ones cannot survive in contested airspace. As the Iranians demonstrated in their shooting down of a Global Hawk on 20 June 2019; this is leading the Americans to re-evaluate the utility of their drones in the new security environment. Making them survivable will make them significantly more expensive, which will reduce their numbers.

Compounding this lack of mass is the reduced availability of these newer more complex platforms; this means that the F-22 Raptor currently has around 60% availability, while the previous generation's F-16 and F-18 achieve 70–80%.

Reduced aircraft numbers, and the resultant lack of persistence, increases the ability of adversaries to employ terrain and tactics to dissipate aerial firepower. At its simplest, seasoned opponents of Western airpower have learnt to wait until aircraft return to base before conducting their operations. Faced with Israeli firepower, Hamas have perfected underground warfare, making it central to all they undertake, including offensive action through tunnelling underneath border defences[87]. The Serbs in the Kosovo crisis showed that these counters were not just the preserve of the irregular fighter. Western airpower faces thinking and adaptive enemies that minimise their *signal* through avoiding the use of technology. Instead of recognising this it has been guilty of focussing on mirror-imaging its own high technology capability; this is not uniquely an air force problem, but its prevalence in this community has resulted in it acquiring its own term: 'conning'[88].

Deep-rooted in the culture of most air forces is the equating of air superiority with the defeat of enemy airpower through air-to-air combat. From the first air-to-air combat was glamorised; World War One aces quickly achieved celebrated status. But it was ground-based air defence that has provided airpower's most persistent and effective challenge. Resulting in supporting ground forces being a significantly more dangerous mission than contesting air superiority. This was particularly so in the last ten months of the Great War, with improvements to air defence guns and effective height/range finders that allowed fuzes to be accurately set. 80 Squadron RAF lost an average of 75% of its pilots every month through conducting close air support[89].

In World War Two, the defeat of the Luftwaffe's fighters over their own homeland – a fight they could not decline as it was combined with the strategic bomber offensive – was a significant strategic success. However, this only halved the Anglo-American Bomber offensive's aircraft loss rate per sortie. Through to the war's end, ground based air defences, with occasional fighter support, shot down 2.6 aircraft per 100 sorties[90]. German anti-aircraft gunners accounted for half of American bomber losses, despite this it was not until 1943 that they identified that *'it is probable that the importance of flak has been under estimated*[91]'.

This emphasis on attrition is due to air defences rarely providing an impenetrable defence against airpower. Instead it seeks through inflicting an unacceptable level of attrition, to force air forces to either change targets or adopt force protection measures. The latter leads to changes in tactics, techniques and procedures that can reduce airpower's operational effectiveness. At its most effective, air defence can make whole capabilities obsolete. Due to the relative failure of faster jet aircraft, the P-51 Mustang was re-introduced to conduct close air support in the Korean War; despite its greater effectiveness, it suffered twice the loss rate – largely from radar controlled anti-aircraft artillery equipped with proximity fuzes – as the faster and more durable jet aircraft. This led to the Mustang's withdrawal. The Israeli Air Force lost 109 aircraft in 1973 War, of which 61 were lost during ground attack against a deadly synergy of surface-to-air missiles and radar-directed multiple-barrel light flak[92]. This effectively removed Israeli airpower from the land battle until ground forces were able to help defeat the integrated air defence system with tank and artillery fire. The Mujahedeen acquisition of Stinger missiles in the Soviet's Afghan War significantly decreased the effectiveness of airpower, in particular their Hind attack helicopters[93]. The loss of an AC-130 in daylight above Iraq in 1991 led to its current restriction to nocturnal operations [94]. In the Kosovo crisis, the undefeated (because it was rarely drawn into combat) Serbian air defences – particularly mobile SA-6 and man portable missiles – by their mere presence degraded the effectiveness of NATO airpower. With the notable exception of Israel's 1982 invasion of Lebanon[95], the defeat of opposing airpower has proved significantly easier than the suppression of their ground based air defences.

Man-portable missiles and mobile cannon currently represent the most pervasive threat to airpower, as they are difficult to counter due to being rarely detected before they engage. But given their range limitations and low lethality, the effect of these weapons is closer to harassment, rather than the denial of airspace. In recent years Western airpower has had ascendency over the longer range more capable systems capable of airspace denial. This is changing with the fielding of more capable integrated air defence systems. The proliferation of these is creating a growing number of 'no-fly' zones that Western air forces may need to face in the coming years if they are to maintain the control of the air that they have exercised for three decades. These modern systems network together missile launchers with early warning and target acquisition radars, through a resilient command and control network (often employing buried landlines or point-to-point UHF communications), all of which benefit from enhanced computing power. The key advantage of ground systems is that they do not face the miniaturisation and integration challenges that apply when these systems are fitted into an aircraft. This allows ground based air defence systems of systems to employ large and heavy components, and disperse individual platforms to avoid any mutual interference issues. This makes it possible to network significantly more powerful radars, and to improve their lethality, while also making them more survivable[96]. Not being weight and space restricted allows Russian integrated air defence weapons to overcome the still-extant Western technological lead.

Compounding the inherent technical advantage of a ground system when faced by an airborne one, is the disinvestment by all major Western air forces – with the notable exception of the US Navy – in anti-radar and jamming-resistant capabilities[97]. Likely foes of the West will continue investing in ground-based air defences to contest Western airpower, rather than trying to symmetrically match their capability through fighter aircraft. The purpose of these air defence systems is to achieve a level of attrition that makes airpower's employment unaffordable, and to force aircraft to operate in a manner that significantly reduces their effectiveness. Once Western airpower is blunted, Chinese and Russian fighters expect to be able to achieve at least localised air superiority.

In the absence of a technical solution or overwhelming numbers combined with a willingness to take losses, defeating a modern integrated air defence system will be problematic, and if successful will most likely require a prolonged integrated joint offensive operation[98]. Without this the most effective response that an aircraft can make to integrated air defence systems will be masking their sensors with terrain through flying low. This will of course make aircraft more vulnerable to man portable surface-to-air missiles and anti-aircraft cannon. Aircraft flying interdiction and strike missions can route themselves away from concentration of these systems; however, such low-level air defence systems are invariably at their densest protecting ground combat forces, leading to significant attrition en route and over the target area when conducting close air support.

In summary, there are several reasons why of all the joint fire systems, aerial-delivered firepower remains the easiest to counter. Firstly, aircraft largely operate as direct fire weapon systems – with the target acquisition and engagement capability in the same platform – hence they have fewer force protection options than the other joint fires systems. Secondly, as well as being actively challenged by air defence systems, airpower's lack of persistence makes passive counters especially effective in avoiding offering a viable target. Finally, even without enemy action, technology is reducing airpower's impact in land warfare through reducing serviceable aircraft numbers. So whilst dominating joint warfighting, in peer engagements the actual battlefield effect of conventional airpower is likely to be significantly less than in recent conflict. This is particularly important for Western ground forces who have grown reliant on air support. In contrast to the increased vulnerability of orthodox combat aircraft, simple unmanned aircraft, over the last few years, have been able to operate largely unchallenged over the battlefields of Ukraine, Syria, Iraq and Nagorno-Karabakh, employing either their on-board weapons or more usually cueing artillery. These unmanned aircraft have realised even more persistent surveillance than was achieved by two-seater light aircraft in the positional warfare of the 1944 Normandy campaign and Korean War. When this is coupled with the enhanced lethality of modern artillery, this combination has dominated recent static combat.

These unmanned aircraft have been largely unchallenged because civilian technology has driven their rapid technical development, while the technical response is reliant upon military procurement. Hence, as at 2020, air defence systems are relatively ineffective against such elusive aerial targets. This capability shortfall is being addressed; but these small aircraft, with an insignificant radar cross section, will remain a challenging target. Especially quadcopters which can hover amongst the low-level ground clutter that will defeat most sensors. The outcome of being largely commercially sourced is greater immunity from Augustine Law's aircraft cost inflation, resulting in them being available in mass.

It follows that the small quadcopter with a simple electro-optic sensor will probably be the most survivable aerial capability in positional close combat. In comparison, more sophisticated bespoke military unmanned aircraft, that were the surveillance mainstay in the West's recent counter-insurgency campaigns, will present an easy target in peer conflict; however, their longer range and more sophisticated sensors will both assist in positional warfare and dominate target acquisition in mobile operations.

Given the need to remain small and stealthy these quadcopters will probably not carry effective organic weaponry. Of course, they can turn themselves into a weapon. Loitering 'kamikaze drones', such as the Israeli Harrop, have sufficient mass to damage air defence systems; however, these are easy battlefield targets, leading to them primarily cueing joint fire systems. Returning airpower to its original Great War role, as a user, rather than provider, of firepower to the land battle. In mobile warfare aircraft are more effective if they combine target acquisition and engagement; which, at least currently, is made more effective by an onboard pilot making the decisions.

In conclusion, in conventional warfighting, the most effective way of employing airpower will remain engaging the opposing ground forces before they reach the direct fire battlefield. Aerial firepower remains essential when ground forces face imminent defeat, but fixed wing aircraft no longer have the monopoly on providing such support. The attack helicopter cannot match the fixed wing aircraft's weight of firepower, but in most circumstances it is more survivable, has greater persistence and a range of weapons that match likely targets. If attack helicopters take-on low level close air support as their primary mission, then fighter-bombers can concentrate on standoff engagement. Making the leap to greater reliance upon attack helicopters for close air support is anyway inevitable, as the technical sophistication of current and future fighter-bombers will not compensate for their reducing numbers and their optimising for precision strike[99]. Furthermore, rather than fixating on close air support, armies and air forces should seek through converging their warfighting to match the most suitable capability to the tactical circumstance. Ground forces should focus their targeting resources on achieving the maximum employment of airpower in front of the direct fire battle. Then, rather than husbanding air force sorties, armies should rely upon the attack helicopter to provide a reserve of firepower to deal with unforeseen circumstances; army operated unmanned aircraft will maximise organic firepower and will partly compensate for limited airforce persistance.

Chapter 8: Aviation Firepower

'the rotor drives a coach and four through conventional military wisdom by putting paid to the linear imperative of movement, and by allowing troops to use ground tactically without depending on it for mobility[1]*.'*

Brigadier Richard Simpkin

Helicopters have revolutionised all aspects of land warfare from reconnaissance to logistics. Their impact has probably been greatest in making troop movement and resupply largely independent of terrain, with the arming of helicopters coming second. This study will restrict itself to armed helicopters, which are general-purpose helicopters converted to deliver lethal effect, and the less common, bespoke, attack helicopters. In its short history, armed aviation has gone from providing improvised armed escorts and area firepower when field artillery is out-ranged, to being land warfare's most potent direct fire weapon system. Aviation's desire to compete with fixed wing aircraft in deep attack is discussed in detail. As is the helicopter's more successful displacement of fixed wing aircraft in delivering close air support. The Soviets and Russians provide a contrast to the Western approach, initially at least, seeing helicopters as a direct replacement for their World War Two armoured ground attack aircraft; this results in a focus on cannon, rockets and gravity bombs. Their latest attack helicopter designs may indicate a shift towards adopting the Western belief in the primacy of the anti-tank role.

Early pioneers and theorists saw the armed helicopter as becoming the decisive weapon in conventional warfare, seeing a parallel with the dominance that armoured warfare achieved over World War Two's infantry-based armies. They expected the helicopter's speed advantage over conventional ground forces would more than compensate for its vulnerability and limited weapon load. The helicopter has not achieved the dominance predicted by its proponents, but it has become a significant contributor to combined arms warfare, and land warfare's most lethal provider of precision firepower, particularly against tanks.

The Introduction of Armed and Attack Helicopters

'Cavalry, and I don't mean horses[2]*.'*

General James M. Gavin, the American aviation pioneer

The fielding of armed and attack helicopters results from a combination of the technical potential of rotor aircraft and the desire of armies, as air forces became more independent, to retain their own organic air support. For both these reasons America has largely led development. For some in the US Army, the Korean War proved that the newly formed US Air Force (this occurred in 1947) could not be trusted to provide effective close air support. They saw this as the outcome of the Air Force's primary focus being nuclear strategic bombing; in the tactical domain it was on achieving air superiority, followed by deep strike and air interdiction[3]. The desire for their own under-command airpower led to the Army fielding of unarmed fixed wing aircraft and helicopters. The distribution of tasks between the two services was agreed in the 1948 Key West Agreement. This saw Army aviation restricted to reconnaissance and medical evacuation[4]. While the arming of fixed wing aircraft was considered a step too far, the rapidly maturing helicopter technology provided opportunities to contravene the Agreement. Obviously, this was opposed by the air force; at time not very rationally. When Lieutenant General James M. Gavin discussed the development of the helicopter with the USAF Director of Requirements, he was told: *'The helicopter is aerodynamically unsound. … No matter what the Army says, I know that it does not need any*[5].' This view may now appear to border on the luddite; but the first helicopter flew in 1907, it was not until 1939 that there was a practical aircraft in Igor Sikorsky's VS-300, and development effectively stalled in World War Two. In addition to getting a valuable fighting platform, the Army also recognised that the fielding of armed helicopters would provide a valuable lever to incentivise the USAF to agree with their position on resourcing close air support.

The French first operationally armed helicopters; the Bell 47 (Sioux H-13) casualty evacuation helicopter was modified by placing infantry machine gunners in its stretcher panniers during the Algerian War of 1954–62. By November 1960 H-13 Sioux were fitted with machine guns and SS-11s anti-tank guided missiles. America's Vietnam War drove an exponential growth in the helicopter's technical capability; air mobility became central to American counter-insurgency tactics. During the War, the US Army and Marine Corps deployed more than 12,000 helicopters.

Responding to the threat from ground fire, the standard transport aircraft the UH-1 Iroquois or 'Huey', had door-mounted machine guns fitted; from early 1962, units in theatre were converting UH-1 into specialist platforms equipped with rockets, grenade launchers, and machine guns; these gunship UH-1s were commonly referred to as 'Frogs' or 'Hogs' if they carried rockets, and 'Cobras' or simply 'Guns' if they had machine guns. The success of these armed helicopters led to the development of the World's first attack helicopter, the AH-1 Cobra. Its bespoke design put survivability at a premium; it was armoured and much narrower than previous helicopters, so presenting a more difficult target from the front, the expected high threat arc. This led to a tandem seat arrangement that has become characteristic of attack helicopters. Removing their troop-carrying function resulted in a higher power to weight ratio, and so a significantly greater weapon load could be carried; being purpose built allowed the weaponry to be fully integrated with the crew.

The arming of utility helicopters continues, as they are cheaper and more versatile than the specialist attack helicopter. In contrast to arming utility helicopters, which retain their troop and logistic carrying capability, the UH-60 Blackhawk has been turned into a bespoke attack helicopter, the AH-60. This is used by US Special Operations Forces. Having an attack and utility helicopter on the same platform simplifies logistics through greater commonality across their fleet; in addition, rather than using an already in service attack helicopter, the AH-60 allows the US Special Operations Forces to optimise their weapons and avionics for irregular rather than conventional operations.

From the first there were varied ideas on the employment of armed and attack helicopters. In the Vietnam War, American helicopters in the aviation battalions and cavalry squadrons provided intimate support for air mobility operations. Separately, at divisional level, there were the aerial rocket artillery units, controlled by the divisional artillery commander, these were not part of all arms formations; instead they were divisional troops who, like artillery, were controlled on the divisional fire support radio net. This allowed the massing of helicopters (12 aircraft were the minimum fire unit) to deliver a weight of firepower that was able to substitute for tube artillery in suppressing an area target. While they may not have been able to match artillery's ability to sustain fire support, armed helicopters were often superior at providing danger close fire support, and they could deliver a much greater initial weight of fire. And of course, their coverage was much greater as it extended to the helicopter's combat radius.

In the Vietnam War helicopters primarily employed the 2.75-inch aerial rocket, supplemented by machine guns, miniguns, and grenade launchers. Faced with a predominantly infantry target, the machine gun's high rate of fire and greater quantity of ammunition was usually preferred to cannon. The cannon's subsequent displacement of machine guns was due to the growing importance of the anti-tank role, and the need for greater standoff due to improvements in air defences. The machine guns greater anti-personnel effect means that it remains the primary close protection weapon of utility and transport helicopters.

Attack Helicopters Primarily Become an Anti-Tank Platform

'[The attack helicopter is] an airborne armoured fighting vehicle, and in intent and purpose [is] more closely related to the tank than the airplane[6].'

Richard P. Hallion, Senior Adviser for
Air and Space Issues, The Pentagon, 1989

At the battle of An Loc, on April 13, 1972, an AH-1 Cobra from Battery F, 79th Artillery became the first helicopter to destroy a tank with a guided missile. Disengagement from Vietnam coincided with the 1973 Arab-Israeli War showing the effectiveness of anti-tank guided missiles and the vulnerability of close air support to ground fire from missiles and guns. Following the Vietnam War, preparing to fight the Soviets became the US military's priority. NATO's new *Active Defense* doctrine, adopted in 1976, gave the attack helicopter the central role of delaying or stopping Soviet armour.

The chief advantage of anti-tank guided missiles is their accuracy at long-range, however in most terrain, intervisibility restricts ground mounted launchers from achieving more than a fraction of their theoretical field of fire. Helicopters can rapidly move to another firing point, or increase their altitude, to overcome obstacles that interfere with their fields of fire. This allows helicopters to dictate the terms of an engagement by exploiting their missile's maximum range. So achieving the standoff that makes them immune to most anti-aircraft systems. Switching roles greatly increased the helicopter's combat worth. Attack helicopters can carry between six (Hind) and sixteen (Apache) missiles; given their missile's high hit and kill probability, this means that even a pair of helicopters could effectively defeat a tank battalion. In comparison, significant numbers of helicopters are required to match artillery's ability to suppress area targets.

With the fire support requirement removed, the aerial rocket artillery battalions disappeared. Despite this, their proven utility in the Vietnam War led the Americans to field more helicopters than any other military. The American Army established a Combat Aviation Brigade in every division, with battalions to provide: service support, combat support (UH-60 Black Hawk and CH-47 Chinook), air assault (UH-60 Black Hawk and attack/reconnaissance (AH-64 Apache). The 101st Airborne Division (Air Assault) has the largest aviation brigade; plus, there are special forces helicopter regiments, a number of Air Cavalry Squadrons attached to armoured cavalry units, and Corps/Theatre Aviation Brigades for deep strike.

The effectiveness of anti-tank helicopters was practically demonstrated in the Israel/Syria conflict in 1982. The Syrians used French-built Gazelles; the 4,000m range of their HOT missiles made them largely invulnerable to ground fire. This allowed them to form a screen which successfully delayed the Israeli advance and destroyed seven tanks[7]. Israel's American-built AH-1 Cobras and Hughes 500MD had missiles with less range and faced more effective Russian supplied anti-aircraft weapons, and so they had to rely upon pop-up engagements from behind mountainous terrain[8].

In the Gulf War's four-day ground phase, attack helicopters predominantly provided fires in front of the armoured forces through operating 'over their shoulder' to exploit the range of the Hellfire missile. The open terrain allowed attack helicopters to excel at reconnaissance. 101st Airborne Division (Air Assault) exploited its airmobility to set up an advanced base within Iraq from which to conduct aviation strikes. This was a partial exploitation of the helicopter's mobility differential that the proponents of airmobility had predicted[9]; however, the pace of the armoured advance, helicopter serviceability in desert conditions[10], and the likely impact on the air component's freedom to engage, have all been cited as reasons why no subsequent operational-level air assault occurred. The exploitation of airmobility to cut off retreating Iraqi forces was proposed, but in addition to the above factors, there was an unwillingness to risk such an unorthodox operation when the war was already won[11].

The 2003 Iraq War provided an opportunity to conduct helicopter deep attack, resulting in the 11th Attack Helicopter Regiment one, that discredited this approach[12]. This led to a debate on whether such operations are conceptually flawed or whether it was merely an instance of inadequate preparation and execution; what is certain is that in damaging 29 out of 30 aircraft, the Iraqis had adapted to the challenge posed by attack helicopters. When employed to provide over-the-shoulder fire support or in offensive reconnaissance, helicopters proved significantly more effective. Subsequently, stabilisation and counter-insurgency operations in Afghanistan and Iraq have resulted in them providing vital fire support, largely with cannon. To achieve precision long-range engagement against personnel, the Hellfire anti-tank missile was converted into a multirole weapon through a thermobaric warhead, and the 70mm (2.75-inch) rocket received laser guidance.

Helicopter Survivability

'because everybody in this country has a weapon. And if they all shoot them up in the air at the same time at every helicopter that flies over, it becomes a very lethal environment for a low-flying aircraft[13]*.'*

Lieutenant General Wallace, the V Corps commander in the Iraq War

From the first the helicopter has been criticised for their loss rate. Over 300 AH-1 Cobra helicopters were lost in the Vietnam War; but only 3.5% of the total battle damage occurred when flying over 1,500 feet above ground level[14]. Only one AH-64 was lost in the Gulf War, to an RPG (Rocket Propelled Grenades) hit at close range; the Apache crashed but the crew survived, (compared to four A-10s, all lost to surface-to-air missiles). Operations by utility helicopters over Mogadishu in 1993 showed that low altitude, combined with hovering, made them particularly vulnerable, leading to the loss of two machines within a few minutes[15]. Open sources suggest that 40% of recent US helicopter losses are due to RPG and 20% due to small arms fire; both of which require low altitude engagement[16]. Flying low, in large formations on predictable routes, makes helicopters vulnerable to most weapons; this makes low-level battalion and brigade helicopter strikes lucrative targets. The very perception of the vulnerability of helicopters prevented their use in the Kosovo War[17]. In recent conflict, even a weak anti-aircraft threat, when coupled with a reduced willingness to tolerate casualties, has severely restricted aviation operations[18].

To counter the threat, helicopters have made considerable progress in masking the five distinct signatures that give them away: visual, acoustic, radar, infrared, and electronic. Modern helicopters have early warning systems, operating in the radar, infrared and acoustic spectrums, to allow helicopters to know they have been acquired. This enables them to respond, this could involve use of active countermeasures: chaff, decoy flares and jammers. If acquired as a target, the helicopter's two most important aids to survivability are physical protection and standoff distance, these are often complementary. Helicopters are increasingly resilient, so even if hit, they can often survive. In the heavy fighting near the city of Al Hillah in 2003, the 101st Airborne Division had eight Apache helicopters which were hit by enemy fire; as they were deployed well behind ground forces, the Iraqi weapons did not overmatch the protection and they remained flyable. As long as a vital part was not hit, even unarmoured helicopters can survive multiple hits from 7.62mm or smaller calibre small arms; surviving 12.7mm rounds is problematic, a helicopter is lucky to survive anything larger. The RPG can defeat any helicopter armour, but its range is limited; as it is unguided, its accuracy declines rapidly with distance, especially if crosswinds are present.

The key to countering most ground fire is standoff distance. In operations against technically limited opposition, this can be simply achieved by altitude. 7.62mm rounds can reach 1,500 feet before arcing over, 12.7mm can achieve twice that altitude. Helicopters can easily fly above this, making man-portable and easily concealed surface-to-air missiles and anti-aircraft cannon the greatest threat. Most shoulder-fired missiles can engage targets up to 6km

(4 miles), this in theory translates into 20,000 feet of altitude. However, these missiles only have sustained flight for a few seconds before their rocket motor burns out, making it possible for an alert and agile helicopter to avoid them at anything but close range[19]. The most famous contribution of anti-aircraft missiles was those in the hands of the Mujahedeen in the Russo-Afghan War. According to Russian sources, 74 helicopters were lost in Afghanistan, with 27 shot down by Stinger and two by Redeye[20]. This attrition caused Soviet helicopters to adopt less effective tactics that improved their force protection through remaining at significantly higher altitudes.

Most man-portable surface-to-air missiles are reliant upon heat-seeking for their guidance. This is a declining threat to modern aircraft, as significant progress has been made in countering this guidance through infrared exhaust suppressors, active infrared jammers and flare dispensers. Of course, some standoff from the opposition is usually required for the defensive aid suites to be effective. Infrared guidance remains more effective for air-to-air missiles because dogfighting jets are significantly hotter. The effective countering of heat seeking guidance is leading to a shift to laser-beam-riding missiles that rely upon an operator continuously tracking the target. Because the data links from the ground to the missile cannot effectively be jammed, the only counter is to attack the firing point or to violently manoeuvre and force the operator to lose his track.

Using altitude to avoid machine guns, cannon and small missiles makes aircraft vulnerable to integrated air defence systems in conventional conflict. Helicopters are more vulnerable than fixed-wing aircraft when flying at medium altitude as they lack speed and agility, their rotors cause a greater radar signature, and they are rarely equipped with as effective counter measures to radar guided missiles. So instead of using altitude, helicopters achieve standoff through horizontal distance from the threat. Of course, operating close to the ground makes them vulnerable to concealed close range threats; this they can overcome through either holding a safe position, or operating behind advancing ground forces (firing over the shoulder). Helicopters are at their most vulnerable when advancing on their own, over enemy-occupied territory, in particular when their speed limits their ability to survey the battlefield and identify potential threats. The networking of increasingly sophisticated sensors – such as unmanned aircraft providing data feeds to attack helicopters – will improve the helicopter's situational awareness. However, it is always easy, in all but the most open terrain, to hide small air defence weapons from a helicopter.

The latest tactical air defence systems out-range most of the missiles on modern attack helicopters. Two of the most capable systems are the Russian 2K22 Tunguska (or SA-19 Grison in the NATO classification) and the 9K331 Tor (or SA-15 Gauntlet). Both systems are highly mobile due to their tracked chassis; they have search and tracking radars that can easily detect a helicopter's high radar cross-section and launch a couple of missiles at the helicopter before it is within its own weapon range. If the helicopter was close (less than 4km compared to the missile's 10km) the Tunguska could alternatively use its 30mm cannon. The 9K331 Tor has an even greater advantage over attack helicopters with its 16km range. These systems have forced Ukrainian helicopters on the Donbas to improvise an indirect fire capability using their rockets pods to engage, relatively ineffectively, from behind cover.

Fitting attack helicopter with longer-range direct fire weapons is a partial answer, but the engagement range will be limited by the inter visibility challenge if the helicopter remains at low level, to achieve force protection through hiding in the terrain. This leads to the requirement for weapons that can engage these air defence systems without exposing the helicopter. To achieve this, the latest Apache mounts its primary sensor – the Longbow fire control radar and the Radar Frequency Interferometer which can locate air defence radars – above the rotor blade to maximise cover. Survivability is further improved by the fielding of fire-and-forget missiles (AGM-114L Hellfire) with a millimetric wave radar seeker that requires no further guidance after launch, they can even lock-on to their target after launch. Going one stage further, the Israelis have fitted the Non-Line-of-Sight Spike missiles to allow their helicopters to engage from up to 25 km (16 miles); its man-in-the-loop guidance allows the operator to identify and destroy air defence systems before closing to direct-fire Hellfire missile range. Alternatively, anti-radiation or sensor-fused munitions could home onto an air defence system's distinctive electronic and physical signatures.

Russian and Chinese Employment of Attack Helicopters

'Using artillery to blast a corridor for helicopters allowing the helicopters to penetrate to deal with targets in depth which are difficult to locate is an obvious example of [Soviet] integrated fire destruction[21].'

Chris Bellamy, Historian

The Soviets are the only nation to develop and employ attack helicopters in a significantly different way to the US. They were already developing an armed helicopter, but the Vietnam War convinced the Soviets of the advantages of a bespoke design, leading to the development of the Mi-24 Hind, making it the second purpose-built attack helicopter[22]. The Soviets had a clear view of the Hind's role: it was to fulfil the same function as World War Two's flying tank – the Il-2 Shturmovik. It largely employed the same mix of munitions: cannon, rockets and unguided bombs. The primary weapon of the Mi-24 is the rocket, initially the S-8 80mm rocket mounted in 20-round packs. While it was designed for anti-tank guided weapons, the Hind was not optimised for standoff engagements, as its low power to weight ratio makes it difficult to hover behind cover; when this is coupled with its large size, the result is an indifferent anti-tank platform. A willingness to accept these limitations may in part have been due to the influence of the open steppe on the Russian psyche; a few years later another extremely large attack helicopter, also with a poor power to weight ratio, haled from the South African veldt.

Given that their usual target set has rarely been tanks, the 80-millimetre S-8 rocket and cannon have been the most used weapons. The need for greater standoff appears to have been the motivation behind the twin-barrelled 23mm and 30mm cannon replacing the earlier Mi-24D's 12.7mm four barrelled machine gun or a single 30mm grenade launcher. The upgraded Mi-24, the Mi-35, employs a twin 23mm cannon, which offers greater lethality against soft targets, at the expense of 30mm's range and superior anti-armour capability. The Russians appear to be content with this trade off, as they see the S-8 rocket (itself a replacement of the 57mm (2.2 in) S-5) as providing greater range and hitting power. The latest attack helicopters also use the 122mm rocket, this offers more range and a larger warhead. Unlike other helicopters, the Mi-24 has made extensive use of bombing; in Afghanistan the Mi-24 routinely carried ten 100-kilogram (220 lb) iron bombs for attacks on camps or strongpoints, while harder targets were engaged with a load of four 250-kilogram (550 lb), or two 500-kilogram (1,100 lb) iron bombs, or fuel-air explosive free-fall bombs.

The Hind's design characteristics are closer to a heavily armed utility helicopter, in that it has a troop-carrying capability. But the Hind was a bespoke design that aimed to span capabilities, rather than being a conversion of a utility helicopter. Leading to it being called the World's only 'assault helicopter' due to its combination of firepower, troop-carrying capability and armour; however, limited use has been made of the ability to carry infantrymen on operations. Afghanistan's hot and high flying conditions challenged the Hind's poor power to weight ratio. This led to the infantry space, if used at all, carrying a mechanic or extra rounds of rocket ammunition, which allowed the crew to land and self-reload in the field. Even in less challenging flying conditions infantry have rarely been carried.

Attack helicopters have three main roles in Soviet/Russian conventional warfighting. In set piece operations they provide fire support, invariably as part of a coordinated fire plan. Attack helicopters usually engage the depth targets in a zone between the maximum range of artillery and where the fixed wing aircraft assume responsibility; if engaging the same target as other means of firepower, then the Hinds' attacks are usually deconflicted by time. Secondly, they support manoeuvring forces, exploiting a break-through by providing an overhead, armoured close air support weapon. Finally, in greater depth, the Hind's combination of firepower, armour and in theory their troop-carrying capability allows them to support air assaulting airborne troops[23]. The firepower of attack helicopters is of a premium when most surface-to-surface fire support is out-ranged. This means that their key role is in the all arms deep battle, in particularly accompanying an exploitation force; of course airborne formations also have high reliance upon attack helicopters, as they expect to be outside the range of the artillery that does not fly-in with the force.

Operationally the Mi-24 has proved popular with ground troops, largely stemming from the persistence that attack helicopters have over the battlefield when compared to fighter-bombers. This enables them to acquire elusive targets and provide fire when needed. With the end of the Cold War, the Russians reassessed their requirements and determined that their Hind's general-purpose characteristics continued to suit the developing character of conflict; The Wars of Soviet Secession have reinforced the need for danger close and area fire support of ground and airborne forces. This led to the Mi-35, a development of the Hind, but with new avionics and communication equipment, an improved tail rotor and a much more powerful engine. This was at the expense of the troop compartment's capacity, which can now only accommodate three. But there was also a recognition that the Hind needed to be supplemented by more specialist designs.

The Soviets initiated, and the Russians have produced, helicopters that are as advanced as almost any Western helicopter. The Mi-28 and the Kamov-produced Ka-50, were originally in competition, but both have been fielded. While they are radically different designs, they are closer to the Western approach, with a greater anti-tank and anti-helicopter capability. The Ka-50 Black Shark (NATO designation Hokum) is unconventional, with contra-rotating coaxial rotors that eliminate the need for a tail rotor assembly, leading to a compact design. The machine has a crew of one pilot, who has a significant workload that involves both flying and acquiring and engaging targets in combat. The Ka-50 has subsequently been developed into the two-seater Ka-52. The latter has a target acquisition capability similar to the Apache. When this is combined with a modern battle management system the K-52's task appears to be to coordinate the activities of lesser helicopters, plus directing other sensors and fires assets; this capability could make Russian helicopter forces significantly more capable of operating independent of ground forces. These Kamov helicopters are slightly smaller and lighter than the Mil Moscow Helicopter Plant's designs, making it more suitable for on-ship operations and being deployed by strategic air transport.

The Mi-28 is the natural successor to the Mi-24/35, but without any ability to the carry personnel. Again, 80mm and 122mm unguided rockets are seen as the primary fire support weapon; laser guidance makes its missiles a more effective anti-tank system, fitting them with thermobaric warheads expands their utility. For close-in work there is a 30mm chin-mounted cannon. It is the World's heaviest attack helicopter, allowing significantly improved physical protection, reduced thermal signature and enhanced avionics. The most advanced version of the Mi-28 is the Mi-28N Night Hunter (NATO designation Havoc), like the AH-64D Apache Longbow Apache it has a mast-mounted target acquisition radar. The Ka-50 attack helicopter appears to be usually employed with airborne, special operations and naval forces, while the Mi-28 appears to be the ground forces attack helicopter.

The switch to helicopters better able to employ terrain masking and conduct standoff attacks reflects changing helicopter tactics; initially Soviet helicopter attack profiles in Afghanistan were similar to the Il-2 Shturmovik dive attack. Reacting to the improved air defence, by the end of the conflict helicopters were attacking at low level, from differing azimuths, with some helicopters remaining at medium altitude in overwatch. Relatively ineffective attacks were also conducted from well above the air defence threat using iron bombs. Cooperation between helicopters and ground forces atrophied with the breakup of the USSR; in the First Chechen War, attack helicopters were ineffective:

> *'In theory their [Mi-24 Hinds] missions were coordinated by air support controllers on the ground, but the lack of trained personnel created problems. Furthermore, aviators complained that there were not enough of them to deploy at battalion level and below. Mi-24 crews often found that they got far better information from their airborne colleges in the Mi-8 than they did from the ground controllers'*[24].

This, coupled with concerns over the enemy's air defences, led to Hinds being largely excluded from combat in urban areas. When the conflict resumed, Russia's aviation tactical groups were controlled by brigade HQ combined air support cells, manned by pilot forward air controllers. There were additional terminal controllers at battalion, and sometimes even at company level, but not enough to match the quantity of aircraft. This led to helicopters largely conducting their own target acquisition, and directly coordinating with manoeuvre forces. They operated in groups of two to four Hinds with one or two Mi-8 Hip utility helicopters; with the latter operating at altitude to acquire targets, and then direct the attack helicopters. To counter the surface-to-air missile threat, the Hinds combined steep diving descents down to tens of metres from medium altitude, with surprise pop-ups from different directions, always with Mi-8 providing overwatch during an attack[25]. The effectiveness of this approach led to helicopters largely supplanting fighter-bomber fire support in the Second Chechen War.

Reacting to the proliferation of surface-to-air missiles, Russian helicopters in the Syrian conflict have approached their targets flying nap-of-the-earth; they gain altitude to fire their weapons, and then exit at extremely low altitude while emitting both flares and chaff countermeasures. Extremely low flying has become one of the characteristics that allows observers to differentiate Russian from Syrian-piloted helicopters, the other being aggression.

The Chinese have successfully merged Russian weaponry with largely Western technology and design philosophy. Their latest attack helicopter, the Z-10, has a millimetric-wave fire-control radar, like the Apache Longbow, and an infrared search and track system[26]. The Z-19 is a light attack and reconnaissance helicopter that has been converted from a Harbin Z-9W, which is a license-built variant of the Eurocopter AS365 Dauphin multi-purpose helicopter. The Z-10 is seen primarily as an attack helicopter and the Z-19 as a scout. The Z-19 is different from other nations' light attack helicopters in having the characteristic tandem cockpit configuration of the purpose-built attack helicopter.

The Chinese see their purpose-built attack helicopters as primarily an anti-tank system. Hence, the introduction of the Z-10 and Z-19 helicopters has led to the retirement of tube anti-tank vehicles. Their rational is that the: *'Anti-tank missiles and helicopters represent the trend of anti-tank warfare. They can form a three-dimensional anti-tank firepower network*[27]'.

Helicopters in the Combined Arms Battle

'Army attack aviation should focus on the missions it has performed so well in major combat and stability operations in Iraq – for example, close support of ground forces, armed reconnaissance, and precision attack in urban areas[28].'

David E. Johnson, RAND Corporation

The attack helicopter, in the right terrain, has become the dominant direct-fire weapon system in conventional land conflict. This does not mean that it will replace the tank. Helicopters cannot match their greater protection, persistence upon the battlefield, and ability to deliver the closest physical and psychological support to infantry that is necessary to seize and hold ground. Instead, the attack helicopter provides significant and discriminating fire support with a range of weaponry that is effective against most target sets. But of course, helicopters are now optimised to engage point targets, with an unmatched anti-tank capability. Despite the effectiveness of their rockets and cannons, helicopters cannot carry sufficient munitions to rival artillery and mortars in suppressing area targets. The West's most recent counter-insurgency operations have played to its strengths rather than exposing the helicopter's limitations. As Dr Afzal Ashraf of the Royal United Service Institute identifies its advantages in terms of perception:

> *'It's much better to use Apaches than fast jets because you can get much more up close and personal, and have time for a target to pop up. Then you can use machine guns, rather than a big 500lb bomb that can cause a lot of civilian damage[29].'*

Attack helicopters, despite becoming more capable, cannot compete with the fixed wing aircraft's advantages of speed, reach and payload. These characteristics make fighter-bombers much more suitable than helicopters in the deep battle. In the close battle, the helicopters have superior danger close fire support ability; the discrimination that helicopters can achieve is due to a combination of munitions, platform and aircrew. They have precise guided and unguided low yield munitions; these are targeted at low level by usually excellent sensors. Finally, aviation aircrew usually have a greater affinity with the ground force perspective than fighter-bomber aircrew. Against sophisticated, unsuppressed, ground based integrated air defences, the only certain counter is terrain masking; this gives the helicopters a distinct advantage over fixed wing aircraft. This adds to the arguments for fighter-bombers to cede close air support to helicopters, as was observed by General Scales in the Gulf War[30], with fixed wing aircraft being employed only when the highest volume of fire is required; this will usually be through precision point attack from medium altitude. Against a peer opponent, only in the most extreme circumstances is it likely that fixed wing aircraft will join helicopters at low level in the contact battle; this would be the most effective way for Western militaries to employ their joint firepower. However, the current lack of organic artillery and mortar firepower means that fixed wing close air support will routinely be required to equalise most tactical encounters against a peer opponent.

The doctrinal and institutional imperatives that have led Western helicopter forces to prefer the deep battle have already been covered; the third factor is the difficulty of integrating aviation into the combined arms close battle. The training required to conduct aviation deep attack is simple in comparison. Invariably with unfortunate results, this has often been made even simpler by failing to coordinate aviation with artillery, electronic fires and air support. Combined arms training is by its nature challenging, the different physical velocities and differing cultures of aviation and ground forces compound this. Operations in Iraq and Afghanistan have provided the imperative and opportunity to perfect fire support techniques. This expertise is now fading in many Western militaries, and this is not the same challenge as integrating aviation into combined arms conventional operations against a peer adversary. Adding to the challenge will be the electro-magnetic spectrum being contested, with jamming of communications and GPS-based navigation.

Maintaining flying skills naturally distances aviators from ground forces training; it can lead to training been conducted in geographically separate training areas. Being safe in the air is obviously the priority; when resources are tight, this can lead to insufficient flying hours for combined training. Simulation provides a partial answer, but most armies limit this to the battalion level. The Israeli Mission Training Centre conducts three days of computer-generated brigade level combined arms battles that fully test the coordination of air and ground forces. Few armies provide the opportunity to live train helicopters as part of an all arms force. The Americans lead with their National Training Centre at Fort Irwin in California, which the Israelis have sought to replicate in the Snir training base in the Golan Heights and the MALA Urban Operations facility in the Negev Desert. However, not all armies are well provided; the British rarely integrate live firing attack helicopters into armoured or dismounted battlegroup training.

Effective combined arms live fire training is essential for helicopters to be trusted to provide close fires to ground troops. In the Gulf War, unless controlled by a forward air controller, fixed wing close air support was kept at least 5km in front of own troops. Given the rapid speed of advance, such a separation was considered essential to ensure safe aerial fires[31]. Less formal, but similar, distances were observed in the 2003 Iraq War. Attack helicopters were trusted to provide intimate fire support because they had previously perfected it in combined arms training, culminating in live fire.

Fully integrating attack helicopters into all combined arms training is an expensive undertaking; until this is resolved, an alternative is to restrict the aviation role to what can safely be undertaken with limited live fire training opportunities. An option is to limit attack helicopters in the close battle to providing fire support using the close air support procedures. In 2003, the US Marine Corps rejected aviation's bespoke close combat attack procedures and incorporated helicopters into their existing fixed wing close air support system. The key difference between the two systems is that in close air support, ground forces authorise aviation firepower, rather than attack helicopters engaging on their own authority. Changing systems need not unduly restrict aviation firepower to individual designated targets; the chain of command, acting through forward air controllers, can authorise aviation to engage areas where there is no chance of collateral damage, such as everything north of a given geographic feature, where all military targets are known to be hostile.

Restricting aviation support to close air support procedures, does not fully exploit the attack helicopter's full potential. Aviation significantly increases the combat worth of manoeuvring armoured formations through providing 'over the shoulder' firepower and surveillance. Integrating attack helicopters into armoured and reconnaissance force training, if this could be made affordable, would significantly add to their combat power; in particular, attack helicopters add significantly to the lethality of forces conducting screening and guard tasks.

If helicopters largely supersede fighter-bombers in providing low level close air support, then the *quid pro quo* should be their ceasing to compete in areas where fixed-wing aircraft are more effective. Recent operations have proved that fixed wing aircraft are better at engaging targets beyond the forward line of own ground troops. Currently many in the attack helicopter community continue to aspire to Cold War-style massed, deep attacks in conventional warfare. This is not required to assert their institutional independence, the helicopter's place on the battlefield is assured – though after considerable investment in aviation since 9/11, the American Army is certainly rebalancing towards surface-to-surface fires[32]. If circumstances dictate that brigade and battalion strikes are necessary, then the key is an all arms approach. Aviation needs support from the other arms to achieve ingress to an area (probably an engagement area or kill box), followed by egress via a different route. In the Cold War the American assumption was that deep strike was a task for specially-trained corps level aviation brigades. And in AirLand doctrine this would be undertaken with the air force and supported by the full range of combat support. In the Cold War there was insufficient training time for formations to be effective in both the conventional close and deep combined arms battle, surely this still applies?

Operationally, the employment of smaller forces of helicopters to raid into the enemy depth has proved to be a more effective approach; it reduces their vulnerability to air defences and makes aviation significantly more agile, given the superior mounting tempo of small raiding forces when compared to battalion and brigade strikes. In addition, these raids are not dependent on identifying a significant target array to justify their launch; employing small numbers of aircraft to infiltrate into the enemy's depth could principally have a psychological rather than physical effect; this is of course a significantly easier training task than battalion and brigade level deep attacks.

This approach might suite existing inventories, but it is American helicopter technology that drives the attack helicopter capability. Their Future Attack Reconnaissance Aircraft programme will both restore the dedicated aerial scout mission that the Army gave up in 2017 when it retired the Bell OH-58 Kiowa[33], and replace half of the 700 AH-64 Apache attack helicopters[34]. For the last few years the Army has had a scouting capability gap that has not been effectively filled by pairing AH-64 Apache with the Textron AAI RQ-7 Shadow unmanned air system. The new aircraft appears to be prioritising speed, range and payload. The two main contenders are the Sikorsky Raider 'pusher' and Bell 360 Invictus. The former has flying characteristics that will close the capability gap with fixed wing aircraft, rather than make more capable the existing attack helicopter capability. Hence if Sikorsky is the eventual winner it is likely to have the qualities that suite deep operations; however, given its capability and ability to network, it is unlikely that such a helicopter needs numbers to mass to achieve effect, and so it could primarily be seen as a 'light cavalry' raider.

Chapter 9: Tube Artillery

'Of the principal arms that could be brought to bear directly on the enemy, infantry, armour, and air were seriously handicapped by the weather and terrain. Through all, however – day and night, good weather and bad – the flexibility and power of our modern artillery were applied unceasingly.'

General Courtney H. Hodges US Army

Cannons remain the close battle's primary means of fire support. This is the result of tube artillery's ability to: provide both sustained and intense fire, employ a wide range of munitions, have the range to achieve both mass and coverage, and deliver guaranteed, responsive fire support. World War One was probably tube artillery's apogee; subsequently with the maturing of the other joint fires systems it has declined in its relative importance. Of course, in absolute terms tube artillery has grown in its power through increased target effect, longer range and therefore greater coverage; plus increased accuracy and consistency, this includes the fielding of terminal precision guidance munitions. This drew the leading scholar of industrial age killing to conclude: *'the big guns determined the strategy and general context in which twentieth century conflict would take place*[1]*.'*

Despite significantly reducing its artillery park following the end of the Cold War, tube artillery numerically dominates in Western armies. Its main task is now fire support of the close battle, with reduced reliance being placed on using it to engage targets not in contact with own forces. In contrast to NATO's armies, as well as the field guns supporting the close battle, the world's other leading armies retain large calibre guns and howitzers designed for the deep battle, though these are being displaced by rocket artillery. This development is being challenged by the experience of recent prolonged conflicts in Syria and Ukraine. This indicates that tube artillery's ceding of the deep battle may be premature, as it retains an unmatched capability to economically place a variety of projectiles onto a target. This has led the Russians to put large calibre artillery back into active use.

Such is the dominance of tube and rocket artillery in the Russian way of war that they are conducting the Russo-Ukraine War without employing any form of airpower. This decision is of course partly motivated by political concerns – to contain escalation and to maintain the fiction of ambiguity over Russian participation – but, it is difficult to see a Western country even contemplating the use of ground force without aerial firepower.

Evolution of the Modern Tube Artillery

'Artillery is not a static factor, a piece on the chess board, or a constant in some sort of military equation. It has evolved continuously and is evolving[2]*.'*

Shelford Bidwell, Gunner and Historian

The 19th Century perfecting of breech loading, rifling and recoil systems led to artillery increasing in range, accuracy and rate of fire; this plus superior munitions, significantly improved lethality. Modern artillery is a confluence of these technical improvements with the tactical innovation of indirect fire – this being the firing of a projectile without relying upon a direct line of sight between the battery and its target. For the first two millennia of artillery's history, target acquisition and the decision to engage was conducted at the catapult or gun position; from the 16th Century there had been isolated incidences of the use of indirect fire. This was a necessity when intervening terrain between a battery and its target demanded high trajectory fire; in time, the protection provided by terrain became sought after for its tactical advantage. At first only mortars were used for higher trajectory fire, but the advantages of combining the direct-fire gun and the mortar led to the first howitzer, a 1690s Dutch invention[3]. Howitzers came to make up around a quarter of an army's field guns; in the age of solid shot, they were valued for their high explosive shell, which could be delivered to almost any target due to their lobbing trajectory. However, except at sieges, howitzers rarely employed indirect fire. The Great War's character of conflict necessitated indirect fire, making what had long been technically possible tactically essential.

In comparison to the revolutionary changes in the other joint fires systems, between World War One and the 1980s artillery developed upon a predictable path. Mechanisation's replacement of horse power led to the introduction of self-propelled artillery; once indirect fire became the standard means of engagement, the distinction between guns and howitzers largely became redundant. This led to the gun-howitzer becoming the standard field piece. Specialist guns continued to meet the long range requirement, but they are challenged by rockets. Other than that, tube artillery merely became bigger and better along this predictable evolutionary route; this should be expected, as tube artillery is a mature weapon system whose technology should follow the law of diminishing returns. However, since the 1980s a spate of innovation has disrupted this orderly progression. Automated loading has led to unprecedented rates of fire for medium and heavy calibres; previously a high rate of fire was the preserve of the smaller, easily manhandled, calibres. Platform and munition innovation has resulted in tripling of the range of artillery within a generation. Exploitation of aerial munition technology has resulted in a similar increase in lethality. Digitisation has fundamentally changed artillery command and control, deployment procedures and conduct of fire missions. By reducing the impact of the variables that cause ballistic inaccuracy, in most circumstances modern artillery can now deliver first round accuracy against impromptu area targets. Similar improvements have been made to consistency; a more stable firing platform and automated laying, so reducing human error are the key factors. The time taken to occupy firing positions has been significantly reduced by a revolution in artillery survey, made possible by GPS plus inertial navigation and orientation. This has led to 'shoot and scoot' tactics and widely dispersed gun positions; both significantly increase survivability against counter-battery fire. This technology also enables quick deployment from the line of march, so enhancing artillery's ability to support advancing manoeuvre forces.

Despite technical change, tube artillery has maintained its traditional advantages. It combines a high burst rate of fire with the ability to sustain a lower rate of fire over a prolonged period; increasing range has provided the ability to cover the expanded areas now occupied by brigades and divisions. Range remains tube artillery's key advantage over mortars; these, even with rocket-assisted projectiles, need constant movement to support armoured battalions in mobile operations. As cannons or guns are now actually gun-howitzers, they can vary their propellant charge and fire high trajectory – or over 45 degrees to the horizontal – which means that unlike rockets or fixed charge low trajectory guns, they can engage most targets regardless of the topography. Tube artillery maintains reasonable ballistic accuracy at most battle ranges; unlike individually aimed aircraft-delivered munitions, once artillery is adjusted onto a target, its rounds will consistently fall around the point of aim, allowing troops to exploit this predictable suppressive effect in the assault or when holding ground.

Tube artillery easily adapts to enhancements in munitions technology, as long as these are designed within standardised ballistic guidelines. This allows tube artillery to meet a variety of indirect and direct lethal and non-lethal fire support tasks; including employing precision and near precision munitions. Furthermore, a wide variety of munitions can be rapidly employed through having them at the platform ready to be loaded; unlike aircraft and multiple rocket launchers, which need them to be pre-selected for a given mission.

All of these features, when combined with the necessary command and control, lead to tube artillery's ability to provide responsive, accurate fire support with a range of munitions across a formation's battlespace. It is the generalist in the joint fires' pantheon. Other systems can be much more effective at individual tasks; this may make them more important in a specific character of conflict, but tube artillery's flexibility means that it can readily adapt to changes in a conflict's character. It is tube artillery's blending of these characteristics that means it continues to be the *primary* means of delivering fire support (as distinct from deep fires) for almost all armies. This does not mean that tube artillery's position is unchallenged. The Russians, for long the possessors of the World's most powerful artillery, have significantly increased their proportion of rockets, and their gun-mortars may be replacing tube artillery in the close support role.

Armoured and Tracked Self-Propelled Guns

'The tanks must not follow on the artillery, but the other way around[4]*'.*

Major General Heinz Guderian

Despite early experimentation[5] the self-propelled gun is effectively a product of World War Two. They were improvised on existing tank chassis, and were either primarily a direct or an indirect fire weapon, in accordance with their nation's warfighting approach. Those primarily designed for indirect fire, being improvised designs could rarely provide their crew with all-round protection. Those chiefly designed as direct fire weapons were better protected, sometimes in excess of contemporary tanks. Self-propelled guns mainly designed as direct fire weapons can be further divided into anti-tank weapons, with high velocity guns, and low velocity larger calibre guns that primarily fired over open sights to support infantry assaults. These 'turret-less tanks' proliferated in the European War, especially on the Eastern Front. The Germans saw the need for an assault gun to accompanying their infantry as one of the lessons of the Great War, leading to the StuG III, their most numerous armoured fighting vehicle. The Red Army started World War Two without a self-propelled artillery arm; by the end of the war self-propelled guns made up 40% of the Soviet armoured vehicle holdings. In contrast to the Germans, Soviet self-propelled guns did not usually accompany the infantry and tanks in the assault, leading to them lacking a machine gun, as they were not intended to close with enemy infantry. The Soviets saw armour and tracks as means of improving the ability of their direct fire artillery to adopt the most suitable firing positions to engage enemy positions; this led to the mounting of their standard field gun on a light tank chassis, making the SU-76; this was the most common Soviet self-propelled gun, with nearly 13,000 being produced. Later designs were more heavily armoured, in response to the increase in the range of German anti-tank guns, which made self-propelled guns vulnerable in their over-watch firing positions.

Despite its prominence, self-propelled artillery formed the minority of World War Two artillery. Only the American armoured divisions fielded solely armoured self-propelled direct support artillery. Since World War Two self-propelled guns have dominated the artillery park of most Western armies. The anti-tank role has been largely transferred to anti-tank guided weapons, or to main battle tanks, who have also taken back the assault gun role. This has led to most self-propelled guns being primarily indirect fire weapons. The exception being the Soviets/Russians, whose 122mm 2S1 is specifically designed for direct support to tanks and motor rifle troops, being equally adept at direct and indirect fire. Its low silhouette, small turret, and considerable on-board ammunition is designed to provide fire support over open sights from overwatch positions. Its ability to elevate to 70 degrees made it ideally suited to urban and mountain operations. Larger calibre Soviet and Russian weapons are principally designed for indirect fire, but they still feature superior direct fire sighting systems to Western cannons, and often bespoke direct fire ammunition. Leading to the employment of 2S3 and 2S19 tracked, and the 2A65 towed, 152mm guns to provide fire support over open sights.

Some modern self-propelled guns are conversions of obsolete tanks, but most are either purpose built or on heavily-modified common chassis that can cope with the radically different firing stresses – a tank's firing stresses are close to horizontal, artillery ones are 25–45 degrees above the horizontal. They usually have a turret, providing both crew protection and the ability to engage targets at any azimuth and up to a high angle of elevation; this is a significant enhancement upon turret-less World War Two systems; these could only engage targets on a limited arc, and outside this required the traversing of the whole vehicle before engagement. Heavier calibre self-propelled guns have often had to compromise, forgoing a turret and protection to remain relatively light and so maintain their mobility; the rationale for this approach is that these longer range guns are less likely to require rapid switches of fire, and achieve protection through out-ranging the opposition.

Most self-propelled guns are now 152/155mm calibre, the major exception being Russia and users of her equipment who keep faith with 122mm. Russia's continued belief in the need for a lighter calibre for direct support is evidenced by the 122mm gun being supplemented, or perhaps being replaced by, the 120mm gun-mortar. The self-propelled gun suits large calibres as its chassis can effortlessly take the weight, and has the power for mechanically-assisted loading to overcome the 152/155mm calibre's traditional disadvantage of a slower rate of fire. By overcoming many of the disadvantages of the towed medium gun, the self-propelled gun has been instrumental in making 152/155mm the standard field artillery calibre. This view led to the replacement by the American Army of the 105mm M108 with the 155mm M109. However, despite being declared obsolete, the M108 continued to serve in the Vietnam War; its lighter platform weight delivered improved mobility and its 105mm round better suited the provision of danger close support to dismounted infantry.

The original driver for the fielding of self-propelled guns was the need for superior mobility, especially cross-country, to enable continuous support to armoured forces. Self-propelled guns have repeatedly proved their utility in even the most challenging terrain. 33rd Indian Corps' advance through Burma in 1945 received significantly better support from self-propelled than towed field guns; their key advantage was that they could always come into action, as a tracked vehicle can create a viable gun platform in almost any topography[6]. Self-propelled artillery equipped the first assault waves on D-Day of Operation Overlord, deploying in the surf to provide fire support. The self-propelled gun excels in urban operations with its greater requirement for direct fire. Given their greater deployability and reduced logistic burden, initially the Russians mainly deployed towed guns to the Chechen conflict. Over time, self-propelled artillery replaced towed guns, until they accounted for 70% of the artillery park. The self-propelled gun's mobility allowed it to transit the largely destroyed city of Grozny, crossing terrain inaccessible to towed guns. This, plus their armoured protection, allowed them to provide direct fire support to individual storm detachments.

Compared to a towed gun, an enclosed armoured platform is of course more resilient to all forms of attack, from small arms to chemical and nuclear munitions. Armoured self-propelled guns provide significantly superior survivability against counter-battery fire. Under fire, they can either continue providing fire support, or rapidly displace to outside the danger zone. The survivability and mobility advantages of self-propelled guns led the Soviets in the 1970s to largely replace their towed guns in their first class armoured and motor rifle divisions[7]. The spur was the recognition that artillery's role needed to change to being able to provide continuous fire support through the full depth of NATO's anti-tank defences. Previously the Soviets focussed upon the break-in battle and the hand-over to the exploitation force; roles that suited their vast towed gun park. In the exploitation they largely relied upon tanks, (obsolete) assault guns and aircraft for firepower. NATO's defences were now perceived as being in such depth that the mobile force would need the ability to employ heavy suppressive fire throughout the advance of the exploitation force.

Given that the Soviets were enthusiastic users of self-propelled artillery in World War Two, their subsequent reliance on towed guns was probably as much resource as doctrine driven. Other large armies face similar challenges, notably the Chinese and the Indians. Approximately a quarter of Chinese artillery is self-propelled; this mainly supports their mechanised formations with 122mm, but there are an increasing number of larger 155mm calibres[8]. The Indians currently lack sufficient self-propelled guns to support all their armoured and mechanized formations. Since the retirement of the 105mm Abbott, and the failure of the 130mm Catapult, their only armoured self-propelled gun is the aged 122mm 2S1. This deficiency is now being addressed by the Korean Samsung Techwin K-9 Thunder, with a 155mm gun and a 52-calibre barrel giving a very long range. As at 2020 the Indians are buying at least 100.

The Americans have continued to modify their versatile M109. Despite updates, the M109A6 used in the Iraq War lacked ordnance range and vehicle speed. Operation Iraqi Freedom (2003) featured high speed advances in combat column formations; this necessitated extremely bold handling of the M109 to ensure continuous fire support for manoeuvre forces. Some battalion commanders in the Iraq War placed a battery behind their lead company, conducting direct fire as well as indirect fire engagements; the conventional placing of artillery at the rear of these formations could have resulted in it being out of range. For the Americans this 2003 conflict confirmed the continuing requirement for armoured tracked guns, as only these have the mobility and protection to provide continuous support. The upgraded M109A7 primarily addresses the A6's lack of mobility, and improves its agility through greater digitization, but it has not increased weapon range, as it still has a 39-calibre barrel[9]. Addressing this is the primary objective of ongoing development of the M109 in the extended range cannon programme.

The German PzH 2000 self-propelled 155mm howitzer sets the performance standard for NATO's armoured artillery, in particular protection, rate of fire and range[10]. It is designed to survive counter-battery fire through a thick armoured roof with several tons of reactive armour to defeat top-attack munitions. Its 60-ton weight reflects this protection; which some see as too much of a good thing; but at least the German designers recognise the danger presented by cluster and sensor fuzed munitions, which are likely to be the counter-battery high-tech weapons of choice. The Russian approach has sought to combine top armour protection with more active defence, including laser detectors and smoke dischargers designed to defeat precision weapons. Armoured artillery in other nations is largely restricted to protection levels sufficient against conventional splinters and small arms.

The current NATO armoured artillery park's major problem is under-investment, the result of their limited employment in recent counter-insurgency conflicts, and a lack of clarity of the required characteristics of a replacement system. This led to the American failure to replace the M109 with the Crusader artillery system in 2002, and then seven years later with the XM1203 NLOS-C. The Crusader was deemed too expensive and too heavy – though at 45 tons it was significantly less than the tank it supported. The NLOS-C was an impressive design that showed the capability that could be delivered in a 27-ton vehicle[11]. Whether a self-propelled gun needs to be constrained to that weight when it supports 60 to 70 tons of tank remains moot, but an armoured wheeled or tracked gun, employing some of the technologies developed for NLOS-C, is a good match to support the medium forces currently being fielded by several Western armies.

In contrast to the West, the Russians have continuously developed armoured self-propelled guns. The 2S35 is a capability step change from the impressive 2S19, it sets the standard for rate of fire and range, combining this with a high level of automation. The Russians are prepared to pay the price in weight and cost. In contrast to the evolution of Russian guns, until recently armoured self-propelled guns were often seen in the Western armies as legacy platforms, unsuited to the current and future character of conflict. Intellectual under-investment has resulted in the current best-selling Western gun – the South Korean Samsung Techwin K-9 Thunder – being in most of its design characteristics a modernised and digitized M109 with 52-calibre barrel. The development of armoured and tracked self-propelled guns fits into the following chronology:

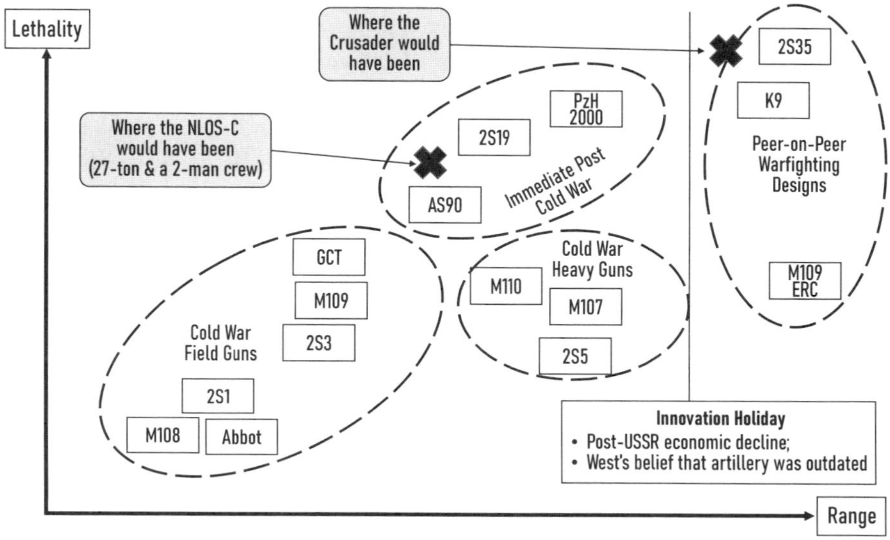

The World's leading armies, with the greatest recent conventional warfare combat experience, aggressively use their artillery to deliver guaranteed fire support to their mechanised manoeuvre forces. The armoured self-propelled gun makes this possible through being able to both keep pace and survive. The greater investment in wheeled and hybrid technology may result in tracks losing their significantly superior performance on soft soils and mud, plus gap crossing[12]; but presently tracks offer the best mobility solution for the 30–40-ton self-propelled guns. Armies wishing to retain their ability to conduct operational-level combined arms manoeuvre against peer enemies are retaining and modernising their armoured artillery. They follow the rationale that the historic trend of ground warfare – increased area of operations, reduced force densities, more lethal counter-fires and increased tempo – strengthens the case for armoured self-propelled guns.

Wheeled Self-Propelled Artillery

'The demand for a portee field gun had originated in July 1942, in the Middle East … It was intended for the normal support of desert columns … Owing to the nature of the terrain, and the distance to be covered, it was to be equipped with wheels.[13]'

Brigadier Pemberton, official World War
Two British artillery historian

The need for greater mobility in the Western Desert in World War Two led to the improvised mounting of towed guns on trucks. Compared to towed guns, it is more challenging for truck-mounted guns to make themselves a more difficult target through using manmade and natural protection. This significantly greater vulnerability led to this improvisation being abandoned.

The first bespoke wheeled self-propelled gun arrived in 1981, with the Czechoslovakian 152mm DANA. It was followed two years later by the South African G6 155mm wheeled gun. These guns have armoured turrets and they have sufficient stability, at most charges, to withstand the recoil of firing through 360-degrees. The DANA achieves this through lowering three hydraulic stabilisers onto the ground prior to firing, which impacts on its out of action time; the South African gun manages recoil chiefly through its 46.5-ton weight – which is heavier than many tracked guns. The Slovaks have developed the DANA, first fitting the standard NATO calibre, and in the most recent version, into the Zuzana 2, with a 155mm 52 calibre barrel. Given these characteristics they should be bracketed with tracked armoured self-propelled artillery. The Swedish Archer also best fits into this category; while it lacks a conventional turret, the 155mm gun's automation means that crew do not need to dismount from their armoured cab to fire.

The other form of truck mounted gun is a lighter design – protection is generally limited to an armoured driving cab. They are cheaper to build, easier to maintain, have lower whole life costs, and greater mobility on roads and in good going. Truck-mounted guns can be deployed by transport aircraft, both into and around a theatre. At 20 tonnes or less they are generally too heavy for most helicopters[14]; this renders these truck mounted guns as not really viable for amphibious or airmobile operations. Not being helicopter transportable can also limit their utility in mountainous and jungle operations.

Unarmoured truck-mounted guns expect to survive on the battlefield through a combination of long range, to keep them out of the range of any weapons seeking to retaliate, together with 'shoot and scoot' tactics. All guns can employ 'shoot and scoot' tactics to improve their survivability, but their quick in and out of action times makes this tactic more effective with self-propelled guns. Constant movement reduces available firepower; but not by a factor of ten, which was identified in one study that appeared to be almost designed to defend the traditional gun position[15]. Truck mounted guns are more survivable when operating within a largely safe area, either behind a front line in linear operations or in a defended position. Their survivability on a non-linear battlefield would be more challenging. Furthermore, unarmoured guns under counter-battery fire cannot sustain fire support to troops in close combat. This also applies to towed guns, but these are much easier to place in protected gun platforms.

Lighter truck-mounted guns either cannot, or are extremely vulnerable, while conducting direct fire. Truck-mounted guns are a much larger target than their tracked equivalents, a significant disadvantage when being drawn into the direct fire battle. This is due to truck-mounted guns requiring: greater suspension clearance; wheel-turning clearance; multiple driveshaft transfer cases and drivetrain components. The difference is in the order of a 28% increase in vehicle volume[16]. Their unsuitability for conducting direct fire is a severe disadvantage, not just for its reduction in self-defence capability, but also because in some tactical circumstances – such as urban warfare – direct fire is the most effective means of providing fire support. Direct fire is also advantageous when a simplified sensor-to-shooter chain is at a premium, such as in very high tempo operations, and in counter-insurgency operations with restrictive rules of engagement.

The truck gun's light weight, high centre of gravity, and powerful gun can present stability problems during firing. For the lightest guns and at the higher charges, fire needs to be conducted along the axis of the chassis, which allows the funnelling of recoil into the ground though spades at the rear of the gun. This means a relatively narrow field of fire without moving the vehicle. This is a disadvantage when compared to self-propelled guns equipped with a turret, but truck-mounting is significantly superior to the towed medium calibre gun, which can need several minutes to move trails that have 'dug-in' as a result of firing. In comparison, lighter towed guns usually have a central pivot mount or platform, so can switch almost as quickly as turreted guns. The advantages of being able to easily switch fire are rarely appreciated in peacetime training, but soon becomes apparent on operations[17].

Despite these disadvantages, the truck-mounted gun is an appealing capability. American artillerymen have questioned whether adding a truck-mounted gun with a 155mm calibre, to their combination of armoured self-propelled and highly deployable towed guns, would better suit some expeditionary scenarios[18]. The Israelis have concluded that their current armoured artillery piece, the M109, cannot economically be further upgraded, a truck-mounted replacement is being considered. This may perhaps be a partial replacement, as its characteristics may suit the less challenging terrain of the southern theatre. A lively debate is on-going; as already identified it appears that the Israelis have recognised that fire support rather than standoff deep fires is their artillery's priority. In 2016, Israel's Chief Artillery Corps Officer believed that there is a continuing requirement for the armoured, tracked, self-propelled gun[19]. He rejected the view that the truck mounted gun's range and deployability compensate for its limitations in supporting armoured forces[20]. The IDF Artillery Corps has defined the characteristics of the new self-propelled gun as being a crew of four[21] and a range of 40km. As a result, Artillery Corps committed to the technology of the Elbit System's ATMOS 155mm/52 calibre truck-mounted howitzer. As of 2020, they have commissioned Elbit to head up a consortium to develop a M109 replacement[22]. This could be on a truck or mounted on a Bradley-type tracked chassis but it appears to have been determined that a 8x8 tank will meet the whole requirment. This seems to be favoured over a solution based on the Artillery Gun Module which uses much of the PzH 2000 technology, but with reduced cost, crew levels and weight. This also can be fitted to either a wheeled or tracked chassis[23].

The French have already decided that armoured tracked artillery is not required to support their armoured forces. The Caesar is a largely unarmoured truck that uses a 52-calibre barrel to achieve its 38km (with extended range projectiles) range, providing excellent coverage. France's in-service version of the Caesar compromises ammunition storage and handling, crew protection and gap crossing capability to achieve lightness. All these issues are addressed in the 8x8 version being fielded by the Danish artillery, leading a weight increase from 18.5 tonnes to 32 tonnes. Its advantages are leading to its fielding to support French armoured forces.

The Chinese have developed the SH11 – a turret-mounted 155mm, 39-calibre gun on an 8x8 chassis – apparently for the export market; the Russians are doing the same. The Polish artillery operates a mixed fleet, as well as DANA and 2S1 122mm howitzers – the Elbit Systems' ATMOS 2000 is mounted on a local truck and called the Kryl. Their second new gun is a heavy tracked self-propelled 155mm howitzer on a local chassis with the British AS90 Braveheart turret and a Rheinmetall gun. The original requirement for a mixed fleet was driven by the need for deployability. Given the current emphasis upon territorial defence, the Poles may be revising their ratio of armoured to lightly protected truck-mounted guns[24]. This may mean that the Kryl is not produced or fielded in reduced numbers.

The original World War Two portee guns were an attempt to improve the mobility of existing field guns. In a similar way, the South Koreans are fielding the EVO-105 self-propelled artillery system, which mounts the World War Two-vintage M101A1-series of 105mm howitzer barrel assembly, recoil system, and breech onto the bed of a Kia KM500 (6×6) 5-tonne truck chassis. Compared to a towed gun, the system is extremely fast into action, requiring less than sixty seconds to stop and shoot, versus four and a half minutes for its towed counterpart; it takes only 30 seconds to displace. Through having simpler and less laborious deployment drills, it requires three fewer crew than its towed counterpart; its lack of range (11km) and light calibre is not a major issue for its infantry fire-support role; it is supplemented by the longer-range divisional level 155mm K9 Thunder guns.

The Americans are considering innovative approaches to improve the survivability of their towed guns. The company Mandus Group have designed a 105mm gun mounted on a HUMVEE called the Hawkeye. They are using soft recoil technology, plus front and rear stabilisers, as a means of allowing longer range guns to be safely fired from a light chassis. This arrangement significantly speeds up time into and out of action, making it more survivable through shooting and scooting than a towed gun. Being on the vehicle rather than being towed behind means that this design significantly reduces rolling resistance, so improving the gun's mobility. The downside is that the method of mounting the ordnance of a M119 howitzer on a HUMVEE makes loading difficult, and the current design achieves three rounds a minute rather than the towed gun's six[25]. They have also developed a soft recoil version of the M777 155mm ordnance on a 5 ton truck. In summary, the wheeled gun capability choice is largely between protection and range:

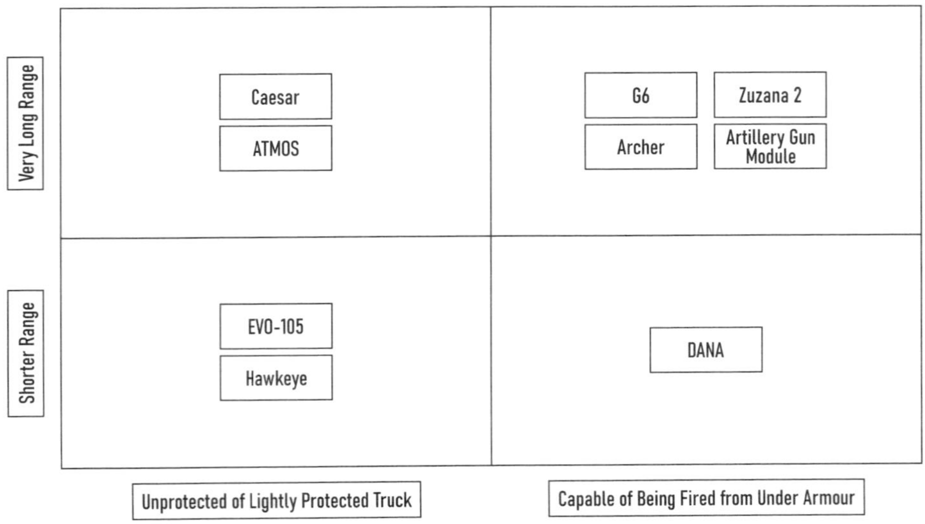

Towed Tube Artillery

> *'Towed guns remain the only field artillery that can be lifted by helicopter. This offers tactical mobility from one site to another, but once dropped they cannot move long distances under their own power*[26]*.'*
>
> Stephen W. Miller

As towed guns are the cheapest means of equipping an artillery force, they make up most of the World's artillery park. In some armies they are the most sophisticated, long range systems. This is usually not the case with armies that are reliant upon armoured artillery; but most of these also have a proportion of towed guns, if only for challenging terrain or rapid deployment tasks that necessitate air transportation. Only towed guns can currently achieve the lightness, with stability, that is necessary to support heliborne light force operations, but the Hawkeye is challenging this.

There are several alternative approaches amongst towed tube guns. Extremely long-range 155mm artillery (35–40km) is currently championed by the Indians; originally the South Africans pioneered this approach. The Russians and Chinese are partly following this path, as are some Arab armies. These are sophisticated and heavy guns, that should be slow into and out of action. However, most have an auxiliary engine to assist in this and allow them to move into position without relying upon their limber vehicle. They achieve force protection through a combination of long range and sufficient mass to silence opposing artillery. The heavy 155mm gun's firepower is assisted by the auxiliary engine also providing the power to mechanically assist loading, resulting in a higher rate of fire. Lack of battlefield platform mobility is not seen as a significant disadvantage, given the expectation that ground operations will be limited to being within the range of emplaced artillery. This approach was considered appropriate in the Cold War by some NATO armies, resulting in the fielding of FH70 – which had a long range for its time. This approach is probably the most cost-effective means of providing tube artillery firepower. These armies supplement these guns with lighter tube artillery for terrain where it is difficult to deploy these heavy 155mm guns, and a lesser number of self-propelled guns to support mechanised forces.

These extended range guns use at least 45-calibre barrels and specialist long-range ammunition. The Indians are converting 300 M46 130mm/52 calibre guns into the M46 Sharang 155mm/45 calibre. With its larger calibre and long-range munitions, these guns can achieve a 36–39km range, compared to the 130mm gun's 27km range. There is of course a weight penalty in upgrading the 152–155mm calibre to 52-calibre lengths. The Russian 2A36 152mm goes one further with a 54-calibre barrel and weighs in at 9,760kg (or about double the M777). While it can fire the OF-59 rocket-assisted projectile, the Russian approach appears to be relying upon having a longer barrel to achieve the required range; judging that this is a better use of resources than expensive bespoke longer-range projectiles. This is a reasonable deduction given the quantity of artillery ammunition actually fired in conflict, as most recently demonstrated in the Russo-Ukraine War.

For armies seeking a highly deployable general-purpose gun, the M777 usually meets the bill. Its versatility allows it to be the sole piece for armies such as the Canadians, Australians and US Marine Corps. The lightweight 155mm M777 gun, which weighs in at under 4,100kg

(9,000 lb) is smaller and 42% lighter, than the M198 155mm gun it replaced. This was achieved through making sacrifices in other design characteristics, including: the retention of the 39-calibre barrel with its limited range; largely manual loading with a rate of fire of 3–4 rounds per minute; restricted tactical movement without helicopters; and through lacking an auxiliary engine, the physical challenge of getting the gun into and out of action, as well any significant shift from centre of arc or base line[27].

The M777 has questionable survivability characteristics against an effective counter battery capability in peer conventional warfighting. With a 39-calibre barrel it lacks the range to standoff from the majority of the threats, and the agility and burst rate of fire to effectively employ 'shoot and scoot' tactics. It has the reputation in certain armies as being a gun suitable for counter-insurgency forward operating bases, and lacking wider utility. Such was the dominance of the counter battery threat at the turn of the millennium that armies who had hitherto relied upon towed artillery, such as the Australians, began to consider switching to self-propelled[28]. Of course, the 9/11 Wars presented a different set of challenges, leading to Australia's adoption of the M777, only for the survivability challenge now to re-emerge.

Making the M777 better suited to the current character of conflict has spurred a series of improvements. The American engineers at Picatinny Arsenal are trying to extend the M777's range; they are aiming at 70km. The first step has been fitting a barrel that is 2.4m longer, this has added 454kg (12%) to the system weight, so reducing its handiness and deployability[29]. This allows more propellant to be used and results in a higher muzzle velocity for the rocket assisted XM1113 projectile. A 25% increase in weight allows the M777 to have an auxiliary power unit and automatic loader, which would partly address its greatest challenge of crew fatigue both during firing and deployment[30]. For a modern 152/155mm towed gun to match the capability of a self-propelled one requires an even greater investment in weight and money. Achieving a comparable rate of fire and reasonable into action time (2-minutes) requires a built-in power unit to allow almost full automation. The General Dynamics European Land Systems 155mm can match most self-propelled guns, but it is almost three and half times the weight of the significantly less capable, but deployable, M777[31].

Pairing 155mm guns with a 120mm mortar has been attractive to armies wanting to combine firepower with deployability. The French Army saw the Caesar truck-mounted 155mm gun, when paired with 120mm mortars, as offering a practical solution to support the full spectrum of capability: armoured, mechanised, marine, mountain and airborne brigades[32]. The original French plan was to dual role all their personnel; the training bill has often resulted in an artillery battalion having two batteries that concentrate on tube artillery and one on mortars[33]. The US Marine Corps have abandoned their gun and mortar combination, again due to an inability to be equally capable with both systems.

Lighter towed guns are significantly more survivable on the modern battlefield than 155mm guns, particularly those which are manually operated. 105mm guns can quickly come into and out of action and manually achieve a high rate of fire; their small size allows them to better exploit terrain for both concealment and protection. The disadvantage of 105mm towed guns is their lack of lethality against hardened targets; in compensation they are superior to heavier guns at infantry close support. Their reliance upon mortars for this form of firepower is questioned by some in the French Army, given its operational deployments often leads to the need to support dismounted infantry. This led to concern over the decision not to replace the HM2 105mm gun with Nexter's LG1 Mark II. This was developed for both the French Army and the export market, and could provide French forces with the highly useful fire support of a 105mm gun[34].

The split between highly deployable towed guns and significantly more capable heavier ones is likely to continue. But the gap will close; survival on the conventional battlefield necessitates highly deployable guns being upgraded to improve their agility and burst fire lethality. Longer-range ammunition will partly address the lack of standoff range. In its more austere configuration, guns such as the M777 will continue to provide a helicopter transportable capability for less demanding conflicts. The qualities of the different towed gun designs allow them to fit into distinct categorises:

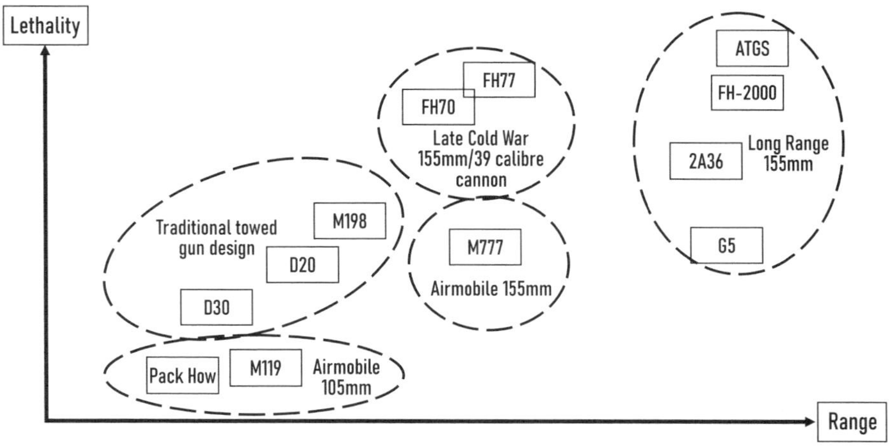

Tube Artillery Calibre

'In peace the cry is for mobility, in war for weight of shell[35].'

Lt Col Alan Brooke

Anything less than a 105mm calibre for field guns is now usually considered to be ineffective at defeating contemporary targets. This view contrasts with that of previous generations of artillerymen, notably World War Two British and Russian gunners, who valued the greater 'number of bangs' that smaller calibre weapons could deliver. They identified that suppression was the primary task of field artillery. In the European Theatre, the British were convinced that their 25-pdr gun/howitzer represented about the ideal weapon. Post-War there was even a view that they could manage with a 20-pdr shell, optimised for fragmentation with limited explosive blast effect. Fragmentation suited the role of providing suppressive fire for an army invariably on the attack, as the British were in the latter stages of the War. The same rationale applied to the Russians in World War Two, who were equally content with 76.2mm as their standard field gun calibre, despite firing a 14-pdr munition. It appears that its post-World War Two replacement by first an 85mm gun, and then heavier calibres, was largely driven by the need to improve its anti-tank performance, rather than its indirect fire capability.

In contrast to the European Theatre, the British Army's experience in the Burma campaign showed the requirement for a larger calibre. Explosive content, in the region of the 100 pounds provided by the 5.5-inch gun, was required to destroy Japanese bunkers[36]. Close support suppression was the role of direct fire tanks, self-propelled guns and recoilless rifles. Faced with similar targets, the Americans in the Pacific Theatre, despite the challenging terrain, also favoured heavier weight of shell, with the 75-mm howitzer being replaced by 105-mm howitzer in direct support units, and divisions receiving 155-mm howitzers for general support[37].

As the American World War Two standard field howitzer was 105mm calibre, this became the NATO field artillery standard, leading to the replacement of lighter calibres. With the fielding of self-propelled guns, the 105mm calibre gave way to 155mm, with field and medium artillery effectively merged for armoured forces. This decision was rationalised by the need for heavier calibres against the likely massed tank targets of NATO's Central Front. The need for a greater weight of shell to be effective against tanks was accepted by even the British in World War Two, as demonstrated by a British infantry battalion trying to consolidate a defence position after an assault over a canal in Holland, in late 1944:

> *'Theoretically the chief risk in these kind of operations is being counter-attacked with armour before the anti-tank guns were in position. So medium artillery was always deployed against such a threat. These guns fired a 100-pound shell and therefore had four times the destructive power of the 25-Pounder, which itself was ineffective against tanks. Their officer [the medium artillery] told me that near Caen his regiment had brewed-up two Tiger tanks and knocked over a third with their first salvo of the campaign[38].'*

The greater effectiveness of medium artillery against armoured targets was demonstrated in trials and in the 1973 War, when the Israelis had considerable success at destroying tanks[39]. With 155mm becoming NATO's standard medium gun calibre, the Alliance had standardised on two further tube artillery calibres: 175mm and 203mm, respectively for the heavy gun and howitzer, until rocket systems largely replaced these. The Americans and the Israelis led the way in the replacement of the 105mm calibre by 155mm artillery, with the British and the French being more conservative and retaining 105mm self-propelled guns into the 1990s. It appears that little thought was given as to whether what had previously been considered a suitable calibre for medium artillery, up until the 1970s, was actually suitable as a field artillery calibre. The need to defeat tanks in the Cold War seems to have overridden the need to engage other targets in support of manoeuvre.

The Russians continued with their policy of relying upon the greater suppressive ability of lighter calibres. They expected suppressing defending infantry to be the most likely task, rather than massed armour. Thus, the 122mm remains their most common close support artillery weapon. A possible like-for-like replacement is the 120mm gun-mortar, a calibre that can be fitted to the same platform. If the Russians follow this approach, they will be trading the superior target effect of the mortar bomb for less range, thus preserving a distinct close fire support weapon. The alternative may be a gradual phasing out of 122mm in favour of 152mm. The Russians have always recognised the need for larger calibres against armoured targets. Marshal Zhukov identified this weakness in 1942:

'the enemy brought up new forces and dug in tanks and self-propelled guns on dominant elevations as strongpoints. These could only be rendered harmless by powerful artillery fire, and we had very few big guns at our disposal at that time[40]'.

Given their doctrinal influence and the success of the Soviet arms industry, many other armies, including the Chinese, make significant use of 122mm calibre guns. These make up almost half of the Chinese artillery park. And most of their self-propelled guns are Soviet built 2S1. The Chinese preference for towed guns to be predominantly of a heavier calibre matches the Indian approach; both armies also field 105mm howitzers for their light and mountain formations[41]. The continued need for specialist light artillery in the most challenging terrain recognises that:

'there was a point at which the price paid for a heavier shell – range, mobility, fatigue or ammunition resupply – becomes uneconomical.[42]'

While for Western forces massed armour has been a rare target, the additional explosive content provided by 155mm round has proved useful in engaging well-protected targets in complex terrain. This was the case in the Second Battle of Fallujah in November 2004 when the M109 Paladins supported their infantry advance through the urban areas with a succession of concentrations controlled by roof-mounted observers. This in effect created a rolling barrage. The 155mm high explosive shells were successful at *'delivering suppressive or interdiction fire and, rather surprisingly, clearing out areas that were mined or booby-trapped by explosive devices*[43]'. In World War One artillery fire was used to clear paths through barbed wire, less successfully in World War Two it cleared mines.

In most Western armies anything greater than 155mm calibre is now considered to be too heavy to be effective. This is for two reasons: 155mm is the heaviest calibre for which one man can easily carry a shell[44], and it is the largest calibre that a land platform can currently practically deliver a burst rate of fire. Russia stands apart from this consensus, as they continue to make effective use of the 203mm gun and the 240mm mortar[45]. These have been upgraded with modern Russian artillery command and control systems, as well as their barrels and recoil mechanisms being refurbished or replaced. These fulfil the traditional 'siege artillery' role: engaging fortifications, bridges and prepared defences, exploiting the significantly greater explosive content of their munitions, aided by the fielding of precision rounds. Turkish artillery faced with defeating the Afrin Kurds in their heavily fortified Syrian stronghold turned to the material destruction provided by the 203mm M110[46].

Standardisation on the 155/152mm calibre has led to the other calibres receiving less investment in munition development. 155/152mm rounds' internal volume is sufficient to carry a large quantity of sub-munitions; this also makes its smoke and illumination rounds significantly more effective than their 105mm equivalents. The calibre is also suited to the bespoke precision shell; the 155mm is sufficiently large for the course correction fuze's canards to be able to steer the shell to near precision accuracy. Designing a 105mm fuze that can be fitted to standard rounds and is capable of delivering near precision capability is significantly more challenging[47]. Producing a bespoke 105mm precision guided shell is not. Russia does not restrict its bespoke laser-guided projectiles to the larger 155/152mm calibre. It fields the 122mm Kitolov-2M, and the 120mm gun-mortar also has similar rounds.

Until recently, except for the most specialised jungle and mountain units, it was assumed that all modern artillery would standardise on the 155/152mm calibre, especially as this had already achieved dominance in self-propelled artillery; this would lead to economies of scale through fielding a single calibre. Standardisation led the American Army Chief of Staff General Edward C. Meyer, in May 1980, to direct that the new light infantry divisions were to use the M198 as their direct-support weapon. Lack of suitable prime movers, and it being too heavy for most support helicopters, prevented this being implemented. The Army then decided to have a new 155mm weapon system designed; meanwhile the light divisions returned to using 105mm guns for direct support. The fielding of an effective lightweight 155mm gun, the M777, which offered the firepower of the larger calibre, at a weight not much more than most 105mm systems, provided the opportunity for complete standardisation of the ammunition system[48]; however, the Americans have did not take this opportunity, they field within their light battalions a single 155mm M777 battery, and one or two 105mm M119 batteries.

There is considerable longevity to this calibre mix; the American artillery had concluded in a 1938 study at Fort Sill, the US Fires Centre of Excellence, that their fire support needs were best met through a 105/155 combination[49]. The merits of both calibres have been reinforced by operations, including the comparative analysis provided by Battery D, 2nd Battalion, 13th Artillery; this sub unit simultaneously operated both calibres in the Vietnam War. The 155mm howitzer was more effective at engaging targets in the triple-canopy jungle; the 105mm was more effective for close-in defence and for delivering rounds at high rates of fire. Over a generation later, some bases in Afghanistan had both types of guns, but often with only sufficient crew to man one system at a time. When there was a choice to be made, the 105mm gun usually supported US troops in close contact; this invariably required danger close fire to neutralise the target. The greater lethality of the 155mm shell was used against targets where destruction was the aim and this could be pursued without significant collateral damage concerns.

In addition to the benefits accruing from the shell, 105mm offers other advantages. Firstly, two guns can be manned with the same number of personnel as a single M777; secondly, it is more responsive, in particular in making large switches of fire. Thirdly it achieves and sustains a much greater rate; finally, the M119 gun, its detachment, essential stores and 100 rounds of unboxed ammunition weighs slightly over half the M777 similarly provisioned[50]. The M777 is a generation newer than the M119; a modern 105mm design, such as Denel Land System's Light Experimental, demonstrates that this ratio can be significantly improved.

Convinced of the utility of the 105mm calibre, the Americans have embarked upon the digitization of their fleet to the new M119A3 standard, with further capability development likely. The M119A3 will also feature a weight reduction programme that ultimately aims at making the gun around 140kg lighter through exploiting more modern materials and design[51]. The British have digitized their similar L118 platforms but have not matched the platform enhancements. Further improvements in the lethality and range of the American 105mm rounds are possible; this will probably not feature a requirement for a precision or near precision capability. The M777 battery in each light battalion, supported as necessary by guided multiple launch rocket systems and airpower, is considered sufficient to meet the point target requirement. American operational experience suggests that while precision engagements could proportionately increase, particularly in irregular warfare, the majority of fire missions will be with unguided munitions. Of all the 155mm rounds fired by the Americans in their recent conflicts in Iraq and Afghanistan, only 0.2% were precision rounds.

To prove that militaries can look at the same factors and determine a different capability approach, the US Marine Corps initially fielded a dual M777 155mm gun and 120mm mortar capability, and the US Army both 105mm and 155mm. The Marine approach has been re-evaluated as part of Expeditionary Force 21, their new concept of fighting. The Army's 105mm gun has been trialled against the Marine's current inventory. This identified the 105mm gun's crucial advantage: the agile direct fire ability, particularly in the urban environment[52]. The American Army is studying a single system replacement for the M119 and M777 towed howitzers currently fielded with the Army's Infantry Brigade Combat Teams[53]; this will test the practicality of meeting the broad requirement with a single calibre. One current proposal is for short and long barrelled 155mm guns. This standardisation is on the pathway of the Fires community's long-term objective of: one sensor, one shooter, and one mission command system. This ultimately aims at one artillery platform, one radar and one mission control system for both field and air defence artillery[54]. Those less wedded to a transformational agenda see the need for equipment suited to different roles in different characters of conflict.

Tube Artillery Ammunition Resupply

'[In Operation Desert Storm] Field Artillery brigades were so low on ammunition, their ability to augment division artillery fires were seriously degraded at wars end. In fact, many of the units were almost out of ammunition when the cease fire was declared[55].'

Major Jesse T. Acosta US Army

Invariably in conventional warfighting the provision of artillery shells is an army's greatest logistic challenge. An exception could be during the pursuit, when the demand for fuel to manoeuvre exceeds that of ammunition. The challenge of resupplying artillery ammunition is being made greater by: larger calibres, increased rates of fire, and the proliferation of ammunition natures. In addition, lighter, more expeditionary platforms and limber vehicles have reduced carrying capacity. Altogether this increases the challenge of ensuring the availability of the correct rounds in the required quantity.

Achieving and sustaining a gun's planned rate of fire ultimately requires a gun detachment and ammunition party large enough to sustain the breaking down of ammunition from storage to firing configuration. The fuze, round and charge then need to be transported into either the gun's breech or magazine. This challenge is compounded by the way munitions are safely and economically packed for peacetime storage and shipment; this makes the challenge of actually using them manpower intensive. Advances in automating guns have masked the fact that this packaging makes the whole process resistant to mechanisation; addressing this requires a redesign of ammunition packaging. Unfortunately, ease of access to artillery ammunition has not had the same priority as that of tank and infantry natures; these users have insisted on the design priority being ease of employment.

The US Army approach to their armoured artillery ammunition resupply is designed for the most challenging counter-battery environment. It recognises the unsuitability of unarmoured truck-based resupply of artillery ammunition direct to the gun position; this is the most dangerous location, as it is the part of the artillery system of systems most easily acquired and engaged. This leads to each gun having a dedicated armoured tracked limber vehicle, allowing the protected transfer of ammunition. The M992 CAT (Carrier, Ammunition, Tracked) ammunition carrier vehicle carries 90 rounds (the M109 carries 39); the CAT vehicle can be reloaded in 15 minutes of manually intensive work; crucially this can be done from a truck in a less vulnerable location.

The Chinese also follow this approach; their equivalent gun to the M109A7 – the PLZ-45 and the PLZ04 – have an ammunition supply vehicle that carries 90 shells to the 30 on the gun; as do the Koreans, whose K-9 gun also has its own armoured limber. The Israelis couple their M109 with the M548 (a version of the M113), as their tracked resupply vehicle. They learnt in their First Lebanon War the importance of protected ammunition resupply:

> *'We solved the ammunition supply problem by converting one of the howitzers into a Field Artillery ammunition support vehicle (FAASV). We also put 70 to 80 rounds on the floor of each SPH [Self-Propelled Howitzer][56].'*

Of course, this approach comes at a price, hence it is admired but seldom copied. In addition, not all artilleries see the operational challenge as primarily being the provision of continuous fire support to manoeuvre forces in a high threat environment. The Russians have always expected their guns to carry sufficient rounds onboard for the most immediate fire support tasks, a tendency reinforced by their emphasis on firing over open sights. They are currently exploring a novel approach to reducing their resupply challenge through significantly increasing their on-board ammunition. The DT-30 comprises two articulated tracked units, with the crew in the front unit, with the engine behind, leaving the rear unit free for a payload. When this unit is fitted with a 155mm gun, up to 200 rounds can be carried.

Other armies rely upon, at best, lightly protected trucks to cover a battery's first line ammunition resupply requirement. Unlike the armoured limber vehicle, the ammunition in trucks usually remains in its storage, rather than its firing, configuration. Trucks and the associated forklift trucks and pallets of ammunition, are extremely vulnerable to incoming counter battery fire if they remain on the gun position once the battery has unmasked. Resupply on the gun position can also make the self-propelled gun more vulnerable, given that most guns rely upon opening a large door to laboriously restock their on-board ammunition. The alternative in high threat environments is to geographically separate ammunition resupply from the firing positions, of course this takes guns out of action and reduces the level of fire support. Armies that follow this incoherent approach to ammunition resupply are likely to compound their challenge as they move towards smaller gun crews over the next decades. Detachments of three or four will be unable to sustain manually breaking down ammunition from its storage configuration through to loading it into the gun in sufficient quantity to sustain the rate of fire required.

Tube artillery's ability to sustain or burst-fire a range of ammunition to deliver lethal and non-lethal effects gives it an advantage over the other joint fires systems. Delivering this requires an array of ammunition natures to be available, including when armoured guns are 'closed down' due to hostile fire. Given that the range of munitions is expanding, and the use of non-lethal munitions (smoke and illumination) has increased on recent operations, rather than declined in accordance with budgetary predictions, a ready-use stock of ammunition of at least 40 rounds of various natures on each platform is prudent. The limited number of rounds ready to fire on the newer truck-mounted guns is a particular challenge – the standard Caesar has only 16 ready rounds. Presumably the design expectation is for either a static deployment, or for relatively few rounds to be used in an engagement, with sufficient time subsequently to reload, or always having a resupply truck on hand.

A working assumption in many militaries is that the greater lethality of modern shells, particularly those with terminal guidance, means that significantly fewer rounds will be fired. Of course, this is a popular position for a range of stakeholders, as fewer shells need to be actually bought, less magazine capacity is required to store them and economies can be made in the force structure. Unfortunately, one of the universal, and seemingly enduring lessons of history, is that the availability of shells never matches the operational requirement. This is usually particular acute for the first two years of conflict (the British 1915 'Shell Scandal' was so serious that it was a key factor in bringing down the government). In the same war, the French lost 600 guns in inadvertent explosions due to hurriedly manufactured 75mm shells and charges[57].

Those arguing against this indisputable historical fact point out that improved weapon accuracy has significantly reduced direct fire ammunition use. In World War Two, a tank required an average of 17 rounds per tank kill; in the Gulf War Abram tanks required 1.2 rounds[58]. If artillery were fired at individual targets, then similar reduction might be possible; however, area suppression remains artillery's primary mission. Despite its stop-start nature and the employment of enhanced lethality rounds, the rate of expenditure in the Russo-Ukraine War has at peak times exceeded previous norms. The 1973 Arab-Israeli War led to NATO significantly increasing its ammunition holdings, as a result of some guns firing 250 rounds per day. Israeli ammunition war reserves were 800 rounds per medium calibre tube; this proved far too low. During the war, the IDF employed all of the available 175mm and most available 155mm and 130mm rounds[59]. In the Ukraine, batteries have fired 300–400 rounds per tube per day. As at mid 2016 it was opined that more ammunition had been fired in the conflict than NATO possesses east of the Rhine[60]. The Americans are reacting to the challenge, the Army's budget proposal for the 2019 fiscal year includes a request for a more than 800% increase in purchases of 155mm high explosive shells alone.

Tube Artillery's Accuracy and Consistency Improvements

> *'the battle opened a new chapter in the life of the Royal Regiment [of British artillery]. Survey was here to stay, the Royal Regiment must now have its own surveyors. Calibration became important to everyone. The artillery doctrine born at [the battle] of Cambrai, stayed unchanged until the end of the War, and lasted well into the 1939–45 conflict. Some principles remained unchanged until the arrival of the computer in the 1960s[61].'*
>
> General Farndale, soldier and historian

By 1917 the artillery system had advanced to the point that predicted fire was becoming the basis of the new all arms battle. Until the last 25 years – when modern computing power has provided impetus to addressing the challenges of the gunnery problem – subsequent increases in artillery's accuracy and consistency have been incremental. The outcome of this recent innovation is that modern artillery can now precisely engage an area target with unguided munitions at current battle ranges. However, dispersion around the target area still significantly increases with range and especially as a cannon approaches its maximum range. This means that beyond 25km achieving consistent accuracy is largely beyond current technology, without employing terminal guidance munitions. Of course, the resource-intensive and inefficient massing of fire to overcome the individual inaccuracies of unguided munitions, remains a combat-proven option to 'shoot-out' the problem of long range.

For unguided munitions, artillery accuracy is a measure of how close to the mean point of impact a group of rounds is to the point of aim. This is the function of the combined errors within the whole indirect fire system. The Americans identify five requirements of accurate predictive fires: accurate target location and size; accurate firing unit location; accurate weapon and ammunition information; accurate meteorological information; and accurate firing data computational procedures[62]. Getting these inputs correct is key, as the most perfect mathematical computation model can only make at best a 7% improvement in accuracy.

Consistency is the dispersion of rounds around that mean point of impact, and is the round-to-round variation in: muzzle velocity, meteorology, gun laying and ramming the shell. This dispersion around the point of aim is a predictable statistical function for a given range and charge. When this dispersion is plus and minus of the mean point of impact along the line of fire it is known as Probable Error Range (PE_R). A much smaller dispersion occurs either side of the line of fire and is known as Probable Error Line (PE_L). This line dispersion is in the order of a seventh of the range dispersion. This means that the area over which a given percentage of rounds will land is elongated along the line of fire – the fall of shot is commonly described as a cigar shape. Direct fire weapons, such as machine guns, call this a beaten zone. Misleadingly it has become common, despite the disparity in the size of PE_L and PE_R, for artillery weapons to be given a circular error probability in line with other modern weapon systems.

Historically the principal means of achieving accuracy has been to correct the mean point of impact of the artillery or mortar fire onto the target[63]. The most accurate fire comes from adjusting each individual battery onto the target. Alternatively, instead of individually adjusting batteries onto a target, the registration process determines the cumulative error and applies a correction. This is established by firing a single battery, then circulating its final firing data to the other batteries that subsequently engage a target. This is more resource efficient and has the possibility of retaining some surprise. Not adjusting a battery onto the target and instead relying on predicting the fire better suits modern warfare, as it delivers target effect from the first round and preserves surprise. This requires all significant sources of error to be precisely measured and accounted for in the firing solution. Obviously, all these variables, and in particular meteorological factors, need to be constantly updated.

The improvements in accuracy and consistency for modern artillery over the last 25-years – at the firing rather than the target end – can be summarised as follows:

Area of Improvement		**Likely Error**		**Principal Reason(s) for the Improvement**
		1990s	**2020**	
Meteorological		300–350m	100–150m	Traditionally meteorological conditions close to the gun position have been measured, this is then applied to the whole trajectory. Greater accuracy is achieved through computer modelling of the meteorological conditions along the whole flight path of the shell. This uses data from multiple military and civil sources.
Survey	Fix	100m	10m	In the 1990s survey determined the battery centre and then made allowance for individual gun locations. This has been replaced by Global Positioning Systems and Inertial Navigation Systems to precisely fix each firing platform.
	Orientation	5mils	0.5mils	Inertial Navigation Systems are now on each firing platform
	Gun Laying	2mils	1mil	Automated laying also reduces mistakes, especially during fire for effect.
Muzzle Velocity	Wear & Adopted Muzzle Velocity	3m/s	2m/s	The fitting of Muzzle Velocity measurement to all guns has resulted in improvement in calibration data.
	Occasion-to-Occasion Muzzle Velocity Variation	3m/s	3m/s	This remains the area where the most improvement can take place through adopting technology and a calibration policy that allows for Occasion-to-Occasion Muzzle Velocity variation.
Measurement of Charge Temperature (Celsius)		4 degrees centigrade	1 degree centigrade	More accurate measuring, coupled with a more rigorous measurement regime, has led to significant improvement.

In addition, improving the quality of the manufacturing process – such as machining the shell outside and inside to strict tolerances rather than employing a forged shell – has reduced dispersion[64]. Modern techniques have also addressed the probability of mistakes through reducing their magnitude and incidence[65]. The British and Canadians at the end of World War Two undertook a systematic study of mistakes[66]. Technology has reduced the probability of some of these mistakes; the manual laying of the gun has been replaced by less error-prone digital weapon sights. Computers have made firing data computation more reliable, however the machine's authority can undermine the culture of conducting independent checks. The remaining mistakes identified in World War Two were incorrect handling of ammunition, and employing the wrong firing data for the shell and its propellant. The latter has not been adequately addressed, as the wrong firing charge for the elevation remains a consistent training error. Technology could certainly help with this (such as bar coding of shell and propellant as an independent check?), but this will not automatically lead to better handling of ammunition.

These technological advances also allow artillery and mortars to break away from traditional battery positions and employ significantly different methods of deployment. Traditionally artillery has required laborious processes before it can conduct indirect fire; surveying a gun position is now a matter of moments. Guns with integrated position and azimuth determining devices permit on-board computation of firing data. These can receive fire missions via radio, quickly occupy a firing position, compute and automatically lay onto their firing data, then quickly displace upon completing the fire mission. This allows modern guns, such as the Paladin to operate in small groups employing 'shoot and scoot', so they do not offer a lucrative battery-size target[67].

Over the last 25 years the improvements in accuracy and consistency have led to the artillery system being able to effectively employ predicted fire on area targets. Technology has made longer range fire more accurate, in particular through the modelling of meteorological conditions along the whole trajectory. The complete answer for accurate engagement of an area target at range is a combination of these improvements to ensure that the shell is on the best predicted ballistic path, with a course correcting fuze that can address most of the remaining error. This combined approach is necessary for efficient cannon fire beyond 25kms.

Naval Gunfire

[At the Salerno landings in 1943] 'When the situation became really serious, battleships were rushed to the scene in spite of the danger of radio-controlled bombs with which the enemy was scoring some success[68].'

Brigadier Pemberton

While there are a range of naval weapons, the general-purpose gun, able to engage air and surface ship targets, remains, at least for now, the most common means of engaging land targets from the sea. The development of bespoke ship-launched land attack weapons might in the future challenge the general-purpose gun's primacy. The most common naval weapon is the American

5-inch (127mm) 54-calibre gun, which can fire its 32kg or 70lbs shell to a maximum range of about 23km (or 14 nautical miles)[69]. The World's navies seem to agree on the need for a range of at least 20km to conduct naval gunfire support. This provides a balance between keeping some distance from the shore for ship self-defence, and coverage of land targets. The 76mm mounted on smaller ships is primarily designed to combat air targets, though bringing the ship close to the shore allows it to provide naval gunfire support, as the Israelis have done.

The aspiration of some Western navies has been to replace 5-inch with 155mm. This allows them to exploit the significantly greater investment made on this calibre's munitions. The US Navy's Advanced Gun System combines the 155mm calibre with the much longer barrel, 62-calibre lengths, that is able to be practically mounted on a ship. (Though in the American quest for longer range, the traditional norms for barrel length on land platforms is being challenged). As well as standard artillery rounds, a specialist long range land attack projectile with a range of up to 109km or 61 miles was partly developed. This uses rocket assistance and deployed canards that allow it to glide for much of its flight path. GPS guidance compensates for the dispersion that is the result of this range. The fielding of only three Zumwalt Destroyers (rather than the planned 32), plus the deferring of the rearming of the rest of the fleet to 155mm calibre, made this bespoke round too expensive for service.

The US Navy is evaluating a step change in capability with its electromagnetic rail gun programme[70], which may be in service in the mid-2020s. The new destroyer's integrated power system can deliver the required electricity; this suggests that even if the rail guns are successful, retrofitting this system to existing ships will be challenging as they may not have the required reserve of power. The Chinese currently appear to be trialling a similar weapon[71].

Increasing standoff distance and accuracy is likely to be achieved by the more cost-effective conventional solution of a longer 5-inch gun barrel and improved munitions with GPS guidance. The experimental rocket-assisted Ex-171 munition that was fired from a modified 5-inch gun with a 62-calibre barrel achieved a range of 63 nautical miles or 117kms. As a modified 5-inch round is easily more affordable than retro fitting 155m guns, this capability route has always been the more likely, especially for the Americans, who are able to exploit the proven technology of the 155mm Excalibur round and re-engineer it into the one-inch smaller naval calibre.

The types of munitions available in the specialist naval calibres are usually limited to high explosive, white phosphorous smoke, and illumination (sometimes called star shells in naval circles). Given their anti-aircraft role, all naval high explosive rounds tend to be proximity fuzed. When these fuzes were uncommon in land warfare, this partly made up for their smaller calibre and invariably naval shells being of an older design. Naval guns can achieve and sustain (due to water-cooling of the barrel and their more robust design) a very high rate of fire. 20 rounds per minute is the 5-inch gun's maximum, it can sustain half that. This is achieved through the automation of fixed rounds; this prevents the trajectory been changed by varying the propellant charge. Therefore, the high velocity naval gun has a low trajectory which can preclude the engagement of land targets that are in the dead ground behind hills. This is partly addressed by a special reduced charge for defilade fire.

Even without GPS rounds, modern warships can deliver highly precise fire support. They fix their own positions primarily through GPS, if this is not available, the alternative is a radar fixation upon a land navigational reference. This reversionary mode delivers good accuracy once the correction to the initial error is determined through a first salvo. Fire support planning and coordination on even the most modern ship is usually accomplished by a plotting team and charts, with voice communications being as common as data. This usually results in the requirement to 'swivel chair' firing information from land to maritime systems, reflecting the secondary nature of this task. Making this system work effectively can necessitate the reinforcement of ships with naval fire support specialists. Effectively employing naval fire ashore requires specialist observers or spotters, plus signals specialists able to establish communications with supporting ships. This expertise can only be replicated through placing a considerable training burden on normal observers; as this is unlikely to be successfully met, the absence of specialist observers will reduce the effectiveness of the capability.

If sea and air control is contested, then ships providing shore bombardment do it at some risk. Of course, there are some circumstances when this is justified, such as when ground forces are in danger of being driven back into the sea, as could have happened at the Salerno landings in 1943. Here this fire support was decisive, including the defeat of the counter-attacking Hermann Goering division before it could close with Allied forces. In other cases, as in the Falklands War, naval firepower was not vital to successful operations on land, and so a different level of risk was appropriate. The ships supported the night attacks – often firing off most of their ammunition – before retiring to a safer distance before daylight. The artillery and mortars were thus able to preserve their ammunition for daylight fire support.

The contribution of naval gunfire continues to be questioned in peacetime. Unfortunately, General Eisenhower's dispatch from the Sicily landings has not been decisive in concluding the argument. His view was that naval fire was: *'so devastating in its effectiveness as to dispose finally of any doubts that naval guns are suitable for shore bombardment*[72]*'*.

Tube Artillery's Future Development

> *'the army, which pinfolds and neglects its Artillery, so to say, lays hands on itself. For every half-kopeck put down from the budget of this kind of weapon, for every omission in the combat training of its units in peacetime, it will have to pay with unnecessary rivers of blood of its Infantry on the battlefields*[73]*.'*
>
> Russian Artillerymen Lieutenant General Alexander Trofimovitch Baumgarten

For such a mature technology, tube artillery's level of change and uncertainty is surprising. Future development will no doubt be on the traditional lines: longer range, higher rate of fire, greater speed into and out of action, greater protection especially against improved munitions, and higher levels of accuracy. But there is some genuine technological uncertainly – in part due to the fielding of novel approaches such as the truck mounted, largely unarmoured, gun. This is compounded by a lack of timely decision-making in determining replacement systems.

This has led to the US Army Lieutenant General H.R. McMaster's warning on 5th April 2016 to the US Senate's Armed Services AirLand subcommittee that the American artillery is already '*outranged and outgunned by many potential adversaries*[74]'. The first step is to acknowledge the need for a new weapon, which the American artillery have traditionally found challenging[75], although their recent study into the next generation of their towed and self-propelled guns shows a new confidence in artillery's future[76]. The current American emphasis is on increasing range, including developing a strategic long-range cannon.

Currently a significant proportion of the Western gun park are over 40 years old. The self-propelled guns are the most ancient, most obviously much of the M109 fleet. In the absence of replacements, countries will continue to extend their existing artillery's service life. These ageing platforms are suffering from the fatigue and wear of their constant use in training and on operations. This is compounded by Western armies often allocating inadequate resources to maintaining their fleet, let alone sustaining their competitive capability. The age of most self-propelled guns means that the extension of capability often requires a complete rebuild. This has been the effectively done for the American M109A7 and the German PzH-2000. Their UK equivalent, the AS90, has not undergone its planned upgrades. The result is that it has not maintained its combat effectiveness and has failed to reduce the cost of ownership through replacing obsolete components with modern, easier sourced, equivalents.

The West's towed artillery fleet is better placed. The 105mm cannon used by the British and Americans is venerable but will soon be completely modernised. Many of the 155mm towed guns are quite modern; however, as identified, the M777 needs to be made more capable, and so heavier, to survive on the conventional battlefield.

Russian and American armies that have done most of the recent high-end fighting still subscribe to tube artillery (or for the Russians gun-mortars) being their primary means of fire support. Both countries see the armoured tracked self-propelled gun as essential to the conduct of mechanised operations. Only it has the mobility and protection to keep up with armoured manoeuvre forces; as well as having the ability to continue providing fire support even whilst being engaged by counter battery fire. Finally, it provides more responsive fire, with a heavier weight of fire than almost all towed guns.

The protected direct fire weapon system's (the tank) obituary is written in every break between conflicts; this is promptly rescinded when actual conventional ground fighting occurs. The same peacetime disadvantages apply to the armoured self-propelled gun: expense, lack of deployability and the logistic challenge. Despite this, when actual warfighting occurs, it should be expected that the armoured self-propelled gun will again show its superiority over the other means of fire support, especially as it is such a superior direct fire weapon.

Recent operational experience has reinforced the importance of direct fire; the Russians and, to a lesser extent, the Americans continue seeing it as the most effective means of employing firepower in a range of circumstances. Both countries also see the requirement for both a lighter calibre artillery (105mm, 120mm gun-mortars and 122mm) optimised for danger close fire support, supplemented by infantry-controlled mortars, and a more general-purpose medium calibre (152mm and 155mm). The countries have two points of difference: the Russians still see a need for heavier tube artillery calibres, and for 120/122mm armoured self-propelled gun-mortar/artillery to shoot-in their mechanised airborne and motor rifle troops. This may in part be legacy; certainly, most Russian resources are going into improving their rocket systems and fielding 152mm guns. While some authorities see the Russians standardising on the 152mm calibre for their armoured ground troops, the efforts that have been put into re-barrelling the 2S1 with a 120mm gun-mortar – possibly not wholly successfully – demonstrates a continued belief in specialist close support guns.

The view that Russia may be standardising on the 152mm calibre is probably encouraged by their fielding an exceptionally capable gun in the 2S35, though perhaps only twelve were in service in 2020. This is reported as having a very high level of automation that results in a crew of three, and a range of up to 70km using precision-guided rounds, and probably 30 km with standard rounds. Reports vary on its rate of fire, but is at least 8 rounds per minute, together with an impressive ammunition load of around 60–70 rounds. Its impressive sustained rate of fire may have been enabled by a barrel-cooling system developed by the Burevestnic research institute in Moscow. If the weapon is this capable, then by a considerable margin it is the World's most effective self-propelled gun[77]. Apparently, a wheeled version is being considered for coastal artillery and export, if so, this is likely to be the World's heaviest wheeled self-propelled gun. It is reported that the first unit to be equipped with the 2S35 is within the 2nd 'Tamanskaya' Guards Motor Rifle Division[78]; this suggests that initially at least, the Russians see their new 152mm gun as being a divisional and not close support weapon.

Regardless of to what extent the 2S35 can actually deliver this level of performance, it and the Korean K9, serve to signpost likely areas for armoured self-propelled gun development. Artillery which fires less than four rounds per minute with a detachment of up to ten members per platform is resource-inefficient and unsustainable over the longer term. This particularly applies given the cost to defence of manpower ownership in developed nations. This makes greater automation inevitable; realising this needs to encompass the whole system, including the packaging and handling of the ammunition, with the aim of maintaining a high burst and sustained rate of fire without wearing out the crew. Sustaining high rates of fire requires a barrel cooling system[79]. It is Russia, with its demographic challenge, that is leading the way on automation.

To match current towed artillery, any new self-propelled gun is likely to need at least 30km of range, unassisted by either base bleed or rocket-assisted munitions. 52- and 55-calibre barrels were considered to be the maximum practical length for land systems. The Americans are using a 58-calibre barrel to upgrade the M109A7 and 55-calibre for the M777. The upgraded barrel on the M109 is hundreds of pounds heavier and six feet longer than the current one. This is made possible by a sturdier design (the XM907 cannon barrel) that can handle more powerful ammunition and propelling charges, without adding too much weight. This Enhanced Range Cannon Artillery (ERCA) is currently seen as a divisional level weapon, rather than an upgrade to the brigade level M109 cannon, which currently are expected to remain 39-calibre. The ERCA's extra propellent, longer barrel, and a rocket assisted shell, leads to a range of over 70km. A further three feet of barrel is being considered[80], but any significant range enhancement, using current technology, probably needs to come from enhanced extended range ammunition. As will be discussed later, munitions with ramjet technology may be the best approach to achieving a range of over 70km.

The American Army are prioritising extending the range of their artillery ahead of other capability areas. This both fits with the recent Western favouring of standoff engagement over closing to decisive range, and the belief that the greatest challenge facing Western conventional forces is overcoming anti-access and area denial weapons as opposed to achieving victory in the close fight. Engaging at these ranges requires some form of precision guidance to overcome the additional dispersion extenuated by base bleed or rocket assisted ammunition. These range extending techniques will reduce munition lethality. Longer ranges also requires higher trajectories that will probably require longer to clear with the air force, so reducing responsiveness.

Change in towed guns will focus on two areas: re-establishing the balance between capability and weight for 155mm calibre guns and whether it is possible to standardise artillery on a single medium calibre. The austere design of the M777 suits expeditionary and recent counter-insurgent operations, but its lack of automation leads to a pedestrian rate of fire and time into and out of action. Closing the capability gap between the M777 and the more sophisticated 155mm guns is ongoing. This does not mean that armies do not want a cannon that can be lifted by their standard support helicopter. The need also to transport the crew and a reasonable quantity of ammunition favours a 105mm cannon. Commonality of ammunition, plus the range and firepower benefits of a 155mm weapon, lead to aspirations for this calibre at close to the 105mm weight. Options to achieve this include a shorter barrel and a soft recoil mechanism to deliver a lighter platform. A short-range light 155mm gun/howitzer may be technically possible, but this does not mean that this is a better means of supporting light forces than smaller calibre artillery.

The established way to increase artillery lethality is to maximise firepower in the brief window of a target's maximum vulnerability. This is the first 10–15 seconds of the engagement. After this the target has the time to improve their protective posture. Lethality was increased in World War Two by the time-on-target (TOT) procedure. This requires rounds from separate batteries, with different times of flight, to all detonate at the same time on their target. Lethality is further increased by maximising the number of rounds able to fire within the first 15 seconds, leading to modern artillery's burst fire capability.

The final technique that appears to offer a further step change in lethality is multiple round simultaneous impacts. This is the employment of different trajectories to create different times of flight from the same gun, with the aim of successive rounds simultaneously detonating on a target. Multiple round simultaneous impacts have been popular at artillery demonstrations since the 1960s. It allows well trained, and crucially, well-rehearsed detachments to demonstrate their skills in perfect conditions. Increased automation, sufficiently different-sized propelling charges, and a fire control system able to calculate the firing data and present it to the gun commander in the right order should allow this technique to be regularly employed on operations. The leading artillery manufacturers draw attention to the ability of their guns to conduct multiple round simultaneous impacts. The South Koreans identify that the K-9's high rate of fire can easily achieve a three-round simultaneous detonation. The Russians call this technique 'simultaneous fire assault' or 'iterative fire strike' and are actively considering its use with the 2S35 Koalitsiya and its predecessor the 2S19 Msta 152mm self-propelled howitzer.

Even if the technology makes it possible, multiple round simultaneous impact has significant disadvantages. Employing a sub-optimum charge and trajectory for an engagement is detrimental to consistency. The number of rounds that can be simultaneously delivered depends primarily on the range, at longer ranges the lowest propelling charge will not reach the target. At shorter ranges high angle is required to achieve the necessary time of flight differential. In addition, different trajectories present a battle space management challenge. Furthermore, while it must be true that three rounds landing virtually simultaneously are better than the same quantity spread over 15 seconds, there is no empirical evidence as to how much better.

The higher the rate of fire, the greater ability a cannon has to put down a lethal weight of fire before displacing to avoid retaliatory fire. The Russians envisage firing 12–15 rounds in a minute and moving before the first round lands. Taking this one step further, the Russians envisage self-propelled artillery pieces able to fire on the move[81]. Current technology, with the right command and control, makes continuous movement allied with short halts for rapid fire missions possible. However, this movement, in the wrong circumstances, could make artillery an easier target to acquire.

A high level of automation is made easier through the use of modular charges. The bulk and expense of the non-modular charge system adds significantly to the logistic burden. The efficiency of modular charges will particularly benefit self-propelled gun designers, who have to provide sufficient space within an armoured compartment for an adequate quantity of on-board ammunition. The introduction of modular charges will result in logistic and financial savings; however, a completely modular charge system cannot fully replicate tube artillery's ballistic properties[82]. The practical compromise is a base charge different from the other modular charges. The Americans are content that the advantage of their 155mm modular charge system outweighs the disadvantages. Entirely replacing propellant charge bags with a more variable system – such as liquid propellant, electric rail gun or an electro-thermal chemical approach – will certainly achieve logistic efficiency and probably improved performance. In addition, their ability to minutely vary the quantity of propellant, and thus the trajectory and time of flight, will significantly increase a gun's ability to achieve simultaneous time on target. It just needs to be made technically possible.

In summary, the uncertainty of tube artillery's place on the battle following the end of the Cold War has been replaced by innovation on almost every front. Tube artillery is not behaving like a mature technology. Instead of experiencing diminishing returns for investment, the latest cannons are significantly more capable than the previous generation. The level of change has resulted in uncertainty as to the most suitable combination of calibre, calibre length, level of protection, level of automation and type of locomotion. Historically designs which provide a balanced approach to these capabilities have better stood the test of time. The capability compromises that delivered the light weight and deployability of the M777 are now having to be addressed. As originally envisaged the US artillery's desire to put range ahead of all other characteristics might have led to a similar unbalanced capability. However, now the project's funding is secure, a more balanced approach is being taken; including increasing the ERCA's rate of fire with an auto loader.

Chapter 10: Rocket Artillery

'On sea and land the fighting raged,
The screaming shells contested in the air,
Then from the forest little Kate would come.
To some familiar landmark, bathed in fire,
Out she creeps, her rockets loaded up,
Against our homeland's dread assailant.
And screams: a company is gone,
And howls again; no regiment[1]*.'*

Poem to the Katyusha ('little Kate')[2]

Given a large enough rocket, longer ranges and heavier payloads can be achieved when compared to conventional artillery, which remains constrained by the tube's length and diameter, and the chamber's volume. By mounting multiple rockets on the same platform, this weapon system can quickly deliver an overwhelming quantity of munitions onto a target. This heavy weight of fire is followed by a long reload time that makes it unsuitable for the majority of routine fire support tasks; but the rocket system's longer range and greater munition weight has led to it largely displacing heavy guns in the deep fire and counter-battery roles. In the close battle it can deliver stunning blows, that can neutralise whole battalions. Without precision guidance, their lower accuracy means that rockets are ineffective against smaller targets; with precision, rocket artillery provides land forces with their organic means of engaging point targets with large warheads[3].

Since the 1930s the Soviets have set the pace in this capability; its importance is recognised by the providers of Soviet and Russian firepower being called Missile Troops and Artillery. In comparison, most Western artillery arms were initially slow in seeing their potential, preferring their tried and tested cannon. Artillerymen have also shown a similar prejudice against the humble, but extremely effective mortar. In the late Cold War, driven by the AirLand doctrine, the Americans fielded the Multiple Launch Rocket System, or MLRS, which given constant munition upgrades now leads in terms of range and accuracy, if not lethality. Most modern armies recognise that tube and rocket artillery have such divergent characteristics that they are complementary. However, the balance may be shifting towards rockets; these are displacing cannons in some armies due to the increased emphasis on deep operations, and the need to engage point targets in the close battle.

Rockets have always been able to deliver a significantly greater weight of fire than tube artillery. A four-launcher battery of World War Two BM-13 launchers can fire in 7–10 seconds a salvo that delivers 4.35 tons of high explosives, making its power roughly equivalent to 72 of the Soviet's standard 76.2mm field gun. This differential has increased over the years. The lethality of shells, the gun's increased rate of fire and its maximum range has not kept up with advances in rocket artillery. The relatively soft launch of rockets, together with their large payload makes them highly suitable for advanced munitions. This allows rocket artillery to lead in the employment of cluster, sensor-fuzed munitions, and mines. Artillery thermobaric munitions is currently only practical with rocket artillery and mortars. The employment of these area effect munitions has encouraged rockets to grow in size.

It is increasingly difficult to separate battlefield rocket artillery from short range ballistic and cruise missiles. The Chinese are leading in converging these two capabilities, reflecting their emphasis on long-range strike systems. This is partly driven by the need for the range to strike across the Taiwan straits; in addition, their rocket force takes on a deep strike role that other militaries would expect to be an air force's responsibility. This study will limit itself to battlefield rockets, which in conventional warfare are usually the multiple barrelled rocket systems. It will work on the assumption that short range ballistic and cruise missiles are likely to be employed beyond the fire support coordination line in the joint battlespace, thus outside the land component's principal area of direct responsibility.

Evolution of the Modern Battlefield Rocket

'Its moral effect is great, especially against savages and cavalry, and owing to the lightness of apparatus required for firing, it can be transported easily in rough terrain[4]'.

War Rocket in the Manual of Gunnery
for Her Britannic Majesty's Fleet (1880)

War rockets predate the use of tube gunpowder artillery, becoming an effective weapon of war in perhaps the 10th as opposed to the 14th century. These primitive designs remained a regular feature of Chinese and Indian armies through to modern times. The medieval Europeans occasionally employed rockets as incendiary weapons, including at the 1408 siege of Liège[5]. Having been exposed to the weapon on the Indian sub-continent, the British improved on the original designs with the longer-range systems pioneered by Colonel Sir William Congreve. These rockets proved to be useful as an area bombardment weapon at Boulogne and Copenhagen, where they successfully set fire to the urban areas. A single troop was used at the Battle of Nations at Leipzig 1813, where it is reported that a brigade surrendered due to the shock of its fire[6]. They were used in the Peninsular Campaign, achieving considerable success in the Pyrenees Mountains where conventional artillery could not penetrate. These primitive rockets may have gained their greatest fame when employed to undermine the morale of the American militia in the War of 1812[7]. The rockets' enduring advantage of a lightweight platform led to their use in 19th century colonial operations when conventional artillery was generally too heavy. The rocket lost ground to tube artillery through the 19th century as cannon became more sophisticated, and above all, significantly more accurate. The British finally took them out of service in 1921, just before the Soviet Union was to revolutionise the weapon.

The Russians used similar rockets to the British in the 19th century, their light weight in proportion to the warhead effect was particularly valued in mountain warfare[8]. Soviet advances in first liquid, and then solid fuel rocket motors led to the fielding of modern multiple barrelled rocket launchers in the 1930s. By 1932, the Soviets identified that rocket motors could fire warheads of any power and at any range[9]. These were not precise weapons, but the Soviets recognised that this weapon system could achieve the level of destruction and shock required by their warfighting doctrine.

In World War Two the Soviets fielded three main systems, the smallest being the BM-8, this was 82mm in calibre with 36 on each launcher. This system's lightness was valued in challenging terrain, such as the Pinsk Marshes, and in accompanying the exploitation force. The most common weapon was the 132mm BM-13, this usually had rails for 16 rockets. The larger 300mm BM-31 had the weight of fire to achieve a destructive effect against even heavily fortified targets. Its blast over-pressure was so great than even a near-miss could kill the occupants of an emplacement[10]. The 300mm rockets were usually fired from static frames, these being assembled to fire at a single target during a set–piece attack. By the end of 1942 the Soviets fielded 216 rocket batteries; these were divided: 21% BM-8 light launchers, 56% BM-13 medium launchers, and 23% BM-30 heavy launchers[11]. The Russians referred to them all as Katyusha, the Germans called them Stalin's Organ. In addition to their physical effect, the Soviets valued their psychological impact on even the Wehrmacht's battle-hardened troops, which partly came from the distinctive howling sound of the rocket flight path[12]. This was one of a number of factors that led the Soviets to favour rocket launchers:

The Germans had also conducted rocket research in the 1930s, and so had a number of rocket batteries in service by 1940. Confusingly, the Germans referred to some of their mortars and all of their rockets as Nebelwerfer or weapons providing the function of 'smoke mortar'. This was because originally, they were designed to deliver poisonous gas and smoke, but high explosive was their usual munition. Almost five and a half million of the most popular 15 cm rockets and 6,000 launchers were manufactured over the course of the war. This rocket's range of 6,900m made it a more useful weapon than the 28/32 cm Nebelwerfer, whose 2,200m range limited the effectiveness of its large warhead. 21 and 30cm designs were also fielded, both capable of the longer range. The short range 28/32 cm Nebelwerfer was usually mounted on an armoured half-track, the rest largely employed a towed carriage derived from an anti-tank gun. Employing a spin stabilised rocket, with a unique design of the rocket motor at the front, it followed a common German practice of being ingenious, but wholly unsuited to ease of manufacture in total war. The Germans recognised that the Russian fin-stabilised rockets were both cheaper and easier to make than their spin-stabilised designs; in addition, they used cheaper launch rails rather than barrels. This led to the Germans making use of captured Soviet rocket launchers and producing copies.

The British and Canadians fielded the 40-barrelled rocket launcher – the Land Mattress – in late 1944 in the Western Theatre. For operations against the Japanese, a 16-barrelled version was developed – this was light enough to be towed by the Jeep, the standard means of motor transport in Burma. The Americans fielded amphibious rocket launchers designed to provide substantial firepower in the final phase of the run-in to an enemy held beach. This role suited rockets given that the required effect was the suppression of a large area, as opposed to any attempt at accuracy. The American 4.5-inch rockets, which were originally produced for use on aircraft, were also used on land in World War Two. The Rocket Launcher T34 (Calliope) had 60 launch tubes mounted on a Sherman tank. In the Battle of Hürtgen Forest in November 1944, First Army's commander General Courtney H. Hodges reported 'excellent results'[13]. However, American artillerymen disliked the rocket's inaccuracies and the smoke and flash that gave away its firing position, and so did not see a post-war role for the war rocket[14].

Post-World War Two Battlefield Rocket Systems

> *'at Zelenopillya, in a combined MLRS fire strike that lasted no more than three minutes, two Ukrainian mechanized battalions were virtually wiped out with the combined effects of top-attack munitions and thermobaric warheads*[15].'
>
> Dr. Phillip A Karber, expert on the Russo-Ukraine Conflict

Post-war the Soviets continued on the same trajectory of developing and fielding rocket systems with larger warheads and greater range. They phased out the 82mm rocket calibre and standardised on a battalion of BM-21 Grad per two or three tube artillery battalions, each launcher with 40 × 122mm rockets. The Uragan or BM-27 entered service in 1975 and was their premier system until it was supplemented by the even more capable Smerch or BM-30 in the late 1980s. Respectively these 220mm and 300mm systems have ranges of 35 and 90km. While the Smerch meets a similar operational requirement to the American MLRS, initially they had a considerable range advantage. The Uragans are now found in artillery brigade rocket battalions, in batteries of 4 launchers, each with 16 × 220mm rockets. The Smerch's 12 × 300mm rockets are in dedicated rocket artillery brigades. Russia's latest launcher, the 9A52-4 Tornado, can fire rockets of any of these three calibres. Hence it could replace all systems; but it is more likely to start replacing the older systems. It can fire a new version of the 300mm rocket with a range of 120km and is being offered for export with a GLONASS satellite navigation system. According to Izvestia newspaper on 8 February 2017, the new missile can hit a metre-sized target[16]. These latest Tornados feature an automated fire-control system and satellite-based platform survey. As well as making the best use of the latest technology, the Tornado is significantly more deployable, due to being close to half the weight of the Smerch.

Only four Western countries made extensive use of multiple rocket launchers before the American MLRS was introduced. The German LARS or Light Artillery Rocket System entered service in 1969; it has 36 rockets of 110mm calibre and was either tracked or truck mounted. The Italian FIROS was a 122mm multiple barrel rocket system that was developed in the late 1970s and is similar in capability to the Soviet BM-21. Both were replaced by the American MLRS. The South Africans fielded either captured versions or copies of the BM-21. The Israelis decided upon the 160mm calibre in the 1970s; its larger calibre gives the LAR-160's 26 rockets a maximum range of 45 km. A light version is also fielded which can be carried by helicopters or towed behind a utility vehicle. That these countries fielded rocket artillery was perhaps the outcome of first-hand experience of using them and being on the receiving end of Soviet systems. As was the case with the Germans and Italians in World War Two, the Israelis fought Arab armies with these systems, as did the South Africans against the Cubans. It was probably also a capability choice that followed from their doctrinal approach; the Germans and Israelis were in the 1960s and 1970s the most manoeuvreist of Western armies. The rocket systems' capacity for extremely heavy weight of fire is an advantage to those who primarily see firepower as a means of achieving and sustaining manoeuvre.

Multiple barrelled rocket systems have proliferated in the Developing World's armies. They are valued for simplicity, mobility, and ability to deliver effective firepower without needing to fully address the accuracy challenge of the gunnery problem, this can be beyond their poorly-trained armies. This is probably the reason behind Russian-backed separatists on the Donbas having a significantly higher proportion of rocket launchers to tube artillery than the regular Russian forces[17]. More effective Developing World armies not only use Soviet systems, but have also produced improved designs, such as India's Pinaka and Brazil's ASTROS system.

The 1980s fielding of the MLRS gave NATO a weapon system able to deliver the AirLand doctrine's deep attack on Warsaw Pact second echelon forces and supporting artillery. The latter were becoming a significantly more challenging target as armoured self-propelled guns largely replaced Soviet towed artillery pieces. The MLRS's bomblet munition lacked range – 32km, comparable to the current in-service NATO heavy guns: the M107 and M110 – but they significantly increased lethality, as each launcher had twelve M77 rockets with 644 bomblets. Twelve rockets could be relatively accurately fired in less than a minute; reducing this down to a two-second interval between each rocket launch was possible, but this reduced accuracy as the rockets flew through the un-dissipated effluence trail of the previous rocket. These dual-purpose fragmentation and anti-tank bomblets were effective against the lightly armoured roofs of self-propelled guns and personnel carriers, and so promised a high level of attrition before the target could displace. The MLRS's secondary impact was to provide evidence as to how vulnerable NATO armies were to the Warsaw Pact's significantly larger arsenal of rocket artillery. The result was a greater emphasis upon shoot and scoot and dispersed positions.

The MLRS rocket's large volume made it an effective carrier of scatterable mines. Terminally guided anti-tank sub-munitions were planned, but were not fielded following the end of the Cold War. For the deeper battle, a single ATACMS could replace the six standard rockets. Its range has progressively been extended from 128km to 165km, then to 300 km (190 miles), this was limited by the legal provisions of the Intermediate-Range Nuclear Force Treaty rather than technical considerations. The first version of the missile had an anti-armour bomblet warhead; later versions had a 500-lb explosive warhead. Due to their expense, the US Army terminated production of further missiles in 2007, while sustaining the current arsenal.

The traditional multiple barrelled systems fire unguided, spin or fin-stabilised rockets; these can be better kept on their ballistic path by a simple cascade inertial guidance system. This is adequate for their original role of delivering a heavy weight of area fire at ranges of up to 40km[18]. Dispersion increases significantly with range; at 40km, twice to three times as many rockets are required to achieve the same target effect as a mid-range engagement. The rocket's inherently less stable trajectory prevents the advances made in the accuracy and consistency of tube artillery having a similar effect[19].

For those nations who do not want to rely upon GPS guidance, active course correction during the flight path offers a way of improving accuracy. A radar monitors the rocket's flight, and orders corrections to ensure that it stays on its planned ballistic flight path. Russian rockets use this to achieve a claimed accuracy of 0.23% of their range, or ~207m at the Smerch's 90km maximum range. The Russians do not seek the same accuracy as Western armies, just sufficient to make their warheads – cluster, thermobaric, sensor-fuzed and minelet – effective when massed against an area target. While the Russians appear to be satisfied with this approach, others question its utility if they have access to cheap and reliable GPS guidance. The fitting of satellite guidance to their latest 300mm rocket may recognise the need to improve accuracy given that its range is 120km, or alternatively that their export customers expect greater accuracy. Rocket accuracy options can be divided as follows:

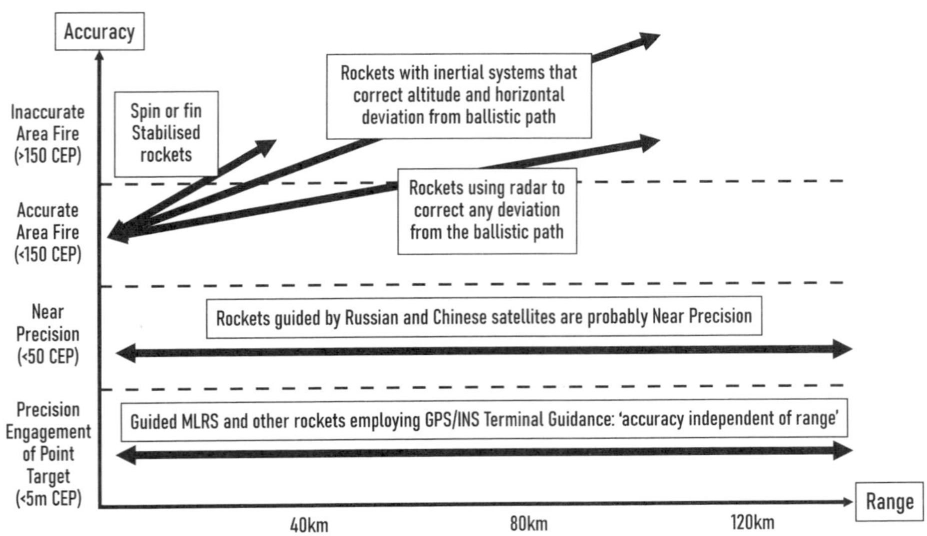

Users of the American MLRS mainly employ guided rockets to engage area targets with cluster and high explosive enhanced with pre-formed tungsten munitions. The unitary high explosive warhead is largely used against point targets[20]. The introduction of precision guidance and a more efficient rocket motor meant that the standard rocket, with its 84km range, could meet many of the ATACM's tasks. This frees ATACMS, also retrofitted with precision guidance, for longer range engagements and where its larger warhead is required. From 2022 extended range rockets will achieve 150km, with a range of warheads. ATACMS will be replaced by the Long-Range Precision Fires (LRPF) rocket. America's withdrawal from the provisions of the bilateral Intermediate-Range Nuclear Force Treaty with Russia means that this is no longer likely to restrict range to 300km. The current requirement is for two of these missiles to replace six standard rockets in a container.

Instead of just fielding a guided American rocket for their MLRS, the Israelis have developed the Romach system. The Romach rocket has a high explosive warhead and GPS-based coordinate-seeking precision. As it is 122mm as opposed to the MLRS's 227mm calibre, there are 18 as opposed to 12 rockets in each launcher. With a quoted range of 35km, it has less than half the range of the most basic American guided rocket, with a significantly smaller warhead. But the Romach fires more rockets per salvo, has a superior response time and a reduced danger area – it has a 20kg as opposed to 90kg warhead – thus making it more suitable for danger close support. The 35km range suits Israel's likely operational theatres, it also avoids any complication in determining where to deploy the launchers, given that the Romach and unguided bomblet munition have similar ranges. Facing the prospect of their opponents denying their airpower access through fielding integrated air defence systems, the Israelis are developing longer range rockets as an alternative deep strike weapon. They see a need for new rockets, with a range of 30–150 km[21]. This could see the formation of a new missile corps, separate from the artillery, to operate these weapons[22].

The Chinese have largely copied Russian rockets; their most common system is the 122mm Weishi-1E, a BM-21 replica. The export version, the SR-5 is a fully computerised and digitised system, that can either fire two pods of 20 × 122 mm rockets or 6 × 220mm rockets. Chinese battlefield equipment is characterised by its long range and large warhead, trading this for quantity of missiles[23]. The 320mm WS-1 has only four missiles, initially with a maximum range of 80km, now enhanced to 180km[24]. The A-100 multiple launch rocket system has six launch tubes for rockets with a diameter of 350mm and a range of 80–100 km[25]. Their reverse-engineered Russian equipment may not be as effective as the original; the Chinese version of the Smerch system is advertised as having satellite guidance. This must be a relatively unsophisticated system as a 200m circular error is claimed – the same as the Russians claims with their radar active course correction[26].

Iran has reverse-engineered Russian rockets and has developed indigenous designs. The Falaq-1 and Fajr-5 rely upon old-style spin-stabilisation systems that lack any means of improving its accuracy despite achieving ranges of up to 75km[27]. This is not a concern for Hezbollah, its most frequent operational user. Their aim is to spread terror amongst Israel's civilian population, which is assisted by their rocket's indiscriminate nature.

There are two battlefield rocket systems which stand aside from mainstream development. The Russians have fielded the TOS-1 or Buratino; this has thirty 220mm rockets mounted on a T-72 chassis. The rockets have large thermobaric warheads, but only a 6km range. They fulfil the role of the World War Two assault flame thrower in urban warfare, but its target effect extends to a whole city block. Recognising that this limited range makes it vulnerable to opposition direct fire weapon systems, the Russians are introducing a 10km range rocket;

this is made possible by a more efficient thermobaric warhead that frees space for propellant without reducing the blast[28].

Placing an infrared and visible spectrum TV camera in the rocket's nose with a real-time data link enables the operator to guide the weapon to the target, or abort if necessary. It combines a high level of accuracy with an ever-improving view of even the best concealed target. The Americans and Europeans worked on this in the 1970s but discounted it in favour of the attack helicopter and conventional rocket combination. The Israelis now lead on this technology with a non-line of sight version of their Spike anti-tank system, with a range in the order of 25–30 km. The missile flies a predetermined flight path to the target but is reliant upon the operator to guide it in the final stages, relying upon the imagery provided by a camera in the missile. The advantage of this man-in-the-loop guidance is high accuracy and reduced risk of collateral damage. The operator visually acquires the target and is able to abort the mission if it does not meet the engagement criteria, making it the most discriminate artillery system. The 70kg missile can be launched from a ground platform or from helicopters, and has both high explosive and anti-tank warheads. As well as the Israeli Defence Force, its operated by the South Koreans[29] and the UK under the name Exactor. Greater acceptance of its effectiveness led to the Israeli Defence Force firing over 250 such missiles in Gaza in 2014. In contrast, in 2008–9, during Operation Cast Lead, only 26 of these missiles were fired[30].

Rocket Artillery Logistics and Survivability

'the very essence and spirit of the Rocket System is the facility of firing a great number of rounds in a short period, or even instantaneously, with small means[31].'

Colonel William Congreve

Their limited recoil, as opposed to the considerable propellant blast, means that rockets do not need the heavy platform a similarly powerful cannon requires. This leads to most multiple barrelled rocket systems being wheeled, but from the first tracked systems have also been fielded[32]. The Soviets mounted their 82mm and 132mm rockets on T-60 and T-70 light tanks to provide the mobility and protection to support their exploitation forces. The Americans initially bucked the trend when they fielded their MLRS solely on a tracked chassis. Subsequently they have fielded a truck-mounted version called the High Mobility Artillery Rocket System or HIMARS. The wheeled version carries only half the number of rockets (a single pod of six 227-mm rockets or one ATACMS), but it has significantly greater strategic and operational mobility. In their most basic form, rockets could be fired from a standard civilian truck – the World War Two Soviets mainly used the American Lease-Lend provided Studebaker truck. Bespoke multiple wheeled chassis are now required for modern heavy rocket systems. Most truck mounted systems have only limited protection against small arms fire and mines, but all need some form of protection against their own rockets' highly toxic effluence. The engaging of fixed positions from static firing platforms was popular in World War Two; it remains a method used by the irregular fighter when employing their indirect fire weapon of choice.

Until recently most launchers were fitted with steel barrels or rails, into or on which the rockets were manually or semi-automatically loaded. More sophisticated rockets now employ containers, pods or modules that are fitted to the launcher. These sealed units are usually loaded at the factory or a specialist logistic facility. They allow a launcher to fire more than one type of rocket, and can be more easily modernised with each new type of rocket. This approach was popularised by the American MLRS and is now employed with the latest Russian systems. Rocket systems present bespoke logistic problems due to their bulk. Only the lightest calibres can be manually loaded, with the rest requiring mechanised handling and specialist reloading vehicles. Whether by hand or crane, reloading seems to take around 15–20 minutes[33].

Launching a rocket results in a trail from the platform along the trajectory, so creating a visual cue for retaliation; in conventional warfighting this vulnerability requires the firer to move immediately to a reload point, to avoid counter battery fire. When promptly executed this makes irrelevant a weapon locating radar's ability to locate the firing point, though it could cue another sensor that might be able to track the rocket launcher following an engagement[34]. Ideally the target acquisition system aims at locating the launchers before firing. The Russian BM-30 or Smerch's engagement sequence shows the challenge: it can fire within three minutes of occupying a platform; all twelve rockets can be dispatched within 38 seconds, it can then move within two minutes of finishing firing. However, if a course correcting radar is used to improve accuracy, it must remain at the firing point until the rockets reach their halfway point. As the Smerch's range is 90km, maintaining continuous surveillance over possible firing points is challenging. The launcher is probably at its most vulnerable during reloading, as this requires at least twenty minutes, but locating this activity will be challenging unless the launcher is tracked from its firing point.

In the absence of an effective counter battery threat, there is no requirement for rocket launchers to move after each engagement. Remaining static allows rocket launchers to be always ready to fire. When this is coupled with long range and precision accuracy, the result is an effective and persistent close fire support weapon in the West's recent counter-insurgencies. Crucially in this character of conflict, the guided MLRS rocket's accurate and discriminate warhead minimises collateral damage. Rockets with man-in-the-loop guidance can be even more effective in counter-insurgency, but currently without the same coverage and lethality.

Rockets in Irregular Warfare

[The 107mm rockets were targeted on] 'objectives having a large area, usually 400m × 400m, such as enemy strongholds, airfields, storage points or towns[35]'.

Captured Vietcong training documents

At the other end of the technology scale, the rocket's importance in irregular warfare continues to grow. Its light weight, long range and lethality is a decisive combination in this mode of warfare. For spin-stabilised rockets, an improvised firing platform can be as little as a slope facing in the direction to the target. Fin-stabilised rockets require a bespoke launcher, but this can be improvised in a village workshop and then abandoned after firing. Of course, makeshift platforms affect accuracy, but this is not significant as these weapons are primarily designed to terrorise military support personnel or civilians. This approach makes use of the observation first made by the British in World War Two that the morale effect of rockets against battle-hardened men was no greater than ordinary artillery, but this dramatically increased against less experienced soldiers[36]. In the guerrillas' hands rockets usually achieve a harassing effect; however, when employed in mass, they can have a strategic effect. The Israelis on the receiving end of rocket firepower see that '*a huge, dark, perpetual forest of Katyusha is blooming in front of us*[37]'.

The Chinese-designed 107mm rocket is most common rocket in irregular warfare. Its light weight – 19kg (42lbs) – means that it can be carried by a two-man crew on a motorbike. Being spin-stabilised, it can be fired from any suitable slope, making it easy for a rocket team to avoid detection while occupying a firing position. License-built in six countries, including noted arms proliferators, it is widely available. Shooting them down is difficult due to their low trajectory. The Israeli Iron Dome system, while claiming an effectiveness of close to 90% against larger rockets, has not proved to be effective in protecting the city of Sderot from the primitive 107mm rocket.

Western forces have faced larger Iranian-designed rockets, with their greater range and lethality. They were easier to use against Coalition forces in Iraq than Afghanistan – due to the former's superior communications and more complex human terrain that aid their concealment. They are much more lethal: the 240mm Falagh-1 rocket has a 50kg warhead compared to the 107mm rocket's 1.3kg warhead. While spin-stabilised rockets are easiest for insurgents to employ, Iraqi armed groups also made extensive use of the 122mm Grad-series rockets. They tolerated the difficulty of concealment, transportation, the need for launch rails, and the challenge of surreptitious launch, in exchange for its longer range and larger payload[38]. The capability of the counter indirect fire operations is usually the driving factor. Iraq was always a more hostile theatre for the rocket teams; as the Afghanistan theatre became more challenging, the insurgents employed rockets that provided a greater standoff distance than the 107mm rocket. When the counter-insurgency's response to the launching of a rocket was sufficiently swift to put the personnel at the firing point in danger, remote firing became standard. This could use a timer or be done by remote control if there was a requirement to engage a target at the specific time, such as an aircraft landing.

The insurgent's rockets usual success has been the steady physical and psychological attrition that they inflicted through their harassing fire. But there has been the occasional spectacular success. In August 1986, a barrage of 107mm rockets triggered an explosive chain reaction that destroyed 40,000 tonnes of weapons and ammunition at an Afghan Army weapons depot near Kabul[39]. Two years later, a rocket attack on the Soviet base in Kalagay reportedly killed at least 100 soldiers and destroyed eight helicopters[40]. The culminative effect of Hezbollah and Hamas rocket attacks has provoked the Israeli invasions of the Gaza Strip and the Lebanon. Turkey has also faced a similar challenge from the Islamic State's rockets, and has also responded through trying to occupy potential launch sites[41].

Future Developments in Battlefield Rocket Artillery

'The disadvantage of rockets remains their long minimum range … It seems probable, however, that there will be an increasing shift of resources from guns to rockets, given the latter's advantage in range … [and that they are] well suited to the delivery of heavy loads of sub-munitions[42]*.'*

Major General Johnathan Bailey

The multiple launch rocket system was invented to produce dense volleys of fire – something tube artillery can only achieve by the simultaneous action of whole battalions – and in this role it continues to be unsurpassed. For less affluent armies it is likely to continue in its unguided form, not least because of the proliferation of existing systems. At least 5,000 of the BM-21 Grad and its derivatives have been built, and it remains in service with over 60 countries. The available upgrades have sought to improve its existing ability to deliver shattering blows, rather than make it suitable for point target engagement.

Unless guided, the rocket lacks the accuracy to provide danger close fires. The MLRS unguided bomblet rocket's accuracy and consistency resulted in a danger distance of 2,000m usually being specified between own troops and a target. With precision guidance the MLRS has become the weapon of choice for point target engagements in combat amongst the civilian populations in Iraq and Afghanistan. Its range of 84km (greater at high altitude) allows a launcher to cover a huge area around its firing location. However, this long range results in a very high trajectory and a long time of flight. The former presents a significant battlespace management issue, and hence needs time-consuming clearance to fire, so compounding the delay imposed by the time of flight. These characteristics challenge the rocket at providing fire support to rapidly manoeuvring forces. The guided rocket excels in the fire support role in the set piece urban battle (where buildings make determining target location easy and engagements can be pre-cleared). In positional warfare it competes on at least an equal footing with close air support in terms of responsiveness and accuracy[43]. It has the significant advantage that its smaller warhead suits danger close fires, and being an organic land asset rocket launchers can provide guaranteed fires.

In more fluid operations, the multiple rocket system's heavy weight of fire makes it ideal for preparatory fire and counter preparation fire. As well as more effectively distributing rockets over the target area, terminal guidance reduces the safe distance between friendly forces and the target. Of course, if a target is to be assaulted, then using bomblet munitions, with their high dud rate and large danger close distance, should be avoided.

The conflict in Ukraine reinforces the view that the multiple launch rocket system remains the pre-eminent means of delivering massed area firepower in conventional land warfighting. The Russians appear to have concluded that their unguided multiple barrel rocket systems are sufficiently accurate for high explosive, bomblet and thermobaric munitions. However, their effectiveness must tail-off at the longer ranges, when rocket inaccuracy cannot be offset by a warhead with a large effective area. Rockets with terminal guidance are equally effective at all ranges when engaging either point or area targets. This will be a key advantage for the West when all its armies match this with ammunition designed to defeat the most challenging conventional warfare targets[44].

Rockets in effect have a single 'charge', in the sense that the rocket has a fixed amount of fuel. Varying their range is done through adjusting the launch elevation. This means that short ranges are achieved with a low trajectory flight path, leading to a large minimum range of usually between 5–15km, and areas behind crests that cannot be engaged. For some of the longer-range Chinese systems, a maximum range of 100km results in a minimum range of the order of 30km. This minimum range can be a limitation in supporting the close battle, but correctly sited, this should not be a factor in the deep battle, except in mountain and urban warfare, where relief could prevent rockets engaging. Primitive rockets can fit drag rings to the rocket nose to change its ballistic properties; of course, this is not an option with pre-packaged rocket munitions. Guided rockets are significantly more flexible, but they also have a minimum range; the result of requiring sufficient flight time and trajectory for the munition to be flown to a target location. But through their use of a high trajectory and a vertical attack profile they are rarely confounded by obstacles between the firer and the target. One limitation on this is that vertical attack is not an option at close to minimum or maximum range.

As with tube artillery, lethality can be increased through the simultaneous impact of a number of missiles, so maximising target effect. Guided rockets can vary their flightpath so creating different times of flight that compensate for their sequential launch. Precision guidance already enables the optimum distribution of rockets over a target area, this could also allow a full load of twelve MLRS rockets to detonate simultaneously.

Improving rocket technology is allowing significantly greater range to be delivered from smaller calibre rockets. Hence long-range battlefield rockets could partly replace the ATACMS, FROG, Tockta and Iskander. These longer-range rocket systems in Western armies can be of assistance to their air components as they can penetrate airspace protected by sophisticated air defence systems without risking a pilot. Current rockets tend to fly a ballistic path; future rockets are likely to be designed to manoeuvre to present a more challenging target for air defence systems.

Operational experience has shown that with the correct targeting cue, a man-in-the-loop guided missile provides a point moving-target engagement capability that can achieve discriminate lethality in both conventional and irregular conflict. The British and Israelis have made considerable use of this system to strike targets amongst the people. The South Koreans see this as a useful counter-battery capability. However, this weapon system raises the same questions that the introduction of the machine gun did at the end of the 19th century in that it '*did not clearly belong to any particular arm or have any particular constituency*[45]'. The parallel goes further, the British saw the machine gun as a colonial (what we would call irregular), defensive weapon. The Royal Artillery marginalised it once it became a rival to the orthodox artillery gun.

Rockets have certainly benefitted more than tube artillery from advances in ammunition technology; due to, greater ability to exploit precision guidance, munition-friendly carrying capability and soft-launch. Precision accuracy has significantly increased rockets' effectiveness in fire support; as a result the traditional balance between tube and rocket artillery – three to one – may be changing to reflect the rocket's increased capability. The Israelis are rebalancing towards rocket artillery, having concluded that a guided multiple launch rocket system offers a more effective means of taking on bunkers[46]. Their new force structure exchanges a M109 battalion for a MLRS one. In the new Russian force structure, the proportion of rocket to tube artillery is increasing[47]. On the Donbas the Russians are exceeding their own doctrinal norms, as the quantity of rockets is close to equal to tube artillery, once separatist rocket batteries are included. However, while this may be a signpost to the future, an alternative explanation is that this character of the conflict suits the rockets as they excel at preparatory and deep fires. The need for danger close fires and in particular covering fire for assaults has declined, as the Russians became unwilling to risk the casualties of close combat. It is probably safe to conclude that close combat remains the purview of tube artillery and the mortar, with rocket artillery providing both its traditional massed preparatory fires, and for those that have invested in precision guidance, its new point engagement role. Rocket artillery is likely to dominate the deep battle when air control is contested and may be key to defeating an opposing integrated air defence system.

Chapter 11: Mortars and Gun Mortars

'The German army uses mortars and Nebelwerfers in large numbers. These weapons are small and difficult to detect from the air; their trajectories make it possible to conceal them completely from ground observation, particularly in close country. The small noise of discharge of the mortar and the ripple effect of the Nebelwerfer make sound ranging difficult. The strain of holding a position and being mortared for days on end is intense. In attack the casualties in forming up areas and on the objective may be very heavy indeed, and are often decisive in throwing back the attack[1].'

21 Army Group's No 2 Operational Research Section

Mortars may be the humblest joint fire system, but when their lethality is compared to their resource bill, they have often been the most efficient. This chapter charts the modern mortar's evolution from being a bespoke reaction to trench warfare into the essential general-purpose infantry support weapon. Compared to the other joint fire systems, over the last hundred years, mortars have largely remained consistent with their original purpose and technology. Incremental improvements have not significantly changed the mortar's nature. As the existing weapon suits its task, the chief capability enhancement has been the enduring infantry concern with reducing weight[2]. Infantry ownership could be seen as contributing to this conservative approach, or alternatively that the mortar is largely optimised for its role and requires little further development.

Currently, the Russians, and armies who follow their capability lead, provide the only significant deviation from the mortar's infantry support role. They employ mortars in roles, which in other armies, would be the responsibility of airpower or artillery. The Russian 240mm mortar provides a precision fire capability against fortifications and urban areas. Other armies have this calibre, and 160mm mortars, in reserve for operations that suit its characteristics. The second deviation is that the Russians have sought to combine the characteristics of the mortar and the close support gun/howitzer, leading to the gun-mortar, in first the 82mm and now the 120mm calibre. These provide their airborne troops with both their battalion and brigade level close support firepower. The gun-mortar is expanding its role beyond battalion support within motor rifle forces.

Evolution of the Modern Mortar

[What the infantry need is] 'some special form of artillery[3].'

Field Marshal Sir John French, Commander of the
British Expeditionary Force, October 1914

A mortar is a short-barrelled weapon that fires projectiles, called mortar bombs, usually at subsonic velocity[4], invariably in a high-arching ballistic trajectory (by definition higher than 45 degrees or

800 mils), so that the bombs fall at a steep angle on the target. It is these characteristics that identify a mortar, rather than whether it is breech or muzzle loading, or the bore is smooth or rifled. Given these characteristics, up until World War One these weapons were largely used in siege operations. Here their high angle of attack allowed besiegers to engage the interior of an enemy's fortification. They were first fielded in significant numbers in the 1540s in response to the revolution in fortifications that necessitated a high angle form of attack[5]. This could require an observer separate from the mortar. Engaging a static target in siege operations made irrelevant the inordinate time that this primitive form of indirect fire took to adjust onto a target[6].

Technically the mortar was ideally suited to World War One's trench warfare. The tactical imperative was provided by the withdrawal of most of the cannons from the front line into indirect fire positions under centralised command; this meant that artillery appeared unresponsive to the needs of front line battalions. Mortars addressed this deficiency and began to meet most of the infantry's routine guaranteed fire support tasks. Their key advantage was firstly an ability to be fired from the (relative) safety of the trench, so avoiding exposure of the mortar crews to all direct and most indirect fire. Secondly the mortar's small size and weight allowed it to be deployed into forward positions. Thirdly, through its high angle trajectory, its bombs could fall into the enemy's trenches. This was one of the century's most significant changes in joint fires, for in a matter of months the mortar was '*transformed from a heavyweight bombardment weapon to a lightweight infantry support weapon*[7]'.

The scale of the mortar's rebirth may have been somewhat of a surprise, but the prescient Germans were well placed to react, with 160 mortars in service in 1914[8]. These were split between 44 mortars of 250mm calibre and 116 of the medium 170mm variant. These were soon joined by the 76mm *Leichter Minenwerfer*, that could be moved around the trenches by its four-man crew. These mortars were the result of preparing to fight through the Belgian and French fortified border zone – the German General Staff analysis of the Siege of Port Arthur determined that a new field weapon was required to destroy bunkers and barbed wire. By the end of the War the Germans had fielded: 1,234 heavy, 2,361 medium and 12,329 light minenwerfer. The French and British were forced to improvise, including employing obsolete weapons such as the French 150mm mortar from the 1840s and using mountain artillery technology to produce an 80mm design. The Germans maintained their technical lead until the British introduced the 3-inch mortar, designed by Sir Wilfred Stokes, in 1915[9]. In contrast to the German Minenwerfer, which were scaled down siege howitzers, the Stokes mortar consisted of a smoothbore tube, a base plate, a bipod mount and a fixed firing pin to ignite the bomb's primer. This weapon set the design standard that has been largely followed by subsequent mortars. Its simplicity in operation and crude design made it the embodiment of industrial total war.

In addition to its defensive excellence, the World War One mortar had the necessary mobility to move forward with the attacking infantry. It both assisted in the defeat of strongpoints holding up the advance, and provided the fire support necessary to deal with the almost inevitable counter-attacks. Initially commanders were reluctant to sacrifice rifle strength to provide parties required to carry these weapons and the ammunition that they so quickly consumed. By 1918 it was standard practice for even 6-inch Trench Mortar to be carried forward by assaulting battalions[10]. The Great War mortar was a result of:

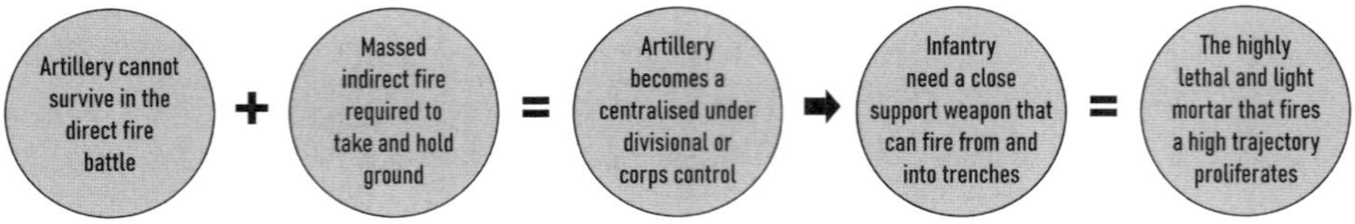

Following World War One, advances in indirect fire techniques improved the mortar's ability to effectively support in more mobile operations. It ceased being seen as a specialist weapon system for trench warfare, and the mortar platoon became the provider of much of the infantry battalion's combat power. British World War Two Operational Analysis determined that each 3-inch mortar caused twice the casualties as a similarly-crewed Vickers medium machine gun (though of course the mortar had a significantly higher logistic burden)[11]. This high lethality was due to combining a very effective anti-personnel round for its calibre with a very high rate of fire. A muzzle-loading 81mm mortar had a maximum rate of fire in the order of a 30 rounds-per-minute and a 16 rounds-per-minute sustained rate of fire. Automatic mortars can quadruple these figures.

Initially the mortar had a rival in the infantry gun. In continental armies, these were either a part of the battalion, or more often the regiment (usually a grouping of three infantry battalions plus support companies). Gradually the mortar was seen as the more efficient weapon, particularly in terms of manpower. However, the direct fire capability of the infantry guns remained a distinct advantage, particularly in urban conflict when there is always a need to punch holes in walls. Following World War Two the infantry gun largely gave way to the mortar, in part because infantry could expect tanks to provide direct fire support[12]. In addition, the proliferation of recoilless anti-tank weapons also offered another means of breaching buildings. Despite all this, the advantages of giving the mortar a direct fire capability led to the gun-mortars subsequently fielded by the Soviets and Russians.

The characteristics of the modern infantry support mortar can be summarised as follows:

Advantages of Mortars	Resultant Disadvantages
Firepower: • High lethality through a trajectory that does not provide enough warning time for the target to take cover. • Given its low velocity, the bomb does not need to be designed to withstand high firing pressures. This allows the bomb to have greater explosive yield than a similarly sized artillery shell. • Ability to engage targets in cover with plunging fire. • A high rate of fire – up to 30 rounds per minute is common – equals high lethality in return for a small crew. • Given that most mortar projectiles are fin-stabilised, their ballistics better suits improving accuracy through course-correcting than artillery shells.	**Firepower:** • Subsonic velocity results in limited range. This can be partly compensated for by rocket assistance, but this results in increased dispersion. • Without Rocket Assisted Projectile (RAP), their limited range requires frequent changes of position to support high tempo armoured operations. • High trajectory fire can easily be detected by Weapon Locating Radar, making mortars highly vulnerable to counter fire. • A high trajectory means that the bomb is greatly affected by meteorological factors: hence it can lack accuracy and consistency. • Simple ground-mounted mortars need to bed-in before they can deliver accurate fire.

(*Continued on next page*)

Advantages of Mortars	Resultant Disadvantages
Survivability: Its size and high trajectory allow it to maximise cover and concealment.	**Survivability:** Except for armoured self-propelled versions, mortar crews are highly vulnerable to counter-fire through being easy to locate and slow to displace.
Simplicity: Easy to operate, mortars can be mastered with a similar ease as other infantry support weapons.	**Simplicity:** Ease of operation contributes to a reluctance to innovate through greater use of technology.
Mobility: They are light for their calibre, and so are transportable over almost any terrain.	**Mobility:** All-terrain mobility requires man-portable design, which can slow deployment into a firing configuration.
Logistics: It is not as burdened by the logistical support artilliery needs.	**Logistics:** Light logistics results in an inability to sustain a high rate of fire.

Some see the mortar's physical lethality as being secondary to their moral impact. There is operational evidence that the mortar's psychological impact is greater than other forms of fire support, although some reports suggest that the effect of airburst artillery fire can be as harrowing[13]. Perhaps the mortar's greater psychological impact is due to its silent flight path and a trajectory that negates most attempts to find protection in gullies or folds in the ground. As Lieutenant Colonel (later Lord) Martin Lindsey observed:

> *'Mortaring is not like shelling; you don't hear the distant whistle of the shell coming slowly from afar. There is a sudden rush and a crack as the first bomb arrives, and you hardly have any time before the other lands*[14].'

In Tunisia in 1943 the British Army attributed 43% of their psychological casualties to the mortar, equal to artillery and air attack combined[15]. Though it must be recognised that the British counted the Nebelwerfer rocket system as a mortar, and by this point of the war tube artillery had ceased being the Wehrmacht's primary fire support system. Research on four British divisions during the first seven weeks of the 1944 Normandy fighting established that mortar and Nebelwerfer fire accounted for 70% of non-fatal casualties – more than 25,000 men[16]. During Operation Protective Edge, in addition to 40% of the Israeli Defence Force soldiers who were injured and killed by Hamas' mortar fire, there were significant numbers who became psychological casualties[17].

As defeating mortars is difficult, this may add to the feeling of impotency experienced by troops under sustained fire, leading, no doubt, to morale implications. The effectiveness of mortars in terms of casualties inflicted, the constraints enemy mortars impose upon own operations, and their impact on morale, provide a salutary lesson to those who take a more theoretical approach to the application of firepower. In particular, the view that the most effective way to employ firepower is to mass it against high payoff targets. This is not the mortar's way, instead available firepower is promptly used against opportunity targets. There is strong case that this may be the most efficient way of using firepower. Both in terms of making it as responsive as possible to the needs of the supported tanks and infantry, and the physical and psychological impact its persistent firepower has upon the opposition. Unfortunately, short of war, the impact of decentralised mortar firepower is less easily quantifiable as massed fire aiming at destruction of individual targets.

Mortar Calibres

> *'[In America's Vietnam war] artillery coverage was so good that many infantry companies went on extended missions without their weighty 81mm mortars[18].'*
>
> Major General Scales

The mortars of World War One suited static warfare, they were a larger calibre and had shorter range than what came subsequently. The British used mortars of 3-inch (the original Stokes Mortar), 4- and 6-inch calibre in World War One, plus lesser numbers of improvised and spigot mortars. By World War Two they used the 2-, 3- and 4.2-inch calibre mortars. Direct support mortars are now largely standardised into these three metric calibre ranges: 50–65mm, 80–82mm and finally 107mm (4.2-inch) to 120mm. Respectively, these calibres are usually employed at the: platoon or company, company or battalion, and battalion or regiment levels. The 4.2-inch mortar has now largely fallen out of fashion; but, the Chinese field a slightly smaller calibre in the Type 89 100mm mortar, which is the battalion level mortar with their airborne, mountain, and specialist light infantry units.

The 80–82mm mortar provides the best combination of range, deployability and lethality for infantry battalion-level dismounted operations. Of course, its bomb is individually less lethal than the 120mm, but this makes it superior at providing covering fire to assaulting infantry. The same advantages of smaller lethal splinter distance and higher rate of fire also applies to close-in defensive fires. Armies who do not wish to deploy another calibre of mortar employ self-propelled 81mm to support their armoured forces. This has the added advantage – when dismounted from a vehicle – of providing a man-portable capability. This is a useful secondary characteristic, but the 81mm mortar is challenged to support armoured operations; it has two-thirds the range of the 120mm mortar, and an ineffective warhead against armoured targets. A rare criticism of the mortar has been its limitations in supporting high-tempo armoured manoeuvre operations, even with the 120mm calibre. The criticism from the 1991 Gulf War – that in their current configuration, mortars lack the range, speed into action and first round accuracy to support armoured operations – has only been partially addressed[19]. In addition, the 81mm calibre so far has not attracted the 120mm calibre's investment in sophisticated munitions and a precision guidance capability.

The 60mm mortar is fielded as either a hand-held direct fire weapon, with the firer also being the observer, or using standard indirect fire procedure. The indirect fire configuration increases the weight from 7kg to 14kg for the American M224, due to a sight, bipod and more substantial base plate. Even in the indirect fire configuration, it is under half the weight of the 81mm mortar. The 60mm's less powerful bomb better suits the mortar's usual task of supporting the infantry battle through providing suppressive fire at the smallest danger close distances. Crucially, the 60mm mortar is a genuinely man-portable system, in that a reasonable quantity of ammunition can also be carried, making it much better suited to operations in the harshest terrain. The 60mm weapon lacks the punch of the 81mm mortar, but with extended range ammunition and increased firing pressures it can almost match its range. For example, the South African Vektor 60mm LR mortar system fires a 2.4kg low-drag bomb to 6,180m. This requires a strengthened bipod and a baseplate which almost doubles its weight (24kg) compared to the standard 60mm mortar. Of course, the 81mm mortar's range can be similarly enhanced, so negating this advantage[20].

There was a view that the grenade launcher would replace the specialist light mortar, experience has disproved this. The Americans, with the M79, pioneered the grenade launcher, but despite its effectiveness, in the challenging terrain of Vietnam they also fielded the company-level 60mm mortars that it was designed to replace[21]. The 60mm had a brief period of popularity with NATO in the Afghan War; subsequently many armies have relegated it to their lightest forces, or hold it in reserve. Some armies see grenade launchers as a substitute.

Despite the suppressive effectiveness of a greater quantity of small bombs, even in counter-insurgency operations the extra range and weight of projectile of larger calibres is a recognised advantage. This led to the re-equipping in 1955 of the British infantry in the Malayan Emergency from 3-inch to 4.2-inch mortars at the battalion level[22]. The lethality of the 120mm bomb means it compares favourably with the 155mm shell, and can present a threat to lightly armoured targets. This led to the 120mm mortar becoming the standard armoured and mechanised battalion level support weapon; however, its weight and considerable danger close distance make it unsuitable for lighter forces. Even when vehicle-mounted or towed into action, deploying and operating a 120mm mortar is a considerable physical challenge; the crucial factor is the effort of muzzle loading 120mm bombs. Hence the popularity of breach loading in this calibre.

The general purpose 81mm mortar remains highly popular, but it is being squeezed between the truly man-portable 60mm calibre and the 120mm mortar. The US Army is currently fielding a modernised 81mm mortar, indicating that the calibre's compromise between firepower and mobility is still appreciated. Alternatively, with a common sighting system, a mortar detachment could operate all three calibres with minimum refresher training, selecting the most suitable calibre for the task. This is the approach of the battalion-level mortar platoons in the US Army's Infantry Brigade Combat Team, who routinely operate both the 81mm and 120mm mortars.

Heavy, Gun-Mortars, Silenced, Low Recoil and Improvised Mortars

'One of the problems of deep penetration forces is that they get held up by strongpoints which they lack the heavy weapons to destroy ... The 240mm mortar could be relied upon to deal with local resistance very quickly, in circumstances where its limited range was not a handicap[23]'.

Chris Bellamy

Several armies have employed mortars of calibres in excess of those suitable for infantry fire support; trading the mortar's lack of range, and therefore coverage, for its significantly greater lethality. Larger calibres accentuate the mortar's advantage over the equivalent-weight artillery system, as increasing the proportion of explosive in the subsonic mortar bomb leads to significantly superior fragmentation. In the Great Patriotic War, the Red Army fielded 160mm and 240mm mortars. Towards the end of World War Two, the Germans recognised the merit of the Soviet heavy mortars and started to introduce the 21 cm Granatenwerfer 69 towed mortar. This illustrated the advantages of the heavy mortar: it fired a warhead 2½ times heavier, from an equipment half the weight of the standard German division-level heavy howitzer. The Russians currently field the 240mm mortar in both towed (M1952) and self-propelled configuration (2S4 or Tulip). The Israelis used the 160mm Soltam towed and self-propelled mortars, these are now probably held in reserve. Other recent users of 160mm mortars include Finland, Singapore, India, Vietnam, China and the Iranians.

Heavy mortars are popular with armies that already favour rocket artillery. Both are means of delivering the greatest weight of fire over the shortest possible period. This allows armies to maximise combat power at the decisive point to achieve and sustain manoeuvre· This makes the limited range of the mortar largely irrelevant, as they can be positioned to support the main effort – this is generally on a single axis – rather than the whole force. In World War Two, the Soviet Army's Breakthrough Artillery Divisions deployed 160-mm mortars in brigades of 32. After eliminating the forward German positions in the initial break-in battle, the 160mm mortars' light weight made them suitable to accompany the exploitation force. In comparison the 240mm mortar was considered too cumbersome; it re-joined the force once fighting ceased being mobile. The Soviets decided that the heavier calibre delivered superior results, and a better-designed 240mm mortar equipped the Cold War Soviet Operational Manoeuvre Groups[24]. This weapon provides the exploitation force with a weight of firepower that could not be as mobile if a conventional tube artillery solution were employed. The current Russian 240mm self-propelled mortar has excelled in the urban fighting in Chechnya, when its limited range was unimportant and its warhead was able to demolish almost any enemy strongpoints[25]. In this specialist role they mainly employ laser-guided projectiles (the *Smelchak* or Daredevil).

Their Chechen experience re-confirmed to the Russians the need for heavy mortars in frontline service. They rediscovered that the 152mm shell lacked the explosive content to cope with well-prepared positions and modern concrete buildings. The 240mm mortar has been decisive in at least two of the set-piece battles of the Russo-Ukrainian War – Luhansk and Donyetsk airports – where its warhead was required to defeat the positional defences[26]. The same laser-guided seeker can also be fitted to the Russian 120mm mortar's bomb, though there are currently no indications that the Russians believe this warhead justifies the fuze's expense. As these operations have been in effect modern day sieges, the mortar has returned to its original role.

With hand-held 60mm mortars it is usual for the operator to also control the target acquisition and engagement. In fluid operations, larger mortars can conduct their equivalent of direct fire[27]. A gun-mortar is different in that it can fire both low and high angle and so can directly aim its barrel at its target. The first operational gun-mortar was the Brandt 60mm Long Range that was fitted to French Panhard armoured cars. This breech-loaded smoothbore weapon used the fin-stabilised bombs of the 60mm infantry mortar, in both direct and indirect fire.

This looked to be a technology dead end until 1977, when the Russians fielded an automated 82mm gun-mortar – the 2B9 Vasilek (Cornflower). The Russians call this type of weapon a combination gun because it can conduct both direct and indirect fire[28]. Its automated loading achieves a rate of fire of 100–120 rounds per minute. It can fire an effective high explosive anti-tank warhead, though given its low muzzle velocity hitting a moving target is challenging. It was fielded as a towed piece, and on an armoured MT-LB chassis.

Experience with the Vasilek convinced the Soviets of the utility of the gun-mortar weapon system, but also of the need for it to be 120mm calibre, with the ability to fire rifled, as well as fin-stabilised, munitions. Rifling probably significantly improves direct fire accuracy as well as providing a longer range. The 2B16 (NONA-K) towed system resembles a normal artillery weapon, but with a very large muzzle brake. This is necessary as the 1,200kg weapon (this is two-thirds the weight of the M119 105mm Light Gun) needs assistance when dealing with low angle recoil; when conducting high angle indirect fire, the ground will absorb most of the recoil energy. The Russians have several self-propelled versions of the 120mm combination gun-mortar, these of course can use the vehicle weight to address the recoil challenge. The 2S9 (on a BMD chassis), provides their airborne troops with both direct and indirect fire support[29]. This is likely to be replaced, or supplemented, by the 2S35 Zauralets-D 120mm self-propelled mortar on a BMD-4 chassis. For the ground forces there is the 2S23 on the wheeled BTR-80 chassis, and the 2S31 on a BMP-3 chassis.

The armoured self-propelled, turreted, gun-mortar combines most of the advantages of the mortar, with a higher degree of protection, and an ability to engage in direct fire from a mobile platform. Of course, these systems approach the cost of self-propelled artillery; in addition, their low muzzle velocity when firing fin-stabilised mortar rounds limits their indirect fire range. Direct fire against point targets with low velocity unguided shells is problematic beyond about 1,000m[30]. This may have spurred the subsequent fielding of laser beam riding guidance for specialist laser-guided shells[31]. In fact, the towed version, the 2B16, is formally designated as an anti-tank gun.

The latest combination gun for the ground forces is the 2S34 Chosta/Hosta, this mounts the 120mm gun-mortar turret on a 2S1 chassis. The fitting of a muzzle brake, despite it being a relatively heavy platform (16 tonnes), signifies that the ordnance's firing pressure cannot be absorbed within the recoil system; this, plus what appears to be a longer barrel, indicates a longer range than is normal for this type of weapon. A Russian airborne artillery commander identified the need for the combination gun to 'extend the range of effective fire for conventional long-range ammunition to 14km, and increase the maximum firing range to 21km through the creation of a new rocket-assisted projectile[32]. A 14km range, without rocket assistance, could only be achieved through firing supersonically; a simpler task with rifled ammunition than fin-stabilised projectiles[33]. Firing supersonically would require mortar bombs to be more streamlined and to be of stronger construction, this reduces their lethal effect. Rather than doing this the Russians use bespoke rifled shells as well as mortar bombs, so they carry munitions able to fire either subsonic or supersonic.

Currently the Russian Army operates a large fleet of ageing 2S1 *Gvozdika* self-propelled howitzers, converting them to the 2S34 standard would extend their operational life. For a slight reduction in unassisted range, the 2S34 has a greater rate of fire (probably double the rate of the 2S1) and more deadly ammunition. The 2S35 can also fire laser-guided munitions. The success of this conversion has been questioned, as it appears that only 30 have been fielded. Plus the orthodox 2S1, with the BM-21, are providing battalions with their fire support in the Russo-Ukraine War. The decision not to deploy the 2S34 has been taken as indicative of its relative failure; however, it may also reflect the requirement for long ranges in the relatively open terrain, which gives the advantage to the 2S1. Or it could simply be a force generation issue, which favours the more familiar weapon system.

Whatever the status of the 2S34, the gun-mortar is in effect the successor to the howitzer, restoring its emphasis upon high angle fire and highly lethal munitions. It stands in contrast to the gun-howitzer that is now the standard field artillery piece. This conflated the field gun and howitzer between the World Wars; high muzzle velocity, giving range, largely trumped other considerations. Like the howitzer, the gun-mortar's low velocity limited the effectiveness of its direct fire against individual targets; but this has now largely been addressed through modern fire control and precision munitions. The Russians and users of their equipment may see the 120mm gun-mortar as a natural successor to their 122mm direct support artillery in the ground forces. Although their new 152mm gun-howitzer – the 2S35 – is such an impressive weapon that it may turn out to be the successor to the 122mm 2S1. With tube artillery standardising on the 152mm calibre and battalions having their 120mm gun/mortars. The resource implications of this level of re-equipment means that the Russians are likely to continue fielding a mixed fleet of weapons and calibres.

At first, China produced simple clones of the Vasilek, under the designation W99. These mortars equip their mountain brigades. They developed the W99 into the SM-4 mortar in the late 2000s; it retains the full-auto fire capability of the W99 but mates it with a longer barrel and heavier projectile that doubles the range. Unlike the Russians the Chinese primarily operate towed guns, towing the SM-4 by a variety of light tactical vehicles – the Dongfeng EQ-2050 4×4 vehicle (a.k.a. the Chinese HUMVEE) seems to be the most common.

Despite favouring combination guns, the Russians still see the need for conventional mortars, fielding their latest version in 2011. The 120mm NONA-M1 towed rifled semi-automatic breech-loading mortar is perhaps the World's most sophisticated 120mm mortar. Its advantage over an equivalent gun-mortar is largely weight; 500kg compared to 1,200kg. This allows it to be broken down into four components convenient for installation on a vehicle, on a parachute-equipped platform, or carriage by the crew in rough terrain. The comparative advantages of conventional and gun/mortars can be understood by comparing the two Russian weapons:

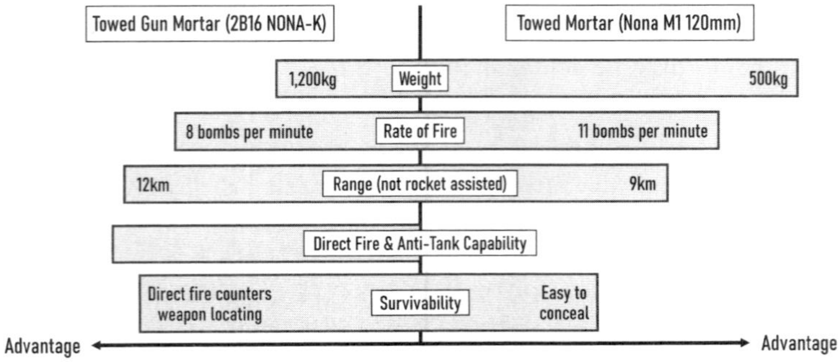

The Russians have also developed the unique 2B25 82mm mortar for their special forces. It is light (13kg), and quick into action (ready to fire in 30 seconds). Its unique feature is its stealth, with virtually no muzzle flash or smoke and the acoustic signature is comparable to an assault rifle. This leads to a limited range of up to 1,200m.

The only other gun-mortar currently fielded in significant numbers is the Swedish AMOS or advanced mortar system, a 120mm automatic twin-barrelled, breech-loading, smooth bore mortar. This is a sophisticated system – whose cost must approach that of a modern self-propelled gun – with a high-level of automation and impressive rate of fire. It can be fitted to a range of armoured vehicles. The Swedes and the Finns see this as primarily an indirect fire weapon, with the direct fire capability being for self-defence. It is a lethal weapon system, but it lacks coverage; given that their bombs are unassisted by rocket propulsion, they have a maximum range of around 10km.

Another area of mortar development is in low recoil technology. A standard 120mm ground-fired mortar generates a recoil of 120 tons; firing a mortar from a vehicle without special firing stabilisers requires this recoil to be reduced to 30 tons[34]. To fire a mortar from a light 4×4 vehicle, such as an easily deployed HUMVEE, requires this recoil to be reduced to 10 tons. This can be achieved using a soft recoil mechanism. Elbit, the Israeli manufacturer, produces such a system and it enables the mortar to be fired from a HUMVEE, that can then immediately depart to avoid retaliatorily fire. However, the soft recoil mechanism adds significantly to the mortar's weight and adds further complication and expense.

Mortar Ownership and Resourcing

'Again, because there was no other place for them to go, the [British] infantry battalions were given platoons of 3-inch mortars, some 2-inch mortars for each company [to reflect the lessons of World War One][35]*.'*

Shelford Bidwell and Dominic Graham, Gunners and Historians

In World War One mortars were largely operated by those corps who led on siege warfare for their respective armies, so a combination of artillerymen, pioneers, engineers and infantry. Heavy mortars are now an artillery weapon, and infantrymen exclusively operate 60mm and in most armies the 81/82mm mortars. The Canadians are a notable exception, their infantry now lack battalion mortars, with their artillery tasked to regenerate a mortar platoon capability at readiness[36]. Or as in the case of their current Enhance Forward Presence deployment to Latvia, they rely upon their Czech allies to provide 120mm mortars. The heavier 120mm mortar, is operated in one of three ways: by the infantrymen in the American and Israeli Armies' mechanized forces; alternatively, by artilleryman who are organic to infantry battalions in the German Army; and, finally, it has been operated by artillerymen, as a secondary more deployable weapon, with their primary equipment being the 155mm gun/howitzer. This is not just a recent development, artillerymen have previously operated mortars in arduous terrain or when deployability trumps all the other characteristics, such as during air assault operations.

It occurred in World War Two in those campaigns in which range was less important than mobility; this included the British in Burma who at certain points of their campaign relied more upon mortars than tube artillery. It also occurred later in the Korean war when the 4.2-inch mortar, which had previously been part of the divisional machine gun regiment, an infantry unit, equipped a battery in each artillery close support battalion. The mortar also provides an easy-to-use secondary weapon for artillerymen whose capabilities are not currently required. This was often the case for Anglo-American anti-aircraft and anti-tank gunners in the last years of World War Two.

The rationale for infantry mortars is to provide guaranteed fire support to the parent battalion. As a result, even if a target is within their coverage, mortar platoons are resistant to employing ammunition against opposition not directly affecting their parent battalion. The resistance to massing mortar platoons to support brigade level operations is at its least in conventional war, when the operational imperative can overcome institutional resistance. Of course, massing mortars is easiest in armies using a permanent regimental organisation that commands three battalions plus support troops[37]. But even armies with independent battalions could, when circumstances provided the driver, mass their mortars. In the Falklands War, the mortars of the 3rd Battalion, the Parachute Regiment, supported their 2nd Battalion's attack on Wireless Ridge.

In both World Wars major armies integrated infantry mortars into their offensive and defensive fire plans. They matched the targets selected with both the mortars' limited range and destructive capability, while exploiting their impressive suppressive effect. The mortar platoon's participation in the fire plan ceased once their battalion was committed to the attack. The ammunition expended upon the fire plan was usually in addition to their first line holdings (applying the artillery principle that ammunition is the reserve), and so the mortar platoon's ability to subsequently support the battalion was not compromised. Given the institutional resistance, this procedure is now rarely practiced by Western armies, leading to them not maximising their available firepower. This is likely to continue until the employment of mortars is primarily addressed from an output rather than an ownership perspective.

The humble mortar proliferates when armies actually fight; conversely it is often disproportionately a target for manpower reductions during peacetime contraction. Some British battalions with largely an Imperial internal security role – such as those based in India – ceased having mortars altogether after World War One. They only began to re-equip once World War Two became inevitable. For the British Army one of the key lessons of fighting the Germans in France and Belgium in 1940 was the inadequate fire support organic to their infantry, and so the number of 3-inch mortars in a battalion expanded from two to six[38].

By the middle years of World War Two, the Germans had switched from seeing tube artillery as their primary means of fire support, substituting mortars and rocket launchers. Their infantry divisions had: 12×120mm and 57×81mm mortars, spread between six infantry battalions and a fusilier (reconnaissance) battalion. In addition, each platoon had a 50mm mortar. The Luftwaffe's Parachute Divisions had additional 120mm mortars in compensation for their lesser artillery park.

Their recent operational experience has resulted in the Israelis determining the need for a mortar platoon in all their battalions, not just the infantry. This is addition to the under-armour

60mm mortar that uniquely equips each Israeli Merkava tank. Their active duty armoured battalions started to be re-equipped in 2016, with the reserve battalions following on. The Israeli infantry will operate Keshet, an M113-based 120mm mortar, for the armoured corps[39]. This is a return to Israel's pre-1967 organisation when tank battalions had infantry-operated mortars[40]. This was a casualty of General Tal's creation of a virtually 'all tank force'.

The US Army's post-Cold War reorganisation – the Division XXI structure – permanently removed the company level mortar (already a casualty in certain units in the Division 86 reorganisation) and reduced the infantry battalion's mortars to four 120mm tubes[41]. Following almost continuous conflict, American battalions currently have ten tubes, divided two per company and four at battalion level. This applies to all their armoured units, which starting in 2005–2006, have reorganised into combined arms battalions, with a mix of mechanised infantry and armour companies.

The Future of Mortars

'The combined effects of these recommendations [addressing meteorological and muzzle velocity error], are estimated to improve the [mortar] system accuracy by as much as 20%[42].'

Raymond Trohanowsky, US Department of Defence Scientist

The humble mortar probably has the most obvious growth potential amongst all the joint fire systems. Technically this could involve improving its accuracy, ease of operation, range, rate of fire and projectile lethality. Tactically, changes in procedures could address its speed into action and fully integrate it into the broader fire support system. If the institutional issues are addressed, this can be readily achieved through implementing technology and approaches that are already standard in artillery. For this to occur, the rational desire for the infantry's organic support weapons to remain as simple as possible needs to be balanced against both avoiding obsolescence, and continuing to employ established but inefficient processes.

Easy-to-identify obsolescence includes the continued employment of optical weapon sights. Sights that employ GPS coupled with inertial navigation systems can deliver more accurate fire and reduce deployment times. This increased agility will assist mortars in avoiding counter fire. This technological enhancement will make the mortar more consistently effective and easier to use.

Lethality is affected by a resistance to systematically applying corrections that address indirect fire's inherent inaccuracy; mortars are often guilty of failing to update meteorological information; this is the major factor in the mortar's inaccuracy, due to the high trajectory and the susceptibility of the finned mortar bombs to cross winds. Calibration to determine the actual muzzle velocity of the bomb as it leaves the tube is rarely effectively done, if at all. The result is that mortars rarely achieve first round accuracy, nor consistently deliver firepower over a target area. This of course extends the duration of an engagement and so increases their vulnerability to counter fire.

The advantages of embracing change can be readily seen. From 2002 the Americans introduced a digital fire control system that delivers improved speed, accuracy and survivability. The M95/96 mortar fire control system has achieved in operational testing 90-seconds between deployment and responding to a fire request. When meteorological, calibration and survey errors are corrected, a circular error probable of about 75m is achieved. In contrast, conventional mortar platoons typically require 8 to 12 minutes to set up and have a circular error probable of 230m for their first round. Of course, this technology better suits less weight-constrained mechanised mortars. Light battalion and company mortars may not suit full digitisation into the artillery-run fire control system. But light mortars can readily employ a weapon sight that employs a lightweight GPS receiver and a tube orientation device to address survey.

Part of this resistance to adopt the advances made by the other indirect fire systems is that mortaring is a discipline that is peripheral to the experience of most infantry leaders. Current procedures have usually proved sufficient in recent conflict and peacetime battalion level training rarely poses a realistic challenge. This can limit itself to ensuring that the mortars can deploy and bed-in, then conduct a standard series of shoots that ensure that their fire is effective on a target. The survivability and fire support challenges of the conventional battlefield are rarely practiced.

Mortars are inherently vulnerable to counter fire as they are easily detected by weapon locating radars. Air defence radars were misemployed and bespoke weapon locating radars were rushed into service in World War Two to deal with the mortar threat[43]. Most mortar rounds are fin stabilised, making it easy for sensors to detect the resultant large radar cross-section. Rifled mortars (no radar reflecting fins), rocket assisted (which interrupts a ballistic flight path) and vehicle-mounted systems (capable of 'shoot and scoot' and when armoured, provide greater protection) make defeating mortars more challenging.

While they add to the survivability challenge, fin-stabilised mortar projectiles are ballistically more suitable than shells for maximising the potential of course-correcting fuzes. These, when fitted to a mortar bomb, can deliver accuracy to within a metre, but only if the other elements of the indirect fire error budget are also addressed; achieving this and conducting precision engagements is a considerable challenge for many infantry mortarmen. Not least is the need for observers to determine a target location to the accuracy required by coordinate-seeking munitions. Undertaking precision point mensuration or similar means of achieving a very accurate target location in a timely manner is challenging, hence laser-guided projectiles may be more suitable for the close battle.

The mortar's infantry support role within the joint fires system-of-systems is well established and largely unchallenged; nor in most armies is it likely that mortars will expand outside this role and take on the function of artillery, due to their lack of range. This leads to a lack of coverage and an inability to mass fires, tube artillery's key attribute. The result is that a gun with a 40km range covers sixteen times the area of a mortar with its 10km range[44]. The exception to this delineation of role is the Russians, who see a niche role for their heavy mortar, both in conducting modern day siege operations, and in providing overwhelming firepower at the point of main effort. As a secondary weapon, artillerymen are likely to continue to operate 120mm mortars in the most challenging terrain, or when deployability trumps other considerations; but the training burden has already led the USMC to abandoning this approach.

It is of course possible for the infantry to continue modernising mortaring and surely this is preferable approach. But some armies have elected to hand over the role of delivering a battalion's mortars to artillerymen. The German Army have made this switch and this will no doubt improve the technical performance of their 120mm mortars. The danger is in pursuit of this objective, artillery mortarmen may lose sight of their need to achieve the closest integration into battalion operations. The Russians have always used artillerymen to operate the infantry battalion's mortars, they make this work within their unique command and control approach and firepower dominated tactics.

While the traditional mortar is not likely to replace field artillery, the gun-mortar is challenging the traditional delineation of tasks[45]. The Russians continue to field orthodox mortars for airborne and special operations forces, but they now see the gun-mortar as a potential replacement for direct support tube artillery as well as providing battalion level support. Fielded with a rifled barrel, as well as conventional mortar bombs, these weapons are able to fire artillery shells at supersonic velocity, enabling them to almost match the range of 105mm and 122mm cannon. Their direct fire capability allows them to provide a useful assault gun and anti-tank capability, made more effective by modern fire control and laser-guided munitions. Where possible the Russians employ armoured self-propelled gun-mortars. Recognising the additional vulnerability of the mortar necessitates mobility and protection. Of course, one of the easiest ways to negate the counter fire threat is to hide the mortar bomb's trajectory within ground clutter. This is of course an easier task for a gun-mortar able to fire low trajectory.

This difference between most armies and the Soviet and now the Russian approach probably stems from their Missile and Artillery Troops controlling and manning fire support from the battalion level upward. This enables the clarity required to see firepower from an outcome basis, rather than focussing upon considerations of ownership, type of equipment, and which trajectory to employ. Armies less encumbered by artificial institutional splits are best placed to embrace the technical possibilities. They might see the 120mm self-propelled, turreted gun-mortar as the most effective means of supporting mechanised forces. This is leading to the introduction of the highly capable of the 2S42 Lotos into their elite armoured airborne forces; it has extended range projectiles, and the ability to fire supersonically, so it can also meet most of the tasks of direct support artillery. Meanwhile the traditional (Stokes) mortar, with an electronic sight that allows for calibration and meteorological variation, continues to provide efficient fire support to dismounted forces.

Chapter 12: Munitions

'Data from the Ukraine conflict show that artillery is producing approximately 80 percent of all casualties. Four trends have emerged that are important for U.S. ground forces: – Russia employs a combination of dual-purpose improved conventional munitions, scatterable mines, top-attack munitions and thermobaric warheads that have catastrophic consequences when used in preplanned, massed fire strikes[1]'.

Doctor Phillip Karber, a long-time
observer of the Russian military

The truism that the weapon of artillery is the shell also applies to all of the joint fires systems. Hence the importance of reviewing current and evolving types of fuzes and munitions, with particular emphasis on terminal accuracy, warhead effect and how to improve range. Historically, improvements in joint fire platforms tend to outpace the munitions they employ; this disconnect is often facilitated by empowering different organisations for each activity. Given the need to closely integrate aircraft and their munitions, this should not be the case with airpower, but general-purpose high explosive bombs, based on World War Two technology, are still used. It can take a major war to replace outdated, with modern, munitions. This takes time, in America's case most of their Vietnam War. General Bailey identified that post-war incremental technical advances – superior casing materials, better fuzes, and more energetic propellants and explosives – failed to keep pace with a changing target set, the result being that:

'The value of the firepower of artillery relative to the other arms declined between 1945 and 1985 … The hitting power of high explosive shells remained almost unchanged, and yet armoured targets became harder and faster and more difficult to attack successfully[2].'

Joint fires munitions started becoming significantly more lethal in the 1960s with airpower's employment of sub-munitions and precision munitions. This technology spread to artillery in the 1980s and from the 1990s, in some armies, to mortars. There has always been a lag in converting aerial munition technology into what can survive the firing shock of launching an artillery projectile.

Factors other than increased lethality have also spurred munition innovation. For certain countries this has included developing munitions to minimise collateral damage, in part to meet national unilateral humanitarian action, but also in accordance with international arms control initiatives[3], including restrictions on cluster munitions. While the prominence given to this requirement varies between nations, even the Russians theoretically recognise the need to restrict the employment of certain types of ammunition in irregular warfare operations[4]. Another driver for change is the requirement for safer ammunition handling in peacetime; this can be mandated by national legislation. There is also the need to adopt new technology when legacy approaches become unobtainable or at least uneconomic; this prompted the shift from mechanical to electronic fuzes.

For lethal munitions, the design challenge is to convert the projectile's energy into target lethality. The cannon ball, the original artillery projectile, wasted most of its energy through embodying it all in a single projectile. While this was spectacular against a human target, this was greatly in excess of the requirement. Hence, except for direct fire weapons, this approach has been discounted; however, it may become an option for hyper velocity munitions[5].

The smooth bore cannon's equivalent to sub-munitions were the canister case and the shrapnel round. The canister split on leaving the barrel producing a spread of shot, which could therefore distribute the munition's energy, over the target. The sacrifice was range, the canister ball's energy was soon dissipated by air resistance; its modern equivalent is flechette. Shrapnel combined the ballistic properties of the cannon ball with, if the fuze was correctly set and the powder burned at the desired rate, the anti-personnel target effect of canister. Originally a niche howitzer capability, the high explosive shell came to prominence in World War One when the need for blast effect against field fortifications became more important than engaging troops in the open. Fitting a fuze capable of airbursting high explosive shells allows them to match the anti-personnel effect of the shrapnel shell. The radar proximity fuze enabled this to be reliably done. The following table traces the development of the major artillery and mortar munitions' ability to inflict personnel casualties:

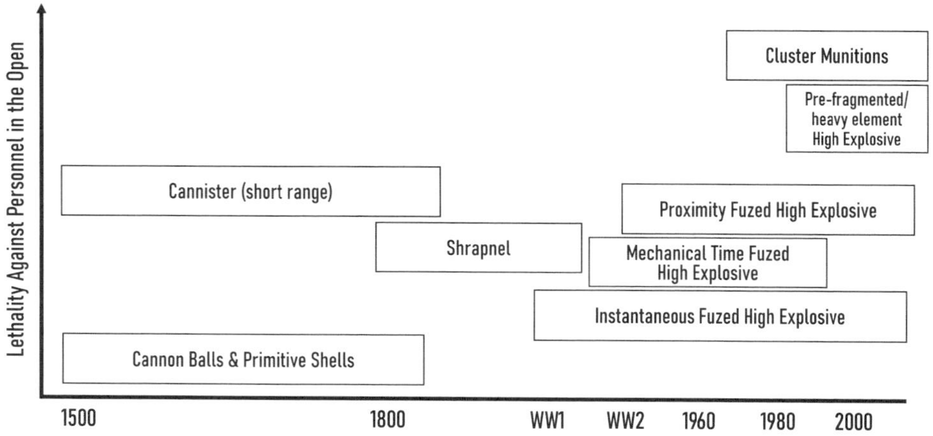

The enduring theme has been the spreading the projectile's energy from a single into multiple projectiles. This has led to the modern employment of sub-munitions. These create multiple points of burst, from which they in turn produce a lethal cloud of splinters.

In their shorter history, aerial munitions have made a similar journey. But as aircraft have focussed on destroying targets predominantly with blast, the high explosive bomb has dominated, either fuzed for point detonating or with a delay to achieve greater penetration. Airburst and cluster munitions have been used when greater area effect is required; thermobaric munitions provide an even more efficient means of attacking a target area.

In some Western air forces most, if not all, air delivered bombs and missiles are now precision-guided. Precision guidance has spread to land rocket systems, and in some nations to artillery and mortars. However, the overwhelming majority of surface-to-surface munitions remain unguided, due to a combination of affordability and their greater operational utility. The employment of terminal guidance delivers significant improvements in accuracy and consistency. Precision guidance assists with retaining lethality as range is extended, making base bleed and rocket-assisted projectiles significantly more effective through counteracting the greater dispersion that comes from how they achieve a longer range. For artillery, maximum and effective range become the same thing.

Lethal Munition Fuzes

'When all armies get this [Proximity] shell, we will have to devise some new method of warfare.'

General George Patton

World War One's replacement of shrapnel with high explosive increased artillery's effectiveness against troops in cover and materiel, but the early fuze designs, plus the manufacturing limitations imposed by total war, resulted in a delay in the initiation sequence that resulted in most of the blast and fragmentation being absorbed into the ground. By the last years of the war fuzes were fielded that were capable of operating instantaneously on hitting a target; these were known as direct action, super quick or point detonating fuzes. This increased fragmentation and was significantly more effective in destroying barbed wire obstacles[6]. A delay in initiating a shell was desirable against some targets; against entrenchments an underground explosion could collapse the trenches; against buildings it allowed the penetration of the wall or roof before exploding. Experimentation determined that a 0.1 second delay was optimum. This also allowed jungle or forest canopy to be penetrated before activating the shell.

Initiating the high explosive shell above the ground further increased the distribution of splinters[7]. Achieving an airburst required an accurate judgment of the time of flight, and an accurate clockwork mechanism in the fuze. Even with this, an observer usually needs to correct the fuze length to get an effective airburst; this is both time consuming and required a high level of training. Even if a fuze had been correctly adjusted, this was often transitory, as any change in the ballistic solution – such as a variation in meteorological conditions – varied the time of flight; hence a good result is a ratio of two airburst shells to a single ground burst shell. Given these limitations, the mechanical time fuze did not significantly improve the high explosive shell's performance. The British in World War Two perhaps had the least faith in this fuze[8].

They also determined that the time-fuzed high explosive mortar bomb was 'practically valueless', as a steep angle of descent meant that any round-to-round variation would result in either ground burst, or it bursting too high in the air[9].

What was required was a fuze that automatically detonated the shell at a set height. The obvious way forward was to fit a radar in the shell's nose that would initiate the shell when the reflection from the ground equated to correct burst height. The optimum height for an air burst was established by British Operational Research in World War Two as 30-feet or around 10m. The theory was easy; practically producing a radar able to fit inside a fuze, survive the firing stresses and be affordable was not. But when this was perfected, the variable time or proximity fuze significantly improved the lethality of the high explosive shell. At first, the priority was production for the anti-aircraft role; in December 1944, field artillery use was authorised, with the Americans leading the way. They made a notable impact in the Battle of the Bulge; with the Germans attacking, their troops in the open provided the ideal target for airbursting shells.

By the end of World War Two, the variable time or proximity-fuzed high explosive shell was established as the most effective combination. But their expense led to the dual-role point detonating and delay fuze numerically dominating, with proximity fuzes reserved for lucrative targets. These include armoured vehicle crews operating with hatches open, soft skin vehicles and of course personnel in the open. Airbursting should in theory be twice as effective as ground burst against targets in slit trenches, but World War Two British trials failed to show this[10]. The minor disadvantage of proximity fuzes is that they can be initiated at the wrong time. In mountainous terrain, peaks along the ballistic flight path can produce sufficient radar reflection for detination. If the target is below trees, then a normal point detonating fuze will burst amongst the trees, so delivering an effective airburst, in contrast proximity will largely harmlessly initiate 10m above the tree canopy. Even the dust thrown up by a prolonged bombardment can result in the proximity radar assuming that this reflection is the ground, and thus detonating ineffectively.

Urban targets and strongpoints are rarely productive targets for proximity rounds, but combining airburst's effectiveness against personnel in the open with its minor effect on adjacent structures proved to be the ideal combination for the Americans while city fighting in Iraq:

> *'In at least one instance, friendly troops were clearing the lower floors of a building when HE [high explosive] Variable Time swept the roof of enemy soldiers. This was confirmed by the infantrymen who looked out the window to see the dead and wounded foe fall past them*[11]*.'*

Mortars have not adopted proximity fuzes with the same energy. Of course, this can be attributed to their greater conservatism, but it also reflects the weapon's different characteristics, which remove much of the incentive to air burst. The mortar's high trajectory results in a close-to-vertical angle of impact. This makes the mortar's ground burst mode much more effective in undulating terrain, when small irregularities in the ground can screen the effect of artillery shells due to their shallow angle of impact[12].

The replacement of mechanical with electronic technology in Western manufacturing led to the adoption of electronic fuzes[13]. Electronic fuzes offered improvements in safety and could deliver all the functions required within a single fuze. Each multi-role or multi-option fuze can be set to deliver point detonation, delay or a proximity airburst detonation. In the rush to exploit this technology mistakes have been made: at least one leading army failed to appreciate the continuing requirement for a delay function. These fuzes can also vary the height of their proximity burst; this can take account of target areas having different levels of radar reflectivity. This allows an observer to adjust the shell burst height to achieve the optimum 10m. It remains questionable whether the additional expense – not least in training, as judging burst height is challenging – is justified.

The switch to electronic fuzes makes artillery vulnerable to electronic counter measures; these can initiate the fuze at a distance away from the target, so rendering its explosion ineffective. The Russian have used the SPR-2 VHF/UHF radio jammer in the Ukrainian War; against artillery shells it claims a radius of protection of 400m, and 280m for mortar bombs. Current Russian and Chinese fuze jammers have the mobility and protection to support a moving armoured formation. So, the optimum multi-role fuze also needs to be jamming resistant and failing that, it must have a non-electronic fail-safe point detonating function.

Artillery, Rocket and Mortar Warheads

'Although personally I am quite content with existing explosives, I feel we must not stand in the path of improvement[14]'.

Winston Churchill

With artillery and mortar munitions, the principal role of the explosive content (the charge) is to impart velocity to their fragmented case. It is effectively spreading fragmentation, rather than blast, that causes most personnel casualties. Approximately 30% of the energy released by the explosive detonation is used to fragment the case and impart kinetic energy to the fragments. The balance of available energy is used to create a shock front and blast effects. For optimum affect against personnel these metal splinters should be around 1/25 ounce (about a gram). Heavier fragments have two main drawbacks: firstly, they produce fewer splinters and so cover less of the target area; secondly, they may present a danger to own troops or third parties, as large splinters can travel up to several hundred metres from the point of impact; this is because all shell fragments initially have the same velocity, but the heavier fragments travel further due to their greater kinetic energy (half mass x velocity squared). An advantage of larger splinters is that they can achieve superior penetration against protected targets. Superior design and manufacture of the container, and more energetic explosive, can achieve a better splinter pattern; this is further improved through pre-formed fragmentation. The outcome is a reduced danger zone and an increased lethal zone:

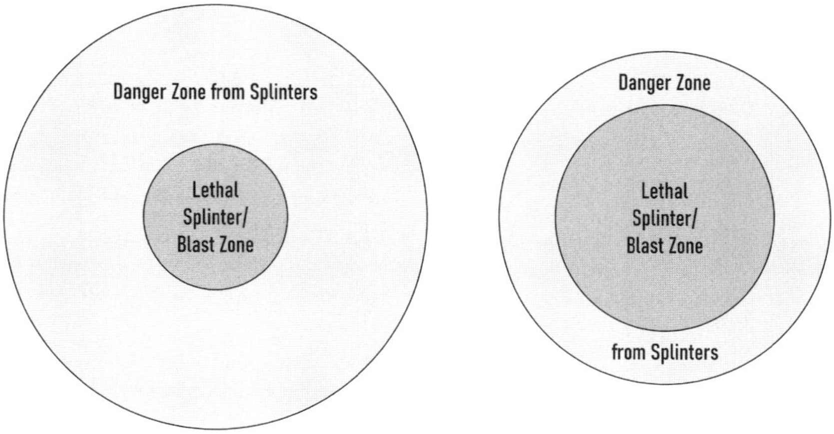

Traditional Munitions with Variable Splinter Weight

Modern Munitions with Optimum Splinter Weight

Blast matters when it comes to the destruction of natural and man-made material targets. With the very largest artillery munitions, blast can have an effective anti-personnel function, particularly in confined spaces such as within buildings, or when the blast wave makes use of local material, in particular glass, to produce a fragmentation effect.

Britain's World War Two Operational Research programme identified that the ratio of the explosive weight to overall shell weight is the crucial determinant of a shell's lethality. It established that for the optimum anti-personnel fragmentation, the high explosive content needs to be 25% of the munition's total weight. The key to achieving this is using higher-grade steel whose tensile strength enables thinner shell walls that can still tolerate the firing pressure. As can be seen from the table below, 25% explosive content has rarely been achieved in operational ammunition, usually because cheaper steel is employed – especially during World War Two with the pressure of total war:

Shell (American if not specified)	Age	High Explosive % of Total Weight	Comments
105mm M1	1930s	<15%	Effective for its age, but the case is prone to produce over-large splinters resulting in an unpredictable danger area.
British 105mm L31 HE	1960s	15%	An ageing, but still effective munition.
British 105mm L50 HE	2000s	20%	Perhaps second to the American M913 and M1130 as the most lethal 105mm shell in widespread use.
South African 105mm M2020	2000s	13%	As a capability choice, payload loses out to range.

(*Contiunued on next page*)

Shell (American if not specified)	Age	High Explosive % of Total Weight	Comments
M913 105mm HERA	2000s	17%	This has less high explosive than the British round, largely due to being rocket assisted. Despite this, its pre-formed fragments lead to the manufacturer claiming that it is 80% more lethal than the M1 HE round against unprotected targets.
M1130 105mm HE-PFF	2000s	15%	Despite its low proportion of high explosive, it has high lethality through combining tungsten spheres and preformed fragments.
Russian 122mm OF-462 FRAG-HE	1940s	17%	A relatively effective round, which has been improved in its slightly more modern version, the 3OF56, this has almost 19% of its shell weight as HE.
Russian 152-mm OF-530	1940s	14%	This World War Two shell is still considered effective enough to be fired by modern guns.
Russian 152mm FRAG-HE 3OF45	1980s	18%	This round is supplemented by the 3OF63 & 64, which have slightly more explosive and superior fragmentation, producing 1.3 to 1.5 times the 3OF45's target effect
155-mm M107	1930s	16%	Always considered a poor performer: payload loses out to range
155mm M795	2000s	24%	Very good lethality due to high explosive content and high fragmentation steel. Reported as 30% more lethal than the M107.
British 155mm L15	1980s	26%	The thin walled L15 contains 64% more HE than the old US M107 and remains one of the most lethal 155mm shell in widespread use.
British 7.2-in	1940s	14%	A poor performer as a result of a very old design
8-in M106	1940s	19%	The large calibre outweighs the old design, so allowing a reasonable proportion of HE
81mm Mortar (M821)	1970s	18%	As can be expected the proportion of HE in a mortar bomb increases with calibre. Being subsonic, these mortar bombs can use material in their case construction that is particularly suitable for fragmentation.
120mm Mortar (M934)	1990s	21%	
Russian 240mm Mortar (2S4 & M-240)	1960s	26%	

The examples chosen show an increase in the proportion of high explosive with calibre. Improved designs have increased the proportion of explosive by around a third since World War Two, but technology cannot overcome the constraint provided by calibre. Hence even the most modern 105mm rounds cannot achieve the optimum 25% of the shell weight being explosives. As the increase in explosive content has plateaued, other means of improving lethality are being pursued.

Through employing more energetic explosives, that can impart more kinetic energy, shells can improve their fragmentation. TNT mixed with less powerful, but cheaper derivatives, such as Amatol filled most World War Two shells. This was replaced by the more powerful TNT/RDX mix[15]. More recently plastic bonded explosives based on RDX have been developed to meet the West's insensitive munition regulations. Nano technology may offer the next leap forward in explosive technology; this could allow the fielding of 'dial-a-yield' weapons, tailoring the destructive effect to the target. This would be determined in the targeting process through balancing the chance of achieving the target effect against minimising collateral damage concerns.

Employing casing materials and designs that improve fragmentation is an easy way of improving lethality. Cast iron as opposed to forged steel shells and bombs are a simple way to increase personnel lethality[16]. The disadvantage is that the casting process requires significantly larger tolerances than forging; the result is a much rougher surface finish, reducing accuracy and range[17]. Cast munitions are also less robust, resulting in thicker cases and limiting firing pressures; therefore, casting suits mortars. World War Two trials determined that the British cast iron (Mark IV) bomb was about 70% more effective than the steel (Mark III) bomb[18]. With limited firing stresses, rockets can also case their explosive in cast iron; aerial bombs also use it.

Preformed fragmentation of a shell or bomb's case ensures that when it fragments it produces the optimum size of splinter[19]. This leads to greater lethality over the target area, and a reduced and more predictable danger area. An example of this is the American 105mm preformed fragmentation shell which has a greater lethal radius that the older US 155mm M107 HE projectile, and at the same time it has a 76% smaller danger area. This makes preformed fragmentation shells highly suitable for danger close fires. However, their more complex manufacturing process makes these munitions more expensive.

Coupling preformed fragmentation with the employment of an element heavier than steel allows the employment of smaller fragments, which nonetheless have the optimum mass[20]. This leads to more fragments and so greater lethality. Tungsten and tantalum – both of which are more than twice as dense as steel – significantly improve fragmentation; a sleeve of Tantalum turned the Hellfire missile from purely an anti-armour weapon into a more general purpose one.

The American MLRS's Unitary and Alternative warheads show what can be achieved with modern technology. The Unitary rocket uses a very energetic and expensive explosive charge to create an intense fragmentation of optimum size splinters. This results in a greater lethality over a smaller danger area than almost any joint fires weapon system, making it ideal for precision strikes against high value individuals in counter-insurgency operations. The Alternative warhead is being fielded as a partial replacement for cluster munitions in that it is designed for area rather than point targets. It maximises its fragmentation through utilising 160,000 preformed tungsten fragments within each 90kg (200lb) warhead.

These techniques allow a modern 105mm round with pre-formed fragmentation and a high percentage of energetic explosive to have a greater fragmentation lethality than older 155mm rounds. The advantage is even greater if one of the denser elements such as tungsten is used. Despite this, as blast is required against better-protected targets, even old 155mm shells are more effective against armour and field fortifications. The optimum calibre to engage most battlefield targets through blast was established by the Germans in World War One, with their fielding of the 150mm Howitzer, *'the outstanding weapon of the whole war'*[21]. Therefore, almost all subsequent medium howitzers have been between 140mm (the British 5.5-inch) and the contemporary 152/155mm weapons.

Air Delivered Blast and Fragmentation Bombs

> *'The psychological effect on the fighting force, especially the infantry, of such a mass of bombs raining down on them with all the force of elemental nature, is a factor that must be given serious consideration. It is not in the least important whether such a carpet of bombs is dropped on good or bad troops. They are more or less annihilated by it, and above all their equipment is ruined*[22]*'*.
>
> Field-Marshal von Kluge on the Allied Heavy Bombers in Normandy in 1944

Dating back to the Italian-Turkish War of 1911–12, bombs are the original aircraft weapon. A container filled with high explosives, delivered by gravity, remains the primary air-delivered weapon. Bombs have been supplemented by guided missiles; these two weapons are now converging given that many bombs can glide to their target. Due to the greater size of their munitions and the absence of firing pressures, aerial bombs can have a significantly greater proportion of high explosive than shells or mortar bombs. This leads to even a small munition such as a 500lb bomb having almost 40% of its weight as explosive. Even the relatively low technology Russian FAB 500M-62 bomb has 207kg of its total weight of 497kg devoted to high explosive. As a rough rule, the larger the bomb the greater the proportion of HE. The specialist large blast bombs can have over 90% of their weight in explosive content.

Blast may be more important for bombs than shells, but it is also complementary to fragmentation in covering a target area. Blast primarily operates along the bomb's fore-aft axis, while fragmentation is concentrated sideways. This combined coverage is almost a circle. Improvements to aerial bombs follow the same path as shells: higher quality steel, more dense material, pre-formed fragmentation, and a higher ratio of more energetic explosive. The latest version of the Mk 82 bomb, the Mod 7, improves its lethality through employing a cast iron ductile case.

Airbursting a bomb above the ground increases the maximum radius of pressure, or impulse, that a blast weapon creates. Air bursting also reduces the quantity of splinters immediately buried into the ground, leading to a 50% increase in the lethal area over the same bomb detonated at ground level. To engage hard targets without resorting to specialist penetrating weapons, general purpose and fragmentation bombs can have their fuzes set to delay. Lacking this facility on their standard munitions significantly reduced the effectiveness of American close air support against Vietnamese bunkers[23].

The most common close support bomb weight is probably 500lb (227kg); since World War Two the 1,000lb bomb has been the most common general-purpose air weapon. The other common sizes are: 250lb, 2,000lb and 5,000lb. Countries operating the metric system follow roughly these sizes, but through 'rounding-up' they have heavier weapons, leading to them employing the heavier 1,000kg bomb as opposed to a 2,000lb one. Larger size bombs are occasionally fielded; the Russians may still have 5,000kg/11,000lb and 9,000kg/20,000lb bombs. They certainly used them in Afghanistan in the 1980s. The US developed a 21,700lb guided bomb for the First Gulf War as a replacement for their Vietnam-era BLU-82 Daisy Cutter. A single point of detonation becomes less efficient the larger the weapon, resulting in the Russians seeing thermobaric munitions as the natural replacement for large conventional blast bombs.

In ascending order: aerial bombs, rockets and missiles, mortar bombs (whose muzzle velocity is almost always subsonic) and finally artillery need progressively stronger containers. The exception to this are the specialist aerial bombs designed to penetrate hardened targets. The Paveway III bomb has a 6-inch (15cm) thick steel nose – in comparison its walls are only 1-inch (2.5cm) thick – to allow it to penetrate the target before initiation. These weapons can employ rocket assistance to increase their impact velocity and therefore penetration. Deep penetration bombs can also use a shaped charge to clear a pathway. More steel leads to proportionately less high explosive, but this is partly offset by penetrator bombs being larger. The Paveway III weighs in at 2,000lb and the Enhanced GBU-28 at 5,000lb.

The anti-concrete shell is the artillery equivalent to the aerial deep penetration bomb. This follows the same design as its air-delivered equivalent, with a hardened nose and a lower proportion of high explosive filling, but being initiated in a confined space increases the effect of the explosive. These are now largely obsolete, as aircraft have taken up the hardened target attack role, as they can deliver significantly greater weight of ordnance than is practical with artillery. But the Russians continue to field them; their G-530 152mm shell is largely conceived as a direct fire munition. In this role, it expects to penetrate 114cm of concrete before exploding, making it useful against structures such as bridges and large buildings. Their specialist 'siege weapon', the 240mm mortar, also employs a penetrating round.

Aerial weapon designers have taken two different approaches to making their weapons more 'usable' through reducing their danger area. One approach is to reduce the explosive content and replace it with an equivalent weight of inert material to retain the bomb's ballistic properties. The more sophisticated approach is the BLU-129/B; this employs a carbon fibre composite weapon case with pre-formed tungsten fragments that combine high lethality with a two-thirds reduction in danger area[24]. Fibre composite can replace a steel case due to the bomb's lack of firing pressure.

As aerial munitions are on the leading edge, it is cost-effective to reverse engineer their technology into surface-to-surface munitions. One proposal for the American MLRS is to replace the M31 rocket's warhead with a Small Diameter Bomb; the rocket delivers the bomb to the target area, and it then glides to its target. The AGM-176 Griffin takes this a stage further in being a lightweight precision-guided (semi-active laser or GPS/INS) munition that is designed to be either ground or air launched. With a 5.9kg warhead (in comparison a Hellfire's warhead is 8–9kg) and precision accuracy, it is a low collateral weapon highly suited to irregular warfare[25].

Air Unguided Direct Fire Weaponry

'Both [North Korean] prisoners and [US Air Force] pilots were asked to rate the effectiveness of air-delivered anti-personnel weapons. Pilots rated napalm as the most devastating, followed by rockets – with strafing a distant last. Prisoners who had been subjected to air attack consistently reversed this order: they stood in greatest fear of strafing, followed by rockets, and with napalm a distant, relatively harmless last. The pilots, quite naturally, appear to have rated weapons effects only on the basis of results visible from the air; since calibre .50 strafing impacts could hardly be seen from the air, pilots thought little of their machine guns[26].'

Pierre M. Sprey, defence analysis

From the first aerial bombs have been supplemented by first machine guns and then autocannon, these being the ideal dual-purpose ground and air target weapon. Machine gun and cannon close air support has proved extremely effective at adding impetus to close assaults that have lost their momentum, as there is a significant morale element to the visible delivery of accurate air support. Their accuracy and limited danger area mean that they can be employed close to own forces. The downside is that strafing exposes an aircraft to ground fire and is difficult to coordinate with manoeuvring forces, otherwise it would be an ideal danger close fire support weapon. In World War One the machine gun was probably the most effective ground attack weapon. Relatively, strafing's effectiveness has declined since then, in part due to better bombs, but also because aircraft speeds have increased at a faster pace than the rate of fire of machine guns and auto-cannons. The result is an increase in the distance on the ground between the impact of successive rounds during a strafing run. By the early 1930s, an aircraft travelling at 250 miles per hour, with a machine gun with a rate of fire of 300 rounds per minute, would place a bullet, rather ineffectively, every 18m along the line of fire[27]. A steep dive attack could reduce the spread. Nonetheless, it required the mounting of up to eight machine guns, together with an improved rates of fire, to restore the effectiveness of strafing.

The auto-cannon steadily displaced the machine gun on fighter aircraft from the 1930s–50s. The French Air Force led, having presciently adopted the 20mm Hispano auto-cannon in the mid-thirties. This conversion was almost complete by the jet age, as significantly more robust jet aircraft demanded the cannon's fragmenting round to inflict serious damage. While superior at air-to-air combat, the aerial cannon may have actually reduced airpower's effectiveness against personnel. This is demonstrated by the retention of machine guns – with their higher rate of fire and superior ammunition supply – by the specialist gunships that are primarily designed to engage area ground targets. These gunships overcome dispersion on the line of fire caused by an aeroplane's forward momentum by circling a target. Of course, this lethality applies to personnel in the open; cannon have the advantage against protected targets.

General-purpose cannon with armoured piercing rounds can penetrate light armour, but penetrating tank armour requires a specialist larger calibre weapon. This led in World War Two to the bespoke tank-busting Stuka armed with two 37mm cannon, and the

Hurricane armed with two 40mm guns. These were effective, but given their cannons' extra weight, these aircraft were slow, un-manoeuvrable and awkward to fly. When coupled with the requirement for close range engagement, these aircraft were extremely vulnerable to ground fire; as a result, specialist cannon-armed aircraft largely gave way to ones armed with the air-to-ground 5-inch rocket, with its greater range and penetration. The Germans retained their cannon-armed Stuka as this remained effective on the Eastern Front's less contested airspace. One key advantage of the rocket was that it did not require a specialist aircraft. Fighters could be easily turned into ground attack aircraft with the fitting of rocket launch rails. The Soviets pioneered aerial rockets and used them against Japan in the 1939 border clashes. Being a specialist aircraft, the Il-2 Shturmovik could combine rockets with a large cannon, which was upgraded from 20mm to 23mm, with the 37mm calibre also fielded[28]. The Soviets also fitted rockets to their fighter aircraft. Soviet rockets were less accurate than the Anglo-American ones, leading to greater reliance upon specialist anti-armour shaped charge bombs.

Despite its widespread popularity with air forces, the effectiveness of the aerial rocket was questionable. The British Army Operational Research team's investigation into its use in the 1944 Normandy campaign led to an inter-Service dispute; the 2nd Tactical Air Force agreed with the evidence, without accepting the implications for their equipment, tactics and operational doctrine[29]. Nor did the trials conducted by the RAF do anything to allay these concerns: 64 rockets were fired by four Typhoons at stationary, captured Panther tanks that were painted white; the result was only three hits.

Rockets were considered to be very effective in the largely uncontested airspace of the Pacific Theatre, particularly against bunkers. In the Okinawa campaign napalm was used to remove camouflage, exposing the fortifications to rocket attack. The rocket was credited with being a significant factor in the greater use of close air support in this operation, partly displacing artillery and naval gunfire support[30]. Two issues are probably at work in the overrating of the rocket's effectiveness; their launch and impact appears impressive to the pilot, and from a wider air force perspective they validated the swing role fighter-bomber doctrine.

Rockets have continued their popularity post-War, particularly with helicopters. The 2.75-inch folding fin aerial rocket became the primary weapon system of the Aerial Rocket Artillery units in the Vietnam War. The UH-1 Huey carried 48 rockets and the more powerful Cobras carried 76. The modern versions of this weapon type, such as Hydra-70, have greater range and accuracy. They come in smoke, illumination, sub-munition and flechette, as well as the high explosive variants; the very latest versions can be laser guided, allowing a high level of affordable accuracy. Fielding fuzes capable of point detonating, airburst or delay overcomes the problem identified by SLA Marshall in Vietnam:

> *'Most of the rockets are HE [high explosive] rounds. Against jungle the ARA [Aerial Rocket Artillery] gets a lot of detonation that is high in the trees. That scares the people below. But it very seldom hurts anybody*[31]'.

Post-war the only ground attack aircraft designed around carrying a large calibre cannon has been the A-10, with its 30mm gun. In comparison, other aircraft carry lighter weapons with less range and penetration, plus a significantly smaller ammunition load[32]. Part of the controversy of replacing the A-10 with the F-35 is that it carries only a fifth of the A10's ammunition load. The F-35's light and more accurate GAU-22/A auto-cannon has a rate of fire of 3,300 rounds per minute, which will be out of ammunition in a four second burst. In addition, being a faster aircraft, it cannot provide as stable a firing platform as the A-10. There can be no doubt that the A-10 is a significantly superior platform for strafing, however as has been argued previously, the proponents of the F-35 see strafing as a rare and retrograde requirement.

Cannon are an essential, but not the primary weapon, of modern attack helicopters. Hovering can achieve superior accuracy and avoids the dispersion that results from a fixed-wing aircraft's forward motion. But the helicopter's lighter airframe and lack of forward momentum cannot offset the firing recoil of a powerful cannon. This leads to the 30mm cannon on the Apache firing a round with less propellant than the A-10's round, leading to a lower velocity and reduced armour penetration. However, a similar ammunition load is carried, making it an effective suppressive weapon.

The auto-cannon's dual role capability is being partly compromised by the fielding of munitions made solely of metal, so without any explosive content. The advantage of the solid round is a superior muzzle velocity, leading to greater accuracy, and of course improved aircraft peacetime safety through fielding a more insensitive munition[33]. This ammunition might be more effective in air-to-air combat, but this is at the expense of its strafing lethality, an interesting capability choice as strafing is probably a more likely role for cannon than air-to-air combat.

Aircraft rockets and guns have incrementally improved since World War Two; of the two, rockets have the greatest potential, not least as their greater range significantly improves aircraft survivability. The recently fielded laser-guided 70mm rocket, coupled with the right warhead, could match the aerial cannon's danger close ability. There are also options to improve their lethality, including laser-guided rockets that burst on their flight path to deliver a shrapnel-like effect. These could offer even greater lethality than current flechette warheads, as could the employment of sub-munitions[34].

Unguided Joint Fires Sub-Munitions

'Cluster bombs are perhaps not good in themselves, but when they are dropped on identified concentrations of Taliban troops they do have a heartening effect'[35].

Christopher Hutchins, polemicist

A single shell, bomb or rocket delivers overkill on the immediate area of detonation; sub-munitions multiply the points of detonation and spread the explosive effect more evenly over an area, so delivering increased lethality[36]. Cluster weapons consist of a container or dispenser and the actual sub-munitions. There are four main categories of sub-munitions: anti-personnel, usually primarily fragmentation; anti-tank and anti-materiel, usually with a shaped charge; dual purpose for use against armour and personnel; and anti-tank or anti-personnel mines. Sub-munitions were first employed by aircraft, due to the absence firing pressures and their ability to carry large ordnance. Following the same logic as other munitions, the technology spread to rockets, and then to artillery. Mortars rarely use bomblets, in part due to their smaller calibre, but also the greater lethality of their existing warhead.

The chief problem of sub-munitions is the unreliability of the individual bomblet, which can result in 5–11% of them not functioning, leading to a significant unexploded ordnance hazard[37]. This is caused by a combination of: the quantity required resulting in cheap build standards, their small size preventing sophisticated fuzing, and their low terminal velocity hindering percussion initiation. This unreliability has led to them being grouped with anti-personnel mines as weapons whose use may pose an unacceptable long-term risk of collateral damage. Fielding a reliable fuze may be uneconomical for anti-personnel sub-munitions due to their sheer quantity and small size, but it is certainly possible for the larger anti-tank munitions.

The Germans in World War Two were probably the first to operationally use aerial sub-munitions, deployed from a container this was nicknamed the 'butterfly bomb'[38]. They were quickly followed by the US, Russia and Italy. While they have been used extensively in almost all conflicts, the key driver for their development and production was the requirement for an effective air and artillery delivered munition to engage Soviet forces if the Cold War went hot. Equipped with an anti-tank warhead, they remain unrivalled amongst unguided projectiles in their effectiveness against massed armour. For a brief period, the dual-purpose anti-armour and anti-personnel bomblet round in NATO artilleries rivalled and then supplanted the high explosive round. US trials indicate that the 155mm bomblet is 6.54 times more lethal than the old M107 high explosive shell against standing personnel in the open. It retains a significant edge over the most modern high explosive rounds. Its lethality advantage is at its greatest against armour, as bomblet anti-tank warheads can penetrate tank top armour.

The effectiveness of cluster munitions is directly proportional to its number of sub-munitions. As larger shells are more efficient carriers, sub-munition technology led to the view that the 155mm would become the smallest effective calibre on the battlefield, especially as only bomblets offered an effective anti-armour capability. Sub-munitions have removed the smaller calibres' advantage against personnel and their greater suppressive effect, as bomblets deliver more bangs[39]. In addition, the 155mm round has the enduring advantage of having more high explosive, making it more destructive against solid targets and is more capable of being fired further. These factors led to the view that the smaller calibres would in the future be restricted to specialist mountain or jungle operations.

Operation Desert Storm was so far the high point in the use of artillery cluster munitions. The US Army's 25 battalions of 155mm M109s fired approximately 43,500 rounds of dual-purpose improved conventional munition bomblets, with their British ally making a further significant contribution. Bomblets accounted for about half of the total American rounds expended[40]. Up to twenty-two allied soldiers were killed and fifty-eight wounded by unexploded sub-munitions – not all of which were artillery delivered – during and after the Gulf War[41].

Of course, it is impossible to determine the casualties to own forces that could have resulted from engaging an enemy without first employing overwhelming firepower. Nonetheless, the employment of these munitions in this and other conflicts resulted in a series of arms control initiatives that culminated in the Convention on Cluster Munitions. As at 2020 there were 110 states who were Parties to the Convention, and another 13 states had signed, but had not ratified the convention. For some nations, the bomblet's withdrawal from service has led to a capability gap, others are developing replacement systems before taking a significant capability reduction. The Americans agreed in the Cluster Munition Policy Memo (19 June 2005) that its munitions would not produce >1% UXO. Those that were not compliant would be removed from the inventory not later than June 2019. This deadline has now been extended, in recognition of the challenge of fielding a cost-effective replacement capability, and the changed geo-political circumstances.

Even without these arms control measures, there are practical issues with tactically employing cluster weapons. First, their much greater dispersion over the target results in a greater danger distance, which makes them unsuitable for providing close defensive fires or shooting-in an assault. Secondly, firing bomblet onto an objective creates a hazard for assaulting troops. Each MLRS rocket contains 644 M77 grenades, a salvo from only three launchers would drop 23,184 bomblets in the target area. With a conservative 5% failure rate, this would leave over 1,000 undetonated bomblets. This dud rate led to V Corps' preference in 2003 for aerial preparatory fire onto objectives that were due to be assaulted[42], followed by artillery covering fire with high explosive in the assault. This led the 3rd Infantry Division's Assistant Divisional Commander to remark:

> *'in hindsight, the division carried too much dual purpose improved conventional munitions and not enough high explosive field artillery ammunition because the actual use of high explosive was much greater than the planning factors predicted[43].'*

High explosive rounds made up a sixth of the division's combat load[44]. When this was expended towards the end of the campaign, bomblet had to be fired. No artillery cluster munition missions were fired in Iraq after the end of major combat operations (1 May 2003), and none at all in Afghanistan during Operation Enduring Freedom. Forswearing these munitions in counter-insurgency conflicts is relatively easy, given the reduced requirement for area fires when compared to conventional warfare.

There is no such reticence to use cluster munitions in many Developing World conflicts or in Russia's operations in Georgia and Ukraine. The Georgians credit rocket delivered cluster munitions with delaying the Russian assault in 2008 by 24-hours. Clearing the unexploded munitions on the road leading from the Roki Tunnel – the only route into South Ossetia from Russia – presented a considerable challenge[45]. Cluster munitions have also been used in the conflicts in Syria, Yemen, Sudan and Libya.

How much less effective the West's joint fires system of systems is without cluster weapons is disputed. Over six years the US Army and Marine Corps conducted five studies, four of these have concluded that the effectiveness of their artillery has been reduced by between 4% and

25%[46]. One study concluded that the total removal of these weapons will have no effect; these variable results can be explained by the design of the scenario, and specifically to what extent the future will be a continuum of the current character of conflict. That is: largely counter-insurgency or against a limited regional power, with air superiority, significantly more joint fire attack assets than actual targets, and the most common target being among complex human terrain which restricts the use of firepower to point targets rather than engaging moving massed armour. Obviously, the prominence given to conventional area targets in the simulation largely determines the capability gap resulting from the removal of bomblets.

Resurgent Russia has clarified the capability requirements and the need to either develop a replacement or continue the fielding of cluster munitions. Replacing bomblet is likely to require two systems; a more effective high explosive capability against personnel, and guided sensor-fuzed munitions against armour[47]. Munitions using a combination of the most effective high explosive, pre-formed fragments and tungsten fragmentation can meet the anti-personnel function. Sensor-fuzed munitions, which can be aimed at individual vehicles probably offer the only realistic alternative to bomblet's anti-armour function, but of course at significantly greater unit cost. One advantage is that this solution, with its larger warhead, is likely to be more effective against the very best armoured targets. Alternatively, a significantly more reliable bomblet fuze could be treaty-compliant. The option for some nations is to tolerate the unexploded ordnance and their tactical limitations, and carry on employing this relatively cheap but highly lethal munition. America is probably taking a twin track approach of maintaining cost-effective cluster munitions for conventional conflict, and fielding munitions that can achieve the same effect – albeit at greater expense – but without the UXO issues.

Man-in-the-loop Terminal Precision Guidance

[The Fritz-X radio-controlled anti-ship bomb] '... generated early anxiety about the future survivability of US surface combatants, particularly aircraft carriers[48].'

Barry D. Watts

The air-launched 1,400-kg (3,100-lb) Fritz X's sinking of the Italian battleship Roma and a hospital ship at the Anzio bridgehead in 1943 signposted a significant change in warfare. As the opening quote identifies, this was immediately apparent within the maritime community but took time to spread to other services. This German weapon relied upon a man-in-the-loop guidance system – it was *flown* through radio commands from the launching aircraft. Early variants of man-in-the-loop guidance include the American Bullpup missile, which like the World War Two example was flown by observing a flare on the back of the missile and steering through a joystick control. Its replacement the Maverick, in its early version, used a nose-mounted electro-optic and then thermal camera, making flying the missile much easier, leading to improved accuracy. Given the operator workload this form of guidance is more effective in uncontested airspace, through deliberate engagement from medium altitude. Another innovation has been the replacing of the radio link with a fibre optic cable (which is thinner than a fishing line) that allows speedier data transfer and significantly reduces the system's vulnerability to counter-measures. Employing fibre optics from aerial bombs is less problematic than with surface-to-surface missiles, which are vulnerable to the ground physically interfering with the data link. Later versions of the Maverick overcame the workload challenge by employing laser guidance, and now fire and forget, with the missile's seeker head relaying the target image to a screen in the cockpit for the pilot to check before launch.

The key advantages of a weapon-mounted camera are that it provides an ever-improving picture as the weapon gets closer to the target, and it allows the tracking of a moving target. In recent operations, the requirement for greater discrimination has seen a move away from 'fire and forget' towards 'fire and observe' weaponry. The operator's ability to abort the engagement right up to its final stages significantly reduces the probability of collateral damage. As a result, there has been some retrofitting of technologies that put an operator back in control of previously autonomous weaponry.

This guidance approach may provide a high level of operator control, but it also poses a considerable challenge for the operator to identify the target and orientate the weapon to the target. This is particularly challenging in a complex urban environment, which may be further compounded by friendly forces within the target area. The Israeli Spike non-line of sight missile leads in this technology area; it is now being offered dual-fitted with semi-active laser guidance. This allows a third party to designate the target for the missile, while the operator, observing through the nose-mounted camera, still has overall control of the engagement.

Laser-Guided Terminal Precision Munitions

'The Copperhead artillery shell, when it comes into service in 1981, will have an impact exceeding that of radar in World War II.'

Dr William J. Perry, US Under Secretary of Defence
for Research and Engineering

Laser-guided weapons made their operational debut in Vietnam, at the famous attack on the Thanh Hoa Bridge on 13 May 1972. These weapons rely on the target being illuminated, or 'painted', by a laser beam, using a unique coded series of pulses from the target designator. Either the aircraft dropping the weapon, a ground team, or a third-party aircraft, can provide this designation. While effective, these Vietnam War vintage weapons were particularly prone to 'wild bombs' and hence they were not used in close air support[49]. While the technology has matured, atmospheric obstructions – cloud, precipitation, or its man-made equivalents such as smoke screens or smog – can still prevent the designator providing sufficient illumination for the seeker. The other significant limitation is that the laser designator needs line of sight of the target throughout the engagement. This can be a considerable tactical challenge, both in terms of aircraft survivability, or the insertion of a ground designation team to achieve visibility of the target.

The fielding of artillery laser-guided weapons was more than a decade behind air delivered ones, partly because of the technical challenge of developing a seeker able to withstand the 9,000g force of being fired from a gun. The other challenge was steering the projectile; laser guidance can be easily retrofitted to aerial bombs as these are much easier to steer than fin-less artillery shells; shells require bespoke designs to achieve the necessary manoeuvrability to steer onto the target. By the early 1980s laser-guided bombs were an established weapon in advanced air forces. In this decade the US Army introduced the M712 Copperhead, a 155mm calibre cannon-launched, fin-stabilized, laser-guided shell. The Russians followed with an equivalent capability, the 152mm Krasnopol, which was subsequently made available in a 155mm variant for export. The Russians claimed a longer range and a larger warhead than the Copperhead. Certainly, the Krasnopol has had more export success, being acquired by at least 12 countries in Africa, Asia, the Middle East, and also China. The latter nation appears to have reverse engineered both it and other Russian guided systems that they bought in small batches[50]. Also in production is the Kitolov shell that can be fired from 120/122mm gun/mortar and artillery systems. The Russians claim up to 90% hit probability for these weapons[51].

Compared to their success as aerial weaponry, the challenges of the ground environment have limited the effectiveness of laser-guided artillery weapons. The primary challenge is that ground-level laser designation is significantly more taxing than with an aircraft. In Europe line of sight of at least two to three kilometres occurs on average around 20% of the time. For ranges over five to six kilometres, this drops to a few percentage points. It is especially challenging to achieve line of sight in *true* urban terrain (this was not the case for the Russians in Chechnya, as the capital is low-density urban sprawl). Adverse weather can make laser guidance problematic, both Chechen conflicts were largely carried out over the winter months, which limited the effectiveness of laser-guided weapons[52]. The Indian employment of the Krasnapol in high altitude trials showed similar weaknesses[53]. The high canopies and ambient moisture levels of the jungle tend to blind the munition's seeker to a ground-based illuminator. Seekers are similarly limited in the desert, becoming inoperative in sandstorms; and the American laser target designators were prone to overheat[54]. These weaknesses should be expected and could probably be tolerated in return for the capability's operational benefits. However, they run counter to an artillery culture that expects guaranteed 24/7, all weather, fire and forget, target engagement.

Terminal control of these systems is challenging, particularly for the Krasnopol: the laser target designator needs to be within 300 metres of the gun-target line (the Copperhead is more forgiving, the controller needed to be within 80-degrees of this line) and the cloud ceiling needs be at least 600 metres above ground level to allow the seeker to acquire the laser. For both systems, achieving an initial relatively accurate target grid is essential given the artillery guided shell's higher velocity and limited ability to correct from its ballistic path. This is compounded when a low cloud base giving the round little time to correct its trajectory. The Krasnopol's ability to correct itself along its ballistic path is so limited that the standard practice is to adjust using unguided rounds onto the target area, and then fire a laser-guided round[55].

Despite the prediction of the opening quote, artillery laser-guided weapons have had a limited operational impact. The Copperhead was fired in the Gulf War, but it was not judged to have been worth the resources devoted to achieving the target effect[56]. It was not employed in the Iraq War, and America and its allies are now reliant upon coordinate-seeking munitions.

The Russians, through not wishing to rely upon satellite navigation, have taken a different path. They identified that their artillery guided weapons' weaknesses were: command and control; the poor synchronisation of the observer's calls for fire with the gun positions; and a lack of knowledge on the gun position at operating these specialist munitions. Instead of trying to get all their artillery competent with laser projectiles, they formed specialist 240mm batteries with dedicated observers. They determined that the 240mm mortar bomb was sufficiently lethal to justify the expense of the fuze, and that it would be used in a deliberate manner against priority targets. The result in the Second Chechen War was: '*the use of correctable Smelchak shells was extremely effective and became the decisive factor in the assault. They destroyed 127 targets*[57]'. This large calibre mortar effectively delivered a siege warfare capability against field fortifications and infrastructure.

Laser-guided munitions have become an essential munition for the most advanced air forces. More problematic is their utility in ground warfare, though the Russians have proved their worth in deliberate operation, against static targets, with specialist operators. While their limitations are obvious, laser guided munitions have considerable advantages; they are: cheap for precision guided munitions, relatively simple to manufacture, accurate, provide a facility to abort at practically the last moment, and can hit slowly moving targets. These advantages mean that they will continue to be widely employed in the air domain, though in the most contested air environments, achieving line of sight for target designation will be problematic. Given the challenges of laser guidance, the attraction of GPS is readily apparent, especially as its potential weaknesses are rarely as obvious in peacetime.

Coordinate-Seeking Terminal Precision Munitions

> *'Everybody is desperately looking for either augmentation to your primary [navigation] system, or GPS, or they're looking for something that's non-GPS. There is no magic bullet that can replace GPS*[58]*.'*
>
> Al Simon, navigation systems marketing manager
> for Rockwell Collins

NATO's Operation Allied Force campaign against Serbia had to contend with dense cloud cover, compounded by smog over the industrialised urban areas, and smoke screens to protect vulnerable targets. This meant that laser-guided bombs often failed to acquire their target or worse, after launch lost their seeker lock, raising the possibility of collateral damage. The Joint Direct Attack Munition (JDAM), an all-weather attack capability not dependent on laser guidance, had already proved itself in the Gulf War. The circumstances of the Kosovo Campaign accelerated the fielding of hybrid multimode seekers that combine laser guidance and grid reference coordinate seeking. Providing airpower with a truly all-weather, day-or-night precision attack capability was a milestone in its evolution. This development was not particularly expensive: retrofitting a standard free-fall bomb to become a JDAM cost in the region of $18,000 at 2016 prices. It was also easy to accomplish; the only challenge being that the munition being upgraded may need some explosive to be removed to achieve a large-enough recess for the new fuze with its seeker and steering canards.

Coordinate-seeking munitions correct their ballistic path to the target through a combination of GPS and the Inertial Navigation System (INS). INS utilises motion sensors – usually three linear accelerators and three rotational gauges (gyros) – to determine the direction and speed of travel. As long it has an accurate starting location, it can precisely track its movement and so calculate its current position and orientation; thus INS compensates for any temporary loss of the satellite signal. Inertial navigation deteriorates with time and distance; GPS updates compensate for this and thus prevent any loss of accuracy. This allows weapons to achieve a circular error probability of below five metres, or sub-metre accuracy with encrypted military GPS.

Aerial munitions can solely use grid coordinate seeking guidance, but they usually combine it with laser-guidance, and sometimes a third sensor such as millimetric-wave radar to do imagery matching. Laser-guidance would be used if the aircraft wished to retain the ability to abort the mission throughout the engagement, or against a moving target. The ability to launch and leave makes GPS guided weapons a preferred means of engagement in contested airspace.

A precision fuze's steering canards can easily steer aerial munitions, non-rifled mortar bombs and rockets because of their lower velocity and large control surfaces (or fins), but the artillery shell's ballistic characteristics make it resistant to being steered from the nose. As a result, the same precision fuze fitted to a finned mortar bomb or rocket delivers significantly greater accuracy than it does with an artillery shell. Larger steering canards can improve accuracy through increasing in-flight steerage, but these need to fit into the internal diameter of the artillery tube. When a small calibre is combined with a high velocity – as in the 105mm gun – a precision fuze cannot make sufficient correction to the ballistic path to significantly improve accuracy. The 152/155mm calibre allows the precision fuze to have larger canards, these deliver sufficient steerage, when coupled with a long time of flight, to significantly improve accuracy, but not to achieve sub-meter precision.

The American M1156 Precision Guidance Kit has been operationally proven for their 120mm mortar and 155mm gun[59]. The original design requirement was 50m circular error probability; the latest versions are achieving less than 30m[60]. Officially the 120mm mortar bomb with a course corrected fuze achieves the same accuracy as the 155mm shell, but in practice it is much more accurate. Certain US Army publications equate mortar bombs with Precision Guidance Kit with the guided MLRS and the Excalibur round; the latter two are specified as having a sub 10m circular error probability[61]. A possible solution to getting precision accuracy from a standard shell is to design a fuze with canards that pop-out once the shell exits the tube and couple this with base mounted fins; these fins could be screwed (or similarly attached) onto the base of a standard shell. The combination of these fins could generate sufficient control surface to steer the munition to a sub-metre accuracy; until this happens, modern tube artillery should expect the following accuracy:

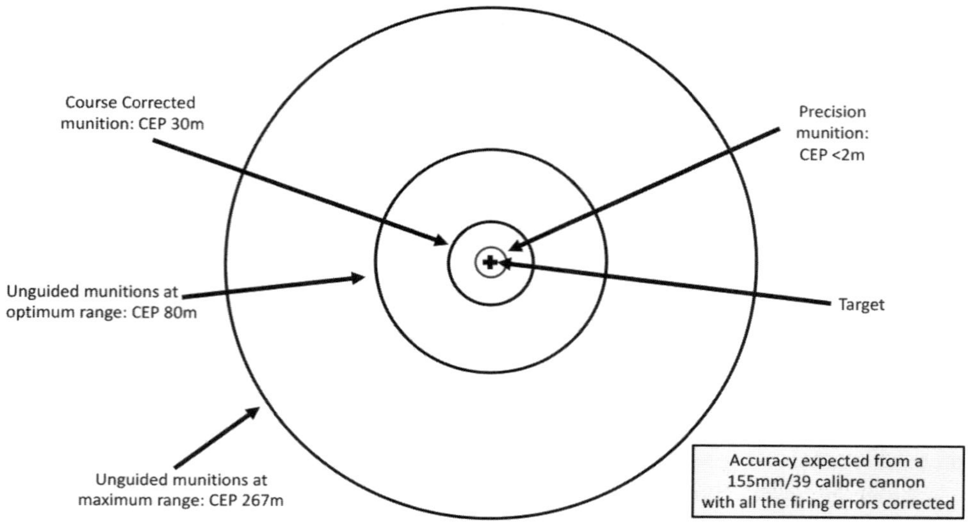

Currently bespoke artillery projectiles are required to achieve true precision with GPS/INS guidance. The American Excalibur 155mm round does not follow a ballistic path, its folding fins allow the projectile to gain altitude before gliding to the target. This design is expensive and sacrifices much of its explosive payload. Making a bespoke 105mm coordinate seeking shell is of course possible, as precision guidance has been fitted to even large calibre small arms rounds[62]. The question is whether the improved accuracy warrants the cost of custom-made munitions with limited payload. The Americans currently expect 155mm to deliver a precision capability, allowing their 105mm cannon to concentrate on area targets.

Future artillery precision weapons may combine laser guidance with coordinate seeking, following the practice of aerial munitions. In June 2013 the manufacturer Raytheon initiated an internally funded program to upgrade the Excalibur so that it also had semi-active laser guidance[63]. During a recent weapons test, the Excalibur round was launched with GPS guidance and then switched to laser-guidance[64]. The munition would make use of the fire support team's extant ability to designate air-delivered laser-guided weapons.

As with laser guidance, armies have not found the employment of coordinate-seeking artillery munitions straightforward. Producing target locations with sufficient accuracy has often been challenging, as has been the battlespace management problem. The human challenge of overcoming these issues is illustrated by the disconnect between the US Marines, who at one stage in the Afghanistan conflict had fired 13 times as many Excalibur rounds as the US Army, despite being the smaller force[65]. This also applied to the guided MLRS; in Afghanistan, the much smaller British Army fired almost as many rockets as the US Army. That these first-class militaries differed so significantly in their adoption of these new weapons is probably due to mature operations developing their own orthodoxies and conservatisms. When there is already an established fire support system based on airpower – as was the case in some of the Regional

Commands in Afghanistan – an organic precision fire capability has difficulty achieving traction. As at 2019 there have been over 1,400 Excalibur combat firings; peaking at over 20 rounds per day in operations against the Islamic State, less than1% of total 155mm rounds.

GPS's greatest vulnerability is its weak signal – this is roughly as powerful as a standard television transmission if this were broadcasting from five times as far away as the moon. This means it can be easily overpowered by a physically closer jammer, resulting in either a total loss of service, or an inability to acquire new satellites, or the replacement of a genuine signal with a false one (spoofing). About eight times more jamming power is required to defeat encrypted military as civilian GPS. In addition, military GPS also operates on multiple frequencies. Despite this, the power advantage lies with the ground-based jammer and not the space-based system[66].

Open source information identifies that the Russian Pole-21 jammer can suppress a non-military GPS signal up to 80km away[67]. The North Korean jamming of a combined US and South Korean exercise in March 2011 provided a rare demonstration of the potential of jammers against military GPS[68]. America's concern over GPS denial has increased incrementally. Only a decade ago the comforting view was that low-powered jammers could be simply countered, while high-powered jammers could be easily found and destroyed[69]. Ten years later, cheap jammers have both proliferated and significantly improved their capability; they are now easily transportable and hence are difficult to target, through say positioning them on a school or a hospital roof, or putting them on a bus following an urban route[70].

The Americans recognise that their vulnerability to GPS jamming cannot be easily resolved. Simultaneously with hardened existing technology, advanced research is examining non-navigational electromagnetic signals (including commercial satellite, radio and television signals), pulsed lasers and tracked lightning strikes to provide precise location updates in GPS-denied areas. The limitations of these technologies mean that most of the on-going work is focussed on reducing the INS's deterioration in accuracy[71].

The INS in current advanced munitions deteriorates at approximately one degree per hour. This means that even if they lose their GPS signal 6km from the target, INS deterioration over the remaining distance will result in an addition of 20m circular error probability. Militarising advanced civilian technology will deliver smaller, cheaper inertial navigation that will significantly reduce this deterioration rate[72]. Moving from the current 1 degree per hour to 0.01 degree per hour may be possible: non-weaponised technology has can already achieve 0.05 degree per hour. Obviously, weaponising this technology will be easier for rockets and free fall bombs. For these, within the next few years this technology is likely to provide sufficient accuracy for short-range weapons (up to 20km?) to be released with an accurate position from GPS, and then purely rely upon INS to get them precisely to the target. Over a slightly longer time frame, it is likely to be possible for artillery to become purely reliant on INS for ranges up to 80km. Superior INS will also make the munition more resistant to GPS spoofing. As accurate inertial navigation will improve the ability to detect a spoof GPS signal that is trying to convince the munition that it is at a different location[73]. Better GPS tracking software, together with multi-element antennas, allow the munition to better capture GPS signals; this will further reduce vulnerability to jamming. The Precision Guidance Kit is vulnerable because it lacks an

INS able to adequately check the satellite signal and has only a single antenna that operates on a single channel. The Americans are overcoming this vulnerability but of course the challenge is fitting a guidance system resistant to spoofing and jamming into the limited space of a normal fuze.

GPS combined with inertial navigation has made airpower a genuine 24/7 near all-weather capability. It provides artillery with either a full precision capability, or course corrected fuzes with the ability to deliver precise fire out to maximum range. This means that GPS denial represents a significant operational challenge. Future technical improvement is likely to limit jamming's impact, but currently, airpower is reliant upon an alternative seeker – such as infrared imaging or millimetric radar – to deliver a standoff capability in a GPS denied battlefield. Artillery may be less reliant upon GPS munitions, but its denial is still significant.

Image and Scene Matching Guidance Precision Munitions

'Bombs that can recognise their targets are back in fashion[74]*.'*

The Economist newspaper, 2016

Image or scene matching compares the image received by the munition's sensor with pre-stored imagery. This technology was first used in the closing stages of the Cold War, before the widespread fielding of GPS systems. The American Pershing II ballistic missile matched the stored image of the target area with that collected through its radar seeker; the Russian SS-12 and OTR-23 theatre ballistic missiles continue to use this technology. The Tomahawk cruise missile used terrain contour matching to navigate to the target area, where it switched to digital scene matching to achieve greater accuracy in the final part of the flight[75]. More modern version of this and similar missiles use GPS for navigating to the target area before switching to high-resolution infrared camera and digital scene-matching area correlation to acquire the target[76]. This approach overcomes target-based GPS jamming, but may be vulnerable to wide area jamming.

A solution is increased quantities of stored imagery; this can now cover the whole route to the target. This is aided by the collection of imagery being less resource-intensive, due to synthesis techniques. However, the creation and maintenance of an imagery library of countless pixels remains a significant task. As a result, scene-matching technology suits countries such as Israel with its defined security threat, close proximity to likely targets and impressive imagery collection capability. The Americans may be behind in this capability, but they are putting considerable resources into further improving their image-based navigation and targeting[77]. However, the timely creation of databases may not always be possible on more expeditionary operations. Civilian technology may be providing at least a partial answer to this challenge; Hydra fusion software can create a high-resolution three-dimension map from ordinary video. Lockheed Martin intends to use this technology in their Northstar optical navigation system[78].

Being reliant upon a single spectrum is a vulnerability; the best munitions can now correlate two or more complementary sensors operating in the visible, infrared and millimetric-wave radar parts of the spectrum[79]. Faced with targets protected by integrated air defence systems and GPS jamming, scene-matching technology can enable the West to retain a standoff precision attack capability. Fitted to a 250-pound air-to-surface glide-bomb, the Israeli SPICE (smart, precise impact, cost-effective) guidance kit employs scene-matching technology to navigate 100km before delivering precision accuracy. An initial accurate GPS fixation is necessary to orientate the inertial navigation and cue the scene-matching technology. The 100km range allows it to be released outside the area affected by even the most powerful GPS jammers[80].

The cheapest form of this technology provides the guidance for anti-armour sensor-fuzed sub-munitions. These munitions are carried to a target area by bombs, rockets and shells[81]. Once deployed, these sub-munitions match the images being detected by their sensors against targets whose characteristics are pre-programmed into their database. Once the seeker acquires a target the sub-munition intercepts and engages with an anti-armour warhead[82]. Most sub-munitions use an explosively formed penetrator warhead that is effective against most tank top armour[83].

The sensor can employ the optical spectrum, but most use infrared with its day and night capability. At significantly greater expense, radar or radio frequencies can provide an all-weather capability. Low frequency radars can even penetrate foliage. The cheapest solution is a fixed infrared seeker, this has a relatively small field of view, with the swing inherent in the parachute descent naturally searching the target area. This may be a cost-effect approach, but only radar can overcome the prevailing low cloud base in likely temperate conflict areas[84]. Being relatively cheap sensors, most employ only a few hundred pixels in their seeker focal plane and have a limited number of targets within their memory. This limited capacity, processing power and time to engage is adequate against armoured vehicles, which usually stand out when compared to their background. If no target is detected, these sub-munitions are designed to self-destruct; this plus having too few sub-munitions, means they are compliant with the convention on cluster munitions[85].

On 21 March 2003, American artillery destroyed two Iraqi tanks with the M898 155mm SADARM (Sense And Destroy ARMour) employing an infrared and millimetric wave radar seeker. Initially this munition was developed for the 8-inch howitzer, the programme shifted to 155mm in the 1980s when it became technically possible to miniaturise the munitions to this calibre. During the Invasion of Iraq, a total of 108 rounds were fired and 48 vehicle kills were claimed. Subsequently, counter-insurgency became the principal challenge and the munition did not achieve full-scale fielding. In addition, the 1,500m danger close distance proved to be a more significant limitation than was envisaged in Cold War defensive operations.

European armies have pursued the sensor-fused munitions route with more energy. The Germans have the 155mm SMArt and the Russian Smerch 9K58 multiple launch rocket system, deploys five MOTIV-3M or Bazalt parachute-retarded munitions per rocket[86]. Faced with a resurgent conventional warfare threat, the US Army is buying the Swedish BONUS system as an interim capability[87]. Simultaneously they have launched their own programme – cannon-delivered area munitions – which aims at delivering an improved capability, particularly in terms of range and improved all-weather target acquisition. The French have fired BONUS shells operationally, largely wiping out an Islamic State armoured convoy. Systems based on the 155mm shell tend to employ two anti-armour sub-munitions. 120mm mortar bombs can have one or two sub-munitions, these have not been extensively fielded.

The Americans and some of their allies (notably the South Koreans) have fielded aerial munitions containing sensor-fuzed sub-munitions. The CBU-97 air-delivered cluster bomb spreads 40 sensor-fuzed projectiles (called Skeets) to search an area of 1,500 by 500 feet (460m × 150m). As an A-10 can carry ten of these bombs this equates to 400 projectiles, each capable of destroying a tank. Proof firing on weapon ranges suggest that this weapon load, under ideal conditions, could account for 40 tanks[88]. An improved version, the CBU-105, has two self-destruct mechanisms and meets the Department of Defence requirement of less than 0.15% UXO on the battlefield. Eighty-eight were used on Operation Iraqi Freedom, and such was the confidence in their reliability that US Air Force invited the Human Rights Watch to examine an Iraqi battery engaged with this weapon, the Watch did not identify any unexploded ordinance[89].

Image matching technology has focussed on delivering two separate capabilities. First, attacking massed armour targets in conventional warfighting. Armoured vehicles provide considerable contrast to their background, especially when moving; so without effective counter-measures, they are vulnerable to sensor-fuzed munitions with even relatively low technology sensors. The lessons that the Russians have drawn from their 21st century conflict is that armoured vehicles should primarily be engaged with sensor-fuzed munitions, with high explosive and cluster rounds being used against softer targets and when suppressing objectives[90].

The second use of this technology is delivering precision-accuracy bombs and missiles without relying upon GPS or laser designation. These weapons employ significantly more sophisticated sensors that enable munitions to be launched at a standoff distance and can overcome a more challenging target acquisition challenge. Their targets are likely to be camouflaged, at least partly concealed in buildings and foliage, and will employ sophisticated decoys and may not have such an easily recognised shape as a tank.

Smoke Munitions

'If nature has failed to oblige us with fog to blind the enemy defensive weapons and observers, the artillery must provide a substitute in the form of smoke[91].'

Major General Heinz Guderian

Artillery smoke munitions were first fielded in 1916 to screen the movement of own forces and deny the enemy observed fire and situational awareness. Artillery and mortars remain the primary means of generating tactical smoke screens as they can provide it at greater range than grenade smoke, and unlike smoke generators they allow considerable freedom in their placement. Aircraft-delivered smoke screens were a feature of World War Two Soviet warfighting, but this is now obsolete[92]. Most smoke shells are optimised against the visible range, but the screening of other parts of the electro-magnetic spectrum is becoming more common.

Smoke munitions have the following secondary roles: adding the suppressive effect of high explosive shells when providing covering fire, serving as a pre-arranged signal, marking a target, and aiding the adjustment of fire when observation is difficult, such as with air observation or in the jungle.

Smoke shells and bombs can be divided into those that eject two, three or four smoke canisters from their base, and those that burst. Base ejection smoke rounds employ a slow-burning compound which is then spread by the wind. It takes around two minutes to build up and so suits the creation of deliberate smoke screens that cover considerable distances. Bursting smoke munitions use an explosive charge to spread white phosphorus or similar material; this spontaneously ignites in contact with air, so rapidly creating a screen and instant obscuration. The intense burning results in the smoke pillaring upward rather than spreading out along the ground, so it cannot provide the same quantity or duration of screening as base ejection smoke. White phosphorous has two further advantages: its mist of liquid droplets scrambles infrared as well as visual radiation, plus it also has an incendiary and anti-personnel effect.

White phosphorous' characteristics are a good match for the infantry's immediate needs in the close battle, so mortars nearly always use it. Tube artillery tends to use both types, as they meet different tactical requirements. They can be complementary; maintaining the integrity of long smoke screens provided by base ejection rounds is easy with white phosphorous munitions to plug any gaps. White phosphorus is also a more effective obscurant in mountainous terrain as the relief can prevent the formation of coherent smoke screens[93]; this challenge is often compounded by smoke canisters rolling down hills.

The requirement for smoke rounds is usually underestimated in peacetime. They accounted for 10% of the 105mm rounds and 8% of the 155mm rounds of the American expenditure in Afghanistan and Iraq between 2003 and 2014[94]. The Israeli artillery fired 34,000 artillery rounds in their 2014 Gaza Strip operation, this split 12,000 smoke, 3,000 illumination, and 19,000 high explosive rounds[95]. For the Blackjack Brigade's direct support artillery, the 3–82 Field Artillery Battalion, smoke constituted 25% of all missions fired in the Gulf War[96]. This level of use contrasts with the normal proportion of 5%, or at the most 10%, devoted to artillery smoke rounds, in most Western ammunition stockpiles.

A fifth of Russian artillery and mortar rounds expended in Grozny in the Second Chechen War were smoke. In complex urban terrain the Russians found it difficult to identify and suppress all Chechen firing points, hence smoke screens were necessary to allow almost all above ground level movement between buildings. The white phosphorous shell could also mark a building as a target, act as an incendiary, achieve attrition, and by creating fires spread terror. This was aided by the toxic white phosphorus smoke's ability to penetrate the filters of most protective mask. Despite this, it is not banned by any of the current chemical weapon treaties.

Target identification in complex vegetation often requires smoke shells to mark targets and objectives. In the jungle-covered hills of the South West Pacific in World War Two, the convention was for individual white smoke rounds to mark the four corners of a target for aerial engagement, while own forces used coloured smoke to show the pilots their own positions[97]. Aircraft-delivered smoke is becoming rare; but it provides an airborne forward air controller with the ability to mark a target for lethal engagement[98].

Smoke shells when mixed in the final rounds of a barrage or concentration indicate that fire will shift onto another target, informing the assaulting infantry to close on the suppressed objective before its defenders can recover. Different coloured smoke shells can assist with this marker function. In World War Two, the British deployed red, yellow, blue and green smoke shells. Given that current ammunition stockpiles are significantly smaller, such variety is uncommon.

Base ejection smoke rounds have also been used as a non-lethal means of indicating future intent, and so seek to modify behaviour. An example was the Georgian smoke bombardment into South Ossetia, on 7 August 2008 at the start of Russo-Georgian War, which was followed by a 15-minute pause for civilians to leave before the start of lethal fires[99]. In doing this, consideration needs to be given to where the carrier shell lands, i.e. its ballistic point of impact, as this lump of metal can be lethal.

Traditionally designed to block the visible spectrum, smoke shells can now burn compounds that produce particles able to block other frequencies. Burning phosphorous has always partly shielded colder emissions behind its screen, adding elements such as aluminium-coated glass fibre exaggerates and prolongs this effect. The carbon in smoke screens already absorbs laser energy, making it an effective counter to laser range finders, designators and sensors. Adding particles of the right size to smoke screens can interfere with ground surveillance radars. In operations against near-peer enemies, the best-equipped armies will require smoke able to block the visual, infrared and near infrared. Given that it is an active sensor, the defeat of radars may be more economically done by offensive action. Armies are trying to determine what proportion of their smoke munitions needs to be multi-spectrum. The evidence of recent operations is that overall smoke should make up at least 10% of artillery munitions, and a higher percentage for infantry support mortars.

Illumination Munitions

'rather than shoot counter-battery with HE [high explosive], we did it with illum [illumination rounds] to let them know we are tracking[100]*.'*

101st Airborne Division's response to a single
mortar attack from an urban area

Since World War One artillery and mortars have provided illumination for the manoeuvre arms when they need additional light. Artillery and mortars, independently of the other combat arms, can also use illumination shells to assist with target engagement. These munitions have also been called star shells, a term that continues in nautical circles. A modern illumination munition ejects a flare that slowly falls beneath a non-flammable parachute, illuminating the area below. The munition's time fuze is set for the flare to achieve a height above ground, of about 600–800 metres for 155mm and 400 metres above the ground for 105mm. The 120mm mortar has a height of burst of 500–700m and the 81mm 200m lower. Mortar bombs usually frontally eject their flare, so avoiding the fins. Larger calibres munitions burn longer and provide more illumination through having greater luminosity. When used in an attack, the flare is ideally positioned behind the enemy to illuminate them while, hopefully it will be sufficiently distant from attacking troops so that they remain in the dark. During defensive operations, these munitions are generally used to illuminate attacking troops for engagement by direct and indirect fire.

The requirement for white light should be declining with the proliferation of night vision devices; however, as these devices can degrade situational awareness, there remains an enduring requirement for white light during complex activities. For example, illumination rounds have been used during the reorganisation phase after a night attack to assist with the speedy identification of wounded and dead, dealing with prisoners, distribute fresh ammunition and reorganise squads and platoons following casualties. Of course, this is a tactical risk versus reward choice, as it would be much safer to do this using night vision devices.

Illumination rounds have a number of secondary roles. They can be used instead of a marker shell and can be more effective as they register in both the visual and thermal spectrum. The intense light of illumination flares can also be used to render early generation night vision devices ineffective. In non-warfighting operations, illumination munitions can serve as a non-lethal indication of intent, so signalling the requirement for a change of behaviour. As with smoke shells, in the non-lethal role, care needs to be taken with the ballistic impact point of the carrier shell. Illumination munition's utility was demonstrated in NATO's deployment to Kosovo:

> *'In one brazen attack that first summer, a Russian soldier was wounded, and the isolated outpost of Russian soldiers was pelted with rocks until American artillery fired six illumination rounds to light the area and the attackers finally dispersed*[101]*.'*

Recently, white light illumination has been supplemented by infrared illumination, which greatly increases the effectiveness of night sights. Infrared illumination burns longer, significantly increases the area of battlefield illumination (in some cases by 2.5 times the diameter of visible light illumination) and it is less sensitive to adverse climatic conditions when compared to the standard visible light illumination.

Improvements in sensors have made aircraft delivered flares less common. Their characteristics are similar to artillery and mortar illumination, but they are significantly more capable. This is due to combining a high candela (they can be twice as powerful as artillery ones), a low dud rate (due to avoiding firing pressure) and the slower sink rate made possible by a larger parachute. The US Air Force made extensive use of flares in the Vietnam War, discovering that the removal of the cover of darkness was often sufficient to defeat an attack[102]. The Soviets in their Afghanistan conflict increased their use following initial failures to effectively track Mujahedeen exiting from a contact[103].

There air force employment may be diminishing, but the continuing usefulness of illumination rounds is demonstrated by their accounting for a fifth of the rounds the US expended in Afghanistan and Iraq between 2003 and 2014. As with smoke shells, this level of operational use contrasts with the 5–10% devoted to illumination rounds in most stockpiles. A deduction from recent operations is that a greater proportion of smoke is required in conventional warfighting; in contrast more illumination is required in counter-insurgency. Modern armies should expect to employ both white light and infrared illumination.

Thermobaric Munitions

> *'The [blast] kill mechanism against living targets is unique – and unpleasant … What kills is the pressure wave, and more importantly, the subsequent rarefaction [vacuum], which ruptures the lungs … If the fuel deflagrates but does not detonate, victims will be severely burned and will probably also inhale the burning fuel. Since the most common FAE [Fuel Air Explosive] fuels, ethylene oxide and propylene oxide, are highly toxic, undetonated FAE should prove as lethal to personnel caught within the cloud as most chemical agents*[104]'.
>
> Human Rights Watch

The development of thermobaric munitions started with World War Two German research that established the practicality of munitions relying upon the atmosphere to provide most of the explosion's oxygen. The Russians weaponised this research and employed these munitions in the Sino-Russian border conflicts and their Afghanistan War; the Americans used them in the Vietnam War. These early weapons were usually known as fuel air explosives. They employed a container of fuel and two separate explosive charges, one to disperse the fuel and the second to ignite it. Given this, they could only be weaponised in the configuration of a large aerial bomb.

Modern munitions have replaced petroleum-based fuel with powdered metals, such as aluminium, ethylene oxide or magnesium. By including an oxidizer in the explosive mixture these munitions do not require the complex detonation sequence of the older weapons. In this form, they are usually called thermobaric. These do not the need the preliminary dispersal before detonation, allowing these warheads to be also employed by rockets, mortars and missiles. The Russians lead in their use; Western nations predominantly employ this technology in aerial munitions, including the Hellfire missile whose thermobaric variant is designed for use against structures. Thermobaric 60mm, 81mm and 120mm mortar bombs have all been developed. Thermobaric technology cannot currently be effectively used by tube artillery, whose terminal velocity, heavy casing and limited internal volume make other forms of explosive a better capability choice.

The Russian 24-barrelled 220mm Buratino rocket system has been specifically developed to exploit thermobarics. A single salvo can achieve destruction over an area 200m by 400m; it is used as an assault weapon against fortified and urban areas. The Buratino is not assigned to the regular Russian Missile Troops and Artillery, instead it is employed by specialised nuclear, biological and chemical warfare troops, as part of a flamethrower battalion. It spearheads assaults; most recently it has proved its effectiveness in Syrian cities from 2015[105].

Conventional explosives are about three parts of oxidiser to one-part explosive fuel. Employing the atmosphere's oxygen allows thermobaric munition to be almost solely fuel. This effectiveness is further increased by more evenly distributing the explosive over the target area. Thermobaric munitions' lethality largely comes from blast, with the rupture of the warhead's light casing providing limited fragmentation. The high proportion of fuel means that the blast wave covers a greater volume, for a longer duration, and has a higher temperature. Thermobaric munitions are particularly effective in enclosed spaces, such as tunnels, urban areas and bunkers, where their blast effect is magnified. The burning of the atmosphere's oxygen can also lead to asphyxiation. The fireball's massive overpressure can kill by crushing. Conversely, the lack of a significant quantity of oxidiser makes these weapons ineffective at high altitude, where there is less oxygen, and in adverse weather when moisture in the atmosphere inhibits the explosion.

Thermobarics are a controversial weapon system as a result of how they kill and injure, leading to repeated calls for their banning. Given that these weapons have largely been used in urban areas, it has been argued that their use is illegal under Article III of the 1980 Convention on Certain Conventional Weapons. This forbids the use of any incendiary weapon on civilian populations. Despite this, their use is likely to proliferate, because in optimum circumstances they deliver an explosive effect equivalent to around seven times their weight of TNT or around four-fold modern military explosives (RDX is one and a half times more powerful than TNT). In addition, the munitions' utility is increasing, with more combat taking place in urban areas, which favours a pure blast weapon.

Specialist Munitions

'The results of the test of the aviation explosive device that have been created have shown that it is comparable with nuclear weapons in efficiency and potential[106].'

General Alexander Rukshin on Russia's
'Father of All Bombs' Thermobaric weapon

Some armies retain specialist direct fire rounds to engage personnel and armoured targets. Flechette, a shell carrying steel darts, has replaced canister as artillery's close-in man killer. A typical 105mm Beehive round has 6,000 darts and at about 50 metres from the muzzle, the carrier shell ejects the darts, which spread, replicating a giant shotgun in their effect against troops in the open. Attack helicopters can use flechette warheads on their rockets as a specialist anti-personnel weapon. Each 70 mm Hydra 70 rocket has a warhead containing 1179 flechette.

To engage armoured targets, in World War Two, artillery replaced the kinetic energy of solid metal rounds with chemical energy munitions[107]. Western artilleries now rarely employ specialist anti-tank warheads, instead relying upon their standard high explosive round. If this achieves a direct hit, then its momentum and blast will impact upon a tank's combat effectiveness through, at a minimum, destroying antenna, sights and external fittings. Tanks are unlikely to survive a direct hit from a 152/155mm shell. Russians and armies that follow their lead, not only employ specialist anti-tank rounds, they also employ modern tank-like fire control systems. This reflects their emphasis upon direct fire and the requirement for artillery to significantly contribute to anti-tank defence, as 2S1s have done in the conflict on the Donbas.

Smoke and illuminating rounds have a secondary function in indicating targets, but the specialist marker round continues to be fielded. Coloured smoke dissipates and illumination burns out after a couple of minutes; in contrast, marker rounds leave a durable coloured mark. They are made by mixing high explosive and coloured dye, it can either burst in the air or on impact. The American 155mm shell comes in four colours: red, blue, purple and orange. As they operate solely in the visible spectrum they are less useful for target indication with the fielding of sensors using other parts of the spectrum. This argument is used against retaining a bespoke marker shell; the real rationale is the financial saving and simplifying of logistics that comes from reducing the stockpile by one nature.

Using artillery to deliver anti-armour and anti-personnel mines allows them to be deployed where they are needed, even if this is in enemy territory, without incurring any risk to the carrier vehicle, whether a truck, helicopter or aircraft. Of course, this means of emplacement cannot achieve the density of more conventional mine laying. In addition, with remote delivery, not all the mines will be effectively orientated. With American scatterable mine munitions, it is expected that 5–15% will ineffectively come to rest on their edge, a percentage that increases in mud or snow.

The greater rate of fire and larger payload of rocket systems allows them to rapidly lay minefields. Each of the sixteen 220 mm rockets on a BM-27 rocket launcher can scatter 312 anti-personnel mines. In Afghanistan a common Soviet tactic was to lay anti-personnel mine fields behind their opponents, to hinder their retreat. In Ukrainian operations the Russians have deployed scatterable mines directly onto the target, combining them with fire strikes of conventional high explosive, bomblet, and thermobaric munitions. The scatterable anti-tank mine fixes the armoured target for its destruction by other munitions. The Europeans see a less offensive role for artillery-deployed mines, seeing them largely as highly portable obstacles.

Given the offensive character of their wars, the Americans have made only limited use of their scatterable mines. In addition, by the 2003 Iraq War the use of any mines – not just anti-personnel – was controversial; this applies even to modern scatterable mines that have a pre-set self-destruct capability and so are treaty compliant. A combination of this and tactical circumstances meant that none were used. In comparison, twelve years previously in the Gulf War, the Americans deployed 118,000 artillery and air delivered landmines. The American Marines used them in response to the attack on Khafji, diverting the Iraqi forces towards defending direct and indirect fire. The Americans plan to primarily use their 155mm howitzers to deliver mines, accepting the need for continuous firing over an extended period to deliver an effective minefield. In compensation, as tube artillery is more responsive, mines can more easily be combined with manoeuvre and other fires.

Aircraft can deliver scatterable mines in greater quantity and at longer range than artillery. The Russians tend to use ground attack aircraft for this role; the SU-25 Frogfoot was the primary platform used to emplace mines on mountain tracks in the First Chechen War[108]. Helicopters conducting mine laying are usually more vulnerable, and so they are normally restricted to friendly territory.

Napalm though first used in World War Two, was most widely used in the Vietnam War[109]. In the popular imagination it has become synonymous with the conflict: '*I love the smell of napalm in the morning*[110]'. Napalm has been used against personnel, tanks, buildings, but it is against fortifications that it is at its most effective. There is no doubt as to its psychological effect against poor quality troops. The Israelis observed that '*the threat of napalm almost always aborted (sic) Egyptians from their tanks and bunkers before it actually hit*[111]'. Its lesser physical effect has led to its lethality being eclipsed by rival munitions[112]. The requirement for low-level delivery makes aircraft vulnerable. As a result, in advanced militaries the user community are largely content with ceasing to use napalm on humanitarian grounds. However, many nations retain stockpiles and it is likely to continue to be used in Developing World conflict.

In addition to napalm, specialist incendiary weapons were extensively used in World War Two, particularly against cities. Though colloquially known as bombs, they do not detonate, instead they are designed to ignite. Modern versions use a mixture of metal powder and metal oxide, which are the hottest burning man-made substances, achieving temperatures of more than 2,200 degrees centigrade, enough to burn through steel or asphalt. The Russians in June 2016 joined the Syrian government in using thermite incendiary weapons against rebel cities.

Some armies have adopted training rounds, in part for economy, but also to address the challenge posed by firing more lethal 155mm rounds onto artillery ranges originally designed for smaller munitions. These training munitions are ballistically matched to the standard round, but have a reduced quantity of high explosive, leading to less energetic fragmentation and a smaller danger area. When employed on operations, they can engage targets for which a standard high explosive round represents over-kill, delivering an equivalent capability to the air forces' low collateral damage bomb. They can also deliver greater operational safety than normal high explosive rounds when adjusting fire. This could be of use in positioning final protective fire, which is invariably within danger close distance, or in war amongst the people to avoid collateral damage. The American version is officially called the low-cost indirect training round; it is more commonly referred to as the *Smurf bullet* due to its blue colour[113].

Air forces have inert (concrete replacing high explosive) bombs to deliver point attacks whilst minimising collateral damage concerns. Another less lethal approach is the American CBU-107 Passive Attack Weapon. This is an air-dropped glide cluster bomb which dispenses 3,750 metal penetrator rods of various sizes, each individually achieving a kinetic effect. This enables the attack of targets where the use of explosives would be undesirable – such as fuel and chemical facilities – due to probable collateral damage concerns[114]. One was used successfully to destroy two roof-mounted antennae without significantly damaging the building in the Iraq War.

Electronic attack usually takes place at the operational level of war, but the selective attack of digital networks by E-Bombs – a term first coined in 1992 – is likely to be a feature of sophisticated land operations. These weapons use the burst of energy from an electromagnetic pulse (EMP) to disrupt or damage electronic equipment of digitally reliant modern militaries[115]. According to a CBS News report, the United States deployed an experimental E-Bomb on March 24, 2003 to knock out Iraqi satellite television and disrupt the broadcast of propaganda[116]. In 2015 the US confirmed that it has an operational system known as the counter-electronics high-powered microwave advanced missile project (CHAMP)[117]. The open source assessment is that E-Bombs could be made by nations capable of developing nuclear weapons, and so most advanced military powers are likely to have an undeclared capability.

The effectiveness of E-Bombs is difficult to quantify, as electronic components may be unexpectedly resistant or conversely susceptible at specific frequencies or polarisations. What is certain is that contemporary military equipment's reliance upon commercial off-the-shelf processing and networking hardware makes it significantly more vulnerable than Cold War era electronics. Vulnerable hardware would make E-Bombs effective disruptive or area-suppression weapons, not least as perhaps uniquely they can seriously degrade military capability without any loss of life[118]. Striking fielded land forces may well be the best way to limit these weapons' greatest weakness, their indiscriminate nature. If they were employed in a populous area they could inflict considerable collateral damage through the destruction of non-military digital capability. Doctrine is evolving in this area; one tactic could be an initial attack with EMP weapons to create maximum confusion, followed by attack with conventional weapons to take advantage of the immediate situation[119]. Countering these weapons can be done, but at considerable expense and in some cases the technology required cannot be practically employed by land formations[120]. Delivery systems – initially at least, given the challenge of weaponising this immature technology – are likely to be freefall bombs, glide-bombs or missiles. Something that can survive tube artillery firing pressures is probably currently impractical.

A more common form of electrical attack is the jamming of electromagnetic signals. Employing artillery and rockets to place a jammer amongst the enemy's transmitters maximises the disruption to their use of the electro-magnetic spectrum, whilst minimising the impact on own use. The size of the jammer necessitates larger calibres. The Russians have the 152mm HS30 and VRS-546 jamming round. The American 155mm jamming round is nicknamed Jabberwocky; the jammer deploys by parachute from the carrier shell, and on landing its antenna elevates to transmit its powerful broadband radio jamming.

There is ongoing development of artillery carrier munitions to deploy target acquisition sensors. An artillery-launched drone's chief advantage is that it can be rapidly deployed to the target area, and penetrate contested airspace with greater surety than a conventional unmanned aircraft. Equipping the drone with a laser designator could allow it to target designate for a follow-on salvo of laser-guided shells or rockets. The Russians are marketing a 300mm rocket containing an unmanned aerial vehicle for their Smerch multiple rocket launch system[121]. Currently there is a capability disconnect; the rocket has a range of at least 90km (56 miles), but the unmanned aerial vehicle can only transmit data to a distance of 70 kilometres (43.5 miles). Fully exploiting this technology may require satellite communications[122]. The Chinese version (AVIC Drone, from the Chengdu R&D department) is claimed to be sufficiently robust to be deployable by artillery shell. The Americans have also done some development work on an unmanned aerial vehicle launched from a 5-inch naval gun, these could offer 15-minutes worth of observation. A further option is fitting a micro aircraft within a 70mm (2.75-inch) unguided rocket pod mounted on a helicopter. The slowness in fielding this capability, despite its obvious potential, is indicative of the technical challenge of designing an unmanned aerial vehicle of sufficient size and robustness. Designing it to survive artillery firing pressures is another order of magnitude of difficulty. Despite the challenge, the ability to rapidly deploy a sensor to an area of interest, and for it to conduct target acquisition and designation, will probably lead to the fielding of this capability, and thus a further significant increase in joint fires lethality.

The reintroduction of artillery nuclear weapons, including tube artillery launched rounds, appears to be the result of the current Russian view that sees them as potentially tactical weapons. As their impact will be strategic, despite a maximum range of around 50km when launched with rocket assistance from their latest 152mm guns, discussion of these rounds will be limited to recognising their existence. One danger is the possibility of confusing them and their use with thermobaric weapons, which can have an effect similar to a a small nuclear weapon. The employment of chemical weapons should also have a strategic impact. Unfortunately, regimes such as Syria's tactical employment of them leads to the requirement for them to be covered in this study. In their weaponised form, chemical agents can be carried in rockets and shells, employing an explosive component to disperse them; or they can be used in aircraft-delivered munitions, which may just be canisters fitted with sprays and then relying upon gravity and the wind for further dispersion.

Chemical weapons were first used in World War One where they were primarily used to injure rather than kill entrenched defenders. Initially the agent was released from static canisters and relied upon the wind to move the gas clouds. The lethality of these weapons increased through the war, with mustard gas being introduced in 1917. Mustard gas did not need to form a dense cloud to be effective, so making shells and mortar bombs the most effective means of dissemination. The mortar, with its munition's large internal volume, trajectory and short range, suited attacking opposing trenches with chemicals, while the artillery took on the deeper targets. Specialist mortars, such as the 8-inch (200mm) diameter Livens projector could fire a gas cylinder containing 30 or 40lb (14 or 18kg) of lethal chemicals up to 1,900m. A battery of these projectors could create a dense concentration of gas.

Countering chemical weapons through personal protection reduces military effectiveness, hence gas shells have been extensively used to suppress opposing batteries. World War One saw the only significant contested use of chemical weapons; subsequently they have been primarily used against unprepared targets, and often against civilians. The shell and the mortar bomb have yielded to the rocket, with its superior volume, as the most effective means of dissemination. The level of lethality of individual chemical agents has increased, which for prepared troops is partly offset by superior individual and crew protection. Chemical agents can be simplistically divided into non-persistent, which is usually used against objectives to be assaulted, and persistent which can provide a long-term danger and therefore suits suppressing fixed installations. Which chemical agent to use, and how to deliver it, and whether to combine it with other joint fires munitions, are the key tactical decisions for anyone employing these illegal weapons.

Extended Range Munitions

'The North Vietnamese Army fully realised the power of the American artillery in support of infantry actions and made every attempt to use their superior range to neutralise the American guns[123]*.'*

Oscar Gilbert, Historian

The desire for greater range has been an endearing feature of warfare. The limitations of inadequate range were most apparent in World War One, when offensive rarely penetrated beyond the coverage of their emplaced artillery. This was effectively fixed by the inability of artillery and ammunition to advance across no man's land in any meaningful quantity. Subsequently, improved platform mobility reduced range's importance. In recent conflict, the Americans have proved that aggressively handled self-propelled artillery and sensors, aided by airpower, can overcome artillery with superior range[124]. Nonetheless, in almost all circumstances improved range adds to the effectiveness of artillery. Its greater coverage allows more targets to be engaged, increases the number of batteries that can be massed onto a target, and improves survivability by permitting artillery to stand further back from the front lines, thus inhibiting at least some of the enemy's means of retaliating[125].

Rockets principally achieve longer range by increasing the quantity of their fuel and so elongating their time under thrust. Increasing the quantity of fuel is more challenging for artillery and mortars, as their velocity is imparted at the very start of ballistic path – with rocket assisted shells and mortar bombs being the partial exception. Increased muzzle velocity is achieved by more powerful propelling charge that increases the gas pressure, coupled with a longer barrel to allow this to be imparted to the projectile for a longer time span. A larger chamber for the propellant and a longer barrel means increased firing stresses, this may require a complete redesign of the carriage and mountings that support the ordnance.

A more economic approach than fielding a new or redesigned gun is to improve the projectile's performance. With ballistic munitions this can be achieved in three main ways, all of which can be combined in the same projectile. First, through elongation, shells can be streamlined to improve range without reducing payload[126]. This can create a storage challenge, particularly for turret stocks in self-propelled guns. The most extreme application of this approach is the sub-calibre shell, which uses a sabot to seat a slim projectile within the barrel. The spike-like Hypervelocity Projectile of the American railgun programme has a streamline design which makes best use of its initial high velocity. The additional range it delivers is leading to it being considered as a possible munition for guns that use gunpowder instead of a massive surges of electromagnetic energy for propellant. As well as expense, its big disadvantage is its reduced lethality, due to the its tapering design leaving little room for high explosives and this being an unsuitable carrier of cluster munitions.

The second approach addresses base drag: the vacuum left behind the projectile due to its blunt base. A small generator of gas, called a base bleed, artificially reduces this aerodynamic resistance by filling this vacuum. This Swedish developed technology increases the range of artillery shells, when combined with streamlining, by about 25–30%. Its disadvantages are: expense, a loss of accuracy caused by the generator's variable burn rate and its provoking of a more turbulent airflow, and a small loss in explosive payload, which is necessary to allow the gas generator to be housed[127].

Finally, the shell can be given its own source of power through a built-in rocket motor that provides additional thrust to that provided by the propellant in the barrel. The additional thrust reduces the slowing down of the projectile due to air resistance, leading to greater range. The rocket-assisted projectile's disadvantages are the same as base bleed, but of a greater magnitude: greater expense, reduced payload and loss of accuracy. Even minor variations in ignition time and rocket power can cause variations in the projectile's trajectory, leading to greater dispersion along the line of fire. When a significantly greater range is required, the best approach is to replace a conventional rocket motor with a ramjet. This requires less propellant through employing atmospheric oxygen, and can provide ranges in excess of 90km. However, the space required for the ramjet means that with current technology almost half of the payload is lost. This technology allows cannon launched projectiles to rival the range of missile systems, and probably at reduced cost. Of course, this range plus a small warhead necessitates precision guidance; the question is whether the resultant small warhead is sufficient for likely targets.

Using conventional rocket technology, the Denel V-LAP shell when fired from a 52-calibre barrel achieves 50km, but this munition has less than half a conventional round's payload. A lesser sacrifice in payload leads to a 40km range with base bleed and 30km for a streamlined boat tail round[128]. The Russian 152mm ordnance of the 2A64 (towed) and the 2S19 (self-propelled) guns fire an unassisted shell to 24.7 km, a base bleed munition to 28.9 km[129], and rocket assisted projectile reportedly achieves 36 km[130].

The loss of accuracy in going for longer ranges can be significant. The base bleed round has in the region of an additional 50% greater circular error probability than an unassisted shell when both are at maximum range. A rocket-assisted projectile has approximately another 50% greater dispersion than the base bleed shell[131]. The following rough order of accuracy should be expected:

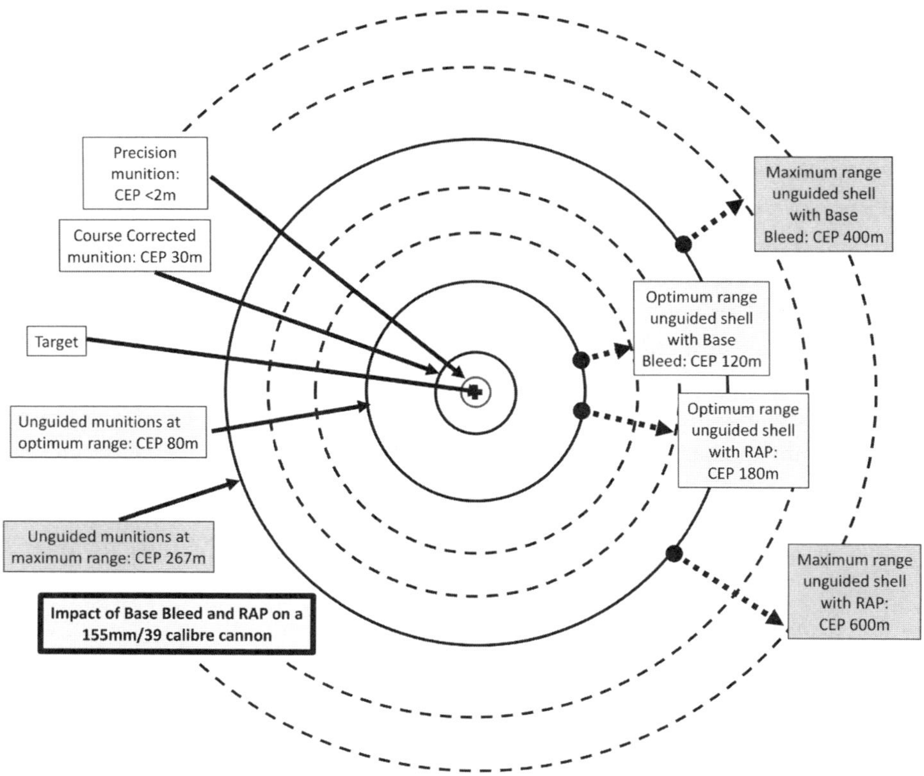

Streamlining subsonic mortar bombs has a reduced ability to increase range. Base bleed is a practical option for rifled but not fin stabilised mortars; rocket assistance can be used with all mortar bombs. It provides a means to extend range beyond 10km whilst preserving the advantages of the mortar bomb remaining subsonic. Without the restrictions imposed on tube artillery by breech loading, shot seating and chamber size, a bespoke rocket assisted mortar bomb can be significantly longer, providing space for a large motor without sacrificing the warhead. This led to the US Marine Corps' RT 120/M327 mortar's standard range of 8.2km increasing to 17km with the Dragon Fire Precision Extended Range Munition. Bespoke guided cannon and mortar munitions also can exploit gliding to extend their range. The Dragon Fire munition employs rocket-assistance plus folding glide fins (like the Excalibur) to provide lift from its trajectory apex to the target. Making gliding the fourth means of extending range.

Employing base bleed and rocket assisted munitions creates inaccuracy that could be avoided through using a longer barrel and a larger chamber to achieve a higher muzzle velocity with conventional munitions. Long range munitions financially appear to have considerable merit when compared to fielding a new or redesigned gun. It is an approach that is particularly attractive in peacetime, although the wartime expenditure of munitions may make it a false economy.

Currently combining all these technologies requires considerable loss of warhead payload; in the future a single 'motor' combining base bleed and rocket assistance will become common; this could control a propellant's output by varying its burn rate, initially to provide thrust through to the top of its ballistic flight path, before switching to a base-bleed effect to reduce drag for the remainder of the flight[132]. This combined motor could double the range of the standard projectile, without further significantly increasing the loss of payload. Rather than these being bespoke shells, the greatest logistical and tactical flexibility could be achieved through being able to affix a combined rocket/base bleed unit onto a standard shell. The standard high explosive shell could be designed to allow such a unit to be screwed onto its base. This is the route being followed by the South Koreans with their 155mm NAMMO High Explosive Extended Range round.

Long range fire, without a form of terminal guidance, results in a level of dispersion that compromises tube artillery effectiveness and prevents it from providing danger close fire support. Base bleed and rocket assistance are significant contributors to dispersion; without adopting terminal guidance, the most effective approach to most close support tasks is a 52-calibre barrel with modern streamlined shells. For longer ranges, a screw-on base bleed or combined base bleed/rocket assistance, with a course correction fuze – if this can be made resilient to jamming and spoofing – offers the best approach. This may be conservative, but it arguably better suits tube artillery's place within the joint fires system-of-systems as the primary means of fire support. It certainly is at odds with the current American approach of seeking to double the range of their tube artillery, which leads to a time of fight of four to five minutes[133]. It is difficult to envisage coordinating fire and manoeuvre with such a time of flight, hence their interest in hypervelocity projectiles.

Chapter 13: Target Acquisition

'If you have imprecise locations or if you just know there's enemy force out there, but you don't have them accurately located, precision doesn't help you much'[1].

General Eric Shinseki, US Army

In the land domain, intelligence, surveillance and reconnaissance collection assets have two main roles: first, to assist with understanding the battlespace in order to effectively direct overall military operations; second, to identify specific points to achieve decisive effect; in conventional warfare, this mainly consists of identifying targets to engage with firepower. This makes target acquisition the detection, identification, and location of a target in sufficient detail to permit the effective employment of lethal and non-lethal means. The air domain does not have such a rigid distinction, as the understand function is largely synonymous with target acquisition; put simplistically understanding where to drop bombs or shoot-down aircraft. The land commander's natural inclination is to emphasise the improvement of his situational awareness through achieving greater understanding of the environment. Or as the Duke of Wellington put it:

'All the business of war, and indeed all the business of life, is to endeavour to find out what you don't know by what you do; that's what I called "guessing what was at the other side of the hill"[2]*.'*

Implicit in the Iron Duke's approach was the acceptance of uncertainty, necessitating the requirement for intuitive deductions from what is known. The promise of technology can seduce modern commanders into expecting greater certainty. Academically this is being addressed, restating the Clausewitzian requirement to tolerate and even to exploit uncertainty[3].

Despite emphasising peer warfighting some Western armies continue to organise their collection and analytical assets primarily around the understand function. This has led to the dropping of target acquisition in the specific description of this activity[4]. Target acquisition is usually a more challenging task than providing information that improves general understanding. Focussing on the understand function leads to intelligence exploitation by continuing to observe, or cue another sensor onto the target; this approach rarely needs to be as time sensitive as when attacking a target, nor do the sensors need to be as accurate, or be accredited for target engagement. Airmen and artillerymen can be criticised for taking a target-orientated perspective, but this approach focuses individual sensors, and the overall target acquisition system, on the timely identifying of discrete targets to achieve a military effect.

With modern weapons, accurately acquiring a target is usually more challenging than actually hitting the target. For weapons designed to engage an area target, a general location of a target is often sufficient, even if the enemy is no longer in view, as the distribution of fire will usually achieve the desired suppressive effect. In comparison, theoretically more effective individually terminally guided precision weapons can be restricted in their utility by the need for an exact location of a still-visible target. This is why area weapon systems are often more effective in the fog and friction of the conventional battlefield than precision weapons. The exception being sensor-fuzed munitions; these require a similar target location accuracy as area weapons, they then individually identify and engage their targets.

Of course, the lethal area of a weapon system can overcome a certain level of target location inaccuracy. This means a 2,000-lb bomb does not need the same level of target accuracy as a 500-lb Small Diameter Bomb to achieve the same effect. In the Iraq War, F-15s used targeting data from the E-8C JSTARS to launch GPS-guided bombs during a sandstorm. The JSTARS radar is a coarse-grain sensor, but given the target size and the employment of 2,000lb bombs, this was effective. Of course, this approach is unsuitable when there are collateral damage concerns, or within the danger close distance of friendly forces. Minimising the chance of collateral damage can lead to the requirement for multiple-source positive identification, and continuous observation of the target area prior to engagement. The dominance of this approach in recent counter-insurgency operations has led some Western militaries, and their political masters, to assume that this standard of target acquisition fidelity can apply to all characters of conflict.

Development of Technical Target Acquisition

'Whereas the [Russian] Armed Forces had only 180 UAV [unmanned aerial vehicles] Systems in 2011, now we have 1,720 state-of-the-art UAVs[5]*'.*

Russian Defense Minister, General
Sergei Shoygu 11 December 2015

Indirect fire transferred target acquisition from the naked eye, possibly assisted by a telescope or binoculars, at the gun position, to an observer at a suitable vantage point. Improving the observer's command of the ground led to balloons, and then to other aerial vehicles. Balloons did not challenge the existing means of communications; exploiting the capability of the aircraft necessitated the development of wireless communications. Interim measures were the order of the day in the Great War, until technology caught up with the requirement. In World War One, the main challenge was passing the target information from the aircraft to the guns. By the next World War, the challenge had shifted to passing target information to aircraft, as aircraft had ceased being largely a user of artillery firepower to becoming the deliverer of much of the ground battle's firepower. Effective, but still fragile and thus unreliable, radio communications in World War Two largely solved the ground-to-air communication challenge, and made possible the overall transformation of joint fires' command and control[6].

Except for poorly sited guns – not behind a hill or similar cover – standard visual means of target acquisition in the counter battery battle were redundant once artillery had withdrawn from the contact zone. Spotting the muzzle flash of guns could lead to their geo-location through triangulation by taking bearings from more than one observer. Sound ranging could detect a firing battery regardless of its cover and concealment. This relied upon a series of microphones (usually 4 to 6) producing a bearing to the source of the sound, the intersection of these bearing being the firing battery's location. Supplementing these methods was the rapidly developing signal intelligence – the direction finding of a radio signal, and its triangulation to determine a target location. It was in the reconnaissance and target acquisition role that aircraft made its most decisive contribution to the World War One land battle. Despite the popular image of World War One militaries, this featured from the start of the conflict: the British first used aircraft to find artillery targets at the Aisne on 13 September 1914. By 1917, 90% of the identification of previously un-located hostile battery observation was done by aircraft using wireless communications[7]. Air photography to identify depth positions rapidly became indispensable. An effective ground forces concealment policy, ideally with air superiority over the battlefield, was essential to maintaining the element of surprise.

Except for the introduction of weapon locating radars in its last year, World War Two target acquisition relied upon further developing existing capabilities – though these were often significantly improved through leveraging civilian know-how[8]. Except on the Eastern Front, the balloon observation platform was largely replaced by light aircraft. The Anglo-Americans employed them in such quantities (ten aircraft per American division, plus more at corps level), that when operations were relatively static, they could maintain persistent daylight and fair-weather observation over the enemy's entire forward areas. By the later stages of the campaigns in Italy and Western Europe, total air supremacy, allowed the unarmed L-5 observation aircraft to range up to five miles behind enemy lines[9]. The main threat to these aircraft came from ground based air defences, leading to anti-flak patrols being used to preserve their ability to provide continuous observation[10].

When battle lines were more fluid, long-range ground reconnaissance patrols could be inserted behind enemy lines. This usually occurred during rapid advances, or where lower force density ratios prevented continuous front lines. The World War Two Soviets led in this area, making extensive use of specialist reconnaissance forces, often in cooperation with partisans, to identify depth targets. In the Western Desert campaign, the open flank provided opportunities for a host of embryonic special operations forces. These focussed on raiding, and rarely achieved the level of integration into the operational level plan that was standard in the Soviet way of war.

Target acquisition radars made a minor impact in the final months of World War Two – they controlled 9% of the American XV Corps' corps-level artillery missions in February 1945. Nonetheless, their effectiveness demonstrated that they would become the primary counter-battery sensor, providing superior persistence, coverage, accuracy and reliability than aircraft, flash spotting and sound ranging. These advantages resulted from its all-weather electromagnetic waves that detect a projectile's trajectory once it has risen above ground clutter[11]. Modern radars achieve a circular error probability of around 0.3–0.4% of range. At best, sound ranging achieves half this accuracy, and this is highly dependent on meteorological conditions.

The radar's chief disadvantage is of course that it actively emits. Against peer opposition, they are more survivable when cued by a passive system, and only emit when there are firing batteries to locate. In irregular warfare, weapon locating radars can permanently emit. This leads insurgents to fire their rockets from close range, to confuse the radar track with ground clutter, and through a short time of flight reduce the target's available response time. Alternatively, the irregular fighter can engage outside the 90-degree arc of surveillance of most radar systems which are designed for conventional operations. Reflecting the need for all-round coverage, the American Army is rationalising its holdings down to two 360-degree systems. They are a lightweight, Humvee-mounted radar and a more sophisticated truck mounted long-range system that in conventional warfare will normally operate on a 120-degree arc to provide range and accuracy[12]. A detection arc of 120-degrees is now replacing 90-degrees as the industry standard: examples are the Israeli EL/M-2084 3D S-band AESA radars and the latest versions of Saab's Arthur radar. The American approach is almost certainly the most appropriate capability response, but most advanced armies have not invested in expensive dual purpose radars, instead optimising for linear conventional warfare. Alternatively, air defence radars, which are usually not required in their primary role in counter-insurgency operations, can deliver a 360-degree coverage. These are capable of acquiring the usual insurgent weapons – rockets and mortars[13] – at short range. The Saab Giraffe radar has been extensively used in this role in Iraq and Afghanistan. As has the radar of the German Modular, Automatic and Network-capable, Targeting and Interception system, without its 35mm guns, on the UN mission in Mali.

Following World War Two, the helicopter largely replaced fixed wing aircraft in providing artillery air observation posts; its ability to operate from a gun position was recognised as a key advantage[14]. The shift to helicopters was accelerated by counter-insurgency conflicts, because without a front line, spotter aircraft were vulnerable to inadvertently flying over enemy ground troops[15]. Unfortunately for the employment of joint fires, most army aviation now sees the air observation as a very secondary role. Reacting to the demands of conventional warfighting, the Americans in the 2003 Iraq War placed a fire support officer in the second seat of a helicopter. The need to restore conventional warfighting capability is seeing a restoration of artillery spotting in Western militaries through qualifying aircrew. The same driver is restoring the airborne forward air control capability.

The manned aircraft is now losing its target acquisition role to unmanned aircraft. They have become the most versatile means of surveillance in land operations. The Israelis pioneered the operational use of unmanned aircraft in 1982, where they were instrumental in delivering targeting information for the subsequent destruction of the Syrian air defences. The NATO bombing of the former Yugoslavia saw the first large-scale use of unmanned aerial vehicles with near real-time sensors. The next significant milestone was the Russo-Ukraine conflict, this being contested between fleets of unmanned aircraft[16]. Hezbollah has the first substantive non-state actor capability. It fields around 200 unmanned aircraft; ranging from Iranian and Chinese versions of armed Reapers that fly from prepared strips, through to small quadcopters.

At the tactical level these unmanned platforms primarily mount electro-optic sensors, providing imagery for immediate use by the operator, and for subsequent intelligence exploitation. The most sophisticated systems can achieve sufficiently accurate target acquisition for first-round area fire engagement. Commercial off the shelf quadcopters can provide a stable target acquisition platform. In contrast, cheap fixed wing aerial vehicles can rarely provide an accurate target location. These less sophisticated systems usually cue another sensor to control an engagement, hence the popularity of a mix of unmanned aircraft.

Unmanned aerial vehicles geographically separate the sensor from the observer. This separation also occurs in aerostats and mast-mounted sensors; these have proved effective in delivering wide area surveillance in relatively static counter-insurgency conflicts. In addition to providing target acquisition, they also conduct intelligence gathering and achieve a considerable deterrence effect. These technologies could assist with the defence of static facilities from a range of threats in conventional war. Remotely sited cameras also provide safe and effective surveillance of potential target areas, leading to their use by specialist observation teams.

Air and space surveillance platforms have significantly improved the ability of land forces to see behind the hill. Satellites provide unrivalled coverage. Air-breathing platforms are timelier and more responsive to land forces' tactical needs. Airborne radars, such as the joint surveillance target attack radar system (JSTARS), provide all weather, day/night and theatre-wide situational awareness. Modern target pods on fighter-bombers can provide an equivalent capability to the most sophisticated unmanned aircraft, but of course they lack their persistence. Ground forces can see the imagery feed of airborne sensors through capabilities such as the American ROVER system. With both ground forces and aircrew seeing the same imagery, they can agree on where aerial firepower is applied. Getting this wrong could dislocate a campaign; as the Djakovica incident almost did in the Kosovo Conflict[17].

Networking sensors can significantly improve sensor effectiveness through fusing and overlaying the same series of images; it also allows multiple users to view and exploit the same imagery. Sharing imagery is bandwidth intensive; currently for most militaries it requires static communication infrastructure, as in recent in counter-insurgency operations. The experience of recent conflict is that sharing, overlaying and fusing of sensors is a more efficient approach than simply investing in additional sensors. This can provide the high level of certainty required by Western nations when employing firepower in war amongst the people. During high tempo conventional operations, forces are less likely to have the bandwidth to access this information. Furthermore, in peer conflict greater autonomy and redundancy between sensors might prove more survivable.

Despite these advances in technical target acquisition, the weapon ranges of organic land strike systems have kept ahead of their organic sensors. This discrepancy between the range and target acquisition capability has existed since the 1980s:

> *'The chief shortcoming of ATACMS [Army TACtical Missile System] in the Gulf [War] was the dearth of deep eyes capable of spotting a lucrative target with sufficient precision and timeliness to justify expending a missile*[18]*.'*

Exploiting the maximum range of such systems depends upon air-based sensors or long-range weapon locating radars. The key challenge for surface sensors is the curvature of the earth, which is why radars that detect the trajectory of the projectile, rather than the weapon's firing point, remain effective at range. Elevating the sensor overcomes the intervisibility challenge. Unfortunately for long range army weapons, the air components tend to favour employing their own assets, employing a simpler single service sensor-decider-shooter linkage, and an established battle damage assessment process. Of course, allocating these land systems to the air component can make them more usable. Despite the challenges, many armies see the need for long-range rockets; the American Army sees the requirement to fire beyond 500km. This is the purpose of the Long Range Precision Fires program, the replacement of the ATACMS. Their strategic long range cannon aims at a range of 1000km.

The Role of Manoeuvre Forces in Target Acquisition

> *'In 1944, before the offensive of the First Ukrainian Front, fifty reconnaissances in force were carried out between 1 May and 12 July, as well three hundred lesser raids and detailed sketches were furnished to all units*[19]*.'*
>
> Raymond L Garthoff, Historian

Despite the advances in technology, and the understandable desire to conduct standoff engagement, manoeuvre forces often prove to be the best means of acquiring and fixing targets. In the Vietnam War, the Americans knew this approach as 'infantry finds, artillery kills[20]'. Despite its proven worth, in that war, such was the surfeit of fire over manoeuvre, that much of American firepower was used without bothering with effective target acquisition. As General Bailey, historian and soldier, identified:

> *'The surest way to identify a target is to make ground contact, to manoeuvre in order to apply fire, yet only 15% of artillery ammunition fired and 4% of bombs dropped in Vietnam were in support of friendly ground actions*[21]*.'*

Joint fires terminal controllers are primarily seen as the means of providing fire support to combined arms manoeuvre, but they can also exploit the target acquisition opportunities resulting from their permanent presence with ground forces.

The World War Two Soviets ruthlessly exploited ground manoeuvre to expose the Germans to their firepower. Specialist reconnaissance forces were sited to observe the preliminary attacks made by disposable penal battalions. These aimed at provoking a response, thus identifying the main defensive positions, unmasking defending artillery and provoking reserve formations to give away their positions. The secondary purpose was to clear away outposts, so allowing Soviet artillery to be sited in range of depth positions. The Soviet aim was to identify at least 70% of their targets prior to their main attack. Identifying the location of German artillery was the most important task. Marshal Zhukov explained to Stalin that an attack on 5 September 1942 failed:

> *'Because we did not have enough time to prepare the offensive and reconnoitre the enemy's artillery positions and therefore could not aim our preparatory fire effectively*[22]*.'*

The Russians continue to task their manoeuvre forces to achieve target acquisition. This is despite the impressive strides made in their technical target acquisition capability, in particular their airborne sensors. On the Donbas, seeking to avoid casualties rather than closing with the enemy, they have often used their ground forces to find and fix the Ukrainians for fire strikes.

Western militaries place greater reliance on technical target acquisition, but their ground forces have also provided the fixing force for the application of firepower. However, this is usually more challenging to achieve than in the Soviet/Russian combined arms battle, as the Western airpower-dominated deep battle is usually temporally and spatially separate from ground operations. The relative failure of NATO airpower in conflicts since the Gulf War has encouraged a more integrated approach between ground forces and aerial firepower; the need to cooperate was reinforced by the failure of largely-airborne target acquisition technology to identify whole Iraqi divisions in the 2003 Iraq War, until they came into contact with Coalition ground forces:

> *'[t]he ability of Iraqis to hide, with some success, from the incredible array of technical intelligence available to the coalition may give pause to those advocating that US forces will be able to develop the situation out of contact and attack from standoff distances*[23]*'.*

This is of course the norm in counter-insurgency, where the guerrillas can usually evade detection until they initiate an engagement. Whatever the character of conflict and the sophistication of sensors, the failure to identify targets until they come into contact with ground forces is likely to continue to be inevitable given war's friction and fog. Therefore, there may be merit in following the Russian approach and formally integrating into the operational design the employment of manoeuvre forces in the target acquisition role.

Contrasting Western and Russian Target Acquisition Approaches

> *'The operation of forcing Georgia into peace showed that we need more effective "battlefield" drones, ones that are capable of not only looking over the nearest hill, but also of seeing dozens of kilometres ahead, giving exact coordinates of targets and allowing them to be targeted not only by the means at our direct disposal, but also by artillery systems that are located 70–100 kilometres away*[24]*.'*
>
> Col-Gen Vladimir Shamanov, Commander of the Airborne Troops

Western intelligence collection and analytical capabilities have been honed in counter-insurgency operations, leading to a focus on the human environment and the acquisition of individual human targets in complex terrain. In contrast, the Russians have retained a more traditional approach, limiting their target acquisition's fidelity to the level required to make firepower effective. They couple this with an emphasis upon surveillance of the whole depth of the enemy's position. This emphasis leads to the Missile Troops and Artillery controlling most army sensors, including unmanned aerial vehicles. Their standard allocation of sensor assets being: 60% acquiring targets for artillery, 35% finding targets for aircraft and the remaining 5% to direct support of ground troops. The current role of the Missile and Artillery Troops is entirely consistent with their Great Patriotic War predecessors:

'to perform efficient and reliable reconnaissance to the full depth of the enemy defence 24 hours a day under any weather conditions; to contribute to the commander's estimation of the situation; to provide mobile, flexible and accurate fire support; to perform accurate and complete destruction of any targets to the full depth of the enemy defence[25]'.

Russia's greater tolerance of collateral damage means that there is less emphasis on accuracy, and they rarely conduct pattern of life surveillance. They seek instead to maximise, to a mathematical certainty, target destruction. This willingness to be less discriminating allowed the Russian Air Force in Syria in 2016 to achieve more weapon releases than the more numerous American-led Coalition[26]. They achieved immediate physical and psychological impact by employing the massed firepower of unguided weapons. Precision weapons were reserved for high priority point targets where accuracy was essential in achieving destruction. Battle damage assessment was seen as a lesser priority.

This target-focussed approach noticeably reduces the demands upon the Russian reconnaissance-intelligence-strike complex. At the tactical level, the information from thermal, radar, acoustic, and visual spectrum sensors is manually fed into battery and battalion level artillery command and reconnaissance vehicles. This is the gateway into the digital fire control system; this system processes this information into targets and determines which weapon systems will engage. This 'swivel chairing' alleviates the need for unmanned aircraft to have the current digital fire control system[27]. The Russians see this as an interim measure; the company developing the next systems (the Uralvagonzavod Corporation) intend to integrate target information produced by unmanned aircraft direct into the digital fire control system[28].

The Russians have not fielded armed unmanned aircraft, but they are expected to from 2021. They see the direct cueing of tube and rocket artillery fire strikes as delivering significantly greater combat power than the few missiles unmanned aircraft can carry. Being unarmed means that that Russian aircraft can carry either more fuel to increase their endurance or superior sensors, both increasing the chance of target acquisition.

The other key difference with the West is Russia's institutional approach to counter-surveillance. Termed *maskarovska*, this is a key component of their system of war and they see it as applicable to all characters of conflict. Western armies are having to relearn this discipline following their years of counter-insurgency. As General McMaster identifies:

'Look at the enemy [the Russians in Ukraine] countermeasures … dispersion, concealment, intermingling with civilian populations … the ability to disrupt our network strike capability, precision navigation and timing capabilities[29].'

Russian sensor technology was certainly found wanting in the 2008 conflict with Georgia, leading to the rapid fielding of a range of unmanned aircraft. These benefitted from the latest

Israeli drone technology. These are fielded in a single company per all arms and artillery brigade; these companies are divided into platoons based upon a single type of aircraft[30]. Following their inability to suppress Georgian artillery, the Russians have modernised, and their modern weapon locating equipment matches Western ones in terms of range and the accuracy of detections. While Russian electronic warfare equipment may not be as good as the best Western technology, like their other target acquisition capability, it benefits from scale and being a permanent part of all-arms and artillery brigades. This means that the Russians may be more effective at integrating their find capability into all-arms operations than Western armies. They are almost certainly better at striking targets.

Target Location Accuracy in the Close Battle

'the biggest problem I've got in the Field Artillery is target location. 10 or 15 years ago, our average target location error at NTC [National Training Centre] was 270 metres. We worked hard and got it down to 250 metres. Ask yourselves, how, with all of the equipment we've got out there, are we still at 250 metres? It gets back to the training strategy. We teach people to guess grids and adjust fire. It is changing[31].'

Major General McDonald, Commanding General
US Fires Centre of Excellence, 2013

Improving target location accuracy is an objective for all joint fire disciplines. This does not mean that all disciplines have been equally enthused at improving 'first round accuracy'. For aircraft 'first round accuracy' is the only accuracy that matters; this is not the case for artillery and mortars, as they routinely adjust rounds or bombs onto the target. Once this is achieved, subsequent rounds are consistently delivered to a given area. This is unlike aerial engagements, when aircraft individually engage their target[32]. This leads to a tension for artillery and mortar men between quickly getting 'rounds on the ground' so they can be adjusted onto the target, and a more considered approach that accounts for all the technical variables. The former approach is favoured by much of the mortar community, in particular when these weapons are infantry operated. Historically most field artillery has favoured speed in opening fire, followed by bold adjustments, over maximising first round accuracy. The employers of longer range guns, with their origin in siege and coastal gunnery, have favoured a more deliberate approach. It was the more technical British Royal Garrison Artillery who in World War One led on the Battle of Cambrai's wholly predicted fire plan. This became the norm in deliberate fire plans, but for more impromptu fire support, adjusting the fire onto the target often dominates. Of course, accurately hitting a point on the ground with artillery fire is a measure of performance. The only true measure of effectiveness is a target ceasing to offer effective resistance due to firepower either achieving suppression or destruction.

Technical advances have addressed or reduced most of the inaccuracy in the joint fires system, leaving the terminal controller's determination of a target's location as the last remaining major source of inaccuracy. The challenge being to be accurate in the hurly-burly of the contact battle. When a cannon battalion fires its standard distribution, the observer's target location error needs to be less than 250m for the rounds to have any effect[33]. Observers deriving inaccurate target locations is generally accepted as the major cause of ineffective target engagement, but there is a lack of recent empirical evidence. The mean target location error was 500m for all exercises at the American National Training Centre in the 1970s and 1980s[34]. This resulted in only a third of predicted fire plans and opportunity target engagements being sufficiently accurate to achieve any effect. From 1988 more artillery was employed on the exercise, making firepower more effective, despite failing to improve accuracy.

The US Artillery has halved the mean first round accuracy error since the 1980s, but, as can be seen from General McDonald's opening quote, they are struggling to deliver further improvement. This is not to say that the Americans are uniquely poor at first round accuracy. It is the product of their highly realistic training regime that replicates the fog and friction of real conflict; this is in contrast to some other militaries, whose tactical training is closer in character to a highly rehearsed demonstration. With observers engaging predetermined targets whose location is known to 8-figure grid reference, or 10m, accuracy.

A slightly later study on the utilisation of mortars at the National Training Centre concluded that for them first round accuracy was not their greatest problem. Instead it was an inability to subsequently adjust fire onto the target, and a failure to correctly utilise and integrate mortars into the manoeuvre plan. The latter was evidenced by the failure to expend their first line ammunition scaling in training. As this was calculated from operational experience, this is likely to better reflect the quantity of fire required for combat success than the training being conducted[35].

The forward air controller's target location challenge can be significantly reduced by passing on the task to the aircraft. With the controller directing the aircraft into the target area, this allows the aircrew to identify the target and conduct the engagement using their own sensors and possibly their own designator. However, talking an aircraft on to a target is unlikely to be a safe option in contested airspace, as aircraft survivability will probably necessitate a standoff engagement. For this an accurate target localition is required. This could involve a ground observer laser designating the target, or employing precision point mensuration to provide an accurate target location for coordinate-seeking munitions.

Technical aids to improve target location usually rely upon improving the bearing and distance calculation from the observer's location to the target. The observer's location is easily determined by GPS; differential GPS, through making successive observations, can further improve this accuracy over time. The cheap and light digital magnetic compass achieves reasonably accurate orientation. Alternatively a resection using terrestrial or stellar (the sun and stars) reference points can achieve greater accuracy. However, the observation of these reference points cannot be guaranteed, and it is also time consuming, making it only suitable for static observation posts. Inertial navigation systems sense the rotation of the earth, determine true north and then convert this into a very accurate grid north. This technology suits mobile operations, but the inertial navigation system's major disadvantages are weight and bulk. Measuring the distance to the target is accurately done by a laser range finder[36].

Current equipment achieves sufficient accuracy for area mortar and artillery fire if a target is in line of sight of a laser range finder. But precision level accuracy (to the nearest metre) requires equipment that is too currently heavy for on-the-man usage. The current alternative to computing a target location from a known point using a bearing and distance is to use precision point mensuration of pre-stored imagery. Of course, this is dependent upon the target location coinciding with a feature on the ground that can be identified on the imagery. This is not an issue in urban operations, but this is a major limitation in warfare in open terrain. In addition, conducting precision point mensuration will often be too slow in the contact battle.

Seeking to improve accuracy, the US Artillery introduced the 80-10-10 targeting standards[37]. These numbers state, as a percentage, the time that a terminal controller should spend training to achieve the required NATO target location standard, defined by categories (Cat) of target location error (TLE)[38]. As can be seen, when the standard was set the technology only partly supported the aspiration, with the weakest element being the on-the-man equipment[39]:

Criteria	Precision Target Grid	Near Precision Target Grid	Non-Precision Target Grid
Frequency	80%	10%	10%
Accuracy	10m TLE (Threshold) Cat 2 6m TLE (Objective) Cat 1	50m TLE Cat 4	200m TLE Cat 5/6
Current Systems	Static and vehicle mounted precision point mensuration or highly accurate laser, orientation and own position fixation.	Older generation static and vehicle systems and the newer on the man equipment.	Reversionary mode: Binoculars, Map, Compass and Protractor.

Delivering a target location error of less than 10m circular error probability can only be achieved when in a static observation post or with precision point mensuration. Achieving the accuracy to fully exploit precision munitions is more challenging in a constantly moving armoured vehicle, and by a dismounted observer given the weight challenge. As well as the technical limitations of the current equipment, the forward observer also faces institutional challenges. These have led to 20 to 30 minutes being required to mensurate a target, because coordinates had to be checked and re-checked by the fire support chain of command before permission was given to shoot a precision munition[40]. This can make this pursuit of accuracy unsuitable for the time-sensitive close battle.

In contrast to their gun position's scientific approach, forward observers tend to be technology averse. Until recently British dismounted observers rarely used anything more than hand-held binoculars together with a projector placed on a map. This is despite being issued with: ground surveillance radar (fielded in 1975), laser range finder and image intensifier night observation device (1976), position and azimuth determining system to deliver inertial navigation (1981) and thermal imagers (1990). This reticence is partly a response to their weight, which largely limits their use to static observation posts. As an example, the American Lightweight Laser Designator Range-Finder, which was fielded in the late 1990s, weighed nearly 32-pds or 14kg. Another deterrent was the restrictions on the use of lasers in training before they were fielded with eye safe modes. But the major factor is that technology will never be able to eliminate target acquisition error in the close battle.

In actual close combat targets rarely remain in the open, so preventing their distance being measured by laser range finders. Precision point mensuration, as well as being too slow – unless this is pre-planned – is reliant upon fixed infrastructure on the ground and in the imagery data base. This makes it extremely effective at the start of urban conflict, and useless once firepower has changed the landscape. Target acquisition in the close battle will remain as much as an art as a science, with terminal controllers exercising judgement in determining likely target locations. An inability to precisely locate most targets, plus the primary purpose of firepower being suppression, means that the engagement of area targets will continue to dominate the contact battle. So while the 80-10-10 targeting standard, or 'grid getting standard' correctly seeks to embrace a shift in culture towards precision, it should not be seen as defining in the provision of fire support in the close battle.

Chapter 14: Company Level Fire Support Elements and Terminal Fire Control

'The issue at the NTC [National Training Centre] is not field artillery, it's fire support – the full integration of manoeuvre with fires … Field artillery is exceptionally good at sending rounds down range and hitting the right point on the ground. The piece we don't do well is to put rounds on a specific target at exactly the right time and event in the battle[1].'

Brigadier General Carter, when he was the
US Army's NTC Commanding General, 1992

In the close battle, fire support elements operating with the infantry and armour execute most of the target engagement, and enable the coordination of fire and manoeuvre. As the opening quote identifies, fire support is the greater challenge. This they achieve through: informing the manoeuvre commander of the joint fire capabilities, influencing the manoeuvre plan, and then ensuring that firepower is integrated into its execution. Many armies see the provision of fire support as beyond the capacity of the artillery personnel they provide to support each company, expecting them to restrict themselves to engaging targets. This clear division of responsibility is rarely possible in actual combat.

More traditional armies restrict the permanent allocation of fire support elements to the battalion level, with companies receiving only *ad hoc* support. This approach can be effective in large-scale warfighting – when most fire support can be pre-planned – but when fire support needs to be decentralised and more responsive, companies need their own fire support elements. Armies that employ terminal controllers at platoon level employ them almost solely in the terminal control role. To simplify this analysis, observers at platoon level are considered to be part of the company fire support system.

There is national variation in the size of company fire support elements. Some teams are too small to carry the equipment that enables 24/7 surveillance, let alone sustain continuous observation. The commander's rank varies between sergeant and captain. Seniority usually translates into greater empowerment to control firepower and conduct fire support. This often reflects as much a military's culture or tradition as any conscious force design considerations. The Americans traditionally favour small teams commanded by junior officers, seeing their company level fires element as assisting the company commander, the designated fire support officer, with technical advice. The Commonwealth of Nations approach employs larger teams commanded by captains. The role of Western forward air controllers has been effectively standardised through the dominance of US airpower and NATO policy. But the rank can vary from corporal to commissioned officer. Mortar fire control is usually provided by one or two sergeants or corporals attached to each rifle company. These are usually empowered to fire at least a section of two or three tubes, and can be further authorised to employ the whole platoon.

All these joint fires observers tend to stand out as targets. This stems from their technical and tactical challenge, the unique signature of their equipment, and their striving for good observation. Attacking terminal fire controllers has often proved to be easiest way of dislocating the opposing fire support system. The Chechens, like many irregular force, lacked a significant counter battery or air defence capability, hence they targeted Russian terminal controllers. This included impersonating Russian controllers, to misdirect close air support missions; more directly they systematically engaged forward air controllers with snipers[2].

In most Western militaries, aviation is the only form of fire support where the terminal controller lacks the power to authorise an engagement, instead attack and armed helicopters engage on their own authority. This was not the case in the Vietnam War, when some helicopters were under a unified centralised divisional fire support system; the change partly reflects aviation's institutional independence. Arguably there is no logical rationale for maintaining these distinctions, but both the American Army and Air Force are determined to continue maintaining the difference between fixed-wing and rotary fire support that they formally articulated in 1975:

> *[The attack helicopter's role is] '... integral to the Army ground manoeuvre unit and an extension of organic firepower ... the attack helicopter does not perform CAS but is intended to complement Air Force CAS capabilities[3].'*

In contrast, the US Marine Corps and the Israelis have both their helicopters and fighter-bombers controlled by the same close air support procedures. Informally in combat, regardless of origin, aviation has regularly engaged using close air support procedures.

Artillery and Mortar Terminal Control

> *'According to French doctrine [in 1940], forward observers did not have to accompany the unit being supported. They remained to the rear, observing from a vantage point ... Apparently the unit being supported had little influence over the artillery fires it received[4].'*
>
> Robert A Doughty, Historian

In World War One, continuous observation was met by rotating battery officers and soldiers through the battery's single forward observation post. Due to the unreliability of communications with the guns, the technical and tactical responsibilities of these observers were often limited to calling for pre-arranged defensive or SOS fire. On the offensive, anchor observation posts tried to ensure that the firepower was correctly executed in accordance with the fire plan. But battlefield obscuration usually prevented these observers from judging whether the barrage was actually supporting the infantry. Observers moving forward with the infantry usually knew what support was required, but as they were rarely in communication with the guns, so they were equally unable to ensure effective fire support.

Between the wars, advances in wireless communication allowed fire support to be better tailored to the needs of manoeuvre. Not all armies in World War Two chose to exploit the opportunity for greater flexibility – in 1940, the French Army had reverted to their rigid artillery practices of 1915–17. This probably stemmed from inadequate peacetime combined arms training, leading to the substituting of the delivery of firepower in accordance with the fire plan as the main training objective, rather than meeting the needs of the infantry.

In their set piece attacks, the Soviets expected their infantry and armour to match their movement to the fire plan. Positions unsuppressed by the fire plan became the responsibility of accompanying direct fire weapons, rather than triggering adjustment to the artillery fire plan. With this limited role, each battery usually had only a single static observation post, with the battery commander directing the fire. Despite doctrine insisting on the co-locating of artillery and infantry commanders, the Soviets identified inter-arm cooperation as their greatest weakness[5].

The American and British in World War Two developed different systems to exploit the fire mobility made possible by portable radios. The American approach was to request fire through providing target information, with most of the fire support decisions being made in a fire direction centre. They believed this offered superior decision-making through being able to take a broader and more considered view, usually with access to superior information. The British generally favoured trusting the man-on-the-spot to determine the manoeuvre arm's fire support requirement. This included allowing senior forward observers to engage with all of the divisional fire assets. These observers usually held the rank of major, while standard parties were led by captains[6]. Both armies expected their officers to use their initiative to modify fire plans to support manoeuvre; this could include shifting the fire plan's superimposed batteries onto opportunity targets, as well as extending or curtailing serials of the fire plan. The different approaches can be understood by comparing the purpose of the fire and the authority of the observer:

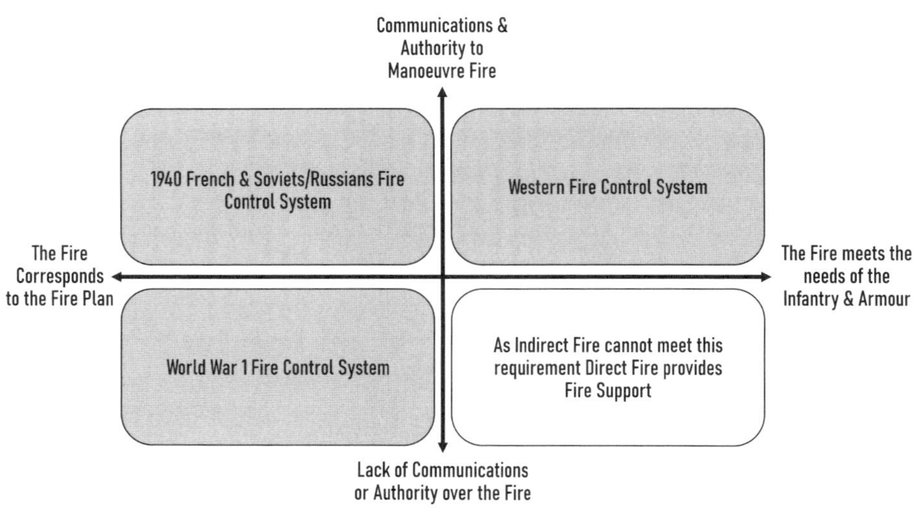

The Americans went into World War Two with the Great War practice of the battery commander being in a static observation post; by the Sicily campaign this had been replaced by the forward observation team approach. Each company was provided with a fire support element, and at times they even had sufficient observers to support companies held in reserve. Force generation of 40 observer teams led to the employment of manpower from many sources – including non-divisional artillery. This challenge was compounded by forward observers not been formally established in the infantry division organisation until after the Normandy invasion. Even then the need was not adequately addressed; the armoured division ended the War with three forward observers in each direct-support battalion, when twelve were required[7]. Naturally the best type of soldier gravitated to these posts and proportionately they suffered the most casualties. This led to most field artillery battlefield promotions being awarded to enlisted men serving as forward observers.

In World War Two, Commonwealth of Nations armies had two observer teams per battery. This forced the constant regrouping of forward observation teams between companies. In compensation, they and their battery commander often had extended attachment to the battalion they supported, in some cases for the campaign's duration. The artillery unit's commanding officer would also have a lengthy period providing similar support to the brigade commander. Commonwealth forward observation officers were captains, with their greater seniority and near permanent affiliation came a different expectation of their contribution[8]. They had the necessary experience to provide broad support to their company commander[9], as Lieutenant General Sir Brian Horrocks observed:

> *'time after time their [the Royal Artillery's] young forward observation officers would step into the breach and take command of some forward infantry unit whose commanders had become casualties*[10]*'.*

The American approach of investing experience in the artillery fire direction centre did not prevent its young artillery lieutenants, in the absence of other officers, from taking command of rifle companies. As was the case in the battle for LZ Bird in the Vietnam War:

> *'It suddenly occurred to this artilleryman [Lieutenant Campenella] that every officer of the rifle company was either dead or out of the fight. As the attached forward observer, he therefore took command of the remnants*[11]*'.*

There were exceptions to the American view that decisions could be better made from a command post. In World War Two, General Collins, then a Corps Commander, directed that more experienced personnel were to be forward, with the infantry, controlling artillery fire. He arrived at this view through having studied at Fort Sill, the Artillery school, and put his views into practice in the North-West Europe campaign:

> *'As infantrymen, we wanted the best artillerymen, irrespective of what their other job was, to be right up there with the front line of the infantry to know what was going on and to adjust fire there … Prior to the Second World War, artillery tables of organization provided for one officer*

> *who was the liaison officer, usually about the lowest second lieutenant. And nobody paid very much attention to him, which was an utter mistake. When it came to fighting we put the best artillerymen up as the forward observers. Battery commanders. People really expert in their job. Not some poor second lieutenant wetting his feet for the first time*[12]'.

General Collins was also concerned that the natural inclination for forward observers was to occupy elevated positions that provided good observation. He preferred them being in the front line to ensure that they were attuned to the fire support needs of the infantry and armour. This emphasis on fire support is not reflected in the current American Army chain of command – brigade and battalion fire support is the responsibility of an attached artillery staff officer; artillery battalion and battery commanders focus on commanding their units.

In World War Two, the American company level fire support element consisted of the forward observer, an officer, plus one wireman and one radioman to provide communications. In the Vietnam War, the American observer party was generally a forward observer who was meant to be a lieutenant, but could be a junior non-commissioned officer, and a radio operator[13]. At this time, the Americans seemed to take pride in having '*the smallest observation party of any army in the Free World*[14]'. The Commonwealth approach has been for four-to-six strong parties. This larger number is sufficient to maintain 24/7 observation or split the party. On the offensive this allows for both an anchor observation post, and an element going into the assault with the company commander. On the defensive it allows more than one observation post to be occupied. Alternatively, the party could split to provide a joint fire observer to each platoon. The French take this one stage further through separating the company level liaison function from target engagement by employing separate teams.

Soviet and Russian artillery battalion and battery commanders conduct fire planning, and they also take on much of the target engagement. Their deputies are with the guns. Russian forward observation teams solely have the task of spotting targets, and are not expected to coordinate fire support. In conventional warfighting forward observers are only attached at company level in exceptional circumstances. Adapting to the challenges of irregular warfare – where every convoy and outpost may need joint fire support – artillery observers have even been provided at platoon level[15]. The Soviets and now the Russians have no standard size of spotter teams; their vehicle determines this. Tracked units have a team of four in the PRP-4A Argus artillery reconnaissance vehicle, which is on a BMP chassis. There is a single spotter squad in each battery and a further two are held at artillery battalion level, for brigade-level tasks. If required, additional ones could be formed from the HQ battery[16].

The Israelis often use a single artillery liaison officer at battalion and company level. Regardless of the individual's ability, the Israelis now recognise that a team better reflects the mission load. This tendency towards larger artillery observation parties is reinforced by them morphing into joint fires teams.

Fire support elements accompanying ground troops provide artillery with the ability to continuously engage the enemy with effective fire. The American artillery's World War Two experience was that forward observers adjusted up to 95% of observed fires[17]. Despite this proven utility, the need for artillery observers at company level has been questioned, most systematically by the Americans; notably in response to new means of target acquisition and the fielding of laser-guided shells in the later stages of the Cold War. A series of studies determined the need for combat observation lasing teams (or COLT) to designate laser-guided precision munitions, and concluded that infantry companies in heavy brigades should lose their forward observers[18]. A RAND study concluded that company forward observers were: '*generally underutilised and initiated only a small percentage of indirect fire missions*[19]'. The rationale behind this conclusion was that the destruction of individual enemy tanks, rather than area target engagement, was considered to be the best use of artillery in the close fight. The eventual force structure the US Army fielded saw the retention of forward observers and the fielding of two combat observation lasing teams in each brigade. These have rarely conducted laser guided missions on actual operations, and can seldom operate independently due to force protection challenges. This has led to them usually being used to provide two additional observation teams in support of manoeuvre units.

In contrast to the varied artillery approaches, either an individual or a pair of mortar observers support most infantry companies. Those with company-level mortars also have platoon-level observers; these are usually infantry junior or senior non-commissioned officers with specialist training. Given that tube artillery and mortars are fundamentally the same weapon system, both call-for-fire procedures should be compatible; however, most armies have allowed their mortars and artillery to adopt different systems. Obviously the most efficient system would be for mortar and artillery fire controllers to be able to fire each other's weapons. As the senior partner within the surface-to-surface joint fires community, the artillery should advocate this.

Another advantage of the having observers integrated with manoeuvre forces is the ability of the infantry and armour commanders to cue fire through the artillery chain of command's communications. This is often overlooked in peacetime, though some armies continue to provide live fire training to infantry commanders; most restrict training to classrooms and simulators. Given the challenge of coordinating fire in mobile operations, this is usually at its most effective when infantry occupy established defensive positions. This allows the infantry to call defensive fire onto known locations through pre-arranged procedures. A forward observer, who served in the Anzio beachhead in World War Two, identified that infantrymen conducted half of the artillery fire missions in his sector[20].

Forward Air Control

> '*a portable radio and radio telephony ground set which is so small and easily set up that one can be carried by two or three men or on the back of a mule, horse, or donkey. In future operations, every unit which has these and every unit should have one – will be in instant communication with the planes – and through them with any other station*[21].'
>
> US Marine Corps Gazette, 1920

Forward air control is the provision of guidance to close air support aircraft to ensure they hit intended targets and do not injure friendly forces. Ground forces in World War One mainly used coloured panels, lights and smoke to indicate their positions to aircraft and so orientate the pilot towards the enemy[22]. Some aircraft were fitted with Morse code receivers that could be used to indicate targets, however this was both unreliable and a time-consuming means of communication. Direct voice communication by wireless telephoning was a better solution, but physically challenging in a open cockpit. Communication to fixed HQ's was possible, but not with ground forces. This meant that aircraft usually acquired their own targets. On the offensive, the forward edge of the barrage was the chief method of target indication, in the sense that anything in front of it was considered hostile.

Advances in radio technology between the wars made possible effective voice communications between the ground and aircraft. Despite this, the Germans largely fought their blitzkrieg campaigns without direct communication between forward ground elements and aircraft. Instead, the Luftwaffe signal detachments attached to army HQs communicated the fire support requirements through the air force HQs to the airfields, with aircrew being briefed prior to take-off[23]. As these signal detachments stopped at the regimental level of command, the Germans fielded additional Luftwaffe teams in armoured vehicles to support the lead mechanised forces. Direct communication with the airborne aircraft was usually limited to marking targets with smoke, while light signals or pyrotechnics marked German positions. These methods proved to be more effective than designating a bombing line in mobile operations[24].

In set-piece World War Two battles, Soviet aircraft were tasked through the fire plan; usually being allocated targets that were out of artillery range. Subsequently aircraft supported a thrust line, ranging in front and to the flanks of the advancing armour. They identified their own targets rather than relying upon close coordination with ground forces. The Eastern Front's reliance on pre-planned close air support reflects the Soviets', and to a lesser extent the Germans', lack of ground-to-air VHF radios; but it also suited the roles both militaries expected of airpower. The Soviets saw aircraft as a subordinate element in the all-arms battle, to be orchestrated in the fire plan like any other means of fire support. Once mobile operations began, like accompanying artillery, Soviet aircraft largely identified their own targets for direct fire engagement. The Germans prioritised close air support to stemming massed Soviet breakthroughs; given the quantity of targets involved, this rarely needed precise ground control. Instead, aircraft largely identified their own targets, often under the control of a lead aircraft operating as an airborne forward air controller. This could be a fighter-bomber or a bespoke light aircraft, such as the Fieseler Storch[25]. As a result, neither side recognised the requirement to invest in the personnel and equipment necessary to deliver the flexibility of the emerging Anglo-American air-ground cooperation system.

By 1942 in North Africa, the British Army and the RAF had established most of the features of the current Western air-land integration system. This employed, like the Luftwaffe, forward air support elements with each brigade. These communicated with an RAF HQ that controlled all air support and tasked the airfields. The novel feature was the employment of mobile fighter controllers who used portable radios to direct airborne aircraft onto targets. These kept pace with the battle in light armoured reconnaissance vehicles. These were subsequently called forward air controllers. They ensured that airpower was employed against the most tactically relevant targets, rather than what had been briefed before the aircraft took off. The air support control HQ sat at the centre of the system, with an all-informed radio net, or 'tentacles', linking all levels of army command, from brigade upwards, with the air force. The employment of this all-informed radio net ensured that air support could be significantly timelier than going through each level of a hierarchical chain of command. Unlike the German system, which allowed Luftwaffe signal detachments to deal individually with squadrons on airfields, this structure facilitated centralised command to achieve massed effect. The system worked as follows:

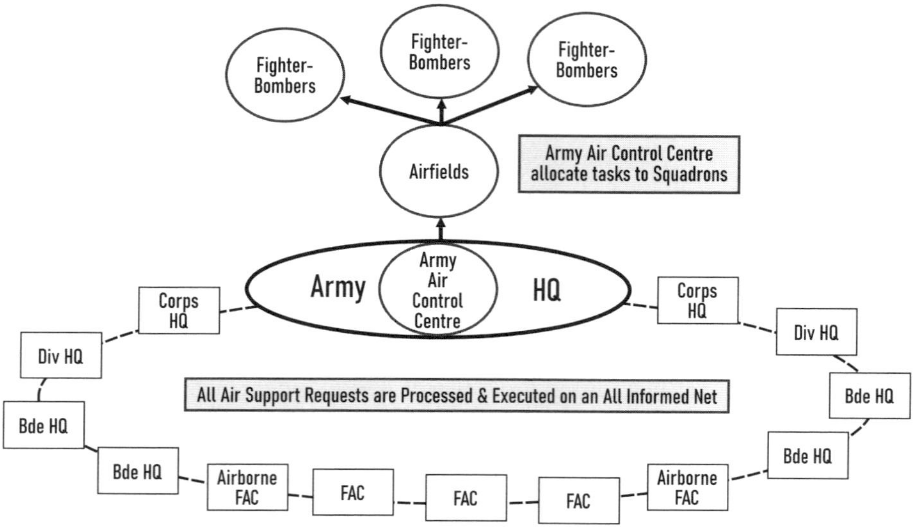

The Anglo-American forces that entered North Africa as part of Operation Torch employed the previous practice of restricting air-ground control parties to higher Army HQs. The impetus provided by combat allowed the superior Western Desert techniques to be rapidly adopted. This practical adaptation did not straight away find its way into doctrine. It was not until 1944 that American forward air controllers directed aircraft onto targets in the South West Pacific Theatre[26]. Practical difficulties included the unreliability of voice communication equipment in that climate, and the challenge for the forward air controller of indicating a target on one jungle-covered hill as opposed to another. In addition, the deliberate nature of operations favoured pre-planned close air support. There were exceptions, in the Battle of Buna-Gona in New Guinea in November 1942, Australian forces used forward air controllers to engage impromptu targets – perhaps drawing upon the experience of compatriots in the Western Desert campaign. In the Burma theatre, lacking artillery and mortars, the Chindits enthusiastically took to close air support, with a forward air controller per column; these largely directed American airpower[27].

In contrast to their current pre-eminence in this area, the US Marine Corps lagged behind in adopting these techniques. In part this was due to the special circumstances of the Battle of Guadalcanal, their first major offensive operation. Initially there was no direct communication between the Marines ashore and their supporting aircraft afloat[28]. When Marine aircraft came ashore, air support requests were processed at divisional level at Henderson Field air base, where the pilots received their target brief before take-off[29]. It was not until the Bougainville landings in November 1943 that the US Marine Corps deployed air liaison parties to every battalion, regimental and divisional headquarters. These were able to both request air support and control aircraft already in the air. By the end of the war these parties had their current title: tactical air control parties (or TACPs). Given the nature of amphibious assaults, the Marines made extensive use of an airborne air coordinator. Flown by experienced pilots – often the squadron commander or executive officer – these aircraft directed fighter-bombers on to their target and conducted rudimentary airspace management[30]. At least one authority sees these tactical developments as coming from the European Theatre[31]. Wherever the ideas came from, the Marine Corps soon achieved a level of effectiveness that led to the US Army expecting them to coordinate close air support for all land forces. This included the campaign to liberate the Philippines, where the American Army predominated.

Operations in Western Europe in 1944–45 saw the full maturing of the Anglo-American close air support system. Army HQs down to task force or brigade level had tactical air control parties, and air and ground forward air controllers exploited the greater availability of aircraft made possible by air superiority. The advance across France benefitted from near-constant air support directed by forward air controllers alongside the lead tanks[32]. The primary technique of forward air control – the indication of a target, information on the target area, and authorisation to engage – has not significantly changed since World War Two. This has been standardised into the '9-Line Brief'. This continuity is despite significant advances in the equipment available to the controller. These included: improved marking of the target through lasers; designation for laser-guided precision weapons; the improved ability to determine target accuracy; and voice control being supplemented or replaced by digital control. Operational experience has shown that fully-digitised fire control may meet the technical requirements, but this does not mean that it addresses the psychological requirements. Specifically, the mutually-reassuring dialogue between controller and aircraft to establish the necessary level of *trust* before weapon release[33]. Digitally-aided close air support appears to be particularly advantageous in multinational operations as it reduces the linguistic challenge. However, it is these operations that also have the greatest requirement to build up *trust*. It will certainly be required in peer conventional conflict when contested airspace will prevent controller and aircraft having a protracted dialogue.

The initial assumption by most militaries was that only aircrew had the 'airmanship' necessary to integrate airpower with ground operations; with the implicit assumption that this meant a fighter-bomber pilot[34]. Over the years there has been a systematic and begrudging retreat from this position, due to insufficient aircrew to meet the requirement. Prior to 1986, only US flying-rated officers were authorised to clear aircraft to use their ordinance[35]. Flyers provided all battalion air liaison officers (or ALOs) for a further twelve years. For a further seven years, only they could deliver the air liaison function in higher HQs[36], with fighter pilots continuing to dominate American air liaison posts filled by aircrew[37]. Manning realities have resulted in further broadening of potential candidates for TACP officers; USAF now allows application direct from civilian life and inter-service transfers. Even the US Marine

Corps has started using non-aircrew officers in these roles[38]. The USMC had very few non-aviator controllers prior to Operation Iraqi Freedom (2003), when it was recognised that two forward air controllers per battalion was inadequate, but force generating more from aircrew proved impossible[39].

Other militaries have undergone a similar transition[40]. This has resulted in armies employing army personnel as forward air controllers. Some countries operate a mixed economy, and seek through employing both soldiers and airmen to benefit from the merging of the ground and air cultures. This is not an option for the Americans as this division of responsibility was formalised with the creation of the Air Force as an independent Service.

In addition to the force generation challenge of employing aircrew in ground posts, there are the aircraft hours required to train and sustain forward air controllers. Sustaining existing trained controllers is often more challenging than creating new ones; the US Marine Corps allocates a third of their aircraft hours to initial instruction and certification; the remaining hours provide controls to maintain qualified joint terminal attack controllers.

The Soviets saw no formal requirement for air staff below regimental level, and the Russians continue to field forward air controllers at a lesser scale than Western armies. This means that their air force liaison officers are almost always qualified pilots; but despite this they rarely dynamically re-task aircraft, instead relying upon pre-planned close air support; though this could involve correcting the point of aim between air attacks. This approach is generally ineffective against elusive foes, who rarely provide static targets, leading to the Soviets and Russians to improvise additional forward air controllers when fighting opponents using irregular warfare tactics. To achieve one controller per battalion the Soviets in their Afghan War were forced to employ non-pilot air force officers and ground officers[41]. Whatever the source, the inability of these forward air controllers to operate within a combined arms grouping has been a recurring feature; often making them ineffective, and sometimes dangerous to their own side, as in the First Chechen War. In the second war, the Russians had significantly improved their coordination of aerial firepower with ground operations. Air/Land integration remains under resourced; the one forward air controller per battalion that was identified as one of the key lessons of Russia's Georgian War has not been achieved[42]. Lack of sufficient forward air controllers is not restricted to the Russians, even the Israelis expect that:

> *'Units and sub-units would use their own commanders or artillery observers as ground-based FACs [forward air controllers], with the coordinator assigning aircraft to them in accordance with the priorities established by the divisional commander[43].'*

By 2009, the Americans fielded twice as many joint terminal air controllers as they had before 9/11. Unfortunately, the laydown of the ground forces in theatre required twice as many more, and as a result they became centrally located at the fixed operating bases and often used artillery and mortar fire observers to acquire the targets. This task was assisted by satellite radio, full-motion video and downlink, and precision weapons[44]. The result was that the forward air controller was rarely at the side of the ground commander when employing aerial fires. Faced with this, the US Army and Marines have sought to improve the training and equipment of their artillery forward observers and mortar fire controllers, to better prepare them to employ aerial firepower. These secondary forward air controllers significantly increase the target acquisition coverage, and close air support can be timelier and more accurate than is possible with untrained personnel operating through a forward air controller. This training has been formalised through the creation of joint fires observers. Lieutenant Colonel Michael Todd, the Joint Fires Observer Course Chief at Fort Sill, identified that:

> *'[The Joint Fires Observer] buys time … He makes what would be a long process to safely request close air support to engage a target, a more timely and efficient process … Afghanistan has shown us how important JFOs are. Because of the mission set and the terrain, it really creates the necessity for that brigade to have JFOs at all levels*[45]*.'*

The joint fires observers are trained to conduct the terminal attack function, under the authority of a forward air controller. They are equipped and authorised to communicate directly with the pilot, so they do not need the joint terminal attack controller to relay their instructions to the aircraft. But qualified controllers retain overall control of the close air support engagement including, crucially, the complex deconfliction of the aircraft with other users of the battlespace. Reflecting their less demanding simulation-based training, unlike an accredited forward air controller, the joint fires observers cannot order the aircraft to engage. Despite some disquiet from the air force, while there is an operational imperative, this procedure is likely to endure, despite the challenges of retaining currency[46]. The US Marine Corps aspires to provide this training to its standard infantry squad leaders, aiming at a Marine infantry battalion of three certified joint terminal attack controllers and 27 joint fires observers.

The French have also created a specific course and qualification; the French national fire observer's role is to provide the necessary information to the forward air controller, so he can forward them in more understandable terms to the pilot in charge of the attack. This lesser ambition is reflected in a week-and-a-half long course, as opposed to the two weeks of its American equivalent. In contrast, most nations take six or seven weeks to train specially selected students as forward air controllers.

There are penalties that result from distancing the forward air controller from the ground commander. In the Korean War the US Marine Corps showed what was possible with a very high level of coordination between air and ground forces:

> *'pilots assigned to a pre-planned mission would frequently visit the ground troops the day before the mission, to look over the terrain and get the commander's views on just how he wanted the strike conducted*[47]*'.*

The technical challenge of terminal control of aerial munitions and airspace management has always been the main challenges facing forward air controllers. However, this cannot be at the expense of understanding the ground battle and how to support it with aerial firepower. It is in this area that operationally they have often been found wanting.

Airborne Forward Air Control

'In the first 18 months of the Mosquitos [the Korean War term for airborne forward air controllers] existence, 93% of all close support sorties were controlled from the air; Mosquitos also became primary source of intelligence for the Joint Operations Centre, and often performed visual reconnaissance both within the bombline and behind the enemy lines[48]*.'*

US Air Force Historical Division

In World War One scout aircraft led ground attack aircraft to their targets, flares were used to indicate specific points of attack. Alternatively, aircraft spotting for artillery could mark a target for air attack through employing artillery smoke rounds[49]. Of course, it was improved radio technology that would allow a controlling aircraft to verbally direct close air support aircraft. In World War Two squadron and flight commanders routinely directed their aircraft to targets. But how effective dedicated target acquisition and engagement aircraft could be was not initially grasped. In February 1943, in Papua, the Australians probably conducted the first close air support mission, controlled by an airborne forward air controller, in a Wirraway light aircraft[50]. The capability grew in sophistication as the war progressed and perhaps reached the apogee of its impact on the enemy in the Korean War. An elevated platform significantly improves target acquisition by making irrelevant much of the cover and concealment that is effective at ground level. It improves overall situational awareness, crucially making it easier to locate friendly forces and any third parties. Aircraft are also a less challenging environment for communication equipment, whose range is improved through being in an elevated position. Finally, being in an aircraft improves the controllers 'air-mindedness', heightening their understanding of the challenges faced by the close air support aircrews.

The chief disadvantage of the controller being in an aircraft is that he is remote from the ground commander and the challenges being faced by manoeuvre forces. This can, in some circumstances, increase the chance of fratricide. Physically dislocating the forward air controller from the other joint fires' controllers can also hinder synergising firepower. This is particularly an issue in mobile operations. In contrast, the lethality of airborne forward air control increases when the front line becomes static and when there is a limited air threat. This allows aircraft to operate with relative impunity over friendly lines at an altitude that allows persistent surveillance of the enemy's positions. Coupling this with a considerable force of fighter-bombers means that the enemy is under constant threat of attack[51].

Despite the advantages significantly outweighing the disadvantages, there has always been a peacetime reluctance to field airborne forward air controllers[52]. This may be due to the capability being made up of varied elements spanning the ground and air environments, rather than being owned by a single proponent. Another factor is that airborne forward air controllers' true forte is engaging targets not in close contact with own forces. Experience shows that the deep battle tends to be marginalised between conflicts. As is positional warfare; which is when airborne observation and target engagement is most effective.

Traditionally, airborne forward air controllers need aircraft able to fly sufficiently low and slow to spot fleeting targets[53]. This is the same requirement as airborne artillery observers, hence the use of the Stinson L-5 Sentinel, the Lysander and the Wirraway for both roles in World War Two and the Korean War. In the early stages of the Vietnam War a similar aircraft, the Cessna O-1 and O-2A[54], were initially used until the fielding of the purpose-built OV-10. Despite logging over half the total hours flown by the US Air Force, these aircraft could not deliver the persistence that was possible when there was a fixed front line[55]. Following the Vietnam War most of these 'slow FAC' aircraft were transferred by the US to friendly governments facing insurgencies. Advanced militaries, if they retain an airborne forward air controller capability, see the helicopter as a more suitable platform. Lacking a dedicated capability, the 101st Airborne Division in the Iraq War placed a forward air controller in the right hand seat of OH-58 scout helicopters[56].

The 'slow' forward air controller's key advantages of persistence and the ability to investigate possible targets can now be better met by unmanned aircraft. Current unmanned platforms have a limited ability to provide their operating crew with the necessary situational awareness to safely and effectively coordinate and de-conflict joint fires, particularly when ground manoeuvre is involved. Despite the challenges, on Operation Iraqi Freedom, controllers used unmanned aircraft to acquire and designate targets for a fighter-bomber with laser-guided bombs[57]. This happened in advance of doctrine and agreed tactics, techniques and procedures[58]. While a manned aircraft is currently undeniably the superior capability, unmanned aircraft probably represent the future of 'slow' airborne forward air control. The future unmanned capability will need to provide superior situational awareness, effective air-to-air communication and the ability to indicate the target, through a combination of laser target marker, infrared pointer, and tracer rounds or white phosphorous rockets[59].

Placing airborne forward air controllers in a high-performance jet aircraft significantly improves their survivability in contested airspace. The US Air Force employ 'Fast FACs' deployed in A-10 Warthogs and F-16 Fighting Falcons. Both aircraft have the sensors, designators and ordnance (including white phosphorous rockets to mark targets) to identify and then pass-off targets to other aircraft. In addition, they are trained to manage a stack of aircraft engaging an individual or series of targets. This leads to a high workload for the pilots of these single seat aircraft. The US Marines initially stipulated that airborne joint terminal attack air controller is a role for two-seat aircraft, a decision made easier by having the two-seat F/A-18D Hornet. Subsequently, in 2005, this was relaxed to allow the single-seat F/A-18C Hornet and AV-8B Harrier to deliver the function. These forward air controllers excel at coordinating engagements in a kill box[60]. They have also shown their utility in recent counter-insurgency operations, delivering danger close air support, often coordinated with army artillery[61]. The US Marine Corps expect half their aircraft to be flown by qualified airborne forward air controllers; achieving an overall ratio of one-third airborne to two-thirds ground based forward air controllers.

Fighting the insurgencies in Iraq and Afghanistan was risk-averse warfare. The saying at the time was 'one bomb will never win the war, but it could sure lose it'. This led to a view that control over air-delivered weapons needed to be exercised by a forward air controller standing at the side of the ground commander authorising the fire support. As we have already seen, lack of forward air controllers led to this being compromised. But given finite resources, most belligerents choose to train ground rather than airborne forward air controllers[62]. So, despite their proven effectiveness in the 2003 Iraq War, outside the USMC and the A-10 community, airborne forward air control has largely been marginalised and is in need of its regeneration.

Combined Joint Fires Support Teams

'With modern artillery and fire support, a pair of eyes backed up by an unjammable radio and perhaps a thermal imager becomes the equivalent of at least a (company) combat team, perhaps a battalion[63].'

Richard Simpkin, soldier and military theorist

Traditionally each element of joint fires has had their own discrete terminal controllers, with their own bespoke procedures and siloed training. This included, for certain armies, separate observers for the company-level 81-mm mortar platoon and the battalion's 107-mm heavy mortar platoon. When all the elements of the joint fires system-of-systems came together in the Vietnam War, the case for a multi-discipline team, able to synergise fires, became unassailable. Blending maximises their strengths and overcomes the weaknesses of each form of firepower. It also assists with deconfliction of firepower to avoid fratricide.

Following the Vietnam War, the US Artillery Centre at Fort Sill, in concert with the USAF, identified how to break down silos or stove pipes by placing all observers in a single fire support team (FIST)[64]. The FIST chief would be responsible to the manoeuvre company commander for the coordination and control of all elements of fire support, with terminal control being the responsibility of the individual accredited observers. The Army approved the FIST concept in 1977[65]. With minor modifications being made in name and organisation in the early 1980s, it continues to the present day. The US Marine Corps also adopted the FIST concept, a change made easier through building upon perhaps the first true joint fire support teams: the Air Naval Gunfire Liaison Companies. These US Marine Corps teams have the added advantage of always having an accredited forward air controller per deployed rifle company[66]. The US Army makes do with at least one Joint Fires Observer per team.

The joint fire team's chief determines the best way to use each form of firepower, coordinates the apportionment of airspace, and then delegates to his terminal controllers the actual control of the fires. This allows the individual terminal controllers to focus on their technical task of getting their weaponry onto the target. The technical complexity of conducting terminal control and airspace management can result in the air controller losing situational awareness of ground operations[67]. The joint fire support team structure seeks to avoid this through having a supervising team chief.

Effective joint fire support teams simultaneously work to both the fires (including air force) and the ground manoeuvre command structures. This presents a considerable career and training challenge. It was a factor in the US Army's decision to permanently assign their artillery-led fire support teams to their combat units. This was expected to improve their all-arms understanding, and so facilitate more effective fire support. However, lacking professional fires oversight and mentoring, their technical skills deteriorated, leading to this initiative being largely recognised as a failure. It would be easy to forgive this as a genuine mistake if it had not happened before. Technical proficiency suffered from General Dever's 1947 decision to make artillery officers '*ground officers first, and gunners second*[68]'. It took the inadequacies exposed by the Korean War to reverse this approach. The warfighting impact of emasculating fire support teams has not been as cruelly exposed, as a counter-insurgency operational environment since 2003 has masked it. However, its negative impact has been compounded by field artillery being employed outside their core technical role, to provide extra infantry, military police or transport in Iraq and Afghanistan[69].

Joint fire support teams are operationally proven in dismounted operations; their equipment and procedures are now fairly mature; there remain challenges when operating under armour on the move. This was significantly easier with older technology; when voice communications, estimation of a target location from a paper map and no requirement for precision grid references were the norm. Many of the technical enhancements of joint fires – networking of sensors, remote target acquisition, laser designation and precision point mensuration of targets from imagery – currently require static employment. The coordination through battlespace management of all air users – shells, bombs, rockets and aircraft – is also significantly easier when static. None of this precludes the teams conducting mounted manoeuvre, but their vehicles need to be specifically designed to support the task, and there is probably an increased requirement to operate at the halt in over-watch positions. The other main challenge is to fully synergise rather than sequence joint fires. Sequencing is easier, as it deconflicts air-delivered and surface-to-surface fires. While it may meet a target-focussed approach, it may not be the best way of supporting manoeuvre, in particular the need for covering fire during an assault.

Future Direction of Joint Fire Terminal Control

> '*[firepower from] fighter aircraft would no longer be employed by a specialist unit. Instead battalion commander and company commanders will be able to communicate with the fighter pilots and employ them only hundreds of metres from the manoeuvring elements, to obtain close air support … We have conducted brigade training exercise at night with live fire, while incorporating tanks, fighter aircraft, attack helicopters, guns and mortars*[70]'.
>
> Colonel Amir Baram, Israeli Parachute Brigade Commander

Advanced armies have radically overhauled the roles and capabilities of their fire support elements. These are now capable of controlling the breadth of joint fires systems. They can employ precision fires on point targets, which was previously the purview of targeteers in HQs. These fire support elements can network with a variety of ground and air sensors; they can conduct fire missions by data as well as voice. Finally, they can control local airspace to safely deliver ground and air fires. Despite all this change, there are significant elements of continuity; the techniques of controlling indirect fire have not significantly changed over its first hundred years, nor has close air support in its fundamentals since World War Two. These processes have been preserved within joint fire teams, which seek to coalesce bespoke systems into a joint solution, rather than breaking down silos.

Despite the effectiveness of the current approach, for those who see warfare as primarily an exercise in process management, there is room for improvement. Their argument being that *empowering* the combat soldier with direct access into the joint fires system must be more efficient than going through the 'gateway' provided by a joint fire controller. The first practical challenge is communications, in particular ground-to-air communications, which invariably require specialist communication equipment. Surface-to-surface fires largely use standard army radios, but are conducted through bespoke voice procedure and fire discipline drills, or their digital equivalent. In addition, specialist target acquisition equipment is required to effectively employ most precision munitions; of course, the equipment issues can be overcome. A greater challenge for a non-specialist is to determine: the priority, correct delivery system, the type of munitions, and the weight of fire to achieve the desired effect on the target. The task of employing firepower in concert with manoeuvre has always been technically and tactically challenging. The joint dimension is making this more so. As the Australian Army has identified: '*The intersection of complexity, mission command, and small-team warfare is increasingly occurring where the land and air domains meet*[71]'.

As well as these practical challenges, joint fires personnel are increasingly being formally made responsible for the application of their firepower. While disciplines and nations vary, most are moving towards greater formalisation of the requirement for their terminal controllers to be accredited as trained, qualified, current and competent. This is at its most stringent for forward air controllers; with Western militaries following the NATO and US Air Force standards. Given the current legal direction of travel towards increased formalisation of duty holder responsibility to manage risk, it is difficult to envisage Western nations not continuing to insist upon fully accredited terminal controllers. Operationally, risk management includes a series of checks and balances that have incrementally developed to deliver greater surety, including the mandatory two-man check of firing data. This is not just within the joint fires system; a common drill for the engagement of impromptu targets is for their grid to be announced over manoeuvre voice command net; silence is consent to fire[72]. Collateral damage incidents and the ineffective application of fires have convinced the Russians of the need for increased checks and balances. Artillery and air force terminal controllers have to independently verify a target's grid reference, rather than rely upon the infantry or armoured commander's target location[73]. Finally, it is difficult to envisage a safe process that can manage battlespace without specialist joint fires elements embedded into each level of command. Despite all these factors, the retention of specialists to conduct fire support will, no doubt, continue to be challenged.

Some armies also believe that the commander needs to have direct contact with the assets providing support, rather than relying upon their fire support element. Chief amongst these are the Israelis, who have recently restored the direct link between ground commanders and the close air support aircraft. This had ceased being common practice after the First Lebanon War in 1982[74]. Of course, all commanders can talk to the pilots through the forward air controller's radios, but other armies do not see this as essential in achieving trust between ground and air elements. The uniqueness of the Israeli approach may be the outcome of how they structure their fire support. The control of aircraft is vested in a single specialist unit; this addresses the required technical skills, but arguably it is less effective at coordinating air fires within the combined arms battle. In addition, the Israeli Air Force's joint terminal attack controllers' course only provides air and ground officers with a mere two weeks of study of each other's environment[75].

The joint fire support team seeks to coordinate the current firepower silos. The alternative approach is to break these down and adopt a single fire control system. Under this, a universal call for fire would replace the discrete methods that have iteratively developed in response to the different characteristics of the weapon systems. A universal system would enable all the fire support team personnel to terminally control all joint fires systems. This approach would certainly be more manpower efficient. However, a universal fire controller is demonstrably impractical in terms of training this span of responsibility, but rationalisation within the joint fires system of systems is certainly possible and desirable. It makes no sense for tube and rocket artillery to employ different call for fire procedures to infantry mortars.

The division between close combat attack and close air support procedures is also largely artificial; this is proven by the Israeli, Russian and the US Marine Corps who all use a single air support system. Rationalisation to two fire control systems – one each for the bespoke needs of the air and ground environments – is a realistic goal. The desire to go further stems from a quite reasonable assessment that technology is making the terminal control of fire easier. Which it does, in terms of placing the munition on to the target; but, if anything, in its totality fire support is getting more complex. The technical challenges include: the multiplying of platforms, munitions and fuze types. Tactical challenges include: more complex rules of engagement; battlespace management of potentially contested airspace; and more complex human and physical terrain.

The need for a single team to control all methods of joint fire support is conceptually incontestable and is aided by the team's equipment increasingly becoming largely agnostic of the firepower's source. A laser designator can control artillery, mortar and air-delivered munitions. Despite multi-roling and some lightening of individual equipment, carrying target acquisition, engagement and communication equipment remains a considerable challenge. It is this, together with maintaining 24/7 operations, that drives a team of five or six personnel, rather than just the need for qualified terminal controllers. Armies are likely to continue having considerable variation in the rank and experience of fire support personnel, particularly of the team chief. Armies content with having their most junior officers in this role need to recognise its increasing complexity, and for the American Army that their predecessors did not always follow this approach in conventional warfighting.

Despite being a battle-winning capability, airborne observers rarely feature in peacetime structures. A combination of airborne and ground-based terminal controllers is required; the elevated platform is more effective at target engagement, but it cannot as effectively coordinate fire support, nor provide the same persistence. In World War Two an American division tried to man forty ground observation parties to ten airborne ones. Currently the US Marines aspire to a ratio of one-third airborne and two-thirds ground-based forward air controllers. The marginalising of the airborne capability is in part due to the demise of the dedicated, low performance, fixed wing aircraft. Helicopters combine greater survivability with persistence and an ability to hover in order to investigate possible targets; however, they are rarely dedicated to controlling either close air support or artillery. The sensor suite and endurance of unmanned aircraft make them suitable platforms, engaging with artillery is relatively easy, but close air support is more challenging; but as unmanned aircraft become more sophisticated and their crews more practised, they should be able to conduct close air support with no greater limitations than that experienced by a controller inside a manned aircraft. In recent conflict, Russian, Turkish and Azerbaijan drones have conclusively demonstrated that airborne target acquisition significantly increases the lethality of airpower and artillery.

All unmanned aircraft are exploiting a window of opportunity presented by inadequate air defences. Allowing them to achieve near persistent surveillance in positional warfare. When this is linked to a responsive firepower system, the result is an opponent unable to effectively operate without a lethal counter to their actions. Of course, like their World War Two and Korean War predecessors in light aircraft, this capability is less effective in mobile warfare. We should expect conventional unmanned aircraft to be countered by air defences in peer conflict. However, small, relatively inexpensive, quadcopter systems are likely to represent an enduring threat through their quantity and ability to use cover to achieve survivability. Hence, it is likely that the quadcopter, supported by small fixed wing unmanned aircraft, when supported by responsive firepower will continue to dominate the frontal zone of the close battle.

Western force employment needs to respond to this in two ways. Firstly, unmanned aircraft greatly increase the fire support elements' ability to acquire targets. Hence the need for each team to have a quadcopter capability. Ideally this should be capable of tethered operations, to minimise its signature, while still improving a team's surveillance by flying above their observation post. Secondly, as fire support elements are fixed to the companies they support there is a need for a capability that independently hunts out targets. The temptation would be to equip this hunter capability with more proficient mini unmanned aircraft. But the primary requirement is survivability through exploiting ground cover. This leads to a small quadcopter with a day/night sight. It requires sufficient range to allow it to infiltrate beyond the line of sight of the troops in contact and their fire support teams. As the key requirement is to cue firepower this capability is best sourced from the artillery, as part of their fire support system.

As identified, American division in World War Two had a ratio of 10 light aircraft to 40 fire support elements. Sufficient aircraft as they operated in daylight at altitudes that aided their observation. The need for 24/7 operations, and the restrictive observation that is due to very low-level flying, suggests equal numbers of fire support elements and hunter quadcopters teams.

Chapter 15: Command and Control of Joint Fires

'[Israeli] Ground commanders would plan their battles in close coordination with their air advisor – likely to be a recently retired and very senior air officer – using the latter's expertise in more or less the same way that they would that of their artillery advisor. Once the plan was settled, the Air Command and Control Centre would be responsible for implementing the aspects of it, just as an artillery staff were responsible for an artillery fire plan … Front commanders and their air advisors were normally within speaking distance of each other, divisional commanders and their coordination would be as close as the operational situation permitted – perhaps in neighbouring vehicles – and at every level of command ground-air communications would be monitored by the next higher level, both as a means of 'reading' the battle, and for rapid redeployment of aircraft according to the exigencies of the situation[1].'

Trevor N Dupuy, soldier and historian

The World Wars identified that a separate artillery chain of command answering directly to the commanding general was the most effective approach to employing firepower in conventional warfighting. While the Russians, and countries that take a doctrinal lead from them, remain true to this, some Western armies have diminished the role of their artillery staff. In contrast, some Western air forces are increasing the responsibility of their officers; moving away from the liaison role to one that sees an air commander and his staff embedded in land HQs. This is occurring at the same time as battlespace management processes that seek to dynamically integrate are replacing restrictive ones that seek to deconflict.

The artillery command and staff structure that moved, deployed and directed the fire of Napoleonic *grandes batteries* did this through traditional personal command and control, usually from the back of a horse; except in mobile operations, when direct fire could be employed, this approach was obsolete by late 1914. The dominance of indirect fire, the split into the close and deep battles, and the need for centralised control over all sources of firepower, required artillery commanders and their staff in every command centre from brigade to the army level. Air and then aviation followed the artillery in establishing specialist staff in land HQs. Though usually not in the same quantity, because in most militaries air and aviation staff officers accepted a lesser responsibility for the coordination of firepower. This was made possible by relying upon the pre-existing artillery command and staff.

The divisional level of command, and its equivalent in non-Western armies, has a key role in joint fires: it is the lowest level of command that can simultaneously conduct the close and deep battles. The end of the Cold War saw a shift from the division to the brigade as the primary level of command for unifying the individual arms to achieve a common mission; this happened when peer inter-state conventional warfare was considered a remote possibility.

Changed geostrategic circumstances are leading to a return to the primacy of the division in conventional warfighting. Restoring the divisional level of command will particularly assist with the effective apportionment and application of firepower.

Integrating air and land fires with manoeuvre presents the greatest challenge to these specialist firepower staffs. This is due to a combination of the physical challenge of coordinating the different velocities of ground and air movement, coupled with the institutional and cultural disconnect between the components. Unfortunately the result, for many militaries, is a transactional relationship, with liaison officers often acting as mediators. The apportionment of aircraft and the target nomination process provide a mechanism to deal with disputes over priorities. This process works, but managing it can detract from the efforts of commanders and staff officers trying to combine air and land operations into joint warfighting.

Historically, the co-location of air and land HQs has made personnel, develop personal, and professional relationships that lead to more effective joint working. The current Western joint warfighting approach has led to physically separate component HQs[2], leading to a joint plan and subsidiary air and land plans. The challenge of knitting together land and air operations at the tactical level has led the Americans and Israelis to appoint senior officers to lead the air staff in army HQs. Most militaries rely upon more junior air force officers; these can only really deliver liaison. As we have seen historically these arrangements have often failed to build *trust* between air and ground commanders.

Inefficient control of the battlespace has been both a cause and a symptom of ineffective air-land cooperation. Both forces have contributed to ineffective joint warfighting; armies through seeking to achieve the greatest level of control over their air support and direct control over the maximum operational area; air forces have contributed to the problem through their desire to directly control all airspace, leading to unresponsive organic land fires. They can compound this by over-resourcing air control to the detriment of the joint mission. The most significant problem occurred in the Gulf War – inadequate battlespace management allowed Iraqi forces to shelter from Coalition firepower – when very linear procedural processes were followed. Errors repeated in the Iraq War, leading to the requirement for a more flexible and dynamic approaches; indicated by the view that '*the US Army must redefine the battlespace based on our ability to influence it*[3].' The current approach has proved effective in recent conflict, but of course is untested in high tempo peer-on-peer conventional warfighting.

Another challenge being faced is adjusting to greater uncertainty of information in conventional conflict. In recent counter-insurgency operations, Western commanders have grown used to access to an unprecedented range of information before choosing a course of action. This has included full motion video of a target area before conducting joint fire strikes. This has been made possible by the provision of lavish point-to-point communications between static locations, and generous satellite communications to support mobile HQs. Replicating this access will be difficult in high tempo manoeuvre operations, particularly against a peer opponent, who will contest information flow. The electronic signature associated with facilitating access to information and communicating orders makes a modern HQ highly vulnerable to being acquired and engaged. This makes generals who seek to exercise real-time command from these HQs as vulnerable as the Mogul generals who sought to improve their situation awareness by riding elephants in the firearms age. This, in the view of a contemporary Persian, made them '*a target for everybody*[4].'

Artillery Commanders and their Staff

> *'There is the employment of fire by command centers, which relies primarily on C2 systems. In recent years it has become more significant, owing to the era of network-centric warfare and the technological evolution. There is another method, that of the maneuvering-assaulting unit… In this situation, what you see is what you attack … Sometimes it may be more convenient to employ fire through display screens, but in the case of maneuvering, there is no replacement for human-controlled employment of fire*[5].'
>
> Colonel Dubi Cohen, Israeli Artillery Corps

Most resources in peacetime are expended upon training the artillery terminal controllers operating with the manoeuvre forces. In actual conflict commanders and their staff in HQs have usually employed most of the firepower. From World War One these HQs have sat at the centre of a web of sensors providing targeting information. In the Great War not only did these HQs take on responsibility for the deep battle, they also controlled much of the firepower used in the close fight. In subsequent conflict, through advances in radio communications, the control over indirect firepower in the close battle shifted to those that could see the targets. In recent years technology has shifted the balance back towards HQs becoming the primary authoriser of engagement. This is the result of giving commanders and their staff real-time access to an expanded range of sensors, crucially including full motion video. Commanders in static HQs during counter insurgency operations with access to networked sensors have had significantly greater situational awareness than commanders on the ground. Of course, there are other intangible factors which mean that most armies still expect the on-the-spot commander to have the final say, particularly in fluid situations.

Prior to World War One, regardless of how senior, artillery generals were in effect staff officers, who exercised command through the commander-in-chief's General Staff. This reflected the reality of most guns being in direct support of the brigades, leaving artillery generals to exercise direct authority over only the heaviest guns. At the start of the Great War, the commanding general, advised by his General Staff, usually determined the plan without the participation of any artillery experts. Once the plan was finalised, the artillerymen were tasked to construct a supporting fire plan. Experience soon showed that that artillery needed to be at least a partner in the planning process. Once it was recognised that artillery was the key resource in solving trench warfare's tactical challenge, the fire plan began to determine the manoeuvre plan.

World War One artillery commanders and their staff executed the traditional responsibilities of personnel, operations and plans, and supply over their soldiers. This was a considerable task as by mid-war the artillery arm had expanded to being around a third of most armies' total strength, and artillery ammunition became the greatest logistic challenge. Responsibility was exercised through an orthodox command and control structure; however, a different approach was possible with the manoeuvring of firepower around the battlefield. Exploiting the delinking of the control of firepower from the standard military hierarchical command system required a separate artillery chain of command, paralleling the existing chain of command. So instead of following a hierarchical command chain, when communications permitted, firepower could be controlled by the observer best placed to engage a target. By 1916 the British had:

> *'created an artillery hierarchy, not for command, for that must always be the responsibility of commander-in-chief, and by his authority, of the General Staff, but for "control", which is a different matter, and for dealing with all questions of artillery policy, doctrine, manning and training*[6]*.'*

By the end of the war, successful armies had large artillery staffs, answering to the commander-in-chief, through a separate artillery command structure, and empowered to control firepower.

Achieving fire ascendency through effective counter-battery fire became the precursor to successful operations[7]. This required the intelligence and artillery staff to direct and interpret sensor information to determine targets for both immediate and future engagement. The corps level of command emerged as the correct level to conduct the counter battery battle. Following the industrial age warfare rationale of tasks further dividing into ever greater specialisation, the process of countering artillery batteries was separated from defeating mortars. In World War One divisions were usually responsible for the counter mortar battle. By World War Two countering artillery and mortars was usually respectively the task of divisions and brigades.

As their way of war depends upon the scientific application of firepower, since World War One the Soviets and Russians have organised their artillery in a separate command chain. The senior Missile Troops and Artillery officer in a HQ is a commander, distinct from officers of similar rank who are in charge of branches, under the chief of staff. This allows him to report directly to the army commander. The artillery commander also has coordination responsibility for other sources of firepower, including battalion mortars, aircraft and even tanks. This leads to the commander-in-chief and his commander of Missile Troops and Artillery expending much of their personal time on the construction of the fire plan, as this drives the employment of manoeuvre forces.

Soviet/Russian training is jointly conducted under the authority of the artillery and combined arms chains of command to ensure that exercises fully practice the centralised and decentralised control of firepower. The tank or motor rifle battalion being exercised receives at least a supporting battery, but more usually an artillery battalion. Once combat becomes mobile and firepower is decentralised, the separate artillery command chain serves as a high-speed channel for guidance and coordination of missile and artillery assets. The Russians seem to achieve this without undermining the authority and responsibility of the combined arms commanders. In contrast, most Western artilleries work through the chief of staff, with as a minimum the General Staff being responsible for the promulgation of orders to artillery units.

Few maintain the purest form of a separate chain of command which allows the artillery commander to answer directly to the commanding general.

There are different approaches to how HQs engage targets, the Soviets had designated complexes to identify and destroy high-value targets in near-real time. At the operational level the reconnaissance strike complex largely employed surface-to-surface missile systems and aircraft-delivered munitions. The reconnaissance fire complex was the tactical equivalent, it linked intelligence data, precise targeting, a fire-direction centre and tactical artillery to destroy high-value targets in near-real time. The Russians have restored this process and have developed and employed their reconnaissance fire system[8]. As Russian airpower is a subordinate part of combined arms warfighting, the artillery commander controls its targeting. Western militaries split this responsibility, with the air force being largely responsible for the conduct of joint targeting. The joint commander partly directs this through nominating time-sensitive targets. Western artillerymen largely conduct tactical level targeting.

While the World War Two Anglo-American approach is now effectively the NATO standard, the constituent armies have their distinct national approaches. Many of these institutionally, if not in formal doctrine, favour artillery being under both the command and control of brigades. This was reinforced by the end of the Cold War's reduced requirement for conventional warfighting's massed fires. The Americans have followed this trend in making direct support artillery battalion organic to their manoeuvre brigades. The overall effect over the last couple of decades has been a decline in artillery institutional independence and the marginalising of its discrete chain of command. This is despite World War One establishing the enduring principle that centralised control by a discrete chain of command achieves the most effective matching of firepower against targets to achieve the commanding general's priorities.

Air and Aviation Command and Staff

'There is a line of command and a chain of control … control must be vested at the level, and in the instrument, that can read the battle, which may or may not fit the line of command[9].'

Major General Dan Tolkovsky Former Commander of the
Israeli Air Force quoting Israeli doctrine in the 1980s

Experience gained using observation balloons to conduct reconnaissance and artillery spotting during the Franco-Prussian War assisted the integration of Great War aircraft into ground operations. But all belligerents had to rapidly improvise mechanisms to command and control aircraft as they expanded into other roles. The short range of World War One aircraft made direct support to the field armies and corps the only effective command and control option. Throughout the war, reconnaissance aircraft remained under local ground formation command. Like reinforcing artillery, the quantity of fighter squadrons allocated to each formation depended on its mission. The Germans were the first to react to the need to organise their air force to contest control of the air. They formed their first specialist fighter squadrons in 1915, and later formed them into wings of four squadrons. The British formed their flying squadrons into brigades that were assigned to each of their armies; practically from the first these were commanded by pilots. The brigade consisted of an army-level wing, responsible for air superiority, bombing and strategic reconnaissance, and a corps-level wing, which undertook artillery observation and ground liaison duties, with one squadron detached to each army corps. The key task of aerial photography led to the French, British and American observation squadrons being permanently assigned '*at the direct orders of the corps commander*[10]'. As a result, air commanders and staff were required in Army and Corps HQs. By 1917 the British were able to fill these corps and army staff posts with experienced flyers. At about the same time, under Colonel Duval's leadership, the *Service Aéronautique* overcame localised resistance and imposed centralised authority over all French aircraft. Previously their brigade and division structure had tended to answer solely to the local ground force commander. Under Duval's command airpower could be massed for the decisive French and American offensives in the closing stages of World War One[11]. The Imperial German Air Force never achieved similar centralisation.

It was soon recognised that airmen needed to be in command if airpower was to achieve its full potential. Achieving real time command and control over their forces required wireless communications. Initially this was unreliable, but by 1918 British aircraft had an effective link by wireless to the Central Intelligence Bureau at Corps HQ, which then tasked artillery and aircraft to engage by passing the targets by landline[12]. In contrast, air-to-air communications remained unreliable, resulting in air command being exercised from the ground.

By World War Two, more portable and longer-range radios enabled air forces to follow the artillery's approach of having an air fire support element at each level of ground command. This grafted onto the existing fire support processes developed by the artillery, but was more extreme in separating of the control of firepower from the traditional hierarchical command structure. Reliable communications – which flourished in the radio-friendly conditions of the Libyan Desert – linked the British Desert Air Force staff officers in the brigade, division and corps HQs with their supporting airpower on a single radio net. The air support HQ was the controlling station, exercising central control by allocating missions to aircraft through direct communication with the airfields. The Desert Air Force commander determined force employment to support a plan jointly agreed with the 8th Army commander.

In each HQ the air staff officers' primary function is to ensure that airpower is correctly employed. This includes, as well as close air support, intelligence, surveillance and reconnaissance, and air transport. In addition, some armies employ supervisory forward air controllers in their brigade and divisional HQs to oversee the practicalities of the terminal control of airpower. Some combine the two functions, notably the Israelis. The air staff officer's key challenge is overcoming the different warfighting approaches of land and air forces, which is an inevitable product of their distinct environments.

Of course, air-land integration works both ways, resulting in a mutual exchange of liaison elements. The need for an army element in the theatre-level air component HQ was recognised in the American Cold War AirLand Doctrine. These individuals were needed to coordinate fire support, integrate air and missile defence, and aid with intelligence sharing, airspace management and airlift. This resulted in a battlefield coordination detachment in each American geographic combat command. This is a requirement in NATO doctrine, though if executed it is rarely done with the right quality of personnel. In addition, many militaries have ground liaison officers at individual air bases to assist with the understanding of the army's requirement.

Even with the correct doctrine, training and education, the challenge of converging air and land operations should not be underestimated, especially without the imperative for cooperation provided by conflict. American airpower was kept busy through the 1990s, but usually without the need to coordinate with land forces. This changed in the post-9/11 wars, with 10th Mountain Division's Operation Anaconda identifying severe shortcomings. Chief amongst these was a failure to appreciate what the divisional air force staff could actually achieve. The division was supported by several US Air Force officers and thirty-plus enlisted forward air controllers. Given their low rank and limited experience they were unable to correctly integrate airpower into the division's operation[13]: The lack of experience was particularly felt below the divisional level of command:

> '*[On Operation Anaconda] The enlisted JTACs [Joint Terminal Attack Controllers] at battalion level were experts at requesting air assets and providing terminal control; however, they lacked the knowledge base to exploit all the air and space assets capabilities fully*[14].'

The ability of air force officers to integrate air and land operations improved throughout the Iraq and Afghanistan counter-insurgencies. However a 2008 fact-finding trip to Iraq noted that US Air Force enlisted controllers assigned to Army units '*are generally unable to contribute significantly to air/ground planning*[15]'. Their challenge is made even greater through a policy of temporary attachments rather than more permanent assignments[16]. This is probably an unfair criticism, as a Joint Terminal Attack Controller is designed to be a terminal controller. A reasonable task for an enlisted airman, but they cannot be expected to adequately represent their service and ensure the correct employment of airpower in the land battle. This is the responsibility of the air staff officers; however, these are also handicapped by their lack of rank and experience.

The artillery commanders are usually one or at most two ranks lower than the commander of the formation to which they are attached. The air force officer is generally three ranks lower at brigade, divisional and corps levels, and usually more at battalion level. This can result in them being too junior in rank for their views to carry sufficient weight with the commander they advise, or alternatively within the HQ's staff processes. In addition, their actual control authority is usually limited to airborne aircraft already allocated to the land formations. This, in part, reflects reluctance for any form of decentralisation that could impact upon airpower's unity of command. Despite this being a central canon of Western airpower theory, the Americans and Israelis are currently shifting towards air officers having command authority in both land and joint sub-theatre HQs. The Israelis are currently the most innovative in their employment of air force officers to improve airpower's integration.

In their 1967 and 1973 Wars the Israeli air force provided battalion and higher levels of command with an officer of similar rank and experience as their artillery advisor. This practice lapsed in the Intifada. The 2006 Lebanon War was the nadir of cooperation, with the air force chief of staff personally authorising individual close air support missions if these were within danger close distance of Israeli ground troops. Reforms followed, including placing a senior air force officer with a supporting staff within the lead ground force HQ. This turned the brigade level of command into in effect a joint HQ. A land service brigadier general commanded, with an Israeli Air Force colonel at his side. Delivering a difference of only a single rank between the army commander and his air force deputy is of course easier in the Israeli system with its veteran reservists.

In Operation Cast Lead against Hamas in 2008, brigade HQs had five air force staff officers supporting the Israeli Air Force colonel. This included at least one attack helicopter pilot from the squadron providing direct support, and a fighter-bomber pilot or weapons system officer. These officers split their duties between the control of aircraft and traditional air staff functions. The brigade's chief forward air controller was either a senior major or lieutenant colonel, with the authority to lead the other forward air controllers and ensure that they made effective use of allocated air assets[17]. This air staff ensured that the brigade's plans and its execution made the best use of airpower. During this conflict the Israeli Air Force's main air operations centre also took on a permanent battlefield coordination detachment of land force officers[18]. In compensation for the increased number of air force personnel required at brigade level, fewer are required at lower levels, as artillery officers have increased their responsibility. Below brigade level, the artillery liaison officer has evolved into the battalion fire support commander. This expanded their responsibility from just mortars and guns to include artillery precision weapons, attack helicopters and fighter aircraft[19].

While the Americans have not been as radical as the Israelis, they are challenging the canons of air theory and doctrine, with the aim of achieving greater synchronisation of the air and land campaigns. This has been described as 'joint interdependence[20]'; which seeks the convergence, and not just integration, of land and air combat. While there were problems at the lower levels of command, Coalition forces in the Iraq War benefited from having the same air component commander – Lieutenant General T. Michael Moseley – as the Afghanistan operation the previous year. The result was an attempt to address the Afghanistan failings through placing a two-star general (Major General Daniel Leaf) within the land HQ controlling the invasion of Iraq. This general had the specific responsibility of reducing the friction between components, and was able to '*offer air and space expertise from the very beginning, from the genesis of the motion, whether it's ever executed or not*[21]'. This was made possible by General Leaf being authorised to speak for the air component commander.

This was doctrinally formalised in 2003 with the establishment of the Air Component Coordination Element within the land HQs. This resulted in an air force operational-level air planning team led by a brigadier general joining the theatre HQ in Afghanistan[22]. This received delegated authority to organise, plan, and direct local Air Force elements and became a 2-star command in 2010[23]. The US Central Command air commander's rationale was that:

> *'Effective integration at all levels requires more than close proximity. The air component coordination element needed, and I gave him, sufficient staff to integrate at all levels, responsibility for forces assigned to the joint operations area … and the necessary authorities to respond to the Joint Force Commander's needs*[24].'

Most armies lack sufficient helicopters to generate enough aviation staff officers to permanently attach them to all their Army HQs. When fielded these tend to be singleton or at best a few officers, who are likely to be overmatched by the task on operations. In some armies this leads to aviation liaison or staff officers being reinforced by itinerant aviation planning teams, when an operation relies upon integrating attack helicopter firepower. Militaries that employ rotor wing and fixed wing close air support procedures can dual role air and aviation staff officers so making force generation easier.

Led by the Americans and Israelis, air staffs in land HQs are evolving along lines that see a convergence with established command and control artillery practice; resulting in an empowered air commander, able to inform and influence the land commander to employ airpower most effectively. The result may be that armies are coalescing around a common joint fires command and control structure, though with specialists covering surface-to-surface and aerial fires. The Israeli approach has proved its effectiveness in their border conflicts, and provides an instructive approach. A single commander and staff controlling fixed and rotary wing firepower joins the artillery battalion commander and his staff in brigade HQ; however, having the air force colonel as effectively the brigade deputy commander may not appeal to all armies. It may not be the Israeli practice in operations involving multiple brigades. The Israeli employment of flying representatives from the force elements most likely to provide direct support leads to greater integration than air staff officers with no previous affiliation. Of course, this requires earmarking flying units to support army formations, which contravenes the traditional air force views on unity of command[25]. The marginalisation of the artillery chain of command by several Western armies adds further complexity, as most airmen rely upon artillerymen to synergise firepower and manoeuvre, especially at the lower tactical levels.

Disconnect between the Joint and Component HQs

'Of all the lessons we learned about tactical air operations, perhaps the most important is that the air commander must have a sincere desire to become part of the ground team. The army must, of course, have the same dedication to reciprocate[26].'

Lieutenant General Elwood 'Pete' Quesada of the IX
Tactical Air Command in 1944

The reliance on aerial firepower in the current Western land warfighting approach necessitates, from the very start of a campaign, highly effective inter-component cooperation. Historically the synergising of air and land operations has proved easiest when HQs have collectively developed the same overall plan, a process greatly aided by commanders and their staff being co-located.

Since the middle of World War Two, the Western command design has been an integrated joint force, commanded by a joint HQs sitting over the land, sea and air components[27]. This seeks to deliver joint warfighting. However, an overarching joint HQ can add another actor to the three environmental components; it comes with its own institutional agenda that may not necessarily aid coherence; it certainly has encouraged a transactional relationship between the air and land HQs. This has been compounded by these HQs usually being geographically separate. Proximity allows components to easily work together, rather than relying upon the coordination provided by the joint HQ and through exchanging liaison officers.

Again, Operation Anaconda provides a lesson of what can go wrong. 10th Mountain Division's Major General Hagenbeck assumed that the acquiescence of liaison officers signified air component support. This and similar failings led the then USAF Chief of Staff to identify that the failure to correctly plan air support was the key lesson from Afghanistan. He stated that: '*We know how to do CAS at a tactical level … we absolutely positively must have the right interfaces at the operational level of war*[28]'. In Afghanistan the air force's special operations forces coordination elements were generally recognised as being more effective, this was due to almost constant cooperation on actual operations, an option that armies usually lack, but they can substitute genuinely challenging training[29].

Effective air and land cooperation may be difficult to achieve in peacetime, but even after several years of warfighting the British forces had not accomplished this in the Western Desert campaign. This led General Montgomery to move his 8th Army HQ to where the Desert Air Force was based. Future plans were then jointly worked out, based on his belief that: '*if you can knit up the power of the Army on the land and the power of the air in the sky then nothing will stand against you, and you will never lose a battle*'[30].

While an enthusiast for a single team, at no point did General Montgomery, nor any of his contemporaries, believe that air and land power were equals. American doctrine – the 1943 FM 100-20, Command and Employment of Air Power – enshrined the principle of an air force, independent and coequal to Army ground forces. But there was clarity that the army commander had overall responsibility[31]. The Desert Air Force's Air Marshal Coningham identified the balance of responsibility as:

> *'The Soldier commands the land forces, the Airman commands the air forces, both commanders work together and operate their respective forces in accordance with the combined Army-Air plan, the whole operation being directed by the Army Commander*[32].'

In North Africa as co-partners in the plan, soldiers did not insist upon maximising close air support if there were higher priorities. Nor did the air force always insist upon air superiority being the priority. Despite this apparent synergy the Allies were still learning how to correctly utilise the air and land team. The result was that land operations were not consciously designed to maximise aerial firepower, instead airpower was often used as an enabler to either extant land operations, or to provide a way out of an emerging military challenge that could not be met by organic land firepower.

The Anglo-American operations from D-Day onwards did not have the clear-cut command and control arrangements that were possible in the Mediterranean Theatre with its purely tactical air forces. As a result, the deciding authority for the employment of airpower and the land HQ were no longer co-located; this probably contributed to the deterioration of personal relationships between soldiers and aviators[33]. The Pacific Theatre largely avoided this through the sequencing of isolated land campaigns, and it was not until the final year of the conflict that significant strategic attack on the Japanese homeland was possible.

Following World War Two joint force theatre command continued in America's regional combat commands. This included the NATO Cold War joint commanders for the European and Atlantic theatres. However, the circumstances of the Cold War prevented this negatively impacting on coordination; air and land commanders were often co-located, in the British case with adjoining offices. Plus, they all shared a mutual understanding of the extant theatre operational plans that had been refined over the decades. This was not of course the case when conflict turned hot, as in the Korean War, the USAF's first. It took time for a joint operations centre to be established in Korea; and for it to establish its authority over Navy and Marine aircraft.

Although not a panacea, co-located working and socialising can lead to a greater degree of cooperation and understanding, if not personal warmth, between commanders and their staffs. Not only can this aid better operational decision-making, it will put the institutional development of air land integration on a firmer footing between conflicts. As one historian identified: '*The lack of dialogue between air and ground leaders had more serious effects on the evolution of CAS [close air support] than on any other aspect of airpower*[34].'

In the age of constantly improving information technology, it can be argued that effective air and land integration does not require co-location of commanders and their planners. Others contend that technology cannot yet overcome the impact of geographically separate HQs[35]. Despite its popularity through COVID 19, the limitations of technology are identified in the civil sector – captured in the expression 'virtual presence equals actual absence'. Part of the new appreciation of the strengths and weaknesses of technology is an increasing understanding of the how information actually flows and decisions are made, identifying the key role of 'side bars' during meetings[36]. Militaries intrinsically know this; otherwise they would not have invested so heavily in joint staff colleges that bring together students from the individual services on a single campus.

Properly harnessing joint firepower not only increases combat power it also avoids the creation of seams between air and land operations that can be exploited by an opponent. The current Western approach may deliver the most effective joint warfighting, but it makes synchronising firepower challenging due to the sequential planning process. In NATO's doctrine, on receipt of the mission the joint task force commander and staff conduct a mission analysis and then develop courses of action. They then send the component HQs a formal warning order; though of course, throughout, there is information sharing and liaison between all these HQs. The next formal step occurs when the joint task force commander promulgates his guidance to the components. The limitations of this approach led one authority on joint warfare to identify that the impact on air and land operations is that '*At no time do the commanders doing the fighting in either element actually interact*[37]'. This approach encourages the almost autonomous development of component plans, which are subsequently integrated in accordance with the joint guidance, rather than these being collaboratively derived[38]. In contrast, the historical experience of co-located HQs is that they facilitate army and air force staff cooperatively creating a single plan. This of course leads to superior integration of joint fires.

Perhaps the most serious impact of the separation of component HQs is that initial land planning often proceeds without being sufficiently informed as to airpower's probable contribution and any limitations. Taking this into account can require the reverse-engineering of an extant plan, one in which the commander and his staff have made personal investments. Overcoming this requires airmen in land HQs to have the necessary rank and authority delegated from the air component commander. They cannot just to be proponents for their own service; as identified by Lieutenant General Mike Hostage, when he instructed his delegated commander to: '*Support the commander of ISAF [International Security Assistance Force] …Help him succeed … by his measures of success*[39].' Of course, the purpose of a single joint plan is to ensure that the land component's measures of success are coherent with the joint ones. However, the land commander will often have a different perspective, this can be influenced by him often being the only commander in theatre.

It is the reduction in its organic firepower in Western armies and their reliance upon aerial firepower, that makes this such as issue. A joint interdependence warfighting approach can only work with the highest level of air and land synchronisation and convergence. If the land component were better able to fight on its own, then the joint HQ could concentrate upon the conduct of the operational level of war and the coordination of component warfighting.

Challenges to the Divisional Level of Warfighting

> '*The traditional twentieth-century concept that field artillery was never in reserve had resulted in pooling resources at the division level and above, allowing flexibility in supporting operations as required … Divisions normally had attached a direct-support field artillery battalion to each of its combat brigades, but the practice became formalised with the modular transformation of the [US] Army [in 2005]*[40].'
>
> Janice E. McKenney, Official US Artillery Historian

The division is the level that traditionally delivers all-arms warfighting. This is the original purpose of this level of command, as by definition this organisation has a part, or division, of each arm and service. The division has the span of command and sufficient staff to sequence tactical engagements, and simultaneously conduct the close and deep battles. This makes it the crucial level of command for joint firepower; despite this, leading armies have moved away from the primacy of the division.

Post the Cold War, a combination of practical and conceptual factors led to this marginalising of the divisional level of command. First there was the force reductions of the 1990s and the realisation that the future would see far more brigade-level deployments than divisional sized ones. Secondly there was the questioning of whether the current corps and divisional structures were too cumbersome for the emerging security environment. This development was popularised in the phrase 'breaking the phalanx[41]'. It was largely led by the US military, who identified the requirement to shift the responsibility for the combining of all the separate arms and services down to the brigade level of command. Divisional HQs were to employ the brigades to fight the battles and engagements. Above them, '*corps conducted large-scale land operations, employing divisions as part of a joint campaign, executing operational level actions to achieve strategic effects*[42]'. Driven by downsizing, rather than doctrine, some militaries decided to be more radical, and removed the divisional level of command[43]. The impact of the marginalisation of the divisional level of war has been to reverse the historic trend for the employment of land firepower to become increasingly centralised. The chain of events being:

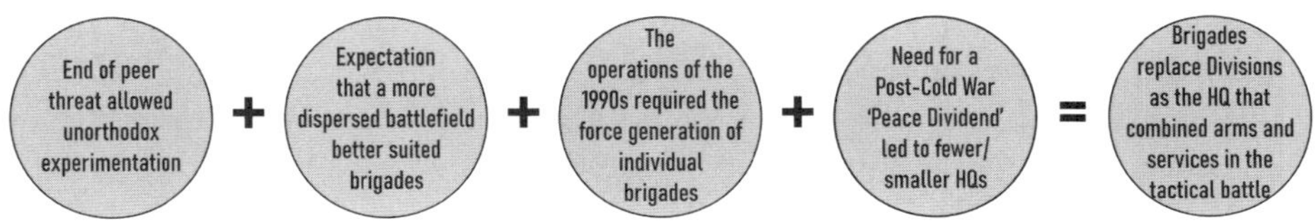

When counter-insurgency was the dominant military task this reorganisation did not appear to be radical. America and her allies were deploying a succession of brigades and battalion groups for operations in Iraq and Afghanistan; this meant that they all received a 'slice' of divisional troops. When divisional HQs deployed they were largely stripped of their firepower, and instead largely focused on policy guidance and oversight of the non-military functions necessary in counter-insurgency operations.

During warfighting, America's new concept required brigade combat teams, with their own organic fires battalion, to conduct the close battle. It was perceived that making artillery organic to the all arms brigades would lead to higher tempo and thus a lesser a requirement for firepower[44]. While fires brigades (renamed back to field artillery brigades in 2014) and aviation brigades, supported by airpower, conducted the deep battle. This change meant that divisional artillery ceased being responsible for resourcing the close fight and conducting the deep battle. As all tube artillery became organic to the brigades, the division could only reinforce with airpower and rocket artillery. This could be effective, but these delivery means could not provide tube artillery's guaranteed area firepower at danger close ranges. This type of firepower is essential in suppressing opposition in the close battle. In extremis, a division could reinforce a brigade with another brigade's artillery battalion. However, the donor brigade will have positioned their artillery battalion to support their formation's forces. This means that it may not be in range to provide divisional reinforcing fires.

By 2011 Russian ground forces were predominantly organised into independent brigades, with only a single division remaining: garrisoning the Kuril Islands[45]. This change did not affect the parallel artillery chain of command; it now reported direct from the brigade level to the 3-star combined arms armies that command tank, motor rifle, air defence, missile and artillery brigades. Nor, unlike the West, did the Russians reduce their artillery holdings. Despite this, the Russians are reintroducing the 2-star level of command. They have identified that this can more effectively employ combined arms, in particular artillery, in conventional warfighting against a peer adversary[46]. They specifically identify that their independent brigades lack the combat power to breach a NATO defence. Independent brigades are being retained, they have a role in less demanding theatres and for more mobile tasks. These new Russian divisions have three tank or motor rifle regiments. These regiments have both tube and rocket artillery, but in a lesser quantity than independent brigades; but this is still a considerable quantity, a combined total roughly equal to that held by the division's artillery regiment. Two divisions are paired with an independent brigade in a combined arms army. This suggests that the divisions achieve the breach and the brigade exploits. As well as providing additional combat power, the divisional staff has the capacity to plan and execute simultaneous tactical actions. This is necessary for a seamless transition between the break-in and break-through battles, and the subsequent exploitation. Enabling this manoeuvre requires the Russian artillery and rocket troops to simultaneously neutralise the opposing artillery[47].

The Chinese have adopted a similar approach to the Russians with their shift towards independent brigades, though with proportionally less artillery[48]; even though they have a total of 8,000 artillery pieces. These largely reside in their two remaining artillery divisions and their 17 artillery brigades[49]. Their expectation for the brigade level of command mirrors that of the Russians in seeking greater agility[50]. While the Russians and the Chinese may have partially moved away from the proven Soviet approach, the Indians did not; retaining the divisional level of command and their faith in highly centralised firepower, a view reinforced by the experience of their artillery-dominated frontier conflicts.

Western armies are restoring the authority of the divisional level of command, notably the Americans, who have re-established artillery HQs in all their divisions. There is agreement on the need for an artillery chain of command to establish and maintain professional standards for all artillery. In late 2020, the debate is on-going over operational control of brigade-level artillery. There are compelling reasons for the Americans to restore centralised command over their artillery. Firstly, they have significantly less artillery than likely peer opponents, and so can ill-afford to have unengaged batteries awaiting tasking from their own brigade. Secondly the US Army and Marines' command and control system is optimised for centralisation, and is relatively ineffective at employing individual batteries. Finally, the flexible use of massed firepower has been an enduring theme of American warfighting and it remains a crucial strength. Deviation away from this approach has historically proved to be short-lived, such as with the 'accompanying artillery' of World War Two; this was soon absorbed into the artillery's centralised fire support system. Decentralising control of artillery significantly contributed to the American reversal at Kasserine Pass on 18 February 1943.

Adopting the primacy of the brigade level of command contributed to the decline of Western artillery, both in terms of quantity and the command and control capability to maximise its firepower. The command and control challenges are being resolved, but without significantly reversing the reduction in organic firepower that followed from the disbandment of much of the general support artillery. The Russian shift to brigade level operations preserved both artillery's quantity and its separate command structure. Their brigades have sufficient organic firepower in most circumstances to permit manoeuvre. When facing a prepared defence, their artillery and missile brigades could provide the reinforcing fire necessary to achieve and then maintain manoeuvre. Russian military science, with its firepower-centric logic, meant that a return to a divisional structure was an inevitable outcome of the need to simultaneously apply firepower over the whole depth of a peer adversary's defensive position. Divisional HQs can both command the quantity of firepower required, and have sufficient artillery staff to ensure that it is scientifically employed.

Joint Fires Battlespace Management

> *'the single greatest issue between the Army and the Air Force during OIF [Operation Iraqi Freedom in 2003] was the old one of battlespace management. Ironically, this issue also surfaced between the various echelons of the ground component ...*[51]*.'*
>
> David E. Johnson, RAND

Management of the battlefield has always been crucial to effective warfighting. Historically it has been done through linear battle formations, with individual units either forming up on the flank of another unit or upon a terrain feature. While the battlefield may be becoming less linear[52], there still remains the understandable human desire for physically protected flanks. Clarity also reduces the chance of fratricide through avoiding ambiguity in tactical responsibility. This leads to the desire for the boundary lines that designate a military body's geographical area of responsibility being established on easily identifiable terrain.

Modern operations are conducted in the all dimensions, domains or environments[53]. Spectrum and cyberspace management are growing problems, but due to its institutional and technical aspects, the managing of airspace remains the greatest battlespace management challenge. Managing airspace has become more complex due to the proliferation of air users, and the greater range and ceiling of army helicopters, drones and missiles. Synchronising air and ground users is usually achieved through segregating users into different airspace. The alternative approach is to let surface-to-surface fires and aircraft share the same airspace and accept a level of fratricide. Ideally, multiple air users can use the same airspace through dynamically separating them by time and space. The tactical battlespace management challenge has increased with the aspiration to employ multiple forms of joint fires simultaneously onto the same target.

American-led coalitions have dynamically managed battlespace in recent limited conflicts without incurring aircraft fratricide. However, it is an order of magnitude more challenging to this in high tempo conventional warfighting against a peer opponent. In theory, through enhancing situational awareness and improving command and control, technology should allow air users to move beyond prescriptive separation. However, the friction and fog of war, coupled with radars being limited by ground clutter, will prevent any surety in managing low level battlespace. As a result, given the tempo, scale and complexity of large-scale conventional warfighting, prescriptive procedural battlespace management is likely to continue in the near term.

In the World Wars aircraft were generally free to engage in front of the limited range of artillery, with often the lead barrage providing a visual indication of this separation. A formal fire support coordination line, or FSCL, originally known as the no-bomb line or bomb safety line, came into use from 1944. Short of this line, ground commanders needed to authorise aircraft weapon release. Tactical aircraft continued to be more dynamically employed, but the line was mandatory when Western strategic bombers supported land operations. In World War Two this no-bomb line was sited at the danger close distance of heavy bombers from own troops; in the 1950s and 1960s it became usual to site this several kilometres beyond the maximum range of tube artillery. No restriction was required to prevent ground forces from firing beyond the no-bomb line as artillery lacked the range[54]. The FSCL was formalised in American doctrine in 1977 and was adopted by NATO, at the time that rockets and attack helicopters were allowing armies to operate in traditional air force battlespace. Reacting to this, the US Army's Cold War AirLand doctrine sought to directly control engagement of the enemy at much greater depth. This led to a FSCL at least 100km in front of own forces, with the US Army controlling the employment of its own organic assets and seeking to control airpower short of this line.

As the extant practice sees the joint commander only assigning battlespace to 'surface' components (land and maritime), since Desert Storm the FSCL has often been used to separate air and land component responsibility[55]. Its siting is the land commander's decision, despite its correct placement and subsequent policing being essential to effective joint warfighting. It has led to considerable inter-component friction, not least because allowing ground forces to assign aircraft to targets short of the FSCL is contrary to the centralised employment of airpower[56]. The result was that during the planning of the location of the Gulf War fire support coordination line:

> *'The dialogue between ground and air commanders soon began to look more like litigation than combined-arms warfare, with each marshalling its evidence and scoring points[57].'*

This was despite the sequencing of the Gulf War, into a 41-day 'air campaign', followed by a 100-hour joint phase, which should have minimised inter-service disputes. But the incorrect placing of the FSCL was subsequently seen as permitting the escape of the most effective elements of the Iraqi Army:

> *'It became clear that the positioning of the [air and land] boundary was one of the most important miscalculations in the final hours of the [ground] War. Moving the line east and north was correct if the Army followed through on the ground. But if the Army attack was delayed, the line should have been moved back so that Allied warplanes could concentrate their firepower on the fleeing forces. CENTCOM [Central Command] did neither. As a result, much of the Iraqi Army was shielded from the sort of punishing bombing raids it endured during its retreat from Kuwait City. A doctrinal technicality and inertia took precedence over common sense[58].'*

Following the Gulf War the Air Force and the Army continued to debate how to divide the battlespace[59]. US Air Force Chief of Staff, General Merrill McPeak, attempted to achieve resolution through redefining the different roles. He proposed a division into 'close, deep and high battles'[60], suggesting that the Air Force took over the last two, while operational control of the close battle would remain the prerogative of 'surface forces' (Army, Navy, Marines). Such an approach would allocate the air component the entire depth of the battlespace, and directly challenged the Army view that airpower's task was to support the 'decisive' ground forces[61]. The impact of this initiative was largely to stoke the inter-service dispute.

The dispute was not satisfactorily resolved in time for the Iraq War. The American V Corps placed the FSCL 100km in front of forward troops[62]. However, the rapidity of the advance combined with delays in implementing FSCL shifts resulted in the actual distance being closer to 55km[63]. The air view that this distance was too great to allow effective joint warfighting was reinforced by 11th Aviation Brigade's ill-fated raid on the night of 23 March 2003. This required an extension of the Corps' battle area that in effect shielded the Iraqi forces from Coalition airpower. 3rd Infantry Division almost overran the FSCL, further highlighting the failure of timely inter-component coordination[64].

A further complication with the current arrangements is that fire support coordination lines are permissive fire control measures. This means that the land component can fire beyond the line without prior coordination with the air component. In the Korean theatre of operations, there is a deep battle synchronisation line, beyond which land assets cannot fire without prior coordination. In the Gulf War the 'Horner Line' – which was set at 30 nautical miles parallel to, and in front of, the fire support coordination line – effectively followed this practice[65].

In the Iraq War the FSCL also proved to be an ineffective means of control when the front line was the lead elements of friendly forces advancing along several axes and there were large pockets of resistance behind these advancing units. Because of this the 1st Marine Expeditionary Force employed its own 'battlefield coordination line', retaining the responsibility for ensuring that it matched the progress of ground operations. In this non-linear conflict, apportioning battlespace by kill box proved to be more effective approach. These three-dimensional areas were either pre-planned or immediate. They can be further divided: purple kill boxes which were open to both surface-to-surface and air-to-surface fires and blue kill boxes – which were generally beyond the range of artillery – for airpower[66]. These kill boxes were closed to aircraft until opened by V Corps' Air Support Operations Center. Once opened, airpower could engage blue boxes without further coordination.

In theory relying upon kill boxes and not apportioning geographic areas to components should allow more flexible use of battlespace, and avoid inter-service confrontation. The contrary view is that in the same way that the joint HQ is the expert in joint warfighting, the individual components are similarly expert within their own environments. It follows that they should have delegated battlespace, rather than needing to operate through a joint construct.

The 2006 Israeli invasion of Lebanon – a ground war they largely blundered into – shows the problems caused by inadequate coordination. They did not formally divide the battlespace; instead they activated kill boxes to employ airpower, but this proved inadequate because:

> *'ground commanders often lacked a clear picture of their battlespace ...airborne aircrews could never be sure that friendly ground troops were not inside a given kill box*[67]*.'*

To add clarity, a 'yellow line' was drawn running east and west parallel to Israel's northern border, with aircrews been given freedom to engage targets beyond this. The air force believed that this line was too far north and interfered with their prosecution of shorter-range rockets. This was disputed by the Northern (ground) Command, resulting in the same disagreement that could be expected with a FSCL. Inadequate coordination resulted in a 'big sky, small plane' approach to airspace deconfliction:

> *'Once the IDF's [Israeli Defence Force] ground involvement began in earnest, aircraft and artillery operated together closely, often even interchangeably. There was reportedly no attempt by the IAF [Israeli Air Force] to deconflict flight operations from artillery fire because doing so with any exactitude would have been, in the words of one IAF officer, "practically impossible" ... With as many as 173,000 or more rounds of artillery fired altogether by IDF ground forces over the course of the 34-day campaign, the avoidance of even a pretence at airspace deconfliction constituted a colossal gamble that an in-flight fratricide event would not occur sooner or later[68].'*

Leaning from this, a more sophisticated approach was taken two years later in operations over the Gaza Strip. Formal deconfliction of shared airspace, resulted in increased combat power by allowing '*attack helicopters into airspace above hot areas on the ground that were concurrently being serviced by bomb-dropping fighters*[69]'. Without these formal measures, aircraft will probably practice informal deconfliction to avoid fratricide; as pilots are likely to over-compensate, this is likely to diminish combat power.

There can be a stark contrast between peacetime deconfliction – with its assured separation of individual aircraft by altitude, time and space – and actual operations when air users unschooled in this – shells and rockets, and to a lesser extent drones and low flying helicopters – are added to the mix. Peacetime air safety is purely airmen controlled; addressing the other wartime air users means working with the ground component, which adds significant friction. The complexity of practising operationally realistic airspace deconfliction in peacetime training deters most militaries from attempting it. Most air forces contend themselves with the overall control of airspace management for the joint commander, rather than focussing on the knotty problem: the management of airspace immediately above land component operations. This has the practical challenge of ground clutter preventing even networked ground and airborne radars from delivering an assured recognised air picture. If complete fidelity were possible, correctly employing this information would require considerable investment in sensors, skilled personnel and advanced communications. The US Army identified the need for over 1,600 trained operators in cells at corps, division, and brigade levels, all linked through the tactical airspace integration system[70]. The actual utility of this is questionable, as most army air users follow a ballistic path rather than flying instructions from an air controller.

Currently this airspace management challenge necessitates procedural control with the allocation of height bands to different air users[71]. Separating rotor and fixed wing aircraft is achieved through a dividing coordinating level. This is normally 3,000 feet above ground level, but a higher divide can provide more room to manoeuvre in helicopter-intense operations, as well as partly making an allowance for a country's rugged relief. This led to the coordination level being set at 5,000 feet during America's Vietnam War. In other circumstances, it can be the likely cloud base or weapon mixes that are the decisive factors[72]. Below this coordinating level, fixed wing aircraft will usually employ bespoke low-level transit routes or will be restricted to operating zones around a target managed by a forward air controller.

Above this coordination level there are different approaches to the management of the airspace above land combat operations. If airspace control authority is not delegated to the land component, then it imposes upon mortars, tube and rocket artillery the need to individually clear their fires with the air component. The resultant delay can emasculate much of the land component's firepower. Alternatively, the land component can exercise airspace control up to a designated altitude; this is a joint endeavour that draws upon the air component's command and control assets, with much of the work being done by air force officers in land HQs. The Americans expect to exercise control up to a coordinating altitude[73] over land formations and horizontally up to the FSCL. This can be a pre-planned airspace control zone; which can be activated (turned 'hot') during periods of intense land combat, such as when a brigade goes into close combat. This allows guns and mortars to fire through this battlespace without pre-clearance. Aircraft stay out of this battlespace unless specifically directed by land force controllers. Effective joint warfighting needs a team approach to managing airspace:

> *'While procedural control methods will remain a mainstay of airspace and fires integration for the foreseeable future, the integration of personnel from both Services who are directing and monitoring ongoing operations permits dynamic coordination, activation, and deactivation of airspace and fire support coordination measures ...*[74]*.'*

The key airspace control decision is whether to improve the response time of organic firepower or maximise airpower's freedom. If the majority of the firepower is expected to come from airpower, then impediments to aircraft should be minimised. This is not likely to be the case in conventional warfighting against a peer enemy; here organic land firepower is likely to dominate. However, the joint commander may need to restrict the land component's freedom within the battlespace above their formations, in the interests of the most effective joint warfighting. Of course, this land/air-controlled battlespace is small compared to the whole theatre, but keeping the coordinating altitude as low as possible reduces the restrictions on airpower. As does minimising the time in which the battlespace is 'hot'.

Land forces only need airspace to a certain height to conduct their fires: this is the artillery maximum vertex height plus an extra 1,000ft of separation (the airspace management safety convention). Calculating the coordinating altitude using artillery's battle or planning range as opposed to maximum range significantly aids joint warfighting. This range also limits the wear on guns through not employing maximum charge and maintains consistency, which significantly tails off at long range. The contrast between using planning and maximum range can be seen for a range of British equipment[75]:

Weapon System	Range Type	Range (m)	Trajectory Vertex Height (feet)	+1000 feet additional separation for a Stay Above Height (feet)
155mm 39-Calibre	Max	24,700	27,000	28,000
	Planning	19,500	10,000	11,000
British 105mm	Max	17,200	17,000	18,000
	Planning	15,000	9,000	10,000
81mm Mortar	Max	5,675	9,000	10,000
	Planning	5,100		

It follows that a coordinating altitude of 11,000 feet is adequate for these typical weapon systems[76]. 14,000 feet was the standard for operations against the Islamic State. In the Gulf War it was set at 18,000 feet. Higher coordinating altitudes are used and they provide greater flexibility for the land component – allowing closer-to-maximum range to be employed and allowing some high angle fire – but this needs to be balanced against the impact on joint warfighting. Crucially, keeping the coordinating altitude low allows aircraft to both transit over and deliver standoff precision fires from above when this airspace is 'hot'. Of course fires above this coordinating altitude need to be individually cleared with the air component. This is another factor in making the MLRS less responsive than tube artillery and mortars.

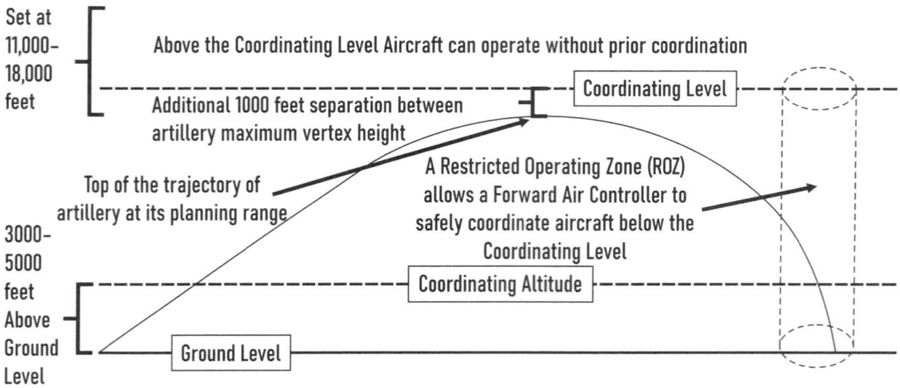

The Soviets/Russians prefer to employ simpler battlespace management techniques. As pre-planned airpower is mainly used against depth targets it usually does not need to coordinate with artillery. When air and artillery/mortars engage the same target, they are usually separated by time. An exception to this is the use of direct artillery and gun-mortar fire, which is of course low trajectory, onto targets already being engaged by aircraft[77].

Improving Joint Fires Command and Control

'The object of future-gazing is not only to predict what organisations, doctrine, and technologies are the right ones, but also to estimate when these three primal warfighting variables [organisations, doctrine and trechnologies] will be mature enough to be applied to create combat units[78].'

Reverting to the traditional levels of organic firepower and centralising its employment will allow Western armies to compete with peer opponents without almost total reliance upon airpower. Of course, matching Russian artillery will take time, but restoring the authority of the artillery chain of command to match the return to divisional level conventional warfighting can be easily implemented. More challenging is better integrating air and ground planning and execution. One approach is to replace the focus on operational-level joint warfighting with one designed to also achieve inter-component tactical synergy; this will deliver immediate benefits in synergising joint fires. Initially co-locating the individual elements of the joint, land and air HQs that need to work together could foster a more collegiate approach. Historically this has led to more integrated operational planning. The land component's command function will then need to go forward with the fighting elements for the plan's execution. But there is no requirement for the majority of their staff, who have a controlling function, to go with them. These can continue to collaborate with their joint and air colleagues in dispersed static locations: so facilitating joint fires.

Senior air force officers, suitably empowered by the air component commander, could improve air/land decision-making in this forward land HQ. In conventional and counter-insurgency warfighting, the Americans have deployed two-star generals into land component HQs. The Israelis have determined that this 'commander air' needs to operate like his artillery opposite number, and thus requires at least the same rank, experience and staff support. This air force staff presence has made their brigade HQs effectively joint when engaged on operations. Of course, this practice may not extend beyond the country's current security challenge. This Israeli development builds upon their broader view of airpower – temporally interrupted by the re-focussing of their military upon the Intifada – that has led to instances of ground commanders personally re-allocating close air support aircraft to air interdiction, despite being in close combat. It is difficult to see this as likely within NATO's more transactional approach to air and land integration.

This risk of relying upon airpower to deliver a significant proportion of land's firepower was compounded by the post-Cold War de-centralising of organic firepower in NATO armies, in particular by the American Army. This led to the neutering of the parallel command structure that allowed the senior artillery commander to work directly for the commanding general in employing firepower. This development runs counter to the previous trajectory of Anglo-American warfighting, with its centralisation allowing the manoeuvring of fire between the close and deep battles. Historically this has provided a balancing mechanism against the understandable tendency of reacting to the close battle's most immediate challenge. This was a feature of World War Two German warfighting with its subordinating of both artillery and air support to tactical-level close combat. Land firepower's decentralisation was in part collateral damage from a policy change that identified a permanent shift in the character of conflict that gave primacy to the brigade level of command. This is now being partly reversed, but without fully restoring the disbanded divisional and corps level artillery units.

Maximising the integration of air and ground operations cannot be solely achieved by employing sufficient airpower expertise in land component HQs. The challenge is for soldiers to have sufficient experience and training to appreciate where airpower fits in. Unfortunately almost all professional education is initially conducted on a single-service basis. This leads to officers being quite senior when they attend the joint staff colleges with their navy, marine and air force peers. The US artillery is putting all junior artillery officers through joint fires officer training, in part to improve its organic ability to direct airpower, but also to make them 'air aware' from the start of their careers.

While the American Army and Air Force conflict over battlespace management has effectively culminated, there is a need to formalise the current arrangements in joint and then NATO doctrine. Otherwise without the catalyst of combat operations the services may return to their entrenched positions. Easy-to-implement reforms are required to reduce the chance of joint battlespace management serving as a vehicle for inter-service dispute and leading to inefficient warfighting. The land component's control of the airspace above ground combat operations needs constant, demanding joint training with live air. This needs to be undertaken on the basis that in conventional warfighting when this battlespace goes 'hot', surface-to-surface fires will engage without further clearing airspace. The established path for Western air forces is for increasingly dynamic management of the airspace; but this is not equally applicable to land component airspace. Air forces need to recognise that different environments result in different approaches to the character of conflict. This led to this French view on the limited impact of improved situational awareness, and its failure to replace procedural control:

> *'in spite of all their capabilities, these types of equipment [the French joint battlespace module[79]] considerably weigh down a battlegroup [staff] for a mere visualization, and an incomplete one, of its air space[80]'.*

If the FSCL is to serve as in effect the horizontal delineation between air and land responsibility, then it needs to cease being a permissive fire control measure. It should be closer to ground troops than has recently been the case. 30–40km is sufficient for most ground sensors and tube artillery. In a rapid advance this divide will need frequent adjustment. Having the line this close to ground forces means that recce, land-operated aircraft and longer-range rocket systems will need coordination with the air component to fully exploit their range. This is probably best done with kill boxes. While this may appear to run counter to achieving tempo, in reality such coordination almost always needs to take place[81].

This would mean that the army would largely cede direct control over corps shaping operations. This was in effect the outcome of the USAF sponsored work following the Iraq War. The overall conclusion was the need to take a more dynamic approach, rather than a straight delineation between air and land battlespace[81], especially as the FSCL often artificially cuts through the corps level battle. But it identified that if the Army were to cede battlespace, it needed greater surety that air operations would meet their shaping objectives.

It is difficult to disagree with the proposition that the air component is the best placed to achieve effect in the deep battle. Partly because fixed wing aircraft have proved to be significantly superior to the combination of attack helicopters and precision surface-to-surface missiles at attacking depth targets. But also because air force HQs are designed for this function, as the 3rd Infantry Division (Mechanised) after action report from the Iraq War identifies:

'The argument seems to be that CFACC [Coalition Force Air Component Command] would not adequately address V Corps' targeting requirements; 3ID (M) violently disagrees. CFACC is a component, manned and equipped to effectively manage this battlespace forward of the FSCL; V Corps is not and has demonstrated their inability to manage said battlespace. 3ID (M) believes CFACC is better prepared to engage targets to effectively shape the battlefield … The U.S. Army must redefine the battlespace based on our ability to influence it[83]*.'*

Inter-component fires have proved to be simple to execute when there is clarity of purpose emanating from the joint headquarters. This usually coexists with certainty of responsibility for a given battlespace. It is easy to sympathise with General Creighton Abrahams – America's *de facto* joint commander for much of the Vietnam War's – views on the need for clarity:

'I have used the word 'flexibility' for the last time. It seems that this is a large general purpose test under which chaos, confusion, and general incompetence are kept well hidden from the public[84]*'.*

Effective battlespace management requires clarity of responsibility; conforming Robert Frost's view that '*good fences make good neighbours*[85]'.

Significant change is required to deliver an approach to joint warfighting that compensates for the West's current shortage of organic land firepower. Historically such radical change, as Barry Posen notes, has generally not been possible without the imperative provided by significant defeat or the concerted efforts of civilian policymakers[86]. But led by America, with the Israelis also providing some innovative ideas, there appears to be a willingness to address the deficiencies of inter-service cooperation.

Chapter 16: Fifty Propositions Towards a Land Firepower Theory

Before Colin S Gray published 'Fighting Talk', the use of maxims, principles, enduring truths and the like was not fashionable in scholarly circles. They are a feature of the military profession; hence they are a natural choice when trying to tersely explain ideas on land firepower. Serving as the book's conclusion, this chapter advances a series of propositions that aim to identify the key issues and make some judgements. To some they may be provocative, perhaps in part due to their novelty or simply wrong; this will serve a purpose if it encourages further examination of the topic. Ideally, these propositions seek to lead to agreed principles, maxims and metrics. They will at least encourage the view of land joint fire's future path as determined by the interconnectivity of the constituent elements. This could assist in determining the right balance between them for a given conflict's character. This is the outcome of advocating for land joint fires to be seen as a system-of-systems. However, for the foreseeable future, most discussion of force employment will probably continue to focus on firepower's discrete elements. Time is probably required for a longer view of land joint fires; after all, it took Americans about a hundred years to stop saying the United States 'are' and begin saying the United States 'is'[1].

Firepower's Role in Warfighting

1st Proposition: Artillery and mortars have become more lethal through the joint fires' century. The proportion of casualties inflicted by indirect fire was around 60% in World War One, this increased to around 70% in World War Two. It may even be as high as 80% in the Russo-Ukraine War. This proportion increases in static combat and reduces when the fighting becomes mobile. Of course, it also depends upon a combatant having the necessary technology. In the Korean War, Communist artillery and mortars accounted for nearly 60% of Americans killed in action; the much more powerful UN artillery must have inflicted an even higher proportion of Communist casualties. Through indiscriminate use, artillery and mortars have often been responsible for most of the casualties in wars amongst the people. The exception to this rule are low technology conflicts, such as those that have predominated in Africa. Another trend is firepower's increased lethality against armoured vehicles. Inflicting casualties may not always directly lead to victory, but it is a key enabler, and a reflection on firepower's ability to both allow and hinder the manoeuvre of military forces. Firepower also directly impacts upon an opponent's morale and thus willingness to resist.

2nd Proposition: Decisive land close combat relies upon combining organic firepower with ground manoeuvre. The other forms of firepower can assist, but this proposition rests upon artillery and mortars providing the covering fires, usually at danger close ranges, that enable close assault. Deep fires assist this by dislocating the opposing firepower and command and control. Actual, or even the threat of, close assault particularly when this comes from an unexpected direction, is the principal means of breaking an opponent's primary group cohesion, and thus their will to fight. Aggressive exploitation of successful close combat can send shock waves that makes an army vulnerable to losing its cohesion. The chances of this are heightened by an effective deep battle that paralyses an opponent's physical and psychological ability to respond. Historically in conventional conflict, a warfighting approach that emphasises the combined use of battlefield firepower and ground close combat has swept aside other approaches. Ways of war, that emphasise measured, cerebral and carefully calibrated effects, such as in sub-threshold operations, are vulnerable to violently executed ground manoeuvre by armies with a clear warfighting ethos. In the same way the armies of the Age of Reason could not cope with the directness and brutality of the French Revolutionary armies.

3rd Proposition: Conventional warfare is more likely to be politically decisive when it overwhelms an adversary in battle; especially when this turns most combatants into prisoners of war. This proposition links the manner in which a conflict is conducted with the nature of its termination. The traditional Western approach has sought to decide wars in battle. Successful close ground combat turns many of the opposition combatants into prisoners. The capturing of significant quantities of prisoners of war greatly aids the defeated side in accepting the political outcome of a conflict, as do stand-up fights that test comparable forces upon the battlefield, as this meets the need for a contest which is hardwired into *homo sapiens*. The West's most recent conflicts have not followed this approach. Post 9/11, the American Coalition eschewed conventional land forces in the defeat of the Taliban, and failed to capture and disarm most of the Iraqi Army. Unsurprisingly, both nations resorted to 'people's war'. The interconnectivity between how conventional warfighting is conducted and its post-conflict impact is still not fully recognised in Western doctrine.

4th Proposition: Since the late 19th century land warfare's pre-eminent battlefield challenge has been surviving firepower; this primacy has been challenged, but not replaced, by information age technology and techniques. Countering modern firepower necessitates the employment of concealment, physical protection, armour, dispersion, constant movement, deception, and has the requirement to pre-empt danger by attacking opposing firepower at source. Some take this one stage further in seeking to use human terrain to hinder target acquisition, and as protection against an opponent's firepower. This is nothing new – the 13th century Mongols systematically used hostage screens. Recent Russian practice in Ukraine is seen as relatively novel in seeking to dislocate firepower by creating a degree of ambiguity as to whether an armed act can be legitimately challenged at the strategic level or targeted at the tactical level. But throughout history aggressors have sought to achieve gain without triggering a violent response. In the last years of the 20th century, the pre-eminence of firepower has been disputed by a rival view that information age technologies and techniques now dominate warfare. More recently war has been seen to have been transformed by aggression that remains below the threshold of a response and the increased use of the non-military forms of state power. While much has changed, this does not add up to a revolution in military affairs. Evidenced by the continuation in militaries of established hierarchical structures and the enduring of industrial age functions. Ultimately it is hard power that sustains Russian and Chinese aggression and ultimately firepower based land power will be required in any geopolitical rebalancing.

5th Proposition: Indirect fire is inherently more lethal than direct fire, and this differential is growing as more accurate and lethal munitions are reducing the effectiveness of counters to firepower. This proposition is derived from indirect fires' greater ability to identify and engage targets. This rests on three main advantages. First, except when aircraft find their own targets, joint fires separates the firer from the controller of the engagement. This allows firepower's terminal controller to occupy the best position, or employ the most suitable technical means, to acquire the target and ensure that the fire is effective. Second, unlike direct fire, indirect fire does not require an uninterrupted line of flight from the 'barrel' to the target. Through employing trajectories that avoid terrain, indirect fire can engage almost any target within range. Finally, joint fire systems are better able to achieve and sustain lethal fire. Part of this is psychological – as joint fires are less affected by human limitations in inflicting violence. More significantly, a greater weight of fire is made possible by it being significantly easier to deliver munitions to a gun position, mortar line or airfield than to troops involved in close battle. These traditional advantages are being supplemented by more accurate and lethal munitions that are reducing the effectiveness of the traditional counters to firepower, in particular dispersion and cover. In addition, by choosing their point of impact, precision munitions reduce the protection afforded by armour and fortifications.

6th Proposition: Firepower is increasingly the dominant partner in conventional combined arms warfighting as its combat power has grown at a faster rate than manoeuvre forces. Firepower's lethality has accelerated since the 1980s. This is due to enhancements in target acquisition, range and coverage, accuracy, responsiveness and munition lethality, especially against armoured targets. This capability increase has not been matched by similar advances in manoeuvre forces, whose execution tempo predominantly remains wedded to the ground combat vehicle's cross-country speed, while the need to achieve line of sight between firer and target limits lethality. Soviet military science expected most combat power to come from firepower; amongst Western armies, the Americans standout in following through with the implications of this paradigm. Specifically, that this inverts the traditional relationship between firepower and manoeuvre. Infantry and tank formations do not advance under the cover of fire support; instead their physical presence identifies and fixes targets for firepower. Then through the threat or delivery of close assault, they make firepower decisive by providing the psychological pressure to break the defender's will to fight. Throughout, firepower provides most of the combat power.

7th Proposition: Area not point engagement remains the most effective means of employing firepower in conventional close combat. Concentrating fire onto identified enemy positions, is, of course, the most lethal means of employing firepower. Precision munitions can make this even more effective through engaging individual point targets. However, while this is technically possible, in the fog and friction of the close battle, it is rarely practical to identify each discrete target and then individually apportion a munition. Instead, in time-competitive close combat, it is more practical to precisely engage an area covering a number of targets. This is not new: the ability to concentrate firepower has always been proportionate to the accuracy of target location, the agility with which firepower can be directed and the ability of munitions to hit their aim. In World War One this led to barrages that could sweep the battlefield for the unidentified machine gun, rather than solely relying upon concentrations on identified enemy locations. Today, it leads to the continued employment of area fires despite precision munitions and technically advanced target acquisition. This proposition recognises that the historic trajectory is towards the more precise employment of firepower. The increased fielding of sub-munitions able to home onto an individual target will probably decisively tilt the balance towards point engagement.

Application of Firepower

8th Proposition. Achieving fire superiority is a pre-condition to effective land warfighting in the same way that air superiority allows the efficient application of airpower. Central to Western airpower doctrine is achieving and maintaining air superiority. This aims to both prevent enemy airpower from interfering with own operations, and create the freedom to engage opposition forces at an advantage. In recent conflicts Western artillery has rarely been systematically countered, and thus has had freedom to conduct fire support and deep fires, leading these nations to underinvest in their counter-fire capability. In conventional conflict, against a peer opponent, achieving firepower superiority has usually been a pre-requisite for successful manoeuvre. Neutralising an opponent's fire system dislocates their combined arms warfighting capability, so providing a decisive edge in close combat. It also, by hindering an opponent's freedom of manoeuvre, prevents them from effectively reacting. Of course, the ideal is to defeat the opponent's fires system; however, history shows that the temporary and local neutralisation of their firepower is usually more achievable. Coinciding this with own manoeuvre allows this to be decisively exploited.

9th Proposition: The attritional application of firepower is the stronger form of warfighting, but with a lesser aim. The systematic orchestration of firepower to incrementally destroy an opponent's fighting power is the key characteristic of attritional warfare. Its execution requires the methodical application of routine processes by intelligence, air and artillery staffs. Commanders need to supervise this application, but they are not required to deliver inspired direction derived from intuitive military genius. This makes it a lower-risk way of conducting warfare; leading to its historical employment by less agile armies confident in their materiel superiority. Its systematic nature facilitates effective all-arms cooperation. As tank and infantry movement is easy to synchronise with fire through fixed fire plans. Efficiently executed, especially when exploiting technical superiority through standoff engagement, it can deliver victory without significant friendly casualties. It can be the best approach when the political objective of the war does not require the total defeat of the opponent's armed forces.

10th Proposition: The manoeuvreist application of firepower is the weaker form of warfighting, but with a greater aim. In manoeuvre warfare, firepower coupled with manoeuvre aims at the systemic collapse an opponent by defeating their will to resist. Achieving this requires the synergising of fire and movement in order to psychologically challenge an opponent. In this doctrine, the destruction of targets has no intrinsic value. When compared to the centralised, systematic, attritional approach, it is inefficient at inflicting casualties. Employing firepower to collapse an opponent's will to fight is more of an art than a science. Its execution requires intuitive command judgement, rather than commanders only capable of supervising staff officers conducting process. Effectively doing this can necessitate a level of decentralisation in decision-making that some armies find uncomfortable. Those armies that espouse a manoeuvreist philosophy, but are uncomfortable with delegating command responsibility, can restrict their subordinates through retaining rules of engagement authority at the highest level.

11th Proposition: The psychological impact of firepower is its dominant characteristic, realistic live fire training can mitigate this, but this is becoming less common. Firepower's impact has led to enduring use of the World War One phrase 'shell shock' to describe war's psychological impact. This is greatest with poorly trained and motivated troops. Despite this, armies continue to invest in technology, novel doctrine and organisations, in preference to effective live fire training that psychologically prepares troops for combat. Recent conflicts show that well trained and led forces, using effective, well understood doctrine, can compensate for deficiencies in equipment. Hence the USMC matches the performance of the US Army despite being less well equipped. Most recognise that it is a false economy to restrict training, as the human dimension remains the most import in warfare. Despite this, exposing troops to joint fires in training has become less common. For some this is because they are unwilling to accept the risk to life of realistic peacetime training. As well as acclimatising troops to firepower, it allows them to understand how close they must be to the fall of shot to exploit covering artillery and mortar fire. The historical experience is that aircraft add to the psychological effect of their firepower by being visible to their target. This training challenge is particularly serious for Western ground forces; since 1943 they have become so acclimatised to air superiority that they have responded with anger, outrange and not infrequently terror if even a few enemy aircraft appear overhead. Hence the importance of exposing troops and their commanders to simulated aerial attack in training.

12th Proposition: The over-reliance of the Western firepower system-of systems upon networked databases, GPS and guaranteed sensor-to-shooter communications will continue until corrected in a 'strategic shock'. Conditioned in their civilian lives to anticipate ever-improving and more pervasive technology, Western soldiers expect guaranteed access to information and communications on the battlefield. However, spoofing and jamming of GPS and communications are both cheap and difficult to counter, while cyber-attacks are becoming an omnipresent threat. Western militaries have made themselves more vulnerable with their reliance upon unhardened civilian technology, distributed decision-making, expectation of information dominance, plus their reliance upon dynamic targeting and precision fires. In contrast, the Russian trust in pre-planned fires, direct fire and non-GPS precision technology; this makes their firepower more resilient when the EMS and cyber domains are contested. Given their hierarchical nature, militaries are perhaps more vulnerable than most professions to 'normalcy bias'. This is the psychological phenomenon whereby people underestimate the danger of their current position, as the alternative is unimaginable. There is a strong case to see this as the condition prevailing in the technological reliance of Western militaries. Unfortunately, the corrective is likely to require battlefield failure.

The Close and Deep Battle

13th Proposition. Despite being both theoretically and practically overlooked, the firepower deep battle has been a facet of land warfare since World War One. Using manoeuvre forces in the deep battle has been an enduring feature of land warfare. It may have gained its greatest prominence in the raiding forces of the American Civil War. World War One created the firepower deep battle, adding this role to the fire support of the close battle. In this war, aircraft were the most capable target acquisition system, but they had to largely rely upon artillery to engage targets. This lack of lethality resulted in them failing to exploit their full range. Technical improvement in sensors, platforms and munitions – particularly in aircraft – led to the Western Allies engaging the Wehrmacht over significantly greater depth. The Soviets in the 1930s created a different type of deep battle. Instead of using firepower on its own, their all arms formations (including tactical aircraft) created a combined firepower and manoeuvre deep battle. The outcome of their air force led deep battle was that Western land warfighting doctrine largely ignored the deep battle until the late Cold War, when in the AirLand Battle doctrine Western militaries reinvented the firepower deep battle, basing it upon high tech weaponry.

14th Proposition: The 'empty battlefield' now extends significantly behind the front line; most rear area troops have not adjusted to this fact. If survivability is not a factor, then massed formations are more effective on the battlefield. Keeping troops together offers an easier leadership challenge, superior control, increases morale through being part of a visible cohort, offers more efficient logistics, and overall makes it easier to deliver firepower or close assault. All these advantages explain why massed formations were reluctantly abandoned in the close battle. But enhanced firepower forced this from the mid nineteenth century. The logic of the 'empty battlefield' now extends over much of the theatre of operations behind the front line. This is due to improved sensors, delivery systems and munitions, coupled with an improved ability to dynamically engage targets. Together these impose upon troops in the rear areas a similar survivability challenge to that faced by those in the line of contact. Reacting to this will be particularly challenging for non-combat arm troops. Combat enforced the tactical changes required to adapt to enhanced direct firepower. If this historical experience is repeated, then rear area forces will not find it easy to make this fundamental adjustment in peacetime training. Again, unfortunately the corrective is likely to be battlefield failure.

15th Proposition: Fire support and deep fires are distinct capabilities that require weapon systems of different characteristics. Fire support and deep fires require target acquisition, platforms and munitions with distinct capabilities. Different approaches are also required in command, control and target engagement procedures. Fire support requires guaranteed availability, accurate and consistent danger close fires, speed of response, and a rate of fire that can provide continuous suppressive fire. Crucially it needs ease of coordination with ground manoeuvre to deliver an effective combined arms team. For deep fires, all these characteristics are secondary requirements to range and lethality. Hence mortars and tube artillery are largely optimised for fire support, while rocket artillery and most aircrafts' strength is deep attack. The specialist close air support aircraft and attack helicopters are the exception, as these are orientated towards the close battle. When rockets, fighter-bombers and bombers are used for fire support, their characteristics makes them more suitable for preliminary rather than covering fires.

16th Proposition: The aspiration to attack the weakest link of the opposing firepower system needs to be tempered by the realism that it is often only the firing platforms that can be acquired as targets. Locating the opposing firepower system in advance and engaging its weakest link is the most effective approach to the counter fire battle. This would result in destruction being focussed on command and control, logistics and the computerised computation system, ideally achieved by airpower that outranges conventional artillery. However, if artillery and mortars employ effective counter-surveillance they are unlikely to be acquired before they unmask. Bespoke weapon-locating sensors will then acquire artillery and mortars by their sound, flash, or identifying the projectile's trajectory once it rises above ground clutter. Acquiring the other elements of the artillery system is significantly more challenging. This means that it is usually the launcher of the projectiles that is engaged. Therefore, the counter fire system needs the ability to locate, process and then assign weapon systems with the responsiveness and lethality to engage mobile and often protected guns. As rocket systems will have displaced from their firing points before they can be engaged, countering them will usually involve cueing sensors to track them for their subsequent defeat.

17th Proposition: Firepower may be able to neutralise opposing artillery and mortars, but it usually requires manoeuvre forces to decisively defeat an opponent's firepower system. This proposition rests upon opposing artillery and mortars being able to survive by choosing not to be drawn into a counter fire contest. Exceptions occur when there is significant imbalance of forces, in terrain which favours target acquisition, or when the option to pull artillery and mortars back out of range does not exist. In contrast, guns and mortars cannot usually avoid the direct fire of tanks, helicopters and infantry, who also have an asymmetric advantage in close combat. This avoids the need for consent that is inherent in the mutual attrition of an artillery duel. Compared to manoeuvre forces, counter battery fire with unguided shells is an uneconomic way of destroying the opposing fire system. Artillery can achieve neutralisation with perhaps a tenth of the ammunition that is required to destroy a battery. And neutralising the opposing fire support system dislocates the combined arms team, so significantly increasing the chance of success in the close battle, so allowing the gun line to be subsequently attacked. The advent of precision munitions may be shifting the balance in the counter fire battle from neutralisation to destruction. Current counter fire sensors cannot determine target location with sufficient accuracy to provide a firing solution for most precision munitions. But sensor-fuzed munitions only need to be delivered to the target area for them to home in on their targets. Alternatively radars and sound ranging can cue fighter-bombers to the source of the fire, for these to acquire and destroy each individual target with their precision munitions.

18th Proposition: While firepower cannot totally replace manoeuvre forces, the two are almost interchangeable in generating combat power in conventional conflict. Whether attacking or defending, the trajectory of land warfare is towards firepower replacing manoeuvre forces. As firepower is not limited by what can be physically massed into a geographic space, deriving most combat power from firepower greatly aids the concentration of force at the decisive point. But firepower cannot totally replace manoeuvre. There needs to be an assault force on the axis of advance, but even a small element that physically closes with a neutralised enemy is capable of psychologically breaking their will to resist. This assault force can be small because it derives most of its combat power from artillery, mortar and aerial fires. Its small size enables it to maximise survivability techniques against defending firepower. This has led to the Israelis employing a limited number of personnel carriers with main battle tank protection. Firepower is even more interchangeable when holding ground. Artillery and mortar defensive fires provide obstacles that few assaulting troops will cross. Because obstacles created through firepower encourage the individual's survival instinct and prevent leaders from moving around to control and inspire their people. This means that an outpost line, with guaranteed firepower, can be as effective as a number of battalions at holding ground. This has been true throughout the joint fire century, hence in wartime infantry battalions' man their support weapons, not their rifle platoons. Modern firepower has merely shifted the balance in the close battle. In the deep battle, firepower can solely deliver combat power; but its impact significantly increases when it is combined with a manoeuvre force, as this adds a psychological to the physical effect.

19th Proposition: Air forces are more effective than armies at conducting deep fires beyond the range of organic land sensors. This proposition rests upon each component being the best at their primary function. Armies are optimised for applying fire and manoeuvre in the close and the relatively shallow deep battle. Only the divisional level of command really has the capacity to simultaneously fight close and deep. This and corps HQs can process and engage only limited numbers of targets. Air HQs are primarily designed around identifying and processing multiple targets, and then tasking aircraft sorties. This makes army command and staff structures inherently less effective, by their design and culture, than their air force equivalents at conducting deep operations. In the Gulf and Iraq Wars, army long range rockets and helicopters attacked only a fraction of the targets engaged by fixed wing aircraft. In part because armies are reliant upon the air component to provide targeting information beyond the range of their ground-based line of sight sensors, and of course it is simpler for air forces to use their own assets. Despite this, armies are investing in long-range rockets and aviation. Making these productive will require them to effectively operate under air component control. They will improve the effectiveness of the joint force: long-range rockets will provide a useful capability against integrated air defence systems. Crucially they increase the army's equity in the deep battle. Exploiting this requires the land component to clearly articulate how they want the battlefield shaped, and ensure that there is a feedback loop that ensures that the air force executes the necessary targets.

Firepower in Conventional and Irregular Warfighting

20th Proposition: The West's post-Cold War reliance upon aerial fires to replace organic land fires has partially proved its effectiveness against second-rate opposition; it remains unproven in peer conflict. The increased capability of aerial firepower was the West's main rationale, post-1992, for significantly reducing their artillery and mortars. Airpower was expected to destroy much of the opposing combat power prior to ground close combat. If organic firepower was insufficient to defeat what was left, then this could be supplemented by guaranteed close air support. In the 1990s this reliance on airpower was reinforced by various information age theories that identified a reduced requirement to conduct ground warfare, and specifically engage area targets. Instead, precision munitions would systemically defeat an opponent through being carefully targeted at identified weaknesses. These post-Cold War information age warfare theories have now been supplemented by an emphasis upon sub-threshold/grey zone operations and the non-military elements of state power that seek to dislocate the use of conventional militaries. These novel means of defeating an opponent lead to structures and force employment approaches that are untested against peer opponents. Even though these novel techniques are attributed to Russia and China, these retain doctrine and force structures that can employ overwhelming land firepower and decisive manoeuvre.

21st Proposition: In conventional conflict, between evenly matched armies, a force structure that has near numerical parity between firepower and manoeuvre has been the most successful. In the World Wars the successful combatant nations had almost as many artillery battalions as infantry and armour battalions. This ratio delivers the level of firepower necessary to facilitate friendly manoeuvre and prevent the manoeuvre of opposing forces. The West largely maintained this ratio in its conventional conflicts through to the Gulf War. The World's other major armies are still organised around this traditional ratio. In addition, uniquely the Russians extend this to their airborne forces. Armies that have been successful despite not following this proposition – the Wehrmacht early in World War Two and the Israelis before 1973 – have required their opponents to be ill-prepared and/or have significantly less fighting power.

22nd Proposition: The joint fires system-of-systems is the iterative result of a century of warfighting; therefore, caution should be applied before radically changing its balance. This proposition recognises that changes to one element of the joint fires system may have an unexpected effect upon the whole system-of-systems. Systems theory explains why the processes, structures, tools and technologies matter in fire support. It provides the theoretical understanding as to why the user of firepower cannot be agnostic of its source. The source determines the degree of guarantee, responsiveness, and the ease with which its fires can be integrated into manoeuvre. Unfortunately, this is often misunderstood, not least because the simulations employed in most operational analysis uses physical destruction as their primary measure of effectiveness. Leading to an underestimation of the importance of factors other than lethality in the firepower system-of-systems.

23rd Proposition: Western force employment and capability development fails to recognise the different demands that urban warfare makes upon the joint fire-system-of-systems. There is a disconnect between the forecasting of the importance of urban fighting, and actual preparation. This particularly applies to organic fire support. Despite the proven requirement for artillery direct fire, armies are fielding weapons limited in this capability. This deficiency cannot be made up by direct fire systems, as their anti-material effect is secondary to their anti-tank capability. Effect against material targets requires medium calibre munitions (152/155mm artillery or 120mm gun/mortar calibre); but even these are being overmatched by reinforced concrete structures. Artillery thermobaric, incendiary, and smoke munitions are required in greater proportions than open warfare. There is also a different target acquisition and command challenge, driven by the deep battle being a few hundred metres in front of the line of contact. Precision munitions have changed the character of urban fighting due to their ability to engage individual buildings and strongpoints. Because an identified strongpoint can easily be destroyed, mobile defence, from multiple fighting positions, has replaced positional defence. On the offensive, joint fires can take on much of the fighting from the infantry. In most armies, this has not triggered doctrinal change. Nor, despite the destruction of cities such as Ramadi and Mosul in Iraq, Raqqa and Aleppo in Syria and Marawi in the Philippines, is the need for conventional fighting in cities seen as unavoidable.

24th Proposition: By separating it from manoeuvre, firepower will continue to be ineffectively employed by Western armies against opponents employing irregular warfare tactics. This proposition probably has a healthy future because even sophisticated militaries fail to apply orthodox military practice to non-conventional characters of conflict, leading to them in counter-insurgency being more concerned with constraining firepower than using it effectively. Current Western counter-insurgency doctrine fails to identify how to separate a mature insurgency from the people. This requires firepower in concert with manoeuvre forces to tactically defeat the insurgent. Success on the battlefield demonstrates the government forces' greater ability to provide security. Attempting this without a decisive firepower advantage leads to either indecisive combat, or unacceptable security force casualties. While firepower needs to be discriminate and proportionate, this does not necessarily lead to the use of minimum force. Demonstrating overwhelming force can accelerate the process of gaining the allegiance of the people, and provides the security essential to the governance, economic and social lines of operations.

25th Proposition: Government forces must possess sufficient firepower to prevent insurgents adopting potentially decisive conventional warfare tactics. The adoption of irregular warfare tactics is invariably a response to the government forces being superior at firepower-dominated conventional warfighting. Irregular warfare's principal attribute is to diminish firepower's effectiveness. However, an insurgency cannot achieve their political objective through sticking to irregular tactics. A successful insurgency needs to seize control of a state, and this requires the open employment of combat power. It is firepower that prevents an insurgent from successfully transitioning to conventional warfare tactics. The timing of this transition is key. The badly-timed Tet Offensive led to Communist forces being decimated by American firepower. Despite this, they struck a psychological blow that eventually led to the American withdrawal; aided by images of excessive use of firepower. Illustrating that government forces need to be equally agile in reducing their use of firepower when the character of conflict switches to one less openly belligerent.

26th Proposition: Decapitation strategies are ineffective against established insurgencies; as attrition is not coordinated with manoeuvre it cannot significantly contribute to winning the allegiance of the people. Ruthlessly pursuing a strategy of leadership decapitation has defeated immature insurgencies. It has failed against insurgencies that are firmly rooted within the people, or are Jihadist in nature. In recent years, the Western decapitation strategy has achieved considerable attrition of insurgent leadership. This attrition has been credited with providing an opportunity for the campaign to progress along the other lines of operations. However, the civil lines of operation, which are essential to achieving progress in the campaign, need to operate within a secure environment. This can only be achieved by conventional government forces separating the insurgent from the people, and then, through their permanent presence, securing the environment. Of course, pursuing a discrete decapitation strategy satisfies the special forces' desire for institutional independence. Furthermore, it can be pursued by Western governments without the scrutiny that conventional operations would attract, while allowing politicians to demonstrate to their populations the appearance of success. However, to be decisive, decapitation must be used in concert with conventional forces that physically secure the population through their permanent presence.

Surface-to-Surface Firepower

27th Proposition: Guaranteeing fire support requires artillery and mortar to have similar levels of mobility and protection as the rest of the combined arms force. Fire support in conventional warfare requires artillery and mortars to keep within range of manoeuvre forces and survive the counter fire threat. In mechanised warfare, there currently is no effective replacement for the armoured, digitised, self-propelled gun and mortar with its combination of protection, mobility, and the lethality of a sustained high rate of fire. These characteristics enable them to deliver timely direct and indirect fire that can rapidly neutralise targets. Whether this self-propelled gun or mortar is wheeled or tracked should be a second order issue; however, the advantage of having similar mobility capability as tanks and infantry fighting vehicles is compelling. Furthermore, tracks have a clear advantage with heavier platforms – the tipping point is generally accepted as between 30 and 40 tonnes, and self-propelled guns are becoming heavier. This is due to: the need for greater firing range, resulting in longer barrels with greater recoil force; automated loading; greater active and passive protection; and more on-board ammunition storage to deal with an expanded range of munitions. Superior battlefield mobility considerably assists with getting the gun into the right place to conduct direct fire. This need may be increasing in importance due to: urbanisation, higher tempo operations within a less dense battlefield, and the challenge of sustaining indirect fire support against electronic attack upon artillery communications.

28th Proposition: The survivability challenge means that towed guns and mortars cannot be employed in their traditional manner in peer conventional warfare. The Russians have concluded that the towed gun and mortar are too vulnerable to be employed against peer opponents. Self-propelled armoured howitzers and gun-mortars now provide almost all close support to their ground and airborne forces. Only the most highly deployable Russian airborne forces retain ordnance that is neither armoured nor self-propelled. Recent conflicts have convinced America and their allies of the utility of the unarmoured towed gun and mortar, largely due to their ability to be transported by helicopter. Against a peer opponent, the survivability of towed cannon and mortars will be largely determined by their ability to come quickly out of action and move following unmasking. This provides significant advantages for smaller calibre weapons which can more easily 'shoot and scoot'. Heavier calibre guns that are largely reliant upon manpower to come into and out of action are less survivable in conventional peer conflict than similar calibre guns with auxiliary power units to enable rapid change of location.

29th Proposition: Rockets have permanently displaced tube artillery in the deep battle because of their inherent technical advantages. The rockets can achieve long ranges with more lethal munitions than tube artillery. Greater range comes from the rocket motor's ability to impart more thrust than can be provided to a shell or mortar bombs by propellent in a tube. Superior lethality comes from the rocket's greater warhead volume and soft launch. Both these make it easier to exploit precision guidance and carry sub-munitions or an equally lethal thermobaric warhead. Most battlefield rocket systems launch multiple rockets, leading to an unrivalled weight of fire. As a result of range and lethality, rocket artillery now dominates land warfare's deep attack. This overall proposition is being challenged. Firstly by the Americans who are developing tube artillery with a strategic range – however, this effectively is a cannon launched missile; secondly by the Russians who have reintroduced heavy tube artillery on the Donbas to provide sustained fire from munitions with a larger blast content than 152mm.

30th Proposition: In actual conflict, most fire support is at danger close distances; making munitions with small danger areas operationally necessary. The current joint fires capability development trajectory is towards improved lethality and greater reach. On actual operations, there is an enduring requirement for the employment of suppressive firepower close to own troops and non-combatants. The effective use of low yield precision munitions in recent counter-insurgency operations has confused the capability requirement. In conventional conflict, precision munitions lack the speed of response and ability to suppress an area target in the close battle. Experience shows that assaulting troops need to be on the objective within two minutes of the fire lifting. The reduced danger area of smaller munitions means that assaulting troops can get closer to the objective before fire support has to cease. The Russo-Ukraine War has demonstrated the vulnerability of lightly armoured infantry fighting vehicles on the modern battlefield, as a result the dismounted infantry attack remains the norm, even between mechanised forces. Their danger area, means it is not possible for dismounted troops to close onto an objective within two minutes if 120mm mortars and 155mm cannon provide fire support.

31st Proposition: As delivering suppression is the key requirement, small calibre guns and mortars are often superior at fire support. Suppression enables own movement and hinders enemy movement. Suppression is a psychological condition that is best achieved through an initial heavy weight of fire, subsequently it is the 'number of bangs' that counts. Denying the ability of leaders to personally motivate their men is probably the most important factor in causing a unit's combat failure. Of course, smaller calibres are more efficient at delivering this high 'number of bangs'. This proposition links with the previous one in making the case for fielding of capability specifically designed for the fire support of infantry on their feet. It is this that has prevented tube artillery being standardised on the 155/152mm calibre and 120mm becoming the standard mortar calibre. But without the operational imperative, the greater lethality and range of heavier calibres is making a more compelling case in most operational analysis. The Americans are now questioning the need for 105mm artillery plus 60mm and even 81mm mortars are now being taken out of service in some Western armies.

32nd Proposition: The need for both mortars and guns in providing close fire support has been successfully challenged. This proposition recognises that gun/mortars can deliver the functions of both mortars and cannons in the close battle. This divide was originally a product of the two weapons having different design characteristics, but it is now a product of their army's doctrine and thus organisation. The Soviets and now the Russians are unencumbered by institutional baggage that differentiates between artillery and infantry ownership of fire support. Leading to them fielding the hybrid weapon: the gun/mortar. They mainly field the 120mm calibre in a turret on an armoured tracked chassis. This provides close fire support to mechanised and airborne forces. It particularly excels in urban conflict as it can employ direct fire at all elevations of the barrel and use high angle indirect fire against targets behind buildings. The greater danger area of its highly effective warhead can be offset by using more accurate and responsive direct fire when shooting in an assault. As direct fire significantly reduces the danger area. Laser guided munitions provide it with an effective point attack capability, including against tanks. With extended range projectiles or the ability to fire supersonically, the gun/mortar can match the range of light artillery. Only the Scandinavians have shown a similar interest in armoured mortars able to conduct direct and indirect fire. However, as they see them primarily for indirect fire they have not fielded an advanced direct fire control system. It would be surprising if there is not more fielding of gun/mortars.

33rd Proposition: Multiple platforms and munitions provide the flexibility to adjust firepower to a conflict's character. This proposition recognises that no individual firepower capability possesses all the characteristics necessary to meet an army's needs. The joint fires system-of-systems both exploits the synergies and masks deficiencies of the individual systems. This variety of platforms and munitions allows armies to adapt to a conflict's character. However, this rarely happens by design, because militaries expect a conflict to fit with their preconceived views, as articulated in their doctrine. Most doctrine shows a bias towards preparing for mobile operations in open terrain. Militaries that plan for a number of challenges – such as the Germans in 1914 who prepared to pierce a fortified zone before open combat – are better placed than those whose doctrine leads to reliance upon a dominant weapons system. This was the case for their French opponents, who relied on the shrapnel firing French 75mm. Of course, peacetime cost-cutting makes it difficult to field more than a limited number of platforms and munitions. The Russians stand aside from this approach. They are equipped with a breadth of weaponry and munitions that will probably provide an advantage in most future conflict. This is the outcome of seeing urban warfare as a force driver. They also recognise that positional warfare may be necessary to defeat a technically superior foe.

Aerial Firepower

34th Proposition: Technology will continue to reduce airpower's limitations, but declining aircraft numbers means that it has probably passed its apogee in determining the outcome of peer-on-peer ground combat. Individual aircraft are becoming more effective through overcoming the limitations imposed by weather and darkness, and by significantly increasing their lethality. However, fewer aircraft means reduced persistence over the battlefield; this limits their ability to engage targets and restrict, by their mere presence, enemy activity. This, coupled with the reduced effect of their munitions against area targets, prevents modern aircraft replicating the constricting impact achieved in the World Wars by masses of aircraft, constantly circling overhead. By largely employing direct fire weapons, massed airpower (the Soviets employed their ground attack aircraft in corps of 500) could provide World War Two ground forces with the suppressive firepower necessary to fix opposing forces and enable their own ground manoeuvre. Modern airpower may be significantly more capable at destroying point targets, but it is less capable of both imposing its will upon ground forces and replacing organic land firepower in the combined arms battle.

35th Proposition: Integrated ground based air defences have inherent technical advantages over airpower. In recent conflicts, following a brief period of achieving air superiority, the only enduring constraint on Western airpower has been the requirement to avoid the contested low level altitudes. This zone is disputed because it is very hard to detect and defeat man-portable surface to air missiles, machine guns and cannon; together these provide an effective low altitude asymmetric challenge. Modern integrated air defence systems have changed this military equation by making all altitudes contested. Ground based air defences have inherent technical advantages over aircraft through not being as constrained by weight and system integration challenges. Defeating a modern integrated ground based air defence system, if it is possible, will take time and require considerable joint resources. The alternative is to force package strike aircraft with other counter-air defence aircraft and other agencies that will provide physical and electronic protection. This approach may suit deep strike, but it will be challenging when conducting close air support to deliver responsiveness and ensure force protection. This will be possible for pre-planned support to major operations when Western forces have the initiative. When emergency close air support is required, this is likely to be where an opponent has his strongest air defences, hindering close air support from delivering its historic mission of preventing ground forces being overrun.

36th Proposition: Aerial firepower will continue to be the most easily countered form of fire support to land forces. This proposition rests upon the proven effectiveness of active and passive counters to aircraft attacking ground forces. While ground based air defence cannot guarantee the protection of land assets, they can inflict a level of attrition that either deters further air attacks or leads to aircraft adopting attack profiles that reduce their lethality. This change can be immediate, through deterring individual attacking aeroplanes; alternatively, this can occur over the duration of the campaign, through convincing air forces to adopt tactics that increase their force protection. This could include finding less well defended targets than ground forces. The Kosovo conflict showed that even if it rarely engages, an extant air defence system hinders the employment of airpower through forcing aircraft to carry self-defence munitions and using flight profiles that improve force protection. Despite technology's diminishing of airpower's limitations, ground forces can still exploit: darkness, weather, human and physical terrain to reduce its effect. Ground forces can add to the effectiveness of this through dispersal, camouflage and concealment. Alternatively, an opponent closing to within the danger close distance of friendly forces has a much greater impact on airpower's lethality than this does on mortars and artillery fire. Ground forces operating against a dominant air force become well practiced at exploiting airpower's lack of persistence. This is made easier by diminishing aircraft numbers. This proposition is being strengthened by the proliferation of integrated air defence systems amongst peer opponents. In addition, many of the non-state enemies of the West are acclimatised to operating under the permanent threat of airpower and have become expert at passive counters.

37th Proposition: Close air support is neither an aircraft nor a mission, it is a capability; reduced numbers of forward air controllers and air staff officers represents the greatest challenge to its effectiveness. The ongoing American debate as to whether close air support requires a specialist aircraft or can be done by fighter-bombers fails to address the need to look at the system in its totality. As well as requiring a platform, munitions and aircrew, close air support requires an effective air and land integration structure. This needs two elements: terminal controllers of the aircraft; and a staff structure, including air force officers, able to effectively employ aerial firepower within the land battle. In the West's recent conflicts, the current structure has proved proficient in using airpower against, at best, third rate opposition. This does not mean it will be adequate in synchronising all the elements air/land cooperation required for success against a peer opponent. Throughout its history, an inadequate air and land integration structure has been the major factor in stymying airpower's impact.

38th Proposition: Viewing all counter-land missions against fielded enemy forces as close air support obscures the correct employment of airpower. In the Cold War, armies expected to receive only limited close air support. Leading to aerial firepower being associated with the requirement to prevent friendly ground forces being overrun. This usually necessitated danger close firepower, initially at least controlled by forward air controllers, and authorised by the local ground commander. The term close air support has now expanded to cover any air attack on land forces. Including: armed reconnaissance; what used to be called battlefield air interdiction; and the use of airpower in the absence of friendly forces against enemy ground forces, as in the Kosovo conflict. Lack of clarity in taxonomy has resulted in a failure to understand the imperative of individual ground attack missions. Specifically, the breadth of the term fails to reflect whether it should have priority over other tasks, such as air interdiction, which might be a more effective way of employing airpower to aid the land battle. Prioritisation is important because the fundamental disagreement between armies and air forces is not over the utility of employing air-delivered firepower in close combat, but its relative guarantee. Returning to the Cold War assumption that close air support was rare, and was only guaranteed for the highest priority tasks could allow the correct prioritisation between missions. Merely attacking opposing land forces lacks the same immediacy and priority. Recognising this is key in judging the risk against reward when operating against unsuppressed air defence systems.

39th Proposition: In peer conflict, by flying nap-of-the-earth and achieving horizontal standoff distance, helicopters are more survivable than fixed wing aircraft when providing fire support to close combat. In the very highest threat environment – being opposed by an unsuppressed integrated air defence systems – flying fast and low, to employ terrain masking, might improve aircraft survivability. The superior approach in almost all other circumstances is achieving distance between aircraft and target. In recent conflict, fixed wing aircraft have largely achieved this through altitude, turning release altitude into weapon range with free fall bombs; with gravity bombs this range can be substantially increased with glide wings; missiles can provide even more standoff. However, integrated air defence systems can engage aircraft seeking to make use of medium level weapon release; preventing fixed wing aircraft translating standoff distance into survivability. Attack helicopters achieve standoff through maximising the horizontal distance to their target; exploiting superior sensors and guided munitions, and, preferably engaging from behind cover that prevents their acquisition by air defence systems. The greater survivability of the attack helicopter has been evident in conventional warfighting since the Gulf War.

40th Proposition: Specialist fixed wing aircraft are neither a cost-effective nor a survivable means of delivering low-level close air support in peer conflict. Most close air support in recent operations has been from medium level with precision weapons. In exceptional circumstances fixed aircraft have employed low-level attack profiles that allow them to identify their targets and then engage, sometimes with cannons. If aerial firepower is required to aid ground forces who are being overrun, then fixed wing aircraft will probably need to engage with direct fire weapons and acquire their own targets. Making this survivable requires specialist ground attack aircraft. Alternatively, attack helicopters – employing horizontal standoff to achieve survivability – are an effective replacement for the specialist aircraft. They cannot of course match the fixed wing aircraft's weight of firepower. Hence, they may need to be supplemented by fighter-bombers operating from medium level. Retaining aircraft optimised to fly low and slow to deliver strafing is an expensive capability choice that probably cannot be justified.

41st Proposition: Despite operational experience showing that attack helicopters are more effective in the combined arms close battle, the Western aviation community will continue to aspire for massed deep attack. Western army aviation has resurrected the Cold War battalion or brigade deep attack on massed target arrays. Identifying such targets within the mounting and execution tempo of massed aviation strikes remains problematic, as is helicopter survivability when advancing rapidly over hostile territory. Small numbers of helicopters stealthily infiltrated into the deep battle have occasionally proved to be effective, but aviation's usual employment has been part of the close combat combined arms team. In this arena they have become the leading tank killer and have often replaced fixed wing aircraft in delivering danger close aerial fire support. Helicopters excel at these operations because they can achieve persistence in the area of a target through hovering. This enables their crews, with their affinity with the ground force's perspective, to employ their excellent sensors to direct their precise and highly lethal munitions.

42nd Proposition: Until effective air defence systems are fielded, the mini unmanned aircraft and artillery combination will continue to dominate positional warfare and will be extremely effective in mobile combat. This proposition rests upon ineffective counters to small unmanned aircraft. The result of civilian drone technology outstripping the ability of military procurement to provide active counters. Quadcopters are particularly survivable through exploiting low-level ground clutter that defeats most sensors. A combination of survivability and mass, due to these aircraft being relatively inexpensive and easy to operate, means that they can achieve persistent surveillance of the close battle. This is a similar capability to the two-seater light aircraft, that through cueing airpower and artillery, dominated positional warfare in the 1944 Normandy campaign and Korean War. Larger unmanned aircraft, with sophisticated sensors, while more vulnerable, are required in mobile conflict and to deliver a deep battle target acquisition capability. Given the challenge of employing close air support in peer conflict, small unmanned aircraft may be returning airpower to its original Great War role, as a user, rather than provider, of firepower to the land battle.

Joint Firepower's Command and Control

43rd Proposition: Having joint fire specialists in an institutionally separate chain of command has historically proved the most successful form of conventional warfighting. As it delivers unity of effort, a single General Staff, responsible for both fires and manoeuvre, should be the best land warfighting approach. However, historically a distinct fires chain of command, paralleling the manoeuvre one, has been the feature of successful warfighting armies. It allows the commanding general to delegate control of firepower to air and artillery commanders who can employ it within the command guidance he provides. In the absence of a separate fires chain of command, control over artillery and airpower follows the hierarchical command structure. This leads to each level of command controlling their own firepower. This enables guaranteed responsive firepower, but this can come at the penalty of penny-packeting firepower to meet the most immediate tactical challenge. Without central control of airpower, ground commanders are likely to prioritise close air support, over demonstrably more effective means of employment, including enabling air superiority. The same can happen with artillery; resulting in, failing to contest the deep battle and probably losing the counter battery battle.

44th Proposition: The Soviet/Russian binary firepower doctrine is intrinsically resilient to modern warfare's fog and friction. The Soviets/Russians centrally control firepower to support deliberate operations. The commanding general authorises his artillery commander to control all sources of firepower down to company level mortars. They jointly produce the fire plan which seeks to neutralise opposing defences through their full depth, in order to enable deep manoeuvre. To limit enemy interference, firepower is often controlled by timed programmes. Following the set piece battle, this centralised control is replaced by ruthless delegation. In mobile operations, tube and rocket artillery battalion fire is controlled by the tank or motor rifle company or battalion commanders. This provides manoeuvre commanders with highly responsive firepower to facilitate high speed manoeuvre. This binary approach is resilient to the fog and friction of war's nature. In particular, it more resistant to the electromagnetic spectrum being contested than the Western system of centralised command and decentralised control that is dependent upon reliable communications.

45th Proposition: Through its ability to switch between the deep and close battle, mass on a single or engage multiple targets, the Western system of centralised command and decentralised control is the most efficient means of employing firepower. The Western command and control system is designed to manoeuvre firepower between formations in the close battle, or alternatively switch it to the deep battle. Firepower is commanded at the highest level with its control being delegated. For artillery, this control is delegated to either individual terminal controllers or fire direction centres. For airpower, terminal engagement lies with the forward air controller. This requires investment in communications, and skilled personnel that possess the situational awareness to make the correct resource judgements. These personnel operate within distinct fires chain of commands whose primary task is to effectively match firepower to targets. This system also requires a command philosophy comfortable with delegating decisions.

46th Proposition. The West's centralised firepower system includes ways that address the need for manoeuvre commanders to 'trust' that they will receive fire support. Centralising firepower may be the most efficient approach, but this impersonal approach does not account for commanders requiring confidence that they will have guaranteed fire support. In the

Western system, centralised firepower systems achieve mass at the decisive point through taking firepower away from lesser priorities. Military cultures generally associate ownership with a level of trust; this is of course the antithesis of the centralised system. It follows that there needs to be compromise within this firepower system's organisation and processes. Trust in the Western firepower system is achieved by a combination of organic battalion-level direct support mortars, and the integrating of air and artillery controllers and staff at each level of command. The latter try to ensure that the needs of manoeuvre forces are sequenced with the availability of firepower. Current Western airpower practice fails to fully address the trust issue. Forward air controllers rarely achieve the same level of training in cooperation that is provided to artillery controllers. This also applies to aircraft apportioned to the 'supported' land contingent commander; leading to ground alert aircraft tasked to close air support remaining under air component control; this leaves the land commander without a guarantee on the use of his most effective reserve of firepower. There are considerable physical challenges in synchronising air and land operations, but it is organisational and cultural factors that explain soldiers' preference for less powerful sources of firepower, that are more responsive and guaranteed.

47th Proposition: Integrated air and land warfighting is handicapped by the current joint approach to command and control. The West's current joint warfighting process leads to the largely autonomous development of air, land and maritime component plans. This results in the land component's initial planning starting without sufficient information on airpower's probable contribution and any limitations. This means that airpower often needs to be reverse-engineered into an extant land component plan, one in which the commander and his staff have often made personal investments. In comparison, World War Two air and land HQs were often co-located to allow them to collectively develop a combined plan. To overcome this challenge, within the current joint warfighting construct, the Israelis and Americans are placing a senior empowered air commander in land HQs. This is usually restricted to limited operations, making this a permanent requirement would significantly increase the effectiveness of joint firepower. An even greater stride could be made by the individual components being co-located to jointly develop their plans. This would start in routine training.

Firepower's Force Development

48th Proposition: Justified by non-military factors many Western militaries will continue to allow their potential opponents a decisive edge in munition lethality. Humanitarian concerns mean that many Western countries are not planning to make significant use of cluster and thermobaric munitions, despite their clear advantages in lethality; replacing the capability provided by dual-purpose cluster munitions requires two completely separate munitions. Pre-formed fragmentation of expensive metal can match cluster munitions' lethality against soft targets. Providing an equal capability against armour requires terminally guided munitions. Fielding both makes this a more expensive and less effective capability choice when compared to cluster munitions. A more sustainable position would be for NATO to adopt a policy of only using cluster munitions for defence of its own territory. Thermobaric munitions provide significantly greater blast. Making them particularly effective in urban operations, the most likely future battlefield. It takes multiple conventional munitions to achieve the same effect. Making ammunition safer to store and handle has led to a further reduction in the lethality of Western munitions through the introduction of more insensitive conventional explosives.

49th Proposition: Through an unrealistic expectation of their lethality, compounded by their expense, precision munitions are accentuating the peacetime habit of inadequate stocks of shells, bombs and rockets. Underestimating their need for firepower leads armies to misjudge the quantity of munitions required in warfighting, leading to inadequate stockpiles that fail to match the intensity and duration of a conflict. Precision munitions provide a ready, but fallacious, rationale for further economising on munitions. More precise munitions leading to reduced quantity has some merit for direct fire weapons, but this approach has been incorrectly extended to include munitions that provide neutralisation of area targets. Even the stockpiles of precision munitions have proved to be inadequate in the West's recent limited conflicts. The Russians have arrived at a balance between employing precision and unguided weaponry that enables them to sustain high tempo combat operations. Western concern with collateral damage has led to precision munitions being employed in their more recent limited conflicts, seemingly whether they are necessary or not. Leading to some NATO air forces having no other munitions. Short of a strategic shock, adoption of this pragmatic Russian approach is unlikely.

50th Proposition: While the Americans have accepted the logic of the changed geo-political situation, most of their allies are resisting the need to field militaries suited for peer conflict. This proposition rests upon the outcomes of inadequately preparing to defeat, and therefore being able to deter, a peer opponent. The failure to recognise the return to great power completion is fundamentally a political one, but some militaries are playing a willing supporting part as it is at odds with the lived experience of post-Cold War armies. Being human organisations, armies tend to be fixated upon their most recent experiences, rather than adjusting to present circumstances and their likely range of future tasks. As this experience has not featured major operations, European militaries have found it easier to adapt to the challenge of strategic competition by focussing on their sub-threshold and non-warfighting capabilities. The outcome of this is that in contrast to America, most of its allies are not addressing their inadequate organic firepower. Nor is their force employment adjusting to the threat presented by opposing modern firepower. Furthermore, in contrast to America's drive to reduce their commitments to provide time and resources for peer warfighting training, European armies continue to dissipate their forces on secondary activity. For almost all in NATO's armies, training for peer conventional conflict is wholly novel. Unlearning the habits of limited war and adapting to the most challenging character of conflict will require intense and sustained training. Achieving this requires a reduction in their other commitments.

Annex: Possible Firepower Approach to a Peer Conflict

Task	Role	Capability	Rationale
Armoured Warfare	Battalion organic support weapon	120mm gun-mortar, turret mounted in the same armoured vehicle as the rest of the battalion. Can fire both mortar bombs and supersonic shells. With GPS/INS sighting system and on-board computation to improve deployment times and accuracy.	• 120mm's lethality, but direct fire overcomes the danger distance by when conducting dismounted assaults. • Precision with course corrected fuze. • Range/coverage matches armoured battalion footprint. • Secondary anti-tank capability. • **Concern:** Vulnerable when providing direct fire support.
	Divisional artillery	155mm cannon with at least 52-calibre barrel on an armoured, tracked vehicle. With enhanced direct fire capability and improved counter-battery survivability.	• Achieves considerable range/ coverage without relying on extended range shells. • Armour and tracks, because: able to keep pace with tanks, sustain fire support under fire and effectively deliver direct fire. • **Concern:** Sustaining ageing platforms.
		HIMARS with full range of 227mm warheads, including laser guided, but without munitions able to range over 100km, unless funded to support the joint battle.	• Given its range and no requirement for direct fire, wheels rather than tracks. • **Concerns:** Long time of flight makes it unresponsive to the close battle and its warhead is too small for some targets.
Light Infantry Warfare (Airborne/ Airmobile/ Amphibious)	Company organic fire support	60mm mortars with GPS and pointing sighting system to improve deployment times and accuracy.	• Most effective danger close capability for assaults and defensive fires. • Range/coverage matches company footprint. • **Concern:** Easy to acquire and unprotected.
	Battalion organic support weapon	81mm with GPS and pointing sighting system to improve deployment times and accuracy. (Dual trained on 60mm mortar, deploying with this when this better meets tactical circumstances).	• Reinforces 60mm in providing danger close capability for assaults and defensive fires. • Range/coverage matches battalion footprint. • **Concern:** Easy to acquire and unprotected.

Task	Role	Capability	Rationale
	Brigade artillery	105mm towed cannon with GPS/INS sighting system and on-board computation to improve deployment times and accuracy. **Or** 120mm towed gun-mortar also with GPS/INS sighting system and on-board computation to improve deployment times and accuracy.	• 105mm reinforces mortars in providing danger close capability for assaults and defensive fires. • Only survivable through shoot and scoot. • **Concerns:** Range/coverage does not match brigade footprint, small warhead and this brigade is likely to lack organic precision. Hence, towed 120mm gun-mortar is an alternative with its greater lethality and precision.
Light Mechanised Warfare	Company and Battalion mortars as per Light Infantry (as dismounted combat is the norm).		
	Brigade Artillery	120mm gun-mortar, turret mounted in the same armoured wheeled vehicle as much of the brigade. With GPS/INS sighting system and on-board computation to improve deployment times and accuracy.	• High lethality. • Precision with course corrected fuze. • High survivability. • **Concern:** Range/coverage does not match a mechanised brigade footprint without using extended range munitions.
Positional Warfare (Urban)	Brigade Artillery	227mm reduced range (10km) but larger warhead rocket on either a light self-propelled wheeled chassis (significantly more deployable) or fired from HIMARS.	• Significantly increased warhead provides required blast to defeat urban targets. • Much shorter time of flight makes it more responsive to the close battle. • **Concern:** Short range, this will usually be sufficient in urban and other positional combat.
		Additional 120mm gun-mortars required to provide every assaulting company with its indirect fire and direct fire able to engage targets at all elevations.	
		Man-in-the loop non-line of sight missile on an agile platform that delivers survivability through shoot and scoot.	• Provides high level of discrimination in war amongst the people. • Range of at least 30km required given dispersion of counter-insurgency. • **Concern:** Problematic effectiveness against more capable opponents able to contest the EMS and conduct effective counter-battery.

(*Continued on next page*)

Task	Role	Capability	Rationale
Munitions	Cannon ratio	• 40% High Explosive. (80% if 105mm). • 30% Bomblet. (Not 105mm). • 10% Sensor Fuzed Munitions. (Not 105mm). • 10% Smoke (Base Ejection). • 5% Smoke (White Phosphorous). • 5% Illumination. • Fuzes: 20% of total fuzes to be Course Corrected to deliver accurate long-range area fires. • Extended Range: Up to 20% of the rounds can be fitted with a screw on combined rocket assisted/base bleed unit.	• The mix preserves danger close fires, while strengthening lethality against armoured vehicles and in positional warfare. • Recognises increased need for obscuration. • **Concern:** Rapid production required to meet additional HE and Illumination needed in counter-insurgency.
	Mortar & Gun-Mortar Ratio	• 50% High Explosive. • 15% Thermobaric. • 25% Smoke (White Phosphorous). • 10% Illumination. • Fuzes: Plus 10% of fuzes are Course Corrected to deliver precision fires and effective area fire at extreme range. • Extended Range: 20% of High Explosive and Smoke rounds are rocket assisted	• Weighted towards danger close fires, but increases lethality. • Recognises even greater need for obscuration. • **Concern:** As per tube artillery.
	Rocket Ratio	Standard Missiles (70% of stockpile): • 20% High Explosive (Unitary/Alternative). • 38% Bomblet. • 30% Thermobaric. • 10% Sensor Fuzed Munitions. • 2% Jamming and/or EMP. Reduced Range Missiles (30%): • 40% High Explosive. • 50% Thermobaric. • 10% Bomblet.	• Significant increase in deep battle lethality, while still providing precision fires to the close fires. • Recognises urban warfare's bespoke requirements. • Provides a non-lethal electronic attack capability. • **Concern:** Balance between point and area target capability is unsuitable for war amongst the people.
Air	Fighter-Bombers	Aviation takes on routine close air support; fighter-bombers provide standoff precision point attack, and in extremis, an unrivalled weight of fire. Airpower devoted to air interdiction.	• **Concerns:** Greatest threat to this capability is lack of investment in air/land integration structures. Plus the lack of artillery firepower and aviation's preference for deep attack may fix NATO airpower into delivering routine close air support.

Task	Role	Capability	Rationale
Aviation	The Apache remains the most effective attack helicopter in the world; how it is employed is key. The primary role must be the close battle, with pairs infiltrating into the deep battle. Both roles require greater integration into other sensors to exploit its firepower and target acquisition capability. But the resource priority is not equipment, it is all arms training.		
Company Level Terminal Controllers	Artillery & Mortars Air & Aviation	Joint fire support teams with the ability to employ all forms of fire support. Able to achieve sub-meter target locations, laser mark and designate targets, all weather surveillance through radar, digital fire control and able to deliver 24/7 observation assisted by integral unmanned aircraft.	• One fire support team per sub-unit. • Fire control system ensures mortars deliver guaranteed support. • Artillery and mortar terminal controllers employ the same call for fire procedures. • Air and aviation both use CAS procedures. • **Concern:** Training challenge.
	'Hunter' Mini Quadcopter	Mini unmanned aircraft able to cue firepower. Focussed on hunting targets beyond troops in contact and their fire support teams' line of sight.	• Purely target engagement not fire support. • **Concern:** Ability to operate in mobile operations so reliant upon effective all arms integration and ability to rapidly launch.
Technical Target Acquisition	Counter Battery	Weapon locating radar with 120-degree coverage and a range of 40km. Supplemented and cued by sound ranging and electronic direction finding.	• Range more important than coverage in peer conventional warfighting. • Sound ranging vital because it is passive and difficult to jam. • **Concern:** Lacks 360-degree coverage for counter-insurgency; but this can be provided by air defence radars.
	Unmanned Aircraft	Runway launched fixed wing aircraft. With high endurance. Primarily using long-range moving target radar and electronic direction finding. Unlikely to ever use their day/night sights and lasers in peer conflict. (Note, once effective air integrated defence systems are fielded, in peer conflict, no role for any unmanned aircraft that does not employ standoff or can fly nap of the earth.)	• In addition to the mini unmanned aircraft a more sophisticated platform is required, especially in mobile operations. • Standoff to achieve survivability. • **Concern:** Survivability against integrated air defence systems requires agile piloting, rather than flying 'race tracks'.

Glossary

Artillery Guns. Guns traditionally have a maximum elevation of significantly less than 45°, employ one fixed or alternatively a low number of charges, a high muzzle velocity and a long barrel. Limited numbers of 'true' guns have survived, these being optimised for long range rather than having multi-role characteristics. The gun's continued utility as dedicated deep fire artillery is challenged by rocket systems. Fixed charge, long barrelled, guns remain the standard naval armament; leading to the challenge of employing these low trajectory weapons in fire support of land forces in hilly terrain.

Conventional Warfighting. Regular or conventional warfighting is a form of warfare conducted using orthodox weapons and battlefield tactics between two or more states, or similar political constructs, in open confrontation. The forces on each side are usually well defined, and they fight using weapons that primarily target their opponent's military.

Eastern Way of War. Analysis of a distinct Eastern way of war have been bedevilled by cultural stereotypes that can border on the racist. Nonetheless, as a broad generalisation, there is an Eastern way of war that is less focussed on the decisive battle and instead adopts a more drawn out approach to achieving the desired political outcome.

Firepower. This is the destructive capacity of a military force, that is, the ability to deliver effective fire, normally through the use of shells, missiles, bombs or other projectiles. While all land force elements are capable of generating firepower, above the sub-tactical level, firepower refers to artillery, mortars, rockets and aircraft that form the joint fires system of systems.

Gray Zone Conflict. A definition of gray zone conflict or competition is that which falls between the traditional war and peace duality. If black is war and white is peace, these challenges are in that gray zone between them.

Guerrilla Warfare. This is a form of irregular warfare that uses ambushes, sabotage, raids, petty warfare, hit-and-run tactics, and mobility, to fight a larger and usually less-mobile traditional military. It can be used by insurgents or unconventional auxiliaries of a government; including the Soviet Partisans in World War Two. Regular special operations forces operating behind enemy lines also use these methods, such as the Special Air Service in the Mediterranean in World War Two.

Gun-Howitzers. The division between howitzers and guns in artillery parks largely survived until the 1930s when most armies began to re-equip with the modern gun-howitzers. This was in response to the lessons of World War One, which demanded a weapon combining both howitzer and gun characteristics in response to the variety of targets on the modern battlefield.

Howitzers. Modern howitzers have a maximum elevation of greater than 45° (usually up to 70°) with a larger range of charges, a low muzzle velocity, and usually a shorter, but larger calibre barrel, for a given size of ordnance. This is at the expense of range.

Insurgency. In most conflicts, insurgents employ irregular warfare tactics, and there is a tendency to conflate the terms. Actually, insurgency is a violent rebellion against a recognised state authority.

Irregular Warfighting. This is the opposite of conventional or regular warfare. This is generally the character of conflict between an insurgent(s) and a state's counter-insurgent forces. Battles are less important and will only be decisive if they lead to the loss of vital personnel or equipment, the demoralisation of the irregular force, or the acceptance within a belligerent population that the insurgents are the losers.

Manoeuvre. This is an organised movement of forces for combat purposes to place themselves in positions of advantage in the battle. Manoeuvre forces are those elements – infantry, armour, cavalry/reconnaissance and for some armies aviation – that seek to use manoeuvre to defeat their adversary. When manoeuvre is opposed it leads to 'fire and movement'. Even when manouevre is not opposed, the very presence of combat forces can exert a psychological effect on an adversary.

New Theories of War. There are multiple, overlapping and in part contradictory new theories of war. One of the earliest polemics of the need for change – Alvin and Heidi Toffler, War and Anti-War: Survival at the Dawn of the 21th Century – still has influence in this desire for transformation. Perhaps Network Centric Warfare has the greatest impact. It is largely an American theory and had its origins in 1997–8. It drew upon business theories and practice that were designed to allow better military decision-making through superior information. It also sought to reduce internal friction in the execution of those decisions, leading to the view that information age armies would thus significantly outperform industrial age armies. Other theories and initiatives to gain traction in the United States and the West include: The New American Way of War, Army After Next (AAN), Force Transformation, Rapid Decisive Operations (RDO) and its nom de guerre *'shock and awe'*, Effects-Based Operations (EBO), Dominant Battlespace Knowledge (DBK), 4th Generation Warfare and Standoff Firepower-based Operations (SFO). While there are different aspects to each of these terms, their common thread is the diminished requirement for ground force manoeuvre (including fire and movement) to physically destroy the enemy's forces. Instead, information is collected to understand the enemy as a system, to usually allow standoff (invariably precision) fire, predominantly from the air, to attack vulnerable nodes.

Revolutionary War. This is a descriptor of the purpose of the military activity. While generally conflated with irregular warfare, revolutionary warfare can also be the outcome of conventional war, such as America's post-9/11 regime-changing invasions. Historically the American Revolutionary War fits this category; it was almost entirely fought by conventional forces. This book uses irregular warfare to describe a character of conflict that seeks to avoid conventional force-on-force match ups; it identifies insurgency as seeking to defeat a state's government by a force, largely using irregular warfare tactics; and throughout it avoids using outcome descriptors, such as revolutionary war.

Soft Recoil. Soft recoil lets the barrel slide forward at the moment of initiation, so that the forward momentum cancels much of the recoil from firing. Soft recoil systems can be up to 70% efficient, as some recoil energy is always required to return the ordnance to the firing position. There is of course a weight penalty in making this complicated recoil system work, but this is more than compensated by having a significantly lighter platform. Its previous use has been stymied by the requirement for exact timing on the initiation and the drop of the barrel and additional movement during firing, resulting in increased range dispersion. Modern technology ensures more precise and consistent movement forward of the barrel.

Terrorism. This is a tactic or method; it is usually a label used by sovereign states and is usually defined within the context of law.

War, Warfare/Warfighting and Battles. Throughout this book the following definitions are used: war is the whole and warfighting is but one part of war. As warfare is but a part of war, it need not always be the most important, nor the most decisive element. This means that war involves grand strategic choices of policy, and warfare the practise of armed coercion and violence used to implement political strategy. Of course, in reality there is an overlap between these two spheres. Battles are condensed warfighting. This makes them invariably the most decisive element in conventional warfighting.

Ways of War. The 'way of war' concept emerged when the former British officer and intellectual Basil Liddell Hart claimed that there was a specific British way of warfare. The concept recognises that throughout history different peoples have fought differently. Obviously, the nature and character of the arms used determines how they will fight, but there are also political, economic, cultural and social factors.

Western Ways of War (Current). America dominates the current Western way of war. At the strategic level the American way of war seeks swift military victory. As this is often independent of strategic policy success, the political and military outcomes do not always align. At the tactical level, the aggressive use of force tries to overwhelm and destroy enough of the enemy's forces to acquire a decisive and quick victory with minimal casualties; achieved though employing well-trained professionals who can exploit speed, manoeuvre, flexibility, and surprise. This method of battle is highly dependent on technology and firepower (mainly airpower), and has large-scale logistical requirements. All efforts are made to ensure that force is both legal and legitimate.

Western v Eastern Way of War. It is easy to overstate the division between the Western and Eastern ways of war, as there is much continuity between the two approaches. For example, the Franco-Vietnamese War was decided by decisive battle, but there is sufficient difference for this concept to aid our analysis, without being drawn into accepting all of the theories advanced by Victor Davis Hanson, its leading advocate.

What is Not War. A Clausewitzian definition of war requires it to be adversarial, violent and it needs to an organised political activity. With this definition there can be no War on Terror, which is at best a public relations locution, like the 'war on poverty'.

Select Bibliography

Johnathan Bailey, Field Artillery and Firepower, AUSA Institute of Land Warfare book. Annapolis, MD: Naval Institute Press, 2004.

Correlli Barnett, Shelford Bidwell, Brian Bond, John Harding and John Terraine, Old Battles and New Defences, Can We Learn From Military History? Brassey's Defence Publications, London, 1986.

Chris Bellamy, Red God of War: Soviet Artillery and Rocket Forces, Brassey's Defence Publishers, London, 1986.

Benjamin Franklin Cooling (Ed), Case Studies in the Development of Close Air Support, Office of Air Force History, United States Air Force, Washington DC, 1990.

Stephen Biddle, Military Power: Explaining Victory and Defeat in Modern Battle, Princeton University Press, Princeton, NJ, 2006.

Shelford Bidwell & Dominic Graham, Fire-Power: British Army Weapons and Theories of War 1904–1945, George Allen & Urwin, London, 1982.

Shelford Bidwell, Gunners at War, Arms & Armour Press, London, 1970.

Phillip Bobbitt, Terror and Consent, The Wars for the Twenty-First Century, Penguin, London and New York, 2008.

Buckley, John, Air Power in the Age of Total War, London: UCL Press, 1998.

Michael Burleigh, Small Wars, Far Away Places, Pan Books, London, 2003.

CE Callwell, Small Wars: Their Principles and Practice, Albion, London 2016.

Carl von Clausewitz, On War, ed. and trans. Michael Howard and Peter Paret, Princeton University Press, Princeton, NJ, 1976.

Anthony Clayton, Paths of Glory, The French Army 1914–18, Cassel, London, 2003.

Christopher Coker, The Improbable War, China, the United States & the Logic of Great Power Conflict, C. Hurst & Co, London, 2017.

Anthony H Cordesman: Lessons of the Iraq War: Main Report, Center for Strategic and International Studies, Washington DC, July 21, 2003.

Martin Van Crefeld, the Age of Airpower, Public Affairs, New York, 2011.

Robert A. Doughty, The Seeds of Disaster: The Development of French Army Doctrine, 1919–1939, Archon Books, 1985.

Etienne de Durand, Benoît Michel and Elie Tenenbaum, Helicopter Warfare. The Future of Airmobility and Rotary Wing Combat, Focus stratégique, Number 32 bis, January 2012.

David Edgerton, Shock Of The Old: Technology and Global History since 1900, Profile Books, London, 2008.

Gil Eliot, Twentieth Century Book of the Dead, Allen Lane, London, 1972.

Colin S Gray, Airpower for Strategic Effect, Air University Press, Air Force Research Institute Maxwell Air Force Base, Alabama, 2012.

Lester W. Grau, The Bear Went Over the Mountain: Soviet Combat Tactics in Afghanistan, NDU Press, Washington, 1996.

Colin S Gray, Another Bloody Century, Future War, Weidenfeld and Nicolson, London, 2005.

Colin S Gray, Fighting Talk, Forty Maxims on War, Peace and Strategy, Potomac Books, Washington DC, 2009.

Bruce I Gudmundsson, On Artillery, Praeger Publishers, Westport CT, 1993,

Von Hardesty, Red Phoenix, The Rise of Soviet Air Power 1941–45, Arms and Armour Press, London-Melbourne, 1982.

Stephen Ashley Hart, Colossal Cracks: Montgomery's 21st Army Group in Northwest Europe, 1944–45, Stackpole Books, Mechanicsburg PA, 2007.
Charles E Heller and Willian A Stofft, America's First Battles 1776–1965, University of Kansas Press, Lawrence KS, 1986.
Jonathan M House, Combined Warfare in the 20th Century, University Press of Kansas, Lawrence, KS, 2001.
David E. Johnson, Learning Large Lessons: The Evolving Roles of Ground Power and Air Power in Post-Cold War Era, Santa Monica, CA., 2007.
Archer Jones, The Art of War in the Western World, University of Illinois Press, Urbana and Chicago, 1987.
Frederick W Kagan, Finding the Target, The Transformation of American Military Policy, Encounter Books, New York, 2006, pp. 310–19.
Robert R. Leonard, The Art of Maneuver, Maneuver-Warfare Theory and AirLand Battle, Presidio Press, New York, 1991.
David Kilcullen, The Dragons and the Snakes, How the Rest Learnt to Fight the West, Hurst & Company, London 2020.
Janice E McKenny, Organizational History of Field Artillery, 1775–2003, Centre for History of the United States Army, Washington, 2007.
MP Manson Guns, Mortar and Rockets, Brassey's New Battlefield Weapons Systems & Technology Series into the 21st Century, Brassey's (UK) Ltd, London, 1997.
Colonel Phillip S. Meilinger, 10 Propositions Regarding Air Power, Air Force History and Museums Program, Washington DC, 1995.
John McGrath, Fire for Effect, Field Artillery and Close air support in the US Army, Fort Leavenworth, Combat Studies Institute Press, Fort Leavenworth, KS, 2007.
Compiled by Brigadier ML Pemberton MC, The Development of Artillery Tactics and Equipment, The War Office, London, 1951.
Bruce R. Pirnie, Alan Vick, Adam Grissom, Karl P. Mueller, David T. Orletsky, Beyond Close Support, Forging a New Air-Ground Partnership, RAND Corporation, Santa Monica, CA, 2005.
Gideon Rachman, Easternisation, War and Peace in the Asian Century, Penguin, London, 2016.
Robert H. Scales Jr., Firepower in Limited War, National Defense University Press, Washington, DC, 1990.
Richard Simpkin, Race to the Swift, Thoughts on Twenty-first Century Warfare, Brassey's Defence Publishers, London, 1985.
Air Marshal of the Royal Air Force, Sir John Slessor. Airpower and Armies, Oxford University Press, London, 1936.
Hew Strachan, Carl von Clausewitz's On War, A Biography, Manjul Publishing House, Bhopal, India, 2011.
Elie Tenenbaum, The Battle over Fire Support. The close air support Challenge and the Future of Artillery, Focus stratégique, Number 35 bis, October 2012.
John Terraine, To Win a War, 1918, The Year of Victory, Sidgwick and Jackson, London, 1978.
John Terraine, White Heat – The New Warfare 1914–18, Leo Cooper, London, 1992.
Tim Travers, The Killing Ground, The British Army, the Western Front, and the Emergence of Modern Warfare, 1900–1918, Pen and Sword, London, 2009.
Mark Urban, The Edge, Is the Military Dominance of the West Coming to an End? Little, Brown, London, 2015,
Russell F. Weigley, The American Way of War, A History of United States Military Strategy and Policy, Indiana University Press, Bloomington and Indianapolis, 1973.
David Zabecki, Steel Wind: Colonel Georg Bruchmüller and the Birth of Modern Artillery, Praeger Publishers, Westpoint CT, 1994.
Georgi K. Zhukov, Marshal Zhukov's Greatest Battles, Harper & Row, New York, 1969.

Notes

Introduction

(1) David Kilcullen, The Dragons and the Snakes, How the Rest Learnt to Fight the West, Hurst & Company, London 2020, p. 246.

(2) Harvey M. Sapolsky, Benjamin H. Friedman, and Brendan R. Green, eds., US Military Transformation and Innovation since the Cold War: Creation Without Destruction Taylor & Francis, London, 2009, p. 7; James Q. Wilson, Innovation in Organization: Notes Towards a Theory, in J. O. Thompson (editor) Approaches to Organizational Design, PA: University of Pittsburgh Press, Pittsburg PA, 1971).

(3) Max Boot, The New American Way of War, Foreign Affairs, July/August 2003. Russell F. Weigley, The American Way of War, A History of United States Military Strategy and Policy, Indiana University Press, Bloomington and Indianapolis, 1973.

(4) Richard K Betts, Pick Your Battles, Ending America's Era of Permanent War, Foreign Affairs, November/December 2014.

(5) Following the taxonomy of US Army's Colonel Arthur Lykke: 'Strategy equals ends (objectives toward which one strives) plus ways (courses of action) plus means (instruments by which some end can be achieved).'

(6) If we look at demography, higher education, military innovation and productivity, then the US is not a superpower in decline. However, it is relative decline is due to the rise of other powers. The challenge America faces is made greater by the actual, rather than relative, decline in military power of its traditional allies, in particular the Europeans. This is partly compensated by increased investment by Asian allies, such as the Japanese. European rearmament in the face of the Russian threat is not of the same level. With the notable exceptions of the Nordics, Balts and Poles.

(7) Gideon Ross, What's Inside, Foreign Affairs, January/February 2019.

(8) David Kilcullen, The Dragons and the Snakes, p. 202.

(9) David Kilcullen, quoted in Michael Puttré, Winning on the Battlefield is Not Enough, The Bridge, May 13, 2020.

(10) Gil Eliot, Twentieth Century Book of the Dead, Allen Lane, London, 1972, p. 133.

(11) The Imperial Japanese military are a notable exception to surrendering being the major cause of combatants becoming hors de combat. Only between 19,500 and 50,000 prisoners were taken by the Western Allies prior to the end of the Pacific War in August 1945. The cause was the indoctrination of Japanese soldiers, which became self-reinforcing as many Allied troops ceased taking prisoners. In contrast to the attritional campaigns of the Western allies, the Soviet Manchurian offensive seized and imprisoned more than half a million Japanese troops.

(12) Randall Collins, A Dynamic Theory of Battle Victory and Defeat, Cliodynamics: the Journal of Theoretical and Mathematical History, Volume 1, Issue 1, pp. 3–25.

(13) Victor Davis Hanson, The Western Way of War: Infantry Battle in Classical Greece, Oxford University Press, New York, 1990 and Victor Davis Hanson, Carnage and Culture: Landmark Battles in the Rise of Western Power, Anchor, New York, 2002. This author traces the Western emphasis on the decisive pitched battle back to the classical Greek hoplites. This author finds irony in the fact that the Iliad, the most important work about how the Ancient Greeks saw themselves, required underhand subterfuge – the Trojan Horse – to achieve victory.

(14) Cathal J. Nolan warns of the danger of expecting decisive battle to deliver quick victories in: The Allure of Battle, A History of How War Have Been Won and Lost, Oxford University Press, New York, 2017. His historical survey identifies the recurring assumption amongst professional militaries that through 'genius' decisive battle(s) will deliver quick victories. This leads to a distorted strategic approach that identifies non-materiel factors as being invariably decisive. Leading to the belief, that a more powerful enemy can be quickly beaten by: operational or tactical skill encapsulated in superior doctrine, greater physical courage or willpower, or even racial superiority leading to greater fighting performance. Professor Nolan's analysis identifies that winning wars is often a matter of resources, as conflicts tend to be decided by drawn-out attrition. Of course, much of this attrition comes from battles. Professor Nolan's has identified a lack of strategic understanding as key to why protagonists have historically failed to make these battles decisive.

(15) The taking of prisoners in the post-9/11 Wars is a controversial issue. But a contrast can be made between 2003 invasion of Iraq and the American Army in World War Two. The latter meticulously planned for the capture of enemy troops in large numbers, and was prepared to sustain them pending a political settlement, whilst maintaining high tempo operations. See Paul Joseph Springer, American Prisoner of War Policy And Practice From The Revolutionary War To The War On Terror, Dissertation, Texas A&M University, May 2006.

(16) Christopher Coker, Rebooting Clausewitz, On War in the 21st Century, Hurst and Company, London, 2017, p. 107.

(17) Stephen Biddle, Military Power: Explaining Victory and Defeat in Modern Battle, Princeton University Press, Princeton, NJ, 2006, p. ix.

(18) Victor Davis Hanson, War's Bitter Laws, National Review, 11 July 11, 2003.

(19) Doctrine is usually written by officers too senior to have had much recent experience of tactical battle. They write for committees consisting of Generals. A better approach would be for the senior leadership to empower sergeants and lieutenants, rather than impose a top down view. This was Timothy T. Lupfer's analysis of the successful German doctrine that underpinned stormtrooper tactics in the Great War. Timothy T. Lupfer, The Dynamics of Doctrine: The Changes in German Tactical Doctrine During the First World War, Combat Studies Institute, U.S. Army Command and General Staff College Fort Leavenworth, Kansas, July 1981.

(20) For a more nuanced view of the Western and Eastern ways of war see: John Lynn, Battle: A History of Combat and Culture from Ancient Greece to Modern America, Westview Press, New York, 2003.

(21) Dr Henry Kissinger, America's Assignment, Newsweek, 8 November 2004.

(22) Emile Simpson, War From the Ground Up: Twenty-First Century Combat as Politics, Hurst, London, 2012, p. 27.

(23) General Sir Rupert Smith, The Utility of Force: The Art of War in the Modern World, 2005, Allen Lane, London.

(24) Of course, On War can be used to justify almost any position. But in book one, chapter one, of On War, Clausewitz identified that two motives lead men to war: 'instinctive hostility and hostile intent'. The former is driven by the primitive passion that Clausewitz subsequently identifies as an equal driver in conflict as politics. The eventual outcome of this debate was a more practical approach to using the German master to understand contemporary conflict. Though at one end of the spectrum, Colin S Gray argued that 'Clausewitz is not holy writ, only canon law'. Christopher Coker, Rebooting Clausewitz, On War in the 21st Century, Hurst and Company, London, 2017, p. ix.

(25) Victor Davis Hanson, War's Bitter Laws.

(26) The phrase revolution in military affairs derives from the old Soviet general staff term from the 1960s that identified military technical revolutions. Technology is identified as the transformational trigger in most of these theories. Max Boot, War Made New: Technology, Warfare and the Course of History, 1500 to Today, Gotham Books, New York, 2006, identifies the gunpowder, the first and second industrialisations and information military revolutions.

(27) Ben Buley, The New American Way of War, Routledge, Abingdon, 2007, p. 87.
(28) Carl von Clausewitz, On War, ed. and trans. Michael Howard and Peter Paret, Princeton University Press, Princeton, NJ, 1976, p. 122.
(29) Bill Owens, Lifting the Fog of War, Farrar, Strauss and Giroux, New York, pp. 9–17.
(30) David A Fulghum, Hi Tech Reassessed, Aviation Week & Space Technology, 10 Nov 2003, pp. 29–30.
(31) The failure to predict the 2008 financial crisis is but one example of greater access to data failing to improve decision-making. Times, London, 4 August 2015.
(32) Gary Klein, Sources of Power, MIT Press, Cambridge, MA, 1999, pp. 3–44.
(33) This is contested, notably by Donald Kagan, The outbreak of the Peloponnesian war, Cornell University Press, Ithaca, New York, 1969, pp. 190–92, 345–47.
(34) Carl von Clausewitz, On War, ed. and trans. Michael Howard and Peter Paret, Princeton University Press, Princeton, NJ, 1976, pp. 81–82. This translation, which has become the accepted standard in the English-speaking World, is used throughout.
(35) Jan Morris, Heaven's Command, An Imperial Progress, Volume 1 of the Pax Britannia Trilogy, Faber and Faber, London, p. 93.
(36) Jeffrey Record, The creeping irrelevance of US Force Planning. Monograph presented to the US Army War College' Strategy Conference, 31 March–2 April 1998.
(37) Colin S Gray, Fighting Talk, Forty Maxims on War, Peace and Strategy, Potomac Books, Washington DC, 2009, p. 156.
(38) The Small Wars Journal has been the usual forum for these views, such as: The US Army's Shift to Irregular Warfare by Michael A. Vane. In addition, there is: Sir Lawrence Freedman, Regular and Irregular War an address to the Canadian International Council on 19 June 2008.
(39) David Betz, Carnage and Connectivity, Landmarks in the Decline of Conventional Military Power, London, 2015, p. 6.
(40) Beatrice Heuser, Victory, Peace and Trinity: The Neglected Trinity, Joint Forces quarterly, 69, 2, 2013.
(41) Seth G. Jones, Waging Insurgent Warfare: Lessons from the Vietcong to the Islamic State, Oxford University Press, 2017, p. 7.
(42) Richard D Hooker Jr and Joseph J Collins (Editors), Lessons Encountered: Learning from the Long War, National Defence University Press, Washington DC, September 2015, pp. 13–14.
(43) Edward Luttwak, Dead End Counterinsurgency warfare as military malpractice, Harper's Magazine, 18 February, 2018.
(44) Barbara F. Walters, International Organization, The Critical Barrier to Civil War Settlement, Vol. 51, No. 3, Summer, 1997, pp. 335–364.
(45) Carl von Clausewitz, On War, ed. and trans. Michael Howard and Peter Paret, Princeton University Press, Princeton, NJ, 1976, p. 88.
(46) Secretary Albright's counter to General Colin Powell, then chairman of the Joint Chiefs of Staff, on a perceived unwillingness to use the American military in the Bosnian conflict. Madeline Albright, Madam Secretary, Harper Collins, New York, 2003, p. 182.
(47) A different analysis is offered in: David Kilcullen, The Dragons and the Snakes.
(48) Victor Davis Hanson, The Second World Wars, How the Global War was fought and Won, Basic Books, New York, 2020.
(49) Sydney J Freedburg Jnr, Tanks up, Choppers Down, Artillery WAY Up In the Army's Old School 2019 Budget, BreakingDefence, February 12, 2018, 5.13pm.
(50) Megan Eckstein, New Marine Corps Cuts Will Slash All Tanks, Many Heavy Weapons As Focus Shifts to Lighter, Littoral Forces, USNI news March 23, 2020 11:28am.
(51) Having been running down their militaries since the Cold War, the European members of NATO have added more than $50bn to their collective annual expenditure since 2015, the year after Russia invaded Ukraine. This is the equivalent of the French or British Defence budget. Defence, The Pan-European Army, The Economist, February 2nd–8th February 2019, p. 31.

(52) The current debate echoes the 'missile gap' that featured in the 1960 American Presidential election. In that Russian and Chinese missiles were considered in isolation from fixed wing airpower. The future President Kennedy was able to argue that America was at a severe military disadvantage due to the failure of the Republican administration. It was in terms of missiles but not in terms of airpower. Commendably the purpose of the current public debate is to resource longer range missiles, but Defence professionals need to be clear that these missiles are put one part of most nations long range strike systems.
(53) Adam Zamoyski, Warsaw 1920, Lenin's Failed Conquest of Europe, William Collins, London, 2014, p. 29.
(54) Eldridge A. Colby and A. Wess Mitchell, The Age of Great-Power Competition, How the Trump Administration Refashioned American Strategy, Foreign Affair, January/February 2020.
(55) Donald Kagan, On The Origins of War and the Preservation of Peace, Anchor/Doubleday, New York, 1995, p. 211.
(56) Barbara W. Tuchman, The Guns of August, Macmillan, London, 1962, quoted in Michael C. Thomsett and Linda Rose Thomsett, The Speakers Treasury Of Quotations: Maxims, Witticisms and Quips for Speeches and Presentations, McFarland and Company, Jefferson NC, 2009, p. 817.

Chapter 1: Firepower's Role in the Current Character of Land Warfare

(1) Professor Michael Howard, The Use and Abuse of Military History, The RUSI Journal, 138, 1993.
(2) Colin S Gray, Fighting Talk, pp. 109–110.
(3) Examples of allies drawing in Great Powers include: the Peloponnesian War, World Wars One and Two. In other circumstances, allies provide the causus belli, as in the Second Punic War.
(4) Christopher Coker, The Improbable War, China, the United States & the Logic of Great Power Conflict, C. Hurst & Co, London, 2017, p. 33.
(5) Gideon Rachman, Easternisation, War and Peace in the Asian Century, Penguin, London, 2016, p. 34.
(6) How militaries learn and adapt: An interview with Major General H. R. McMaster by Andrew Erdmann, McKinsey and Company, April 2013.
(7) Frederick W Kagan, Finding the Target, The Transformation of American Military Policy, Encounter Books, New York, 2006, pp. 310–19.
(8) Lucas Kello, The Meaning of the Cyber Revolution, Perils to Theory and Statecraft, International Security, Volume 38, Number 2, Fall 2013, pp. 7–8.
(9) A prescient counter to the view that we are in a World dominated by inventions and innovations is provided by: David Edgerton, Shock Of The Old: Technology and Global History since 1900, Profile Books, London, 2008.
(10) Sean McFate, Why high-tech weapons may be worthless in the wars to come, Linked In, Published on February 1, 2019.
(11) Nicholas Bloom, John Van Reenen, Charles I. Jones and Michael Webb, Are Ideas Getting Harder to Find? July 26, 2019 – Version 4.0.
(12) John Lynn, Battle: A History of Combat and Culture from Ancient Greece to Modern America, Westview Press, New York, 2003, p. 124.
(13) The term Blitzkrieg was probably coined by an American journalist following the Polish campaign. Originally it might have been a translation of the Italian notion of Lightning War. When Hitler first heard it, he considered it to be 'a very silly word'. The Germans saw their approach as rooted in their extant doctrine of the rapid operational level approach, or Bewegungskrieg. Its purpose was to avoid drawn-out wars through the employment of tactics designed to achieve encirclement and the annihilation of the enemy, or Kesselschlacht. It was never a coherent doctrine but a 'German phenomenon based on the traditions and heritage of German military history', Murray, German Military Effectiveness, Nautical & Aviation Pub. Co. of America, Baltimore, 1992, pp. 99–140.

(14) Deputy Secretary of Defense Bob Work, The Third U.S. Offset Strategy and its Implications for Partners and Allies, speech delivered at the Willard Hotel, Washington, DC, US DoD, January 28, 2015.

(15) The Thirty Years War is traditionally seen as a watershed between confessional and secular motivations for European war. This historical view has been modified by recent academic research motivated by the religious element in recent conflict. This has identified a strong religious element to much of the resistance to the French Revolutionary and Napoleonic armies in South Italy and Spain, with Roman Catholic priests providing much of the leadership. Subsequently Spain suffered from a series of conflicts where religion was a significant factor in delineating the opposing forces.

(16) David Betz, Carnage and Connectivity, Landmarks in the Decline of Conventional Military Power, London, 2015 p. 22.

(17) William S Lind and Lt Col Gregory A Thiele USMC, 4th Generation Warfare Handbook, Castalia House, Kouvola, Finland 2015, pp. 4–5.

(18) The term major or great powers may seem to be an anachronism; it is increasingly returning to the fore given the end of American pre-eminence. The World's multi-polar construct has a number of emerging, previously regional powers (some with more global ambitions, as illustrated by the naval building programme of several Asian powers) that merit a term that differentiates them from the other states. See Cheng Li interview, A New Type of Major Power Relationship? Georgetown Journal of International Affairs, 26 September 2014.

(19) Phillip Bobbitt, Terror and Consent, The Wars for the Twenty-First Century, Penguin, London and New York, 2008, p. 85.

(20) Charles Tilly and Gabriel Ardant. The Formation of National States in Western Europe, Princeton University Press, Princeton, 1975, p. 42.

(21) Max Weber, Politik als Beruf (Politics as a Vocation), Lecture 28 January, 1919.

(22) David Edgerton, Shock Of The Old, pp. 139–42.

(23) G.P. Pisano, You Need An Innovation Strategy, Harvard Business Review, 93, No 6, June 2015.

(24) General Electrics and McDonald's are cited as traditional organisations who are effectively adapting to the digital age. See Andrew McAfee and Eric Brynjolfsson, Machine, Platform, Crowd: Harnessing Our Digital Future, Norton, 2017.

(25) Cyberspace was coined by the science-fiction writer William Gibson in the 1982 short story 'Burning Chrome'. Of his creation, Gibson later said 'it seemed like an effective buzzword … evocative and essentially meaningless. It was suggestive but had no real semantic meaning, even for me.'

(26) Unpeace is a term coined in Lucas Kello, The Virtual Weapon and the International Order, Yale University Press, 2017.

(27) Graham Allison identifies one possible scenario of cyber conflict escalating out of control in his Destined for War: Can America and China Escape Thucydides' Trap? This scenario postulates that America's dismantling of China's cyber-walls that denies its citizens free access to the Internet is seen as regime threatening. Leading to cyber-attacks on American infrastructure, escalation into naval skirmishes in the South China Sea, and then into space conflict through pre-emptive attacks on Chinese satellites to prevent their targeting of America's carriers. He believes that avoiding such a conflict requires a self-restraining commitment not to employ information technology to challenge each other's sovereignty.

(28) General Sir Richard Barrons quoted in Lucy Fisher, Battle of ideas over conflict in the 21st century, Times, London, 25 Aug 20.

(29) Stephen Biddle, Military Power, p. 206.

(30) Air-to-air combat provides the classic example of one side that is reliant upon unproven new technology being bested by a proven, more primitive, approach. American fighter aircraft were equipped with the first-generation air-to-air missiles in the Vietnam War. Their opponents countered this advance in technology by choosing to dogfight with their 'primitive' cannon. This led

to American pilots not being given the opportunity to undertake combat in the circumstances for which they were trained and equipped, and hence they suffered disproportionate losses. Rectifying this required the fielding of aircraft more suitable for close aerial combat. Crucially, it also needed the training of aircrew to operate in such environments leading to the establishment of the Top Gun and Red Flag schools of aerial combat.

(31) Proponents of an information-focussed approach identify a cycle of turning data into information, leading to knowledge and wisdom. This broadly similar to some military cycles that see information leading to intelligence, understanding and action.

(32) Brian Nichiporuk, Jerome Bracken, John Gordon, and Richard E. Darilek, Measures of Effectiveness for the Information-Age Army, RAND Corporation Santa Monica, 2001, p. 109.

(33) Christopher Clark, Sleepwalkers How Europe Went to War in 1914, Penguin Books, London, 2012, p. 203.

(34) The shape of the technology lifecycle is often referred to as S-curve, or the Law of Diminishing Returns. Much of land firepower capability is at the mature point of the curve, where performance improvements are minor, due to technology reaching its limits. Aviation technology, being significantly newer, continues to evolve at a faster rate and equally significant developments in munitions are on-going. Aerial munitions lead the way, and then their technology trickles down into ground systems.

(35) Aleksandr Svechin quoted in General Valery Gerasimov, February 27, 2013, Military Doctrine, Military-Industrial Kurier, translated by Robert Coalson June 21, 2014.

(36) Carlos Ospina Ovalle, Insights from Colombia's Long War: Counter-insurgency Lessons Learned, Counterterrorism 12, Number 3, Fall 2006, p. 29.

(37) Martin van Creveld in Modern Conventional Warfare: An Overview identifies nineteen conventional wars, which he defines as armed conflicts openly waged by one state against another by means of their regular armies. There are the 'three Indian-Pakistani wars of 1947, 1965, and 1971. Next come the five Arab Israeli wars of 1948, 1956, 1967, 1969–70, and 1973. Others were the Korean War of 1950–53; the Indian-Chinese War of 1961; the Iran-Iraq War of 1980–88; the war between Ethiopia and Somalia (1978); the Chinese attack on Vietnam (1979); the Falklands War (1982); the Kosovo Campaign (1999); and, of course, the two wars against Iraq (1991 and 2003). Even if we add the so-called "Kargil War" of 1999 (when 500 Pakistani irregulars entered a few hundred yards into India and had to be expelled), and the Israeli-Syrian clash of 1982 (which lasting all of three days, was but a by-product of the invasion of Lebanon) …' The conflict between Sudan and South Sudan – which subsequently became a recognised state – can be added. The Croatian Operation Storm against the Serbs followed the grammar of regular more than irregular warfare, despite being within the internationally recognised borders of Croatia. A superior understanding of the defeat of the Taleban in Afghanistan in 2001 recognises that it was mainly decided by conventional conflict. Subsequent conflicts to the compiling of van Creveld list include the Russia's attack on Georgia in 2008. Operations against the self-declared Islamic State and the wider conflict in Iraq and Syria that have been largely conventional in character. To these can be added those when airpower rather than the full range of military power was employed to support indigenous ground forces, such as Libya in 2011. Of course, regular warfare tactics have featured in conflicts otherwise dominated by irregular warfare; including the Vietnam War, which ended in 1975 with North Vietnamese armoured forces capturing Saigon.

(38) LV Gorka and David Kilcullen, An Actor-centric theory of War: Understanding the Difference Between COIN and Counter-insurgency, JFQ/issue 60, 1st quarter 2011, p. 15.

(39) The Relevance of Air Power in Irregular Wars, Pathfinder, Issue 213, Canberra, Australia: RAAF Air Power Development Centre, December 2013.

(40) Some would justify Russia's aggressive actions as a defensive response to: the broken promises not to enlarge NATO following the collapse of the USSR; a subsequent undertaking not

deploy Western forces in former Warsaw Pact states; the detachment of Kosovo from Serbia, so demonstrating Western appetite for regime change, justified as humanitarian intervention; and a belief that the West has supported separatists in Chechnya and is conspiring to undermine the Russian Federation.

(41) Timothy Snyder, The Road to Unfreedom: Russia, Europe, America, Tim Duggan Books, New York, 2018.

(42) Oriana Riana Mastro, The Stealth Superpower, How China Hid Its Global Ambitions, Foreign Affairs, January/February 2019.

(43) Bear F. Braumoeller, Only the Dead: The Persistence of War in the Modern Age, Oxford University Press, 2019.

(44) Norman Angell, The Great Illusion: A Study of the Relation of Military Power in Nations to their Economic and Social Advantage (First ed.), G.P. Putnam's & Sons, New York, 1910, retrieved 22 January 2018.

(45) Richard Ned Lebow, quoted in David Betz, Carnage and Connectivity, Landmarks in the Decline of Conventional Military Power, London, 2015, p. 32.

(46) Steven Pinker, The Better Angels of Our Nature: Why Violence Has Declined, Viking Books, New York, 2011.

(47) Conrad C. Crane, The Lure of the Strike, Parametres 43(2) (Summer 2013): p. 5.

(48) Henry Kissinger, The Vietnam Negotiations, Foreign Affairs, Volume 47, January 1969, p. 214.

(49) Stathis N. Kalyvas, The Logic of Violence in Civil War, Cambridge Studies in Comparative Politics, June 15, 2006.

(50) Counter-insurgencies willing to be ruthless in achieving victory include: Sri Lanka (the Liberation Tigers of Tamil Eelam, also known as the 'Tamil Tigers'), Peru (the Maoist organisation known in the West as the 'Shining Path'), Malaya (a communist faction within the Chinese minority), the Philippines (Muslim separatists), Hafez al-Assad's crushing of the Muslim Brotherhood in Hama, and the Soviet eradication of Ukrainian nationalists (1944–59). Other, insurgencies have also been defeated largely through political measures and without significant civilian casualties. Examples include the Philippines in the time of President Ramon del Fierro Magsaysay, the Khalistan issue in India, and the Thai communist movements. Developing World regimes generally succeed in their objective: remaining in power.

(51) Sándor Fabian, Irregular Warfare, The Future Military Strategy For Small States, 17 Feb 2015.

(52) Friedrich Engels, Revolution and Counter-Revolution in Germany, 1852, chapter 17. Winston Churchill had by 1901 experienced the 2nd Anglo-Boer War and he identified that: 'The war of the people will be more terrible than those of kings'.

(53) The Chinese century, Well under way, The Economist, October 27th 2018, p. 89. Much of the increase has been in air and maritime forces. Between 2014 and 2018 China launched naval vessels with a total tonnage exceeding that of the entire Indian or French navies, according to the International Institute of Strategic Studies.

(54) Thucydides, The History of the Peloponnesian War, translator Richard Crawley, Pantianos Publishers, First published 1914, p. 1.23.

(55) Graham Allison, Destined for War: Can America and China Escape Thucydides' Trap, Scribe, Australia, 2017.

(56) President John F. Kennedy, Commencement Address at American University, Washington, D.C. June 10, 1963.

(57) Between 2016 and 2020 the US has funnelled $20 billion across the Atlantic for the European Deterrence Initiative. The comparable Maritime Security Initiative for Asia got a paltry $425 million over five years – less than Ukraine alone.

(58) George F. Kennan on Organizing Political Warfare, April 30, 1948, History and Public Policy Program Digital Archive, Obtained and contributed to CWIHP by A. Ross Johnson. Cited in

his book Radio Free Europe and Radio Liberty, Chapter 1 number 4 – NARA release courtesy of Douglas Selvage.

(59) Military thought is bedevilled by a simplistic linear progression between two polarised extremes; with manoeuvre and attrition being an example. Attempts to add greater depth to these concepts through use of phrases such as mosaic of conflict to replace spectrum of conflict have not been wholly successful. More sophisticated – even if he over employs it – is Carl von Clausewitz's use of threes. The most important are elevated in status to trinities. These trinities allow a position to be established between three 'magnetic poles'. This work will attempt to avoid linear dialectics, as a third element can through adding depth hopefully achieve nuance, and so improves understanding. Clausewitz's tendency to 'seeing issues in threes', is identified in: Hew Strachan, Carl von Clausewitz's On War, A Biography, Manjul Publishing House, Bhopal, India, 2011, p. 85.

(60) George F. Kennan, Lectures at the National War College 1946–7, Measures Short of War (Diplomatic), Edited by Giles D. Harlow George C. Maerz, NDU Press, Washington, 1991, p. 3. George Kennan, The inauguration of organized political warfare, Policy Planning Memorandum, May 4, 1948, National Archives and Records Administration, RG 273, Records of the National Security Council, NSC 10/2.

(61) Benjamin Jensen, The Cyber Character Of Political Warfare, The Brown Journal of World Affairs, Fall/Winter 2017, Volume XXIV, Issue 1.

(62) Disinformation and democracy, The rhythm of struggle, The Economist May 16th 2020, p. 73.

(63) Frank Hoffman, On Not-So-New Warfare: Political Warfare Vs Hybrid Threats, War On The Rocks, July 28, 2014.

(64) Philip Meilinger, The Mutable Nature of War, Air and Space Journal, 28, 4, 2010.

(65) Thomas Rid, Cyber War Will Not Take Place, C. Hurst (Publishers) Limited, London, 2017, pp. 12–13.

(66) Ross Babbage, Winning Without Fighting, Chinese and Russian Political Warfare Campaign and the West Can Prevail, Volume 1, Centre for Business and Strategic Assessment, 2019, p. 73.

(67) A good definition of frozen conflict is a situation in which active armed conflict has been ended, but no peace treaty or other political framework resolves the conflict to the satisfaction of the combatants.

(68) Peter Mattis, China's 'Three Warfares' in Perspective, War on the Rocks, January 30, 2018. Peter Navorro, Chinese Non Kinetic 'Three Warfares' against America, The National Interest, 5 January 2016.

(69) Thomas Rid, Active Measures, The Secret History of Disinformation and Political Warfare, Farrar, Straus and Giroux, New York, 2020.

(70) Deterring Terror, How Israel Confronts the Next Generation of Threats, English Translation of the Official Strategy of the Israeli Defence Forces, Belfer Centre, Havard Kennedy School, August 2016.

(71) Christopher Coker, The Improbable War, p. 44.

(72) Eric Hobsbawm, Age of Extremes: The Short Twentieth Century, 1914–1991, Abacus, London, 1994.

(73) David E. Johnson, Military Capabilities for Hybrid War, Insights from the Israel Defense Forces in Lebanon and Gaza, RAND Corporation, Santa Monica, CA, 2010.

(74) General Joseph L. Votel, The Gray Zone, United States Special Operations Command, White Paper, September 9, 2015.

(75) Voyenno Promyshlennyy Kuryer, November 28, 2018.

(76) General Valery Gerasimov, February 27, 2013, Military Doctrine, Military-Industrial Kurier, translated by Robert Coalson, June 21, 2014.

(77) Thucydides. History of the Peloponnesian War, 5.89.

(78) Norman Stone, The Atlantic and Its Enemies, London, 2010, p. 16.

(79) Gideon Rachman, Easternisation, Bodley Head, London, 2016, pp. 104–107.

(80) Thomas Schelling, Arms and Influence, Yale University Press, New Haven, CT, 1967.
(81) Christopher Coker, The Improbable War, p. 137.
(82) Sergey Minasyan, 'Hybrid' verses 'Compound' War: Lessons From The Ukraine Conflict, Ponars Eurasia, 11-2015.
(83) An example of America's denial that war's purpose is ultimately political was the view of General Marshall, Chief of Staff of the US Army, on whether to try and reach Berlin before the Soviets in World War Two: 'Personally, and aside from all the logistic, tactical and strategic implications, I would be loath to hazard American lives for purely political purposes'. Quoted in Niall Ferguson, The War of the World, Penguin Books, London, 2006, p. 586.
(84) Thomas E Ricks, The Generals, Penguin Books, New York, 2012, p. 237.
(85) Colin McInnes, The British Army's New Way in Warfare: A Doctrinal Misstep?, Defense & Security Analysis, 23:2, DOI, 2007, p. 132.
(86) Edward Luttwak, Dead End Counterinsurgency warfare as military malpractice, Harper's Magazine, 18 February, 2018.
(87) Hew Strachen, On War: A Biography, discusses in its chapter two (pp. 68–106) Clausewitz's didactic process which resulted in the recognition of two sorts of war.
(88) Eliot A. Cohen, The Mystique of US Airpower, Foreign Affairs, Volume 73, Number 1, January/February 1994, p. 109.
(89) Robert A Pape, The True Worth of Air Power, Foreign Affairs, March/April 2004.
(90) David Betz, Carnage and Connectivity, Landmarks in the Decline of Conventional Military Power, London, 2015 p. 15.
(91) Robert A Pape, The True Worth of Air Power, Foreign Affairs, March/April 2004.
(92) Frederick W Kagan, Finding the Target, p. 320.
(93) Jeffrey Goldberg, The Obama Doctrine, Atlantic Magazine April 2015.
(94) Bob Woodward, Bush at War, Simon and Schuster, New York, 2003, p. 230.
(95) M. Djilas, Conversations with Stalin, Harcourt Brace and Company, New York, 1962, p. 114.
(96) J. C. Wylie, Military Strategy: A General Theory of Power Control, Annapolis, 1989, p. 72.
(97) Liddell Hart, Thoughts on War, Faber and Faber, London, 1944, p. iv.
(98) Gil Eliot, p. 133.
(99) Valery Havard and John Van R. Hoff, reports of Military Observers Attached to the Armies in Manchuria During the Russo-Japanese War, Government Printing Office, Washington DC, 1906, p. 31.
(100) Zaritskiy, V.N, Missile forces and artillery: reforming problems, March 1, 2002; Military Thought Article Archive, HighBeam Research.
(101) Napoleon, the military genius behind most of Clausewitz's writing, takes a different view in believing he never had enough artillery. He wanted 5 guns per 1,000 men. The original Grand Army had only 2 guns per 1,000. In 1807–9 it had risen to 3 and later achieved 3.5 per thousand by issuing the infantry with battalion guns.
(102) Carl von Clausewitz, On War, pp. 287–8.
(103) Paddy Griffith, Battle Tactics of the American Civil War, The Crowood Press, Marlborough, Wiltshire, 1987, pp. 177–9.
(104) Shelford Bidwell & Dominic Graham, Fire-Power: British Army Weapons and Theories of War 1904–1945, George Allen & Urwin, London, 1982, p. 57.
(105) By way of an example of the impact of this approach, the Soviet General Staff by the end of the Great Patriotic War had compiled a 60-volume study of the conflict. The purpose was to rigorously learn the lessons from each operation. See: translated by Harold S. Orienstein, Soviet Documents on the Use of Their War Experience, Frank Cass Publishers, London, 1993.
(106) Christopher Donnelly, Red Banner, The Soviet Military System in Peace and War, Janes's Information Group, Alexandria, VA, 1988, p. 230. In the Motor Rifle Division the total number of artillery and mortars went from 162 to 222, and in the Tank Division from 96 to 180.

(107) Robert H. Scales Jr., Firepower in Limited War, National Defense University Press, Washington, DC, 1990, p. 73.
(108) Derek M. C. Yue, Deciphering Sun Tzu: How to Read The Art of War, Oxford University Press, New York, 2014, p. 84.
(109) Sir Lawrence Freedman, Regular and Irregular War an address to the Canadian International Council on 19 June 2008.
(110) E.N. Luttwak, Dead end: Counter-insurgency warfare as military malpractice, Harper's Magazine, February 2007, pp. 33–42.
(111) CE Callwell, Small Wars: Their Principles and Practice, Albion, London 2016, pp. 75–76.
(112) Colin S Gray, Irregular Enemies and the Essence of Strategy: Can the American Way of War Adapt, 2006, p. 23.
(113) Victor Davis Hanson, War's Bitter Laws, National Review, 11 July 11, 2003.
(114) Max Hastings, Vietnam An Epic History of a Tragic War, Williams Collins, London, 2019, p. 640.
(115) The British – who had already agreed to leave Malaya – were fighting a minority within the minority ethnic Chinese population. The Americans in Vietnam faced a successful and popular national liberation movement. The British were in control of the state, while the Americans worked through a succession of deeply flawed South Vietnamese leaders. Malaysia is an isolated peninsula, in contrast Vietnam's borders could never be sealed, with neighbouring countries providing resupply and safe havens. The Chinese and Russians provided significant materiel support to the North Vietnamese, in contrast Malayan guerrillas largely relied upon their own resources.
(116) Robert H Scales, Firepower in Limited War, p. 61.
(117) Though most historians do not have the same certainty, such as: Mark Boden, Hue 1968: How one battle changed minds about Vietnam, Grove Press, London, 2017.
(118) At the Battle of Ocotal on 16 July 1927, the Sandinistas (Nicaraguan insurgents) suffered over 150 people killed and wounded. Five American aircraft, armed with machine guns and four 25-pound bombs, provided dive-bombing support to government forces. The Sandinistas never did another massed attack.
(119) Christopher A. Lawrence, Airpower: Just Part of the Counter-insurgency Equation, Small Wars Journal Article, 18 January 2016 – 12:03pm. An effective counter to this view is: James Corum, Wray Johnson. Airpower in Small Wars: Fighting Insurgents and Terrorists, University Press of Kansas, Lawrence, 2003.
(120) Maoist insurgency theory is the clearest in this area, as it sees the transition as being the only means of both overthrowing a state and replacing its government. It identifies three 'phases' of insurgency: political work, guerrilla warfare and then conventional war, which Mao refers to as 'orthodox warfare'.
(121) Mark Urban, Task Force Black: The Explosive True Story of the SAS and the Secret War in Iraq, Little Brown, London: 2010, p. xvi.
(122) The decapitation strategy has historically proved to be effective against ideological and nationalist organisations. Sendero Luminoso, which terrorized Peru in the late 1980s, was diminished by the arrest of their founder Abimael Guzman in 1992. Palestinian Islamic Jihad became less effective after its founder Fathi Shqaqi was assassinated by Israel in 1995. Its effect on the current Islamist threat is not yet established. Statistical analysis suggests that decapitation strikes on religiously-motivated terrorist groups tend to be followed by more lethal attacks. There is a lack of suitable metrics and data on the impact on the overall organisation. Aaron Mannes, Testing The Snake Head Strategy: Does Killing or Capturing its Leaders Reduce a Terrorist Group's Activity? The Journal of International Policy Solutions, Volume 9, Spring 2008, p. 40. For its basis as a theory see: Gideon Brough and Alun D. Williams Decapitation Strategy, Published Online: 13 November 2011.
(123) Assassinations States are finding new ways of killing enemies abroad, Economist, Mar 15th 2018.

(124) Captain Brett Friedman, US Marine Corps, Clausewitz and Comprehensive Counter-insurgency Creeping Death, Military Review, January-February 2014.
(125) William C. Martel, Victory in War: Foundations of Modern Military Policy, Cambridge University Press, 2006, p. 71.
(126) Heraclitus of Ephesus, the Greek philosopher of the sixth century BCE.
(127) Armeiskiy sbornik [Army digest], September 1996, 46. Quoted in Mr. Lester W. Grau, Artillery and Counter-insurgency: The Soviet Experience in Afghanistan, May–June 1997 Field Artillery Journal. Colonel Litvinenko commanded an artillery regiment and was the chief of the 201st Motorized Rifle Division artillery during 1984–1986 in Afghanistan.
(128) David Fitzgerald, Learning to Forget: US Army Counterinsurgency Doctrine and Practice from Vietnam to Iraq. Stanford University Press, Stanford, 2013, p. 39.
(129) Thomas P. Hohler, Imagination and Reflection: Intersubjectivity: Fichte's Grundlage of 1794, Springer Science + Business Media, Dordrecht, The Hague, 1982, p. 18.
(130) John Shy, First Battles in Retrospect, in Charles E Heller and Willian A Stofft, America's First Battles 1776–1965, University of Kansas Press, Lawrence KS, 1986, p. 327.
(131) Jan Morris, Heavens Command, p. 6.
(132) Bill Gates observed: 'Success is a lousy teacher. It seduces smart people into thinking they can't lose. And it's an unreliable guide to the future'. Bill Gates, The Road Ahead, Penguin Readers, New York, 2008.
(133) Combat Studies Institute, the Operational Leadership Experiences interview with Brigadier General (Retd.) Shimon Naveh smallwarsjournal.com/documents/mattmatthews.pdf
(134) Dennis E. Showalter, Military Innovation and the Whig Perspective of History, in Harold R. Winton and David R. Mets, (Eds), The Challenge of Change: Military Institutions and New Realities, 1918–1941 Lincoln, NE: University of Nebraska Press, 2003, p. 229.
(135) Russel W. Glenn (Ed), Capital Preservation: Preparing For Urban Operations in the Twenty-First Century, Proceedings of the RAND Arroyo-TRADOC-MCWL-OSD Urban Operations Conference, March 22–23, 2000, RAND Corporation, Santa Monica, CA, p. 61. Views echoed by: Lieutenant General Paul K. Van Riper, USMC and Major General Robert H. Scales, Jr, U.S. Army, Preparing for War in the 21st Century, Parametres, Autumn 1997, p. 4.
(136) Christopher Duffy, Frederick the Great: A Military Life, Routledge, Abingdon, 2016, p. 301.
(137) Robert H Scales, Forecasting the Future of Warfare, War on the Rocks, 9 April 2018.
(138) Ralph Peters, Fighting for the Future: Will America Triumph? Stackpole Books, Mechanicsburg, PA, 1999, pp. 171–172.
(139) Christopher Paul, Confessions of a Hybrid Warfare Skeptic: What Might Really Be Interesting but Hidden Within the Various Conceptions of Gray Zone Conflict, Ambiguous Warfare, Political Warfare, and Their Ilk, Small War Journal.
(140) Colin S Gray, Another Bloody Century, Future War, Weidenfeld and Nicolson, London, 2005, p. 22.
(141) General Omar Bradley, May 15, 1951, at the Senate hearings on President Truman's firing of General MacArthur from his Korean command. New York Times Archives.
(142) Professor Sir Michael Howard quoted in Julian Lindley-French and Yves Boyer, The Oxford Handbook of War, Oxford Handbooks in Politics & International Relations, Oxford, 2012, p. 373.

Chapter 2: Firepower Dominated Total War

(1) Geoffrey Till, The Maritime Strategy and the Nuclear Age, Palgrave Macmillan, London, 1982, pp. 224–5.
(2) David Chandler, The Art of War in the Age of Marlborough, Hippocrene Books, New York, 1976, p. 142.

(3) Air Marshal of the Royal Air Force, Sir John Slessor. Airpower and Armies, Oxford University Press, London, 1936, p. x.
(4) Forward air controller is normally used in this publication. The alternative term joint terminal attack controller (JTAC) is used by the US armed forces and is gaining traction amongst allied forces. Both refer to a qualified controller who, from a forward position, directs the action of combat aircraft engaged in close air support and other offensive air operations. The difference in terminology reflects America's unique challenge of multiple air forces and ground forces pursuing their own policies on air land integration. Joint terminal attack controllers are qualified to control Air Force, Navy and Marine aircraft in accordance with inter-service agreement. The term became effective in the US on 3 September 2003 with the publishing of Joint Publication (JP) 3-09.3 Close air support.
(5) David Boucher and Teresa Smith Editors, R. G. Collingwood: An Autobiography and other writings: with essays on Collingwood's life and work, OUP Oxford, 12 December 2013, p. 114.
(6) Clausewitz, Strategie aus den Jahr 1804, p. 66. Quoted in Hew Strachan, Carl von Clausewitz's On War, A Biography, Manjul Publishing House, Bhopal, India, 2011, p. 97.
(7) C. Decker, Die Schlactern and hauptgefeche des Siebjahringen Kriegs … mit vorherrschender Bezugnahme auf den Gebrauch der Artillerie, Berlin, 1837, p. 6. Quoted in Christopher Duffy, The Army of Frederick the Great, David & Charles, London,1974, pp. 100–101 and 110.
(8) Christopher Duffy, The Army of Frederick the Great, pp. 100–101.
(9) Antoine Henri de Jomini, The Art of War, Arc Manor, Rockville, MD, 2009, p. 238.
(10) Fairfax Downey, The Guns at Gettysburg, McKay, New York, 1952, p. 214.
(11) Paddy Griffith, Battle Tactics of the American Civil War, p. 165.
(12) Donald A. Carter, On Target: Henry Hunt – Union FSCOORD, Forward Observer, The Newsletter of the US Field Artillery Association, October 1990, p. 1.
(13) The Battle of Colenso was fought between British and Boer forces from the independent South African Republic and Orange Free State in and around Colenso, Natal, South Africa on 15 December 1899. In the battle, two batteries of field guns deployed in the open well within rifle range of the nearest Boers. Intense Boer fire resulted in the detachments of 16 and 44 Batteries Royal Field Artillery becoming either casualties or being driven from their guns. With great gallantry (four Victoria Crosses were awarded) and loss, two of the twelve guns were rescued.
(14) Field Marshal Earl Kitchener, letter to Pandeli Ralli during the Boer War, 1900.
(15) The principle of indirect fire was published in an article by Russian Lieutenant Colonel Karl G Guk in 1882. The Germans introduced the first indirect fire sight in the Ritchtflache in the 1880s, which the Russians soon copied.
(16) JFC Fuller, The Conduct of War, 1789–1961, Da Capo Press, New York, 1961, p. 142.
(17) Valery Havard and John Van R. Hoff, reports of Military Observers Attached to the Armies in Manchuria During the Russo-Japanese War, Government Printing Office, Washington DC, 1906, p. 31.
(18) Allan R. Millett and Williamson Murray (Eds) Military Effectiveness, Volume 3, The Second World War, Cambridge University Press, New York, 2010, p. 34.
(19) John Terraine, White Heat – The New Warfare 1914–18, Leo Cooper, London, 1992, p. 95.
(20) Cited in Anthony Clayton, Paths of Glory, The French Army 1914–18, Cassel, London, 2003, p. 17.
(21) War Department, Office of the Chief of Staff, Field Service Regulations, United States Army, 1914, corrected to 31 July 1918, Government Printing Office, Washington, DC, 1918, p. 13.
(22) Tim Travers, The Killing Ground, The British Army, the Western Front, and the Emergence of Modern Warfare, 1900–1918, Pen and Sword, London, 2009, p. 255.
(23) Barbara Tuchman, The Guns of August, p. 207.
(24) Quoted in Gunther E Rothenberg, The Art of Warfare in the Age of Napoleon, Indiana University Press, Bloomington, Indiana, 1980, p. 145.
(25) John Terraine, To Win a War, 1918, The Year of Victory, Sidgwick and Jackson, London, 1978, p. 35.

(26) Quoted in Lee Kennett, The First Air War, 1914-1918, Free Press, New York, 1999, p. 31.

(27) Charles Messenger, The Day the War Was Won, Turning Point at Amiens 8th August 1918, Phoenix, London, 2008, p. 55.

(28) Balloons were first used in warfare by France on June 26, 1794, at the Battle of Fleurus. They were subsequently prominent in the American Civil and the Franco-Prussian Wars when operations became sufficiently static to allow their use.

(29) Colin S Gray, Airpower for Strategic Effect, Air University Press, Air Force Research Institute Maxwell Air Force Base, Alabama, 2012, pp. 93 and 99.

(30) Riley Sunderland, Evolution of Command and Control for Close air support, Office of the Air Force History Headquarters, United States Air Force, March 1973, p. 1.

(31) The best background is: James Pugh, The Royal Flying Corps, The Western Front and the Control of the Air 1914–1918, Routledge, Abingdon-on-Thames, 2017.

(32) Anthony Clayton, Paths of Glory, The French Army 1914–18, Cassel, London, 2003, p. 125.

(33) Stephen Budiansky, Air Power, Penguin, New York, 2004, p. 66.

(34) Correlli Barnett, Shelford Bidwell, Brian Bond, John Harding and John Terraine, Old Battles and New Defences, Can We Learn From Military History? Brassey's Defence Publications, London, 1986, pp. 7–8.

(35) Cited in Anthony Clayton, Paths of Glory, The French Army 1914–18, Cassel, London, 2003, p. 27. In this case change was assisted by unavailability of the red dye, this was made in Germany.

(36) CS Forrester's World War One novel, The General, provides an accurate parody of this approach:

> 'In some ways it was like the debate of a group of savages as to how to extract a screw from a piece of wood. Accustomed only to nails, they had made one effort to pull out the screw by main force, and now that it had failed they were devising methods of applying more force still, of obtaining more efficient pincers, of using levers and fulcrums so that more men could bring their strength to bear. They could hardly be blamed for not guessing that by rotating the screw it would come out after the exertion of far less effort; it would be a notion so different from anything they had ever encountered that they would laugh at the man who suggested it.'

(37) Andrew Rawson, Somme Campaign, Pen and Sword, Barnsley, South Yorkshire, 2014, p. 8.

(38) Perhaps the origin of barrages was the Boer War, as the first recorded use was by the Royal Artillery at the Tugela River in 1900. There were many forms of barrage. The most common is the moving or creeping barrage. A standing barrage was static and was designed to prevent enemy troops moving. A variation of this is the box barrage. Three or four barrages form a box around a position to isolate it. This outlasted the other forms of barrages, as it provides a very effective form of pre-planned defensive fire to secure a recently captured objective. The Soviets/Russians call barrages curtain fires, dividing them into fixed protective curtain fires, the equivalent of defensive or final protective fire, and moving curtain fire, the equivalent of a rolling barrage.

(39) Charles Messenger, The Day the War Was Won, Turning Point at Amiens 8th August 1918, Phoenix, London, 2008, p. 55.

(40) Brigadier ML Pemberton MC, The Development of Artillery Tactics and Equipment, The War Office, London, 1951, pp. 235–7.

(41) Anthony Clayton, Paths of Glory, The French Army 1914–18, Cassel, London, 2003, p. 127.

(42) The defeat of the enemy's ground based joint fires systems is also termed counter fire and counter bombardment. An over-literal interpretation of the term counter battery is that it is limited to engaging opposing artillery pieces. Counter fire is currently used by some nations, as its proponents believe that it better reflects attacking the whole indirect fire system. The term counter-mortar, a separate process in World War Two, after that war merged with counter-battery to become counter-bombardment. This term subsequently has fallen from favour.

(43) Brigadier-General James Edward Edmonds and Lieutenant Colonel R. Maxwell-Hyslop, Military Operations: France and Belgium, 26 September – 11 November: The Advance to Victory. History

of the Great War based on Official Documents by Direction of the Committee of Imperial Defence. Volume V, HMSO, London, 1947, p. 574.

(44) We would now recognise shell shock as a type of post-traumatic stress disorder. It was a reaction to the intensity of the bombardment and fighting that produced a helplessness appearing variously as panic and being scared, flight, or an inability to reason, sleep, walk or talk.

(45) Carl von Clausewitz, On War, p. 231.

(46) Colonel Georg Bruchmüller rapidly emerged as the de facto chief artillery advisor to the High Command and having established his reputation on the Eastern Front at the Battle of Riga in 1917, he oversaw the fire planning of most subsequent major offensives. His methods are recorded in his two books: Artillery in the Attack in Position Warfare and The German Artillery in the Break-through Battles of the World War by a German Field Artillery officer.

(47) WO 33/723: Notes on Close Shooting by Guns and Howitzers, registration of targets and calibration.

(48) Calibration, nigelef.tripod.com/p_artyint-cb.ht. Accessed 5 November 2018.

(49) Captain Erich Pulkowski combined metrological data and a velocity correction to improve accuracy. This was strongly resisted, but by the start of 1918, Bruchmüller (when still only a lieutenant colonel) insisted on its use by the German Army. How effective this was is questionable, the German use of long preliminary bombardments provided time for the fire to be adjusted onto the target. Preparatory fire was never reduced below two hours; the British and later the French with their superior accuracy could dispense with this and rely solely upon covering fire.

(50) Artillery in Offensive Operations: SS157, Report on the Overseas Artillery School, Salisbury Plain, May 1917, Issued by the General Staff.

(51) The technical excellence achieved by the British Army in World War One was largely due to the Royal Garrison Artillery; the branch of the artillery responsible for the heavy and coastal guns. The Royal Field Artillery was the separate home of the more dashing and glamorous field and horse artillery. Progress was made through the War in merging the two traditions, though even in 1917, the British General Staff identified that:

> 'The standard of technical knowledge in the R.G.A. [Royal Garrison Artillery] is very considerably higher than in the R.F.A. [Royal Field Artillery]. There is, however, just as great need for science in one branch as the other.'

As the Royal Garrison Artillery-trained officers dominated Britain's artillery schools this gap continued to be closed through the last year of the War. The key outcome of having different branches of the Royal Artillery was a culture gap that prevented a single dominant view on the employment of artillery. There was not, in Britain, anything like the doctrinal dominance within the French Army that led to the 75mm Quick Fire Gun meeting all their fire support requirements. German artillery was also organized into two different branches. The field artillery primarily used light guns to support manoeuvre. The foot artillery manned fixed fortifications, and used heavy howitzers and siege mortars. This did not result in a similar creative friction, perhaps due to the dominance Colonel Bruchmüller had in the German Army. David T Zabecki, Der Durchbruchmueller, Field Artillery, August 1990, p. 14.

(52) Colonel Repington, The First World War, 1914–1918, Constable, London, 1920, p. 160.

(53) David Zabecki, Steel Wind: Colonel Georg Bruchmüller and the Birth of Modern Artillery, Praeger Publishers, Westpoint CT, 1994, pp. 10–11.

(54) L. Van Loan Naisawald, Grape and Cannister – The Story of the Field Artillery of the Army of the Potomac, 1861–1865, Oxford University Press, Oxford, 1960, p. 536.

(55) Johnathan Bailey, Field Artillery and Firepower, AUSA Institute of Land Warfare book. Annapolis, MD: Naval Institute Press, 2004, p. 267.

(56) Most Russian divisions started the war with 48 76mm (3-inch) guns. Two divisions made up a corps which also had 12 122mm howitzers. In addition, they started the war with 20 battalions of both 152mm howitzers and 107mm guns. These battalions usually had 12 guns or howitzers.
(57) Brigade Commander Georgii Samoilovich Isserson, The Evolution of the Operational Art, translated by Bruce W Menning, Combat Studies Institute Press US Army Combined Arms Centre Fort Leavenworth, Kansas, 2013, p. 34.
(58) Anthony Clayton, Paths of Glory, The French Army 1914–18, Cassel, London, 2003, pp. 121–3.
(59) Jonathan Bailey, The First World War and the Birth of Modern Warfare, in MacGregor Knox and Williamson Murray (ed.), The Dynamics of Military Revolution, 1300–2050, Cambridge, Cambridge University Press, 2001, p. 147.
(60) General Oskar Hutier captured Riga in July 1917 with assault troops using what are now known as infiltration tactics, at the time the Germans knew them as Hutier tactics. Trevor N Dupuy, A Genius for War, Nova Publications, Yateley, England, 1997, p. 172.
(61) Extract from letter sent by Churchill to Montgomery, February 1943. Winston S Churchill, The Second World War, The Grand Alliance, Huston and Mifflin Company, Boston, 1950, p. 495.
(62) Frederick Myatt, The British Infantry 1660–1945, The Evolution of a Fighting Force, Bradford Press, Poole, Dorset, 1983, pp. 194–6.
(63) The 1920s saw a French doctrine debate in which the proponents stressed different lessons and periods of the Great War. Ferdinand Foch's followers praised manoeuvre and aggressiveness, while Philippe Petain's disciples preached firepower and defence. Petain's vision prevailed because it better suited France's damaged society and diplomatic posture.
(64) Young, The Strategic Dream: French Air warfare in the Inter-War Period, 1919–39, Journal of Contemporary History, 9(4), October 1974, p. 63.
(65) War Department, Report of the Hero Board, CARL No. AD A161 150, 9 December, 1919, p. 1.
(66) Martin Van Creveld, Technology and War, from 2000 BC to the Present, The Free Press, New York, 1991, p. 193.
(67) Robert H Scales, Firepower in Limited War, p. 12.
(68) The Germans in World War Two called air interdiction indirect support to differentiate it from battlefield direct support of close air support.
(69) Chris Bellamy, Red God of War: Soviet Artillery and Rocket Forces, Brassey's Defence Publishers, London, 1986, p. 47.
(70) Benjamin Franklin Cooling (Ed), Case Studies in the Development of Close Air Support, Office of Air Force History, United States Air Force, Washington DC, 1990, p. 104.
(71) Buckley, John, Air Power in the Age of Total War. London: UCL Press 1998, pp. 126–127.
(72) Buckley, John, The Air War in France, in Bond, B., and Taylor, M.D. (eds), The Battle for France and Flanders 1940: Sixty Years On, Leo Cooper, Barnsley, 2001, p. 111.
(73) General Paul Deichmann, German Air Force Operations in Support of the Army, USAF Historical Study Number 163, Maxwell AFB, Alabama, 1962, p. 140. Alistair Horne, To Lose a Battle, France 1940, Penguin Books, UK, 2007, pp. 162–163.
(74) Buckley, J., The Air War in France, p. 123.
(75) Most historical studies take the Wehrmacht's military excellence as a given. Van Crefeld in Fighting Power, Praeger, Santa Barbara CT, 2007 examines why.
(76) Michael Burleigh, The Best of Times, The Worst of Times: A History of Now, Macmillan, London, 2017, p. 161.
(77) Benjamin Franklin Cooling (Ed), Case Studies in the Development of Close Air Support, p. 115.
(78) Colonel N Zavgorodniy, Combat Use of Fighter Aviation, p. 19, quoted in Benjamin Franklin Cooling (Ed), Case Studies in the Development of Close Air Support, Office of Air Force History, United States Air Force, Washington DC, 1990, p. 126.
(79) The remaining portions are: air superiority (35–45%), interdiction (4–12%) and reconnaissance (2–13%) as quoted in Marin Van Creveld, The Age of Airpower, Public Affairs, New York, 2011, pp. 431–2.

(80) Von Hardesty, Red Phoenix, The Rise of Soviet Air Power 1941–45, Arms and Armour Press, London-Melbourne, 1982, p. 222.
(81) Chris Bellamy, Red God of War, p. 55. Despite being smaller, by calibre, Soviet guns were longer ranged than their Western equivalents.
(82) Lt.-Col. R. Kent Lauchbaum Synchronizing Airpower and Firepower In The Deep Battle, Pickle Partners Publishing 6 November 2015, p. 9.
(83) Von Hardesty, Red Phoenix, p. 87.
(84) The last major World War Two German offensive Operation Frühlingserwachen or Spring Awakening was conducted in Hungary from 6–16 March 1945. It was largely defeated by Soviet defences relying upon artillery. In contrast, in Western Theatre, airpower provided most of the firepower in the Battles of Mortain and the Bulge (in the latter case this had to wait until the adverse weather had cleared). Historians who have drawn attention to the excellence of the Wehrmacht's operational art in responding to the Soviet offensives have failed to give due weight to this being made possible by the limited ambition of Soviet airpower. There are no examples on the Eastern Front similar to the delay and attrition imposed on the Hermann Goring Panzer Parachute Division and the Panzer Lehr Division following Operation Overlord. In both cases air attacks on infrastructure on the line of march were more effective than direct attack. Notably, in the Panzer Lehr case with the destruction of all but one of the bridges across the river Orne. In contrast, airpower achieved little in terms of physical attrition of German armour. See Major General Michael Reynolds' Steel Inferno, 1st SS Panzer Corps in Normandy, Sarpedon, New York, 1997. This draws upon Operational Report on Allied airpower during the Normandy Campaign, which show that few German tank casualties were due to tactical airpower. Richard C. Anderson, Artillery Effectiveness versus Armour in Volume 1, Number 6 of The International TNDM Newsletter, concludes that airpower inflicts around 8% of tank casualties.
(85) Eduard Mark in Aerial Interdiction: Air Power and the Land Battle in Three American Wars, Centre for Air Force History, Superintendent of Documents, US. Government Printing Office, Washington DC, 1994, p. 2.
(86) William J., Dalecky. Major, USAF, Battlefield Air Interdiction by the Luftwaffe at the Battle of Kursk, 1943, U.S. Army Command and General Staff College, Fort Leavenworth, Kansas, 6 June 1980, p. 42.
(87) Hermann Plocher, The German Air Force Versus Russia, 1943, USAF Historical Series, Number 155, USAF Historical Division, Maxwell AFB, AL, p. 66.
(88) Klaus Uebe, Russian Reactions to German Airpower in WW II, USAF Historical Series, Number 176, USAF Historical Division, Maxwell AFB, AL, 1964, pp. 69 and 81.
(89) Ibid., p. 82.
(90) Paul Deichman, German Air Force Operations in Support of the Army, reprint, Arco, New York: 1968, p. 101.
(91) From 1942 the German Army High Command (Oberkommando des Heeres) exercised de facto command of the Eastern Front, rather than the Supreme Command of the Armed Forces (the Oberkommando der Wehrmacht).
(92) Ferdinand Otto Miksche, Attack: A Study of Blitzkrieg Tactics, New York, Random House, 1942, pp. xv & 97–99.
(93) MacGregor Knox, Hitler's Italian Allies: Royal Armed Forces, Fascist Regime, and the War of 1940–1943, Cambridge University Press, Cambridge, 2000, p. 57.
(94) Matthew Powell, The RAF Must Fly the Flag: The British Army's Interpretation of Tactical Air Power during the Battle of France, 1940, University of Sussex Journal of Contemporary History 16, University of Birmingham, 2015, p. 64.
(95) Lieutenant Colonel Michael J. Janser, US Army. Cognitive Biases in Military Decision Making, U.S. Army War College, 2007.
(96) Daniel R Mortesen, A Pattern for Joint Operations: World War II Close air support, North Africa, Office of Air Force History and U.S. Army Centre of Military History, Washington, DC 1987, p. 55.

(97) A pamphlet was sent to every ranking officer in North Africa following the Casablanca Conference, this confirmed that airpower would now operate under the Desert Air Force system. Subsequently this would form the basis of a new US Army Field Manual.
(98) Robert Frank Futrell, Ideas, Concepts, Doctrine; A History of Basic Thinking in the United States Air Force 1907-1964, Air University, Maxwell AFB AL, 1971, pp. 121–122.
(99) In the Normandy campaign the UA Army Air Force claimed to have destroyed the following: Motor transports 1,945; armoured fighting vehicles 155; locomotives 194; railroad cars 2,117; bridges 32; gun emplacements 34; logistic dumps 4; railroad cuts 107; vessels and barges 3; and horse drawn vehicles 365. The key issue is not the exact numbers, but the proportions, showing that effective air interdiction is not the physical destruction of high value army equipment, such as guns and tanks, but rendering them logistically unsustainable.
(100) Sebastian Cox, The Air/Land relationship – an historical perspective 1918–91, Royal Air Force, Airpower Review, Volume 11, Number 2, Summer 2008, p. 5.
(101) Powell, M., A Forgotten Revolution?: Army Co-operation Command and Artillery Co-operation, 1940–42', Canadian Military History Volume 23, Number 1, Winter 2014, pp. 71–88.
(102) Eduard Mark, Aerial Interdiction: Air Power and the Land Battle in Three American Wars, Centre for Air Force History 1994, p. 2.
(103) German Evaluation of Allied Air Interdiction in World War II Sub-Study II. A Study prepared for Headquarters of USAF, Assistant Chief of Staff, October 1969.
(104) Shelford Bidwell & Dominic Graham, Fire-Power, pp. 269–70.
(105) Dr Richard P Hallion, Battlefield Air Support, A Retrospective Assessment, Airpower Journal, Spring 1990.
(106) Martin Lindsay, So Few Got Through, Pen and Sword, London, 2008, p. 54.
(107) FH George, Cybernetics, The English University Press, London, 1971, pp. 8–9.
(108) Johnathan Bailey, Field Artillery and Firepower, p. 258.
(109) On 11 November, 1918, the US Army's artillery was 462,163 strong. By 30 June, 1920 it was 12,560 strong.
(110) D. M. Beere, Lessons of the War as Affecting American Artillery, Particularly Divisional Artillery, Field Artillery, Journal, 11, September-October, 1921, pp. 444–5.
(111) Artillery Command in the German Army, Tactical and Technical Trends, No 29, US War Department, General Staff, 15 July 1943.
(112) John Ellis, Brute Force: Allied Strategy and Tactics in the Second World War, Andre Deutsch, London, 1990, pp. 46–8.
(113) RAC Parker, The Second World War, A Short History, Oxford University Press, 1989, p. 67.
(114) Tactics & Fire Control of Russian Artillery in Attack and Defense During 1941, 1942, and 1944. And their Development In Recent Times By Oberst (I.G) Hans-Georg Richert, In Recent Times PDF, ePub eBook, Accessed 16 February 2017.
(115) Wray, Timothy A., Standing Fast: German Defensive Doctrine on the Russian Front During World War II, Combat Studies Institute, U.S. Army Command and General Staff College, Ft Leavenworth, Kansas, p. 87.
(116) Shelford Bidwell & Dominic Graham, Fire-Power: British Army Weapons and Theories of War 1904–1945, George Allen & Urwin, London, 1982, pp. 242–5.
(117) Gil Eliot, Twentieth Century Book of the Dead, p. 133.
(118) Shelford Bidwell & Dominic Graham, Fire-Power, p. 258.
(119) In the 1920s, Fort Sill, the American artillery school, determined that fire control would have to be centralised at battalion level, creating a fire direction centre (FDC) on the battalion staff to process fire missions. This was changeover was complete by 1934, but it was the invention of a new graphical firing table in 1940 that really speeded the calculation of massed fire. With war looming in 1941, the War Department finally approved the FDC system for the divisions.

(120) Russell A Weathersby, The Field Artillery Group in Support of the Corps and Field Artillery, 1943–53, thesis, US Army Command and General Staff, 1965, pp. 93–96, 112–33; Bernard S. Waterman, The Battle of Okinawa, An Artillery Angle, Field Artillery Journal, September 1945, pp. 523–28; Robert Ross Smith, Triumph in the Philippines, Office of the Chief of Military History, Washington, DC: 1963, p. 291.
(121) RAC Parker, The Second World War, A Short History, Oxford University Press, 1989, p. 190.
(122) Major General George C. Kenny quoted in Samuel Milner, Victory in Papua, The United States Army in World War II: The War in the Pacific, originally 1957; reproduced, US Army Centre of Military History, Washington, DC, 1989, p. 135.
(123) Samuel Milner, Victory in Papua, US Army in World War Two series, Washington DC, 1957 cited in Jonathan M House, Combined Warfare in the 20th Century, University Press of Kansas, Lawrence, KS, 2001, p. 165.
(124) The force deployed to New Guinea consisted of the four brigades of the Australian 7th Division and two regiments (126th and 128th Infantry) from the US 32nd Infantry Division. The latter deployed without their two field artillery battalions and also left behind about a third of their infantry battalions' organic 81-mm mortars. The decision to effectively fight without organic fire support was motivated by: the limited air and sea transports; a willingness to accept the risk of being without artillery due to perceived Japanese weakness; the availability of air support; and that the Australians already had guns deployed in New Guinea.
(125) War Department, Field Manual 31–20, Jungle Warfare, Government Printing Office, Washington, DC, 1941, paragraph 28, quoted in Robert C Gildart, Artillery on New Georgia, Field Artillery Journal, May–June 1944, p. 83.
(126) Brigadier ML Pemberton MC, p. 313.
(127) Preceding World War Two there was little urban conflict outside civil wars, as regular armies avoided this character of conflict. The Prussian Army did not attack Paris, but the Franco-Prussian War was followed by the inter-French street fighting that led to the defeat of the Paris Commune. Prior to World War Two the most significant modern urban fighting was between the Napoleonic French and the Spanish in the City of Saragossa.
(128) Louis A DiMarco, Concrete Hell: Urban Warfare from Stalingrad to Iraq, Osprey, Oxford, 2012, p. 81.
(129) Major Jeffrey D. Noll, U.S. Army Restraint In Urban Warfare: The Canadian Attack On Groningen, Netherlands, 13–16 April 1945, Fort Leavenworth, Kansas, 2013, pp. 61–3.
(130) In their 1944 organisation, the ten Soviet artillery divisions had 190 guns and howitzers to 168 rockets and mortars. In response to German defensive positions' greater depth and improved fortifications, they featured a greater proportion of heavy long-range tube artillery than previous organisations. They were usually reinforced by a Guards Mortar Division, which were equipped with rocket launchers to provide most of the area target suppression. The necessity of this pairing resulted in these artillery divisions being grouped into Breakthrough Artillery Corps, with a total weapon count of around 1,000 guns and launchers.
(131) One British survey calculated that naval gunfire was almost thirty times more effective than aircraft at hitting a point target. Captain JC Downward RA, Army Operational Research Report No 299, The Westkapele Assault on Walcheren, October 1945, pp. 64–67.
(132) Russell F. Weigley, The American Way of War, 1973, p. 308.
(133) GD Sheffield, Leadership and Command, The Anglo-American Military Experience Since 1861, Brassey's London and Washington, 1997, p. 135.
(134) James R Holbrook et al, Tactical Responses to Concentrated Artillery, Combat Studies Institute, IS Report, US Command and General Staff College, Leavenworth, Kansas, 1989, pp. 100–102.
(135) Shelford Bidwell & Dominic Graham, Fire-Power, p. 290.
(136) Field Manuel 6-20 Field Artillery Tactical Employment. War Department, 5 February 1944.

(137) Russell F. Weigley, The American Way of War, p. 286.
(138) The 2nd US Division, which had a significant contingent of World War One veterans, used the only American rolling-barrage of World War Two in North West Europe. Major David S. Wilson, Evolution Of Artillery Tactics In General J. Lawton Collins' US VII Corps In World War II, Pickle Partnering Publications, 2015.
(139) Major James F. Gebhard, The Petsamo-Kirkenes Operation: Soviet Breakthrough and Pursuit in the Arctic, October 1944, Combat Studies Institute, U.S. Army Command and General Staff College Fort Leavenworth, Kansas, 1990, p. 133.
(140) Chris Bellamy, Red God of War, p. 58.
(141) Ibid., p. 73.
(142) Opinions vary as to what extent the actual Soviet World War Two practice followed the doctrine developed by Tukhachevskty and the other theorists of deep penetration between the wars. Some believe it was abandoned in the 1937–1938 purges and that the Soviet forces' actual way of the war was developed pragmatically. Others, including the author, see considerable parallels between the theory and Soviet deep operations once they had the initiative after the Battle of Kursk.
(143) The failure of the Anglo-Americans in the pursuit was not due to a lack of theoretical study. Clausewitz recognised the importance of exploiting battlefield success, as was shown by his analysis of the 1815 campaign in which the pursuit to Paris (which he identifies as the French centre of gravity rather than Napoleon's army) gets twice the coverage as the battle of Waterloo. Christopher Bassford, Daniel Moran, and Gregory W. Pedlow (editor/translator). Carl von Clausewitz and Arthur Wellesley, 1st Duke of Wellington. On Waterloo: Clausewitz, Wellington, and the Campaign of 1815, Clausewitz,com, 2010, chapters 39-43 as opposed to chapters 53–58.
(144) The German Army favoured an elastic defence in depth, but often could not implement it due to other factors, such as the severe weather in the Winter of 1941/42, manpower and supply shortages, unsuitable terrain and of course Hitler's orders. Major Timothy A. Wray, Standing Fast: German Defensive Doctrine on the Russian Front During World War II – Prewar to March 1943, Pickle Partners Publishing, 2015.
(145) For the evolution of the Great Patriotic War Mobile Group evolution into the Cold War Operational Manoeuvre Groups see Chris Bellamy, Red God of War: Soviet Artillery and Rocket Forces, Brassey's Defence Publishers, London, 1986, p. 57. Shimon Naveh, In Pursuit of Military Excellence, Cummings Centre Series, Routledge, London, 1997.
(146) At this point in World War Two British armoured division had only 24 organic self-propelled guns and equal number of towed guns. In comparison US armoured division had 54 self-propelled guns of a heavier calibre, plus six tanks armed with 105mm howitzers in each tank battalion, resulting in a total of 72 armored tracked guns.
(147) Heinz Guderian, Panzer Leader, Penguin, London, 2009 and Maj Gen FW von Mellenthin, Panzer Battles, Spellmount, Staplehurst, UK, 2008.
(148) Raymond L Garthoff, How Russian Makes War, Soviet Military Doctrine, G. Allen & Unwin, London, 1954, p. VII.
(149) Raymond L. Garthoff, Soviet Military Doctrine, Glencoe, The Free Press, Illinois, 1953, p. 174.

Chapter 3: The Firepower's Continued Dominance in the Cold War

(1) Shelford Bidwell & Dominic Graham, Fire-Power, p. 295.
(2) Bevin Alexander, Korea the First War We Lost, Hippocrene Books, New York, 2003, p. 122.
(3) James R Holbrook et al, Tactical Responses to Concentrated Artillery, Combat Studies Institute, IS Report, US Command and General Staff College, Leavenworth, Kansas, 1989, p. 112.
(4) Janice E McKenny, Organizational History of Field Artillery, 1775–2003, Centre for History of the United States Army, Washington, 2007, p. 199.

(5) During the Soyang battle, the equivalent of twenty artillery battalions fired 381,136 rounds from 17 to 26 May 1951, more than 17,400 tons of ammunition. In comparison, thirty-five battalions at Bastogne from 22 to 31 December 1944 fired only 94,230 rounds. Janice E McKenny, Organizational History of Field Artillery, 1775–2003, Centre for History of the United States Army, Washington, 2007, p. 201.
(6) Conrad C. Crane, American Airpower Strategy in Korea, 1950-1953, University Press of Kansas, Lawrence, Kansas, 2000, pp. 14–39, 74–75, 80–92, 127.
(7) Benjamin Franklin Cooling (Ed), Case Studies in the Development of Close Air Support, p. 396.
(8) Lieutenant General Nam Il, Senior Red Delegate, August 1951, quoted in Robert Frank Futrell, The United States Air Force in Korea, 1950–1953, Air University Press, Department of Defence, Washington DC, 1983, p. 345.
(9) Ibid., p. 345.
(10) Indicative of a superior air/land intergration structure is that during the month of September 1951, 5th Air Force flew 2,451 CAS sorties; 1,664 of those were flown in support of X Corps.
(11) John Schlight, Help from Above: Air Force Close Air Support of the Army 1946–1973. Air Force History and Museums Program, Washington, DC, 2003, pp. 120–122.
(12) William T, Y' Blood, Down in the Weeds, Close air support in Korea, Air Force History and Museum Program, Air Force Historical Studies Office, Air Force Pentagon, Washington DC, 2002, p. 43.
(13) James R Holbrook et al, Tactical Responses to Concentrated Artillery, Combat Studies Institute, IS Report, US Command and General Staff College, Leavenworth, Kansas, 1989, p. 108.
(14) Field artillery missions in the Korean War divided as follows: Harassing and Interdicting 22%; Counter Flak 6%; Observed Fires on Targets of Opportunity and Defensive Fires 21%; Offensive Fires 5%; Counter mortar 20%; Counterbattery 10%; Registrations 9%; and the remaining 7% divided between minor tasks.
(15) Office of the Secretary of Defence, 2000 Report to Congress: Military Situation on the Korean Peninsula, Washington, DC, September 12, 2000.
(16) Office of the Secretary of Defence, Military and Security Developments Involving the Democratic People's Republic of Korea 2013, Washington, DC, February 15, 2013. Quoted in Timothy M. Bonds, Michael Johnson, Paul S. Steinberg, Limiting Regret, Building the Army We Will Need. RAND Corporation, Santa Monica, CA, 2015, p. 5.
(17) Stalin to Mao, June 5, 1952, Cold War International History Programme, Bulletin 77–8, Winter 1995/96, p. 59.
(18) Andrew F Krepinevich Jr, The Army and Vietnam, The Johns Hopkins University Press, Baltimore, 1986, p. 197.
(19) Paul Ely, Les Enseignements de la guerre d'Indochine, Rapport du général Ely, Tome 1, Vincennes, Service Historique de la Défense, 2011. p. 55 quoted in Elie Tenenbaum, The Battle over Fire Support. The Close Air Support Challenge and the Future of Artillery, Focus stratégique, Number 35 bis, October 2012.
(20) Colonel VJ Croizat, A translation from the French, Lessons of the War in Indo-China, Volume 2, RAND Corporation, Santa Monica, CA, 1967, p. 35.
(21) Robert H Scales, Firepower in Limited War, p. 42.
(22) Quoted in Michael Burleigh, Small Wars, Far Away Places, Pan Books, London, 2003, p. 237.
(23) Riley Sunderland, Evolution of Command and Control for Close air support, Office of the Air Force History Headquarters, United States Air Force, March 1973, p. 59.
(24) Randy EM Foster, Vietnam Firebases, 1965–1973, Osprey, New York, 2007, p. 14.
(25) Johnathan Bailey, Field Artillery and Firepower, p. 374.
(26) Quoted in Dave Richard Palmer, Summons of the Trumpet: U.S.-Vietnam in Perspective, Presidio Press, San Rafael, CA, 1978, p. 48.

(27) Quoted in Max Hastings, Vietnam An Epic History of a Tragic War, Williams Collins, London, 2019, p. 279.
(28) Thomas E Ricks, The Generals, pp. 268–9.
(29) House Hearings on Cost Escalation in Defense Procurement Contracts and Military Posture, HR 6722, 93d Cong., 1st sess. 1973, p. 868; Colonel Charles E, Canedy. From ACCB to the 6th Cavalry Brigade (Air Combat), US Army Aviation Digest 21, May 1975, p. 3.
(30) David R. Woodward, World War I Almanac, Infobase Publishing, New York, 2009, p. 340.
(31) John J. Sullivan, Overlord's Eagles: Operations of the United States Army Air Forces in the Invasion of Normandy in World War Two, McFarland and Company Publishers, Jefferson, North Carolina, p. 128.
(32) Stephen Budiansky, Air Power, Penguin, New York, 2004, p. 302.
(33) Eduard Mark, Aerial Interdiction: Air Power and the Land Battle in Three American Wars, Centre for Air Force History, US Government Printing Office, Washington DC, 1994, p. 409.
(34) In the Vietnam War: a helicopter was shot down once every 13,000 sorties, the AH-1 Cobra once every 5,700 sorties and fixed-wing aircraft every 3,000 sorties. The relatively high loss rate of fixed wing aircraft was in part due to close air support being their primary mission. Headquarters Pacific Air Forces, CHECO Division, Project CHECO Southeast Asia Report: Army Aviation in RVN, pp. 42–43.
(35) Operation Rolling Thunder started on a small scale, by June 1966 the bombing of North Vietnamese oil storage had begun, by August the average was over 10,000 sorties per month.
(36) Benjamin Franklin Cooling (Ed), Case Studies in the Development of Close Air Support, p. 168.
(37) General Bruce Palmer, Jr., The 25-Year War: America's Military Role in Vietnam, University Press of Kentucky, 1984.
(38) Thomas E Ricks, The Generals, p. 234.
(39) Major General David Ewing Ott, Field Artillery, 1954–1973, Department of the Army, Washington DC, 1995, pp. 142–3.
(40) Keith William Nolan, Battle for Hue, Tet 1968, Presidio Press, Novato California, 1983, p. 183.
(41) Johnathan Bailey, Field Artillery and Firepower, p. 379.
(42) John Michael Hawkins, The Limits of Fire Support: American Finances and Firepower Restraint during the Vietnam War, http://hdl.handle.net/1969.1/151185.
(43) Colin S Gray, Fighting Talk, p. 113.
(44) Quoted in Andrew F Krepinevich Jr. The Army and Vietnam, The John Hopkins University Press, Baltimore, 1986, p. 197.
(45) Thomas E Ricks, The Generals, p. 288.
(46) Military History Institute of Vietnam Translated by Merle L. Pribbenow, Victory in Vietnam, The Official History of the People's Army of Vietnam, 1954–1975, University Press of Kansas, 2002, pp. 238–39.
(47) Christopher D. O' Sullivan, Colin Powell: A Political Biography, (Biographies in American Foreign Policy) 2009, p. 16.
(48) Robert H Scales, Firepower in Limited War, p. 148.
(49) Max Hastings, Vietnam, p. 525.
(50) Avigdor Kahalani, The Heights of Courage: A Tank Leader's War on the Golan, Praeger, Westport Connecticut, 1975, p. 32.
(51) Israel has fought six interstate wars: the 1947/48 War of Independence, the 1956 Sinai Campaign, the 1967 Six-Day War, the 1969/70 War of Attrition, the 1973 Yom Kippur War, and the 1982 Lebanon War (against Syria). It has also fought five wars against its non-state adversaries in the Lebanon and the Gaza Strip. In addition, it has nearly continuously engage in counter-insurgency campaigns and special operations.
(52) The Battles for Abu Agheila in the 1956 and 1967 Arab-Israeli Wars, Research Survey Number 7, Combat Studies Institute, Fort Leavenworth, Kansas, 1990, p. 24.

(53) George W Gawrych, Key To The Sinai: The Battles For Abu Agelia In The 1956 And 1967 Arab Israeli Wars, Pickle Partners Publishing, 2014, p. 104.
(54) Interview with General Uzi Narkiss, Sept. 1996. Narkiss was the commander of Israel's Central Command during the war, the front responsible for conquering the West Bank from Jordan. Kenneth M Pollack, quoted in Air Power in the Six-Day War, The Saban Center for Middle East Policy at the Brookings Institution, Washington, DC, USA, The Journal of Strategic Studies, Volume 28, Number 3, June 2005, pp. 472–473.
(55) Air Power in the Six-Day War, The Saban Center for Middle East Policy at the Brookings Institution, Washington, DC, USA, The Journal of Strategic Studies Volume 28, Number 3, June 2005 p. 485.
(56) Quoted in M J Armitage and R A Mason, Air Power in the Nuclear Age (Urbana III), University of Illinois Press,1983, p. 27.
(57) Dr Sanu Kainikara and Russell Parkin, Pathways to Victory, Air Power Development Centre, Tuggeranon, ACT, Australia, 2007, p. 17.
(58) Ne'eman, Yuval: This War of Our Resolution and how to Safeguard its Achievements, pp. 15–16.
(59) Johnathan Bailey, Field Artillery and Firepower, p. 397.
(60) In addition to their infantry mortars, in 1973 the Israelis had seven battalions of self-propelled M-68 160mm mortars, 12 battalions of self-propelled 120mm mortars, and up to 12 battalions of towed 120mm mortars.
(61) Kenneth S. Brower, The Israel Defense Forces, 1948-2017, Security and Policy Studies No. 150, The Begin-Sadat Center for Strategic Studies Bar-Ilan University, Mideast p. 57.
(62) Martin Van Creveld, The Sword and the Olive: A Critical History Of The Israeli Defence Force, Public Affairs, New York, 1998, p. 232.
(63) James R Holbrook et al, Tactical Responses to Concentrated Artillery, Combat Studies Institute, IS Report, US Command and General Staff College, Leavenworth, Kansas, 1989, p. 136.
(64) Avrahan Adan, On the Banks of the Suez, Presidio Press, Navota, California, 1980, pp. 23–4.
(65) In 1973 an armoured division had a planned tank to armoured infantry company ratio of 24:14. In 1987 the enlarged armoured division had: 27 tank, nine armoured infantry, six reconnaissance and three combat engineer manoeuvre companies. A current division probably has the following ratio: 18 tank, 18 mechanised infantry, six armoured infantry, seven reconnaissance, and six armoured engineering companies. The armoured infantry and engineers are in vehicles with protection similar to tanks.
(66) Brigadier General (Reserves) Arie Mizrachi, IDF, Israeli Artillery Tactics and Weapons – Lessons Learned in Combat, Field Artillery, February 1990, p. 7.
(67) Kenneth S. Brower The Israel Defense Forces, 1948–2017, Security and Policy Studies No. 150, The Begin-Sadat Center for Strategic Studies Bar-Ilan University, Mideast p. 25.
(68) John Clements, Air Defense Mythology, RUSI, September 1982, pp. 27–32.
(69) The armoured formations and artillery destroyed 11 batteries. Although this was only a third of what the Israeli Air Force destroyed, they were mainly SA-6s and with a hole in the missile belt established the rest could be rolled-up. Edgar O'Ballance, No Victor, No Vanquished: The Arab-Israeli War, 1973, Novato, CA, 1997, pp. 248–249 and 303.
(70) Martin Van Creveld with Steven L Canby and Kenneth S Bower, Airpower and Manoeuvre Warfare, Air University Press, Maxwell Air Force Base, Alabama, 1994, p. 228.
(71) Ariel Levite, Offensive and Defensive in Israeli Military Doctrine, JCCS Number 12, Boulder, Colorado, Westview Press, 1990, p. 119.
(72) Ervin J. Kis, Techniques of gaining Israeli air superiority in the 1973 War, better known as 'The Yom Kippur war', Miklós Zrínyi National Defence University, Budapest, Hungary, p. 414.
(73) David Rodman Review Essay: The Israel Air Force and the Evolution of Arab/Israeli Warfare, Small War Journal, Oct 14 2013 – 12:45am.

(74) Brigadier General Arie Mizrachi, Israeli Tactics and Weapons – Lessons Learned in Combat, Field Artillery, February 1990, p. 7.
(75) Ali Ahmad Jalali and Lester W. Grau The Other Side of the Mountain: Mujahideen Tactics in the Soviet Afghan War, Frank Cass Publishers, London, 2003, p. vii.
(76) The one deviation from Soviet wartime practice was that self-propelled gun ceased to be a priority. Leading to World War Two guns continuing in service after the war regardless of their limitations. The SU-76, was a hastily designed and mass-produced mounting of the standard 76mm field gun upon a barely modified T-70 tank, but at least it had the elevation for indirect fire. The equally primitive SU100 was best employed as an anti-tank gun, while the ISU-122 and ISU-152 were best used as assault guns. It was not until the 1970s that with the introduction of a series of self-propelled guns and mortars – in 122mm, two types of 152mm, 203mm and 240mm calibres – that the Soviets fielded modern mobile indirect firepower.
(77) The Russian General Staff, translated and edited by Lester G. Grau and Michael A. Gress, The Soviet-Afghan War, How a Superpower Fought and Lost, University Press of Kansas, 2002 p. 172.
(78) Joseph A Jackson, Moving Artillery Forward: A Concept for the Fight in Afghanistan, Small Wars Foundation, 2010, p. 6.
(79) Lester W. Grau, Artillery and Counterinsurgency: The Soviet Experience in Afghanistan, Field Artillery Journal, May-June 1997.
(80) Johnathan Bailey, Field Artillery and Firepower, p. 422.
(81) The Russian General Staff, translated and edited by Lester G. Grau and Michael A. Gress, The Soviet-Afghan War, How a Superpower Fought and Lost, University Press of Kansas, 2002 p. 172.
(82) The Russian General Staff, translated and edited by Lester G. Grau and Michael A. Gress, The Soviet-Afghan War, How a Superpower Fought and Lost, University Press of Kansas, 2002 p. 175.
(83) Suvorov, Inside the Soviet Army, Mass Market Paperback, 1988, p. 198.
(84) Robert H Scales, Firepower in Limited War, p. 170.
(85) Lester W. Grau, The Bear Went Over the Mountain: Soviet Combat Tactics in Afghanistan, NDU Press, Washington, 1996, pp. 14–18.
(86) Soviet counter measures such as carbon dioxide injection into engine exhaust ducts initially proved effective against the early single colour Stinger seeker, but were useless against the later two-colour seeker.
(87) Etienne de Durand, Benoît Michel and Elie Tenenbaum, Helicopter Warfare. The Future of Airmobility and Rotary Wing Combat, Focus stratégique, Number 32 bis, January 2012, p. 16. Ian Passingham, RUSI lecture Helicopters in Vietnam, London, 24 July 2009, quoted Colin S Gray, Airpower for Strategic Effect, Air University Press, Air Force Research Institute Maxwell Air Force Base, Alabama, 2012, p. 181.
(88) Max Hastings and Simon Jenkins, The Battle for the Falklands, W.W. Norton and Company, New York, 1983, p. 237.
(89) Victor Flintham. Air Wars and Aircraft, Facts on File, New York, 1990, p. 81.
(90) Arthur D. Davis, Guerrilla Warfare and Airpower in Algeria, 1954–1960, Air University, Maxwell AFB, AL, 2005, p. 39.
(91) Charles Christienne and Pierre Lissarague. French Military Aviation, translated by Francis Kianka, Smithsonian Press, Washington DC,1986, p. 430.
(92) Jerome Klingman, Light Aircraft Technology for Small Wars, in Low-Intensity Conflict and Modern Technology, editor, David J. Dean, Air University, Maxwell AFB, AL 1986, p. 129.
(93) Johnathan Bailey, Field Artillery and Firepower, pp. 387–8.
(94) David Mannall, Battle on the Lomba 1987: The Day a South African Armoured Battalion shattered Angola's Last Mechanized Offensive, Helion and Company, 2014 edition, pp. 48–92.
(95) Ian Beckett and John Pimlott, Counter Insurgency: Lessons from History, Pen and Sword, London, 2011, pp. 178–9.

(96) Robert H Scales, Firepower in Limited War, pp. 199–200.
(97) The inadequate quantity of artillery and mortar munitions was due to the lack of logistic support. The mortar bombs were carried by the parachute soldiers who marched to the battle. Twelve helicopter sorties were dedicated to the artillery. These sorties provided one lift for the 28-men, three lifts for the guns, and eight lifts for the ammunition.
(98) Daniel Kon, Los Chicos de La Guerra, New English Library, London, 1984, p. 124. Quoted in Robert H Scales, Firepower in Limited War, National Defence University, US Government Printing Office, Washington DC, 1990, p. 232.
(99) Robert H Scales, Firepower in Limited War, p. 230.
(100) Colonel SLA Marshall, Men Against Fire, William Marrow and Co, New York: 1947 p. 191. Robert H. Scales, Jr. Yellow Smoke: The Future of Land Warfare for America's Military, Rowman & Littlefield Publishers, 2003, pp. 57–58.
(101) Admiral Sandy Woodward, One Hundred Days: The Memoirs of the Falklands Battle Group Commander, Annapolis, 1992, pp. 18–19.
(102) Johnathan Bailey, Field Artillery and Firepower, p. 392.
(103) Anthony H Cordesman and Abraham R Wagner, The Lessons of Modern War, Volume 1, The Iran-Iraq War, Westview Press, Boulder, Colorado, 1990, Chapter 9.
(104) Williamson Murray, Kevin M. Woods, The Iran-Iraq War: A Military and Strategic History, Cambridge University Press, Cambridge, UK, 2014, p. 297.
(105) Gordon, Yefim and Alan Dawes. Sukhoi Su-25 Frogfoot: Close air support Aircraft. London: Airlife, 2004, pp. 133–149.

Chapter 4: The Post-Cold War Divergence into the Firepower and Information Centric Warfighting Approaches

(1) Sheila Rule, Reagan Gets A Red Carpet From British, New York Times 14 June 1989.
(2) Department of Defence, Conduct of the Persian Gulf Conflict: An Interim Report to the Congress, July 1991, pp. 1–4.
(3) Angelo Codevilla, Commentary, Commentary Inc, New York, April 1992, p. 20. More controversially Jean Baudrillard argued that the Gulf War was an atrocity that masqueraded as a war: Jean Baudrillard, translated by Paul Patton, The Gulf War Did Not Take Place, India University Press, Bloomington and Indianapolis, 1995.
(4) James H. Collier, Scientific and Technical Communications: Theory, Practice and Policy, Sage Publications, New York, 1997, pp. 364–366.
(5) John Mueller, The Perfect Enemy, Assessing the Gulf War, Security Studies, Vol 5, No 1, Autumn 1995, pp. 77–117.
(6) Thomas E Ricks, The Generals, p. 273.
(7) A figure of 5% precision weapons is provided in: CENTCOM Operations Order 91–101, dated 17 January 1991. Cited in Rick Atkinson, Crusade; The Untold Story of the Persian Gulf War, Boston: Houghton Mifflin, 993, pp. 20–21. The figure of 8% precision weapons is provided in: Robert C. Owen, Operation Deliberate Force: A Case Study on Humanitarian Constraints in Aerospace Warfare, presented at Humanitarian Challenges in Military Intervention workshop, Washington, DC, November 29–30, 2001, p. 62.
(8) Third ROKA Air Liaison Report, 8 December 1993, Subject F-18 LGB Bombing Accuracy. Quoted in Robert H Scales, Firepower in Limited War, National Defence University, US Government Printing Office, Washington DC, 1990, p. 241.
(9) Air Power in the Six-Day War, The Saban Center for Middle East Policy at the Brookings Institution, Washington, DC. Quoted in The Journal of Strategic Studies, Volume 28, Number 3, 471–503, June 2005, p. 493.

(10) Historical Evaluation and Research Organization, A Historical Analysis of the Effectiveness of Tactical Air Operations Against, and in Support of Armoured Forces, NOVA Publications, McLean, Va, 1980. pp. 36–42.
(11) Robert H Scales, Firepower in Limited War, p. 253.
(12) Stephen Biddle, Military Power, p. 2.
(13) Quoted in Diane T. Putney, Airpower Advantage: Planning the Gulf War Air Campaign, 1989–1991, Air Force History and Museums Program, Washington, DC, 2004, p. 147.
(14) Gordon M. Wells, Deep Operations, Command and Control, and Joint Doctrine: Time for a Change? Joint Force Quarterly, Winter 1996–1997, pp. 102–103.
(15) Robert H Scales, Firepower in Limited War, p. 292.
(16) Paul Westermeyer, The Battle of al-Khafji, Marine Corps History Division, Washington DC, 2008, p. 32.
(17) Thomas A Kearney and Eliot A Cohen, Revolution in Warfare?: Air Power in the Persian Gulf, Annapolis Naval Institute Press, MD, 1995, p. 96.
(18) Robert H Scales, Certain Victory, The US Army in the Gulf War, Potomac Books, Washington DC, 1997, p. 226.
(19) Robert R. Leonard, The Art of Maneuver, Maneuver-Warfare Theory and AirLand Battle, Presidio Press, New York, 1991, p. 287.
(20) Major Andrew S Groenke, Close Air Support, Interdiction and Attack Helicopters, Thesis, Naval Postgraduate School, Monterey, California, June 2005, p. 69.
(21) Sanu Kainikara, Red Air: Politics in Russian Air Power, Universal Publishers, Irvine, California, 2007, p. 312.
(22) Ibid., p. 332.
(23) Stephen Biddle, Military Power, 2006.
(24) Lieutenant Colonel Scott C. Farquhar (General Editor), Back to Basics. A Study of the Second Lebanon War and Operation CAST LEAD, US Army Combined Arms Center, Combat Studies Institute, Fort Leavenworth, KS, 2009, p. 19.
(25) Michael Herzog, New IDF Strategy Goes Public, Policywatch 2479, The Washington Institute, August 28, 2015.
(26) Ron Tira, Shifting Tectonic Plates, Basic Assumptions on the Peace Process Revisited, Strategic Assessment, No 91, Vol 12, No 1, June 2001, p. 102.
(27) Gabriel Sarboni, The Military Campaign in Lebanon, in Brom and Elran (Eds.) The Second Lebanon War: Strategic Perspectives, Tel Aviv: Institute for National Security, 2007, p. 66.
(28) Benny Mehr, The Lessons Regarding Statistical Artillery, IsraeliDefence, 20 June 2018.
(29) Interview with General Halutz, IAF Headquarters, Ha'kirya, Tel Aviv, March 26, 2008. Quoted in Benjamin S. Lambeth Air Operations in Israel's War Against Hezbollah: Learning from Lebanon and Getting It Right in Gaza, RAND Corporation, Santa Monica, CA, p. 290.
(30) Quote by a former F-15 squadron commander, Colonel (Reserve) Dror Ben-David at a presentation to an air warfare conference sponsored by Israel's Fisher Brothers Institute for Air and Space Strategic Studies in May 2007. Israel Air Force Seeks Joint Ops, Middle East Newsline, Montreal, May 15, 2007.
(31) IDF Report Card, Jerusalem Post Online Edition, 24 August 2006, online at http://www.jpost.com.
(32) Timur Goksel, the former chief spokesperson for the UN forces in Lebanon quoted in Captain Daniel Helmer, Not Quite Counter-insurgency: A Cautionary Tale For Us Forces Based On Israel's Operation Change Of Direction, Australian Army Journal, Volume V, Number 2, p. 117.
(33) Dr Carlo Kopp, Post Afghanistan – Where to next with Western land warfare capabilities, DefenceToday, September 2001, p. 2.
(34) David E. Johnson, Military Capabilities for Hybrid War, Insights from the Israel Defense Forces in Lebanon and Gaza, RAND Corporation, Santa Monica, CA, 2010, pp. 10–11.

(35) 13 soldiers killed in Gaza; PM says Hamas tunnels could have caused 'catastrophe', The Jerusalem Times, 22 October 2014. http://www.timesofisrael.com/writers/ricky-ben-david/
(36) Kenneth S. Brower, The Israel Defense Forces, 1948–2017, Security and Policy Studies No. 150, The Begin-Sadat Center for Strategic Studies Bar-Ilan University, Mideast p. 28.
(37) The Israeli Artillery Corps describes itself as comprising of five main arrays:

- The Cannon Array: As the main unit in the corps, the array is responsible for the operation of the self-propelled cannon.
- The Rocket Array: This array operates the rocket launchers of the Artillery Corps.
- The Positioning Array: This system operates advanced equipment for positioning and targeting in the field.
- The Unmanned Craft Array: The system operates the Hermes 450 Squadron and the special unit Sky Rider.
- The Precise Armament Array: This includes the Meitar unit as well as the special unit Moran with the non-line of sight Spike missile.

(38) Barbara Opall-Rome, Gaza War Leaned Heavily On F-16 Close-Air Support, 15 September 2014 – 06:34pm.
(39) Brigadier General Amikam Norkin, Israel Air Force chief of staff, quoted in Barbara Opall-Rome, Gaza War Leaned Heavily On F-16 Close-Air Support, Sep. 15, 2014 – 06:34pm, Defence News.
(40) One Israeli opinion poll reported that only 4% believed that excessive force had been used, compared to 87% who supported continuing the military action. Mark Urban, The Edge, Is the Military Dominance of the West Coming to an End? Little, Brown, 2016, p. 56.
(41) Jeffrey White, The Combat Performance Of Hamas In The Gaza War Of 2014, Combating Terrorism Centre, West Point, Volume 7, Issue 9, September 29, 2014.
(42) Mitch Ginsburg, A year on, Army looks to last Gaza war for lessons on fighting the next one Israel has watched Hamas change tack, so it may have a chance to prepare better for a seemingly inevitable future conflict, Jerusalem Times, July 7, 2015, 8:46pm.
(43) Israeli Artillery Corps Revamping Doctrine, Israeli Defence, 12/3/2015.
(44) Providing armoured units with their own mortar platoon makes them more suitable for urban warfare and breaking into fortified zones than the old tank heavy units. The latter were optimised for mobile operations against enemy armour and operational level exploitation.
(45) Anne C Aldis, The Second Chechen War, Strategic and Combat Studies Institute, Camberley Conflict Studies Research Centre RMA Sandhurst, UK, 2000.
(46) Dmitri Trenin, Russia, Polity Press, Cambridge, UK, 2019.
(47) Restructuring the Tactical Russian Army for Unconventional Operations, Red Diamond, Fort Leavenworth, KS Volume 5, Issue 2, February 2014, p. 1.
(48) Andrew Scobell, Roy Kamphausen, David Lai (editors), Chinese Lessons from Other Peoples' Wars, Strategic Studies Institute, U.S. Army War College, Carlisle PA, November 2011, p. 304.
(49) Jacob W. Kipp, The Russian-Georgian Conflict as Analysed by the Centre of Analysis of Strategies and Technologies in Moscow, Publication: Eurasian Daily Monitor Volume 7 Issue 16.
(50) Retired General Makhmut Gareyev, in Roger N. McDermott, Russia's Conventional Armed Forces and the Georgian War, U.S. Army War College, Parameters: United States Army War College Quarterly, Spring 2009, p. 72.
(51) Paul Rich (editor), Crisis in the Caucasus: Russia, Georgia and the West, Oxford, UK: Routledge, 2010, p. 159. The lack of impact from their air force was more about correct employment rather than any lack of resources. The Russians assembled a force of some 300-combat aircraft, including the Su-24, Su-25, Su-27, and Tu-22. Georgia's small air force of eight Su-25 attack aircraft and around 25 helicopters, played no role in the War after the first day. The Georgian air force did not contest air superiority; the result of their decision to try and preserve their aircraft.

(52) Roger N. McDermott, Russia's Conventional Armed Forces and the Georgian War, U.S. Army War College, Parameters: United States Army War College Quarterly, Spring 2009, p. 73.
(53) Paul B. Rich Crisis in the Caucasus: Russia, Georgia and the West, Routledge, Abingdon, Oxford, UK, 2010, p. 227.
(54) Colonel-General Anatoliy Nogovitsyn, Deputy Chief of the Russian General Staff, Interfax, 12 August 2008. Quoted in Roger N. McDermott, Russia's Conventional Armed Forces and the Georgian War, U.S. Army War College, Parameters: United States Army War College Quarterly, Spring 2009, p. 66.
(55) Michael Kofman, Russian Performance in the Russo Georgian War Revisited, War on the Rocks, 4 September 2008.
(56) Timothy Snyder, The Road to Unfreedom: Russia, Europe, America, Tim Duggan Books, New York, 2018.
(57) Keir Giles, Russia's 'New' Tools for Confronting the West, Continuity and Innovation in Moscow's Exercise of Power, Russia and Eurasia Programme, Chatham House, The Royal Institute of International Affairs, March 2016, p. 16.
(58) Col. Liam Collins, A New Eastern Front: What the U.S. Army Must Learn from the War in Ukraine, Association of the United States Army, 16 Apr 2018, www.ausa.org
(59) Russia, The Ride of the Mercenaries, The Economist, November 4th 2017, p. 36.
(60) Joe Pappalardo, The Right (and Wrong) Way to Use Artillery: Ukraine Edition, When Russia-Ukraine becomes an artillery war, everyone loses, 18 Sep 2014. www.popularmechanics.com
(61) Dr Phillip A. Karber Lessons Learned from the Russo-Ukrainian War, Draft Personal Observations, Johns Hopkins Applied Physics Laboratory & U.S. Army Capabilities Centre, 8 July 2015.
(62) Presentation to NRDC-Italy by Dr Phillip A. Karber, 25 May 16, slide 86.
(63) Philip Karber, Presentation to the US Army Fires Conference, Fort Sill, 2–4 May 2018.
(64) Dr Phillip A. Karber Lessons Learned from the Russo-Ukrainian War, Draft Personal Observations, Johns Hopkins Applied Physics Laboratory & U.S. Army Capabilities Centre, 8 July 2015.
(65) The protection standard of lightly armoured vehicles has been driven by the need to defeat small arms fire and artillery splinters. Recent upgrading has largely concentrated upon defeating mines, improvised explosive devices and man portable anti-armour weapons. The original conventional warfare force protection criterion has been overtaken by events and is no longer valid against a sophisticated foe equipped with sensor-fused and cluster munitions.
(66) Brigadier Ben Barry, Senior Fellow for Land Warfare at IISS is quoted in Ukraine and IS Conflicts Emphasise the Importance of Artillery Developments, Defence IQ, February 2015.
(67) By David Eugene Johnson, Adam Grissom, Olga Oliker In the Middle of the Fight: An Assessment of Medium-armoured Forces in Past Military Operations, RAND Corporation, Santa Monica, CA, 2008, p. 122.
(68) The Russian displayed the T-15 Armata Heavy Infantry Fighting Vehicle, which is based on the T-14 tank, at the Moscow Victory Parade in 2015. Development of better-protected infantry fighting vehicles was initially in response to the losses to Chechen rocket propelled grenades in urban fighting. The Ukrainians have developed heavy infantry fighting vehicles based on T55 and T64 tanks.
(69) Lieutenant Colonel Zygulskiy quoted in the presentation to NRDC-Italy by Dr Phillip A. Karber, 25 May 16, slide 113.
(70) Tor Bukvoll, Russia's Military Performance in Georgia, Military Review, November-December 2009, p. 59.
(71) Sydney J Freedberg Jr, Russian Drone Threat: Army Seeks Ukraine Lessons, Breaking Defence, 14 October 2015.
(72) Jeffrey Carr, The GRU-Ukraine Artillery Hack That May Never Have Happened, Medium, January 3, 2017.

(73) Mr Laurie Buckhout, former chief of the US Army's electronic warfare division, now CEO of the Corvus Group quoted in Joe Gould, Electronic Warfare: What US Army Can Learn From Ukraine, DefenseNews, 12:42 pm. EDT August 4, 2015.

(74) Valeriy Gerasimov, 'Based on the Experience of Syria' [in Russian], Voyenno-promyshlennyy kuryer, March 9, 2016.

(75) Quoted from Konstantin Sivkov interviewed about the Russian operation in Syria, The Saker, 24 October, 2015. thesaker.is/konstantin-sivkov-interviewed-about-the-russian-operation-in-syria.

(76) Russian Military Weakness Increases Importance of Strategic Nuclear Forces. Cdi.org. 11 June 2009. Retrieved 31 Mar 2016.

(77) The Syrian Civil War provides an object lesson in this approach. Max Fisher, Syria's Paradox: Why the War Only Ever Seems to Get Worse, The New York Times, 26 August 2016.

(78) Maria Tsvetkosa and Alexander Winning, Army map suggests presence of Russian artillery unit in central Syria, Reuters, Wed Nov 18, 2015 4:02pm EST.

(79) Before the civil war, the Syrian government was equipped with: D-30 (122mm towed howitzer), M-46 (130mm towed field gun), 2S1 (122mm self-propelled howitzer), 2S3 (152mm self-propelled howitzer), S-23 (180mm long-range gun) and both the BM-21 and BM-27 rocket systems. The Russians have re-equipped them with: TOS-1A heavy flamethrower systems, further BM-27 and the BM-30 Smerch rocket systems, the 2A65 (towed 152mm howitzers) and the 2S19 (152mm self-propelled armoured guns).

(80) Quoted from Konstantin Sivkov (First Vice President of the Academy of Geopolitical Problems) interviewed about the Russian operation in Syria, The Saker, 24 October, 2015.

(81) Mikhail Klikushin, Putin's Army Demands 'NATO Soldiers! Hands Up! Lay Down Your Weapons!, Observer, August 19, 2016.

(82) Quoted in Daniel L Bryman and Matthew C Waxman, Kosovo and the Great Air Power Debate, International Security, Vol 24, No 4, Spring 2000, p. 5.

(83) Robert H Scales, From Korea to Kosovo: How America's Army has Learnt to Fight Limited Wars in the Precision Age, in Future Warfare Anthology, US Army War College, Carlisle Barracks, PA, Revised Edition, pp. 96–101.

(84) Phenyo Keiseng Rakate, The shelling of Knin by the Croatian Army in August 1995: A police operation or a non-international armed conflict? 31-12-2000 Article, International Review of the Red Cross, Number 840, https://www.icrc.org/eng/resources/documents/misc/57jqta.htm

(85) The other key factors were: the Bosnian/Croat alliance (making it a two-sided rather than a three-sided fight); the growing international unanimity for an end to the violence; and that the conflict was beginning to culminate as its protagonists lacked the physical and moral resources to continue fighting.

(86) William M. Arkin, Operation Allied Force: The Most Precise Application of Air Power in History, in Andrew J. Bacevich and Eliot A. Cohen, editors., War Over Kosovo: Politics and Strategy in a Global Age, Columbia University Press, New York, 2001, pp. 9–10.

(87) Daniel L. Byman and Matthew C. Waxman, Kosovo and the Great Air Power Debate, International Security, Volume 24, Number 4, Spring 2000, p. 5.

(88) NATO leaders were briefed on the 19 May 1999 that the bombing campaign had destroyed 31% of Serbia's heavy forces in Kosovo (312 tanks, artillery pieces, and armoured vehicles among 556 pieces of equipment). Don Vandergriff, The Myth of Mission Command, How 'Synchronization Warfare' has removed the Human from Modern Warfare, Fortuna Corner, 31 March, 2014.

(89) Department of Defense, Report to Congress: Kosovo/Operation Allied Force After Action Report DoD, Washington, DC, 2000, p. 86.

(90) Robert C. Owen, Operation Deliberate Force: A Case Study on Humanitarian Constraints in Aerospace Warfare, presented at Humanitarian Challenges in Military Intervention workshop, Washington, DC, November 29–30, 2001, p. 62.

(91) Department of Defence, Report to Congress: Kosovo/Operation Allied Force After Action Report DoD, Washington DC, 2000, p. 86.
(92) Historical Evaluation and Research Organization, A Historical Analysis of the Effectiveness of Tactical Air Operations Against, and in Support of Armoured Forces, NOVA Publications, McLean, Va, 1980. pp. 36–42 and 59.
(93) Ivo H. Daalder and Michael E. O'Hanlon, Winning Ugly: NATO's War to Save Kosovo, Brookings Washington DC, 2000, p. 154. History Branch, Israeli Air Force; Historical Evaluation and Research Organization, A Historical Analysis of the Effectiveness of Tactical Air Operations Against, and in Support of Armoured Forces, NOVA Publications, McLean, Va, 1980. pp. 36–42. Quoted in Air Power in the Six-Day War, The Saban Center for Middle East Policy at the Brookings Institution, Washington, DC, USA. The Journal of Strategic Studies Volume 28, Number 3, June 2005 pp. 502–503. Michael G. Vickers, 'Revolution Deferred: Kosovo and the Transformation of War,' in Bacevich and Cohen, 2001, p. 198.
(94) Bruce R. Nardulli, Walter L. Perry, Bruce Pirnie, John Gordon IV and John G. McGinn, Disjointed War: Military Operations in Kosovo, RAND Corporation, Santa Monica, CA, 1999.
(95) Benjamin S. Lambeth, Task Force Hawk, Air Force Magazine, Volume 85, Number 2, February 2002, p. 80.
(96) Nikolas K. Gvosdev and Christopher Marsh, Russian Foreign Policy: Interests, Vectors, and Sectors, CQ Press, Thousand Oaks, CA, p. 226.
(97) Carl von Clausewitz, On War, p. 77.
(98) Anthony H. Cordesman, The Lessons of Afghanistan: War Fighting, Intelligence, and Force Transformation, Center for Strategic and International Studies, Washington, DC, 2002, p. 152.
(99) Major General Jagjit Singh, Battle-Winning Role of the Gunners in Kargil War, Indian Defence Review, 21 February, 2014.
(100) The Mughal Emperor Babur probably introduced tube artillery to India, and its use appears to have been decisive as early as the Battle of Panipat in 1526. The Sikhs in particular favoured massed artillery and formed Napoleonic style Grande Batteries to achieve a decisive effect on the battlefield. European observers, from the first, identified the employment of large calibre guns in the field.
(101) Rahul Bedi, Paying to Keep the High Ground, Janes Intelligence Review, 1 October 1999, pp 31. Group Captain Anant Bewoor, Close air support in the 1962 War, Bharat Rakshat, https://www.bharat-rakshak.com/IAF/history/1962war/1019-bewoor.html
(102) Rahul Bedi, Paying to Keep the High Ground, Janes Intelligence Review, 1 October 1999, p. 31.
(103) Occurring barely a year after the South Asian subcontinent's nuclearization, the 1999 Kargil conflict was the moment when India and Pakistan came the closest to an all-out conventional war that could have developed into a nuclear exchange. Ashley J. Tellis, C. Christine Fair, and Jamison Jo Medby, Limited Conflict under the Nuclear Umbrella: Indian and Pakistani Lessons from the Kargil Crisis," RAND, MR 1450-USCA, on-line at <www.rand.org>, accessed 2 November 2015.
(104) Marcus P. Acosta High Altitude Warfare: The Kargil Conflict and the Future, Thesis Naval Postgraduate School, Monterey, June 2003, p. 57.
(105) The Bofors gun could achieve a 24km maximum range at sea level, which extended beyond 40-km in the thin air of Kargil. However, with longer range came increased dispersion of the fall of shot, which needed to be compensated for by employing massed fire.
(106) Prasun K. Sengupta, Mountain Warfare: The Kargil Experience, Asian Defence Journal, Volume 10, October 1999, p. 44.
(107) Ibid., p. 46.
(108) In Afghanistan the Soviets also used the unarmoured BM-21 multiple-rocket launcher in direct fire to dislodge the well-protected enemy forces. Recognising its vulnerability, they usually moved the BM-21s into direct firing positions under the protection of an air strike. The destructive effect of forty 122mm rockets was usually sufficient to allow the launcher truck to safely withdraw and reload.

(109) Brigadier Lakhwinder Singh, Commander 8th Mountain Artillery Brigade. Quoted in Maj Gen Jagjit Singh, Battle-Winning Role of the Gunners in Kargil War, Indian Defence Review 29 October, 2015. Gurmeet Kanwal, Colonel, Indian Army, Heroes of Kargil, Army Headquarters, New Delhi, 2002, p. 128.
(110) Observations made by the Kargil Review Committee Report, as quoted by Ashok Kalyan Verma in, Kargil, Blood on the Snow: Tactical Victory, Strategic Failure – A Critical Analysis of the War, Manohar Publishers, New Delhi, 2002.
(111) As at 2020, India has 22 of the indigenous swathi weapon locating radar in service. A further five are on order.
(112) Brigadier (Retired) Gurmeet Kanwal, Future artillery concepts – Neutralisation to destruction, Indian Strategic, June 2013.
(113) Arunkumar Bhatt, New artillery doctrine aims at destruction, The Hindu, India's National Newspaper, Monday, February 21, 2000, p. 10.
(114) Elaine M. Grossman, Anaconda: Object Lesson in Ill Planning or Triumph of Improvisation? Inside the Pentagon, 19 August, 2004.
(115) The most significant battles were: Chapchall on 23 October, 2001; Sayed Slim Kalay on 2–4 December, 2001; Highway 4 on 2–6 December, 2001; and the critical action in the War's northern phase was the breakthrough battle near the village of Bai Beche on 5 November, 2001. Stephen Biddle, Military Power, Explaining Victory and Defeat in Modern Battle, Princeton University Press, Princeton NJ, 2006, p. 8.
(116) Stephen D. Biddle, Allies, Airpower, and Modern Warfare. The Afghan Model in Afghanistan and Iraq, International Security, Volume 30, Number 3, Winter 2005–2006, p. 169. Richard B. Andres, Craig Wills, Thomas E. Griffith Jr., Winning with Allies: The Strategic Value of the Afghan Model, International Security, Volume 30, Number 3, Winter 2005/2006, p. 129.
(117) Richard B. Andres, Craig Wills, Thomas E. Griffith Jr., Winning with Allies, p. 129.
(118) Richard B. Andres and Jeffrey B. Hukill, Anaconda: A Flawed Joint Planning Process, Joint Forces Quarterly, Number 4, 2007, pp. 135–140.
(119) Elaine M. Grossman, Left in Dark for Most Anaconda Planning, Air Force Opens New Probe, Inside the Pentagon, 3 October, 2002.
(120) Richard L. Kugler, Michael Baranick, and Hans Binnendijk, Operation Anaconda Lessons for Joint Operations, Center for Technology and National Security Policy National Defense University, Washington DC, 2009, pp. 25–26.
(121) Anthony H. Cordesman, The Ongoing Lessons of Afghanistan: Warfighting, Intelligence, Force Transformation, and Nation Building, Center for Strategic and International Studies, Washington DC, 2004, p. 34.
(122) Quoted in Rebecca Grant, The Clash About CAS, Doctrinal bias and organizational concerns can make the Army an unhappy customer even in the age of precision weapons, Air Force Magazine, January 2003.
(123) Major General Franklin L. Hagenbeck, Afghanistan: Fire Support for Operation Anaconda, interview by Robert H. McElroy and Patrecia Slayden Hollis in Field Artillery, September-October 2002, p. 6.
(124) Transporting into the Afghanistan theatre of four 120mm mortars, supporting personnel, and equipment takes one and one-half C-17 loads. Six 105mm howitzers, supporting personnel, and equipment requires two C-17 loads. The difference is greater for operational moves within theatre by helicopter, as is the resupply challenge. Joshua D Mitchell, A Case for Howitzers in Afghanistan, Field Artillery, November–December 2003, pp. 7–9.
(125) Christopher F. Bentley, Afghanistan: Joint and Coalition Fire Support in Operation Anaconda, Field Artillery, September–October 2002.
(126) Joseph Jackson, Moving Artillery Forward: A concept for the Fight in Afghanistan, Small Wars Journal, 2010, p. 9.

(127) Virgil Ney, The Evolution of the US Infantry Battalion 1939–68, HQ US Army Development Command, October 1968, p. 14.
(128) Richard L. Kugler, Michael Baranick, and Hans Binnendijk, Operation Anaconda: Lessons for Joint Operations, Centre for Technology and National Security Policy, National Defense University, Washington DC, 2009, p. 10.
(129) Jonathan M. House, Combined Arm Warfare in the Twentieth Century, University of Kansas, Kansas, 2001 provides perhaps the best single volume treatment of modern combined arms warfare. Archer Jones, The Art of War in the Western World, University of Illinois Press, Urbana and Chicago, 1987, identifies the centrality of combined arms through two and half millennia of armed conflict.
(130) Tommy Franks, American Soldier, Regan Books New York, 2004, pp. 395–396.
(131) Harlan Ullman and James Wade Jr., Shock and Awe: Achieving Rapid Dominance, National Defence University, Washington, DC, 1996.
(132) Jeffrey H. Michaels, The Discourse Trap and the US Military, From the War on Terror to the Surge, Palgrave Macmillan, New York, 2013, p. 81.
(133) Thomas Ricks, The Generals, p. 128.
(134) Marisa Linton, First step on the road to Waterloo, History Today, Volume 65, Issue 6, June 2015.
(135) Stephen Biddle, Iraq and the Future of Warfare: Implications for Army and Defence Policy, presentation by the United States War College to the United States House Committee on Armed Services, 21 October 2003.
(136) Major General Robert Scales, Artillery's Failings in the Iraq War: United States Must Focus on Range and Precision, Armed Forces Journal, November 2003, p. 44.
(137) U.S. Army Field Artillery Relevance on the Modern Battlefield Marine Corps University, Marine Air-Ground Training and Education Centre, Marine Corps Combat Development Command, Quantico, VA, p. 8.
(138) Russell A. Weatherby, The Field Artillery Group In Support Of The Corps And Field Army, 1942–1953, Monograph, US Army Command and General Staff College, 1965: pp. 1–2 and 30.
(139) The doctrine was written by Harlan K. Ullman and James P. Wade in 1996 and is a product of the National Defense University of the United States.
(140) David J Gibson, Shock and Awe: A Sufficient Condition for Victory? United States Naval War College, Newport, 2001, p. 17.
(141) David E Johnson, Learning Large Lessons, The Evolving Roles of Ground Power and Air Power in the Post-Cold War Era, Santa Monica, CA, 2007, pp. 116–17.
(142) Final Report of the Defence Science Board Task Force on Integrated Fire Support in the Battlespace, Office of the Under Secretary of Defence For Acquisition, Technology, and Logistics Washington, DC 20301-3140, October 2004, p. 2.
(143) Aaron W Clark and J. Brad Reeves, Reality Check. Close air support detractors are clinging to outdated concepts, Armed Forces Journal, 1st February 2011.
(144) Tony Holmes, US Marine Corps and RAAF Hornet Units of Operation Iraqi Freedom, Osprey, Bloomsbury Publishing, London, 2012, pp. 40–41.
(145) British Ministry of Defence, Operations in Iraq: First Reflections, London, Her Majesty's Stationary Office. July 2003, London, Her Majesty's Stationary Office, London, July 2003, p. 21. Christian Lowe, Joint US Training Vital to Close air support, Defense News, 16 June 2003, p. 38.
(146) Patrecia Slayden Hollis, Trained, Adaptable, Flexible Forces = Victory in Iraq, Field Artillery, Number 5, October 2003, p. 6.
(147) Anthony H. Cordesman and Arleigh A. Burke, The Chronology of the Iraq War, Center for Strategic and International Studies, Washington DC, 2003, p. 21.
(148) Rowan Scarborough, Myers Says Annihilation of Iraqi Army Wasn't Goal, Washington Times, June 30, 2003.

(149) In the early 1990s at the National Training Center, it took an average of seventy-two minutes following a day or night occupation for a battery to be ready to fire. In contrast, the most successful units (about 30% of the cohort) averaged fifteen-minutes to become ready to fire. US Army, Centre for Army Lessons Learned, National Training Center Take Home Packages: 90–1 through 94–7, U.S. Army Combined Arms Training Activity, Fort Leavenworth, KS.

(150) Lieutenant Colonel Pitts, U.S. Army Field Artillery Relevance on the Modern Battlefield, Marine Corps University, Marine Air-Ground Training and Education Center, Marine Corps Combat Development Command, Quantico VA, 2004, p. 17.

(151) Commanding General, 1st Marine Division, Operation Iraqi Freedom (OIF): Lessons Learned, MEF FRAGO 279-03, May 29, 2003.

(152) The Amphibious Assault Vehicles (AAV) were designed for amphibious assault not land operations, it provided some armoured mobility and firepower as did the Light Armoured Vehicles (LAVs). But neither were in the same class as the Bradley and Warrior fighting vehicles supported by main battle tanks.

(153) Anthony H Cordesman: Lessons of the Iraq War: Main Report, Center for Strategic and International Studies, Washington DC, July 21, 2003, p. 284.

(154) Office of the Under Secretary of Defense For Acquisition, Technology, and Logistics, Report of the Defense Science Board Task Force on Integrated Fire Support in the Battlespace, Washington DC, October 2004, p. 21. Anthony H Cordesman: Lessons of the Iraq War: Main Report, Center for Strategic and International Studies, Washington DC, July 21, 2003, p. 226.

(155) Walter L. Perry, Richard E. Darilek, Laurinda L. Rohn, and Jerry M. Sollinger (Editors), Operation Iraqi Freedom, Decisive War, Elusive Peace, RAND, Santa Monica, CA, 2015, p. 91.

(156) Warrant Officer Brian L. Borer and Lieutenant Colonel TC Noel T. Nicolle, Acquisition!: 3d ID Counterfire in OIF, Field Artillery 8, Number 5, September-October 2003, p. 46.

(157) David Rowland. The Stress of Battle: Quantifying Human Performance in Combat, (Part 2) Op Research on Urban Battles, Defence Science and Technology Laboratory, May 2006. This statistical analysis establishes, though admittedly in circumstances with limited anti-tank defence, that armour support results in 80% fewer casualties for attacking infantry. Whilst the greater proliferation of hand-held anti-tank weapons are likely to reduce armour's effectiveness, tanks when working in close cooperation with infantry, will continue to be decisive in urban operations.

(158) U.S. Army 3rd Infantry Division, Third Infantry Division (Mechanized) After Action Report: Operation Iraqi Freedom, Fort Stewart, Ga, 2003, p. 22.

(159) David Rowland. The Stress of Battle.

(160) Anthony H Cordesman: Lessons of the Iraq War, p. 214.

(161) Rowan Scarborough, Apache Operations a Lesson in Defeat, Washington Times, April 22, 2003, p. 1.

(162) Maj. Gen. David H. Petraeus, commanding general, 101st Airborne Division (Air Assault), 101st Airborne Division Commander Live Briefing from Iraq, May 13, 2003.

(163) Colonel (USA) William Wolff, Commander, 11th Attack Helicopter Regiment, interview with RAND staff, V Corps Headquarters, Heidelberg, Germany, April 7, 2004. Cited in: Walter L. Perry, Richard E. Darilek, Laurinda L. Rohn, and Jerry M. Sollinger (Editors), Operation Iraqi Freedom, Decisive War, Elusive Peace, RAND, Santa Monica, CA, 2015, p. 83.

(164) Colonel Gregory Fontenot, Lieutenant Colonel E. J. Degen, and Lieutenant Colonel David Tohn, On Point: The United States Army in Operation Iraqi Freedom, Center for Army Lessons Learned, Fort Leavenworth, Kansas, 2004, pp. 192–195.

(165) The most successful were a two-battalion aviation attack near Karbala on 28 March 2003, and a one-battalion mission near Ramadi on 5 April 2003. The first attack claimed to have destroyed more than 200 enemy vehicles and weapons systems and the second more than 70 without the loss of any Apaches.

(166) Bruce R. Pirnie, Alan Vick, Adam Grissom, Karl P. Mueller, David T. Orletsky, Beyond Close Support, Forging a New Air-Ground Partnership, RAND, Santa Monica, CA, 2005, p. 16.

(167) David E. Johnson, Learning Large Lessons, p. 121.
(168) Major Darren W. Buss, US Army, Evolution of Army Attack Aviation: A Chaotic Coupled Pendulums Analogy, U.S. Army Command and General Staff College, 100 Stimson Ave. Ft. Leavenworth, KS, 23 May 2013. This provides a greater analysis of the factors behind the debate on aviation deep attack.
(169) David E. Johnson, Learning Large Lessons, pp. 159–163.
(170) Jody Jacobs, David E Johnson, Katherine Comanor Lewis Jamison, Leland Joe and David Vaughan, Enhancing Fires and Manoeuvre Capability Through Greater Air Ground Joint Interdependence, RAND, Santa Monica CA, 2009, p. 24.
(171) Lieutenant Colonel TG William Wallace, Commander V Corps, interview by Colonel MacLean, V Corps' Command Historian, 15 April 2003.
(172) Janice E McKenney, The Organization of the Field Artillery: 1775–2003, p. 319.
(173) Lieutenant Colonel Pitts, U.S. Army Field Artillery Relevance on the Modern Battlefield, Marine Corps University, Marine Air-Ground Training and Education Center, Marine Corps Combat Development Command, Quantico VA, 2004, p. 12.
(174) In addition to the reductions in corps and divisional artillery the quantity of howitzers supporting each brigade has declined. Twenty-four cannons supported a 1980s American heavy brigade, eighteen were required in the 1990s, and there were only sixteen Paladins in each brigade fires battalion in 2013. Major Sherman C. Watson Jr United States Army, Artillery is Here to Stay – For Now. School of Advanced Military Studies United States Army Command and General Staff College Fort Leavenworth, Kansas, 2013, p. 22.
(175) Colonel Robert Killebrew, quoted in Thomas E Ricks, Fiasco: the American Military Adventure in Iraq, Penguin Press, New York, 2006, p. 195. While the quote referred specifically to the US in Vietnam it equally applicable to other counter-insurgencies.
(176) This people-centric doctrinal approach was formalised with the publication of US Army's and Marine Corps' Counter Insurgency Field Manual (Army FM 3-24 and Marine Warfighting Publication 3-33.5) in December 2006.
(177) The concept of following an attritional approach to jihadism has gained the most traction in Israel. Israel has been identified as following a 'mowing the grass' strategy against hostile non-state groups, designed primarily to debilitate the enemy capabilities through attrition. This is the Israeli reaction to a protracted intractable conflict, where force is not intended to fulfil unattainable political goals. Efraim Inbar and Eitan Shamir, 'Mowing the Grass': Israel's Strategy for Protracted Intractable Conflict, journal of Strategic Studies, Volume 37, Issue 1, 2014, pp. 65–90.
(178) Stephen J. Maranian, Field Artillery Fires in the Mountains of Afghanistan, Fires, September 2008, pp. 34–36.
(179) Sinclair, Edward J. Posturing Army Aviation: Aviation Task Force Initiatives, Army Aviation, May 2004.
(180) Etienne de Durand, Benoît Michel and Elie Tenenbaum, Helicopter Warfare. The Future of Airmobility and Rotary Wing Combat, Focus stratégique, Number 32 bis, January 2012, p. 34.
(181) David E. Johnson, M. Wade Markel and Brian Shannon, The 2008 Battle of Sadr City, RAND, Santa Monica CA, p. 18.
(182) Robert A. Johnson, Reconsidering Future War, Predicting Future War, Parametres 44(1) Spring 2014, p. 67.
(183) Thomas R Hicks, Our generals failed in Afghanistan, The United States military failed America in Afghanistan. It wasn't a tactical failure. It was a failure of leadership, FP, July 6, 2017, 9:32am.
(184) DJ Elliott, Iraqi Field Artillery: The missing link, The Long War Journal, January 21, 2009.
(185) Dave Kilcullen, Two Schools of Classical Counter-insurgency, Small War Journal, 27 January 2007.
(186) Lt. Gen. H.R. McMaster, U.S. Army Continuity and Change, The Army Operating Concept and Clear Thinking About Future War March-April 2015 Military Review, p. 9.

(187) In 2004 the US State Department contracted DynCorp International, a private military company, to build Liberia's army. It is now rated as one of the most effective in the region. Private military companies are successful in part due to their lack of institutional baggage. Allowing them to create a military which suite the environment that they operate within.

(188) Eliot A. Cohen, The Mystique of U.S. Air Power, Foreign Affairs, Vol. 73, No. 1, Jan–Feb, 1994, p. 109.

(189) Elie Tenenbaum, The Battle over Fire Support. The close air support Challenge and the Future of Artillery, Focus stratégique, Number 35 bis, October 2012.

(190) United States Activities in Libya, White House, 15 June 2011.

(191) Will Laidlaw, Apache Over Libya, Pen & Sword Aviation, Barnsley, UK, 2016, p. 168.

(192) Royal Aeronautical Society – Lessons Offered from the Libya Air Campaign, A Specialist Paper by the Royal Aeronautical Society, p. 12.

(193) Karl P. Mueller (editor), Precision and Purpose: Airpower in the Libyan Civil War, RAND, 2015, p. 171.

(194) In this conflict, with its uncontested control of the sea, naval artillery could be considered as providing persistent fire support, just like its ground counterpart. This was not the case in the 1982 Falklands War where the destroyers and frigates often had to cease providing support to defend themselves. As Royal Navy fire could not be provided at a high level of guarantee it was usually 'superimposed' onto a target already being engaged by field artillery or mortars.

(195) Isabel Coles and Maggie Fick, Kurds Report More Chlorine Attacks, Iraq Pauses Tikrit Offensive, Reuters, 16 March 2015.

(196) Defence Department spokesman Peter Cook quoted in Andrew Tilghman, Forward-deployed US Troops in Iraq ID Targets for Airstrikes, MilitaryTimes, 12 November, 2015.

(197) Mike Benitez, 21st Century Forward Air Control: The Roots to rebuild, War on the Rocks, 1 March 2017.

(198) Alan Lockerby, SCAR-C over Libya – to war in an Aurora, Canadian Military Journal, Vol. 12, No. 3, Summer 2012, p. 64.

(199) Anthony Cordesman, The Real Lessons of Mosul (and Sixteen Years of War in Afghanistan, Iraq, and Syria), Centre for Strategic and International Studies, July 19, 2017.

(200) Mike Benitez and Mike Pietrucha, Political Airpower, Part III: Books Off the Ground, War on the Rocks, 31 January, 2017.

(201) Captain Ra'ad Qarim Kassem, an ISOF Najaf Battalion officer, told IHS Jane's on 28 January 2016, cited in Lessons learned as Mosul operation intensifies, ihs.com, 19 Feb 2017, p. 4.

(202) Mattias Altus, The Many Lessons from the Battle of Mosul, July 16, 2017, www.mtkander.com.

(203) The French fire support coordinator is the head of the Observation and Coordination Liaison Detachment and is in charge of coordinating the use of supporting fires at the battlegroup level. This was authorised by the Joint Doctrine Publication PIA 3.3.5, in June 2011. On subsequent operations this policy was not followed. As will be discussed later, air forces by their nature tend to see doctrine as less binding and expect a greater degree of improvisation than armies. The Air Force chain-of-command view was that the insertion of tactical air controllers was essential. They wanted these to be outside of the Observation and Coordination Liaison Detachment, in a parallel chain. The Afghan experience and the increased dependence of ground forces on air support resulted in these being under the direction of the Fire Support Coordinator. The term 'direction' reflected the French Air Force's refusal to see an air force officer under the command of an artilleryman. The airman had to be responsible directly to the battlegroup chief. Naturally, this does not necessarily mean that both cannot get along when advising the commanding officer. Of course, inter-Service disputes are common and generally healthy in that they reflect different perspectives due to the differing environment and culture.

(204) Douglas Porch, The French Army and the Spirit of the Offensive 1900-1914, In War and Society: A yearbook of Military History, ed. Brian Bond and Ian Roy, NY, 1973, p. 137.

(205) France's War in Mali: Lessons for an Expeditionary Army, RAND, Santa Monica CA, 2014, pp. 41–42.
(206) Anthony Cordesman, The Real Lessons of Mosul.
(207) Doctor Can Kasapoglu, ANALYSIS – Five key military takeaways from Azerbaijani-Armenian war, 30 October 2020.|
(208) Robin Forestier-Walker, Nagomo-Karabakh: New weapons for an old conflict spell danger, Aljazeera.com. Retrieved 30 November, 2020.
(209) Michael Kofman and Leonard Nersisyan, The Second Nagorno-Karabakh War, Two Weeks In, War on the Rocks, 14 October, 2020, Retrieved 30 November 2020.
(210) Colin S. Gray, Thucydides was right: Defining the Future Threat Strategic Studies Institute and U.S. Army War College Press.
(211) Colonel William A. Turner, The Field Artillery Reorganization to Conduct Operational, Joint, and Multination Fires, Fires Bulletin, July–August 2014, pp. 6–7.

Chapter 5: Firepower's Grammar and Challenges

(1) Christopher Duffy, The Army of Frederick the Great, pp. 100–101 and 111.
(2) Gunners is what the Dutch call a 'beggar name' – an epithet proudly adopted by those it was intended to insult.
(3) Gunther E Rothenberg, The Art of Warfare in the Age of Napoleon, p. 74.
(4) Quoted in E Longford, Wellington the Years of the Sword, Harper & Row, New York, 1969, pp. 401–2.
(5) Some historians see General Lee as the land commander of this type, destined to be defeated by the systematic command style of General Grant and his talented team of subordinates. Others see General MacArthur as the last truly heroic commander in chief.
(6) Jacques Ellul, Translated from the French by John Wilkinson, The Technological Society, Vintage Books, A Division of Random House, New York, 1964, p. xvi.
(7) Of course, the more egalitarian United States avoided this challenge; its initial officer training was in theory all arms, but it was largely military engineering. As a result, in the 19th century the top West Point cadets usually pursued a career in military engineering. The closure of the Royal Military Academy at Woolwich in 1939, which originally provided separate initial training to British artillery and engineer officers, who were joined later by the new technical arms, was a decisive step for this army's creation of a single officer corps. Of course, combining this training could lead to an overall reduction in education standards: prior to World War One 1 the French trained their artillery and engineer officers at the Paris Ecole Polytechnique which maintained a significantly higher academic standard than the École Spéciale Militaire de Saint-Cyr.
(8) Chris Bellamy, Red God of War, pp. 207–9
(9) David Fraser, Alanbrooke, Bloomsbury Reader, London, 2013, p. 22.
(10) JW Appel and GW Beebe, Preventive Psychiatry, Journal of the American Medical Association, volume 131, number 18 1946.
(11) NATO Indirect Fire Systems Tactical Doctrine AArtyP-5(A).
(12) Norman Stone, A Short History of World War One, Penguin, London, 2013, pp. 41–42.
(13) James Edmonds, Military Operations in France and Belgium 1918, volume 4, His Majesty's Stationary Office, London, 1947, p. 23.
(14) Richard Simpkin, Race to the Swift, Thoughts on Twenty-first Century Warfare, Brassey's Defence Publishers, London, 1985, p. 138.
(15) Chris Bellamy, Red God of War, p. 138.
(16) Richard Simpkin, Race to the Swift, p. 168.
(17) Ibid., p. 137.
(18) Johnathan Bailey, Field Artillery and Firepower, p. 10.

(19) Billy Congreve's Diary, 1 November 1914, in I.H. Thornton and P Fraser, eds, The Congreves, Father and Son, Murray, London, 1930, p. 247.
(20) Carl von Clausewitz, On War, p. 184.
(21) The nature of the target is the key factor determining effectiveness. During World War Two British researchers concluded that for point detonating artillery munitions the relative risk was: men standing – 1; men lying – 1/3; men firing from trenches – 1/15 to 1/50; and men crouching in trenches – 1/25 to1/100.
(22) Robert H Scales, Firepower in Limited War, p. 228.
(23) Fire Support in Operation Veritable, Effect on Forward Defensive Positions Report Number 26. WO 291/496 Anti-personnel effect of small HE shells.
(24) Tanks employing indirect fire to thicken artillery fire was common in World War Two. The Russians have revived the training of their tank crews in this technique: James Bingham, Russian ZVO tank crews train in indirect fire, Jane's Defence Weekly, 28 February 21018, p. 13.
(25) Brigadier ML Pemberton MC, The Development of Artillery Tactics and Equipment, p. 264.
(26) Chris Bellamy, Red God of War, p. 60.
(27) The Report of the Inter-Service Committee on Fire Support of Seaborne Landings against a Heavily Defended Coast, COS (43) 770/0. (Also known as the Graham Report after the name of its chairman).
(28) Shelford Bidwell & Dominic Graham, Fire-Power, p. 287.
(29) Lt Col Tubeuf, Stellungskampf bei Montdidier, 1932, quoted in J.F Williams, Corporal Hitler and the Great War, 1914–18, London, which is then quoted in Benjamin Franklin Cooling (Editor), Case Studies in the Development of Close Air Support, Office of Air Force History, United States Air Force, Washington DC, 1990, p. 190.
(30) Phillip S. Meilinger, Trenchard, Slessor, and Royal Air Force Doctrine before World War II in The Paths of Heaven: The Evolution of Airpower Theory, ed. Phillip S. Meilinger, School of Advanced Airpower Studies Air University Press, Maxwell Air Force Base, AL, 1997, p. 51.
(31) Alistair Horne, To Lose a Battle: France, 1940 Little, Brown and Company, Boston: 1969, pp. 332–35.
(32) Quoted in Milton Shulman, Defeat in the West, London, Secker and Warburg, London, 1947, p. 148.
(33) R. von Pohl, Anti-Air Protection of German Supply Routes in Italy, Military Affairs, volume 17, number 3, Autumn 1953, p. 133.
(34) Brigadier ML Pemberton MC, The Development of Artillery Tactics and Equipment, p. 228.
(35) Mitch Ginsberg, Israel's artillery corps torn between precision and power, The Times of Israel, 12 October, 2014 quoting an unattributed Israeli artillery officer.
(36) Brigadier ML Pemberton MC, The Development of Artillery Tactics and Equipment, The War Office, London, 1951, pp. 235–7.
(37) James Hazlett, Just-in-Time Warfare, in Stuart E Johnson and Martin C Libicki (editors), Dominant Battlespace Knowledge, National Defence University, Washington DC, 1996, pp. 54–55. He actually goes further and suggests lean business practices, such as just-in-time services and that other forms of synchronisation are equally applicable to warfare as to the commercial sector. Of course, while there is merit in adopting civilian sector best practice, these practices have never been fully tested against warfare's Clausewitzian nature in peer conflict.
(38) Colonel Phillip S. Meilinger, 10 Propositions Regarding Air Power, Air Force History and Museums Program, Washington DC, 1995, p. 41.
(39) Vice Admiral Arthur K. Cebrowski, U.S. Navy, and John J. Garstka, Network-Centric Warfare: Its Origin and Future, Naval Institute Proceedings, Magazine, Volume 124/1/1/139, pp. 28–35.
(40) Douglas Heaven, Why deep learning AIs are so easy to fool, Artificial-intelligence researchers are trying to fix the flaws of neural networks, Nature 9 October 2019.

(41) General Robert Lennox, deputy chief of staff for programs quoted by Greg Grant, Army Determines Precision Indirect Fires Not All That Important in Current Wars, Military.Com, 14 May 2010.

(42) Kenneth S. Brower The Israel Defense Forces, 1948–2017, Security and Policy Studies No. 150, The Begin-Sadat Center for Strategic Studies Bar-Ilan University, Mideast p. 48.

(43) General Valery Gerasimov, Chief of the General Staff of the Russian Federation, Military-Industrial Kurier, February 27, 2013, Rough translation by Robert Coalson June 21, 2014, LINK to original: http://vpk-news.ru/sites/default/files/pdf/VPK_08_476.pdf)

(44) Russia has shown in their operations in Syria the advantages of cheap free-fall fragment bombs. The Russians mainly use the OAF 250-270, costing around $25,000 each. This about one-sixth the price of the American guided bombs and missile. As the Russians often employ larger warheads to compensate for their reduced accuracy they can achieve similar target effect. Of course, this could result in a level of collateral damage unacceptable in the West. When Russia actually needs to hit a point target accurately, to ensure its destruction, it uses the satellite-guided KAB-500.

(45) Paddy Griffith, Battle Tactics of the American Civil War, p. 169.

(46) Infantry in Battle, The Infantry Journal Incorporated, Washington DC, 1939.

(47) The author sees little difference between: attritional theory (the incremental destruction of combat power); synchronized warfare (the desire to harmonise and orchestrate warfare); and position theory (from the propensity to seize and hold a piece of ground in order to employ firepower).

(48) Richard Simpkin, Race to the Swift, p. 19.

(49) Lawrence Freeman, Strategy: A History, Oxford University Press, 2013, p. 22.

(50) Tooke and Lamar, Blending Manoeuvre and Attrition, Volume 90, Number 2, March–April 2000, Military Review.

(51) JFC Fuller. The Dragon's Teeth, A Study in War and Peace, Constable and Company Ltd, London: 1932, p. 213.

(52) PRO, WO106/4348 pp. 184–52 OR'S Memo 7, Morale Effect of Artillery.

(53) SLA Marshall, Men Against Fire, Peter Smith, Gloucester, Mass, 1947 – Reprinted 1978, p. 84.

(54) Stephen Ashley Hart, Colossal Cracks: Montgomery's 21st Army Group in Northwest Europe, 1944–45, Stackpole Books, Mechanicsburg PA, 2007, p. 88.

(55) Interesting Sun Tzu's writings makes effectively the same point in 'invincibility lies in the defence, the possibility of victory in the attack'. From a list provided in: Principles of War in Brassey's Encyclopaedia of Land Forces and Warfare, Brassey's, Washington and London 1996, p. 856.

(56) Viscount Montgomery of Alamein, The Memoirs of Field Marshal Montgomery, Pen and Sword Military, Barnsley, South Yorkshire, Reprint 2007, p. 235.

(57) Edward Luttwak, The Operational Level of war, Strategy and History: Collected Essays II, Translation Books, New Brunswick, NJ, 1985, p. 177.

(58) One of the problems with successfully implementing the manoeuvreist approach is the limitations imposed by military career structures. Almost every other form of human endeavour divides those required to deliver the necessary strategic vision from those responsible for its practical delivery. For example, in a major construction project, the architect and the site manager are products of two separate career paths. Having only a single career stream, militaries rarely identify and promote those unique individuals that can conceive manoeuvreist military operations and then translate these concepts into understandable methods for their subordinates to practically deliver.

(59) General Field Marshall Erwin Rommel, Rommel – Infantry Attack, Greenhill Books, London, 1990, pp. 160–1.

(60) Major Marvin Knorr Jr. USMC, The Development Of German Doctrine And Command And Control And Its Application To Supporting Arms, 1832–1945, Pickle Partners Publishing, 2015, p. 285.

(61) Robert H Scales, Firepower in Limited War, p. 15.

(62) Christopher Bellamy, The Evolution of Modern Land Warfare, p. 16.

(63) Edmund J Dugan, Dominant Land Forces for 21st Century Warfare, The Land Warfare Papers No 73, Association of the US Army, September 2009, p. 50.
(64) As a theory the manoeuvreist approach traces its origins to the practices of the nineteenth century Prussian Army. It was designed to ensure that commanders who were out of communication could, through understanding the commanding general's intent, act in a unified manner whilst preserving the freedom to employ their initiative. Modern surveillance and communications challenge these freedoms by allowing commanders to be always contactable.
(65) Antoine Henri, Baron de Jiminy: Précis de l'Art de la Guerre, 1838, quoted in Jay Luvaas, Napoleon on the Art of War, Simon and Schuster, UK, 2001, p. 43.
(66) Greek mythology tells the tale of Herakles and his fight against the giant, Alcyoneus. Herakles was unable to beat Alcyoneus until Athena, the goddess of wisdom, identified that the giant was invulnerable when in his home country of Phlegra. Herakles therefore carried him off his home soil and slew him. The 'Alcyoneus's Principle', as defined by Robert Leonhard in his book The Art of Manoeuvre, is all about moving your foe into situations that expose vulnerabilities.
(67) Bruce I Gudmundsson, On Artillery, Praeger Publishers, Westport CT, 1993, p. 163.
(68) Shelford Bidwell & Dominic Graham, Fire-Power, p. 260.
(69) Johnathan Bailey, Field Artillery and Firepower, pp. 269–70.
(70) Mikhail Tukhachevskty, New Problems In Warfare, U.S. Army War College Art of War Colloquium: Soviet Operational Concepts by Various Soviet Authors, U.S. Army War College, Carlisle Barracks, PA, November 1983, pp. 7–8.
(71) Daniel Coetzee and Lee W Eysturlid editors, Philosophers of War: The Evolution of History's Greatest Military Thinkers, Praeger, 2013, Volume 2, Santa Barbara, California, pp. 289–290.
(72) Stalin seems to have coined the phrase 'artillery offensive' to distinguish artillery support from merely a preliminary bombardment that lifted once infantry and tanks assaulted the enemy's defences. In contrast, the 'artillery offensive' provided continuous fire support throughout the enemy depth during the entire duration of the offensive. It had the aim of shocking the entire enemy defensive system.
(73) ARMY Magazine, Volume 51, Number 5, May 2001.
(74) Robert R. Leonard, The Art of Maneuver.
(75) Bruce W Watson, Military Lessons of the Gulf War, Greenhill Books, Barnsley South Yorkshire, 1993, p. 111.
(76) U.S. Army Field Artillery Relevance on the Modern Battlefield, Marine Corps University, Marine Air-Ground Training and Education Centre, Marine Corps Combat Development Command, Quantico, VA, 2004, p. 11.
(77) William S Lind, Manoeuvre Warfare Handbook, Routledge, New York, 2016, pp. 19–21.
(78) Johnathan Bailey, Field Artillery and Firepower, p. 16.
(79) Richard E. Simpkin, Deep Battle: The Brainchild of Marshal Tukhachevsky, Fort Leavenworth, KS: U.S. Army Command and General Staff College, 1991, pp. 125–134.
(80) Most Western doctrine divides offensive fire support into preparation fire before the assault begins and covering fire as the troops close on their objectives. Defensive fire support is divided into counter-preparation fire; this occurs before the enemy assault begins. Once the enemy are attacking, fire support is divided into distant and close defensive fires. Close defensive and covering fire can result in firepower being used within the danger close distance of friendly ground forces.
(81) The best guarantee of accurate fire is to see rounds land on a target. In the offensive this is now usually done before the troops start the assault. For less technically adept armies, the practice in the World Wars was to adjust onto target in pre-H-Hour preliminary fire. Alternatively, a long assault distance may also allow adjustments after H-Hour. If close defensive fires are to be fully guaranteed, then own troops may abandon forward positions during the adjustment to avoid fratricide. Fratricide is subsequently an acceptable risk when defeating an assault needs the employment of close defensive fires.

(82) Brigadier Vinod Anand, Modernizing Artillery Retrospect and Prospect, India Strategic, February 2010.
(83) Quoted in Maj Gen Jagjit Singh, Battle-Winning Role of the Gunners in Kargil War, Indian Defence Review 29 October, 2015.
(84) This was the judgement of Justin Bronk, Research Fellow for Airpower and Technology at RUSI, in the oral evidence he provided the UK's Parliament's Defence Committee in June 2018.
(85) Lieutenant Colonel TG William Wallace, Commander V Corps, interview by Colonel MacLean, V Corps' Command Historian, 15 April 2003.
(86) John Monash, 8 September, 1918, quoted in the Official History of Australia in the Great War 1914–18, Dr CEW Bean, Angus and Robertson, vi, 1942, p. 936.
(87) Virgil Ney, The Evolution of the US Infantry Battalion 1939-68, HQ US Army Development Command, October 1968, p. 14.
(88) Shelford Bidwell & Dominic Graham, Fire-Power.
(89) Janice E. McKenney, The Organisational History of Field Artillery, p. 170.
(90) CAB 106/112 30 June 1944. (British Cabinet Office files).
(91) Schnabel, Policy and Direction: The First Year, Center of Military History, United States Army, Washington DC, 1992, p. 97.
(92) Bruce I Gudmunsson, On Artillery, Praeger, West Port CT, 1993, p. 145.
(93) Boyd L. Dastrup, Modernizing the King of Battle, 1973–1991, US Army Field Artillery Center and School, Fort Sill, Oklahoma, 1994, pp. 56–57.
(94) In the Gulf War, the British 1st Armoured Division had six armoured and armoured infantry battalion sized battlegroups and an armoured reconnaissance battalion to three battalions of 155mm guns, one with 203mm and a multiple launch rocket system battalion. Giving a ratio of five field artillery to seven manoeuvre battalions. Their supporting American artillery brigade provided a further two battalions of 203mm tube artillery. Making the overall artillery to manoeuvre battalion ratio one to one.
(95) Major General Robert Scales, Artillery's Failings in the Iraq War: United States Must Focus on Range and Precision, Armed Forces Journal, November 2003, p. 44.
(96) Michael D Maples, FA Priorities After OIF, Field Artillery, US Army Field Artillery Center and School, Fort Sill, Oklahoma, September–October 2003, p. 5.
(97) The Spanish artillery are a notable exemption, retaining three tube artillery battalions for corps and divisional operations. In addition, their brigades have their direct support artillery battalions.
(98) Urban terrain with its easily-identifiable buildings allows soldiers on the ground to readily employ precision munitions that rely upon precision point mensuration. The MLRS guided missile's accuracy and small yield warhead (in comparison to aerial weapons) allows individual rooms to be separately attacked. Varying the weapon's fuze setting allows a choice to be made about on which floor detonation occurs. Hence for assaulting troops an aerial photograph with pre-mensurated targets, plus reliable communications back to the launcher, or aircraft if a larger yield warhead is required, represents a considerable increase in urban warfighting capability.
(99) Michael Barabanov (Editor), Russia's New Army, Centre for Analysis of Strategies and Technologies, Moscow, 2011, p. 23.
(100) The equipment of the Russian airborne forces appears to be adjusting to the recognition that they, rather than the ground forces, will often be Russia's lead land warfighting service. They are no longer just its specialist early entry force. Given the need to be more capable they appear to be being equipped with main battle tanks. The future fielding of heavy tube and rocket artillery cannot be discounted. Of course, this is at the expense of deployability.
(101) Michael Barabanov (Editor), Russia's New Army, p. 31.
(102) The Military Balance 2013, The International Institute for Strategic Studies, Routledge, London, p. 226.
(103) Jane's Defence Weekly, 24 November 2017, Vol 54, Issue 48, p. 28.

(104) Von Hardesty, Red Phoenix, p. 181. Actually, the number of Soviet guns was higher, as self-propelled guns were counted as tracked vehicles.
(105) James J. Schneider, The Loose Marble – and the Origins of Operational Art, Parameter, March 1989, p. 95.
(106) Wilhelm von Scherff, The New Tactics of Infantry, (studies in), translated by Colonel Lumley, Cornell University Library, Graham, London, 1873.
(107) The ill-trained reserve corps used by the Germans at the First Battle of Ypres appeared to their British adversaries to be employing mass formations, whether deliberate or not. As up to 75 percent of the manpower of the reserve corps were student volunteers with virtually no training, their defeat is known to the Germans as the Kindermord (massacre of the innocents).
(108) Stephen Biddle, Military Power, p. 3.
(109) James J Schneider, The Theory of the Empty Battlefield, Journal of the Royal United Service Institute, 1987, pp. 37–44.
(110) The empty battlefield challenges commanders and command systems reliant upon personal intervention as opposed to those reliant upon direction from HQs. Most of the 78 British generals killed in World War One were visiting their troops. Frank Davies and Graham Maddocks, Bloody Red Tabs, Pen and Sword, London, 2014, pp. 22–24. For the last years of World War Two, the German generals were largely restricted to their HQs due to Anglo-American firepower. Field Marshal Rommel in the West, continued to rely upon personally seeing the developing situation, and as a result was severely injured by Allied fighter-bomber aircraft when moving around the battlefield.
(111) National Research Council Staff, Reducing the Logistics Burden for the Army After Next: Doing More With Less, Committee to Perform a Technology Assessment Focused on Logistics Support Requirements for Future Army Combat Systems, National Research Council (U.S.), 1999, p. 64.
(112) Benjamin S Kelsey, a US Army Air Force B-17's escort fighter pilot's observations, interview with the author in 1979, Von Hardesty, Red Phoenix, The Rise of Soviet Air Power 1941–45, Arms and Armour Press, London-Melbourne, 1982, p. 215.
(113) Presentation to NRDC-Italy by Dr. Phillip A. Karber, 25 May 2016.
(114) Trevor Dupuy, Understanding War: Military History And The Theory Of Combat, Leo Cooper, New York, 1986, p. 84.
(115) Colonel Jay Peterson, deputy commandant of the US Army Infantry School. Quoted in Eric Tegler, An Empty Battlefield? Will precision weapons proliferation limit land force engagement in future conflicts? DefenceMediaNetwork, 8 June 2012.
(116) Avrahan Adan, On the Banks of the Suez, Presidio Press, Navota, California, 1980, pp. 141–2, 198, 202–3, 221–5.
(117) Richard Simpkin, Race to the Swift, p. 169.
(118) Ibid., p. 137.
(119) Chris Bellamy, Red God of War, p. 174.
(120) Attributed to Colonel General (later Marshal) Kirill Moskalenko, (Commander of the 38th Army), On South-Western direction, 1943–1945, Moscow, Science, 1972.
(121) Robert R. Leonard, The Art of Maneuver, p. 179.
(122) Air-Land Battle Primer, HQ USAFTAC/USATRADOC Pamphlet (ALFA Agency), June 1978, p. 49.
(123) An alternative explanation is that artillery divisions are merely the continuation of the Chinese practice of centralising capabilities into formations with a single purpose. This leads them to having anti-tank and anti-aircraft divisions.
(124) Lieutenant General (Retired) Harold Moore and co-writer Joseph L. Galloway, We Were Soldiers … Once and Young. Quoted in: Major Matthew R. Myer, Danger Close: Calculating Risk Within the 'Last 100 Yards', Infantry Magazine, Fort Benning, Georgia, May/June 2013.

(125) Lester W. Grau, Soviet Artillery Planning in the Tactical Defence, Department of the Army, Soviet Studies Office, Fort Leavenworth, Kansas, September 1990, p. 9.
(126) Most armies employ common danger procedures. Firstly, when a terminal controller knows that he is engaging a target within the trigger distance, he orders danger close within the opening request for fire. This leads to specific procedures on the guns/mortars and in the fire direction centres to improve accuracy and consistency. Secondly, the terminal controller directs the rounds at fire for effect at beyond the trigger distance. This is to ensure that the rounds are consistent, before they are incrementally brought closer to the target. At any time, if any individual gun or mortar is not firing consistently will be given end of mission and ceases to participate. In addition, the terminal controller will maximise own troop safety by ensuring that they take cover prior to the rounds landing.
(127) The Russian General Staff, translated and edited by Lester G. Grau and Michael A. Gress, The Soviet-Afghan War, How a Superpower Fought and Lost, University Press of Kansas, 2002 p. 185.
(128) Captain James T. Cobb, First Lieutenant Christopher A. LaCour and Sergeant First Class William H. Hight, TF 2-2 IN FSE AAR: Indirect Fires in the Battle of Fallujah, Field Artillery, March–April 2005, p. 24.
(129) Headquarters, Department of the Army. ATP 3-09.32 JFIRE Multiservice Tactics, Techniques, and Procedures for the Joint Application of Firepower, HQDA, Washington DC, 2014, p. 143.
(130) REDs employ a casualty criterion of a prone soldier in winter clothing and helmet being physically incapacitated for at least 5-minutes. Other militaries use variations on the RED methodology including using different friendly casualty criteria, such as level of ballistic protection or assuming they are standing rather than prone. This results in different national distances for the same ordnance.
(131) The actual fall of shot of artillery and mortars is an ellipse along the axis of fire and not a circle. By turning an ellipse into a circle, the circular error probability assumes the worst case. This is of course the safest approach when soldiers do not know the line of fire of supporting fire.
(132) Lethality distances are based upon the type of munition, their fuze setting, and the nature of the ground. However, to avoid the process becoming unwieldy all these factors are not individually considered. But we should recognise that air bursting will increase, and delaying a munitions' detonation until it has buried into the ground will decrease, the munition's lethality. Allowance should also be made for environmental differences such as target elevation, terrain, buildings and trees. For example, rounds landing below an infantry position, say a riverbed, are less lethal than ones being detonated on the same level. When using cannon and rockets the aircraft's axis of attack is a factor. The least dispersion occurs when strafing is parallel to the friendly force's disposition. No system that is usable in combat situations can take in to account all these variables. Hence the need for expert judgement within the fire support element.
(133) RED figures are on open source; hence they do not provide risk estimate distance for terminally-guided precision and near-precision weapons.
(134) The relative maximum ranges are: 60mm mortar 3,500m; 81mm mortar 5,600m; 120mm mortar 7,200m; and for the American 105mm gun 14,100m (19,500m can be achieved with rocket assisted rounds, but this is not a munition suitable for danger close) and the British 105mm gun 17,100m.
(135) The Soviets/Russians employ the following minimum safety distances: free-flight rockets 1000m; helicopter cannon 500m and helicopter machine guns 300m.
(136) Advanced Precision Kill Weapon System II (APKWS II) Goes to War – Defense media network.com, 9 July 2012.
(137) If the 0.1% chance of incapacitation represents the edge of the danger area, then 10% chance of incapacitation represents the edge of the lethal zone. If we look at the ratios between the distances at which 0.1% and 10% chances of incapacitation apply with aerial munitions, then there are significant differences between cluster and conventional munitions. Cluster munitions have a ratio of 16:9 between these two distances, while conventional bombs a ratio of 16:4. The difference with artillery munitions is not as pronounces in the REDs tables, but the same logic applies.

(138) Lieutenant Colonel Charles R Shrader Lieutenant Colonel USA Amicicide: The Problem of Friendly Fire in Modern War. Fort Leavenworth, KS: Combat Studies Institute, U.S. Army Command and General Staff College,1982, p. 17.
(139) David Betz and Hugo Stanford-Tuck, The City is Neutral: On Urban Warfare in the 21st Century, Vol 2, Iss 4, October 2019.
(140) Robert Scales, Forecasting the Future of Warfare, War on the Rocks, University of Texas, 9 April 2018.
(141) Mark Urban, The Edge, Is the Military Dominance of the West Coming to an End? Little, Brown, London, 2015, p. 61.
(142) Julian Corbett, Some Principles of Maritime Strategy, Naval Institute Press, Annapolis, MD, 1988, p. 57. Quoted in Michael I Handel, Masters of War: Classical Strategic Thought, Routledge, London, 2005 p. 223.
(143) Luis Simon, Demystifying the A2/AD Buzz, 4 January 2017, War on the Rocks.
(144) Daniel L. Davis, Seduced by Success, Armed Forces Journal, February 10, 2014.
(145) Meir Finkel, On Flexibility, Recovery from Technological and Doctrinal Surprise on the Battlefield, Stanford University Press, Palo Alto, California, 2011.
(146) BH Liddell Hart (Editor), The Rommel Papers, Easton Press, Norwalk Connecticut, 1953, pp. 521–23.
(147) Norman Stone, A Short History of World War One, Penguin Books, London, 2007, p. 88.
(148) Edward Mead Earle (Editor), The Makers of Modern Strategy, Princeton University Press, Princeton, New Jersey, 1943, p. 100.
(149) Victor Davis Hanson, War's Bitter Laws, National Review, July 11, 2003.
(150) Colleen Bell, Civilianising warfare: ways of war and peace in modern counter-insurgency, Journal of International Relations and Development, 2011, pp. 14 and 309–332.
(151) Dillon, Michael and Julian Reid The Liberal Way of War: Killing to Make Life Live, Routledge, London, 2009, pp. 3–6.
(152) Christopher Coker, The Warrior Ethos: Military Culture and the War on Terror, Routledge, New York and London, 2007, p. 8.
(153) David Kilcullen, Twenty-eight Articles: Fundamentals of Company Level Counter-insurgency, Military Review 86(3), 2006, p. 104.
(154) Richard B. Johnson, Major, US Army, The Biggest Stick: The Employment of Artillery Units in Counter-insurgency, Command and General Staff College Fort Leavenworth, Kansas, 2011, p. 140.
(155) General Sir David Richards, IISS Conference in Geneva, 2008.
(156) Just War theory has two components, labelled in Latin jus ad bellum (literally, rightness or justice in going to war) and jus in bello (rightness or justice in the conduct of war). Most authorities identify seven jus ad bellum criteria: Just Cause, Right Authority, Right Intention, Proportionality of Ends, Last Resort, Probability of Success, and Proportionality. Proportionality is often cited as the driver for the requirement to make firepower more discriminate. Of course, it is always about context and interpretation, rather than technologies such as low-yield precision weapons. Proportionality seeks to balance the impact on non-combatants of the legal use of force against combatants, to achieve advantage from attacking a legitimate military objective.
(157) Vincent M. Messbarger MD, The Hanson Legacy, Cocheta Publishing, 2012, p. 38.
(158) Peter Tsouras, Greenhill Dictionary of Military Quotations, Greenhill Books, 2000.
(159) Barry D Watts, The Evolution of Precision Strike, Centre for Strategic and Budgetary Assessments 2013, p. 17.
(160) United States Air Force Scientific Advisory Board. Air Force Operations in Urban Environments Volume 1: Executive Summary and Annotated Brief, Government Printing Office, Washington DC, 2005, p. 13.
(161) 'Blair statement in full,' BBC, 7 October 2001, http://news.bbc. co.uk/1/hi/ukpolitics/1585238. stm (accessed 9 December 2014).

(162) Robert Perkins, Under Fire, Israeli Artillery Policies Scrutinised, research and publication sponsored by the Government of Norway, 2014, p. 15.

(163) Though, of course, certain states and other political entities have seen war as an end in itself. Whether for political, religious or societal purposes. The so-called Islamic State saw the establishment of a Caliphate as leading to near-permanent struggle, as did Nazi Germany.

(164) The Bible, Book of the Revelations of St John the Apostle, Chapter 6, Verses 1–8.

(165) John Stuart Mills, Dissertations and Discussions: Political, Philosophical, and Historical, Volume 1, Longmans, Green, Reader and Dyer, London, 1868, p. 26.

(166) Major Richard B. Johnson, Biggest Stick: The Employment of Artillery Units In Counterinsurgency, Pickle Publishing, Halstad, Minnesota, 2015, p. 11.

(167) Stephen Biddle, Military Power, p. 4.

(168) Yaneer Bar-Yam, Making Things Work: Solving Complex Problems in a Complex World, Knowledge Press, Cambridge, 2004, p. 28. Quoted in Major Jeffrey S. Wright United States Army, Field Artillery and the Combined Arms Team: A Case for the Continued Relevance of American Fire Support. School of Advanced Military Studies, United States Army Command and General Staff College Fort Leavenworth, Kansas January 2015.

Chapter 6: Joint Firepower Military Thought, Doctrine and Force Employment

(1) John Keegan, History of Warfare, Random House, New York, 1993, p. 6.

(2) Paul AL Ducheine, Michael N. Schmitt, Frans PB Osinga (editor), Targeting: The Challenges, of Modern Warfare, Springer, 2016, p. 2.

(3) Clausewitz's other two means of countering friction are operational experience, or failing that very testing training, and a commander of genius, who can master friction, Napoleon was his role model for this.

(4) Colonel JFC Fuller, The Foundations of the Science of War, Hutchinson and Company Ltd, London, 1926, p. 254.

(5) The stressing of the importance of theory is a conscious rejection of Ralph Peters' view that theory belongs in the sciences, and not the areas of human endeavour, in particular warfare. Ralph Peters, In Praise of Attrition, Parametres, Summer 2004, pp. 25–25.

(6) Isabel V. Hull, Absolute Destruction: Military Culture and the Practices of War in Imperial Germany, Cornell University Press, Ithaca, New York, 2004, p. 97.

(7) Colin S Gray, The Strategy Bridge: Theory for Practice, Oxford University Press, 2010, p. 18.

(8) William 'Billy' Mitchell, Winged Defence, The Development and Possibilities of Modern Air Power – Economic and Military, University of Alabama Press, Tuscaloosa, Alabama, 2009, p. 20.

(9) David MacIsaac, Voices from the Central Blue, Chapter 21 in Peter Paret (Ed), Makers of Modern Strategy from Machiavelli to the nuclear age, Princeton University Press, Princeton N.J. 1986, p. 624.

(10) Eric M Bergerud, Fire in the Sky, The Air War In The South Pacific, Westview Press, Oxford, 2001, p. 6.

(11) David MacIsaac, Voices from the Central Blue, p. 643.

(12) While not exhaustive some of the recent fashionable trends in land fires are: unprotected truck-mounted guns; addressing individual elements of precision accuracy without applying the same rigor in the whole system; failing consider survivability through ease of displacement when fielding towed artillery; deploying longer range weapons without adequately addressing either target acquisition or terminal accuracy; and the fielding of 120mm mortars in light forces despite them being unsuitable for danger close fire support of dismounted troops.

(13) Pursuing capability developments that lead to dead ends is unfortunately a common military phenomenon. The British cavalry school perhaps provided the best riposte when they named a road 'Mounted Infantry' in one of their barracks; it was of course a cul-de-sac.

(14) Hew Strachan, Strategy or Alibi? Obama, McChrystal and the Operational Level of War, Survival, October-November 2010, p. 160.
(15) Thomas E Ricks, The Generals, p. 345.
(16) The American Army has had the following doctrine since World War Two: 1950s – pentomic doctrine; 1960s – counterinsurgency doctrines; 1970s – Active Defense doctrine; 1980s AirLand Battle Doctrine; 1990s1 Full-Dimensional and Full-Spectrum Operations; post 9/11 – counterinsurgency doctrines; the Army's Unified Land Operations concept of the 2011–2012 articulated in Field Manuel 3.0 Full Spectrum; and now Multidomain Operations or MDO.
(17) DePuy, Field Manual 100-5, Position Paper, Sep 76, Field Manuals File, USAFAS, Office of the AC, MSTL Archives.
(18) Lespinasse, Essay on the Organisation of the Artillery Arm, quoted in David G Chandler, The Campaigns of Napoleon, Volume 1, Chandler, David G. The Campaigns of Napoleon, Volume 1, Simon and Schuster, New York, 1966, p. 340.
(19) Colonel H.C.B. Rogers, Artillery through the ages, Seeley, Service & Co., Ltd, London, 1971, p. 39.
(20) Shelford Bidwell, Gunners at War, Arms & Armour Press, London, 1970, p. 21.
(21) Kevin Killey, Ultimo Ratio Regum, Organization, Tactics, and Employment of Artillery in the Grande Armee, 1800–1815, Part 3: The Organization and Battle-Tactics of French Artillery, The Napoleon Series, 2001.
(22) Artillery Notes on Attack by Canadian Corps, August 8th 1918, WO95/1060.
(23) Laurie Burkitt, Andrew Scobell and Larry M. Wortzel The Lessons of History: The Chinese People's Liberation Army at 75, Strategic Studies Institute, U.S. Army War College, Carlisle, PA, pp. 355–359.
(24) Shelford Bidwell & Dominic Graham, Fire-Power, pp. 126–7.
(25) John Monash, 8 September, 1918, quoted in the Official History of Australia in the Great War 1914–18, Dr CEW Bean, Angus and Robertson, 1942, vi, p. 936.
(26) Richard Simpkin, Race to the Swift, p. 150.
(27) The Canadian Army provides the exception to the near-universal acceptance of the need for battalion fire support weapons. They need to re-role their artillerymen from manning 155mm guns to provide a battalion level mortar capability.
(28) Johnathan Bailey, Field Artillery and Firepower, p. 159.
(29) Shelford Bidwell, Gunners at War, Arms & Armour Press, London, 1970, p. 77.
(30) Bruce I Gudmundsson, On Artillery, Praeger Publishers, Westport CT, 1993, pp. 43–59.
(31) This was enshrined in: Provisional Instructions for the Tactical Employment of Larger Units, 1921. This defence-oriented approach saw casualties being minimised by artillery. Robert A. Doughty, The Seeds of Disaster: The Development of French Army Doctrine, 1919–39, Stackpole Books, Mechanicsburg, PA, 1985, pp. 9–10.
(32) Jeffrey A. Gunsburg, The Battle of the Belgian Plain, 12–14 May 1940: The First Great Tank Battle. The Journal of Military History, 56, April 1992, p. 221.
(33) Shelford Bidwell, Gunners at War, p. 209.
(34) W E, Murphy, 2nd New Zealand Divisional Artillery, New Zealand Historical Publications Branch, Wellington, 1966, pp. 402–4.
(35) General Horrocks, quoted in Shelford Bidwell & Dominic Graham, Fire-Power, p. 289.
(36) Report by 1st RHA on the Priest, as edited by Major General Royal Artillery, Middle East Forces, 23 September December 1942. Quoted in Brigadier ML Pemberton MC, The Development of Artillery Tactics and Equipment, The War Office, London, 1951, p. 139.
(37) FM 100-5, Field Service Regulations – operations, Department of the Army, Washington DC, 1949, p. 22.
(38) War Department, Study 64: Field Artillery Gunnery, Report of the General Board, U.S. Forces, European Theater, February, 1947, pp. 30–34.

(39) CN Donnelly, The Wind of Change in Soviet Artillery, International Defence Review 15, No 8, 1982, p. 79.
(40) Chris Bellamy, Red God of War, pp. 20–21.
(41) Ibid., p. 18.
(42) V Ye Savkin, Colonel, Candidate of Military Science, The Basic Principles of Operational Art and Tactics (Osnovnye Printsipy Operativnogo Iskusstra I Taktiki), Military Publishing House Moscow, 1972. Quoted in Joseph D. Douglass Soviet Military Strategy in Europe, Pergamum Policy Studies, 1980, p. 127.
(43) Stephen Ashley Hart, Colossal Cracks: Montgomery's 21st Army Group in Northwest Europe, 1944–45, Stackpole Books, Mechanicsburg PA, 2007, pp. 13–15 and 81.
(44) VK Triandafillov, Character of the Operations of Modern Armies, 1929. Quoted in James R Holbrook et al, Tactical Responses to Concentrated Artillery, Combat Studies Institute, IS Report, US Command and General Staff College, Leavenworth, Kansas, 1989, pp. 100–102.
(45) Chris Bellamy, Red God of War, p. 65.
(46) Attached artillery is under command of the assigned manoeuvre force commander. This is normally excusive, except when the senior artillery general, on behalf of the overall commander, integrates their firepower into a fire plan. In support artillery remains under command of the artillery chain of command but it collocates its HQ with the supported manoeuvre unit HQ. Its fire is not exclusively reserved for the supported manoeuvre unit.
(47) Lester W. Grau, The Soviet Combined Arms Battalion – Reorganization for Tactical Flexibility, Fort Leavenworth: SASO Blue Book, September 1989, p. 66.
(48) V. Litvinenko and S. Voronkov, Artillery Fire and Maneuver: The Role of New-type Tactical Artillery Elements in Armed Conflicts of the late-20th, early-21st Centuries, Army Digest, February 2017, p. 34.
(49) Report by 201 Guards Brigade, 9–18 September 1943, quoted in Brigadier ML Pemberton MC, The Development of Artillery Tactics and Equipment, The War Office, London, 1951, p. 188.
(50) Stephen Biddle, Military Power, p. 3.
(51) BH Liddell Hart, The Rommel Papers, Collins, Glasgow, 1953, p. 7.
(52) Shelford Bidwell & Dominic Graham, Fire-Power, p. 206.
(53) Elie Tenenbaum, The Battle over Fire Support.
(54) Bruce I Gudmundsson, On Artillery, Praeger Publishers, Westport CT, 1993, p. 112.
(55) Brigadier ML Pemberton MC, The Development of Artillery Tactics and Equipment, pp. 37–8 and 139.
(56) Shelford Bidwell & Dominic Graham, Fire-Power, p. 225.
(57) Historical Evaluation and Research Organisation, Modern Artillery Experience in Combat, Dunn Loring, VA, 1977.
(58) Charles Messenger, The Art of the Blitzkrieg, Ian Allan Ltd, Shepperton, Surrey, 1976, p. 219.
(59) The Advanced Field Artillery Tactical Data System (AFATDS) is the fire support command and control system employed by the U.S. Army and U.S. Marine Corps units. It provides automated support for planning, coordinating, controlling and executing fires and effects. Like all American fire support systems since the 1940s, it is primarily designed for massing fires on priority targets.
(60) V. Litvinenko and S. Voronkov, Artillery Fire and Maneuver: The Role of New-type Tactical Artillery Elements in Armed Conflicts of the late-20th, early-21st Centuries, Army Digest, February 2017, p. 34.
(61) Anthony Clayton, Paths of Glory, The French Army 1914–18, Cassel, London, 2003, p. 77.
(62) Artillery Intelligence and Counter-Battery, nigelef.tripod.com/p_artyint-cb.ht. Accessed 13 February 2018.
(63) In November 1944, the weakest link for the concrete-protected coastal artillery batteries on Walcheren Island proved to be the dyke walls holding back the sea. Destroying these and flooding the batteries proved much easier than destroying individual casements.

(64) Quoted in Winston Churchill, The World Crisis; The Eastern Front, Thornton Butterworth, London, 1931, p. 271.
(65) Attempts to employ dispersion, cover, concealment, constant movement and deception are made redundant by artillery opening fire. The act of firing a projectile, which rises above the clutter of the ground, allows weapon locating radar to backtrack along the trajectory to its point of origin. Alternatively, its flash or acoustic signature gives away the battery's location. Rockets also provide a visual indication of their launch point through their effluence left along their flight path.
(66) Artillery, Amiens Canadian Corps, August 1918, RG, 9, III, v.4807, folder 175, 3, NAC. Quoted in Dean Chappelle The Canadian Attack at Amiens, 8–11 August 1918, Canadian Military History, Volume 2, Number 2, Article 11, University of Ottawa, 2012.
(67) Chris Bellamy, Red God of War, pp. 49–50 and 58.
(68) Boyd L. Dastrup, Modernizing the King of Battle, United States Army Field Artillery Centre and School, Fort Sill, OK, 1994, p. 23.
(69) Ibid., p. 4.
(70) Stephen Biddle, Military Power, p. 135.
(71) Dr. Phillip A. Karber, 'Lessons Learned' from the Russo-Ukrainian War, Draft Personal Observations, Johns Hopkins Applied Physics Laboratory & U.S. Army Capabilities Center (ARCIC) 8 July 2015, p. 20.
(72) Col John A. Warden III, The Air Campaign: Planning for Combat, Pergamon-Brassey's, Washington, DC, 1989, p. 95.
(73) German aircraft losses amounted to 27,637 by all causes, in comparison France lost 52,640 and Great Britain lost 35,973. The Aircraft of World War 1 – Statistics. Thearodrone.com. Retrieved 3 September 2018.
(74) John Terraine, White Heat: the new warfare 1914–18, Guild Publishing, London, 1982, p. 215.
(75) Stephen Budiansky, Air Power, Penguin, New York, 2004, p. 69.
(76) Colin S Gray, Airpower for Strategic Effect, 2012, p. 93.
(77) It is having an institutionally independent role, rather than being a separate service that matters. The Israeli Air Force illustrates this; in theory, it is just an element in the Israeli Defence Force, with the same status and independence as any of the ground forces branches, such as the Artillery Corps. But it has always operated as a separate component. Most see it as Israel's the dominant warfighting force. The same can be said for the US Army Air Corps in World War Two.
(78) Giulio Douhet, The Command of The Air, translated by Dino Ferrari, Air Force History and Museum Programme, Washington, DC, 1998.
(79) In Warden's theory, the opposing country is classified as a system organised into five concentric rings. Airpower can bypass the outermost ring, military forces, to achieve greater effect against the innermost rings. In contrast to earlier airpower theorists, who largely emphasised attacking the enemy's war-making and sustaining capabilities through industrial targeting, Warden's principal target was the enemy's strategic command and control, with the aim of achieving total physical paralysis.
(80) Air Marshal of the Royal Air Force, Sir John Slessor. Airpower and Armies.
(81) Daniel R Mortensen (Editor), Airpower and Ground Armies: Essays on the Evolution of Anglo-American air doctrine. 1940–1943, Air University Press, Air Force Research Institute Maxwell Air Force Base, Alabama 1998, p. iii.
(82) Coningham Despatch: Operations carried out by the Second Tactical Air Force between 6 June 1944 and 9 May 1945, PRO AIR 37/876, p. 42.
(83) Legitimacy and legality issues arise in engaging targets within Warden's four inner rings. If airpower focuses on economic warfare then almost inevitably civilians will become casualties. Even with greatly increased accuracy, the issue of collateral damage from air attacks remains a central concern in military planning. Hence the attacking military forces (the outer ring) can become the default option when airpower is used to coerce an opponent.

(84) Ochmanek, David, Ted Harshberger, David E. Thaler and Glenn A. Kent. To Find, and Not to Yield: How Advances in Information and Firepower Can Transform Theatre Warfare, RAND Corporation, Santa Monica, CA: 1998, p. xviii.
(85) Robert A Pape, Bombing to Win: Air Power and Coercion in War, Cornell University Press, Ithaca and London, 1996, p. 74.
(86) Thomas Schelling, Arms and Influence, Yale University Press, New Haven, 1966, pp. 2–3.
(87) Robert L. Sherrod, History of Marine Corps Aviation in World War II, Combat Forces Press, Washington, DC: 1952, p. 32.
(88) Maj Michael D. Becker Command and Control of Marine TacAir In Joint Land Operations, originally published October 1988, accessed through Marine Corps Association and Foundation.
(89) Von Hardesty, Red Phoenix, p. 218.
(90) Ibid., p. 218.
(91) Coningham Despatch: Operations carried out by the Second Tactical Air Force between 6 June 1944 and 9 May 1945, PRO AIR 37/876, p. 42.
(92) Len Cacutt, Great Aircraft of the World, Colour Library Books, 1988, p. 288.
(93) Hermann Plocher, The German Air Force Versus Russia, 143, USAF Historical Study, No, 155, Arno Press, New York, 1967, p. 270.
(94) Sir Anthony Beevor, Stalingrad 75 Rears On, Urban warfare Conference, 2 February 2018, RUSI, p. 5.
(95) Cited in Von Hardesty, Red Phoenix, p. 105.
(96) Ibid., p. 217.
(97) The Russian Air Force is called the Voyenno-Vozdushnyye Sily, (or VVS), the army aviation Aviatsiya Sukhoputnykh Voysk (ASV) or Armeyskaya Aviatsiya and previously independent Air Defence Force Voiska Protivivozdushnoi Oborony (or VPVO). The exception to this centralisation is the Russian Navy and the Internal Troops of the MVD who retain command of their own aircraft. The drive to consolidate air assets into a single force in December 2003 resulted in the transfer of the helicopter assets to the air force. Their poor performance in the Caucasus led to this being reversed.
(98) Benjamin S Lambert, The Continuing Crisis of Russian Air Power, RAND Corporation, Santa Monica, CA, 2001, p. 3.
(99) Laurie Burkitt, Andrew Scobell and Larry M. Wortzel The Lessons of History: The Chinese People's Liberation Army at 75, Strategic Studies Institute, U.S. Army War College, Carlisle, PA, pp. 106–109.
(100) Missions of the PLA Air Force in Richard O Hallion, Roger Cliff and Philip C. Saunders, Editors. The Chinese Air Force Evolving Concepts, Roles, and Capabilities, Center for the Study of Chinese Military Affairs, National Defense University, Institute for National Strategic Studies, Washington DC, 2012, p. 135.
(101) Richard O Hallion, Roger Cliff and Philip C. Saunders, Editors. The Chinese Air Force Evolving Concepts, Roles, and Capabilities, Center for the Study of Chinese Military Affairs, National Defense University, Institute for National Strategic Studies, Washington DC, 2012, p. xi.
(102) Dr Carlo Kopp, China's Second Artillery Crops, LandWarfare, October 2012.
(103) Richard O Hallion, Roger Cliff and Philip C. Saunders, Editors. The Chinese Air Force, p. 35.
(104) Quotes for the Air Force Logistician, Volume 1, Air Force Logistic Management Agency, Maxwell Air Force Base, Alabama, 2006, p. 99.
(105) Arthur Tedder, With Prejudice: Memoirs of Marshal of the Air Force Lord Tedder, Cassel, London, 1966, p. 175.
(106) Command and control of airpower in irregular warfare. Available from: ttps://www.researchgate.net/publication/44279148_Command_and_control_of_airpower_in_irregular_warfar. Accessed 22 Mar 2016.
(107) Curtis E. Lemay Centre for Doctrinal Development and Education, Annex 3–60, Execution the Planning Cycle, Updated 9 November 2012, p. 3.

(108) Major Mustafa R Koprucu, USAF, The Limits of Decentralization: The Effects of Technology on a Central Airpower Tenet, master's thesis, Air University, Maxwell Air Force Base, Alabama, 2001.
(109) Don Vandergriff, The Myth of Mission Command, How 'Synchronization Warfare' has removed the human from modern warfare, excerpted from Path to Victory: America's Army and the Revolution in Human Affairs at https://medium.com/the-bridge/the-myth-of-mission-command-78b81d7f7987, accessed 13 Sep 2016.
(110) Daniel R Mortensen (Editor), Airpower and Ground Armies: Essays on the Evolution of Anglo-American air doctrine. 1940–1943, Air University Press, Air Force Research Institute Maxwell Air Force Base, Alabama, 1998, p. vi.
(111) IB Holley Jr, A Retrospect on Close air support, in Benjamin Franklin Cooling (Editor), Case Studies in the Development of Close Air Support, Office of Air Force History, United States Air Force, Washington DC, 1990, p. 535.
(112) Brig Gen Alex Grynkewich, The Future of Air Superiority, Part 1, the Imperative, War on the Rocks, 3 January 2017.
(113) LF Ellis, Victory in the West: The Defeat of Germany, HMSO, 1968 Official History, p. 430.
(114) Benjamin S. Lambert, Air Power against Terror, RAND Corporation, Santa Monica, CA, 2005, p. 341.
(115) Von Hardesty, Red Phoenix, p. 169.
(116) John J McGrarth, Fire for Effect: Field Artillery and Close Air Support in the US Army, Combat Studies Institute Press, US Army Combined Arms Centre, Fort Leavenworth, Kansas, 2012, p. 73.
(117) David K. Gerber, Major, USAF, Adaptive Command and Control of Theatre Airpower, master's thesis, Air University, Maxwell Air Force Base, Alabama, 1997.
(118) Colonel Gregory S. Marzolf, Command and Control of Airpower – A New Paradigm for the Future, Air War College, Maxwell Air Force Base, Alabama, February 2009, pp. 41–43.
(119) Robert H Scales, Certain Victory, p. 369.
(120) Richard Simpkin, Race to the Swift, pp. 118–132.
(121) General von Senger und Etterlin quoted in Richard Simpkin, Race to the Swift, p. 117.
(122) The decision to form an aviation branch was not without detractors, particularly from a group of retired generals that included Howze, who was practically the father of American Army aviation. Their rationale was that Army aviation leaders would first lose their understanding of ground operations and aviation's role gained through serving as ground soldiers before becoming aviators. Secondly, like the Air Corps before it, they thought that the new branch would seek out an independent role (deep attack) separate from the combined arms tradition of the other ground branches. John J. McGrath Fire for Effect: Field Artillery and Close Air Support in the US Army, p. 141.
(123) Major General Rudolph Ostovich III, Army Aviation in AirLand Battle Future, Military Review February 1991, p. 28.
(124) Robert H Scales, Certain Victory, pp. 157–160.
(125) The attack is covered elsewhere in greater detail. In sum, the corps-level brigade executed a deep attack against elements of the Iraqi Medina Division south of Baghdad. The intent was to interdict the enemy before they could engage friendly ground forces. In the end the attack was a complete failure, with one helicopter shot down, and all but one of the remaining aircrafts damaged, without any appreciable damage being be done to the Medina Division.
(126) Bruce R. Pirnie, Alan Vick, Adam Grissom, Karl P. Mueller, David T. Orletsky, Beyond Close Support, Forging a New Air-Ground Partnership, RAND Corporation, Santa Monica, CA, 2005, p. 16.
(127) Major General David H. Petraeus, Commanding General, 101st Airborne Division (Air Assault), 101st Airborne Division Commander Live Briefing from Iraq, May 13, 2003.
(128) Steven Komarow, General Recounts Key Moments in Baghdad's Fall, USA Today, April 14, 2003, p. 5.
(129) David E. Johnson, Learning Large Lessons, p. 117.

(130) U.S. Department of the Army, FM1-100, Army Aviation Operations, 1997, p. 3.
(131) Johnson, David E. Learning Large Lessons, pp. 157–174.
(132) Dr Christopher R. Gabel, Seek, Strike and Destroy, US Army Tank Destroyer Doctrine in World War 2, Combat Studies Institute, U.S. Army Command and General Staff College Fort Leavenworth, Kansas, September 1985, p. 2.
(133) Richard E. Simpkin, Tank Warfare London: Brassey's Publishers Limited, 1979, p. 11. Major Vincent K. Brooks Back to the Future: Using Attack Helicopters to Restore Shock to the Battlefield, School of Advanced Military Studies, Fort Leavenworth, Kansas, pp. 37–39.
(134) Etienne de Durand, Benoît Michel and Elie Tenenbaum, Helicopter Warfare. The Future of Airmobility and Rotary Wing Combat, Focus stratégique, Number 32 bis, January 2012, p. 19.
(135) F.M. von Senger und Etterlln, 'New Operational Dimensions', RUSI Journal, London: Royal United Services Institute, 2 June 1983, p. 12.
(136) Carl von Clausewitz, On War, p. 265.
(137) Archer Jones, The Art of War in the Western World, University of Illinois Press, Illinois, 2001, p. 600.
(138) Dr. Phillip A. Karber 'Lessons Learned' from the Russo-Ukrainian War, Draft Personal Observations, Johns Hopkins Applied Physics Laboratory & U.S. Army Capabilities Center (ARCIC) 8 July 2015, pp. 34–35.
(139) Richard A. Gabriel, Operation Peace for Galilee: The Israeli-PLO War in Lebanon New York, NY: Hill and Wang Publishers, 1984, p. 212.
(140) Chris Bellamy, The Future of Land Warfare, New York, NY: St. Martin's Press, 1987, p. 29.
(141) Steven Z Starr, The Union Cavalry in the Civil War, Volume 2, Louisiana State University Press, Louisiana, pp. 426 and 432.
(142) Paddy Griffith, Battle Tactics of the American Civil War, pp. 186–8.
(143) Matthew Allen, Military Helicopter Doctrines of the Major Powers, 1945–1992: Making Decisions about Air-Land Warfare, Westport, CT: Greenwood Press, 1993, p. 74.
(144) Ibid., p. 94.
(145) Etienne de Durand, Benoît Michel and Elie Tenenbaum, 'Helicopter Warfare. The Future of Airmobility and Rotary Wing Combat', Focus stratégique, Number 32 bis, January 2012, p. 7.
(146) Department of the Army, Field Manual 1–111, Aviation Brigades, Department of the Army, Government Printing Office, Washington DC: 1997, Table of Contents; Field Manual 3-04.111, Aviation Brigades, Department of the Army, Government Printing Office, Washington DC, 2003, pp. 3–6.
(147) Geoffrey A. McLaughlin, Steven M. Pierce, and David A. Smith, Army Aviation's Evolution to Sustained Operations, Army, June 2004, pp. 62 and 64. AC Schilleci, A Deadly Combination: Integration of the AH-64D M-TADS and High Altitude Tactics on the Modern Battlefield, Infantry, May-June 2008, pp. 21–22.
(148) Jomini, Baron de., Summary of The Art of War, or A New Analytical Compendium translated. Major O. F. Winship and Lieutenant E. E. McLean, New York: Putnam, 1854, p. 41.
(149) Judges 1.19 describes the Philistine advantage in conventional warfare, on the open plains, as due to superior conventional weapons, including chariots. This forced the Israelites to rely upon guerrilla tactics from the hills.
(150) Vincent J Goulding Jr, Back to the Future with Asymmetric Warfare, Parameters, 30, Number 4, 2000, pp. 21–30.
(151) Clausewitz's earlier lectures on small wars (the Kleinkrieg) and guerrilla warfare (the Volkskreig) are integrated into his short passage 'The People in Arms'. Werner Hahlweg, Clausewitz and Guerrilla Warfare, in Clausewitz and Modern Strategy, ed. Michael Handel, Frank Case, London, 1986, pp. 128–131. Also, Carl von Clausewitz, On War, ed. and trans. Michael Howard and Peter Paret, Princeton University Press, Princeton, NJ, 1976, pp. 479–483.

(152) Dave Kilcullen, Two Schools of Classical Counter-insurgency, Small Wars Journal, SWJ Blog Post 27 January, 2007 – 9:32pm.
(153) Calibrating the use of force is not specific to counter-insurgency; it is central to the whole, largely Western, tradition of moderating war's impact. It is necessary to counteract war's enduring nature, which encourages escalation. Carefully applying firepower so that a political objective is achieved without undue casualties, of course aids the transition to peace, the ultimate purpose of war. Calibrating force is the rationale behind the pyramid of escalation – display, show and then finally use of force – that has considerable utility in limited conflicts, such peace support operations.
(154) Army FM 3-24 and Marine Warfighting Publication 3-33.5, pp. 1–38.
(155) The war diary of Gunner James Daniel Lamb, F Troop, 93rd Fd Bty, 25 Regt RA, accessed 1 Oct 2017. www.britains-smallwars.com/malaya/ Malaya-25field%20reg/25_fieldregt.html.
(156) Riley Sunderland, Army Operations in Malaya, 1947–1960, Rand, Santa Monica, California, 1964, pp. 152–155.
(157) Major Scott R. McMichael Historical Perspective on Light Infantry, Research Survey, 1987, p. 115.
(158) Riley Sunderland, p. 238.
(159) Ibid., p. 224.
(160) Robert Taber, War of the flea: the classic study of guerrilla warfare, Brassey's, 2002, pp. 140–1.
(161) Robert Jackson, The Malayan Emergency and Indonesian Confrontation: The Commonwealth's Wars 1948–1966, Pen and Sword, London, 2008, pp. 28–3.
(162) Charters, D., & Tugwell, M. From Palestine to Northern Ireland: British adaptation to low-intensity operations: A comparative analysis. London: Brassey's Defence Publishers, 1989, p. 195.
(163) Clutterbuck, Richard, Conflict and Violence in Singapore and Malaysia 1945–83. Singapore: Graham Brash, 1985.
(164) David French, The British Approach in Counter-Insurgency 1945–67, Oxford, 2011, pp. 215–18.
(165) Karl Hack, The Malayan Emergency as Counter-insurgency Paradigm, Journal of Strategic Studies 32, Number 3, 2009, p. 22.
(166) Richard B. Johnson, Major, US Army, The Biggest Stick: The Employment of Artillery Units in Counter-insurgency, Command and General Staff College Fort Leavenworth, Kansas, 2011, p. 191.
(167) Bill Bailey, Hearts and Minds, Psuedo Gangs and Counter Insurgency: Based upon Experiences from Previous Campaigns in Kenya (1952–60), Malaya (1948–60) & Rhodesia (1964–1979), Australia Counter Insurgency Conference, 2010, p. 7.
(168) Frank Kitson, Low Intensity Operations, Faber and Faber, London, 1973, p. 136.
(169) Doctor Christina Goulter, Counter-insurgency: a Question of Victory, Defence-in-Depth, King's College London. She identifies 71 counter-insurgencies since World War Two. Largely enemy-centric counter-insurgency tactics were used in a one-third of these conflicts. Only about a half of the insurgencies were defeated. Notably, enemy-centric counter-insurgencies has a superior conversion rate to long-term peace and stability than the more people-centric approach.
(170) Greek communist guerrilla forces numbered less than 20,000 armed men. They successfully cut the country in two. Its defeat required a Greek army of several hundred thousand men, with significant foreign support. A crucial factor was the decision by Yugoslavia to cease providing a safe shelter to the insurgents. The three years of military and political pacification, and of economic reconstruction, cost about $2 billion. This was somewhere between 100 and 1,000 times what the Communists had spent.
(171) Michael Burleigh, Small Wars, Far Away Places, Pan Books, London, 2003, pp. 197–8. See also: Benjamin Grob-Fitzgibbon, Imperial Endgame, Britain's Dirty Wars and the End of Empire, London, 2011, pp. 6 and 150–1.
(172) D Galula, Counter-insurgency warfare: theory and practice. Westport, CT, USA.: Praeger Trade, 2006, p. 64.
(173) CE Callwell, Small Wars: Their Principles and Practice, Albion, London 2016, p. 91.

(174) David H. Ucko and Robert Egnell, Counter-insurgency in crisis: Britain and the challenges of modern warfare, Columbia University Press, 2013, p. 99.
(175) Mark Urban, Task Force Black.
(176) David Betz, Carnage and Connectivity, Landmarks in the Decline of Conventional Military Power, London, 2015, p. 111.
(177) Army FM 3-24 and Marine Warfighting Publication 3-33.5, 9–43.
(178) Patrick B Johnston, The Effectiveness of Leadership Decapitation in Combating Insurgencies, Quarterly Journal: International Security, Harvard Kennedy School, 2012. Daniel Byman, Do Targeted Killings Work? Foreign Affairs 85, no. 2, March/April 2006, pp. 95–111. Bryan C Price, Targeting Top Terrorists: How Leadership Decapitation Contributes to Counterterrorism, International Security 36, no. 4 Spring 2012, pp. 9–46.
(179) Michael Burleigh, Small Wars, Far Away Places, Pan Books, London, 2003, p. 17.
(180) Boyd L. Dastrup, King of Battle, p. 283.
(181) Bruce I Gudmundsson, On Artillery, 1993, p. 151.
(182) CE Callwell, Small Wars: Their Principles and Practice, p. 433.
(183) The three principal tactics employed by insurgents are: the propaganda of the deed, the creation of a parallel state structures to replace government authority and the strategy of provocation.
(184) Robert Perkins, Air power in Afghanistan How NATO changed the rules, 2008–2014, Action on Armed Violence, p. 23.
(185) Airpower caused 552 of 2,118 total civilian deaths in 2008, compared to 118 of 2,959 total civilian deaths in 2013. Afghanistan: Annual Report 2013: Protection of Civilians in Armed Conflict, UNAMA, February 2014, http://unama.unmissions.org/Portals/UNAMA/ human%20rights/ Feb_8_2014_PoC-report_2013-Full-report-ENG. pdf (accessed 22 December 2014).
(186) Raymond L Garthoff, How Russian Makes War, Soviet Military Doctrine, G. Allen & Unwin, London, 1954, p. 20.
(187) Ibid., p. 11.
(188) Sir Robert Grainger Ker Thompson, Defeating Communist Insurgency: The Lessons of Malaya and Vietnam: Studies in international security, Chatto & Windus, London, 1966, p. 51.
(189) Insights and Best Practices Focus Paper on Integration and Synchronization of Joint Fires, fourth edition, J7 Deputy Director for Joint Training, July 2018, p. 3.
(190) Quoted in Brian Farrell, Churchill and the Lion City: Shaping Modern Singapore, NUS Press, 2013, p. 101.
(191) The Chairman of the Joint Chief of Staff, General John M Shalikashvili, US Army, created America's first joint doctrine directive in the summer of 1994. British Defence Doctrine was first published in 1996.
(192) Center for Army Lessons Learned, Deep Battle Observations Part 1, 1992, 26, On-line. Internet, 19 December 1996. Available from http:/www-leav-akn.army.mil:1100/efsweb/ webfile/call.html.
(193) Stephen Biddle, Military Power, p. 51.
(194) Robert H Scales, Certain Victory, p. 174.
(195) Dr Richard P Hallion, Battlefield Air Support, A Retrospective Assessment, Airpower Journal, Spring 1990.
(196) Robert Leonhard, The Principles of War for the Information Age, Random House, New York, 2009, preface.

Chapter 7: Fixed Wing Aircraft Delivered Firepower

(1) Cyril Falls, The Nature of Modern Warfare. OUP, New York, 1941, p. 28.
(2) Karl Builder, Icarus Syndrome, Air Power Theory and the Evolution of the Air Force, RAND Corporation, Santa Monica, CA, 1994.

(3) The historian Norman Stone sees the 1911 War as having greater significance, opining that Italy's invasion of Ottoman Libya was the starting-pistol for World War One. Norman Stone, A Short History of WW1, Penguin, London, 2013, p. xvii.
(4) US 12th Army Group, 12th Army Group Report of Operations, (Final After Action Report), Vol II, Anti-Aircraft Artillery, Armoured, Artillery, Chemical warfare and Signals Sections, United States, 1945, p. 61.
(5) Cited in Amy Butler, USAF Eyes New Era Of Close Air Support, U.S. Air Force's campaign to reinvent CAS, Aviation Week & Space Technology – Defense Technology Edition, 30 March 2015.
(6) Susan Mercer Williams and Frank J. Mirande, When the Chips are Down.... A Historical Sketch of Close Air Support, Lockheed Aeronautical Systems Company, Marietta, GA, 1988, p. 1.
(7) John McGrath, Fire for Effect, p. 39.
(8) Shelford Bidwell & Dominic Graham, Fire-Power, p. 142.
(9) Jonathan M House, Combined warfare in the 20th Century, p. 45.
(10) Correlli Barnett, Shelford Bidwell, Brian Bond, John Harding and John Terraine, Old Battles and New Defences, pp. 29–30.
(11) Stephen Budiansky, Air Power: The Men, Machines, and Ideas That Revolutionized War, from Kitty Hawk to Gulf War II, Penguin Group (USA), New York, 2004, p. 305.
(12) Colin S Gray, Airpower for Strategic Effect, p. 280. An insight he attributes to Philip Meilinger.
(13) Stephen Biddle, Afghanistan And The Future Of Warfare: Implications For Army And Defense Policy, Strategic Studies Institutes, London, 2002, pp. 26–33.
(14) David E. Johnson, Learning Large Lessons, p. 24.
(15) John Schlight, The War in South Vietnam: The Years of the Offensive, 1965–1968, Office of Air Force History, Washington, DC, 1988, p. 215.
(16) Examples of the failure of largely airborne surveillance in the Gulf War include the capture of Khafji in Saudi Arabia by Iraqi forces that had occurred before Coalition forces reacted. The same can be said for the counterattack on the US Marines at Burqan, and the movement of a five-division strong blocking force against VII Corps. In the Iraq War, the most significant failure was the undetected movement of three Iraqi Republican Guard divisions around Baghdad; this went unnoticed until they contacted the American V Corps.
(17) Peter A. Costello, A Matter Of Trust: Close air support Apportionment and Allocation for Operational Level Effects, A Thesis Presented to the Faculty of the School of Advanced Airpower Studies, Air University, Maxwell Air Force Base, Alabama, 1995, p. 91.
(18) Rebecca Grant, The Clash About Close Air Support, Air Force Magazine Online, January 2003, pp. 3–4.
(19) Cited in Merrill A McPeak, Presentation to the Commission on Roles and Missions of the Armed Forces, Chief of Staff US Air Force, Washington, DC, 1994, p. 117.
(20) Rebecca Grant, The Clash About close air support, p. 5.
(21) Arthur P. Brill Jr., Close air support: More improvement is needed, Seapower, November, 2003, p. 1.
(22) T. Michael Moseley, Lt Gen, USAF Commander, United States Central Air Forces. Operation Iraqi freedom – By The Numbers. Assessment and Analysis Division, Prince Sultan Air Base, Kingdom of Saudi Arabia: CENTAF, 30 April 2003, p. 5. Colonel Gregory Fontenot, Lieutenant Colonel E. J. Degen, and Lieutenant Colonel David Tohn, On Point: The United States Army in Operation Iraqi Freedom, Center for Army Lessons Learned, Fort Leavenworth, Kansas, 2004, pp. 249–250.
(23) Ahead of the line of contact there are a number of control methods; NATO largely uses 'kill-boxes' to provide battlespace to the air component for them to freely prosecute targets. Sandra I Erwin, Close Air Support Tactics Sharpened in Iraq, National Defence, June 2003.
(24) Charles E Kirkpatrick, Joint Fires as They Were Meant to be: V Corps and the 4th Air Support Operations Group During Operation Iraqi Freedom, A National Security Affairs Paper Published

on Occasion by The Institute of Land Warfare, Association of the United States Army, Arlington, Virginia, 2004, pp. 12–18.
(25) Major Michael H. Johnson, USMC, Cleared to Engage, Improving the Effectiveness of Joint Close Air Support, Air & Space Power Journal Summer, 2008.
(26) Mike Benitez, How Afghanistan Distorted Close Air Support and Why it Matters, War on the Rocks, 29 June 2016.
(27) Cited in Peter C Smith, Dive Bomber, Aircraft, Techniques and Tactics of World War Two, Stackpole Books, Mechanicsburg, PA, 1982, p. 5.
(28) Weapons and Ordinance PS106IS Armed Forces Primer (v 1.0), p. 12. www.army.mil.
(29) Benjamin S. Lambeth, Airpower Against Terror, RAND Corporation, Santa Monica, CA, 2005. http://www.rand.org/content/dam/rand/pubs/monographs/2006/RAND_MG166-1.pdf.
(30) Michael Peck Did Russia Really Build a Smarter Smart Bomb? The National Interest, March 14, 2016.
(31) Pierre M. Sprey, Notes on Close air support, Intrec Inc. Internal Study, Potomac, MD, May 1974 p. 9.
(32) Benjamin Franklin Cooling (Ed), Case Studies in the Development of Close Air Support, p. 136.
(33) Kenneth T. Stefanek, Major, USAF. The Accuracy of the Joint Direct Attack Munitions in an Operational Environment. Master of Aeronautical Science graduate research project, Embry-Riddle Aeronautical University, Nellis Air Force Base Campus. 1997, p. 9.
(34) Benjamin S Lambert, The Transformation of American Airpower, p. 78.
(35) TA Hughes, Overlord, General Pete Quesada and the Triumph of Tactical Airpower in World War II, Free Press, New York, 1991, p. 130.
(36) A study of P-47 fighter-bomber attacks on the Savio River bridges established: against no flak a CEP of 60 yards (55m) could be expected, this resulted in one bomb out of 30 hitting a bridge; a medium level of flak pushed this up to a CEP to 100 yards (92m) and 84 bombs to achieve one hit on the bridge; while heavy flak pushed up the CEP to 140 yards (128m) and 164 bombs per hit. Stephen Budiansky, Air Power, Penguin, New York, 2004, p. 305.
(37) Bill Sweetman, The Great Book of Modern Aircraft, Portland House, New York, 1987.
(38) Pierre M. Sprey, Notes on Close air support, Intrec Inc. Internal Study, Potomac, MD, 1974, p. 24.
(39) United States Air Force Major Greg Defoe quoted in Sandra I Erwin, Close Air Support Tactics Sharpened in Iraq, National Defence, June 2003.
(40) Raoul Archambault and Thomas M. Dean, Ending the Close Air Support Controversy, Naval War College, Newport, Rhode Island, 21 June 1991, p. 5.
(41) Karl-Heinz Frieser, Le mythe de la guerre-éclair, Paris, Belin, 2003. Cited in Elie Tenenbaum, The Battle over Fire Support. The close air support Challenge and the Future of Artillery, Focus stratégique, Number 35 bis, October 2012, p. 370.
(42) Elie Tenenbaum, The Battle over Fire Support, p. 432.
(43) Robert H Scales, Firepower in Limited War, p. 18.
(44) John J. Sbrega, Southeast Asia, in Benjamin Franklin Cooling (Ed), Case Studies in the Development of Close Air Support, Office of Air Force History, United States Air Force, Washington DC, 1990, p. 411.
(45) Benjamin S Lambert, The Transformation of American Airpower, p. 22.
(46) Pierre M. Sprey, Notes on Close air support, p. 12.
(47) Dr Richard P Hallion, Battlefield Air Support, A Retrospective Assessment, Airpower Journal, Spring 1990.
(48) Martin Van Crefeld, the Age of Airpower, Public Affairs, New York, 2011, pp. 431–2.
(49) Bruce R. Pirnie, Alan Vick, Adam Grissom, Karl P. Mueller, David T. Orletsky, Beyond Close Support, Forging a New Air-Ground Partnership, RAND Corporation, Santa Monica, CA, 2005, p. 21.

(50) Benny Mehr, The Lessons Regarding Statistical Artillery, IsraeliDefence, 20 June 2018.

(51) Michel Goya, Les Fantômes Furieux de Falloujah. Opération Al-Fajr/Phantom Fury (Juillet-Novembre 2004), Paris, Centre de Doctrine d'Emploi des Forces, Ministère de la Défense, 2006, p. 100. Cited in Elie Tenenbaum, The Battle over Fire Support. The close air support Challenge and the Future of Artillery, Focus stratégique, Number 35 bis, October 2012.

(52) IsraeliDefense, The Ground Forces can utilize all the Capabilities of IAF. 3/06/2015.

(53) Mike Benitez, How Afghanistan Distorted Close Air Support and Why it Matters, War on the Rocks, 29 June 2016.

(54) Benjamin Fernandes, The future of close air support is not what the air force thinks, War on the Rocks, 18 June 2015.

(55) Joint Publication 3-09.3 Joint Tactics, Techniques, and Procedures for Close air support. The conditions for effective close air support are: (1) effective training and proficiency, (2) planning and integration, (3) command, control, and communications, (4) air superiority, (5) target marking and acquisition, (6) streamlined and flexible procedures, (7) appropriate ordnance, and (8) favourable weather.

(56) Von Hardesty, Red Phoenix, p. 252.

(57) An Air Force study conducted in the 1960s concluded that the ideal close air support aircraft should have the following qualities:

- Able to operate out of short, primitive airfields.
- Reliable and easy to maintain in the field under wartime conditions.
- Able to carry large amounts of ordnance and specifically must be able to kill armour.
- Have sufficient range to loiter 'on call' near the battlefield, and when needed it should have enough remaining endurance to find the target, identify and confirm that it is, indeed, enemy rather than friendly, and then destroy it.
- Must fly at least 350 knots but be manoeuvrable enough to turn tightly over the battlefield so that the pilot will not lose sight of the target when visibility is low.
- It must be survivable; it should be able to take damage from ground fire and still return to base with a healthy pilot.
- It should be a low-cost airplane in comparison to the price of a supersonic jet fighters.

Source: William L. Smallwood, Warthog: Flying the A-10 in the Gulf War, Brassey's, New York, 1993, pp. 10–11.

(58) Yefim Gordon and Alan Dawes, Russian Air Power, Airlife, 2002, p. 31.

(59) Thom Shanker, Russians Melded Old School Blitz With Modern Military Tactics, New York Times, August 16, 2008.

(60) Dan Goure, Jihadi Terror Creates New Global Market For Close Air Support Aircraft, 9 May 2016, The National Interest.

(61) Adolph Galland, The First and the Last, Henry Holt & Company, New York, 1954, p. 29.

(62) Kenneth A. Steadman, A Comparative Look at Air-Ground Support Doctrine and Practice in World War II, Combat Studies Institute, US Army Command and General Staff College, Fort Leavenworth, Kansas, 1 September 1982.

(63) James A. Huston, Tactical Use of Air Power in World War II: The Army Experience, Military Review 31, Number 7, July 1952, pp. 166–68.

(64) The capability step change was the fielding by the Americans of the Lantirn pod set. This comprised of a Navigation Pod containing an advanced J-band terrain-following radar, and navigation Forward Looking Infra-Red projecting on to the HUD, and a Targeting Pod with a two field of views bore-sighted with a laser designator/rangefinder. By fitting two pods fighter-bombers acquired a similar precision attack capability as a dedicated bomber, such as the F-111 fitted with Pave Tack.

(65) Dave Majumdar, The Russian Air Force Was Always Behind the West in One Key Area (Until Now), The National Interest, 11 May 2016.
(66) Benjamin Franklin Cooling (Ed), Case Studies in the Development of Close Air Support, p. 329.
(67) John J. Sullivan, The Botched Air Support Operation Cobra, Parametres 18, Number 1 March 1988.
(68) Dr Richard P Hallion, Battlefield Air Support, A Retrospective Assessment, Airpower Journal, Spring 1990.
(69) William L. Smallwood, Warthog: Flying the A-10 in the Gulf War, Brassey's New York, 1993, p. 205.
(70) Benjamin S Lambert, The Transformation of American Airpower, p. 124.
(71) Riley Sunderland, Evolution of Command and Control Doctrine for Close Air Support, Office of Air Force History, Washington DC, March 1973, p. 10.
(72) Lt Col Eric E. Theisen, Ground-Aided Precision Strike: Heavy Bomber Activity in Operation Enduring Freedom, Air University Press, Air Force Research Institute Maxwell Air Force Base, Alabama, 2003, p. 1.
(73) Air Force Chief of Staff Mark Welsh quoted in Amy Butler, USAF Eyes New Era Of Close air support, U.S. Air Force's campaign to reinvent close air support, Aviation Week & Space Technology – Defense Technology Edition Mar 30, 2015.
(74) Critics Accuse Air Force of Manipulating Data to Support A-10 Retirement by Dan Sagyan May 22, 2014 at 2:50 PM EST. This article records the dispute over the evidence provided by Air Force Secretary Deborah Lee James provided the House Armed Services Committee.
(75) John Matsumura, John Gordon IV, Randall Steeb, Defining an Approach for Future Air Support Capability, RAND Corporation, Santa Monica, CA, 2017, pp. 9–12.
(76) Mike Benitez, 21st Century Forward Air Control: The Roots to rebuild, War on the Rocks, 1 March 2017.
(77) During the Wars of 9/11, to achieve competence, the American Red Flag wargames and the Air Force's Weapons School were changed to emphasise close air support. All types of aircraft now participate in the Army's Air Warrior exercises to both improve their skill and increase the level of trust that ground forces have in air support from outside the A-10 community. The fighter-bomber and in particular the B-1 and B-52 communities learnt from the expertise within the A-10 pilot community.
(78) Christopher Robbins, The Ravens: The Men Who Flew in America's Secret War in Laos, Crown Publishers, New York, 1987, p. 411.
(79) Dr Richard P Hallion, Battlefield Air Support.
(80) Richard Lewis, The Art of Strafing, Air Force Magazine, July 2007.
(81) John T. Correl, ed., More Data From Desert Storm, Air Force Magazine 79, Number 1, January 1996, pp. 62–66.
(82) Benjamin Franklin Cooling (Ed), Case Studies in the Development of Close Air Support, p. 15.
(83) Sydney J Freedberg Jr, Russians Close the Gap for A2/AD, Air Force Gen. Frank Gorenc, Breaking Defence, on September 14, 2015 at 10:36am.
(84) Martin Van Crefeld, the Age of Airpower, pp. 423–426.
(85) Martin, How Much Does the F-35 Cost? Producing, Operating and Supporting a 5th Generation Fighter, https://www.f35.com/about/cost, accessed 30 Sep 18.
(86) Norman R Augustine, Augustine's Law, Penguin, New York, 1986, p. 143.
(87) Mitch Ginsburg, A year on, army looks to last Gaza war for lessons on fighting the next one Israel has watched Hamas change tack, so it may have a chance to prepare better for a seemingly inevitable future conflict, The Times of Israel, July 7, 2015, 8:46pm.
(88) David Gates, Sky War: A History of Military Airspace Power, Reaktion Books, London 2003, p. 22.
(89) Peter C. Smith, Close Air Support: An Illustrated History, 1914 to the Present, NY, 1990, p. 8.

(90) As an example, the US 8th Air Force Lost/Damaged Aircraft per 100 Sorties over Germany was:

Time Period	Total Lost	Hit by Enemy Fighters	Hit by Enemy Flak
January–June 1943	5.5	14.2	16.8
June–December 1943	4.1	7.4	21.4
January–May 1944	2.6	2.2	23.3
Source: W.A. Hewitt, Planting the Seeds of SEAD, Air University: Maxwell Air Base, 1992, p. 5.			

(91) Donald Nijboer, Flak in World War II, Stackpole Books, 2018, p. x.
(92) Dr Richard P Hallion, Battlefield Air Support.
(93) The Russian General Staff Translated and Edited by Lester W. Grau and Michael A. Gress, The Soviet-Afghan War, How a Superpower Fought and Lost, Modern War Studies, University Press of Kansas, 2002, p. 213.
(94) Bill Sweetman, Close Air Support: What Works and What Doesn't, Defense Technology International, October 2008.
(95) In 1982 the Israelis claim of 80 Syrian planes in air-to-air combat for no loss, and the destruction of 30 Syrian anti-aircraft missile batteries – for the loss of only a single aircraft. A significant reversal from ground based air defence's superiority over aircraft in the 1973 War.
(96) Dr Carlo Copp, Surviving the Modern Integrated Air Defence System, Air Power Australia, 3 February 2009.
(97) Elie Tenenbaum, Death From Below: New SAM Threats and the Future of Western Airpower, Airpower Leading Edge, Ultimo Ratio, 26 May 2015.
(98) Major Peter W. Mattes, USAF, What is a Modern Integrated Air Defense System, Air Force Magazine, 1 October 2019.
(99) Martin Van Creveld makes a similar point about the actual strategic effect of land fighting systems: 'though today's Abrams and Leopards and Challengers and T72 are individually much more powerful that the Shermans and Tigers and Cruisers and T34 of World War II, as instruments of war and conquest they may be less effective'. His reasons include a mix of tactical and technical changes, but mainly their reduced numbers. Martin Van Creveld, Technology and War, From 2000BC to the Present, The Free Press, London, 1991, p. 282

Chapter 8: Aviation Firepower

(1) Richard Simpkin, Race to the Swift, p. 130.
(2) James Gavin, Cavalry and I Don't Mean Horses, Harper's, April 1954, pp. 54–60.
(3) For the culture of the newly formed US Air Force see: Benjamin S. Lambeth, The Transformation of American Air Power, Ithaca, Cornell University Press. For the American Army reactions see: Elie Tenenbaum, The Battle over Fire Support.
(4) The Key West Agreement is the colloquial name for the policy paper Function of the Armed Forces and the Joint Chiefs of Staff drafted by James V Forrestal, the first United States Secretary of Defence. Its enduring feature was the division of air assets between the Army, Navy (who represented the USMC), and the newly created Air Force that, with modifications, continues to provide the basis for the division of these assets in the U.S. military today.
(5) Cited in Lieutenant General James M. Gavin, War and Peace in the Space Age, Harper & Brothers, NY, 1958, pp. 109–11.
(6) Richard P. Hallion, Battlefield Air Support: A Time for Retrospective Assessment, Headquarters Air Force Systems Command/SDP Andrews Air Force Base, Md, 17 February 1989, p. 37.
(7) Roger J. Spitter (General Editor), Combined Arms in Battle Since 1939, U.S. Army Command and General Staff College Press Fort Leavenworth, Kansas, 1992, p. 35.

(8) Jonathan M House, Combined warfare in the 20th Century, p. 238.
(9) Etienne de Durand, Benoît Michel and Elie Tenenbaum, Helicopter Warfare. The Future of Airmobility and Rotary Wing Combat, Focus stratégique, Number 32 bis, January 2012, p. 19.
(10) In Gulf War, Apaches had a mission capable rate of 30% due to problems with sand. In comparison, in normal conditions the AH-64A averages 80% availability and the AH-64D 84%.
(11) Michael R. Gordon and Bernard E. Trainor, The General's War, Little Brown and Company, Boston, 1995, pp. 403–404.
(12) Anthony H. Cordesman, The strengths and Weaknesses of the A-64 Apache and other attack helicopters, The Iraq War, Strategy, Tactics and Military Lessons, CSIS, Washington, 2003, pp. 317–332.
(13) Steven Komarow, General Recounts Key Moments in Baghdad's Fall, USA Today, April 14, 2003, p. 5.
(14) Department of the Army, Army Concept Team in Vietnam: Final Report, Evaluation of the AH1G, pp. II–6.
(15) Mark Bowden, Black Hawk Down: A Story of Modern War, New York, Atlantic Monthly Press, 1999.
(16) Dr Carlo Kopp, Helicopter combat survivability, DefenceToday, 2009, ausairpower.net, p. 39.
(17) Bruce R. Nardulli, Walter L. Perry, Bruce Pirnie, John Gordon IV and John G. McGinn, Disjointed War: Military Operations in Kosovo, RAND Corporation, Santa Monica, CA, 1999, p. 95.
(18) Colin S Gray, Airpower for Strategic Effect, p. 236.
(19) Marvin B. Schaffer, Concerns About Terrorists With Manportable SAMS, RAND Corporation Reports, Santa Monica, CA, October 1993.
(20) Nikolay Yakubovich, Russia's combat helicopters. From Omega to Alligator, Moscow, Yuza & Eksmo, 2010, pp. 164–173.
(21) Chris Bellamy, Red God of War, p. 198.
(22) The Mi-24 Hind's official acceptance into the Soviet military in 1972 follows the Cobra (1967) by only 5 years and predates that of the Apache (1986) by 14 years.
(23) Richard Simpkin, Race to the Swift, p. 126.
(24) Olga Oliker, Russia's Chechen Wars 1994–2000: Lessons from Urban Combat, RAND Corporation, Santa Monica, CA, December 2000, p. 56.
(25) Marcel de Haas, The Use Of Russian Airpower In The Second Chechen War, Conflict Studies Research Centre, January 2003, pp. 6 and 20.
(26) Z-10 Attack Helicopter, China, Army-Technology.com.
(27) Zhao Lei, Tank Destroyers Targeted by Modernization, China Daily, 17 November 2015.
(28) David E. Johnson, Learning Large Lessons, p. 76.
(29) Ben Farmer, US throws Apache helicopter gunships into fight against Isil, Daily Telegraph, 15 June 2015.
(30) Robert H Scales, Certain Victory, p. 369.
(31) Ibid., p. 369.
(32) Sydney J Freedburg Jnr, Tanks up, Choppers Down, Artillery WAY Up In the Army's Old School 2019 Budget, BreakingDefence, February 12, 2018, 5.13pm.
(33) The original OH-58A was fielded in 1968 as an interim replacement for the cancelled Hughes OH-6 Cayuse. Later the Army cancelled the high-speed Lockheed AH-56 Cheyenne as costs rose steeply. Three decades later, the Army also cancelled the Sikorsky Boeing RAH-66 Comanche. This was followed by a failed conversion of the Bell 407 into an armed reconnaissance helicopter. Subsequent plans to launch the Armed Aerial Scout (AAS) acquisition programme also were scrapped by the Army. Finally, the OH-58D was retired without, as at 2020, a direct replacement.
(34) Meet the Army's New Helicopter: Future Attack Reconnaissance Aircraft, The National Interest, March 27, 2019.

Chapter 9: Tube Artillery

(1) Gil Eliot, p. 133.
(2) Old Battles and New Defences, Corelli Barnett, Shelford Bidwell, Brian Bond, John Harding and John Terraine. Brassey's Defence Publications, p. 115.

(3) Christopher Duffy, The Army of Frederick the Great, p. 120.

(4) Major General Heinz Guderian, Achtung-Panzer! The Development of Armoured Forces, Their Tactics and Operational Potential, Brockhampton Press, 1999, p. 169.

(5) The self-propelled anti-aircraft gun led the way, with commercial models available from Ehrhardt and Krupp from 1906. The Italians fielded a significant number of 75mm road-bound truck mounted guns in World War One. Late in the War, the Americans, British and French converted tanks to carry artillery across no-man's land. Colonel HCB Rogers, Artillery Through the Ages, The Military Book Society, 1971, pp. 170–171. In the 1920s the British experimented with the Birch Gun, an 18pdr mounted on a pedestal allowing 360-degree engagement and elevation up to 90 degrees, on top of a tracked chassis. Its cancellation was more the result of financial than design considerations. Shelford Bidwell & Dominic Graham, Fire-Power: British Army Weapons and Theories of War 1904–1945, George Allen & Urwin, London, 1982, pp. 173–4.

(6) Brigadier ML Pemberton MC, p. 312.

(7) In 1973 the 152mm 2S3 was introduced; the next year the 122mm 2S1. By the end of the decade there were self-propelled versions of the 203mm gun (2S7) and 240mm mortar (2S4). The long-range 130mm gun was supplemented and then replaced by the 2S5, a turretless 152mm gun on a tracked chassis.

(8) Anthony H. Cordesman and Martin Kleiber, Chinese Military Modernization and Force Development, August 2006, pp. 45–46. IISS Military Balance, 1985–2015.

(9) The M109 A7 or Paladin Integrated Management (PIM) is on a new chassis featuring substantial commonality with the Bradley family of vehicles. In addition to this automotive enhancement it has the following improvements on the current M109A6 Paladin:

- Electric elevation and traverse mechanisms and electric rammer;
- Improved force protection and survivability with capacity for add-on armour (belly and side);
- Fully network capable; and
- Traverse modifications allowing significantly faster pivot steer (by about 30 seconds) when firing out-of-sector missions than the M109A6.

(10) Krauss-Maffei Wegmann Pazerhaubitze 2000 (PzH 2000), Jane's Armour and Artillery, updated February 7, 2012.

(11) The NLOS-C had an auto-loader (from the Crusader), a more modern 155mm gun, a hybrid-electric engine (to reduce fuel consumption), and a 2-man crew compared to 5 in the contemporary M109 and the 4 in its latest version. Of course, it is debatable whether a 2-man crew can sustain round the clock operations, plus maintenance, standing guard and resupply. The latter is particularly challenging given that the gun's on-board ammunition load was only 24-rounds. Nonetheless it demonstrates a step towards making artillery more manpower efficient.

(12) Wheeled vehicles are becoming closer in performance to tracked ones largely due to commercial investment in technological improvements. This has led to ride-height-adjustable, independent suspensions, central tyre inflation, antilock braking systems, stability control, and lockable differentials.

(13) Brigadier ML Pemberton MC, p. 139.

(14) The CH-53E heavy-lift helicopter can lift the Caesar when it reduces from its combat weight of 18.5 tonnes to its airmobile weight of 16.2 tonnes. The crew, support tools and crucially ammunition will of course be in another load.

(15) Alan J. Vick, David T. Orletsky, John Bordeaux and David A. Shlapak, Air Power's Contribution Against Light Infantry, 1996, RAND Corporation, Santa Monica, CA, p. 49. This works on the assumption that takes between five and ten minutes to occupy a new position and recommence engaging a target.

(16) IHS Jane's Defence Weekly, volume 53, issue 22, 1 Jun 2016, p. 37.

(17) Brigadier ML Pemberton MC, p. 313

(18) 18th Airborne Corps Artillery's Brigadier General Mark T. Kimmitt initiated an operational needs statement on 19 February 2003 for a truck mounted medium-weight, highly deployable field artillery

system capable of providing direct and general support to any contingency or follow-on manoeuvre force. Following an extensive debate, the Americans decided to keep their tracked/towed mix.

(19) Israeli Armour, Artillery Corps Shifting Emphasis Revamp Agendas in Common Bid To Boost Firepower, Manoeuvre Defence News Mar. 9, 2014 – 03:45am.

(20) Israeli companies vie for $1B artillery upgrade contracts, UPI, Defence News, OCT. 29, 2013/ 2:20pm.

(21) Being short of manpower, Israel has always been interested in reducing crew size. In 1977, they developed an improvement of the M109 based on a Merkava chassis (Sholef) whose key characteristic was its self-loading ability, which reduced the number of crewmen from 7 to 4. The project's high cost prevented its introduction.

(22) Yuval Azulay_Elbit selected to develop IDF artillery capability, Globes [online], Israel Business News – www.globes-online.com – on April 4, 2017.

(23) IsraeliDefence, New Self-Propelled Gun for the IDF, 18/09/2016.

(24) Queen of Battles: Poland's New Artillery Programs (2014 snapshot), 4 September 2014, 20:19 UTC by Defence Industry Daily staff.

(25) Brad Howard, VIDEO: Watch the Army Test The New 'Hawkeye' Humvee-Mounted Howitzer, The National Interest, August 7, 2018

(26) Stephen W. Miller, Asia's Artillery Renaissance, Asian Military Review, April 2017.

(27) Switching fire through a 360-degree arc is easy for well-balanced towed-guns designed to quickly move off centre of arc or base line, such as the 105mm M119 Light Gun with its box trail plus platform. However, a box trail and platform is impractical for 155mm guns given their size and recoil. Hence most 155mm guns are only capable of 30 degrees of traverse from their centre of arc without repositioning the gun's trails. The M777 gun, due to its platform layout, can only achieve 23 degrees of traverse either side of centre of arc. This is likely to be a considerable challenge in non-linear battlefields.

(28) Dr Carlo Kopp Artillery for the Army Precision Fire with Mobility, Defence Today magazine.

(29) Picatinny engineers seek to double range of modified howitzer – ARDEC.Army.mil, 21 March 2016.

(30) This deduction is based on the Singapore Lightweight Howitzer Pegasus' characteristics, which are almost identical to the M777, but it is 3,000-lbs heavier, as it is equipped with a unit that powers an automatic loading system.

(31) Advanced Artillery System: SIAC 155/52, brochure, Madrid: General Dynamics European Land Systems, January 2012.

(32) As at 2020, the French have the 32 AUF1 155mm armoured tracked gun in service with one of their combined arms brigades, but this is planned to be replaced by the Caesar gun.

(33) Jane's International Defence Review, Vol 51, May 2018, p. 26.

(34) Elie Tenenbaum The Battle over Fire Support, p. 54.

(35) Lt Col Alan Brooke, The Evolution of Artillery in the Great War, Part 1, RAI, Col LI, No 5, 1925.

(36) Brigadier ML Pemberton MC, The Development of Artillery Tactics and Equipment, The War Office, London, 1951, pp. 319, 320 & 330.

(37) Janice E. McKenney, The Organizational History of Field Artillery 1775–2003, pp. 168–9.

(38) Martin Lindsay, So Few Got Through, Pen and Sword, London, 2008, p. 123.

(39) George A. Durham, Who Says Dumb Artillery Rounds Can't Kill Armour? Field Artillery, November–December 2002.

(40) Georgi K. Zhukov, Marshal Zhukov's Greatest Battles, Harper & Row, New York, 1969, p. 138.

(41) IISS Military Balance, 1985-2015, and reporting by IHS Janes. Adapted by Anthony H. Cordesman and Steve Colley at the Centre for Strategic and International Studies.

(42) Brigadier ML Pemberton MC, p. 319.

(43) Michel Goya, Les Fantômes Furieux de Falloujah. Opération Al-Fajr/Phantom Fury (Juillet-Novembre 2004), Paris, Centre de Doctrine d'Emploi des Forces, Ministère de la Défense, 2006, p. 100. Quoted in Elie Tenenbaum, The Battle over Fire Support.

(44) A standard HE 155mm projectile weighs 95lbs, its charge bags weighing 15lbs. The 175mm shell weighs over 150lbs and the 203mm was over 200lbs, with a proportionate increase in the weight of the charge bags.
(45) Michael Peck, The Big Guns are Here: Russia is Bringing Back Its Cold War 'God of War' Heavy Artillery, The National Interest, September 20, 2018.
(46) Jeremy Binnie, Turkish call in heavy artillery against the Kurds, Jane's Defence Weekly, 7 February 201, p. 10.
(47) As will discussed later in greater detail, ideally a precision shell would be steered from its tail. This is effectively the approach taken by dedicated precision rounds such as Copperhead and Excalibur. Course corrected shells are significantly cheaper because they are retrofitted onto existing shells. This necessitates steering a shell from canards from within the fuze at the shell's nose. These can provide limited steerage in 155mm shells; 105mm shells are inherently more difficult to steer. This is due to: their higher muzzle velocity, shorter times of flight, and the greater rotational spin imparted by the rifling that is necessary for their inflight stability. The challenge is compounded by the canards being much smaller; without which the fuze would not fit in the barrel.
(48) Suzann W. Voigt, Much Ado About Something, Field Artillery Journal, July–August 1986, pp. 28–30.
(49) Janice E. McKenney, More Bang for the Buck in the Interwar Army, Military Affairs 42, April 1978, pp. 80–86.
(50) The M777 weighs 4,100kg (9,000lb), almost double the M119 105mm cannon (it weighs 2,130kg or (4,690lb)). The M777 also requires double the crew and of course its ammunition is individually three times heavier. There are also essential stores and camouflage netting. The M119's essential stores and camouflage is about the same weight as two ammunition pallets (72 rounds) or about a hundred unboxed rounds.
(51) As well as digital fire control the American upgrades include; increased low temperature capability, the M20 breech and the upgrading the howitzer's legacy recoil system, which in the past has been plagued with reliability and maintainability issues. This will include redesigns of: the gas equilibrator, recoil system, a titanium spade design and a lower carriage redesign. Colonel (Retired) Donald C. DuRant Training and Doctrine Command Capability Manager Brigade Combat Team Fires: The One-Stop-Shop for All Things Cannon, Fires, March April 2013, p. 39.
(52) Hope Hodge Seck, After Afghanistan, Marines Seek Lighter, More Agile Artillery, 2016 Military.com, 2016, accessed 30 March 2016.
(53) Next Generation IBCT/SBCT Howitzer, Solicitation Number: W15QKN-18-X-01KQ, Agency: Department of the Army, Office: Army Contracting Command, FEDBIZOPPS.GOV, Feb 14, 2018 10:15 am.
(54) Major General John G. Rossi, The State of Fires, Fires Bulletin, January–February 2016, pp. 1–4.
(55) Major Jesse T. Acosta, Field Artillery Brigade Ammunition Resupply in Operation Desert Storm US. Army Command and General Staff College, 5 June 1992, p. 4.
(56) Brigadier General (Reserves) Arie Mizrachi, IDF, Israeli Artillery Tactics and Weapons – Lessons Learned in Combat, Field Artillery, February 1990, p. 9.
(57) Anthony Clayton, Paths of Glory, The French Army 1914–18, Cassel, London, 2003, p. 69.
(58) Robert H Scales, Certain Victory, p. 81.
(59) Kenneth S. Brower The Israel Defense Forces, 1948–2017, Security and Policy Studies No. 150, The Begin-Sadat Center for Strategic Studies Bar-Ilan University, Mideast p. 25.
(60) Presentation to NRDC-Italy by Dr. Phillip A. Karber, 25 May 16.
(61) General Farndale, History of the Royal Regiment of Artillery. Western Front 1914–18.: Western Front, 1914–18, Royal Artillery Institution, 2nd edition, 1987, p. 258.
(62) The adoption by the Americans of the M18 field artillery digital automatic computer (FADAC) in 1964 marked a major milestone in attempts to improve firing accuracy and to reduce response

times. The computer could quickly make allowance for: angle of sight or azimuth of lay, altitude, meteorological conditions, powder or charge temperatures, variations in projectile weights, and a range of other factors. Its use improved firing data, allowed quicker engagement and reduced human error.

(63) MP Manson Guns, Mortar and Rockets, Brassey's New Battlefield Weapons Systems & Technology Series into the 21st Century, 1997, Brassey's (UK) Ltd, pp. 22–24.

(64) The Norwegian Nammo's 155mm HE Extended Range projectile quotes a circular error probability deviation of +/- 30m from target, for the 1960's US M107 HE projectile this figure is +/-80m. Unfortunately, sufficient trialling has not been conducted for the constituent elements of the improvement to be broken down. Christopher F Foss, Smart ammo: precision-guided munitions for field artillery: Field artillery is increasingly employing precision-guided munitions in order to engage targets with greater accuracy, Jane's Defence Weekly, IHS Global Limited, 2015.

(65) In artillery terminology errors are inaccuracies inherent in the guns, instruments, ammunition and external conditions, and thus can be quantified, mistakes are due to bad drills, applying faulty data, engaging the wrong target and other failings.

(66) This was the work of the Field Artillery Working Group of the Standing Committee on the Accuracy of Artillery Fire.

(67) John S Matsumura, Randell Steeb and John Gordon IV, Assessment of Crusader, The Army's Next Howitzer and Resupply Vehicle, RAND Corporation, Santa Monica, CA, 1998, pp. 3–4.

(68) Brigadier ML Pemberton MC, The Development of Artillery Tactics and Equipment, The War Office, London, 1951, p. 188.

(69) Other weapons with similar capability are the British 4.5-inch (115mm) gun, with its 55-calibre barrel, it fires a 21kg round 22km. The Russians predominantly use the 130mm, 70-calibre gun which fires a 33.4kg shell to a range of 23km, and the 100mm, 70-calibre gun that fires a 15.6kg shell to a range of 21km.

(70) Ronald O'Rourke Navy Lasers, Railgun, and Gun-Launched Guided Projectile: Background and Issues for Congress, Congressional Research Service, 1 August, 2018, p. 11.

(71) David Axe, China's Navy Railgun Is Out for Sea Trials. Here's Why It's a Threat to the U.S. Navy, January 6, 2019, The National Interest.

(72) Samuel Eliot Morison, Sicily – Salerno – Anzio, January 1943–June 1944, History of the United States Naval Operations in World War Two, Volume 9, University of Illinois, 2002, p. 118.

(73) Quoted in VA Kezhayez, Russian Artillery: the evolvement of the command and control system, January 1, 2006, Military Thought Article Archive, HighBeam Research.

(74) Sydney J Freedberg, Jr, McMaster: Army May Be Outnumbered AND Outgunned in the Next War, Breaking Defence, 6 April, 2016.

(75) The post-War failure of the Americans to field new tube artillery has resulted in their current towed artillery being British designed and their self-propelled M109 gun-howitzer being on its seventh version, with the M109A7 rebuilding much of that which was not rebuilt with the M109A6. Part of the reasons for this conservative approach is their over-loyalty that their current equipment engenders. An example of this is the 105mm howitzer. The supporters of the World War Two-vintage M101 105mm howitzer defended it against the new M102 by identifying the following superior features: a waist-high breech that made it easier to load; a higher ground clearance when in tow; and that it was cheaper and proven. This was despite its replacement – the M102 – being by far the better weapon. It was only 60% of the M101's weight: a vital consideration given its introduction during the Vietnam War, when the usual means of deployment was by helicopter. In addition, its platform allowed it to rapidly shift of centre of arc or base line without needing to shift the trails, again important in Vietnam with no fixed front line.

(76) Next Generation IBCT/SBCT Howitzer, Solicitation Number: W15QKN-18-X-01KQ, Agency: Department of the Army, Office: Army Contracting Command, FEDBIZOPPS.GOV, Feb 14, 2018 10:15am.

(77) 2S35 Koalitsiya-SV Self-Propelled Howitzer. globalsecurity.org. Retrieved 16 Oct 2018.

(78) Igor Bozinovski, Russia's Koalitsiya-SV SPHs undergoing state trials, Jane's Defence Weekly, 28 February 2018, p. 13.

(79) Barrel heating has become a significant problem with increasing rates of fire and the use of more powerful propellant. This can lead to increased erosion and wear, reduced accuracy and can cause the charge to in avertedly cook-off. This can be partly addressed through modifying the propellant charge, together with projectile and gun barrel design. Given the performance increase, the use of active cooling solutions and changed firing drills to minimise cook-off are likely to feature in cannons with high rates of fire. The problem also applies to mortars, particularly the larger ones which use significant quantities of propellent. Firing five rounds at top charge in two minutes increases the barrel temperature by 40 degrees Celsius in a 120mm mortar.

(80) The longer the barrel, the more it bends when firing, especially with powerful extended range propellant charges. It may also flex more during transit, especially in off-road conditions. This can all reduce the barrel life . To counter this the barrel can be strengthened to increase rigidity, at a weight penalty.

(81) V. Litvinenko and S. Voronkov, Artillery Fire and Maneuver: The Role of New-type Tactical Artillery Elements in Armed Conflicts of the late-20th, early-21st Centuries, Army Digest, February 2017, p. 38.

(82) Currently most armies inefficiently use a combination of propellant charges to achieve a given range; those not used are thrown away. While inefficient, this approach allows the quantity of slow or fast burning propellant to be matched to the range. Modular charge systems are designed to allow the quantity of propellant required for a given range and trajectory to be assembled from common individual charges. It can result in compromises on performance. This leads to modular charges providing less charge overlap than bespoke charges. Charge overlap is the ability of different charges to achieve the same range through using different elevations. This allows significant adjustment from the opening grid reference without having to switch to a different charge. This can improve accuracy, as changing the charge can add a new variable, that may not always be adequately compensated for in the fire control system. As bespoke charges are better at delivering a variety of trajectories to engage a given target, they are more effective in mountains, due to their ability to avoid an intervening ridge through a variation in trajectory.

Chapter 10: Rocket Artillery

(1) Chris Bellamy, Red God of War, p. 151.

(2) In contrast to the other quotations, which seek to add real value to the following discussion, this appears to be decorative. However, it seeks to draw attention to the strange fasciation, and almost inspiration, that multiple rocket launchers engender. In addition to this poem there is Katyusha by Sean O'Brien, inspired by the Hamas use of rockets (published in the UK Guardian Newspaper 2 January 2009). Plus, there are the individual nicknames that rockets attract; most famously Katyusha, the diminutive of Kate, but also Stalin's Organ, and the British called the Nebelwefer Moaning Minnie, from its acoustic sound in flight.

(3) When a rocket is guided, strictly speaking it should be referred to as a missile; for purposes of clarity this convention has not been followed.

(4) Admiralty, Manual of Gunnery for Her Majesty's Fleet, Her Majesty's Stationery Office, 1880.

(5) Nicholas Michael and G A Embleton, Armies of Medieval Burgundy 1364–1477, Osprey, Oxford, 1983, p. 21.

(6) Colonel HCB Rogers, A History of Artillery, Seeley Service & Company Ltd, London, 1971, pp. 195–6.

(7) Fame in the sense that it features in the American National Anthem: the stars of the Star Spangled Banner being the back-drop of British rockets to the flags flying over the American forces. This was an early example of the enhanced psychological impact made by rocket artillery.
(8) Chris Bellamy, Red God of War, p. 26
(9) Ibid., p. 151.
(10) Ibid., p. 152.
(11) Steven J. Zaloga and James Grandsen Soviet Tanks and Combat Vehicles of World War Two, Weidenfeld, London, 1984, p. 155.
(12) Paul Carell, Hitler's war on Russia: the story of the German defeat in the East. Harrap & Company, London, 1964, p. 98.
(13) As quoted in Lida Mayo, The Ordnance Department, Washington, DC: Office of the Chief of Military History, United States Army, 1968, pp. 333–34.
(14) Janice E. McKenney, The Organizational History of Field Artillery 1775–2003, p. 174.
(15) Dr. Phillip A. Karber 'Lessons Learned', p. 18.
(16) 9A52-2 BM-30 Smerch/Tornado 300-mm Multiple Rocket Launcher, GlobalSecurity, 14 Feb 2018.
(17) An estimate in May 2016 was that the separatists operated 472 multiple rocket systems to the Russian regular Army's 92. The separatists operate 372 to the Russian regulars' 172 tube artillery pieces. Presentation to NRDC-Italy by Dr. Phillip A. Karber, 25 May 2016, slide 38.
(18) MP Manson Guns, Mortar and Rockets, Brassey's New Battlefield Weapons Systems & Technology Series into the 21st Century,1997, Brassey's (UK) Ltd, p. 114.
(19) The technical improvements that have reduced the calibration, survey and meteorological error in modern tube artillery, which have made it precise at its battle ranges, cannot achieve the same accuracy improvements in rocket artillery. The inherent inconsistency of the rocket system is compounded by its longer range. Its longer time of flight makes it more vulnerable to crosswinds given a rocket's larger surface area. Crosswinds can in particularly have a significant impact at launch. The large longitudinal cross section – especially for those rockets with large fins – plus low launch velocity makes them susceptible to being turned off their planned flight path. While it only has a minor impact on the rocket's accuracy, the key advantage of modern survey (satellite and inertial navigation, fixation and orientation plus automated fire control and laying) has been the reduction of the time needed to be ready to fire, so reducing the system's vulnerability to counterfire.
(20) Due to the dominance of counter-insurgency post-9/11, the M30 precision-guided rocket, with its 404 improved dual-role sub-munitions, became a lesser operational priority to the precision M31 Unitary munition. The Unitary munition's 200 lb (91kg) predominantly blast warhead, multiple fuze settings – including a delay setting that allows a building to be penetrated before warhead initiation – allowed it became the weapon of choice when avoiding collateral damage was the key concern. Concerns over the usability of cluster munitions led in 2012 to the alternative warhead (fielded as the M30A1 Advanced Warhead) program. This combines long range and precision with an area target attack capability that avoids an unexploited hazard.
(21) Anna Ahronheim, IDF Acquiring New Rockets to Hit All Targets With Unprecedented Precision, The Jerusalem Post, 27 August 2019.
(22) Yaakov Katz, Analysis: IDF's New Missile Corps Will Revolutionize How Israel Wages War, The Jerusalem Post, January 31 2019.
(23) The Chinese military appear to have an enduring fascination with large missiles with corresponding large warheads to offset inaccuracy. This has led to their nuclear missiles having significantly larger warheads than other powers.
(24) The island of Taiwan is separated from the southeast coast of China by the Taiwan Strait; engaging it from mainland China requires ranges from 220km at its widest point to 130km at its narrowest.
(25) Anthony H. Cordesman and Martin Kleiber, Chinese Military Modernization and Force Developmnt, August 2006, p. 47.

(26) SCAIC 400mm WS-2 Multiple Rocket Weapon System, Jane's Armour and Artillery, updated July 22, 2013.
(27) 333mm Fadjr-5 Iranian Rocket, Jane's Armour and Artillery, updated February 5, 2013.
(28) HIS Jane's International Defence Review, January 2017, Vol 50, p. 15.
(29) DefenceNews Israel's Precision Strike Portfolio Grows Worldwide, by-line by Barbara Opall, 21 January, 2014 – 08:11am. South Korea's Defence Acquisition Program Administration announced 'it would equip new AgustaWestland AW159 Wildcat maritime attack helicopters with Rafael's non-line-of-sight (NLOS) Spike missiles, the international brand name for the Israeli Tammuz. Officials in Seoul quoted by the South Korean press said the Israeli missiles launched from helicopters or Humvees would support targeting operations against rocket launchers, artillery tubes and commando forces attempting to invade from the north'.
(30) Mitch Ginsberg, Israel's artillery corps torn between precision and power, The Times of Israel, 12 October, 2014.
(31) Colonel HCB Rogers, A History of Artillery, Citadel Press; Secaucus, NJ, 1975, p. 197.
(32) Comparing platform weight to projectile weight provides a comparison of the advantage of a rocket system over tube artillery. The M109 howitzer fires a 43kg shell and weighs 28,780kg. The MLRS weighs 24,950kg and HIMARS weighs 10,900kg; both these can fire a range of munitions from the standard 300kg rocket up to the 1,670kg ATACMS.
(33) The BM-21, BM-27 and BM-30 all employ a tube-based rocket system that can only be reloaded one rocket at a time, rather than in sealed pods as with MLRS and HIMARS, and other modern systems. If the Russians can consistently achieve these reload times then it is a case of their less sophisticated technology achieving superior results to the admittedly less manpower intensive Western approach.
(34) Radar is the primary locating method as the rocket's acoustic signature is insufficiently loud and distinctive to allow it to be accurately located by sound ranging at conventional battlefield ranges. The alternative approach is to detect the rockets flightpath. The Microflow AVISA Mobile Sound Ranging Array claims to be capable of this; this delivers sufficient accuracy to cue a finer grain sensor. The rocket's trail can make flash spotting very effective. Crater examination, a favoured method of artillery schools, tends to be little used in battle conditions, where probing about in a recent crater is not recommended.
(35) US Military Assistance Command, Vietnam, Countermeasures against Stand-off Attacks, Combat Experiences: Lessons Learned, Number 71, May 1969, p. 12.
(36) Brigadier ML Pemberton MC, The Development of Artillery Tactics and Equipment, The War Office, London, 1951, p. 248.
(37) Ben Kaspit, First, Let's Win, Ma'ariv, Tel Aviv, August 11, 2006. Quoted in Benjamin S. Lambeth, Air Operations in Israel's War against Hezbollah, Learning from Lebanon and Getting It Right in Gaza, RAND Corporation, Santa Monica, CA, 2011, p. 330.
(38) Matt Schroeder, Rogue Rocketeers Artillery Rockets and Armed Groups, A Working Paper of the Small Arms Survey, Small Arms Survey, Graduate Institute of International and Development Studies, Geneva, 2014, p. 20.
(39) Bearden, Milton and James Risen. 2003. The Main Enemy: The Inside Story of the CIA's Final Show-down with the KGB. New York: Presidio Press, pp. 221–22
(40) Dan Biers, Believe Soviets Suffered Worst Losses in Explosion at Ammo Dump, Associated Press. 24 August.1988.
(41) Aaron Stein, ISIS and Turkey: The Rocket Threat to Kilis, Atlantic Council, April 26, 2016.
(42) Jonathan Bailey, Field Artillery and Firepower, p. 520.
(43) David E. Johnson et al, The 2008 Battle of Sadr City, RAND Corporation, Santa Monica, CA, 2011, pp. 18, 24; also, see Jeffrey A. Braco, Fire Support for Irregular Warfare, Monterey, Naval Postgraduate School, 2008, pp. 69–70.
(44) Mr. Jeff Froysland and CW4 Scott Prochniak Training and Doctrine Command Capability Manager – Fires Brigade, Fires March-April 2013, pp. 41–42.

(45) Tim Travers, The Killing Ground, p. 63.
(46) In their 34-day 2006 War in Lebanon the Israelis fired some 120,000 155mm shells at Hezbollah bunkers to little effect.
(47) Most current Russian all arms brigades have the traditional ratio with six tube batteries (in two battalions) to two rocket ones (in one battalion, with a weapon-locating battery providing the third battery). The actual ratio in Ukraine is two to one, due to the ordnance provided by reinforcing artillery brigades, which predominantly have the heavier, longer-range, rocket systems, and separatists holding a higher proportion of rockets.

Chapter 11: Mortars and Gun Mortars

(1) Operational Research in Northwest Europe: The Work of No. 2 ORS, Mimeographed Report, 1945, p. 224. Cited in Terry Copp, Counter-Mortar Research in the 21 Army Group, Canadian Military History: Vol 3: Is. 2, Article 5, 1994.
(2) For example The American M252 81mm mortar's replacement, the M252A1, is 22% lighter. This is made possible through the use of: Inconel 718, a nickel-based alloy optimised for the lesser firing shocks of the mortar's tube, a carbon fibre reinforced composite baseplate and a lightweight material for a new bipod. Through a similar programme the Americans expect to get a 20% weight reduction in their 60mm mortar. Other sources quote a lesser weight saving of 14% once enhancements are factored in.
(3) Quoted from G. D. Sheffield, War on the Western Front, Osprey Publishing, 2007, p. 201.
(4) Through restricting the amount of propellant used, the mortar's muzzle velocity is usually limited to below the speed of sound (around 310m/s). If the mortar bomb were to fire supersonically then mortar bombs would need different ballistic characteristics. This would both reduce their lethality and increase their price. Employing more propellant to achieve supersonic speeds requires a stronger barrel and platform. At an optimum elevation of 45 degrees, keeping the muzzle velocity subsonic gives a theoretical range of just under 12km in vacuum; this translates in air to a maximum range of around 10km.
(5) Christopher Duffy, Fire and Stone, The Science of Fortress Warfare 1660–1860, Greenhill Books, London, 1975, p. 11.
(6) Ibid., pp. 154–5. While fictitious, CS Forrester's Hornblower novel, The Commodore, Penguin Books, 2004, provides a first-rate explanation of the challenge of employing 19th century mortars in indirect fire, in the story's case from two ships.
(7) John Norris, Artillery a History, The History Press, Stroud, Gloucestershire, 2012, p. 203.
(8) Mark Strong and Saunders Marble, Artillery of the Great War, Pen and Sword, Barnsley, England, 2011, p. 7.
(9) Christopher Duffy, Through German Eyes, The British and the Somme 1916, Phoenix Press, Sale, England, 2008, p. 283.
(10) Mark Strong and Saunders Marble, Artillery of the Great War, Pen and Sword, London, 2013, p. 203.
(11) 'WO 291/904 Morale effect of bombardment' also determined in at least one case that the casualty-producing value of an 81mm mortar might be nearer to four than three machine guns, though this varied with tactical circumstances. In an assault, with artillery preliminary and covering fire, it appears that the effectiveness of each weapon system became similar. Experience during the initial assaults on the Normandy beaches suggested that one 81mm mortar had the same casualty-causing effect as a single machine gun ('WO 291/946 Effects of bombardment – present state of knowledge').
(12) Mahon and Danysh, Infantry, pp. 53–54, 63–64, 66–67; General Board, USFET, 'Organization, Equipment, and Tactical Employment of the Infantry Division,' Study Number 15, pp. 5–6, copy in CMH files.

(13) Arty. Lessons, Eight Army, El Alamein to Sousse, issued by MGRA, MEF, on 9 August 1943.
(14) Martin Lindsey, So Few Got Through, p. 233.
(15) Brigadier ML Pemberton MC, p. 169.
(16) Terry Copp, Montgomery's Scientists: Operational Research in 21 Army Group, Waterloo, 2000, p. 24.
(17) Israeli Defence, War of Artillery, 17/08/2014.
(18) Robert H Scales, Firepower in Limited War, p. 91.
(19) Robert R. Leonard, The Art of Maneuver, p. 287.
(20) Increasing range involves a longer barrel, more propellant, lighter payload and a heavier design. The Chinese W91 81mm mortar has an 8km range but weighs 65kg (compared to 41kg of the American equivalent) and it also fires a lighter bomb than most of its contemporaries. Giving a 3km longer range.
(21) Virgil Ney, The Evolution of the US Infantry Battalion 1939–68, Fort Belvoir, Virginia, Headquarters, United States Army Combat Developments Command, October 1968, p. 39. Virgil Ney, The evolution of the US Army infantry mortar squad: the Argonne to Pleiku, Fort Belvoir, Virginia, Headquarters, United States Army Combat Developments Command, 1966, p. 65.
(22) Riley Sunderland, Organizing Counter-insurgency in Malaya, 1947–59, RAND Corporation, Santa Monica, CA, 1964, p. 238.
(23) Chris Bellamy, Red God of War, p. 198.
(24) The Cold War Soviet Operational Manoeuvre Group (OMG) is the descendant of the Great Patriotic War mobile group. Its aim is to thrust fast into the enemy operational depth, shifting the focus of combat to the enemy rear and thus increase the rate of advance of the main force.
(25) Lester W. Grau, Technology and the Second Chechen Campaign: Not all new and not that much, pp. 105–106. AF Bulatov, Methods of taking cities and how to use them. Military Thought, March 2001, p. 1.
(26) Dr. Phillip A. Karber 'Lessons Learned', pp. 40–41.
(27) In one instance of urban conflict at An Nasiriyah, 23 March to 2 April 2003, 1st Battalion, 2nd Marines mortars directly engaged a target 150m from the mortars and 50m from friendly forces.
(28) Chris Bellamy, Red God of War, p. 147.
(29) Russian Airborne Forces (VDV) are a heavily mechanised force but their equipment is usually about half the weight of similar equipment in the Ground Forces. Airborne Forces in the Cold War were equipped with the bespoke ASU57 and ASU-85 self-propelled guns (the calibre of the gun is the number next to ASU designation in mm). They primarily fired over open sights and provided a significant anti-tank capability. They were phased out of service from 1969, when it was apparent that guided missiles could provide a better anti-tank capability weapon. This allowed the gun-mortars to take on the fire support role. Fielding a large calibre gun-mortar allows the anti-tank missile to be tube launched. The Russians are partly returning to a self-propelled, high velocity, anti-tank gun with the 125mm gun- equipped 2S25 Sprut-SD; but currently only 24 have been fielded.
(30) MP Manson Guns, Mortar and Rockets, p. 52.
(31) Dr Carlo Kopp, Artillery in the digital age, DefenceToday, October 2010, p. 44.
(32) Yuriy Avdeyev, 'Tsar-Cannons of the Winged Guard,' Krasnaya Zvezda Online, 02 November 2015, quoted in Operational Environment Watch, Foreign Military Studies, Army, December 2015, p. 45.
(33) MP Manson Guns, Mortar and Rockets, p. 50.
(34) Not all systems need to worry about recoil pressure. The 2S9's BMD chassis can be lowered so that it is flush with the tracks. This design feature was required to make the vehicle robust during air drops; it now allows the mortar to transmit the firing pressures direct to the ground.
(35) Shelford Bidwell & Dominic Graham, Fire-Power, p. 194.
(36) Alex Haynes. The Slow Demise of the Canadian Infantry Corps. Ducimus: Canadian Infantry Association, p. 5.

(37) In World War Two, the Soviet rifle battalion's 82-mm mortar company, with nine tubes, usually fired as a single fire unit for battalion level targets. It could also be centrally controlled either as part of a scheduled offensive fire plan or when in defence, through combining the three mortar companies of a rifle regiment into a provisional battalion. Thus, it was able to mass concentrations of fire on any point of regimental frontage, or on occasion, range permitting, fire in support of adjacent regiments. The Russian military continues this practice with their brigades and regiments and regularly practice massed mortar fire, in concert with other forms of fire support, especially on the defensive.
(38) Brigadier ML Pemberton MC, p. 38.
(39) Israeli Armour, Artillery Corps Shifting Emphasis, Defence News, Mar. 9, 2014 – 03:45am.
(40) Edward N Luttwak and Daniel Horowitz, The Israeli Army – 1948–1973, p. 363.
(41) Jonathan M House, Combined warfare in the 20th Century, p. 277.
(42) Raymond Trohanowsky, 120mm Mortar System Accuracy Analysis, US Army RDECOM-ARDEC Picatinny, International Infantry & Joint Services Small Arms Systems Annual Symposium, Exhibition & Firing Demonstration, 17 May 2005.
(43) Terry Copp, Counter-Mortar Research in the 21 Army Group, Canadian Military History: Vol 3: Is. 2, Article 5, 1994, p. 47.
(44) The 120mm mortar's 10km range translates into 300km^2 of coverage. The 155mm cannon's 40km range translates into 5,000km^2 of coverage.
(45) John Boatman, Murray Hammick, and Gérard Turbé, Mortar Moves, International Defense Review, Volume 25, December 1992, pp. 1157–1162.

Chapter 12: Munitions

(1) Cited in Dan Goure, Will the US Army Get Serious About Revolutionizing Long Range Fires? The National Interest, August 19, 2016.
(2) Johnathan Bailey, Field Artillery and Firepower, pp. 481–2.
(3) JBS Haldane famously argued that it is inconsistent to prefer one method of killing to another. But the desire to restrict weaponry on humanitarian grounds endures.
(4) Nefedyev, S.A. Combat employment of missile troops and artillery in internal armed conflicts, July 1, 2004; Military Thought Article Archive, HighBeam Research.
(5) The return of the purely kinetic warhead may result from the introduction of the rail gun or similar technology. Due to the ability of their projectiles to reach speeds of up to 5,600 miles per hour (a speed at least three times as fast as existing weapons), it is assumed that they will employ solid warheads, with no explosives. The utility of the electromagnetic hyper velocity projectile as a point attack weapon against protected targets is obvious. Its ability to engage the breadth of land targets with a range of munitions is less so. This is why it has not just been the power required by rail guns that has led the World's navies to lead in fielding this technology.
(6) The fuze 106 played a significant role in allowing more flexible British tactics from 1917 onwards. Its super quick fuze exploded on impact with the barbed wire, making it significantly more effective at clearing routes for assaulting infantry through these obstacle belts. Previously an extended bombardment had been necessary to breach these defences, which stopped any chance of surprise.
(7) Bruce I Gudmundsson, On Artillery, Praeger Publishers, Westport CT, 1993, p. 111.
(8) Because of the training difficulties implicit in creating a citizen army and the inadequacies of the Fuze No 210, the Royal Artillery decided not to field variable time fuzes in World War Two. Fortunately, at the insistence of the Canadians, this decision was changed, although appropriate fuzes did not appear in quantity until 1944. Brigadier ML Pemberton MC, The Development of Artillery Tactics and Equipment, The War Office, London, 1951, p. 170.
(9) WO 291/129 Lethality of 3" mortar HE bomb.
(10) WO 291/113 Lethal effect of artillery fire.

(11) Colonel William L. Greer and others, 101st Division Artillery: Fighting with Artillery Fires in an Urban Environment, Field Artillery 8, Number 5, September–October 2003, p. 17.
(12) WO 291/138 Influence of ground cover on performance of HE projectiles.
(13) Regardless of the official belief of most weapon procurement organisations, it is technology, rather than an official requirement supported by doctrine, that is the normal precursor to innovation in military technology. After all, the Wright Brothers' first flight preceded the creation of airpower doctrine. As the civil sector now dwarfs the military research and development budget, armed forces will increasingly follow civil technology.
(14) Graham Farmelo, Churchill's Bomb: A Hidden History of Science, War and Politics, Faber & Faber, London, 2013, p. 190.
(15) RDX is the organic compound with the formula $(O_2NNCH_2)_3$. and started to appear in small quantities in 1945. As RDX is about 70% more powerful than TNT, mixing it into a predominantly TNT filling improves anti-personnel fragmentation by about 25%.
(16) A Hurlich, Review of Soviet Ordnance Metallurgy, Paper Presented at Meeting on Trends in Soviet Metallurgical Development, CIA, Washington DC, 16 April 1953. Declassified 21 November 1979.
(17) The Soviets made considerable use of cast ammunition. Their ammunition was known for rough surfaces, this reflects a total war manufacturing approach. A practice that continued in the Cold War. Non-critical surfaces were left rough while critical surfaces were well-machined to a standard comparable to the West. This can be seen on Soviet shells where the borrelets and rotating bands, the critical points of contact, are well machined.
(18) WO 291/129 Lethality of 3" Mortar HE bomb.
(19) G. Tanapornraweekit, W. Kulsirikasem, FEM Simulation of HE Blast-Fragmentation Warhead and the Calculation of Lethal Range. World Academy of Science, Engineering and Technology, Vol 6 2012-06-27, p. 388.
(20) For the theory see: Dennis Grady, Fragmentation of Rings and Shells: The Legacy of N.F. Mott, Springer, New York, 2004, p. 211.
(21) John Terraine, Indirect Fire as a Battle Winner/Loser in Old Battles and New Defences, p. 8.
(22) Air Historical Branch Specialist Monographs/II/116/22 Air Support, p. 157.
(23) Pierre M. Sprey, Notes on Close air support, p. 25.
(24) Precision Lethality Responds to Urgent Operational Need. AF.mil. 9 January 2105.
(25) William Matthews, Smaller, Cheaper, Lighter, Defense News, 31 May 2010.
(26) Pierre M. Sprey, Notes on Close Air Support.
(27) Benjamin Franklin Cooling (Ed), Case Studies in the Development of Close Air Support, p. 35.
(28) Von Hardesty, Red Phoenix, pp. 83–88 and 153. Benjamin Franklin Cooling (Ed), Case Studies in the Development of Close Air Support, p. 36.
(29) Terry Copp, Montgomery's Scientists: Operational Research in 21 Army Group, Waterloo, 2000, p. 24.
(30) V. J. Croizat, Close air support Procedures in the War Against Japan, RAND Corporation, Santa Monica, CA, 1967, p. 144.
(31) SLA Marshall, Battle in the Monsoon, Grand Central Publishing, New York, 1967, p. 67.
(32) The A-10's 30mm GAU-8 cannon has 1,174 rounds of either high explosive fragmentation or armoured piercing rounds, including depleted uranium. The Russian specialist close air support aircraft, the SU-25 Frogfoot also has a 30mm gun, but they have only 250 rounds of ammunition, hence it relies upon rockets as their principal direct fire weapon.
(33) An example of this approach is the 27mm Mauser cannon that uses a 'frangible' in-situ plastic-moulded tungsten alloy core with integrated driving band. Due to its discarding sabot approach, the ammunition has a very high muzzle velocity, giving a flat trajectory and a short time of flight, which significantly increase the hit probability in air-to-air combat. However, its reduced mass and lack of high explosive fragmentation means that it is less effective at ground targets.

(34) Amy Butler, USAF Eyes New Era Of Close Air Support, U.S. Air Force's campaign to reinvent CAS, Aviation Week & Space Technology – Defense Technology Edition, 30 March, 2015.
(35) MIRROR.CO.UK, Christopher Hitchens: the top 10 quotes from the author, journalist and atheist, 09:41, 16 DEC 2011, Updated 13:54, 15 MAR 2012.
(36) Bombs, missiles and shells that rely upon sub-munitions are variously known as cluster, bomblet and for the Russians case shells. Slang terms for them include butterfly, firecracker and popcorn due either to their design or small explosive content.
(37) The dud rate is a highly contested figure, understandably given the heated nature of the debate. Regardless of what figure is arrived at, all parties agree that it is too high, whether from a humanitarian viewpoint or the operational perspective that any duds reduce a munition's lethality. Operational experience suggests that the dud rate varies considerably with the ground, with few duds on hard surfaces such as roads, while considerably more than 5% could be expected on soft ground. See: Rae McGrath, Cluster Bombs, military effectiveness the impact upon civilians of cluster munitions, Landmine Action, Calvert's Press, London, 2000, pp. 5–6.
(38) Paul Deichman, German Air Force Operations in Support of the Army, Arco, New York, 1968, pp. 4l–49.
(39) This table shows that the 155mm high explosive shell, despite being three times the weight of the 105mm shell, is only one and half times as effective against troops in the open. 155mm bomblet is twice as effective as its high explosive equivalent. The increase in lethality of bomblet is even greater against armoured targets. The advantage of bomblet is even more pronounced for 203mm shell, which of course creates considerable over kill with its single point of detonation.

Shell Calibre	**Weight in 105mm Shell Equivalents**	**Quantity of Bomblets in American Munitions**		**Effectiveness in 105mm Shell Equivalents against troops in the open**	
		1st Gen	**2nd Gen**	**High Explosive**	**2nd Gen Bomblet**
105mm	1	18 (M444 round)	Not fielded	1	
155mm	3	60 (M449)	88 (M483A1)	1.5	2.9
203mm	6	104 (M404)	195 (M509)	2.5	5.9

(40) John S Matsumura, Randell Steeb and John Gordon IV, Assessment of Crusader, The Army's Next Howitzer and Resupply Vehicle, RAND Corporation, Santa Monica, CA, 1998, p. 2.
(41) Paul Wiseman, Ground Forces Won't Use Improved Cluster Bombs Until At Least 2005, USA Today, 11 December 2003, p. A7.
(42) Charles E Kirkpatrick, Joint Fires as They Were Meant to be: V Corps and the 4th Air Support Operations Group During Operation Iraqi Freedom, p. 25.
(43) Brigadier General Louis Weber, Assistant Division Commander (Support) 3rd Infantry Division in Operation Iraqi Freedom, interview by Mr. Fontenot of the Operation Iraqi Freedom Study Group, 24 September 2003. Quoted in U.S. Army Field Artillery Relevance on the Modern Battlefield, Marine Corps University, Marine Air-Ground Training and Education Centre, Marine Corps Combat Development Command, Quantico VA, 2004, p. 27.
(44) The breakdown of ammunition in an American artillery battalion e Gulf war was: 60% Dual Purpose Improved Conventional Munition bomblet, 21% scatterable mines, 16% HE, 3% white phosphorous. 1% Copperhead Laser Guided and 1% Illumination shells. Robert R. Leonard, The Art of Maneuver, Maneuver-Warfare Theory and AirLand Battle, Presidio Press, New York, 1991, p. 287.
(45) Official Georgian Government Timeline, released August 21, 2008, p. 14. Quoted in Ariel Cohen and Robert E. Hamilton, The Russian Military and the Georgia War: Lessons and Implications, Strategic Studies Institute, Carlisle PA, 2011, p. 93.

(46) Michael Jacobson, Why Cluster Munitions Must be Replaced, War on the Rocks, 2 September 2014.
(47) The War on the Rocks, Why Cluster Munitions Must be Replaced, Michael Jacobson.
(48) Barry D. Watts, The Maturing Revolution in Military Affairs, Centre for Strategic and Budgetary Assessments, Washington, DC, 2011, p. 21.
(49) Pierre M. Sprey, Notes on Close air support, p. 13.
(50) Bill Gertz, Russia sells China high-tech artillery, The Washington Times, July 3,1997, p. A1. France to evaluate Russian guided artillery round, Jane's International Defence Review, May, 1997, p. 6.
(51) James Lilley and David L. Shambaugh, China's Military Faces the Future, Routledge, Abingdon, 2016, p. 177.
(52) Major Richard D. Wallwork, Artillery In Urban Operations: Reflections On Experiences In Chechnya, US Army Command and General Staff College, 2004, p. 69.
(53) In March 2007 Defence Minister A.K. Antony admitted in the Lok Sabha (the Indian Lower House of Parliament) that the Krasnopol rounds bought from Russia in 1999–2002 had failed to perform to the desired standards in high-altitude areas.
(54) Lester W. Grau, The High-Precision Tulip: Development and Combat Employment of the Soviet Laser-Guided Mortar Round, Defence Technical Information Centre, 2006, p. 5.
(55) In June 1985, Senior Lieutenant A. Beletskiy employed his 2S4 battery against a Mujahedeen stronghold that artillery otherwise could not engage. Having determined the target location, he adjusted conventional high explosive rounds onto the target area, to ensure that when a guided munition was fired, both its ballistic impact point and the actual target were within the precision guided weapon's footprint. He then illuminated the target with his designator and fired a laser-guided Smelchak round. The 2S4 battery destroyed the Mujahedeen stronghold with twelve rounds. Quoted in Mr. Lester W. Grau, Artillery and Counter-insurgency: The Soviet Experience in Afghanistan, May-June 1997 Field Artillery Journal.
(56) Timothy R. Puckett, Copperhead, Field Artillery Journal, October 1994, pp. 20–23.
(57) Matyash, Vladimir. Artillery in Chechnya assessed. Moscow Krasnaya Zveada (Red Star), 17 May 2000, p. 4. Quoted in Major Richard D. Wallwork, Artillery In Urban Operations: Reflections On Experiences In Chechnya, US Army Command and General Staff College, 2004, p. 65.
(58) Cited in: Joe Gould, Guided-Bomb Makers Anticipate GPS Jammers, DefenceNews, 1:59 pm. EDT June 1, 2015.
(59) In addition to the already combat proven American system, several armies are fielding or trialling course corrected fuzes, including the Israelis who are evaluating Top Gun by IAI and Silver Bullet by Rokar, a subsidiary of the BAE Systems Group. Israel Defence 14.08.2015.
(60) In training an artillery unit fired 22 course corrected rounds which landed in a circular area of less than 36 metres, which is a significantly better performance than a 30m circular error probability (that is 50% of the rounds within 30m of the point of aim). Captain Steve Thomas, Integrating Indirect Fires in a Non-Combat Mission, Fires, July–August 2015.
(61) 4 April 2014 FM 3-09 2-111 Field Artillery Precision-Guided Munitions, Fire Support, Chapter 2.
(62) Course corrected sniper bullets are currently at the experimental stage with both the US Sandia Experimental Laboratories and the Defence Advanced Research Projects Agency. The Economist November 21st–27th November 2015.
(63) Raytheon Unveils Excalibur with Dual GPS and Semi-Active Laser Guidance – Deagel.com, 20 June 2013.
(64) Kris Osborn, The U.S. Navy's Lethal New Precision-Guided Artillery, The National Interest, 15 May 2016.
(65) Over the six-month period from October 2010 to April 2011, Army used the Excalibur M982 in Afghanistan only 11 times while the USMC commanders used it 149 times. Employment of M982 in Afghanistan, US Army and Marine Corps difference, Fires, January–February 2102, p. 17.

(66) Pavel Zavelokin, On the Electronic Front Line, Krasnaya Zvezda Online, 18 September 2015, quoted in Operational Environment Watch, Foreign Military Studies, Army, November 2015, p. 47.
(67) Smart weapons, the vision thing, The Economist, December 3–9 2016, p. 67.
(68) This incident and similar, but less, serious ones have been widely reported: Washington Times August 23, 2012.
(69) The Precision Revolution: GPS and the Future of Aerial Warfare by Michael Russell Rip and James M. Hasik. Naval Institute Press, Annapolis, Maryland, 2002.
(70) Joe Gould, Guided-Bomb Makers Anticipate GPS Jammers, DefenceNews, 1:59pm. EDT June 1, 2015.
(71) Interview with U.S. Defence Secretary Ashton Cater on April 24 2015, reported in: Franz-Stefan Gady, Is the Pentagon Getting Ready to Dump GPS? The Diplomat, April 29, 2015.
(72) Micro-electro-mechanical (MEMS) technology means that inertial measurement units are more robust, smaller (around 2 cubic inches) and cheaper (around $1,200) than previous technology. Their silicon solid-state design, which eliminates mechanical or electro-optical components, can 'pull' 12,000g, making them suitable for cannon launch. As they are widely used on the commercial markets (car air bag and anti-skid systems, gaming and in photography) they are likely to both advance in design and become even cheaper.
(73) Final Report of the Defence Science Board Task Force on Integrated Fire Support in the Battlespace, Office of the Under Secretary of Defence For Acquisition, Technology, and Logistics Washington, DC 20301-3140, October 2004, p. 29.
(74) Smart weapons, the vision thing, The Economist, December 3–9 2016, p. 68.
(75) Introduction to Scene Matching Missile Guidance Technology, National Air Intelligence, ADA315439, 13 Aug 1996.
(76) Dylan Eklund, Dylan, Fire and Brimstone: The RAF's 21st Century Missiles, RAF Magazine, 2006, pp. 19–25
(77) Richard Scott, Air-Launched Weapons, USAF to test image-based navigation and precision targeting on SDB I glide bomb, IHS Jane's Missiles & Rockets, 15 January 2016.
(78) Smart weapons, the vision thing, The Economist, December 3–9 2016, p. 68.
(79) Joe Gould, Guided-Bomb Makers Anticipate GPS Jammers, DefenceNews, 1:59 p.m. EDT June 1, 2015. Of note is that laser detection and ranging (LADAR) has not been fielded, probably due to its expense.
(80) New Israeli Missile Streaks Through Enemy Defences, United with Israel Staff, 14 January 2015.
(81) Full precision guidance is not required, but at longer ranges, some guidance may be required to get the sub-munition canister to the target area. The Americans have upgraded their free fall CBU-97 to the wind-corrected bomb CBU-105 standard. Russian long-range rockets use mid-course correction.
(82) Final Report of the Defence Science Board Task Force on Integrated Fire Support in the Battlespace, Office of the Under Secretary of Defence For Acquisition, Technology, and Logistics Washington, DC 20301-3140, October 2004, p. 31.
(83) An explosively formed projectile is a short rod that is formed by explosively deforming a metallic dish- shaped liner. This is projected downwards on to the roof of its target with a typical impact velocity of ~1800 m/s; this allows it to penetrate most tank deck armour.
(84) For much of Northern Europe and the Korean peninsula the average cloud ceiling is between 0.3 and 0.5km above ground level. This means that due to this cloud a non-radar sensor has only 300–500m of descent to search the target area before target engagement takes place.
(85) To be compliant with the convention on cluster munitions, sub-munitions must have a self-destruct fuze and have fewer than 10 warheads below a certain weight, and that these sub-munitions need to independently select and engage individual targets. This means that munitions such as the SMArt 155 and the BONUS shells are compliant.
(86) John Pike 9A52-2 BM-30 300mm Multiple Rocket Launcher, GlobalSecurity.org. R.

(87) Matthew Cox, Army Concerned Over Ban on Cluster Munitions, Land Mines, 2 May 2017, Military.Com
(88) Ochmanek, David, Ted Harshberger, David E. Thaler and Glenn A. Kent. To Find, and Not to Yield: How Advances in Information and Firepower Can Transform Theatre Warfare, RAND Corporation, Santa Monica, CA, 1998, pp. 93–94.
(89) Off Target: The Conduct of the War and Civilian Casualties in Iraq. By Human Rights Watch (Organization), 2003, p. 111.
(90) V. Litvinenko and S. Voronkov, Artillery Fire and Maneuver: The Role of New-type Tactical Artillery Elements in Armed Conflicts of the late-20th early-21st Centuries, Army Digest, February 2017, p. 36. Lester W. Grau and Charles K. Bartles, The Russian Way of War: Force Structure, Tactics and Modernization of the Russian Ground Forces, FMSO: Leavenworth, 2017, pp. 243–250.
(91) Major General Heinz Guderian, Achtung-Panzer! The Development of Armoured Forces, Their Tactics and Operational Potential, 1999 Brockhampton Press, p. 193.
(92) Von Hardesty, Red Phoenix, p. 137.
(93) The Russian General Staff, translated and edited by Lester G. Grau and Michael A. Gress, The Soviet-Afghan War, How a Superpower Fought and Lost, University Press of Kansas, 2002, p. 172.
(94) The American expenditure of ammunition in Operation Enduring and Iraqi Freedom (up until July 2013) was:

- 155mm – Paladin & M777: 333,210 rounds fired, divided into 71% high explosive missions, 8% smoke missions, 21% illumination missions, and 236 Excalibur rounds were fired.
- 105mm – M119: 217,101 rounds fired, 70% high explosive missions, 10% smoke missions and 20% illumination missions.

Quoted in Fires Journal, July–August 2013, p. 15.

(95) Mitch Ginsburg Israel's artillery corps torn between precision and power, The Times of Israeli, 7 November 2014.
(96) Major Allen W. Batschelet, Challenging the Heavy Brigade Direct Support Artillery Paradigm for the Brigade Close Fight, School of Advanced Military Studies United States Army Command and General Staff College Fort Leavenworth, Kansas First Term AY 94–95, p. 11.
(97) Benjamin Franklin Cooling (Ed), Case Studies in the Development of Close Air Support, p. 332.
(98) Ibid., p. 548.
(99) Independent International Fact-Finding Mission on the Conflict in Georgia, Volume II, September 2009, p. 209.
(100) Lieutenant Colonel Randall Barnes, Commander of 3rd Battalion, 320 Field Artillery, 101st Airborne Division in Operation Iraqi Freedom and others, interview by Lieutenant Colonel Pitts of the OIFSG, 24 May 2003. Quoted in U.S. Army Field Artillery Relevance on the Modern Battlefield, Marine Corps University, Marine Air-Ground Training and Education Centre, Marine Corps Combat Development Command, Quantico, VA, 2004, pp. 18–19.
(101) Jeffrey J Clarke, Operation Joint Guardian, The U.S. Army in Kosovo, 23 Feb 1999, p. 26.
(102) Benjamin Franklin Cooling (Ed), Case Studies in the Development of Close Air Support, p. 558.
(103) Lester W. Grau, The Bear Went Over the Mountain, p. 85.
(104) Backgrounder on Russian Fuel Air Explosives ('Vacuum Bombs'), Human Rights Watch, 1 February 2000. Retrieved 23 March 2018.
(105) Dave Majumbar, Russia's Lethal Thermobaric Rocket Launchers: A Game Changer in Syria? The National Interest, 2 December 2015.
(106) Adrian Blomfield, Russian army 'tests the father of all bombs', London: Daily Telegraph, 2007-09-13. Retrieved 13 April 2015.
(107) The most common type of chemical energy anti-tank munition is the high explosive anti-tank (or HEAT) round, which burns a narrow path through armour. The alternative approach is employing

the high explosive squash head (HESH) round's chemical energy to rupture a tank's armour and detach a 'scab' of armour that will have a devastating effect inside the vehicle.

(108) Dorian D'Aria and Lester W. Grau Instant Obstacles: Russian remotely delivered mines, an article in Red Thrust Star January 1996. Marcel de Haas, The Use Of Russian Airpower In The Second Chechen War, Conflict Studies Research Centre, January 2003, p. 6.

(109) About 388,000 tons of napalm bombs was dropped on Indochina between 1963 and 1973, compared to 32,357 tons used over three years in the Korean War, and 16,500 tons dropped on Japan in 1945.

(110) Quote from the character Lieutenant Colonel Kilgore in the 1979 movie Apocalypse Now.

(111) Interview with Major General Mordechai Hod, Tel Aviv, 16 Jan 1984 quoted in Benjamin Franklin Cooling (Ed), Case Studies in the Development of Close Air Support, p. 490.

(112) Pierre M. Sprey, Notes on Close air support, p. 26.

(113) Command Sergeant Major Dennis J. Woods, The World Dynamics are Changing, Everything is Growing or Dying, Nothing Remains the Same, Fires, May–June 2013, p. 51.

(114) Air Force Developed Bombs Capable of Destroying Syria's Chemical Weapons – Defensetech.org, 30 August 2013. Retrieved 13 April 2015.

(115) In terms of 'warhead' designs there appear to be several technical options. The one-shot Virtual Cathode Oscillators (Vircators) may be more powerful than High Power Spark Gaps and explosively-pumped rare earth magnets. These gigawatt-class weapons could potentially affect area footprints of many square miles.

(116) Joel Roberts, US Drops 'E-Bomb' on Iraqi TV, CBS, March 25, 2003, 10:41pm. Retrieved 18 May 2015.

(117) On 15 June 2015 the Air Force Research Laboratory Commander Major General Tom Masiello confirmed that it has 'an operational system already in our tactical air force'.

(118) Dr Carlo Kopp, E-Bombs vs. Pervasive Infrastructure Vulnerability, Pacific Theatre Air, Sea, Land Battle Concept: IO/EW/Cyber Operations International Conference Information Operations Institute and the Association of Old Crows, October 2012. Dr Kopp is the leading, at least open-source, authority in this area and this section relies heavily on his work.

(119) Dr Carlo Kopp, A Doctrine for the Use of Electro Magnetic Pulse Bombs, Air Power Studies Centre Paper No 15, Royal Australian Air Force, July 1993, p. 14.

(120) Measures of countering EMP include: protecting computer hubs through placing them in Faraday cages (more practical for fixed sites), use optical fibres for data, isolate power feeds with transient arrestors, use non-electrical power feed schemes, use electromagnetic 'air locks' and above all shielding must be comprehensively applied to the whole system.

(121) Russia Develops Rocket with UAV for Smerch Multiple Rocket Launch System, Tass Defense; published June 14, 2016.

(122) The disconnect between the rocket's range and the ability to control and use an unmanned aerial vehicle underlines the point that it is the data link which represents the greatest challenge, particularly when operating these systems in a contested environment. Communication is not only required to send back information, pending significant improvements in AI technology, the unmanned aerial vehicle also needs navigational instructions from the ground control post.

(123) Oscar Gilbert, Marine Corps Tank Battles in Vietnam, Casemate, Newbury, UK, 2007, p. 75.

(124) The American-led coalition's approach against Iraq of getting close to make firepower decisive is arguably more in tune with the Western way of war. Other examples include: Frederick the Great's artillery in the Seven Years War, Prussian/German artillery against the French in 1870 and the British against the Sikhs in the 1840s.

(125) Major General J.F.C. Fuller identified five weaponry attributes: range of action, accuracy of aim, striking power, volume of fire, and portability. Of these, he considered range to be the attribute that 'dominated the fight'. His analysis probably endures.

(126) Streamlining began with the replacement of round shots with shells. Until the 1950s it was believed that the in-flight stability required a calibre to length ratio of 1:3.5 to 1:4.5. This was reflected in the stubby World War Two shell designs. With this convention challenged, and access to quality steel, longer more streamlined shells are now the norm. As well as greater range, longer streamlined shells have more explosive filling and superior fragmentation.

(127) Munition manufacturers usually point out that through modern design and materials, these extended range designs can achieve the lethality of standard design. But, of course they are comparing their newest products to the previous generation of shells. A modern rocket assisted or base bleed shell cannot be as lethal as an equally modern orthodox shell. Their reduced payload and the loss of accuracy that goes with long range means that these extended range munitions will be relatively ineffective unless employed in mass against an area target, unless they use terminal guidance.

(128) Denel 155mm V-LAP, Jane's Ammunition Handbook, Jane's, 25 January 2013.

(129) The standard OF45 high-explosive projectile weighs 43.56 kilograms, it has a maximum muzzle velocity of 823 metres per second. It can be fitted with different rear ends including a screw-on boat tail. If fitted with a base bleed rear end it becomes the OF61 projectile making the shell weigh slightly less at 42.86 kilograms and thus a slightly higher maximum muzzle velocity of 828 m/s. This gives a slight increase in range but most of the additional 4.2km of extra range comes from the base bleed.

(130) The Russian and South African guns achieve an extra 4–10km through base bleed and an extra 11–20km through rocket assistance. The Koreans' K-9 gun overall achieves slightly more range than the South African guns. It fires a standard shell to 30km, base bleed produces a range of 38km, extra streamlining at the expense of lethality gives a further 3.6km, and base bleed, rocket assistance and streamlining will give somewhere between 52–56km.

(131) The M864 155mm Base Bleed Bomblet round has a circular error probability of 186m at 28km while a M549 155mm Rocket Assisted Projectile has a circular error probability of 267m at 30km. In comparison the 105mm Leo towed gun claims a <120m circular error probability with base bleed at 30km. With a standard boat tail shell, it has a circular error probability of <80m at its maximum range of 24km.

(132) Cassandra Mainiero, Army researchers add power, range to artillery, Picatinny Arsenal Public Affairs, November 16, 2015.

(133) Picatinny engineers seek to double range of modified howitzer – ARDEC.Army.mil, 21 March 2016. Retrieved 15 January 2017.

Chapter 13: Target Acquisition

(1) Congressional testimony of Army Chief of Staff General Eric Shinseki, quoted in Shuger, Outgunned: What the Crusader Cancellation Really Means to the Army. MSN.Com, URL: <slate.msn.com/id/2066158/>, November 2003.

(2) Nicholas Rankin, Churchill's Wizards, A Genius for Deception: How Cunning Helped the British Win Two World Wars, Faber and Faber, London 2009, p. 18.

(3) Antoine Bousquet, The Scientific Way of War: Order and Chaos on the Battlefields of Modernity, Hurst, London, 2011, p. 242.

(4) Reconnaissance, intelligence gathering, surveillance, and target acquisition (RISTA) and intelligence, surveillance, target acquisition and reconnaissance (ISTAR) have largely been replaced in the Western military lexicon by intelligence, surveillance and reconnaissance (ISR). ISR has considerable longevity in the air domain, but as has already been identified, the primary purpose of airborne sensors is to identify targets for engagement, in the land domain there is greater requirement to understand the battlespace.

(5) Vitaly Kuzmin, Modernized Artillery Reconnaissance Vehicle for Russian Federation Army May Get a UAV, TASS Online, 19 November 2015.

(6) Despite the advances in command and control made possible by radio technology the use of wire continued to be extensively used, in part due to its superior security, but mainly due to the unreliability and scarcity of radios in World War Two. The German artillery in particular suffered from a lack of radios, as the Luftwaffe and Panzer forces had the priority. This was a factor in their failure to innovate in joint fires command and control.

(7) Shelford Bidwell and Dominick Graham, Fire Power, pp. 101 and 143.

(8) At the start of World War Two American civilian experts identified that the Army's sound-ranging equipment was ten years behind the commercial equipment used by oil companies. Flash spotting had no civil application and so saw little technical development between the wars; leading to American sound ranging technology being assessed as ten times more effective than flash spotting. As well as superior sound ranging technology, there were other factors in limiting the effectiveness of flash spotting: the adverse terrain and weather of Western Europe, and the German use of flashless powder and decoy flares. On the Eastern Front, particularly on the Ukrainian plains, flash spotting proved to be particularly effective. As it still does, to the point of deterring night firing in the Russo-Ukraine conflict.

(9) Benjamin Franklin Cooling (Ed), Case Studies in the Development of Close Air Support, p. 546.

(10) Major Scott R. McMeen US Army, Field Artillery Doctrine and Development 1917–45, Master of Military Art and Science, Fort Leavenworth, Kansas 1999, p. 65.

(11) Weapon locating radar intercepts a shell/rocket/mortar bomb on its upward trajectory and calculates from this ballistic flight path the point of origin. A modern system requires around 8 radar intercepts to detect an incoming round and 20 intercepts to produce a highly accurate grid of the source. Achieving sufficient intercepts on a projectile's trajectory requires a couple of seconds. Detection can happen on a projectile's downward path, but greater accuracy is made possible by detecting the ascending flight path. The quoted range of a weapon locating radar is therefore in relation to a projectile's upward trajectory. Artillery shells, rockets and mortar bombs each have different trajectories. The mortar bomb is close to a parabola, as is tube artillery when firing at high angle (above 45-degrees). The artillery shell, when firing below 45-degrees, ascends for most of its range before rapidly descending. The ballistic rocket ceases climbing and starts to descend just after halfway through its range. To Western forces, the most challenging – but rarest – of the possible opposition multiple launch rocket systems is the Russian-built BM-30 Smerch. This has a range of up to 90km; when firing to its maximum range, it is on an upward trajectory for around 50km of the rocket's flight path. This means that weapon locating radars can detect a Smerch launcher despite it being physically located outside their stated location distance.

(12) In the Vietnam War, the Americans used the AN/TQP-4A radar. See Major General David Ewing Ott, Field Artillery, 1954–1973, Department of the Army, Washington DC, 1995, p. 323. In Afghanistan and Iraq, the American used the AN/TPQ -36 and 37 firefinder radars. All three radars observe a 90-degree arc in order to achieve the range and accuracy for conventional warfare. The latter two radars were later supplemented by the AN/TPQ-48, which is a 360-degree lightweight counter mortar radar (LCMR). The new American radars are the AN/TPQ-50 lightweight counter mortar radar, which is mounted on the Humvee, and the significantly larger, truck-mounted, AN/TPQ-53 Radar.

(13) The radar cross section is one of the key determinants of a radar's ability to detect a projectile. Typically mortar bombs (largely due to the fins) have ten times the radar cross section of an artillery shell. Rockets with fins usually exceed the radar cross section of mortars.

(14) Brigadier ML Pemberton MC, p. 239.

(15) Major General David Ewing Ott, Field Artillery, 1954–1973, Department of the Army, Washington DC, 1995, pp. 96, 179 and 228.

(16) Sydney J Freeburg, Russian Drone Threat, Army Seeks Ukraine Lessons, Breaking Defence, 14 October 2015.

(17) The 14 April 1999 bombing of Albanian refugees near Djakovica (Serbian) or Gjakova (Albanian) occurred when NATO planes responding to Serb attacks on ethnic Albanians mistakenly bombed refugees on the road, killing 73 Kosovo Albanian civilians. Subsequently the air component commander authorised his pilots to fly at lower altitudes to assist in target acquisition.
(18) Robert H Scales, Firepower in Limited War, p. 260.
(19) Raymond L Garthoff, How Russian Makes War, p. 263.
(20) Bruce I Gudmunsson, On Artillery, p. 151.
(21) Johnathan Bailey, Field Artillery and Firepower, p. 379.
(22) Georgi K. Zhukov, Marshal Zhukov's Greatest Battles, p. 138.
(23) Colonel Gregory Fontenot, Lieutenant Colonel E. J. Degen, and Lieutenant Colonel David Tohn, On Point: The United States Army in Operation Iraqi Freedom, Center for Army Lessons Learned, Fort Leavenworth, Kansas, 2004, p. 422.
(24) Orlan Drones – The Sea Eagle of St Petersburg – InformNapalm.org, 09/03/2015. Accessed 16 September 2016.
(25) SV Sheremet, Some ideas about improving reconnaissance in the interests of destruction of the enemy by Rocket Troops and Artillery. October 1, 2006, Military Thought Article Archive, HighBeam Research.
(26) Barbara Opall-Rome, Israeli Air Force: Russian Air Power in Syria Remains Robust, Defence News, 11:37 am. EDT March 28, 2016.
(27) Operational Environment Watch, Foreign Military Studies, Army, January 2016, p. 39.
(28) Vitaly Kuzmin, Modernized Artillery Reconnaissance Vehicle for Russian Federation Army May Get a UAV, TASS Online, 19 November 2015. Accessed 16 November 2016.
(29) US Army Studies Russian-Ukraine War for revolution in tank and drone warfare for modern close combat war lessons, 23 May 2016.
(30) Lester W. Grau and Charles K. Bartles, The Russian Way of War: Force Structure, Tactics and Modernization of the Russian Ground Forces, FMSO: Leavenworth, 2017, p. 373.
(31) Major General McDonald, Fires, July–August, 2013, p. 15.
(32) Strategic bombers in World War Two are an exception to this rule. They bombed as a unit, relying upon the lead aircraft to initiate the pattern, which meant that they could be consistently accurate or inaccurate. Formation bombing, often aided by radar guidance, was also used in the Korea and Vietnam Wars.
(33) Scott McClellan, Get a Grid Excellence in Precision Targeting, Fires Mar–April 2013, p. 26.
(34) Martin Goldsmith, James Hodge, Marion l. Burns III, Applying the National Training Centre Experience: Artillery Target Accuracy, RAND Corporation, Santa Monica CA, April 1990, pp. v–viii.
(35) Stephen J. Kirkin, Marion Goldsmith, Mortar Utilization at the Combat Training Centre, RAND Corporation, Santa Monica CA, April 1992, pp. v–viii.
(36) Though it must be recognised that laser range finders can be accurate to plus or minus five metres due to atmospheric conditions and computation times, and are susceptible to false readings from objects located relatively close to the intended target.
(37) United States Army Field Artillery School (USAFAS), The United States Army Field Artillery 2017 Training Strategy, p. 28.
(38) Expressed as circular error probability the NATO Target categories (Cat) are:

Cat 1	0-6m	Cat 4	31–91m
Cat 2	7–15m	Cat 5	91–305m
Cat 3	16–30m	Cat 6	>305m

NATO follows the US lead in this area, as expressed in: Chairman of the Joint Chiefs of Staff. Joint Publication 3-09.3 Close air support, Chairman of the Joint Chiefs of Staff, Washington DC, 2009, V-4.

(39) Headquarters, Department of the Army. DIVARTY: Division Artillery, Fort Sill Fires Centre of Excellence Internet, available from http://sill-www.army.mil/USAFAS/_img/801010.png, accessed 16 November 2014.
(40) Boyd L. Dastrup, Artillery Strong Modernizing the Field Artillery for the 21st Century, Combat Studies Institute Press Fort Leavenworth, Kansas, 2018, p. 258.

Chapter 14: Company Level Fire Support Elements and Terminal Fire Control

(1) Brigadier General Carter, Synchronizing Combat Power at the NTC, Field Artillery Journal, August 1992, p. 5.
(2) Jim Hedge, Air war over Chechnya, World Air Power Journal, No 42, Autumn/Fall 2000, p. 22.
(3) A letter from the American Army and Air Force Chiefs of Staff to the Chairman of the House Armed Services Committee in September 1975, United States Air Force: Basic Documents, 403. Quoted in Major Michael H. Johnson, USMC, Cleared to Engage, Improving the Effectiveness of Joint Close Air Support, Air & Space power Journal Summer 2008, p. 73.
(4) Robert A. Doughty, The Seeds of Disaster, p. 99.
(5) Chris Bellamy, Red God of War, pp. 207–9.
(6) Shelford Bidwell, Gunners at War, p. 149.
(7) Boyd L. Dastrup, King of Battle, p. 220.
(8) The British artillery switched the role of their officers between World War One and World War Two. In the first war the experienced officers were usually on the gun line. In the Second World war experienced captains and majors directed the fire from the front. This was because the artillery school educated lieutenants were superior at the technical duties on the gun positions. Shelford Bidwell & Dominic Graham, Fire-Power, pp. 252–254.
(9) Though this difference can be overstated, as the high-quality manpower required to conduct the forward observation task inevitably found itself assisting an infantry company with a range of tasks regardless of the actual rank of the observer. In the Vietnam War the American forward observation officers: 'commonly navigated for the company, directed the fires of organic infantry mortars, and assisted the company commander in numerous other ways. On occasion the forward observer, by virtue of his rank and the absence of other company officers, found himself second in command succession to the company commander'. Major General David Ewing Ott, Field Artillery, 1954–1973, Department of the Army, Washington DC, 1995, pp. 96, 179 and 228.
(10) Lieutenant General Sir Brian Horrocks, A Full Life, Leo cooper, Barnsley, UK, 1960, p. 190.
(11) SLA Marshall, The Battle for Bird, The Battery Press, Tennessee, 1968, pp. 106–7.
(12) Number 5 Conversations with General J. Lawton Collins, transcribed by Major Gary Wade, Combat Studies Institute, U.S. Army Command and General Staff College, 1983.
(13) Janice E. McKenney, The Organizational History of Field Artillery 1775–2003, p. 287.
(14) Vietnam Studies, Field Artillery 1954–1973, Department of the Army, 1975, p. 236.
(15) Scott S McMichael, The Soviet Army, Counter-insurgency, and the Afghan War, Parameter, December 1989, pp. 26–7.
(16) Chris Bellamy, Red God of War, pp. 186–9.
(17) Ulrich G. Gibbons, Let's Use Forward Observation, Field Artillery Journal, May 1946, p. 269.
(18) U.S. Army Field Artillery School, Close Support Study Group I, II, IV, Field Artillery School, Fort Sill, OK, 1980, 1984, 1989).
(19) RAND Corporation, Applying the National Training Centre experience: Artillery Targeting Accuracy, RAND Corporation, Santa Monica, CA, 1990, p. 42.
(20) Dale Van Hyning, FO Comments from the Beachhead, Artillery Journal 34, July, 1944, p. 403.
(21) Cunningham, Alfred A, Value of Aviation to the Marine Corps, The Marine Corps Gazette 5, Number 3 September 1920: p. 221.

(22) Riley Sunderland, Evolution of Command and Control for Close air support, Office of the Air Force History Headquarters, United States Air Force, March 1973, p. 1.
(23) Benjamin Franklin Cooling (Ed), Case Studies in the Development of Close Air Support, p. 98. Richard Hallion, Strike from the Sky: the History of Battlefield Air Attack, 1911–1945. Smithsonian Institution Press, 1989, p. 39.
(24) Benjamin Franklin Cooling (Ed), Case Studies in the Development of Close Air Support, p. 99.
(25) Richard Hallion, Strike from the Sky, p. 229.
(26) Benjamin Franklin Cooling (Ed), Case Studies in the Development of Close Air Support, p. 332.
(27) Chindits – A Reappraisal, Pathfinder, Volume 1, Air Power Development Centre, Canberra, 2005, pp. 101–105.
(28) Alexander. A. Vandegrift, An Evaluation of Air Operations Affecting the U.S. Marine Corps in World War II. Quantico: Marine Corps Schools, 1945, pp. III-13–15.
(29) W. E. Sullivan, History and Development of Close Air Support, The Marine Corps Gazette 40, Number 11, November 1956, p. 20.
(30) V. J. Croizat, Close air support Procedures in the War Against Japan, RAND Corporation, Santa Monica, CA, 1967, pp. 141–143.
(31) Rasmussen, Richard A., Marine Corps Close Air Support Development from Guadalcanal to Okinawa, 3 May 2011, Master of Military Studies Research Paper, USMC Command and Staff College, p. 11.
(32) RA Mason, Strike from Above: The History of Battlefield Air Attack 1910–1945, Smithsonian Institute Press, Washington, 1989, pp. 181–182.
(33) In Western militaries the authority to order the aircraft to engage is known colloquially as 'owning the bomb'. The joint terminal attack controller is formally authorised to employ aerial munitions, for which he holds personal responsibility. However, in recent counter-insurgency operations a dual ownership approach has become common. This reflects aircrew usually being of a higher rank than the controller, aircraft at medium altitudes having greater situational awareness and often in recent counter-insurgency operations that there has not been a time imperative that necessitates immediate engagement. When airspace is uncontested, a dialogue can take place between ground and air, resulting in the aircraft identifying the target, determining the location of friendly forces and third parties, and then in effect taking over the engagement from the forward air controller. Of course, when air is contested this option will rarely be available and aircraft will operate in a more conventional manner with the terminal controller 'owning the bomb'.
(34) A comparison can be drawn with the 'piloting' of unmanned aircraft. Air forces largely apply the same standards to this as with manned flight, on the assumption that only these personnel have the necessary 'airmanship'. Organisations that do not have this culture – such as the CIA – are more willing to determine the requirement from first principles.
(35) Mark Raymond Wisher, Can a Non-Rated Officer Effectively Fill the Position of a USAF Air Liaison Officer? Graduate Thesis, Embry-Riddle Aeronautical University Extended Campus Fort Campbell Resident Centre, Ft. Campbell, Ky., September 2004, p. 9: http://handle.dtic.mil/100.2/ADA463295.
(36) The dates quoted refer to the regular element of the air force. The US Air National Guard displayed a greater agility in reforming to meet the operational requirement. Since 1990 it has provided non-aviators for the Air Liaison Officer roles, mainly at battalion and increasingly brigade level, including operational deployments.
(37) In 2006 the proportions of active duty American Officers in Air Liaison Officer posts were: 62% fighter pilots, 10% bomber pilots, 7% bomber navigators, 11% fighter navigators, and 10% air battle managers. Thomas Manacapilli, Steven Buhrow, Improving the Theatre Air-Ground System, RAND Corporation, Santa Monica, CA, 2008, p. 4.
(38) In 2003 the US Marine Corps opened up Air Liaison Officer positions to non-aviators. Lubold, Gordon, Marines Open Air Controller Field to Enlisted Personnel, Air Force Times, May 19, 2003: http://www.airforcetimes.com/legacy/new/0-AIRPAPER-1845582.php.

(39) Marine Corps Combat Development Command. Predictors of Success Among Joint Terminal Attack Controllers. 12 August, 2010, p. 2.
(40) Captains Mike Squire, James Groves and Chris O'Brien, Australian Artillery After Afghanistan, Volume X, Number 1, Australian Army Journal, p. 65.
(41) The Russian General Staff, translated and edited by Lester G. Grau and Michael A. Gress, The Soviet-Afghan War, How a Superpower Fought and Lost, University Press of Kansas, 2002 p. 340.
(42) Roger N McDermott, Russia's Conventional Armed Forces and the Georgian War, Parameters, Spring 2009, p. 73.
(43) T. N. Dupuy, Elusive Victory, The Arab-Israeli Wars 1947–74, Harper & Row, New York, 1978, p. 608.
(44) Mike Benitez, How Afghanistan Distorted Close Air Support and Why it Matters, War on the Rocks, 29 June 2016.
(45) Caitlin Kenney, Joint Fires Observers make battlefield impact, US Army, 27 September 2012. https://www.army.mil/article/88014/Joint_Fires_Observers_make_battlefield_impact.
(46) Master Sergeant Timothy Ryan, Keeping it Real: Don't Let Joint Fires Observer Skills Deteriorate, Fires, January–February 2011.
(47) Benjamin Franklin Cooling (Ed), Case Studies in the Development of Close Air Support, p. 541.
(48) U.S. Air Force Operations in the Korean Conflict, 25 June–1 November 1950, US Air Force Historical Division, 1 October 1952, p. 195.
(49) Shelford Bidwell & Dominic Graham, Fire-Power, p. 144.
(50) Airborne Forward Air Control, a first for the RAAF, Pathfinder, Volume 1, Air Power Development Centre, Canberra, 2005, pp. 101–105.
(51) J Farmer and M.J. Strumwasser, The Evolution of the Airborne Forward Air Controller: An Analysis of Mosquito Operations in Korea, RAND Corporation, Santa Monica, CA, October 1967, p. v.
(52) Major Michael H. Johnson, USMC, Cleared to Engage, Improving the Effectiveness of Joint Close Air Support, Air & Space Power Journal Summer 2008, p. 78.
(53) J Farmer and M.J. Strumwasser, The Evolution of the Airborne Forward Air Controller: An Analysis of Mosquito Operations in Korea, RAND Corporation, Santa Monica, CA, 1967, pp. 68–77.
(54) The Army Cessna O-1 Birddog was underpowered and vulnerable to small arms fire, and hence suffered high casualty rates. From the end of 1967 the larger and faster Cessna O-2A, also known as the Milspec C-337 Skymaster, superseded the Cessna O-1 Birddog, before in turn the purpose-built Rockwell OV-10 Bronco replaced it.
(55) Charlie Potock, Jim Gordon, Jerry Allen and Charlie Heidel, A Brief History of Forward Air Controlling, 2008, p. 8.
(56) Bruce R. Pirnie, Alan Vick, Adam Grissom, Karl P. Mueller, David T. Orletsky, Beyond Close Support, Forging a New Air-Ground Partnership, RAND Corporation, Santa Monica, CA, 2005, p. 72.
(57) Lieutenant Colonel Jay Stout, Close air support Using Armed UAVs, The Naval Institute Proceeding, Military.com, July 2005.
(58) Major Michael H. Johnson, USMC, Cleared to Engage, Improving the Effectiveness of Joint Close Air Support, Air & Space power Journal Summer 2008, p. 74.
(59) Kevin L Digman, Unmanned Aircraft Systems in a Forward Air Controller (Airborne) Role, Air Command and Staff College University, April 2009, pp. 11–17.
(60) In the Gulf War, each airborne forward air controller had a 30 × 30 mile box, defined by latitude and longitude. These were selected to coincide with Iraqi Army formations. Largely using imagery, through the targeting process individual enemy locations were identified within these boxes. The airborne forward air controller and attacking aircrews were provided with these target locations, accurate at best to 100m (6-figure grid reference). The airborne forward air controller's chief role was to manage the turning of this target information into targets destroyed.
(61) David Leone, The F16 and the Forward Air Controller Mission, Aviationist, 28 August 2014.

(62) Mike Benitez, 21st Century Forward Air Control: The Roots to rebuild, War on the Rocks, 1 March 2017.
(63) Richard Simpkin, Race to the Swift, p. 169.
(64) Paul F. Pearson, FIST!, Field Artillery Journal, May–June 1976, p. 7.
(65) Boyd L. Dastrup, King of the Battle, pp. 295–296.
(66) Jonathan N. Sims, Marine Corps FIST: An Inter-Organizational Analysis of the Fire Support System and its Environment, MBA, Naval Postgraduate School, Monterey California, pp. 16–19.
(67) Amy Butler, USAF Eyes New Era of Close air support, U.S. Air Force's campaign to reinvent close air support, Aviation Week & Space Technology – Defense Technology Edition Mar 30, 2015.
(68) Boyd L. Dastrup. The Field Artillery: History and Sourcebook, Greenwood Press, Westport, CT, 1994, p. 246.
(69) Sean MacFarland, Michael Shields, and Jeffrey Snow, White Paper: The King and I: The Impending Crisis in Field Artillery's ability to provide Fire Support to Manoeuvre Commanders (np:np): memo sent to the Chief of Staff of the Army, 2007.
(70) Commanders will Control Aircraft providing Close air support to Forces, IsraelDefense 03.09.2015.
(71) Scott Hopkins (Ed.), 2006 Chief of Army's Exercise Proceedings, Land Warfare Studies Centre, Canberra, January 2007, p. 9.
(72) U.S. Army Field Artillery Relevance on the Modern Battlefield, Marine Corps University, Marine Air-Ground Training and Education Centre, Marine Corps Combat Development Command, Quantico, VA, 2004, p. 11.
(73) Lester W. Grau, The Bear Went Over the Mountain, pp. 14–18.
(74) Commanders will Control Aircraft providing Close air support to Forces, IsraelDefense 03.09.2015.
(75) Israeli AF Lifts Veils on JTAC Roles and Missions, 03/28/2017, armscom.net. armscom.net/news/israeli_af_lifts_veils_on_jtac_roles_and_missions.

Capter 15: Command and Control of Joint Fires

(1) T. N. Dupuy, Elusive Victory, The Arab-Israeli Wars 1947–74, Harper & Row, NY, 1978, p. 608.
(2) Sebastian Cox, The Air/Land relationship – an historical perspective 1918–91, Royal Air Force, Airpower Review, Volume 11, Number 2, Summer 2008, p. 11.
(3) U.S. Army 3rd Infantry Division, Third Infantry Division (Mechanized) After Action Report: Operation Iraqi Freedom, Fort Stewart, Ga., 2003, p. 108.
(4) Nader Shah, leader of the Persians who defeated the Mughals in 1739 at the Battle of Karnal. Thomas R. Trautmann, Elephants and Kings: An Environmental History, University of Chicago Press, Chicago and London, 2015, p. 296.
(5) Ami Roykes Dombi, A New Operational Concept for the IDF Artillery, IsraelDefence, 15 January 2019.
(6) Shelford Bidwell & Dominic Graham, Fire-Power, p. 164.
(7) Ibid., p. 99.
(8) Lester W. Grau and Charles K. Bartles, The Russian Reconnaissance Fire Complex Comes of Age, Changing Character of War Centre Pembroke College, University of Oxford, May 2018.
(9) Interview with Major General Dan Tolkovsky taped at Tel Aviv 1984, quoted in Benjamin Franklin Cooling (Ed), Case Studies in the Development of Close Air Support, p. 498. Hebrew adds a mind word to command (piked) and control (bakara), this is shlita. This third focus is a combination of perspective and authority. The officer with shlita possesses both the big picture and the authority to direct the overall action.
(10) Final Report of Chief of Air Service, AEF, in Report of CINC, AEF, Staff Sections and Services, Washington, DC, 1948, p. 230.
(11) Anthony Clayton, Paths of Glory, p. 185.

(12) Shelford Bidwell & Dominic Graham, Fire-Power, p. 144.
(13) Richard L. Kugler, Michael Baranick, and Hans Binnendijk, Operation Anaconda: Lessons for Joint Operations Center for Technology and National Security Policy National Defense University, March 2009, p. 15.
(14) Michael W. Isherwood, Five Years After Operation Anaconda, Challenges and Opportunities, issue 47, 4th Quarter, 2007, p. 142.
(15) Air Force/ Marine Tiger Team CENTCOM Trip Report, January 8–20, 2008, p. 10.
(16) Bruce R. Pirnie, Alan Vick, Adam Grissom, Karl P. Mueller, David T. Orletsky, Beyond Close Support, Forging a New Air-Ground Partnership, RAND Corporation, Santa Monica, CA, 2005, p. 32.
(17) Benjamin S. Lambeth, Israel's War in Gaza, A Paradigm of Effective Military Learning and Adaptation, International Security 37:2, p. 109.
(18) Ibid., p. 93.
(19) Ami Roykes Dombi, A New Operational Concept for the IDF Artillery, IsraelDefence, 15 January 2019.
(20) General Dempsey and Admiral Greenert described 'joint interdependence' as: 'a deliberate and selective reliance and trust of each Service on the capabilities of the others to maximise its own effectiveness'. JP Clark, In Defence of a Big Idea for Joint Warfighting, War on the Rocks, 22 December 2016.
(21) Elaine M. Grossman, Anaconda: Object Lesson in Ill Planning or Triumph of Improvisation? Inside the Pentagon, 19 August 2004.
(22) Maj Gen Kenneth S. Wilsbach and USAF Lt Col David J. Lyle, USAF, NATO Air Command–Afghanistan, The Continuing Evolution of Airpower Command and Control, Air & Space Power Journal, January–February 2014, p. 12.
(23) Maj Gen Charles W. Lyon and Lt Col Andrew B. Stone, Right-Sizing Airpower Command and Control for the Afghanistan Counter-insurgency, Air and Space Power Journal 25, Number 2, Summer 2011, pp. 5–11.
(24) Ibid., p. 9.
(25) Mike Benitez, How Afghanistan Distorted Close Air Support and Why it Matters, War on the Rocks, 29 June 2016.
(26) Thomas Alexander Hughes Overlord: General Pete Quesada and the Triumph of Tactical Airpower, The Free Press, New York, 1995, p. 296.
(27) In actual warfighting this joint structure has rarely been fully implemented. Generals and Admirals have usually been unwilling to fully delegate command over their parent service. An example being General Eisenhower who also exercised land command over his army groups from late 1944. A notable exception was Admiral Mountbatten as Supreme Allied Commander South East Asia, who worked through air, sea and land commanders-in-chief, as should be expected from a former chief of combined operations with a well-developed ability to delegate. The result was that the size, remoteness and relevance of his strategic joint HQ was questioned.
(28) Grant, Rebecca. The First 600 Days of Combat. Iris Press, Washington, DC, 2004, p. 81.
(29) Jody Jacobs, Gary McLeod, and Eric V. Larson, Enhancing the Integration of Special Operations and Conventional Air Operations – Focus on the Air-Surface Interface, RAND Corporation, Santa Monica, CA, July 2007.
(30) The National Archives [British], Air 37/876.
(31) Daniel R Mortensen (Ed.), Airpower and Ground Armies: Essays on the Evolution of Anglo-American air doctrine. 1940–1943, Air University Press, Air Force Research Institute Maxwell Air Force Base, Alabama 1998, p. vii.
(32) Quoted in Christopher Shores and Giovanni Massimello, with Russell Guest, Frank Olynck and Wilfried Bock, A History of the Mediterranean Air War, 1940–1945. Volume 3: Tunisia and the End in Africa, November 1942–May 1943, Grub Street, London, 2016, p. 332.

(33) Sebastian Cox, The Air/Land relationship – an historical perspective 1918–91, Royal Air Force, Airpower Review, Volume 11, Number 2, Summer 2008, p. 4.
(34) Lee Kennett, Developments to 1939, in Benjamin Franklin Cooling (Ed), Case Studies in the Development of Close Air Support, p. 58.
(35) Maj Gen Kenneth S. Wilsbach and USAF Lt Col David J. Lyle, USAF, NATO Air Command–Afghanistan, The Continuing Evolution of Airpower Command and Control, Air & Space Power Journal, January–February 2014, p. 12.
(36) Steven Johnson, Where Good Ideas Come From: The Natural History of Innovation, Riverhead Books, New York, 2010.
(37) Michael P Noonan and Mark R Lewis, Conquering the Elements: Thoughts on Joint Force (Re) Organization, Parameters, Autumn 2003, p. 40.
(38) Johann Price, Operation Enduring Freedom: Commands and HQs June 1, 2002, Order of Battle, 23 June 2002.
(39) Maj Gen Charles W. Lyon, USAF Lt Col Andrew B. Stone, 2011, p. 11.
(40) Janice E. McKenney, The Organizational History of Field Artillery 1775–2003, p. 322.
(41) Douglas A. Macgregor, Breaking the Phalanx, A New Design for Landpower in the 21st Century, Praeger Publishers, Westport Connecticut, 1997.
(42) Field Manual (FM) 3-94 (initial draft), Echelons Above Brigade (Washington, DC: Headquarters Department of the Army, October 28, 2011), 3-2, paragraphs 3-1.
(43) In 1999 the French Army removed the divisional level of command and reorganized into independent brigades, a decision which was reversed in 2016. The new organisation consists of two armoured divisions each with three brigades, which each have a single artillery battalion, plus air defence and deep fire battalions at divisional level.
(44) Janice E. McKenney, The Organizational History of Field Artillery 1775–2003, p. 321.
(45) This change was well heralded, when the Russian Army was formed in 1992: 'the General Staff was attempting a major change in the army's force structure by introducing a "Corps-Brigade" structure to replace the traditional "Army-Division-Regiment" chain of command'. Michael Orr, The Russian Armed Forces As A Factor In Regional Stability, Conflict Studies Research Centre, 1999.
(46) The Russian Airborne Forces, who are a separate service to the ground forces, never abandoned the divisional level structure. In 2020 there are four two-regiment divisions and four independent airborne/air-assault brigades, one for each military district.
(47) Operation Environment Watch, Foreign Military Studies, Army, June 2016, pp. 38–9.
(48) Modernization of the Chinese Army. http://www.indiandefencereview.com/news/modernization-of-the-chinese-army
(49) DoD, Annual Report to Congress: Military and Security Developments Involving the People's Republic of China 2015, April 2015, p. 78.
(50) Chinese Strategy and Military Modernization: A Comparative Analysis October 5, 2015 p. 206.
(51) Johnson, David E. Learning large lessons, p. 130.
(52) As it is difficult to envisage a logistically independent ground force, linearity will continue to apply to lines of communication. Historically armies have broken with their lines of communication – perhaps most famously General Sherman's March to the Sea in the American Civil War – but largely 'living off the land' is no longer an option for modern mechanised forces. In contrast, there is evidence for reduced linearity in the front line. Such as the risk taken in the 2003 invasion of Iraq when the advancing forces consciously exposed their flanks. Given the rate of advance, the state of the opposition and security provided by airpower, this risk was considered acceptable.
(53) A definition of the battlespace is that it encompasses 'all aspects of a joint operating area within which military activities take place' and has 7 dimensions: maritime, land, air, space, information, electromagnetic, and time. Quoted from the British Joint Doctrine Publication 3–70 dated June

2008; this is largely consistent with US doctrine and NATO's practice, though the Alliance lacks a single body of recognised battlespace management doctrine.

(54) Maj David H. Zook, The Fire Support Coordination Line: Is It Time to Reconsider Our Doctrine? Fort Leavenworth, Kans., 1992, p. 42.

(55) William R. Fearn, Major, United States Marine Corps, Joint Force Fires Coordination: Towards a Joint Force Answer, Naval War College Newport, RI, Advanced Research Project, 1997.

(56) Johnson, David E. Learning large lessons, pp. 140–141.

(57) MR Gordon and Lieutenant General BE Trainor, The Generals' War, Boston: Little, Brown and co. 1995, p. 320.

(58) Ibid., p. 472.

(59) Harold R. Winton, Partnership and Tension: The Army and the Air Force Between Vietnam and Desert Shield, Parameters, Spring 1996, p. 10.

(60) Benjamin S. Lambeth, The Transformation of American Air Power, p. 277

(61) Ibid., 274–278.

(62) U.S. Army 3rd Infantry Division, Third Infantry Division (Mechanized) After Action Report: Operation Iraqi Freedom, Fort Stewart, Ga., 2003, p. 102.

(63) Michael B. McGee, Jr., Air-Ground Operations During Operation Iraqi Freedom: Successes, Failures, and Lessons of Air Force and Army Integration, thesis, Air War College, 2005, p. 17.

(64) Bruce R. Pirnie, Alan Vick, Adam Grissom, Karl P. Mueller, David T. Orletsky, Beyond Close Support, Forging a New Air-Ground Partnership, RAND Corporation, Santa Monica, CA, 2005, p. 20.

(65) Lewis, Richard B. H. Desert Storm-JFACC Problems Associated With Battlefield Preparation. Carlisle Barracks, PA: U.S. Army War College, 1993, p. 23.

(66) Douglas Musselman, Joint Fires Battlespace Deconfliction, op. cit., pp. 10–12; Karl E. Wingenbach, 'Kill Box', Field Artillery, July–August 2005, pp. 13–15.

(67) Benjamin S. Lambeth, Air Operations in Israel's War Against Hezbollah, Learning from Lebanon and Getting It Right in Gaza, RAND Corporation, Santa Monica, CA, 2011, p. 188.

(68) Ibid., p. 193.

(69) Benjamin S. Lambeth, Israel's War in Gaza, A Paradigm of Effective Military Learning and Adaptation, International Security 37:2, p. 118.

(70) Curtis V. Neal, Robert B. Green, and Troy Caraway, Bridging the Gap from Coordination to Integration, JFQ, issue 67, 4th Quarter 2012, p. 68.

(71) There are two means of conducting airspace management, positive and procedural. Positive control requires communication with aircraft and a means of locating and identifying all airspace users. Procedural control relies upon pre-planned airspace control measures. Land components lack the ability to completely conduct positive control. Perhaps some of the challenges will be overcome, such as: improving the recognised air picture and the provision of fighter control personnel to manage airspace. Mortar and artillery fire cannot be redirected after launch; hence they will always need procedural control.

(72) The Israelis set the airspace management division at a 3,000-foot ceiling, which for the 2008 Gaza Strip operations was usually below the cloud deck, employing attack helicopters and unmanned aerial vehicles beneath it. Fighters with precision weaponry hold station in orbits high above the cloud deck. Benjamin S. Lambeth, Israel's War in Gaza, A Paradigm of Effective Military Learning and Adaptation, International Security 37:2, p. 104.

(73) The coordinating altitude is not currently NATO doctrine, although America's closest allies have adopted it, it should expect that this will be eventually adopted. The major challenge is having a sufficiently empowered air staff at the corps or divisional level. Currently many of the European nations of NATO have resisted the empowering of their Air Operations Coordination Centres to become Air Support Operations Centres able to control aircraft operating in airspace assigned to ground formations.

(74) Curtis V. Neal, Robert B. Green, and Troy Caraway, Bridging the Gap from Coordination to Integration, JFQ, issue 67, 4th Quarter 2012, p. 68.
(75) Note. these ranges assume that the topography does not require a lower charge and higher trajectory to overcome relief.
(76) There is a rough rule of thumb for calculating a safe altitude. The artillery vertex height, in feet, is four times the time of flight in seconds squared, and then add a thousand feet. Hence a time of flight of 25 seconds results in a stay-above altitude of 11,000 feet for the aircraft.
(77) The Russian General Staff, translated and edited by Lester G. Grau and Michael A. Gress, The Soviet-Afghan War, How a Superpower Fought and Lost, University Press of Kansas, 2002 p. 173.
(78) Robert H Scales, Forecasting the Future of Warfare, War on the Rocks, 9 April 2018.
(79) The equipment in question is France's surface-to-air missile platform/terrain, which in concert with the MARTHA coordination system delivers a joint battlespace module (known as CMD3D).
(80) Christian Vladich, 'La coordination 3D aux petits échelons tactiques', Doctrine, Number 14, January 2008, p. 94. Quoted in Elie Tenenbaum, 'The Battle over Fire Support. The close air support Challenge and the Future of Artillery', Focus stratégique, Number 35 bis, October 2012.
(81) Systems such as the American Guided MLRS will always need to be coordinated with other air users due to their high vertex altitude. In addition, it would be challenging for aviation conducting deep operations not to be supported by fixed wing suppression of enemy air defence.
(82) David E. Johnson, Learning Large Lessons, pp. 72–73.
(83) U.S. Army 3rd Infantry Division, Third Infantry Division (Mechanized) After Action Report: Operation Iraqi Freedom, Fort Stewart, Ga., 2003, p. 108.
(84) General Creighton Abrahams, Military Review 4/1985.
(85) Robert Frost, Mending Walls, North of Boston, Henry Holt and Company, New York, 1924. The poet identified that this phrase has at least 17th century provenance. Its reflection on the human condition can be seen by variations in other cultures. In Norway 'there must be a fence between good neighbours', in Germany 'between neighbours' gardens a fence is good', in Japan 'build a fence even between intimate friends' and in India 'love your neighbour, but do not throw down the dividing wall'. See Robert Frost: Poems Summary and Analysis of Mending Wall, The poetry of Robert Frost, 1914, Gradesaver.
(86) Barry R. Posen, The Sources of Military Doctrine: France, Britain, and Germany Between the World Wars, Ithaca, N.Y.: Cornell Univ. Press, 1984.

Chapter 16: Fifty Propositions Towards a Land Firepower Theory

(1) Richard White, The Republic for Which it Stands: The United States During Reconstruction and the Gilded Age, 1865–1896, Oxford University Press, 2017.

Index